DATE DUE

A16700 565276

SEP - 8 1995

ALSO BY C. D. B. BRYAN

P.S. Wilkinson

The Great Dethriffe

Friendly Fire

The National Air & Space Museum

Beautiful Women; Ugly Scenes

The National Geographic Society:
100 Years of Adventure and Discovery

Close Encounters of the Fourth Kind

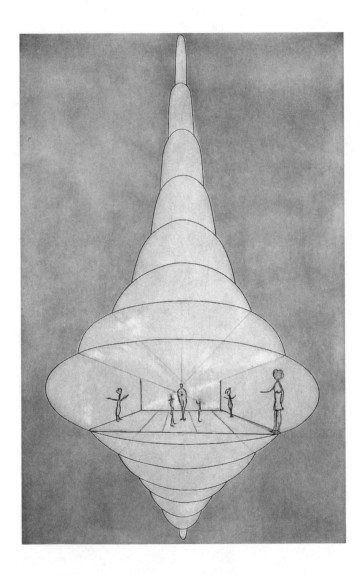

CLOSE ENCOUNTERS
OF THE
FOURTH KIND

---

*Alien Abduction, UFOs, and
the Conference at M.I.T.*

C. D. B. Bryan

ALFRED A. KNOPF   *New York*   1995

THIS IS A BORZOI BOOK
PUBLISHED BY ALFRED A. KNOPF, INC.

Copyright © 1995 by Courtlandt Dixon Barnes Bryan

All rights reserved under International and Pan-American Copyright Conventions. Published in the United States by Alfred A. Knopf, Inc., New York, and simultaneously in Canada by Random House of Canada Ltd., Toronto. Distributed by Random House, Inc., New York.

Frontispiece: Louise Bourgeois, *The Puritan, plate 1, variant.* 1990. Engraving with *chine collé*, with pencil and ink additions; plate: 16¾ x 10¹⁵⁄₁₆". The Museum of Modern Art, New York. Gift of the artist. Photograph © 1995 The Museum of Modern Art, New York.

Owing to limitations of space, all permissions to reprint from previously published material can be found immediately following the index.

ISBN 0-679-42975-1
LC 95-76563

Manufactured in the United States of America
First Edition

For Brandon and Mary Anne

HOLYOKE COMMUNITY COLLEGE
ELAINE NICPON MARIEB LIBRARY

When you have eliminated the impossible, whatever remains, however improbable, must be the truth.

—SHERLOCK HOLMES,
in Arthur Conan Doyle's
The Sign of Four

Contents

Acknowledgments

I wish to acknowledge the kindness shown me by various people during the writing of this book, beginning with Brenda Helen Cummings, R.D.T., who first alerted me to the 1992 Abduction Study Conference at M.I.T. and then introduced me to some of the key written sources.

Next would come those I met and interviewed in Cambridge and afterwards: the conference's co-chairmen, Harvard psychiatrist John E. Mack, M.D., and M.I.T. physicist David E. Pritchard, Ph.D., who graciously permitted me to attend and, subsequently, openly shared their thoughts about the abduction experience with me.

I am grateful, also, to Budd Hopkins, the phenomenon's pioneering chronicler, who was extraordinarily generous in sharing his data, techniques, and information; Temple University historian David M. Jacobs, Ph.D., who provided both a historical context for, and an often amusing sense of perspective about, the UFO movement in addition to the structure of abductions; and folklorist Thomas E. Bullard, Ph.D., whose erudite scholarship made my task so much the easier.

I wish to thank, as well, John G. Miller, M.D., and Richard J. Boylan, Ph.D., both of whom contributed more of their time and thoughts than I had any right to expect; journalist Linda Moulton Howe, whose sense of wonder was infectious; Keith Basterfield and Jenny Randles for their diligent "foreign correspondings"; and John S. Carpenter, M.S.W., whose example inspired me to strive for a similar blend of professionalism and caring in this work.

I am grateful also to the abductees who permitted me to interview them—especially "Carol" and "Alice"—whose confidences and trust I have tried to deserve.

In addition, I would like to thank my editor, Vicky Wilson, who gives the lie to John Cheever's observation that "the relationship between a writer and his editor is that of a knife-to-the-throat." Vicky's elegant surgery was limited to the page and her encouragements made this book a pleasure to write.

I would be remiss, too, if I did not here express my appreciation to my agent, Lynn Nesbit, for her continuing efforts on my behalf.

And this is as good a place as any to acknowledge those writers I have not already mentioned who have gone before me—Keith Thompson, Fred Alan Wolf, Timothy Good, Howard Blum, and J. Allen Hynek, in particular—whose works and ideas I looted like an Attila the Hun.

Finally, there are reoccurring phrases authors use to express their gratitude to their spouses and children for putting up with them through the writing of a book. No words adequately convey, however, how gratified I am by my wife and family's continued enthusiastic support and willingness to stick around.

Close Encounters of the Fourth Kind

CHAPTER I

Background

"Dear Colleague," the letter dated February 28, 1992, began. "We are organizing a scientific conference to assess the similarities and differences in the findings of various investigators studying people who report experiences of abductions by aliens, and the related issues of this phenomenon.

"One of the features of this conference," the letter continued, "will be an abductee panel with abductees drawn widely from the community. If you have investigated an abductee who is articulate and thoughtful and has had particularly interesting and/or manifold experiences, please send us his/her name and address and a brief paragraph about why this person would be a desirable participant."

The five-day conference, the letter explained, was to be held at the Massachusetts Institute of Technology from June 13 through June 17; its co-chairmen were M.I.T. physicist David E. Pritchard and Harvard psychiatrist John E. Mack. The letter's return address was Pritchard's office in the physics department at M.I.T., the university at which the fifty-one-year-old Harvard Ph.D. professor has taught and pursued research in atomic and molecular physics since 1968. In 1991 Pritchard was presented the prestigious Broida Prize, awarded biannually for outstanding experimental advances in the fields of atomic, molecular, and optical physics.

John E. Mack, M.D., Pritchard's co-chairman, is a sixty-three-year-old *cum laude* graduate of the Harvard Medical School and former head of the Department of Psychiatry at the Cambridge Hospital, Harvard Medical School, where he has been a professor of psychiatry for the past twenty years. He is the founding director of the Center for Psychological Studies in the Nuclear Age, has won acclaim for his studies on suicide, and has testified before Congress on the psychological impact of the nuclear weapons competition on children and adolescents. In addition to having authored or co-authored over 150 scientific papers that have appeared in learned psychiatric and academic journals, textbooks, and other publications, Dr. Mack wrote the 1977 Pulitzer Prize–winning biography of Lawrence of Arabia, *A Prince of Our Disorder: The Life of T. E. Lawrence.*

One might reasonably except that a "scientific conference" on such a subject as people who have reported their abductions by "little green men" ought to be dismissed out of hand. And it certainly would have been but for the credentials of those chairing it, the site of the conference—that "high church of technology," as the *Whole Earth Catalog*'s Stewart Brand has called M.I.T.—and the disturbing credibility, generally speaking, of the hundreds of individuals who, uncontaminated by exposure to any previous unidentified flying object lore or to each other, have so hesitantly, reluctantly, *timidly* come forward with their utterly incredible accounts of having been abducted and examined in UFOs not by "little green men" but rather, for the most part, by spindly-limbed, 3½-to-4½-foot-tall telepathic gray creatures with outsized foreheads dominated by huge, compelling, tear-shaped black eyes. And it is in the similarities of these abductees' stories and the consistency of their details that the true mystery lies. For, as John Mack would ask at the Abduction Study Conference, "if what these abductees are saying is happening to them *isn't* happening, what *is?*"

Those invited to the conference were asked to read two publications prior to attending. The first was David M. Jacobs's *Secret Life: Firsthand Accounts of UFO Abductions,* a detailed, quasi-scholarly examination of the abduction experience testimony of some sixty individuals whom Dr. Jacobs, an associate professor of history at Temple University, had interviewed over a four-year period. In the course of that study, Jacobs uncovered approximately three hundred abduction experiences.

The central focus of the alien-abduction program is, according to Jacobs, the collection of human eggs and sperm. He, like his mentor, the New York artist and abduction-phenomenon authority Budd Hopkins, supports the most sinister explanation for the aliens' presence among us: they are, as Hopkins wrote in his book *Intruders,* engaged in "an ongoing genetic study," and "the human species, itself, is the subject of a breeding experiment."[1]

"One of the purposes for which UFOs travel to Earth is to abduct humans to help aliens produce other Beings," Jacobs wrote in *Secret Life.* "It is not a program of reproduction, but one of *production.* They are not here to help us. They have their own agenda, and we are not allowed to know its full parameters. . . . The focus of the abduction is the production of children."[2]

Early in his book Jacobs reviewed what is probably the most famous abduction case, that of Barney and Betty Hill, whose story, as written by John Fuller, appeared first in *Look* magazine in 1966 and later that same year as the book *Interrupted Journey.*

The Hills were an interracial couple; he was a black member of the NAACP and the New Hampshire Civil Rights Commission; she was a white social worker. They were solid, respected, devout members of their community. According to the Hills' story, in 1961, while driving at night along a remote stretch of road en route from Montreal to Portsmouth, New Hampshire, they observed a bright, luminous object in the sky. The object initially appeared to be stalking them from a distance, but later drew closer until it was hovering overhead. The Hills heard two beeping sounds, then saw the disk no more. Upon their return home, they discovered their arrival was two hours later than it should have been. They could not account for the passage of missing time.

The Hills remembered having thought they had seen a UFO, but nothing more. During the next several months, however, they were so distressed by bizarre dreams of being taken aboard an alien spaceship that they sought psychological counseling. They were referred to UFO skeptic Dr. Benjamin Simon, a reputable psychiatrist adept in hypnosis.

Under hypnosis, the Hills separately and singly recalled having been abducted from their automobile by small, hairless, ashen-colored Beings with large heads and eyes, small noses and mouths. The Beings brought the Hills inside a stationary UFO, isolated them from each other in individual rooms, and performed medical examinations upon them. During her examination, a long needle was inserted into Betty Hill's stomach as part of, the Beings told her, a "pregnancy test."

A larger Being, whom Betty took to be the "leader," communicated with her telepathically. At one point the Beings seemed mystified that Betty Hill's upper teeth could not be removed as Barney Hill's could. Barney wore an upper denture.

There followed various other "medical procedures"—skin scraping and the like—and then the Hills were permitted to leave the spacecraft and watch it depart. After a second series of beeps, their memories of the experience were erased. Only a vague sense of unease remained.

Since the Hills' abduction hundreds of other abduction cases have been catalogued and studied, a figure which Dr. Jacobs and others in the field believe is only a *fraction* of the number of abductions actually carried out.

As Abduction Study Conference co-chairman John E. Mack wrote in his introduction to Dr. Jacobs's *Secret Life*, "The idea that men, women, and children can be taken against their wills from their homes, cars, and schoolyards by strange, humanoid beings, lifted onto a spacecraft, and subjected to intrusive and threatening procedures is so terrifying, and yet so shattering to our notions of what is possible in our universe, that the actuality of the phenomenon has been largely rejected out of hand or bizarrely distorted in most media accounts. This is altogether understandable, given the disturbing nature of UFO abductions and our prevailing notions of reality. The fact remains, however," Mack continued,

> that for thirty years and possibly longer, thousands of individuals who appear to be sincere and of sound mind and who are seeking no personal benefit from their stories have been providing to those who will listen consistent reports of precisely such events. Population surveys suggest that hundreds of thousands, and possibly more than a million, persons in the United States alone may be abductees, or "experiencers," as they are sometimes called. The abduction phenomenon is, therefore, of great clinical importance if for no other reason than the fact that abductees are often deeply traumatized by their experiences. At the same time the subject is of obvious scientific interest, however much it may challenge our notions of reality and truth.
>
> The relevant professional communities in mental health, medicine, biology, physics, electronics, and other disciplines are understandably skeptical of a phenomenon as strange as UFO abduction, which defies our accepted notions of reality. The effort to enable these communities to take abduction reports seriously will be best served through scrupulously conducted research by investigators who bring a scholarly and dispassionate yet appropriately caring attitude to their work. In this way patterns and meanings may be discovered that can lead to fuller and deeper knowledge and, eventually, to the development of convincing theoretical understanding.

"Dr. Jacobs's findings will, I believe," Mack went on to say, "impress those who are open at least to the possibility that something important is happening in the lives of these individuals and countless others that cannot readily be explained by the theories and categories currently available to modern science. . . ."[3]

Jacobs is not new to the UFO field; in 1975 Indiana University Press published his *UFO Controversy in America,* with a foreword written by J. Allen Hynek—like John E. Mack, a gentleman with sterling credentials. A former professor of astronomy at Ohio State University and later chairman of the Astronomy Department at Northwestern University, Hynek was brought in by the United States Air Force in 1949 to be scientific consultant for its Project Sign, later Project Grudge, and still later Project Blue Book, the Air Force's effort to gather evidence that UFOs either did or did not exist. For the next twenty years Hynek served as consultant to the Air Force on UFOs. During that period Hynek went from being an astronomer who, prior to his association with the Air Force, had (in his own words) "joined my scientific colleagues in many a hearty guffaw at the 'psychological postwar craze' for flying saucers that seemed to be sweeping the country and at the naivete and gullibility of our fellow human beings who were being taken in by such obvious 'nonsense' "[4] to becoming a man who would demand that the scientific community undertake a "respectable scholarly study of the UFO phenomenon."[5]

In an August 1966 letter to *Science* magazine, the official organ of the American Association for the Advancement of Science, Hynek attempted to refute the most common misconceptions about UFO reports:

1. *Only UFO "buffs" report UFO sightings.* Almost the exact opposite, Hynek pointed out, is true. "The most articulate reports come from obviously intelligent people"[6] who had not previously given UFOs much consideration and were shocked and surprised by their experience. UFO buffs and "believers" of the cultist variety, Hynek added, rarely make reports, and when they do, they are "easily categorized by their incoherence."[7]

2. *UFOs are never reported by scientifically trained people.* "On the contrary," Hynek wrote, "some of the very best reports have come from scientifically trained people. Unfortunately, such reports are rarely published in the popular literature since these people usually wish to avoid publicity and request anonymity."[8]

3. *No UFO has ever been picked up on radar or by meteor-and-satellite-tracking cameras.* Not so, Hynek reported. These instruments had, indeed, tracked "oddities" that defied identification, and because of this Hynek was "unable to dismiss the UFO phenomenon with a shrug."[9]

Pointing out that twentieth-century scientists tended to forget that there would be a "21st-century science, and indeed, a 30th-century science, from which vantage points our knowledge of the universe may appear quite different," he concluded that "we suffer, perhaps, from temporal provincialism, a form of arrogance that has always irritated posterity."

In his 1972 landmark book, *The UFO Experience: A Scientific Inquiry,* Hynek originated the term "Close Encounters," subsequently popularized by the Steven Spielberg film *Close Encounters of the Third Kind.* He did so in order to distinguish between those reports in which a UFO is seen at a distance and those involving sightings at close range.

The more distant UFO reportings he divided into three categories: *Nocturnal Lights,* those UFOs seen at night; *Daylight Discs,* those seen in the daytime (Hynek was cautious to add that he refers to these UFOs as "discs" because "the prevalent shape reported is oval or disc-like, although it should be understood the term is rather loosely applied"); and *Radar-Visual,* those reportings made through observations on radar accompanied by visual sightings.

Close-range sightings Hynek also broke down into three types:

Close Encounters of the First Kind. This category is the simple Close Encounter in which the reported UFO is seen at close range but there is no interaction with the environment (other than trauma on the part of the observer).

Close Encounters of the Second Kind. These are similar to the First Kind except that physical effects on both animate and inanimate material are noted. Vegetation is often reported as having been pressed down, burned, or scorched. Tree branches are reported broken; animals are frightened, sometimes to the extent of physically injuring themselves in their fright. Inanimate objects, most often vehicles, are reported as becoming momentarily disabled, their engines killed, radios stopped, and headlights dimmed or extinguished. In such cases, the vehicles reportedly return to normal after the UFO has left the scene.

Close Encounters of the Third Kind. In these cases the presence of "occupants" in or about the UFO is reported. Here a sharp distinction must be made between cases involving reports of the presence of presumably intelligent beings in the "spacecraft" and the so-called contactee cases.[10]

The "contactees" Hynek was referring to were individuals such as "Professor" George Adamski (*Flying Saucers Have Landed,* 1953; *Inside the Space Ships,* 1956), "Doctor" Daniel Fry (*White Sands Incident,* 1954), Truman Bethurum (*Aboard a Flying Saucer,* 1954), Orfeo Angelucci (*Secret of the Saucers,* 1955), and Howard Menger (*From Outer Space to You,* 1959), each of whom had emerged in the 1950s to peddle accounts of not only having seen UFOs but also of having been in close contact with their occupants.

Adamski's 1952 photographs of "scout craft" from a Venusian "mother ship" bore an uncanny resemblance to chicken brooders readily available from mail-order catalogues. Prior to his notoriety, Adamski had been a handyman in a four-stool California café.

Fry had an undisclosed job at New Mexico's White Sands Proving Ground when an "ovate spheroid" allegedly landed near him and whisked him to New York City and back in thirty minutes. Fry's saucer's occupants told him they were the survivors of a great war between Atlantis and Lemuria, and that they had contacted him instead of someone more highly placed because it would upset the "ego balance" of the Earth's civilizations if they were to reveal themselves.

The captain of Bethurum's "space scow" was Aura Rhanes, "queen of women," whose "smooth skin was a beautiful olive and roses." Aura's planet, Clarion, Bethurum reported, was in our solar system, but because it was always on the opposite side of the sun from us, we have never seen it.

Angelucci, an aircraft mechanic, recounted seeing a saucer land in a Los Angeles field. While inspecting it, he was told by a "space brother" that Earth's "material advancement" was threatening life's evolution. Angelucci's subsequent meetings with the aliens took place in a Greyhound bus depot.

And Menger, a self-employed sign painter, wrote of having been given a tour of the Moon's cities and other wondrous sights by his alien hosts, who subsequently informed him he had been a Jupiterian in a previous life and had been placed on Earth to do good deeds for mankind.

Not surprisingly, Hynek considered the contactees to be "pseudoreligious fanatics" with "a low credibility value" and dismissed their accounts. "It is unfortunate, to say the least," Hynek wrote, "that reports such as these have brought down upon the entire UFO problem the opprobrium and ridicule of scientists and public alike, keeping alive the popular notion of 'little green men' and the fictional atmosphere surrounding that aspect of the subject.

"The typical Close Encounter of the Third Kind," Hynek emphasized, "happens to the *same* sorts of persons who experience all other types of UFOs, representing the same cross section of the public. The experience comes upon these reporters just as unexpectedly and surprises them just as much as it does the reporters of the other types of Close Encounters. These reporters are in no way 'special.' They are not religious fanatics; they are more apt to be policemen, businessmen, schoolteachers, and other respectable citizens."[11]

The Abduction Study Conference to be held at M.I.T. would be an examination of Close Encounters of the Fourth Kind, a category Hynek seemingly had not anticipated. Such a case might be defined as one in which

> personal contact between an individual or individuals is initiated by the "occupants" of the spacecraft. Such contact may involve the transportation of the individual from his or her terrestrial surroundings into the spacecraft, where the individual is communicated with and/or subjected to an examination before being returned. Such a close encounter is usually of a one-to-two-hour duration.

The second pre-conference reading assignment was "On Stolen Time: A Summary of a Comparative Study of the UFO Abduction Mystery" by Thomas E. Bullard, Ph.D.

In this paper, privately published by the Fund for UFO Research in 1987, Dr. Bullard noted that of the nearly three hundred alien abduction cases whose locations were known, 132 came from the United States and 50 from the remainder of the English-speaking world. In addition, there were

69 cases in Latin America, 28 in continental Europe, and 3 from the Soviet Union.

Who experiences abductions? "Just about anybody," Bullard reported. "Abductees come from all walks of life, all levels of education, and all lines of work, though people whose jobs keep them outside at night run a higher risk than average. Two-thirds of abductees in this sample are male and one-third female. Out of 309 cases, 76% are single-witness cases while 49 cases include two other witnesses and 12 cases three. A remainder of 12 cases involves more than three. . . ."[12]

Bullard's most surprising discovery was that "abductions are a peril of youth. If you once pass 30 without ever being abducted," he wrote, "you have little to worry about. A periodicity shows up in the age distribution with peaks at age 7, again at 12–13, 16–17 and 20, lending support to the possibility that the captors keep tabs on a subject over the years. The range of abductions is lifelong, from infancy to age 77, but the frequency plunges in a striking way after 30."[13]

Although both the Jacobs book and the Bullard summary were considered seminal to the meeting at M.I.T., it became apparent as the conference proceeded that there was considerable disagreement as to both the import and the meaning of those abductions they describe as having taken place.

CHAPTER II

_____

At the Conference

Day One

For the Saturday, June 13, 1992, two p.m. opening of the Abduction Study Conference, John E. Mack wears a dark, loose-fitting suit, a white shirt, and a conservatively striped tie. He has been sitting sideways in a front-row seat in the large M.I.T. lecture hall in which the conference is being held, room 6-120. He is scanning the audience as it assembles, waiting until everyone is settled. I choose a row about two-thirds of the way up the steeply banked classroom. The cushioned seats fold up and down like in a theater, a small, comma-shaped writing desk lifts out of the right-hand armrest.

A few moments later, Dr. Mack rises, walks to the front of the room, and stands looking up at us. There is a triptych of green blackboards behind him, a heavy table and an overhead projector to his right. He runs his long, thin fingers through his thick, dark hair and says, "Welcome to this extraordinary event!"

Mack has the stooped posture of a tall, thin academician whose failing eyesight has left him permanently bent from having spent so much time straining to decipher his handwritten lecture notes. Mack at first speaks too fast to allow accurate transcription. I hear him say something about "our chance to bring together scholars who are working in this field" and something about distinguishing between "all the dramatic, sensationalist stuff that flows around and gets merged with this subject." And then, as if he were really seeing the assembled audience for the first time, he says with surprising emotion, "I just want to acknowledge the heroic, courageous—I won't quite say 'foolhardy,' but that was the word going through my head—work of Dave Pritchard in all of this. He has put himself on the line. . . ." And then there is something about "taking a stand" and moving "science and human thought along."

Mack remarks upon the "politics of mindset," the "politics of ontology." He has a way of answering one question with another: "Does the alien

abduction phenomenon require that we create a new scientific paradigm?"
. . . "Do we need only to stretch our minds to conceive of physical and psychological technology of which other species are capable, but that are beyond
our capacities at the present time?" . . . "Is consciousness, and all that consciousness perceives, but itself the play of some divine or cosmic technology?" He lets these questions hang in the air and sits down.

If Mack's visage is furrowed and darkened by the anguish of contemplating nuclear holocausts, his studies of suicide—real and, for his participation in a conference on people who believe they have been abducted by
alien crews from UFOs, perhaps academic—along with the inevitable
wounds and distresses that have surfaced in forty years of psychiatric practice, his co-chairman Dave Pritchard's boyish features seem as ebullient as
the forces of light upon the atoms he has studied. Pritchard's brow, beneath
its hotel-barbershop cut of gray hair, is unlined. He lopes to the front of
the hall with unbridled enthusiasm electric in his powder-blue slacks and
white short-sleeved shirt, its breast pocket filled dweeb-fashion with dif-
ferent-colored marking pens. His eyes flash behind gold wire-framed
glasses; he strides back and forth behind the desk, explaining how the conference came about, that "in trying to deal with the abduction phenomenon" he had been frustrated by "the lack of a comprehensive and sane
review." He tells us that at first he had considered writing a book, "but then
I said, 'No, that's no good, what I really want is a critical analysis and an
exploration of all the possibilities, and the best way to get it is by having a
conference with lots of discussion.' " He lifts a commonplace white plastic
kitchen timer from the table beside him and explains how each speaker will
be rigorously limited to the time allotted and that when the timer rings, he
or she must stop. He speaks a little about the funding for the conference
and how "We've tried to keep the crazies out." And then Pritchard pauses
to emphasize that while this is a conference being held *at* M.I.T. it is not
an M.I.T. conference. It is a distinction Pritchard pointedly made when
I spoke with him fourteen days before. "It's not that M.I.T. endorses
the conference," he had told me at that time, "it's that they endorse the
principle that the faculty should be given enough rope to make fools of
themselves. Many of them," he added with a little laugh, "think I'm doing
just that."

Pritchard did not disguise his nervousness over the exposure he might
get from media attending the conference. "You have to understand my reluctance to be thrown into the spotlight here," he had told me, then cor-
rected himself: "I see it more as a swimming pool full of sharks. But I'm
going to have to face this anyway. I mean, you can't keep walking down this
path without at some point it going public."

What he would be "going public" with, however, was still in question. At the time of our conversation, with only two weeks until the conference began, its organizers—Pritchard among them—were still "just trying to figure out what we would agree the characteristics of this phenomenon are," as he said. "Lots of explanations will be considered: the extraterrestrial hypothesis, individual psychoses, various kinds of collective mental phenomenon that might be culturally induced in relation to other borderline things, fantasy-prone individuals, the phenomenon's similarities to the Near-Death Experience. But as to the actual 'What are the aliens up to?,' we're not sure a third of us will even think it's aliens by the time we get to that point in the conference."

Pritchard's co-chairman John Mack, for example, had already aligned himself in print with those who argued against a simple extraterrestrial explanation for the phenomenon. In his introduction to David Jacobs's *Secret Life,* Mack had pointed out, "A literalist extraterrestrial hypothesis must account for the relative paucity of solid physical evidence—the lack of photographs of the beings, for example—and the virtually insurmountable problems related to accounting for the location, origins, and lives of the aliens themselves within the framework of the physical laws of our space/time universe."[1]

Mack's contention was not that the extraterrestrial explanation was wrong, only that it might not be enough. Right or wrong, however, the existence of the conference and its assigned reading of *Secret Life* was a solid indication that the extraterrestrial hypothesis would not be dismissed.

Following Mack's and his own opening remarks, Pritchard introduces the conference's first speaker. He is Mark Rodeghier, director of investigations for the Chicago-based J. Allen Hynck Center for UFO Studies (CUFOS), the most prominent of the UFO research organizations. Rodeghier's topic is "A Set of Selection Criteria for Abductees."

Rodeghier has been given three minutes to speak and two minutes to answer questions. While Pritchard sets the timer, Rodeghier dims the lights and moves within the shadows cast by the brilliant overhead projector. He slaps his first transparency onto the glass plate. "In order to qualify as an 'abductee,' " Rodeghier says, pausing to focus the projector's lense, "a person must be (a) taken against his or her will, (b) from terrestrial surroundings, (c) by nonhuman Beings."

He swiftly replaces his first transparency with a second. "The Beings," he says, "must take a person to (a) an enclosed place, (b) nonterrestrial in appearance, that is (c) assumed or known to be a spacecraft by the witness."

Next transparency. "In this place," Rodeghier continues, "the person must either be (a) subjected to a physical examination, (b) engaged in communication, verbal or telepathic, or (c) both."

Fourth transparency. "These experiences may be remembered (a) consciously or (b) through methods of focused concentration, such as hypnosis."

There are no questions, and Rodeghier hurries back to his seat. He was as straightforward and succinct in his presentation as a game umpire establishing the rules. He has, I realize, in fact done just that: he has spelled out what an abductee *is*.

Rodeghier is replaced by the second speaker, Thomas E. Bullard, whose presentation is an update of his now five-year-old "On Stolen Time: A Summary of a Comparative Study of the UFO Abduction Mystery."

Bullard, whom everyone calls Eddie, is best-known among "ufologists" as a cataloguer of other investigators' findings and not as an originator of new abduction material: in other words, he does not go out and find abductees and investigate their experiences himself. But Bullard is considered a "heavyweight thinker" by ufologists, and his writings on the folkloric dimensions of the UFO phenomenon are rigorously intellectual, scholarly, amusing, and concise. In addition to being a cataloguer, Eddie Bullard appears to serve another function as well: he is the movement's amanuensis and its witness.

Bullard announces that the number of cases he has catalogued since his 1987 summary has now risen to 725; but he is less rigid than Rodeghier about what should be considered an "abduction." He reports coming across about 80 cases where individuals have seen luminous or glowing orbs in their rooms; and he has also recorded what he calls "psychic abductions": lengthy narratives by people that are "close" to being abductions but are not exactly physical events. In addition, there are what he calls "voluntary entry" cases. These, too, pose a problem, since the individuals, in these instances, apparently welcome visitation, and for that reason, Bullard says, "they shade into 'contactees' in that they develop a long-term, nonprofit relationship with the aliens."

There is a slight ripple of disdainful laughter among the audience at Bullard's mention of "contactees." He smiles in acknowledgment and shares with us that there are certain cases he has had to dismiss; one such, he says, was the man who wanted to tell him "about his tour of duty with the Space Marines."

Following Bullard's presentation there is a thirty-minute coffee break in the Eastman lobby just outside the lecture hall's lower-level doors. A bronze bas-relief portrait of George Eastman is affixed to the marble wall; his nose has been polished to a high gloss by countless student caresses. I take a careful look at my fellow conference attendees. I find myself disappointed by how *normal* we appear. I cannot initially tell who among us are the abductees. But then I notice some of the assemblage are identified on their nametags only by a first name, presumably for the sake of anonymity. These individuals, it becomes clear, are the abductees.

The speaker after the break is Budd Hopkins.

Hopkins is the dean of the UFO abduction investigators, with about fifteen hundred cases to his credit. He is the author of *Missing Time* (1981) and *Intruders: The Incredible Visitations at Copley Woods* (1987); *Intruders* has just been made into a two-part television miniseries broadcast by CBS the month before. He is also a talented painter and sculptor whose works are part of the permanent collections of the Whitney, the Guggenheim, the Hirshhorn, the Brooklyn Museum, and the Museum of Modern Art.

Hopkins is a tall, gentle, silver-haired man with expressive features; his topic today is "Acquisition"—how the aliens acquire their abductees. But before he gets into that, he suggests that UFO abductions may be more common than UFO sightings and that they are "the most portentous phenomenon science has yet to face"—a pronouncement P. T. Barnum himself would have been proud to have produced.

"The acquisition most commonly takes place at night when people are sleeping," Hopkins reports. "The person is first paralyzed—although there seems to be different degrees of paralysis, people can generally move their eyes." The vast majority of abductees Hopkins has dealt with are then either lifted up a beam of light or floated up accompanied by "entities" into the awaiting spacecraft—a journey that for the most part, it seems to me, goes astonishingly unnoticed by people outside whom one might otherwise expect to witness it. Hopkins tells of an Englishman he interviewed who spoke of having been floated through closed doors. A woman reported having been floated past eleven people at a Cape Cod cocktail party; the guests were all "frozen" as if in a state of suspended animation.

Three weeks before, Hopkins says, five people were taken from a Manhattan apartment: a mother and father, their sixteen-year-old and three-year-old sons, and their elder son's sixteen-year-old friend. At the time of the abduction the little boy was sleeping in the main bed with his father, the mother was on the couch in the living room, and the two teenaged boys were sharing a bedroom. All five awoke at 4:20 a.m. with simultaneous nosebleeds. Nosebleeds, we now know from our reading of Jacobs's *Secret Life*, are a common symptom of an abduction.

During the question period someone asks Budd Hopkins what red flags might indicate an obviously disturbed person. Hopkins tells of the individual who came to see him with an abduction story and "had some of the details right" but then had added that at night, the aliens had gone into downtown Toronto and rearranged the buildings. "Common sense is a good indicator of when to stay away from a case," Hopkins concludes.

John Mack rises to point out that among the abductees who have sought his counseling, none showed a "desire to be perceived as an experiencer." (During the course of the conference "experiencer" evolves into the favored identification for an individual who has endured an abduction.) He tells of the university administrator who came to him to tell him his abduction story and, as Mack listened, became increasingly distressed. "Why are you so sad?" Mack asked. "Doctor," the administrator responded, "I had hoped you would tell me I was crazy. Now I have to deal with the fact that something real has happened to me, and that scares me! It scares me because I don't know how to deal with it and I don't know what this is!"

The next presenter, Tom Benson, a neatly dressed middle-aged UFO researcher from Trenton, New Jersey, spells out the initial sequence of events directly preceding an abduction based on approximately one hundred cases over the last forty years in which drawings by the abductees are available. "Analysis of the details," Benson says, "reveals a pattern comprised of the following stages. First, the percipient's attention is drawn to a bright light that may be flashing or pulsing, or hears an unusual sound." The saucer's "humming," Benson tells us, might serve to focus the individual's attention upon the UFO. "Is it a tool for gaining access to a person's mind prior to an abduction?" he asks.

"Second," he continues, "the object is usually noticed in close proximity. Third, the percipient has a strong urge—or even a communicated command—to move to another nearby location. Fourth, the object is seen to land. No entity is observed." Many abductees, the investigator points out, describe the saucer's color as an "orange-red" and say that its "glowing effect is both external and internal." Although the size of the lights on the disc's rim may vary, he says, it is generally agreed that they rotate counterclockwise.

"Fifth," he continues, "an entity appears. The craft may either be on the ground or hovering. Sixth, the percipient is taken on board."

Benson concludes his short presentation stating that "further research is required to test the hypothesis that a typical UFO close encounter is highly correlated with abductions—a result that has long been suspected by researchers."

David E. Jacobs, author of *Secret Life*, is next. He is to discuss what commonly happens to an abductee once he or she has been brought aboard the alien craft.

Jacobs is in his early fifties, a pink-cheeked, mustached, portly man in a carefully tailored charcoal-gray suit. He wears his tightly curled gray hair in a modified Afro, but he would not be out of place in muttonchops. He exudes an air of self-confidence which, I later learn, antagonizes some of the conference members, who read it as self-importance. He has recently completed a successful tour for *Secret Life* and has become a recognized UFO authority. But being a historian, he has also developed an academician's fervor for facts that support his point of view.

In his five years of investigation into abductions, Jacobs tells us, he has performed more than 325 hypnosis sessions with more than sixty abductees. Although the abductees for the most part did not know each other, they told strikingly similar stories containing strikingly similar details. They were abducted by small (3½ to 4½ feet tall), thin, strange-looking, grayish-colored Beings with disproportionately large heads. These Beings floated or led the abductee to an examining table upon which the individual was laid supine. The Beings then subjected their victims to a variety of "medical procedures" before returning them to the place from which they had been taken. The abductees were powerless to prevent what was happening to them; and the moment they were returned, they forgot everything, or nearly everything, that had occurred.

Jacobs reports that while listening to their stories (sometimes recalled through regressive hypnosis, at other times through conscious memories), he began to notice how "structured" the abduction scenario seemed to be: certain procedures were nearly always followed by certain other procedures. Based on this perceived structure, Jacobs tells us, he devised a "common abduction scenario matrix" consisting of three tiers: "*Primary* experiences, which involve procedures that the aliens perform the greatest number of times on the greatest number of people. *Secondary experiences,* which occur less frequently, not during every episode. Among these secondary experiences," Jacobs adds, "might be some procedures that are never performed on some abductees. The third tier I call *ancillary experiences*—those involving specialized sexual procedures or irregular procedures that happen infrequently to the abductee population as a whole."

The first tier of primary experiences, Jacobs explains, establish the framework for all those procedures that follow. These procedures begin once the individual has been taken aboard the spacecraft and laid out on a table seemingly designed specifically for the examination of human beings. Abductees, Jacobs notes, consistently described the table as roughly rectangular, unipodal, long enough to hold an adult-sized human. The lower third of the table might also be opened into a Y and slanted. Sometimes a light-scanning instrument is attached to the table, or perhaps a device for the collection of sperm.

The first stage of the primary experience is the physical examination, Jacobs explains. Abductees describe the small Beings as "probing, poking, feeling, flexing" their bodies. Part of the exam seems to commonly consist of pressing upon a prone abductee's vertebrae one by one from the top of the spine to the coccyx. At other times, the Beings' fingers dance over their captives. One of Jacobs's female abductees said it felt as though someone were "playing a piano" upon her body. Another felt they were "typewriting" on her.

Tissue samples, Jacobs reports, are generally taken during the physical examination, frequently from behind the knee. This is followed by the insertion or removal of an implant. Abductees, he tells us, report having had a narrow instrument with a tiny, round, seemingly metallic ball at its end pushed far up their noses. They would hear a crunching sound, the instrument would be withdrawn, and the ball would be missing.

"The object is as small as or smaller than a BB," Jacobs had written in *Secret Life:*

> and it is usually smooth, or has small spikes sticking out of it or has holes in it. The function of this device is unknown: It might be a locator so that the targeted individual can be found and abducted; it might serve as a monitor of hormonal changes; it might facilitate the molecular changes needed for transport and entrance. . . . Sometimes nosebleeds occur after this procedure. Both child and adult abductees have seen physicians for nosebleed problems, and have discovered odd holes inside their noses.[2]

Alternate implant locations, Jacobs tells us at the conference, are the legs, arms, and genitals, but the most common sites are the sinuses, tear ducts, and ears.

After the physical examination, the small, gray Beings step aside and are replaced by a Tall Being, who might be anywhere from a few inches to a full head taller than the Small Beings.

Whereas the Small Beings' skin is reported to be soft, poreless, with a rubbery or plastic feel to it, the Tall Beings' skin is rougher, more leathery. Neither type of Being has hair, musculature, skeletal structure, or any distinguishing marks such as warts, moles, or discolorations. For the most part, abductees describe the aliens' skin colors in varying shades of gray, from a dark gray to chalk white; if an abductee reports a different color (brown, purple, yellow, orange, blue, and green have all been mentioned), that color will most often be linked with gray: grayish blue, charcoal brown, etc.

Jacobs's abductees describe the Tall Being as having an air of authority; they often refer to the Tall Being as "the Doctor." Although the Small Beings can and do act independently of the Tall Beings, when the Tall Beings give the Small Beings an order, the Small Beings carry it out.

After the physical-examination segment of the primary experience has been completed, the taller Being commences the mental phase. "Mindscan is the focus of his attention," Jacobs says. "Nose-to-nose staring takes place."

During Mindscan, the abductee is still on the table; the Being bends over him or her, comes so close their foreheads might touch. The Being then looks deeply, penetratingly into the abductee's eyes. "The abductee may experience feelings of love, trust, calm, fear, dread," Jacobs says. Abductees commonly sense some sort of information is being extracted from their minds. What sort of information, and what is done with it, Jacobs doesn't profess to know. "It may be some sort of bonding procedure that is taking place."

During the next stage, the Tall Being might sexually arouse the abductee. "Sexual arousal is delicate to discuss," Jacobs tells us, "but profoundly important to understand." He points out that from "time to time the aliens will induce rapid, intense sexual arousal and even orgasm in a woman as part of their Mindscan procedures. Abductees typically complain, 'I hate it when they do this.' " The women feel violated, raped, angry that such a thing was done to them against their will.

When Mindscan is completed, or sexual arousal is at its peak, Jacobs continues, "the Tall Being immediately commences a set of gynecological procedures designed to collect and implant eggs, or urological procedures to remove sperm. Women feel that something is put in them. They are told, 'Now you are pregnant.' They wake up the next morning and feel pregnant. They test positive for pregnancy. It doesn't make any sense. Usually, they are abducted again and are told, 'We're taking it out now' or 'It's time now.' They feel that something is being removed from them, that they are no longer pregnant," Jacobs reports. "There is very strong anecdotal evidence to support this."

Jacobs steps down and is replaced by Yvonne Smith, an attractive hypnotherapist from La Crescenta, California. She has had two cases, she reports, involving a female and a male abductee. The female, a housewife, described a drilling sensation in the back of her head and felt her skull being opened up. She smelled a burning odor, and then her head was resealed. During the procedure she was aware of a pressure on the top of her skull, as if her head was strapped down with a band across her brow. She described a needle and a laser beam having been used inside her ear. In addition she felt a discomfort, some sort of pressure in her left eye. She could not see anything while the examination was going on because her face was half-covered.

The male, Smith tells us, is a member of the Los Angeles Police Department. He became extremely agitated describing an incision made in the back of his head.

Someone asks if, after alien physical examinations, there are any indications of healing. Smith replies, "I have an HIV-positive abductee who now tests negative."

Tests negative? Is she telling us the aliens have a cure for AIDS? Curiously, there is no follow-up question.

Jenny Randles, director of investigations for the British UFO Research Association, is up next. She has written fifteen books on UFO-related subjects. She is small, stocky, indomitable; there is something of the Miss Marple British character actress amateur detective in her stance and delivery.

Randles announces she has studied twenty-six cases documented at the end of the 1960s and during the 1970s in Great Britain—"eighteen achieved without hypnosis, eight with," she reports. "In 60 percent of the cases," she tells us, "the entities did offer some sort of explanation: they were 'conducting long-term surveillance of our planet'; they were 'making repeated visits'; they were 'collecting life profiles'; there was 'some sort of emergency coming.' " In the 1980s, Randles continues, abductees reported a building toward some sort of cosmic ecology; they were being told, "You are special. You will be called on at some future time."

Exposure to popular UFO lore in Britain is limited, she states, and confined largely to Whitley Strieber's autobiographical *Communion* and the movie *Close Encounters of the Third Kind.*

Randles concludes her short presentation saying, "Medical examinations during the 1960s were rare." She also reports that, "In Britain the smell of cinnamon is associated with the entities." (In this country, I later learn, the odors are ammonia, sulphur, lemons, and almonds.)

Randles steps down and David Jacobs returns. His presentation is a continuation of his abduction-scenario matrix taken from his book *Secret Life.* Having covered the primary experiences, he now discusses the next stage, the *secondary procedures.*

"After the abductee has undergone the physical, mental, and reproductive procedures," Jacobs says, "he or she is often subjected to a number of secondary procedures which involve mental examinations—imaging, envisioning, staging, testing—presumably designed to measure psychological reactions to prearranged scenes and situations."

During *imaging,* Jacobs explains, the Beings bring the abductee into a room separate from the examining room. There he or she is shown images on a screenlike apparatus. The images may be scenes of nuclear holocaust, environmental disaster, familial trauma; or they may be sexually charged, romantic, pleasing. While the abductee is viewing the scenes, the Tall Being stands to one side staring deeply into the person's eyes. "The focus of the aliens during the imaging," Jacobs reports, "is not the images but the emotions those images evoke. The scenes themselves do not have any prophetic value."

In *envisioning*, scenes take place not on a screen but in the viewer's mind, often while he or she is still on the examining table. The scene might involve a close friend whom the abductee is made to believe is present in the spacecraft with them. The abductee's interaction with the friend is closely studied. The "friend," however, is really a Small Being who has been made to seem like the friend in the abductee's mind.

Staging is a combination of envisioning and alien "playacting." Jacobs recounts the story of the female abductee who was made to believe that behind the "closed door of the office" her husband's boss was seated at his desk. She also was made to believe that the employer had just severely and unfairly chastised her husband. As a result, she burst into the boss's office and angrily berated him. Once she began to calm, the image of her husband's employer shimmered and disappeared. In his place were a group of Small Beings and a Tall Being observing her closely.

Occasionally an abductee is subjected to *testing;* he or she is given a task to perform and is observed carrying it out. Jacobs mentions an abductee who was placed in front of an instrument panel and told to keep some sort of needle centered between two moving red lines. In this, as in the other mental procedures, the aliens seemed interested only in studying the abductee's emotional response.

"After these secondary procedures involving mental examinations," Jacobs says, "the abductee may be walked into a special room where he or she sees scores of fetuses in the process of incubation." The fetuses may be floating upright in a liquid solution within glassy containers, or they may be horizontal "in either dry or liquid environments," Jacobs tells us. "Some abductees have reported seeing as many as one hundred fetuses gestating in this room. Others see toddlers, youths, adolescents. All seem to be hybrids, crossbreeds. We do not see 'young' Beings. When we see young adults or adolescents," Jacobs continues, "they are helping the Beings in these procedures and they look human, but they have no eyebrows."

An abductee rises to relate having seen one of the "nurse" Beings rubbing what looked like apple butter on a hybrid infant's chest; then a light came on above the child. Worried, the abductee had asked, "What are you going to do—*bake* him?"

"No," the abductee reports being told. "It helps him digest."

During the questioning period one West Coast therapist asks with a trace of exasperation, "Dave, is it always this consistent?" Jacobs replies that with abductions and UFOs everything is a matter of patterns.

Another therapist states that he has seen three dozen abductees and does not think Jacobs's scenario is the norm of his experience. Marilyn Teare, a California therapist with silver hair and a youthful face, adds to the debate that has just now seemingly surfaced between those who accept the somewhat rigid Jacobs/Hopkins/Bullard abduction-pattern scenario and those who don't. "I see a tremendous variance among my patients," she reports. "We must be careful to understand that things are not what they seem."

Someone else adds, "What is the purpose of this? We don't know what the ultimate purpose is. All our abductees ask, 'Why are they doing this?' The answer is we have no solid knowledge of why."

The conference breaks for dinner. We have been given a group rate at the Sail Loft and spill out of the lecture hall onto the M.I.T. campus, now awash in the late-afternoon sun. At the restaurant I seat myself to the right of a young Massachusetts couple who are abductees. They have a notebook filled with drawings they have made of the half-dozen different types of aliens they have encountered.

"Do these aliens have names?" I ask the wife.

"Generally, we refer to them either by their names, or by a nickname, because their language is such that we couldn't pronounce their real names," she says. "So we have agreed on nicknames or the names other human beings have already given them, and they tell me what that name is."

"Do you have any examples?"

"Do you remember Whitley Strieber, who wrote *Communion?*" she asks. "Well, we met his alien, the blue one. And the white one. Did you see that movie?"

"I'm sorry," I say, "which movie was that? *Intruders* was the only abductee movie I've seen."

She looks down at her plate pensively. "I don't think we've met any from that movie. But we're in the process of meeting an organized group of worlds that work together. And some of their names are their real names and some of them are titles. The first one we met is the head of the project, and we call him Zar."

"Zar?" I ask.

She spells it out for me, then explains, "That's the name he gave us to call him. I don't know if that's a proper name or if that's his title, but that's what everybody calls him. And the second one we met was the blue one, the same one from *Communion.* We just called him The Blue."

"How did you know he was the same one from *Communion?*" I ask.

"We thought he was right away," she says. "But later we were told that he was."

"Who told you?"

"Zar did, I think."

"And did you just call him 'Blue'? Or was he 'The Blue'?"

"When we met him we were just saying 'The Blue One' to differentiate between who we were talking about as opposed to Zar. We didn't really think they had names, so we just called the white one 'The White One' or 'The White.' But when we met the next one we found out that he did have a name and we went back and wanted to know what to call The Blue. He said 'The Blue' as a proper name was okay, he was happy with that, and that it was fine to call him that."

"And when you talk to the white one, what do you call him?"

"The White," she says matter-of-factly.

" 'The White,' " I say, an inadvertent bubble of laughter escaping my lips.

"Those aren't their real names," she adds. "And they aren't titles, either. They're just sort of reference names."

"What are some of the others?"

"There are a lot of others. I don't feel comfortable just rattling off names, because they're personalities. These Beings are important to us. We are dealing with an organization. The difference between what we've found so far and what we've found with other people is that we are aware of dealing with an organization of worlds—not unlike our own UN, where people from different countries work together and try to get along together. The aliens out there have been doing it much longer and are much better at it."

"Is this the 'project' you mentioned earlier?"

"Yes, it is. And Zar, like I said, is the head of the project. And then we systematically started to meet other alien Beings. And we found that some of the ones we were meeting were members of a council. They sit on a council not unlike a school board. Everything that goes on in the project goes through the Council. It's very organized and very diligent."

"Is the Council all different types of aliens?"

"We've met many different types. We've also seen others who look just like them on their ships, their crews and their families."

"Who's got the haddock?" a waitress asks.

While we are eating, the woman tells me about the afternoon her husband saw a bright light emanating from within their garage. "That was the first experience," she says. "He was by himself. It wasn't until a couple of weeks later that somebody else saw that very, very bright light with him. There was a doorway cut out of the air—there was no door frame, just a doorway shape—and behind it, through it, he could see that there was a room within that bright light. And that room, he later found out, was actually a room on a ship—which is just a science and technology above what we commonly know."

She tells me their four children, ranging in age from three to fifteen, have "open relationships" with the aliens. "They're all experiencers," she says. "The two girls are not as aware of it as the boys are, because the boys are older, and because we only became aware of this while the boys were young. So the girls remember a little of it, but it's important that they can still do their day-to-day lives without being overly interfered with."

"How many experiences have you had?" I ask her.

"We have daily contact. It started when we were children," she says. "Two years ago we first became aware of it. And looking back on our lives, we realized it had been happening our whole lives and we just didn't realize what it was. That's what happens to most people," she adds. "Two years ago we realized we were meeting with an organization of thirty worlds. And that organization is growing. I don't know how many it is now."

"Do you and your husband sit on the Council, or are you just there as visitors?"

"No. The Council is made up of physical Beings. There are Beings of light, too, but every Being on the Council has to be physical. They're from different worlds, and none of them are human. There's nine of them. And we've met about fifteen different worlds."

"Any idea where these worlds are?"

"I have an idea where one of them is," she says. "Zar said that when he was a ball of energy—he doesn't have a physical body; in his raw form he's energy—he said he could travel at greater-than-light speeds by himself without a ship and reach his star in eleven days. He lives not on a planet but a star. That sounds really far out, I know, but you should hear some of the other stuff!"

"That" and "the other stuff" is what I've come to the conference to hear.

After dinner, I take the long way back to the M.I.T. campus. At the President's House, on the corner of Ames Street and Memorial Drive, I turn right, past the tennis courts and the library, so that I can stroll along the Cambridge side of the Charles. I turn right again, away from where the Harvard Bridge spans the river, past the Henry L. Pierce Engineering Laboratory and the Pratt School of Naval Architecture, then climb the marble steps and pass between the double row of marble columns and through the doors of 77 Massachusetts Avenue, the main entrance to the long corridor that connects the Rogers, Homberg, and Macleurin buildings to the Eastman Laboratories, in which our lecture hall is situated.

I walk past deans' offices and a door lettered in goldleaf DEPT. OF ALCOHOL DISTRIBUTION, OTTUS VAN STUBBLE, his shade discreetly drawn. I pause at a huge framed tribute to Norbert Weiner, who graduated from high school at eleven, cum laude from Tufts at fourteen, and was a mathematician and philosopher on the M.I.T. faculty for forty-five years. Finally I reach the end of the corridor and turn right to the marble Eastman lobby with its bronze bas-reliefs of Huygens, Newton, Rumford, Fresnel, and Galileo on one wall, and on the opposite, Voyle, Lavoisier, Wöhler, Jabir, Ko Hung, Zosimos, Cannizzaro, and Mendeleyev.

I had taken this walk because it seemed important to me to remind myself I was in the center of one of America's great scientific universities. I had come to M.I.T. determined to be objective, open-minded; but during dinner I had had to fight the steadily growing conviction that my abductee dinner companion was crazy as a loon. As I joined the others milling about the lobby before the lecture hall's doors, I steeled myself to remain nonjudgmental. Zar, I told myself, would want that.

The first speaker after dinner is one of the up-and-coming hypnotherapists in the abduction field: John S. Carpenter, a thin, balding, thirty-seven-year-old Menninger Clinic–trained, licensed clinical social worker working in Springfield, Missouri, where he provides individual, marital, family, and group therapy for hospitalized psychiatric patients.

Carpenter interests me. Unlike some of the other investigator/therapists attending the conference, he seems not to have any specific agenda. He simply reports what he has seen without attempting to evaluate or interpret its significance. I subsequently learn that Carpenter has worked closely with a number of other psychiatrists in trying to treat a host of psychiatric maladies, including Multiple Personalities and other dissociative disorders, and through hypnotism has achieved many positive and lasting changes.

Carpenter had only a passing interest in the UFO phenomenon until he read of psychiatric professionals who were employing hypnosis to unlock the memories masked by the amnesia so commonly encountered in individuals who had reluctantly come forward to report having observed a UFO. Carpenter, like John E. Mack, had become "intrigued" that these individuals' stories seemed "remarkably alike from persons so vastly different in their backgrounds." In 1988 Carpenter volunteered his psychiatric experience and hypnotic skills in the service of investigating these UFO reports.

"Although I thought I might manage to participate in at least one interesting case," Carpenter later wrote,

> I fully expected to have to wade through a variety of psychological issues first—including fantasies of hysterical individuals, dramatic confabulations from Borderline Personality Disorders, dissociative episodes as with Multiple Personalities, attention-seeking antics of sociopathic characters, intricately-woven psychodynamics of those traumatized in childhood, and the space-age delusions of insecure individuals, influenced by extraterrestrial themes and speculations in all of the media.

But "to my astonishment," Carpenter admitted, "none of these expectations has become valid in my research so far." Carpenter had interviewed schoolteachers, policemen, businessmen, college professors, and community leaders who claimed to have had abduction experiences, and, as he wrote, he had "found no psychopathology which would even begin to explain these reports."[3]

In his presentation to those of us gathered after dinner back in the huge M.I.T. lecture hall, Carpenter, wearing a short-sleeved shirt and tie but no jacket, delivers a brief report on a case of his, that of "Eddie," a twenty-year-old male abductee who, while already in therapy with Carpenter to explore his past abduction experiences, had an additional abduction encounter. In the course of that abduction Eddie's color blindness was allegedly cured by the aliens.

"During a physical examination by the Beings, Eddie's right eye was removed. He felt it pulled out and replaced," Carpenter reports. "Afterwards there was a redness, a physical soreness. He did not feel they were implanting anything behind his eye, only that they were 'fixing' him. The side benefit of this operation appears to be enhanced colors. The procedure was clearly for their purposes, not for Eddie's, but the partial accidental cure of his lifelong color blindness was a side effect." Carpenter is in possession of a statement from Eddie's doctor attesting to his having had "a green lack and now having a blue-yellow." What was "profound color blindness," Carpenter relates, "had improved up to green color blindness." He returns to his seat.

Like Yvonne Smith, the California hypnotherapist who earlier had reported an HIV-positive abductee who now tested negative, Carpenter, too, seems to have come across a miraculous cure.

––––––––

Eddie Bullard, the cataloguer of UFO lore, steps to the podium again to report on "The Rarer Abduction Episodes"—those in which conferences, tours of the spacecraft, worldly and otherworldly journeys, or theophanies occur before the abductee is returned.

Although the Beings seem "uptight, businesslike during the exams," Bullard says, "they are more relaxed afterwards." During these postexamination conferences, Bullard reports, the aliens are "all talk (telepathic) and no action. Beings ask the abductee a question, then let the abductee ask one, although their questions are rarely answered. Or the Beings give peculiar responses and tell everybody a different story. "For example," Bullard continues, "to the abductees' question 'Where do you come from?' the Beings have answered, 'A small galaxy near Neptune,' 'A hundred and sixty-three million miles away,' or 'We come from a small planet of no particular significance.' To the question 'What are you doing here?' they say, 'We're to bring back data on human emotion.' Sometimes they give warnings or prophecies about the future of the Earth—"*but*," Bullard emphasizes, "*none of these prophecies have ever come true!*"

Another rare episode might include a journey. "Sometimes witnesses report being carried to another place," Bullard states. "This other world is either dark, dim, with an occupied city lit by a red sun, or it is a desolate, subterranean, self-contained environment. These journeys take place in an instant: gone post-breakfast, back before dinner." Bullard pauses, then asks, "What are we dealing with? Alternate realities? Universes around the country? Could these be 'staging' or 'imaging' procedures? Sometimes, in fact *often,* the aliens give false and misleading information. Or it's a complete fantasy. Or the abductees understand wrong. The misinformation may be due to the fact that messages are transmitted telepathically and not verbally."

Bullard is questioned about his "well-ordered abductions": "Do you and Dave Jacobs have the same scheme? Or is it a different scheme?"

"Examination, capture, return seem parallel in widespread episodes," Bullard replies. "Certainly the same things seem to be going on, but we may not have them necessarily in the same order. There are two distinct differences. The Mindscan and Staring procedures—Dave Jacobs had it; I failed to recognize it. The baby presentation," he continues, "aliens curled up asleep in bottles—I found that less prevalent than Dave did. And I know of only a few reported cases where children were seen running around the ship."

Jacobs steps again to the front of the lecture hall. In recognition of this being his third and final appearance as a presenter at the conference, he opens by joking, "Well, after this talk you won't have Dave Jacobs to kick around anymore."

His talk is on the physical description of the aliens. According to Jacobs the vast majority of the descriptions of the aliens by abductees are consistent with one another—the most common type being what has come to be called at this conference the "Small Grays."

A Small Gray is 3½ to 4½ feet tall, with an overly large head, its bulging cranium tapering down to a pointed or near-nonexistent chin. Small Grays are smooth featured, although some seem to have a "furrowed brow." They have no hair on their heads or their bodies, leathery skin, no ears (which, Jacobs adds, is "consistent with telepathy"), a slightly raised ridge of a nose with two nostrils, and a lipless slit-mouth that does not move. "The most striking feature," Jacobs says, "are the two large black eyes: they are enormous and compelling." They do not blink, or seem to move in their sockets. These eyes come in various shapes, but most common are the large, almond-shaped, pupil-less, cornea-less, iris-less, wet-looking, all-black, wrap-around eyes which a few abductees think might actually be a covering for an eye within—like goggles.

The aliens' bodies are flat, paunchless. Their chests are not bifurcated; they have no nipples. Nor does the chest swell or diminish with breathing. "Even with the nose-to-nose Mindscan," Jacobs says, "no one has felt any breath on his or her face, and they do not seem to be air-breathing Beings."

The lower part of their anatomy does not contain any stomach pouch or genitals; it just comes to an end. "We don't know how they reproduce," Jacobs comments. "They have no hips. There is no triangulation to the body as there is with humans. Instead, it seems to form just a straight line down all the way to the ground."

The Small Gray's body appears frail, with thin limbs and no musculature or bone structure. There are no "knees" or "elbows" as such, and legs are the same diameter from the top of the thigh to the bottom of the calf. Nor are there clearly defined "ankles" or "wrists." "Small Grays have three or four long, thin fingers with pads at the ends," Jacobs tells us. "Frequently abductees report seeing only three fingers; and if there is an opposable thumb it is not immediately apparent."

From the back the Beings have "no buttocks, no bifurcation," Jacobs continues, "just a ridge that marks the end of the trunk. Males and females look alike; but abductees seem to sense who the females are because they are more gentle and graceful."

Abductees see no eating quarters, sleeping quarters, no evidence of food or drink aboard the crafts. "What do we make of this?" Jacobs asks, then answers, "A humanlike figure which under its skin is very, very different. They do not appear to breathe or ingest food or water."

Someone from the audience remarks, "Everything you have described sounds more like machinery than biology." Another adds, "Maybe that little horizontal ridge on their bottoms is where they change the batteries." His comment is greeted with punchy laughter; it is nearly ten p.m.

"Are the larger aliens the intelligence behind it?" someone asks. "Could the Small Grays be robots?"

"Both Beings seem able to make decisions and do," Jacobs replies. "They both deal with crises. They both act like sentient Beings that are, perhaps, biologically based."

The next speaker is Joe Nyman, a Boston-area hypnotherapist, whose topic is "The Familiar Entity and Dual Reference."

The "familiar entity" is a reasonable enough concept—that is, if one is able to accept that *anything* said so far at this conference is not totally off-the-wall. Abductees, Nyman suggests, see the same Being again and again. Zar, for example, would presumably be my earlier dining companion's familiar entity. But the "dual reference" premise is startling.

" 'Dual reference,' " Nyman explains, "is a term that has been coined to describe unexpected imagery articulated by experiencers in latent-encounter investigations." He is referring to images that the experiencer has of himself or herself as being "of the same form and kind as those conducting the en counter."

Is Nyman telling us that the abductee, too, is an alien—or may have been one in a previous life or lives?

"The abductee," Nyman says, "tends to see him- or herself engaged in long-term experiences."

Before reading from a May 1989 hypnotic-regression session transcript of a case of a young man who recalls being watched in the woods as a child by aliens, Nyman discloses that the young man thought he was one of them. " 'They're looking at me from behind the trees,' " Nyman reads. " 'They are watching me. I see their faces. I think they want me to come. . . . They touch me! . . . Maybe it's all in my mind. *They've got me!* They're all touching me!'

"I ask him, 'Where do you go?' " Nyman says.

" 'Into a sphere of light! It's all white!' "

Nyman mentions another of his subjects, who recalls being in his crib looking through its bars. A tall figure was leaning over looking at him. "Two aliens are holding this jar," the witness told Nyman. "It has a light in it and I am the light!"

I am mystified. Is Nyman saying that to be an alien is to be some form of light?

During the question period one of the therapists attending the conference accuses Nyman of "leading" his patients during hypnosis. "Are you a psychologist, Joe?" the therapist asks him.

"No, I'm an engineer," Nyman responds.

The young thirty-something-ish woman on my left wears only her first name, "Mary," on her nametag. She whispers to me that she was one of Nyman's abductees and went back into hypnotic regression with him. What she saw, she said, she wasn't willing to tell him—not until she felt safe.

"What did you see?" I ask.

Mary shakes her head. She certainly won't tell me, either.

John Carpenter returns to the podium. According to the program he will speak on "Other Types of Aliens."

"Although the gray aliens may be the most commonly reported and/or discussed variety of extraterrestrial entity," Carpenter says, "there may be other types worth mentioning. There is a growing consistent pattern of data in regard to what some refer to as the 'Tall Blond' or 'Nordic type.' He is six to seven feet tall, handsome, with blond shoulder-length hair. His blue eyes are kind and loving. He is paternal, watchful, smiling, affectionate, youthful, all-knowing, and wears a form-fitting uniform. This Robert Redford/Scandinavian type," he says, smiling, "is like a guardian angel. They have been seen on board with the Small Grays.

"In addition to the Grays and the Scandinavian type, there is a third type," Carpenter continues, "a smooth, lizard-skinned, reptilian, six-to-eight-foot-tall creature with a somewhat dinosaurish face. It has a four-clawed hand with brown webbing between the fingers. This reptile type has catlike eyes with gold, slit pupils. This Being is sinister and deceptive in manner, half human and half reptile."

Carpenter points out that although both the Reptilian and Nordic types could arguably be psychodynamic in origin, the slowly emerging pattern of data does not support this interpretation as yet.

He asks the audience how many have heard of, or seen, the tall, blond type. Hands shoot up all over the lecture hall.

"Who has heard of, or seen, the Reptilians?" he asks. About half as many hands are raised.

During the questioning period Jenny Randles reports that the "guardian-angel types are popular in Britain."

A therapist says she has a six-year-old subject who has seen reptiles for years.

And an abductee rises to report that a six-foot Nordic type tried on her high-heeled shoes.

Her comment undoes me! *What possible reason could the woman have to make up an incident like that?*

My response to this detail of the high-heeled shoes is the same as the reaction I had to the incident in the Barney and Betty Hill story where, because of Barney's false upper plate, the aliens had pulled on his wife's teeth. Neither of these details strikes me as the sort one could expect a victim to have fabricated.

Eddie Bullard replaces Carpenter at the front of the lecture hall to continue with an even greater "Variety of Abduction Beings."

"Out of the 203 cases in which beings are described," he says, "137 are humanoid, 52 human, and 14 nonhuman." Most humanoids, he continues, are the familiar kind: "tall, blond Nordic types working with the most common Small Grays, but some are mummy types, Michelin-man types. Others are hairy dwarfs, or trolls."

Abductees, he says, describe the gray alien faces as looking like those of grasshoppers and praying mantises. The Nordics have "vivid blue eyes," Bullard reports, and adds, "They all seem to look alike!" Clones?

He makes the interesting point that among those Beings seen by abductees, "genuine monsters are scarce and concentrated in the less reliable cases. If Hollywood is responsible for these images," Bullard asks, "where are the monsters? Where are the robots?"

Mary, seated next to me, nods and says, "*Yes!*"

Martha Monroe, from nearby Framingham, next shows slides of "New Types of Aliens." Her presentation strikes me as patently ridiculous. Her first slide depicts what she calls a "Spock type" after Leonard Nimoy's *Star Trek* character. The Spock figure in the slide, she says, is a self-portrait drawn by a Dual Referencer who believes he was an alien. "There is a 'Court Jester,' " she says, throwing up the next slide, a Being with a heart-shaped head. Someone else, she tells us, had a "familiar entity with a head shaped like a football," then adds, "Eared entities also function telepathically." Next slide: "This is a Cloaked Being," she reports. "Cloaks and capes come up quite a lot. . . . The hooded entity seems to be an authority figure."

During the question period someone rises to report that in France there have been "fifty-four instances of a silver-suited variety seen."

Someone else rises to take issue with Jacobs, whose aliens seem confined largely to Small Grays and Taller Beings and who has imposed "too narrow a restriction on the type of information. There are growing, evolving energy types." Conference co-chairman John Mack agrees. He points out that "rigorous scientific evaluation at this point is impossible. Do not screen out *any* possibilities," he insists.

The Saturday session ends at 10:30 p.m. I scoop up my notes and head out into the night. A cool breeze is blowing down the Charles River as I start across Harvard Bridge to my hotel on the Boston side.

As I cross the bridge, downtown Boston, to my left, is alight; to my right the brilliant, bubbling lights of the Citgo sign brighten the western nighttime sky. I walk aware of my ambivalence about the conference. Maybe it's fatigue, but I feel that my open mind is beginning to close and that the first seeds of disappointment have been sown.

Is it because of my resistance to quasi-scientific efforts to present a topic that seems to defy reason? I am naturally suspicious of men who use numbers to shore up irrational conclusions. When Eddie Bullard begins to catalogue the numbers of alien types and abduction reports—rare or otherwise—I am reminded of Nixon's speeches as President to justify the invasion of Cambodia and Laos.

I am leery, too, of Dave Jacobs's attempts to impose a historian's order on what, to me, appears utterly chaotic: the abductees' efforts to come to grips with what they believe has happened to them. And John Mack hasn't impressed me much, either. So far, his most telling comment has been "If this *isn't* happening, what *is* happening?"

So it isn't the scientists, the historians, the intellects, the researchers who interest me—not yet. It is the abductees. There is my dinner companion and her familiar entity, Zar. There is Mary from the conference, whose sharp exhalations and groans at Nyman's doubters are indications of how emotionally she is involved. There are a couple of male abductees I hope to talk to at some later point.

But the most interesting are two women from Maryland, Alice and Carol. During the coffee break I had sat on a stone bench outside the Eastman lobby with them while they smoked. I introduced myself and saw them freeze at learning I was "media." They were both clearly scared to death—not by me, I am quite sure, but by what they were learning at the conference.

Their terror was heartfelt, real, and so palpable and raw I am concerned for their emotional well-being.

CHAPTER III

At the Conference

Day Two

I am sitting alone at a small table in my Boston hotel having breakfast when Dave Jacobs enters the dining room and sits with me. We are then joined by Robert Bigelow, the Las Vegas entrepreneur who is one of the financial backers of this conference.

Budd Hopkins, Jacobs tells me, has investigated about 1,500 cases; he himself has studied about 350; John Carpenter and John Mack have studied approximately 50 cases each.

"The numbers are very important," Jacobs stresses, then adds ruefully, "But if you study this phenomenon, your reward is ridicule from your colleagues." He hesitates for a moment, as if in acknowledgment of the risk, then reconsiders his appraisal. "No," he says, "it's the reward of discovery, and the thought that you are doing something important—in a therapeutic sense. People who come to me feel relieved. When a person walks into my office, it may involve four to five hours. By the time it ends, I'm fairly certain of what they think happened to them. Some abductees go into a New Age group or channeling. It's a normal psychological dissociative state. For some of them that makes sense. Channeling is almost always happy. It lends the feeling that one is part of a grand philosophical design. But Budd Hopkins, John Mack, and myself are the end of the line. Those who have *proper* analysis," he says, "think the abductions are a catastrophic, disastrous relationship for them."

I ask Bigelow what he thinks is happening. He responds matter-of-factly, "Either it's a new psychiatric phenomenon, or it's true." It is the answer of a man who has spent his life studying the odds.

Budd Hopkins enters the dining room and joins us, too. While we are finishing our coffee Hopkins tells an astonishing story about a woman who was lifted from her bed at 3:15 in the morning and floated out of her twelfth-story Manhattan apartment building's closed living-room window into a hovering spacecraft. She was seen rising up a beam of light by two separate carloads of witnesses, Hopkins says. One witness was a woman whose automobile had been disabled as the UFO hove into view; her car's headlights had flickered and gone out, its engine had died, and she had coasted to a stop on the Brooklyn Bridge. The other witnesses were "an important international figure and his two security agents," who were driving up South Street near the East River when their car's mechanical equipment, too, had failed.

"Since these abductions, I gather, are not normally witnessed," I say, "Why do you think these people—the important international figure, particularly—were permitted to see it?"

Hopkins responds, "I think it was a deliberate sign."

I start to ask him more questions, but he holds me off, saying that he is going to discuss the case in detail the following day.

As the four of us make our way across the Harvard Bridge to the morning's first conference session, joggers puff by and bicyclists dodge young skaters on Rollerblades. The city is alive; buses wheeze past, private helicopters thud overhead. Below us, on the river, a cormorant, balancing on a small rock to spread its wings to dry, warily watches the single-man shell sculling against the current toward him. As I take in the world around me, I suddenly realize I am making what psychologists at the conference refer to as a "reality check."

The Sunday session begins sharply at 8:00 a.m. with a quick review of what is missing from the alien craft. The ships have no bathrooms, beds, or kitchens. There are no decorations, no "photos from home." It is noted that the aliens don't seem to eat or sleep, get angry or joke.

The next speaker is John G. Miller, a board-certified emergency physician practicing in the Los Angeles area. Miller looks to be in his early forties. He has dark, neatly brushed hair and a kind face. His quiet, modest, somewhat shy and questioning demeanor is surprising considering the bedlam and trauma I presume he is immersed in at his job.

"As a physician," Miller begins, "the most consistent impression I get from accounts of alleged alien examination techniques and 'medical' procedures, whether from written reports or my own witnesses, is that I'm not hearing about our kind of medicine. I mean *our* kind of medicine in the broadest sense: modern terrestrial medicine. The most consistent feature in these reports is the *difference* between reported alien techniques and procedures and our own.

"'The differences," he continues, "are great enough to invalidate any theory of the origin of these reports that is based on the idea that they somehow originate in the witnesses' own past medical experience or knowledge."

The doctor's point, I feel, is an important one. If the abductees' stories of the "medical procedures" carried out upon them by the aliens were a screen memory for previous traumatic surgery, or a fantasy stemming from their own unconscious, the procedures would not be so foreign to terrestrial medical procedures.

Miller observes that the alien physical examination tends to ignore the cardiovascular, respiratory, lymphomatic, and internal systems from the umbilicus to the thorax. "They seem for the most part unconcerned about the upper abdominal contents, including the liver, spleen, stomach, and pancreas," Miller says, "which are often of great concern to the human physician. . . ." In other words, the aliens seem to have no interest whatsoever in the major life-sustaining components of our bodies.

"By most accounts the cranium is a great focal point of the aliens' exam," Miller continues. "But their techniques are strange! We human doctors don't generally stand at the periphery of our patients' visual field and stare at them. We have no Mindscan procedures; we have to ask questions. . . .

"As some systems are seemingly shortchanged by the aliens, the dermatologic type [of exam] seems grossly exaggerated. Aliens are often reported to inspect the entire skin surface minutely. Additionally, they are reported to become startled or agitated when they find scars or new marks.

"Although female witnesses frequently report gynecologic-type exams by the aliens," Miller continues, "I don't recall ever hearing a witness report of a bimanual pelvic exam, the absolute mainstay of the human gynecological exam."

Miller tells of cases where needle marks reportedly appear overnight, "some in a triangular formation." But I don't get the impression that he himself has seen this.

Miller spends some time discussing the abductees' stories of needles being inserted in their navels, similar to what had been reported thirty years earlier by Betty Hill. And he distinguishes between the alien device and the contemporary Earth laparoscope, which "is much greater in diameter than a mere needle" and "requires a small incision to insert."

Miller points out that he has never heard of aliens using gloves, tongue depressors, EKGs. "Everywhere you look in these abductees' accounts," he continues, "they are fundamentally different from human medicine. These stories are not merely those of human medical techniques seen through the distorted mirror of dreams or fantasies. At every turn, the aliens' alleged modus operandi is fundamentally different from human practice. This suggests to me," he concludes, "that these stories do not arise from the medical experience or knowledge of the witnesses."

Miller is replaced by Joe Nyman, whose previous presentation had been on familiar entities and dual references. This time he discusses the "composite encounter model" he has worked out to describe the abductees' psychological stages during an abduction.

"In working with people over the last fourteen years as they attempted to relive their latent encounter experiences," he reports, "similar images emerged that could be grouped as states of mind." He places a transparency on the overhead projector listing four psychological stages in the abductees' states of mind:

  1. Anxious anticipation of something unknown. Forewarning.
  2. Transition of consciousness from one's normal awake state.
  3. Psycho-physical imposition and interaction.
  4. Overlay of positive feelings and reassurance.

Nyman gives as an example of the first stage a witness making excuses to leave a gathering. "She arrives home and goes through the rooms of her house looking for someone, looking out the windows. She feels a sense of urgency, a sense that someone is coming or that something is going to happen. It is a premonition," he says, "that something is going to happen in a very short time."

During the second stage, Nyman continues, the witness "notices the presence of lights in the room that become a figure," or lights outside. He or she may have an out-of-body experience or become "caught in a beam of UFO light." The transition, he says, can be described as "unusual phenomenon marking changes of consciousness from the normal awake state."

During the third stage, Nyman says, the psycho-physical imposition and interaction is similar to what Dave Jacobs reported, but may also include emergency procedures to correct implants.

Once the physical procedures are completed, Nyman says, "stage four begins: the overlay of positive feelings and reassurance. A sense of source and purpose is given. A 'positive bias' is imposed to make the memory a positive experience." He gives as examples a tour of the ship, a trip to the "nursery" or to an alien landscape, a screen viewing, a meeting with the Council.

"The aliens may become involved in the witness's mission," Nyman says, "such as healing, restoring, health-making through crystals."

Could Nyman be New Age?

He replaces his first transparency with a second:

5. Transition of consciousness to normal waking.

6. Rapid forgetfulness of most or all memory of the experience.

7. The marker stage.

8. The cycle interval.

"The final stages," Nyman says, "are: (5) Transition of consciousness to normal waking—an after-sense of fear or pleasure or happiness or longing. (6) Rapid forgetting of most, or all memory of the experience. (7) The marker stage: what little is remembered is remembered as an incongruity, with unresolved conscious memories and repetitive dreams. And (8) the cycle Interval. These experiences are repetitive, lifelong," he concludes. "The cycle may be as short as one day, as long as one year, or years."

During the question period an investigator rises to point out that at the onset of an encounter, "dogs may bark wildly, then cut off. The dog won't be the same for weeks. It may not go into the room from which the abduction took place."

Budd Hopkins follows Nyman with the observation that although the procedure for returning the abductee to his or her normal environment is usually similar to that of the abduction itself, "sometimes they make unusual mistakes that can present the abductee with a puzzling set of anomalous circumstances." Quoting Murphy's Law, "If anything can go wrong, it will," Hopkins explains that a person might not be returned to exactly the same place, and gives as an example a case of his where a woman was taken from her bedroom and returned to the middle of the woods almost a mile away from home. Her feet, at that time, were not tender. But when she had made her way back to her house, finding her way slowly and returning freezing cold, her feet were badly bruised and cut.

Another of Hopkins's cases: A five-year-old girl awakens outside her house screaming that she had been taken into a "big machine in the yard." All the doors in the house are locked, deadbolted from the inside. Her mother asks her how she got out. The child responds she was taken through the walls.

Jenny Randles tells about an English police officer who was abducted in his patrol car and then he and the car were returned upside-down on a narrow country road.

Hopkins tells of an individual returned in his car to the woods with no tire tracks to show how it had arrived there.

Jacobs rises to tell of one of his cases, where a woman awoke in her car in the middle of a cornfield with no crushed or broken stalks to indicate where she had driven in or out. She sat looking around, then suddenly fell back asleep. When she came to, she was turning into her driveway. "The aliens had made a mistake," Jacobs says, "and set it right."

"These are very much in the small minority of cases," Hopkins adds, "maybe in the range of 4 to 5 percent." He concludes by saying there is a "paucity of physical traces of mistakes, but mental trace-cues are always there to point out to a witness that they have been through an abduction experience."

John Carpenter returns to discuss the "Resolution of Phobias from UFO Data." A phobia, he explains, is "a psychological problem which reaches deeply into a person's emotional feelings. It neither develops nor vanishes without a significant emotional experience attached." To treat a phobia successfully, Carpenter says, one must focus directly on its source.

He tells of a female patient of his who, at four years old, had developed a phobia about her dolls: she thought they "moved at night." The following day she had all her dolls destroyed. Even as an adult, she could not permit her daughter to have dolls. During hypnotic regression, Carpenter explains, it was revealed that "this intense trauma arose from confusing memories of being with hybrid children aboard a UFO, one of whom, she believes, was evidently her hybrid sister." Carpenter points out that, interestingly, his patient had not heard about hybrid children prior to this realization. Once she recognized the source of her phobia, the woman "felt more comfortable and was able to feel good about dolls."

He concludes his presentation saying, "To get to the cause of the phobia is how you help them to get on with their lives."

Across the aisle from me Alice and Carol, the two women from Maryland, are urgently whispering together.

John Miller, the California emergency physician, follows Carpenter. "In my day-to-day practice of emergency medicine, the question of why a person decides they are ill and needs to be seen in an emergency department is often one of the key features of a case. Some cases are, of course, self-evident," Miller says, "e.g., a broken leg. But in a person with some ongoing, long-term medical condition, this issue is often especially important as a source of information about the case.

"In abduction cases," he continues, "I think it is likewise important to try to determine what caused the person to come to the belief that they have been abducted by nonhuman Beings. The answer to this question varies in the cases I have seen, but I think there may be some rough patterns—especially if the witness can identify a discrete moment of special insight. I have come to regard this moment of development of insight as the *Realization Event*, or RE: that event or moment that forces a person to suspect or decide that they have had an abduction experience." Such an event, Miller reports, can be triggered by physical signs: recent scars, bruises, punctures that provide the witness "with personally tangible evidence that something strange *did* happen," Miller says.

Prior to the Realization Event, Miller continues, an abductee may have been able to explain away "a lifetime of strange experiences" as having been dreams, or may have rationalized the experiences in such a way as to make them appear normal. But after the RE the reality of the experiences forces its way into the abductee's consciousness, and the individual, newly aware, "may experience a sudden flood of previously unrecalled abduction memory fragments that provoke anxiety and a desire to explore these further."

Miller gives as an example a case of his, a young woman whom he calls Annie J., who awoke while floating down onto her couch with a tall alien standing over her. The moment she touched the couch the Being disappeared. She got up feeling "unclean," "anxious," and saw that it was now two-plus hours later than when she had glanced at the clock "a moment earlier."

Annie J. would have passed off this episode as just another bad dream, Miller points out, "until she stepped into the shower and discovered a large, painful bruise on her left hip. The mark had three sets of two possible puncture wounds over it. This was her realization event," Miller declares. "Suddenly she couldn't make the 'dream' be a dream anymore."

Annie J. searched her house looking for a table or countertop she might have struck herself on to have caused the bruise, but none was at the right height. At that point "a lifetime of strange memory fragments and images flooded over her and she felt she was now facing a horrible reality she had always avoided in the past. She experienced severe anxiety and panic-attack-like symptoms."

The realization experience might also be triggered by exposure to other witnesses, Miller says. Annie J. discussed what had happened with her roommate, who "recalled fragmentary memories of small alien beings and odd nocturnal events such as awakening to find the bedroom filled with blinding blue light and feeling fear, which was immediately replaced by a profound sense of calm and the awareness 'It's all right. This is for Annie; it's not for me.'" After Annie J. and her roommate had thoroughly discussed these occurrences, the roommate "came to believe she, too, had experienced abduction-type events. This was her realization experience."

REs can also be triggered by exposure to books and movies and as a result of hypnosis, Miller points out. He discusses a subject, "Rob," who has always been aware of his abduction experiences and who felt that his childhood friends, "Jack" and his sister "Sue," had had experiences, too. Jack "had long suspected he had had abduction experiences," Miller explains, "but his conscious memory was only that of an afternoon close encounter with a disc device, with possible missing time, as he and Sue walked home one day from school." Many years later Jack decided, after talking with Rob, to seek hypnotic regression. "What emerged," Miller declares, "was a typical abduction experience in which Sue was aboard also." Jack's Realization Event was the result of his hypnosis.

Sue, as an adult, "has become a highly religious person," Miller says, "and believes these experiences were caused by demonic forces. She will not discuss these events with anyone. She has had no RE, but understands her apparent experiences in a way that feels safe to her."

During the coffee break in the Eastman lobby I overhear one woman abductee describing to another the ball of light that had entered her bedroom and turned into a Being. "I said to the Being, 'I'm glad you're here,' " she tells the other woman. " 'I want to ask you something. Where are you from?' "

The Being, taking her hands in his, did not answer.

"Do you come from a different time?" she asked him.

"No, it's the same time," the Being responded.

"How can that be?"

"If we were home now," the Being told her, "you would understand."

"Does that mean I come from somewhere else?"

According to the woman, the Being evidently did not—or would not—answer her.

The first speaker after the coffee break is Keith Basterfield, the research officer for UFO Research Australia. A thoughtful, amiable, thin, dark-haired man without any obvious Australian accent, Basterfield proposes that a correlation may exist between UFO events (including abductions) and paranormal phenomena such as poltergeists, apparitions, and psychic healing.

Witnesses, he reports, appear to have "an incredible history of psychic phenomena which might explain why they were abducted." The question, he suggests, is "chicken and egg": Are people abducted because they have a long history of psychic ability, or is the psychic ability the result of a long history of being abducted? Is a certain type of person more likely to have paranormal and abduction experiences?

Basterfield mentions an apparent correlation between abductees and microwaves or TVs turning on and off, streetlights blinking out, and computers shutting down.

Alice, the Maryland abductee across the aisle from me, stiffens in her seat.

At 11:30 Sunday morning the first abductee panel assembles to discuss long-term changes in their outlooks and interests and their subsequent lifestyle adjustments. The panel consists of five women, in their late thirties to mid-forties. Their remarkableness lies in how utterly unremarkable they appear.

First to speak is a petite, delicately featured, forty-two-year-old self-employed businesswoman with two children, ages seventeen and twenty-one. In October and November of 1989, she tells us, she had two encounters with alien Beings during which she was taken aboard a space-craft. She explains that she had had no previous interest in UFOs, had neither heard of the Betty and Barney Hill case nor read science fiction, and that the abduction experiences altered her life.

One reaction, she says, smiling, is that after the abductions she changed her name to "Star" and everyone she knows now tells her, "Oh, yes! That name is *you!*"

Prior to the abductions Star had been in sales and marketing; but she made an abrupt and unexpected career change between nine and ten months after the encounters when she enrolled in a massage-therapy school. The name change, she says, came from the alien Beings who told her "Star" was a good name for healing. She has since discovered that she is a "natural" massage therapist, and that her therapy is "good not just for relaxing her clients, but for deep healing and adjusting their auras."

She reports that she can see auras, that she can feel a client's blocked energy vibration and return that vibration to normal, "which is what we call healing."

Star, I subsequently discover, was involved in one of the most interesting abductions and will herself be the subject of a John Carpenter presentation later on.

The next speaker is "Jennifer," a moon-faced, curly-haired woman in a bright red dress. She has been aware of her abduction episodes since she was a small child. From the ages of three to six, she tells us, she slept for protection with her head either under the covers or beneath her bed. Later, she would hide at night in her closet with the light on or sleep under the dining-room table or behind the living-room couch. Following her marriage and the birth of her daughter, she lived in a house protected by deadbolt locks and an attack dog. Because she found herself growing increasingly frightened that someone would steal her daughter, she began taking courses in the martial arts.

In 1982, Jennifer continues, her daughter disappeared from their home. Jennifer frantically searched the house, in vain, only to have the little girl mysteriously reappear fifteen minutes later, crying hysterically that there were "monsters" in her bedroom. As a result, Jennifer reports, the child now has the same fears she has.

After that experience, Jennifer and her family moved to nine acres outside the city. Their new property is ringed with lights and guarded by three attack dogs. Her fear, she says, is gradually being replaced by an acceptance of what has been happening to her. She has continued her study of karate, because, she says, she needs to feel some control over herself and her life, and is now nearly a black belt.

"Margaret," a neatly dressed, carefully made-up brunette in her late thirties, is married to a physician. She experienced a Missing Time episode with her two small children during which she awoke in a disc and saw a greenhouse filled with trees. During her second abduction she was taken into a large room where she was shown scenes of ecological disasters. What started as "several disturbing events," Margaret says, has been transformed into a "unique learning experience" that has brought her a growing concern for the environment. She now considers what happened to her a "positive experience" which has created within her "an expanded ecological awareness."

Margaret reports that her internist husband "is in total denial" and that as a result of the "events," she thinks, a biochemical change may have occurred in her body. She would prefer to call her alien contacts "events," she adds, instead of "abductions."

"Jane" is a conservatively dressed government secretary with a high security clearance. Because of her experiences, she says, she has become "more tolerant of strange things," but admits that it is difficult to lead "a life filled with secrets." She asks, "How do you open a conversation with 'Oh, by the way, I was abducted by aliens'?"

She says she has learned not to talk about her abduction experiences outside her house. She had two close friends, she tells us: one accepted what Jane told her; the other couldn't handle it, and cut Jane out of her life.

"Brenda," a commercial artist, has gone public with her experiences. She sells "alien T-shirts" that she has designed, and has made several appearances on television relating her UFO stories. "There is a temptation to edit one's experiences if you don't feel they will be accepted," Brenda says, then adds, "We weren't born believing in UFOs. The fear is beyond anything you could imagine! The kind of panic—I can't describe it! Don't mistake the fact that because we're dealing with this in a matter-of-fact manner that we aren't—or weren't—*horribly* panicked!"

I am wondering how I would behave if I thought something like what the women have described was happening to me. I suspect that I, too, would be careful with whom I spoke; I, too, would try to deal with it in a matter-of-fact manner. I, too, would be scared out of my wits.

A suntanned Arizona psychologist next presents a brief report on the abductions of children based on the case histories of a California psychologist/ordained minister who was unable to attend the conference:

Christopher, age eight, has been visited by an "orange-skinned man" and a "gentle, gray alien."

Kevin, age eight and a half, also saw a "well-built orange man."

Warren, age twelve, was visited by a small, bald, round-headed, gray-looking Being with a neon-green glowing ball.

In two other instances children described "glowing balls of light."

Jonathan, age five, was floated through his window into "a round thing" that had appeared in the park across his street. Later, during the child's examination, the psychologist showed him the "coloring book" images designed in 1990 by Budd Hopkins that comprise the Hopkins Image Recognition Test (HIRT) for Children. These eight-by-ten images, taken from the "real world" of images familiar to children, are: Santa Claus, Batman, a clown, a policeman, a little girl, a Ninja Turtle, a little boy, a witch, and a skeleton. A tenth image, that of a typical Small Gray, is inserted between the Ninja Turtle and the little boy. They are generally displayed to a child in that order. When Jonathan was shown the Small Gray he exclaimed, "You know my friends!"

The Arizona psychologist notes that the California psychologist thought it interesting that the young children's descriptions of the Beings were very similar despite their being seen on opposite coasts.

Budd Hopkins rises to report that his test has been used by mental health professionals and UFO investigators with great success and tells of a case of his own in which one little boy was going through the cards and when he came to the alien said, "Mommy, that's the man who comes into my room and beams me up into the spacecraft. I saw you there, too, and you were naked on a table."

"Small children do not recognize the alien figure," Hopkins continues, "*unless . . .*"—and his voice trails off.

John Mack tells of a child he was treating who blanched when he came to the Hopkins drawing of the alien and said, "That's the man who's taking me up on the ship!"

Several psychologists rise during the questioning period to complain that Hopkins's "standardized" drawings are neither standardized nor scientific. I am struck, nevertheless, by the children's ability to recognize the Small Gray's face. Where would they have seen one before? They bear no resemblance to the alien creatures in movies, television, comic books, or computer games.

After lunch Budd Hopkins discusses "The Roper Poll on Unusual Personal Experiences." Robert Bigelow, the wealthy Las Vegas entrepreneur who sat with Jacobs and me at breakfast this morning, had approached Hopkins the year before, in January 1991, at a conference on anomalous phenomena they were both attending in Philadelphia. There Bigelow had suggested to Hopkins that if he and Jacobs were to create a questionnaire that might be used in conjunction with a Roper Organization nationwide survey to ascertain what percentage of the United States population may have experienced UFO abductions, he, Bigelow, would pay for the publication of its results.*

It would not have been enough, Hopkins tells us at the conference, to simply ask "Are you a UFO abductee?" since such a query would not necessarily reveal "the extent of those with potential abduction experiences. Many people, as has been pointed out, do not have enough conscious recollection of these events to answer affirmatively." Hopkins and Jacobs instead designed their survey questions to measure "unusual experiences which research indicated were closely associated with abduction histories."

Three separate Roper "Omnibus" polls, involving a total of 5,947 adults, were taken, in July, August, and September, 1991. Eleven Hopkins/Jacobs–designed questions were seeded among the regular in-home service Roper Reports questionnaire. Such a Roper Poll normally contains a mixture of questions on topics such as lifestyle, behavior, attitude, activities during the past week, optimism/pessimism about our country's future, and other political, social, and economic issues.

According to the Roper Organization, every effort was made to place the Hopkins/Jacobs questions "within the preset questionnaire in such a way as to eliminate question order bias and allow the questionnaire to 'flow' smoothly."[1]

Roper interviews were conducted face-to-face in the respondent's home and usually took about fifty minutes. The poll taker presented the eleven abduction-related questions to those being surveyed as follows:

> This card contains a list of things that might have happened to you at some point in your life, either as a child or as an adult, or both. I'd like you to read down the card, and for each item tell me, to the best of your knowledge, if that has happened to you more than twice, once or twice, or never.
>
> a. Seeing a ghost
> b. Feeling as if you left your body

* Another sponsor of the questionnaire is rumored to be the Crown Prince of Liechtenstein.

c. Seeing a UFO

d. *Waking up paralyzed with a sense of a strange person or presence or some-thing else in your room* [my italics]

e. *Feeling that you were actually flying through the air although you didn't know why or how* [my italics]

f. Hearing or seeing the word TRONDANT and knowing that it has a secret meaning for you

g. *Experiencing a period of time of an hour or more, in which you were ap-parently lost, but you could not remember why, or where you had been* [my italics]

h. *Seen unusual lights or balls of light in a room without knowing what was causing them, or where they came from* [my italics]

i. *Finding puzzling scars on your body and neither you nor any one else re-membering how you received them or where you got them* [my italics]

j. Having seen, either as a child or adult, a terrifying figure—which might have been a monster, a witch, a devil, or some other evil figure—in your bedroom or closet or somewhere else

k. Having vivid dreams about UFOs.[2]

The five questions I have put in italics (d, e, g, h, i) were considered "key indicators" designed to elicit experiences related to abductions. Two others, questions c (Have you ever seen a UFO?) and f (TRONDANT) were con-sidered "check questions": the first permitted comparison with other, previ-ous surveys, and the question concerning TRONDANT—a fictional word invented by Budd Hopkins—had no meaning, secret or otherwise; it was included simply to determine how many respondents might answer yes to any odd or paranormal question. Approximately 1 percent answered yes to the TRONDANT question—a figure from which one can extrapolate a corresponding 1.9 million adult Americans. (The responses of that 1 percent were not included in the findings.)

Seven percent of the respondents answered yes to having seen a UFO—a figure corresponding to 13.3 million adult Americans. Interestingly, 11 per-cent—20.9 million—reported they had seen a ghost.

Eighteen percent (34.2 million) said they had experienced "waking up paralyzed with a sense of a strange person or presence or something else" in their rooms one or more times.

Thirteen percent (24.7 million) said they had experienced missing time one or more times.

Ten percent (19 million) had experienced the feeling that they were ac-tually flying through the air, although they didn't know why or how.

Eight percent (15.2 million) had seen unusual lights or balls of light in a room without knowing what was causing them or where they were coming from.

Eight percent also reported finding puzzling scars on their bodies for which neither they nor anyone else could remember a cause.

In the study's conclusion the Roper Organization reported that its research on behalf of the Bigelow Holding Company produced results that were "unexpected . . . chiefly because the number of people reporting occurrences of items on the list far exceeded what was anticipated, and also because the answers cut across most demographic subgroups."[3]

At the conference, Hopkins points out that 2 percent of those surveyed responded yes to four out of five of the indicator questions, which, he says, "shows that mental-health specialists have drastically underestimated the number of people who have had unusual personal experiences." That 2-percent positive response, Hopkins says, would indicate that 3.7 million Americans might qualify as probable abductees. Only 18 of the 5,937 persons surveyed answered all five indicator questions positively; but even this figure, Hopkins explains, would suggest that at a minimum 560,000 American adults might be abductees.

Following Hopkins's Roper Poll presentation, the M.I.T. lecture hall is in an uproar. Scientists in all corners of the large room protest that the survey is "full of holes!"; that is was "a waste of time, money, and opportunity"; that "your whole findings are based on the assumption that your 'key indicators' will strongly predict who might be abductees, and these 'indicators' do not have any scientific basis to suggest they are sound"; that "no systematic pre-tests were carefully done to find out how the respondents interpret what they've been asked." When someone insists that because of the looseness of the questions and the conclusions drawn from them, the need exists for experts to design questions for future polls, John Mack responds somewhat plaintively, "How can we get our colleagues to validate the poll when they totally reject the concept?"

I later speak with D. C. Donderi, an associate professor in McGill University's Department of Psychology, who is also attending the M.I.T. conference. Donderi agrees with those who complained that the poll was not valid. "None of the respondents were interviewed at length to determine whether or not further investigation would indicate real abductions," Donderi says. "And no preliminary study established a quantitative relationship between answers to the poll questions and the probability of a real abduction experience."

And because there is no validating evidence to support Hopkins's and Jacobs's claim that the Roper Poll answers indicate possible alien abductions,

Donderi insists, "the response of any scientifically informed reader, who follows the absolutely essential scientific criteria of conservatism and demonstrability, will then be to ask why he or she—or any other scientifically competent person—should pay any attention to unvalidated poll data."

Donderi believes that the Roper Poll's salvation lies in the fact that respondents who indicated a desire to participate in further studies recorded their addresses and phone numbers, thus enabling researchers to "carry out a systematic follow-up of the original data using volunteer respondents at their own request." Extensive interviewing and testing of a subsample of these volunteers would result in "an assigned probability of actual abduction for every level of responses to the critical questions in the poll." Donderi calls for the development and implementation of a careful, scientifically proven, step-by-step procedure of interviewing and psychological testing of those volunteer Roper Poll respondents, which would include mailings, telephone interviews, scoring and blind coding of test results, and follow-up contacts and personal interviews. "Each successively more detailed interview stage will be used to validate the data from the earlier stage," Donderi points out. "Each more detailed stage will constitute the validity criterion for the less detailed stage."

Donderi's project would be to obtain blind, unbiased evidence on the probability that Americans have experienced UFO abductions, and it would relate that evidence to the results of a nationwide randomized poll. "Only under conditions where a hypothesis can be tested *and can fail*," Donderi insists, "will corroborating evidence—that high Roper Poll scorers without serious personality abnormalities actually *do* have a high probability of reporting a UFO abduction experience—be acceptable to the scientific community."

Donderi is quick to recognize that even a validation study such as the one he proposes would "not by itself convince the scientifically educated audience that the UFO phenomenon is worthy of serious consideration."

Although Professor Donderi, it seems to me, is properly skeptical about the findings of the Roper Poll, his presence at the conference suggests he is not prepared to discard the extraterrestrial hypothesis entirely.

Donderi was fifteen years old when he started his freshman year at the University of Chicago as a Ford Foundation Early Entrance Scholar; he received his B.A. in liberal arts from that university at eighteen, and his B.Sc. in biopsychology at twenty-one. He earned his Ph.D. from Cornell five years later, in 1963. Donderi's doctorate was awarded in experimental psychology, an area that, he explains, "includes questions of human perception, memory, and how one understands the world—in other words, how do we get input about the world, how do we interpret it, and what brain mechanisms and psychological processes can be used to explain how we do that?

"So twenty or thirty years ago, when I first began hearing that people were reporting UFOs, I was intrigued," he tells me. "I was intrigued simply because while I'm aware that it is certainly possible for people to fool and mislead themselves and each other about this kind of thing, there was a certain kind of consistency to these observers' reports—that is, a lot of people were reporting this kind of experience, and they were fairly concrete experiences. Now," he continues, "it was clear to me from the profiles of the people reporting UFOs that they were not all mentally unstable people, or people with social needs to fulfill by telling these stories—and those were, of course, the two theories about who reported this phenomenon used to explain away or dismiss the whole UFO thing."

In 1966, "basically out of curiosity" but also because of the substance and quantity of the UFO evidence being presented, Donderi joined the National Investigation Committee on Aerial Phenomena (NICAP). "When I get independent corroboration of multiple witnesses of the same thing, and they more or less match, then it doesn't take too many of those reports to convince me that these people have *seen* something, and that the 'something' is outside of them and *not* a mental aberration." Even if 85 percent of those sightings could be attributed to a meteorological phenomenon, a misperception of Venus, a misidentified aircraft or its landing lights, "it's the 15 percent left over," Donderi explains, "often with photographic or radar evidence, that is the basis for the UFO phenomenon."

In 1968 NICAP asked Donderi, as part of a scientific panel, to investigate a set of six abduction reports. "Maybe two or three were convincing," Donderi tells me, "and the others had what appeared to be obvious problems—mainly with the witnesses." In his report to NICAP, Donderi concluded that he "couldn't on the basis of the written evidence find any *a priori* reason to discount the credible witnesses." And their stories, though incredible, "as far as they went, would have to stand."

Twenty-five years later, does Donderi still think people are being abducted by aliens in UFOs?

"People *are* being abducted. That's a reasonable conclusion when you look at the evidence," Donderi tells me. "I can't say that with the same certainty I can say there are UFOs out there—which there are. But the evidence is good, whether it's 'scientific' or not. Budd Hopkins is a bright man. And so are Dave Jacobs and a lot of others—John Mack and John Carpenter, just to name a few. They're smart enough not to be guilty of self-deception. Most of the abductees are very convincing; they're not people with axes to grind, or anything to gain from telling absurd stories. Nor do I think this is all some sort of hypnotic confabulation egged on by investigators, which is the common critical response to this phenomenon.

"*I think it's happening.* But," he continues, "the fact is, I can't prove it. And nobody in their right mind would bet the store on abductions without better proof."

Later in the afternoon Jenny Randles speaks of "an interesting study in which individuals were asked to describe imaginary abductions." She explains that if such a study indicated there were significant similarities between a "fantasized abduction" and an actually reported one, then it could be argued that "actual" abductions must be fantasy as well.

The study's test group consisted of eleven male and nine female subjects; 90 percent of the group provided graphic descriptions of how they entered the spacecraft, 10 percent did not. Their methods of entrance, Randles reports, "were totally different from those described by abductees. They were brought on board by aliens carrying ray guns or they were drugged."

The occupants of the spacecraft were described by 55 percent of the test group as small, 25 percent as tall. In the United Kingdom 35 percent of the abductees describe the occupants as tall, 12 percent as small. None of the imaginers in the group described Small Grays; nor did any describe being given a medical exam, whereas 90 percent of the U.K. abductees routinely report medical examinations. Seventy-five percent of the test group imagined being questioned; 40 percent of the U.K. abductees said they were questioned. Thirty-five percent of the imaginers said they were brought aboard the spacecraft to be helped; no U.K. abductee feels he or she has been brought aboard for any beneficial reason.

Perhaps in partial reflection of British xenophobia, a sizable percentage of the test group thought the aliens were visiting as tourists.

Jenny Randles's findings strike me as significant: people who are asked to describe imaginary abductions do *not* come up with the scenarios, sequences, or Beings described by the overwhelming majority of abductees. The "medical examination," such a major, recurring aspect of the abductees' stories, is totally absent from the imaginers' accounts. I am reminded of what Dr. John G. Miller had earlier pointed out: abductees' accounts of the medical procedures carried out upon them by the aliens are so different from our own terrestrial medicine that it is extremely unlikely the origin of the abductees' reports lies anywhere in the abductees' own past medical experience or knowledge. In other words, if one of Randles's imaginers had been asked to make up a story of an alien medical examination, it is likely that such an examination would have a discernible basis in our own kind of medicine.

And from Miller's and Randles's speculations, it is but a small associative step to Eddie Bullard's question of the night before concerning the origin of the aliens' physical descriptions: "If Hollywood is responsible for these images, where are the monsters? Where are the robots?"

During dinner Sunday night I sit with Alice and Carol at Legal Seafood. Both of them are to take part in the abductee panel scheduled for later that night, and both are clearly apprehensive about it. We talk about their horse farm and stay clear of conference topics.

The first speaker after dinner is co-chairman Dave Pritchard, who is going to discuss a suspected implant. The major problem with this whole issue of alien abductions, Pritchard acknowledges, is that there is no "hard evidence." If, as one of the conference attendees suggested earlier, all these implants are being done, why aren't they showing up on X-rays and MRIs with the frequency one might expect?

"Physical evidence probably provides the best way to bring into scientific consideration the hypothesis that there are extra intelligences present on earth," Pritchard says. "By itself, physical evidence is not likely to put abductions on the mainline scientific agenda, but it might, rather, serve as a powerful independent corroboration of the physical reality of some of the abduction testimony. Therefore the pedigree, or link between the evidence and the abduction phenomena which is alleged to have caused it, is crucial."

The "pedigree" of the alleged implant Pritchard examined seems to him to be relatively sound. It came from abductee Richard Price, who says it was placed in his body—actually midshaft in his penis—by aliens and over the years worked its way out. Price says he has conscious memories of the object being implanted in him; that, on some sort of magnified viewing screen, he watched the Beings wire it up; and that a friend of his later took a photograph of the implant device protruding partway out of Price's skin.

Price's implant, Pritchard reports, is amber-colored and measures one by four millimeters. Pritchard examined it under a high-powered microscope and, according to him, it appeared to have a core of translucent material with a collagen sheen about it as a result of having been inside Price's body for an extended period. Projecting up from the object were three little appendages eighteen microns wide, or approximately one-quarter the width of a human hair. Pritchard's analysis of the object's elements indicated carbon, hydrogen, and oxygen were present, along with slightly less nitrogen than might be expected. What that means, he explains, is only that it *might* be something that grew in Price, and that what is really needed is some sort of interdisciplinary team of biologists, chemists, material scientists, and the like who would really be able to look at a supposed physical artifact and evaluate what it is.

"In any case," Pritchard says, "I don't have anything conclusive. What I have is just what you usually get in this business: it will provide more beliefs for the believers and will be instantly skeptified by the skeptics, and it's not very good evidence if it won't move the lines at all. The point is to convince the jury. . . ."

There is a short break to give the abductee panel time to seat themselves in front of the triptych blackboard and the conference audience. The panel consists of two men and five women—including Alice and Carol.

The first to speak is "Virginia," a small, intense, pretty, dark-haired woman in her late thirties. She tells us she has had numerous experiences, including bedroom visitations, materializations, life flashes, phone programs, and blankets pulled off, and once met a man in public who, she thinks, might have been an alien.

Virginia also has two childhood memories that she believes relevant. She remembers screaming in her sleep, waking up with blood all over her pillow, and her mother telling her not to touch her nose. The Beings, she now believes, implanted something in her nose to monitor and study her.

Her second memory, Virginia tells us, is that of hiding in a closet and looking up at two men with pointed faces and black shoes. They told her, she says, about "people who live in a house in the sky and that I would go up into that house in the sky and have babies and that they would take my babies to a different place." She remembers the Beings telling her when she was nine years old of her reproductive cycle and universal motherhood. During one abduction, she says, she was "introduced in the sky house to my sister, who looked exactly like me. She was a clone."

Through hypnotic regression Virginia recalled being seated inside a "birthing room" aboard a spaceship, where she was shown hybrid children. The Beings told her to sing and hum to the fetuses and to touch the hybrid children around her. She "dreamed a baby was brought to her in a white blanket. The baby," Virginia reports, "was three months old and conversed telepathically."

During another abduction, a "naked, almond-eyed woman" showed her images of nuclear war and told her the threat could be diminished through understanding. She was also told that pollution could cause genetic mutations. She says there are multilevel messages in the cosmos and that the Beings told her "I could work with them—that they were not going to invade us and that if they had wanted to they could have done that a long time ago.

"There are many different kinds of entities," she says. "We are part of a universal consciousness. We are no longer spectators but are part of the universal awareness. We should explore the mysteries of life our universe offers us."

Virginia, I later learn, is one of Joe Nyman's abductees.

The second speaker, "Harry," is a handsome, thirtyish young man whose dark brown hair is pulled neatly back into a ponytail. He is wearing well-tailored black slacks and a black silk shirt. He has only recently come forward with his abduction stories as a result of starting therapy with John Mack; he now believes he has been taken up into alien craft at least three times. Harry reports that medical procedures were performed on him and that these procedures specifically "several times involved explorations around my genitals." Harry is clearly embarrassed, uncomfortable talking about this. "I have been reluctant to tell my story because I haven't wanted to say, 'Yes, this happened to me.' "

He looks down at his hands folded on the desktop in front of him. "My first conscious memory," he says, looking up, "was in 1988, when I was living and working in the British Virgin Islands. I woke up one morning agitated, afraid, with strange markings behind my ear. Subsequently I recalled lying naked on a table paralyzed, but aware of my surroundings. A Tall Being was standing next to me, watching and monitoring me. I could feel my testicles being pulled to one side and a small tube entering me where my left testicle would have hung. I was aware they were after something specific." In regression, he says, he suffers overwhelming feelings of humiliation and cowardice.

In 1990, while still in the Virgin Islands, Harry returned to his house to take a nap and was abducted a second time. On this occasion friends heard an intense humming sound emanating from near his building and saw something "unexplainable." During the next few months, Harry began to remember having seen the Tall Being before and that the Being had told him, "This is the only time we will do this to you." A machine was placed over his penis, forcing him to ejaculate into a funnel. He felt "only rage. I realized what they have always taken from me is my seed. At first I thought it was just an acute, realistic dream. But it was much more *severe,* more real than a dream."

He pauses again, obviously distressed. Then he continues: "Our trauma is that our consciousnesses are stretched beyond our abilities to understand. We are left in a state of disbelief and shock. We have no way of integrating what we perceive into our reality."

In January, February, and March of this year, Harry suddenly, unaccountably found himself terrified, weeping. He had sought out Dr. John E. Mack.

"I think the Beings are trying to understand our emotions," Harry says. "Our ability to feel, our deep spirituality—these are our gifts to the universe. No matter how invasive their behavior, we are not psychologically damaged. We are now participating willingly, I believe, and are part of a plan for some future interaction."

Carol is next.

Carol Dedham is the forty-three-year-old manager of Alice's 180-acre Maryland horse farm. Carol attended junior college, has lived up and down the East Coast, and writes and paints in her spare time. She is tall, nearly six feet, thin, green-eyed, with short, feathered, auburn-colored hair; she is very attractive in a leggy, raw-boned sort of way.

Carol's hand trembles slightly as she lifts a rolled-up cardboard poster onto the desktop in front of her. She clears her throat and, in a surprisingly strong voice, begins: "I have not had hypnotic regression, but I have had conscious memories since 1991 and recall things that happened in my childhood.

"Several inexplicable events have occurred in the past several months: marks, vehicle disturbances, wounds and bruises.

"According to my father," Carol continues, "even as a young child, I would be missing for several hours. My father has admitted to me that he had always known where and when to find me, but now feels he failed to protect me.

"My first conscious memory was in 1954 at age five. I went on a car trip with my father to Doylestown, Pennsylvania, for a meeting he had to attend. It was a late afternoon in mid-July, but it wasn't sunset by any means. We were on this dirt road, kind of a shortcut my father knew, and the car just died. It was a new Plymouth station wagon and he couldn't get it started again. There were empty fields on both sides of us, and ahead of us a big oak that put the front end of the car partially in the shade, because the sun was fairly low.

"It was a miserable, stinking, hot day," Carol continues, "and I remember I didn't want my father to get out of the car. I asked him not to get out, but he said it was okay. I was on the passenger's side in the front seat. The car window was down—we didn't have air conditioning in cars in those days. He got out, closed the car door, went around to the front of the station wagon, and when he lifted up the hood, all of a sudden I felt this real cold air.

"It was cold enough to scare me, because it happened so fast! It wasn't like a wind," Carol explains. "It was like somebody had removed the hot air and replaced it with cold air in the snap of a finger, and it scared me. I started crying, yelling to him, 'Daddy! Daddy! Daddy! Come back!'

"He closed the hood, came around to the driver's side, and leaned into the window to say, 'It's okay, it's okay. Everything's okay.' He said something

else, I don't remember what. And then he got back in the car. He was trying to comfort me," Carol continues. "I was still crying and carrying on. I
was so *scared*! And even now I don't know *why* I was so scared. I didn't *see*
anything! I don't remember anything strange, except for that real cold air. I
was so cold! I was shivering and crying, and he was twisted on the bench
seat, his right arm over the back of the seat, his left hand holding my shoulder trying to comfort me. He was turned toward me saying, 'It's okay, Carol,
it's okay,' and the car *started*.

"He hadn't touched the ignition," she says, "The car just started by itself!
And that scared me again. I was really upset by that point. But he just turned
back in his seat, took the steering wheel, and drove away like it was nothing!
Obviously I quieted down, and all I remember is that we pulled into
Doylestown, drove to the office building where my father was supposed to
meet this guy, and it was nighttime. It was dark. The building was dark and
everything, and there was a note on the door saying, 'Sorry I missed you.'

"We couldn't figure out what was going on," Carol continues. "My father glanced at his watch and said, 'Geez! What happened to the time? I had
no idea it took so long!' It was nine o'clock, nine-thirty, something like that.
From where we were when the car stalled to Doylestown was probably
about a forty-minute drive, and yet when we got there it was dark! So we
figured we were missing about an hour and forty minutes, maybe.

"Neither of us knows what happened. My father remembers me
screaming and crying and carrying on. He remembers the car starting. He
says he doesn't know why that didn't scare him, but it didn't. He just
thought it was weird.

"I've always remembered that story," Carol tells us. "It seems like a
pretty clear memory, and I never discussed it with my father until these
other things started happening. I talked to him about it just recently and he
remembers it exactly the same way."

Carol mentions unexplained scars on her legs, the "scoop marks" on her
shinbone and near the corner of her eye. She speaks briefly about an incident that happened last December 15. She was driving home to the Maryland horse farm after visiting her parents in Hagerstown when she saw three
bright white lights in a horizontal line through the tops of the trees. She recognized them, she tells us, from the time she and Alice had seen them near
their farm fifteen months before. She stopped the car, got out and walked
forward to get a closer look, and suddenly the light on the right, nearest to
her, zoomed toward her and halted directly overhead, "so close I felt I could
reach up and touch it.

"The light was blindingly bright," she continues. "I think I saw blue
lights, one on the left side and one on the right side of the craft." But the

light was so brilliant it hurt her eyes. She looked away to see if the other two objects were still there, blinked, and the next thing she knew, she was five miles away in her car, making a right-hand turn onto the dirt road that led to Alice's horse farm with no idea of how she got there. She arrived back missing three-quarters of an hour's time.

Carol next tells about an incident that occurred two and a half weeks later, on January 2. She was driving the farm's pickup truck back from a business dinner in town with a gaily wrapped, shoebox-sized Christmas gift of homemade brownies, fruitcake, cookies, and fudge when she saw the three bright lights overhead once more. This time, she tells us, she knew what to expect. "I think I shouted, 'Oh, no—oh, no! Not again! Please, not again!' I remember I blinked, and when my eyes opened I was eight miles away, four miles on the other side of the farm." In a panic, Carol pressed the accelerator to the floor. She was again frightened, disoriented. When she arrived back at the farm, the contents of her briefcase were scattered about the floor of the truck cab; the truck's interior had the "heavy" atmosphere of a "greenhouse on a hot summer night"; and the Christmas gift had been unwrapped and resealed with masking tape, as if a child had rewrapped it. Once again she was missing time. During a subsequent "flashback," she tells us, she saw the Christmas gift in something's hands

Carol briefly mentions an open, bleeding triangular wound she awoke with in Pennsylvania on January 12 and a third missing-time incident in March, during which she saw a strange Being in a four-foot-wide Stetson hat.

And then she is saying how she recently learned from her father that her grandfather, too, had possibly had "experiences," and that she now has reason to believe her son and granddaughter have had them, too. She unrolls the poster she has brought and explains it was drawn two weeks before by her four-year-old granddaughter, Stacy, when the child and her parents were visiting the horse farm.

"I was talking to my son and daughter-in-law and not really paying much attention to Stacy," Carol tells us, "and when she finished her drawings, she held it up and said, 'Look, Grandma!'

"I looked at it and I took a deep breath thinking, I don't want to interpret this! I thought I knew what I was looking at, but then I just thought my imagination was running away with me and that I should just let her explain it. So I said, 'Tell me what you drew, Stacy.'

"She said, 'You can see what it is.'

" 'I want you to tell me,' I said. 'Can you tell me what you drew?' "

In the center of the poster, outlined in blue Magic Marker, there is a triangular object with its point straight down. At the top right- and left-hand corners of the triangle, in red Magic Marker, are smiling faces, and between

them, a red circle drawn over and over again. Stacy explained that the triangle was "a flying machine up in the sky" and that the red circle was "a red
light in the middle that's on all the time. And these up here," the child had
said, indicating the smiling faces, "are faces looking out of windows in the
flying machine. And this green part down here," at the pointed bottom of
the triangle, "is a green light, except when it opens up and it's a door, and
you can go in and of out the flying machine through this doorway. And
when they close it, it's a green light again."

Within the triangle Stacy had drawn a small kite in pencil. The child
had explained she had drawn it in pencil because "that just shows it's up in
the sky and flies like a kite, but it's not part of the flying machine so I didn't
want to do it in color." Scrawled in Magic Marker above the top of the triangle were a series of red, black, blue, green, and red horizontal lines.
"These are lights, too," Carol was saying, "but Stacy said she had drawn
them like that to show that they moved—rotated. They weren't stationary
like the red light at the top of the craft and the green one at the doorway at
the bottom."

Carol then points to the left side of the poster, where there is a drawing
of what looks like an elongated gourd outlined in red. At the bottom of it is
a small figure, also in red. "Stacy said this is a long tunnel," Carol explains,
"and her imaginary friend, Nu, takes her through this long tunnel, and that
it was very, very red all over inside, like red light. And these green lines in the
tunnel were green marks on the walls on both sides, and there was a long
green stripe on the ceiling all the way all the way down this tunnel. I didn't
ask her about the figure entering the tunnel. It looks like it's wearing some
sort of helmet or has its hands over its head. I didn't ask and she didn't
volunteer. . . ."

Carol is beginning to relax; she is holding up well.

She turns to the two separate drawings on the right-hand side of the
poster. The upper one is of a small grimacing figure outlined in black Magic
Marker with its arms outstretched; its trunk is colored blue. "Stacy told me
this is a picture of Nu," Carol says. "He was normally all in gray, she said,
but I hadn't given her a gray marker, so she used a blue marker. But Stacy
didn't think the blue was quite right, either, so she discarded the blue
marker and switched to black."

Carol points to Nu's "sleeves," outlined in black. "Stacy left this white,
she said, because his arms are so skinny she couldn't outline them. His legs
are skinny, too, she says, and he has square feet. When she got to Nu's head
I said, 'He's got big ears!' And she said, 'Those are not ears! Those are part
of his hat.' "

Carol pauses to explain that one night two weeks before Stacy had drawn the poster, the child had mentioned Nu the first time. Stacy didn't want her grandmother to say anything about Nu to her parents, because, the four-year-old said, "Mommy and Daddy don't like him and when I put my drawings of Nu on my wall Daddy takes them down." Carol had promised Stacy that Nu would be their secret. That night, while Carol was putting the child to bed, Stacy had told Carol that Nu was "gray all over," had "big eyes," and wore a flat hat on his head. Nu played with her all the time, Stacy continued, and said good night to her every night. While Carol was tucking her granddaughter into bed, Stacy had suddenly turned to her bedroom door and said, "Good night, Nu!"

Startled, Carol had wheeled around to look, but the doorway was empty. She glanced back down at her granddaughter, who was still staring at the door. "Nu says good night to you, too, Grandma," Stacy said.

At the bottom right-hand corner of Stacy's drawing, below her sketch of Nu, there was a small, red female figure inside a solid black rectangle. On the two sides of the rectangle there were red stripes. Carol explains that in the original drawing there had just been the figure with the red lines on either side and that Stacy had said it was herself and then fallen silent.

"I asked, 'What are the red lines?' " Carol continues. " 'What is that?' And Stacy said, 'That's a fence.' I asked . . . I asked . . ." Carol pauses for a moment, trying to collect herself. She has had a sudden, vivid, overpowering memory of herself as a child hiding in a closet. She can feel the image coming back, and she doesn't want to see it.

"I asked Stacy, 'Why did you draw a fence?' " Carol says, fighting the image that is growing stronger in her mind. She is thinking, Not now! Not now! Can't do this right now! Clearly struggling to speak, she forces out, "And Stacy told me, 'It protects me!' "

But Carol, in her mind, is no longer at the conference. Suddenly Carol is a small child hiding terrified inside her bedroom closet. Carol recognizes she is in the home she lived in from the time she was four until she was eight and a half. She has been inside this closet a lot, she knows. She is scared because she feels trapped and knows no one is going to help her. She is desperately tearing all the clothing off the hangers in her closet and stuffing them into the cracks of the closet's old, glass-handled, wooden door. She is filling the cracks so the brilliant blue-white light on the other side of the door won't come through. She believes if the light doesn't touch her she'll be safe. She is jerking her clothes off the wire coat hangers, urgently wedging skirts, pants, blouses, winter coats into the openings at the sides and bottoms of the old closet door. *Can't let the light touch me! Can't let the light touch me! Can't let the light touch me!* She has to do it immediately—right now, so she'll be okay.

There is a stillness in the M.I.T. lecture hall except for Carol's little keening sounds. She is rocking in her seat, her eyes fixed, staring at something only she can see. The poster curls forgotten in her hand. A few of the abductees have tears in their eyes. They, better than any of the rest of us, *understand*. They are leaning forward, willing her to come back to us. Alice, next to Carol, gently lays her hand on Carol's arm.

"Stacy told me the fence was to protect her," Carol says, recovering abruptly. "And before I could ask her why, she grabbed the black marker pen and, really upset and tense, began hurriedly coloring in every little inch, every little speck of white surrounding her, making sure she had covered every bit of it. It was sort of scary, and I asked, 'Why did you do that?' you know—'Why did you cover all that in black?'

"And she said, 'I made a box,' " Carol continues, her voice strong again. " 'I'm in the box and I have a key and I can lock myself in the box and nobody can get in because I have the key.' And I asked, 'But why would you want to lock yourself in a box?' And Stacy said, 'Because that way, when Nu wants to take me somewhere I don't want to go, he can't make me go because I have the key.' "

Carol starts rolling the poster back up. "Well, now, to me, this is real clear," she says. "It also tells me that this may have been going on for a while, and only very recently has Stacy been becoming upset by it. She doesn't want to go or do things with Nu anymore. . . ." Carol pauses for a moment, then concludes her presentation, saying, "There were questions I would have liked to ask Stacy, but I didn't want to influence her. If this was indeed a product of her imagination, I didn't want to add to that imagination by giving her ideas to put into it—especially since all this other stuff was going on in very close proximity. That and because it was somewhat of a surprise revelation. I mean, until I came to this conference I didn't know about generational stuff. I had not heard about children's events, and I wouldn't have imagined in a million years she would have had any such experiences—or even that she has had them."

It is Alice's turn to speak next. Forty-one-year-old Alice Bartlett is the owner of the Maryland horse farm and an employee of the Environmental Protection Agency in Washington. She possesses a bachelor of science degree in experimental psychology from a small, private southern college and a master's degree in forestry from Michigan State. Alice's Scandinavian ancestry is evident in her pale complexion and the thick blond hair that falls halfway down her back. The first time I saw Alice I was struck by how much she resembled the woman in Andrew Wyeth's earlier portraits of Helga:

fine-boned but sturdy, soft curves but strong muscles. What Alice lacked was Helga's seeming placidity. Alice's face is taut with fear.

She begins by telling how she hired Carol to be her barn manager and they became close friends. "Although our personalities are quite different," Alice says, "we think a lot alike. We finish each other's sentences. We've shared experiences."

Alice tells about the first experience she and Carol had of the three bright lights over the horse farm. It had occurred in September 1990, two years before. The lights, Alice says, had been "acting in very strange ways. And what was odd about the whole thing was Carol and I have different memories of seeing them. Carol remembers a cluster of three lights with one of them zipping off to one side, then the others disappearing. I remember there being five lights. Three in a triangle and two to the left. I do remember one from the triangle shooting off at a very, very fast rate of speed, and then I remember walking into the house and sitting down and watching television until it was over. Carol remembers me being outside with her the whole time."

Alice next tells of seeing a six-foot Being in her bedroom and how when she turned on the light, nothing was there. She tells of incidents commuting back and forth in the dark to her job in Washington and how banks of overhead streetlights would flicker and go out on the Beltway as she passed.

She describes an incident that took place only a month before the conference during which she and Carol shared the same dream: a Tall Being peeking around their bedroom doorways and two Small Gray Beings at the foot of their beds.

"I don't know what's real and what isn't anymore," Alice says in a stricken voice. "I don't know what are dreams and what aren't. *I just don't know!*" she says, and she begins to cry.

The next speaker, "Robert," is a burly, bearded man in his late thirties. He was in Brooklyn, driving a cab, he says, and his dispatcher sent him to a house. When he arrived at the house he saw aliens behind its windows. The next thing he knew, it was three hours later; his dispatcher had been trying to reach him for an hour and a half. His wife, when he returned home, noticed three marks on his back, by his right shoulder. A doctor subsequently looked at the marks and thought Robert had suffered "some sort of radiation burn."

Under hypnosis Robert recalled two glowing objects that had come through his cab windows. One went to the front of the cab and the other to the back. His taxi had suddenly begun to spin around as though on a turntable. Everything went dark, and then the cab was inside something huge. Some creatures next led him out of the taxi to a chair, where a cloth was wrapped tightly around his chest. The Beings, Robert says, then began discussing the wavy lines that appeared on a screen nearby.

Afterwards, Robert tells us, he was taken back to his taxi; it again started to spin, and "the cab with me in it was back on the street. A creature pointed his finger at me, I felt a pain in my right shoulder, and then he was gone."

On Robert's right sits "Pat," a pretty, blond-haired woman married to a dentist in the Midwest. She has three children: a daughter aged twenty, another, aged six, and a thirteen-year-old son.

Pat tells us that when she first began to realize she was in contact with aliens, she was confused; she didn't know if she should tell anyone. "Put yourself in my shoes," she says. "If you were one of the few in the world who could see color and most others could only see black and white, how could you explain 'red'? I felt others wouldn't understand."

A year ago Pat's older daughter started having "vivid dreams." The young woman, who had not until then had any interest in aliens, Pat tells us, was upset because her dreams had appeared so real. "They seem like dreams," Pat's daughter had told her, "but they're not. They're too real to be dreams."

"I really felt sorry for her," Pat continues. "I understood what she was going through. My daughter remembers going up in a spaceship, and she said, 'Mom, you were there!' She recalls my telling her and the rest of the family, 'Don't be afraid. We're safe.' My daughter was nineteen at the time. She has continued to have real-like dreams. Sometimes there is a light in her room at night, she told me, and she has to shut her eyes because it hurts her eyes.

"I have heard my son, who was eleven at the time, say to the Beings, 'I don't think I really want to go with you now,' " Pat tells us. "He didn't sound angry or frightened. He just a couple of times repeated that he didn't want to go with them. And I remember getting out of bed and going to my son and saying, 'It's okay. You don't have to go if you don't want to.'

"My son tells me he feels that he's flying a lot at night."

Pat reports that one night her husband awoke and "jumped clear out of bed" to attack an alien in their bedroom. She found her husband on the floor "dazed and confused."

"What are you doing?" Pat asked him.

"They were *here!*" he said, picking himself up from the floor. "They were *in* here! They're not supposed to be in here. This is *my* house!"

Pat asked her husband if the aliens had done anything to him.

"I don't think so," he said.

"What bothered you so much about them?"

"I just didn't like them being here. This is *my* house. *My* room. It's *my* property. They shouldn't be here! Somebody's invading my property!"

Pat remembers her husband tossing and turning in his sleep all night, and the next morning, she tells us, "he was mad at me because it seemed to him like I should have done something. He told me he thought I was bringing aliens into our bedroom at night and yelled at me to get them out. I think he's afraid he's going crazy."

It was just after this, Pat says, that "some small bluish-gray aliens with three folds in their forehead entered my room at night, and I remember waking up and seeing them looking at me like they were angry or something." (They looked "angry," she later tells me, because they had no eyebrows, "just the three lines across the forehead, which gave them a stern look." One of the Beings was standing beside the bed, and all Pat could see was his head. The bed, she explains, was about three feet high, so the Being was about four feet tall. He had no hair, no ears, and almond-shaped eyes.)

Their presence, Pat is saying, began to annoy her, because she believed these were the same aliens her husband had tried to attack when they had bothered him. "At one point," she tells us, "I grabbed one's arm just above his hand, but after I saw how I had frightened him, I let him go. I have not had any intrusions or any of those experiences with them since then, and my husband hasn't told me about anything else happening. So those ones haven't returned."

(When I later ask Pat what the Being's arm had felt like, she says, "I did not feel a lot of heat coming from it. It had neither a cold nor warm body temperature. If you can imagine a snake without scales. . . . You wouldn't feel the bones inside a snake, so it wasn't totally squishable in your hands." The arm was firm but very thin; about an inch and a half to two inches in diameter. When she grabbed its arm, Pat says, the Being did not recoil or try to pull away; it just seemed "surprised." And then when she released it, the Being "turned around and there was a globular light where the wall should be and he just walked through it.")

"My experiences with the aliens have been good," Pat tells us at the conference, "and I have cooperated in every way. They have taught me a lot of things and have never deceived me. I appear to have a connection with these particular aliens and an ongoing lesson in my life. I experience with them a place where time doesn't seem to exist. It makes no difference to me if I can't convince other people this is true; I only know I have had the experience. The truth is the truth," she says in conclusion, "and it will still be there when science is ready to see it, or is equipped to validate it."

The last abductee to speak is "Ann," an East Coast single woman in her mid-thirties. Ten years ago in August, Ann says, she "dreamed" a Small Gray opened for her the hatch of a 7-foot-long, 4-foot-wide, 4½-foot-high egg-shaped silver vehicle. At that time she had no idea UFOs existed, nor had she ever read any UFO literature. She tells us she entered the craft, a two-seater, and in front of her was "a red button, a pedal, and a pull bar." The Small Gray told her to push the red button, so she did. "I felt as though I had been struck by lightning," Ann tells us. "I was flattened against the seat. All I saw was a horizontal band of light and then I was descending through dark gray clouds toward a dark gray sea."

The craft landed on a narrow spit of land and she climbed out onto a surface composed of uniformly rounded stones, all 3½ inches by 1 inch by 1½ inches high. Ahead of her was a forest, its foliage a ruddy orange. There was some leaf litter on the floor of the forest, she says, and some smaller trees and brambles. In a clearing were other Beings, one of whom was "part bovine, part reptilian." She also saw, she reports, "very large, foot-wide snakes which appeared to have wings." In the clearing she found another human, a male, who appeared somewhat "out of it," she says. "I took his arm and guided him back to the craft. We got in, I reversed the buttons and flew us back." The next thing she knew she woke up alone in her bed.

The following morning, Ann continues, she began to remember another "dream." "It was intensely, physically realistic," she tells us. "I was swimming toward a brilliant green shore in water which, like the air, felt thick and warm. In fact, there did not seem to be any sharp demarcation between where the water ended and the air began. Nor was there any definition between where the water ended and the sandbar began. There was a very small beach on the shore," she tells us, "which showed no evidence of tidal action. Ahead of me was a little field of neon-green grass and beyond that a very, very steep hill with a wooden observation tower on top containing other humans. I slowly climbed up the hill," Ann says, "and I was so exhausted by the effort I promised myself to start exercising."

Eight years later, in February 1990, Ann and several others with her sighted a triangular-shaped UFO with other little craft circling about it. "Oh, I know them!" Ann heard herself saying. "I've been in one." She began seeing a therapist and told him her story. Some months later, her therapist told her to contact an abductee in the Midwest. According to Ann, the abductee asked her, "Do you remember that planet with the funny water, the neon-green grass, and that teeny-tiny beach? And oh, by the way, have you started exercising yet?"

Ann seems as puzzled by her account as I am. What is one to make of such a story?

During the questioning period John Mack asks the abductee panel, "Do you arrive at an interpretation of your experience through cues related by your investigator?" They all deny being influenced by their therapists.

In response to another question addressed to the panel, we learn that with the exception of Virginia, none of the abductees had any prior interest in UFOs. Virginia, who as a child was introduced to her cloned sister in the Beings' "sky house," admits she has been fascinated by UFOs and the paranormal since she was thirteen.

Budd Hopkins asks the abductee panel if they remember any childhood experiences.

Harry, who was taken by the aliens on the British Virgin Islands, says that as a child he felt he had a "guardian angel in the sky" and remembers thinking it was due to his Catholicism. "Now," he says, "I'm not so sure."

Carol says that as a child she had "an imaginary dog who took me for walks to places where children couldn't go."

"What color was the dog?" Hopkins asks her.

"Gray," Carol answers without thinking. And then, suddenly, she looks surprised. "*Oh!*" she says. It has dawned on her that the gray dog could be a "screen memory" for a Small Gray Being.

Pat tells of having had two Small Beings who would sit with her when she was a child. Once they told her to picture in her mind what she wanted and it would come to her. She imagined her mother bringing her a drink of water; her mother appeared carrying a glass of water. "Okay," Pat tells us she recalled saying to herself, "let's make it a little tougher." She pictured in her mind a diamond. The next morning, a neighbor brought her a diamond-shaped piece of glass.

Someone asks the panel, "What do you need from your therapists?"

"I'm having difficulty taking that first step," Carol responds. "I don't want to accept that all this might be *real*. I need to know that there is someone qualified to help me cope with the fear and to deal with the panic, stress, and fear reactions I feel."

Alice, who has been very quiet, says, "The last six months of dealing with the outside world have been very difficult. One morning I wake up and I can't stop crying. The next morning I wake up and I'm twinkling. I have to interact with all these people at the horse farm and I can't tell them anything! It's all a *secret*!"

Marilyn Teare, the lovely silver-haired California therapist, rises and in a gentle voice says to Alice, "I'm a horse person, too." She asks the abductee panel if they ever notice anything strange or abnormal prior to the appearance of the Beings. Several of the abductees report they do sense in advance when the Beings are about to come. Pat reports she feels heat on one side of her face and a ringing in her ears. Ann, too, says she hears a ringing in her ears, and sees flashes and patterns of light on the ceiling.

Marilyn Teare reports she has a ringing in her ears right now. One of the abductees says she has a headache. A young woman in the audience says she feels sick to her stomach.

The panel is excused.

Carol is desperate to escape the lecture hall. She wants to be alone; but as she steps out from behind the row of desks, Budd Hopkins catches up with her to ask some questions. Hopkins explains he is currently researching cases of multigenerational abductions and wants to talk to Carol about her granddaughter.

Carol is too upset to talk. She tries to brush by him; and when Hopkins persists, she tells him, "Budd, I really can't talk to you now. Can't you see I'm upset?" When Hopkins says something more to her, Carol simply pushes him aside and rushes out of the lecture hall.

That night, while Carol is driving Alice and herself back to their motel in Framingham, one of the banks of orange lights on the Massachusetts Turnpike goes off as they approach it and pops back on as they leave. Carol glances over at Alice, who just shrugs. "It's not something I can control," Alice says. "It's not something I do consciously. It's just there."

CHAPTER IV

At the Conference

Day Three

Early Monday morning, before the third day of the conference begins, I meet with Pat, the member of the previous evening's abductee panel whose husband had accused her of bringing aliens into their bedroom at night. We meet in the courtyard outside the Eastman lobby. She looks freshly scrubbed and rested, young and utterly ingenuous.

Although, Pat tells me, she lives in a small, quiet midwestern town where almost everybody knows everybody else, very few people in the community are aware of her contacts with the aliens, "because," she explains, "it's just not necessary to tell them. I don't want to talk about what has happened to me because I can put myself in the other person's shoes: it's a really hard thing to understand or believe."

I ask Pat how many "experiences" she has had. She thinks for a moment, then says there have been at least five that she has consciously recalled, but she has known ever since she was an infant that "something—at that age I wasn't aware enough to call them 'aliens'—was coming to visit me. I felt a real sense of family with them. I remember waking up in the crib with the anticipation that they were coming and grabbing hold of the bars of the crib and waiting."

"You weren't scared?" I asked.

"No."

"What did they look like?"

"They had the typical features of typical Grays, except, to me as a child, they looked illuminated."

"Illuminated? As though there were a light from within them? Did they glow?"

"Yes," Pat says. She again thinks for a moment, then adds, "They were maybe an offshoot of the Small Grays we've heard about at the conference. Of the same family, but a little different."

The Beings, she tells me, had slit mouths and spoke with her telepath-ically.

"And when you went to their spaceship," I ask, "how did you get there?"

"At that age I don't remember ever going to a ship," she says.

"Can you tell me about a typical experience?"

Pat pauses once more. It is clear she wants to answer my questions as honestly as possible. "A typical experience now would be if, during the day, I got riled up about something I didn't want to be angry about—I'm seek-ing peace in my life, that's my goal," she adds in explanation—"and if I got riled up and couldn't sort it out in my head, I'd have like a discussion with them. They come and I might ask them, 'Well, why do humans behave this way?' And we kind of kick it around between ourselves. Usually they reply with a question to me like, 'Well, why do *you* think they behave this way?' and so on. I think they were showing me there's a different way of life, an easier way to achieve your goal. The term 'way shower' seems to be a real good fit here. They gave me suggestions and they sparked my interest in things that are not part of this physical world."

"So these discussions would take place in your home?"

"Not all the time. Sometimes it's in the ship. Most of the time it's in a quiet area. It seems like it's a desert, or it just looks like it's a desert."

"When you're aboard the ship, how big is it?"

"I haven't had a whole lot of what some people describe as tours of the ship. That's not my experience. I really couldn't tell you its size."

"Can you tell me anything about it?"

"Well, they're very tidy little individuals," she says, laughing. "You don't see any clothing around the floor. You don't see food—or at least I didn't. You don't see a lot of paraphernalia around. Either it's in the walls—and I'm assuming this, because I don't know where they store their instru-ments, since I've never experienced any examinations—or they don't have a lot of stuff. I did see a table, but there was nothing on it. And the walls are really strange. I've thought about this. They look like if you could so-lidify water."

"You can," I say. "We Earthlings call it ice."

"Well, this isn't ice," she says thoughtfully. "It's still. Motionless. Like water in a glass."

"Would it be solid if you touched it? Or would your hand go through it?"

"The wall would be solid."

"What about doors?"

"I didn't see any except for the entrance I came in. I entered through just a hole at the bottom," she says, then hesitates. Pat isn't sure how she actually entered the spacecraft. She doesn't recall any steps or ramp; she remembers floating up, but doesn't recall a beam of light.

I ask her if she ever saw any babies on board the ship.

"I remember one time seeing a room filled with containers with light emanating from inside them," she tells me. "I remember seeing little embryo-type things in the light. I don't recall seeing them in different stages. I know one of them caught my attention and that's the only one I remember. I'm assuming the reason *possibly* that one caught my interest is because maybe *I* had something to do with it myself."

"Because eggs were taken from you?"

"It's not so much eggs," Pat says. "I think it's genetic tissue that's taken and spliced together."

"And how would they have acquired this tissue?"

"I guess either they do it through scrapings of the skin, or . . ." Pat pauses. "Sometimes I wonder about hair clippings."

"Did they clip your hair?"

"No, but it's something I've been wondering about. I really couldn't tell you how they do it."

"But you believe it was some sort of cloning?"

"That's what I feel is present—not to say that they don't take eggs, but I don't think I've had any eggs taken from me."

It is almost time for us to file into the lecture hall for the morning's first presentation. But there is one more question I want to ask Pat. I am curious what her thoughts are about the conference. What has she gotten out of it so far?

"It has helped me to understand the investigators' point of view better," she says. "If I were an investigator, I wouldn't be gullible, either. It's hard to accept something that's been totally dismissed. Sometimes you feel like a patient who has two surgeons go off into a separate room to discuss your case. You don't know what they're going to do and you have the feeling they're hiding something from you. But *here*," Pat continues, "it's like the patient gets to watch and listen to the surgeons talk about what they want to do, and you can hear their disagreements. This is an opening up *to* the experiencer what they, the investigators, believe is going on, or what they don't believe is going on, and I think that's great."

I decide that for the time being the point is not whether *I* believe what Pat has told me is true but that *Pat* believes it is true. And of that there is no question in my mind.

Psychiatrists will often speak of how a patient "presents," referring to the general impression of well-being the individual gives. To me, in both the manner in which she spoke of her experiences and the details she provided, Pat came across as normal as she would have if, in other circumstances, I had asked her what it was like to be a small-town dentist's wife—in other words, straightforward, open, and eager to help me understand.

The first speaker of the morning is Jenny Randles, who, because of her machine-gun delivery, has become one of my favorites. Again, her presentation is precise, reportorial. She has studied forty-three abduction cases in Great Britain, she tells us. The information from twelve cases was gained through hypnosis; seven were "dreams"; six were "creative visualizations"; and eighteen were spontaneous or conscious recollections.

Out of the forty-three incidents, she states, thirty-seven were single events. There were 1.29 witnesses per case, compared with 2.56 per UFO sighting; 53 percent of the abductees were female and 47 percent were male. Their average age was 28 years (compared with 27 in the United States, 27.5 in Europe). They came from all occupations: police officers, factory workers, university professors, artists, etc. Twenty-five percent of the abductions took place in the open air; 51 percent in the bedroom; 24 percent in a car. At the time of the abductions, the experiencers were idling, relaxed. Twenty-two percent reported "information implants"; none reported physical implants.

"At the start of the experience," Randles continues, "55 percent saw a UFO; 30 percent saw a bright light; 12 percent saw a Being. The experience occurred 43 percent of the time between midnight and 0600; 7 percent between 0600 and 1200; 22 percent between 1200 and 1800; and 28 percent between 1800 and midnight. The most common time was between 0300 and 0500.

"Physical description of the entities is as follows," Randles continues. "In Great Britain they are 12 percent Grays, 35 percent Nordics, and 44 percent of normal height, as compared to United States, where 73 percent are Grays, 6 percent Nordics, and 12 percent are normal height, which is comparable to Europe, which is 48 percent Grays, 25 percent Nordics, and 15 percent are normal height."

Over 25 percent of the sightings and/or abductions took place in three ten-mile-square zones, Randles reports—Pennine, Northampton, and Weaver, which, she points out, are where the crop circles occur.

"One final note," Randles says. "Witnesses in Great Britain, too, report the 'Oz Factor'—" the ufologists' term for alterations of the surrounding environment—"traffic vanishing, birds stop singing, everything slows down, the cessation of sound and feeling. Thank you."

Two weeks after the conference Jenny Randles responds to some queries I sent her. "I think the case for continuity of evidence is overstated," she wrote in a very small, precise script remarkable only for the flamboyant swoop of its Fs:

The abduction experience has marked differences with the UFO phenomenon. (Note my figures in one of my papers that 2.56 witnesses per case see UFOs on average—which is not much different to a figure for witnesses to bank robberies, incidentally—but 1.29 experience abductions. . . . That alone shows fundamental distinctions.)

It is perfectly possible to consider that UFOs and abductions are two separate phenomena linked by an accident of social context. In my view the evidence is overwhelmingly that UFOs are a variety of things and there are some quite exciting research projects which have nothing to do with aliens and which may well be leading us towards the areas of science they reflect (e.g., plasma vortex studies, bioelectrical and neurophysiological field effects or microwave pollution research). Abductions are established subjectively as real experiences, but their objective reality is much more in doubt. I don't think this emerged from the conference. It was very much an American-oriented event. (I think only 3 or 4 non-Americans were invited.) In fact, UFOlogy outside of the USA is very different and does *not* presume the alien origin of the data.

No case is perfect. 95%+ of UFO sightings have conventional solutions. I've seen very impressive data crumble on proper investigation (which it rarely gets). But there is some residue and we have good photograph and trace case data. (My two prime examples would be the Trinidad Island photographs taken by a scientific survey team during the I.G.Y.— See my book, *Science & the UFO's* Basil Blackwell, Inc.—the book that [Whitley] Strieber credits in *Communion* with triggering his memory— and the Trans-en-Province, France, landing where a massive scientific investigation funded by the French government, Gendarmerie, and the Space Centre in Toulouse provided major radiation-inspired changes in the soil and plants which followed clear physical rules.)

I've written 15 books about UFOs, all published by reputable publishers, and I'm still struggling to get to the answers.

"P.S.," Jenny added, "Presently I am trying to explain to befuddled journalists 7 years of research just conducted into spontaneous human combustion. You may be surprised to hear that a link with UFOs emerged quite unexpectedly in this research. UFO researchers need to broaden their perspectives away from little grey men!"

I wondered if Randles knew about Louis Joseph Vance, the author of the best-selling *Lone Wolf* stories (about a gentleman crook), who died in

1933 apparently of spontaneous combustion while sitting quietly in his New York apartment. The press reported that his head and upper torso "looked as if they had been pushed into a blazing furnace," yet his lower torso was hardly burned at all; nor was anything else in the room burned but his chair, which was totally consumed except for the frame.[1]

Following Jenny Randles's presentation, Keith Basterfield, the research officer for UFO Research Australia, speaks about his country's abduction experiences, which, he tells us, "were very much the same kind of experience as the U.S., but on a numerically smaller scale." He reports that 55 percent of the Australian abductions take place in the bedroom; 35 percent in a rural, outside environment. "Yes, we do have some interesting cases," he says, "but we're way behind you on research."

Basterfield's most striking story concerns the marvelously named Maureen Puddy, a thirty-seven-year-old housewife from Rye in Victoria whose experience he offers in direct refutation to David Jacobs's assertion that "in the abduction phenomenon, abductees are never physically in place when they have an abduction experience. . . . Researchers have not collected a single case of an abduction in which the victim was actually in a normal location while the abduction was occurring."[2]

Mrs. Puddy's experiences began at 9:15 p.m. on July 3, 1972. She was driving home from a visit to her son, who was hospitalized south of Melbourne, when, according to Basterfield's report, "just after passing over the railway crossing, the roadway was lit up by a blue light. Thinking at first that the light was coming from a helicopter similar to the one which had taken her son to hospital, [Maureen Puddy] did not take too much notice, even though later she recalled hearing no noise at all. Realizing that even though it may have been a helicopter," Basterfield continues,

> it was too low for a normal flight, she accelerated away trying to get out of the blue light. However, she was unable to do so. She therefore slowed down, thinking that the pilot may be trying to get her attention. The light stopped with her.
>
> At this time she decided to stop the car—a thing she would not normally do on such an isolated stretch of road, devoid of streetlights. Shielding her eyes against the light, she looked up to see an unusual object present. She panicked, for it was shaped like two saucers, lip to lip. It appeared stationary, some 20–30m [50–75 feet] behind the car, at an angular elevation of 45°, some 20–30m above the ground. The road at this point was about 8m [20 feet] wide, and the object appeared 4–5 times wider than this and some 5–6m [12–15 feet] in height.
>
> There were no seams visible; no windows, no aerials, or in fact protuberances of any kind. A silver-blue light radiated from it, appearing iri-

descent in nature. It was this light which lit up the road. A low humming noise, likened by Maureen to an elevator moving, was heard while she was outside of the car looking at it.

Standing there, looking at the object, her reaction was to get away from it as fast as she could so she returned to the car and drove away at high speed. As she was driving she noted that the object was visible out of the right hand side (driver's) window, and that by leaning forward and looking out of the top of the windscreen, the object appeared to be keeping station over her vehicle. This pursuit continued for 13 km [nearly 8 miles]. Then the object moved backwards, there was a streak of light and it was gone.

Mrs. Puddy drove to the nearby Rosebud police station and reported the event. The next day, she telephoned the Royal Australian Air Force and reported the incident to them. The RAAF sent her out a form which she completed and returned.[3]

On Monday, July 24th, Mrs. Puddy would normally again have gone to the hospital to visit her son, but did not because of a gasoline strike. On several occasions that day she heard someone calling her name. Her husband and daughter heard nothing. Throughout the night she was unable to sleep because she kept hearing a voice inside her head calling, "Maureen . . . Maureen . . . Maureen." She even went outside the house to look, but saw nothing.

On Tuesday, 25th July 1972, Maureen was again driving home alone from the hospital, when at the same location, and the same time, another incident occurred.

At the railway crossing, she stopped her car to let a man leading a cow cross the road. A few hundred metres further on, the road was lit up with a blue light.

She recalled her thoughts as being, "My God, it's back!," then: "I'm not stopping for anything." She accelerated her vehicle away from the location.

However, suddenly the vehicle's engine cut out as if stopped by turning off the ignition key. Thinking that the engine had stalled, she turned the key, but this had no effect. The car slowed down and came to a halt, all by itself at the side of the road. During the period it was slowing, Maureen turned the steering wheel, but it did not alter the direction that the car went in. Pumping the brake had no effect. Putting the gears through all their positions did nothing either. However, the car's lights [stayed] on all the time.

She maintained that there were no road bumps as the car came to a halt. There was, in fact, no sensation of the road being under the car at this stage. By this time she was terrified.

All of the normal sound: "drained out of the air," and there was an eerie silence. She felt: 'like I was sitting in a tube—a completely closed vacuum tube.' Then she felt that she was receiving some audio transmissions, but she could not understand them.

She thought to herself: "I don't understand." The audio impressions were then understandable in "perfect English." She later related that this voice or impression sounded: "Too perfect," just like a ". . . machine recording," and that they also appeared to be inside her head, not like a normal voice from outside.

The voice said: "All your tests will be negative." This was followed by a 2–3 second pause, then, "Tell the media, do not panic, we mean no harm." There was another pause estimated as a minute long, then finally: "You now have control."

During this period, which lasted perhaps a minute and a half, she had remained seated with her hands clutching the steering wheel. She believed she could have moved if she wanted to, but she decided to remain still. As the audio impressions finished, the vehicle engine started itself; the blue light went out, and the object was suddenly gone. It had been visible, the same thing as on the third, out of the top of the windscreen, but was suddenly no longer there. This departure coincided with the approach of another road vehicle.

(She again reported the incident to the police and to the RAAF, who sent her another form to complete.)

The next day, puzzled as to whether to tell the media she finally decided to telephone 3 television stations and one interviewed her. Radio station 3 AW had her speak on an open line program, on which 2 other callers confirmed having seen something unusual in the area at the time.

Firstly, the wife of the man leading the cow called in to say her husband had seen a blue light but did not go back to take a look. Secondly, a couple reported having seen a blue light in the sky.[4]

And then there occurred the "abduction" that Basterfield felt refuted Jacobs's assertion that there was "not a single case" of abductees remaining in "a normal location" while an abduction was taking place. Basterfield's report continued:

On or about the 22nd February 1973, Mrs. Puddy related that she had again heard a voice calling her first name, all night long. In the morning she said she felt an "eerie presence" around the house and she: "caught a message" telling her to "Go back to the same meeting place."

She telephoned the Victorian UFO Research Society and two members [Judith Magee and Paul Norman] agreed to meet her at the spot where Maureen's car had stopped all of its own accord.

On the way alone to the spot, an entity just suddenly appeared in the car's front passenger seat. Mrs. Puddy almost crashed her car in surprise.

The entity had long blond hair and wore a ski suit. This suit was white in colour, and was tucked in at the wrists, and went over his feet. Just as suddenly, the "man" disappeared from her side.

Arriving at the nominated spot all 3 people then sat in Maureen's car. Suddenly, she saw the same "man" had appeared just outside the vehicle. Neither of the other 2, Judith Magee or Paul Norman, could see anything unusual present. Maureen says that the "man" was beckoning her to join him outside the vehicle. She refused to get out of the car.

Suddenly, according to the others present, Maureen "fainted." She began a verbal description to them whilst she was in this state of apparent unconsciousness.

She related that she was in a round room somewhere, which was lit, but there was no visible source of illumination. This scene was indistinguishable from the consensus reality that we call "real life." The "man" just appeared in the room, in which there was also a mushroom shaped object rising up from the floor. This was stemmed, with a broad domed top. There appeared to be an inner hemisphere, wobbling around, and it was covered with what looked to be hieroglyphics on it.

The "man" told her to describe what she could see, and this she did, to be heard by the 2 in the car. She could see no doors, or windows in this room, and so began to be scared. She started to cry, then woke, still in the car, with tears in [her] eyes, saying she could not remember anything that had just occurred. The 2 in the car filled her in on what had transpired.

About a week after this abduction, Mrs Puddy was driving with her son. He was sitting in the front passenger seat, when all of a sudden the same "man" appeared, sitting between them on the bench seat. The weather conditions were of rain, and low visibility. Yet while the "man" was there the scene in front of her, which should have been of rain and cloud, cleared abnormally, and she could see for kilometers. The "man" simply disappeared and the rain and bad visibility just reappeared.

All who interviewed [Maureen Puddy] stated that she was a normal, healthy individual. She was absolutely perplexed by the entire series of events. She received nothing but ridicule from people for reporting the episodes; yet no one was ever able to describe her as other than (her words) "an average housewife."[5]

Keith Basterfield stresses that these events occurred in 1972 and 1973, before the subject of abductions was "known to any wide degree in Australia;" and that they occurred to a "witness of impeccable character" who was "totally perplexed by the episodes" and "apparently subjected to an escalating sequence of events terminating with an abduction, then a 'visitation' a week later." Basterfield himself spoke to Maureen Puddy ten years after these events, and she remained adamant that what she had described had been "real." "However," he says, "and this cannot be stated clearly enough, she never physically left the presence of UFO researchers Judith Magee and Paul Norman during the abduction."

In response to a letter I wrote Basterfield after the conference, asking him what he thought was going on, he replied:

> In looking at, and working with, Australians reporting abductions my first response has been to explore potential psychological explanations. Hence a look at such topics as lucid dreams, transient memory disorders, hypnogogic and hypnopompic imagery, and fantasy-prone personality theory. All these are currently in mainstream psychology.
>
> Interestingly, these do not appear to be able to explain abductions, in totality. Next, on to psychiatric disorders. Again, nothing to date can explain abduction claims in totality. In summary, conventional psychology and psychiatry fall short of providing an explanation.
>
> So, what next? In my opinion, there still remains much work to be done. In terms of understanding altered states of consciousness. Conventional wisdom has not, in the main, conducted research into altered states. Who knows what we may learn? It is this area I believe that we need to tackle next in the abduction context, before taking a quantum leap to "aliens visiting us." Thus my viewpoint on abductions is that we need much more research before "going public"; and declaring "they" are here.
>
> On the question of hard evidence for "aliens abducting human beings." The more I examine the evidence for such things as implants and missing fetuses, the more nebulous it becomes. Abduction research lacks hard evidence, or we would still not be debating the issue. However, it is tantalising enough to continue to research.[6]

Psychologist Gilda Moura, the Brazilian representative to the conference, reports that most abductions in her country occur in the south and southeast, and that there are fewer in the northeast. The major difference between Brazil and the United States, she tells us, is that the majority of abductions take place outdoors. In a study of 137 abductions alleged to have taken place in Brazil, 67 percent of the abductors were Small Grays, 19 percent were Tall Beings. The purpose of the abductions seems to be genetic manipulation. This manipulation, she points out, is an indication of alien interference in human development, and the message is that this is not the first time such interference has occurred.

Moura reports a case similar to Basterfield's Maureen Puddy account, in which a native woman describes taking a long journey underwater to a cave site during an abduction without ever leaving her chair.

Spiritualism plays a much greater role in Brazilian abduction accounts, Moura explains, than in the United States.

"The phenomenon is global in scope," former NICAP acting director Richard Hall says, summarizing the morning's international reports, and warns that "we can't make too much of differences in alien types in different countries until a better data base is achieved."

Hall reports he is surprised to find that there seems to be "an amazing amount of description of machinery and equipment" on board the spacecraft: "tables, overhead gadgets, examining equipment." Six different investigators in the United States, plus investigators in Great Britain, Argentina, and Spain, report an "overhead scanning device on rails or tracks moving above the person," Hall says, adding that the gadget apparently makes a "clicking sound." In addition, there are similar reports of "hand-held instruments" or devices with lights at the ends that seem to be some sort of illuminated probes.

There are also numerous reports of skin scrapings, nail clippings, and blood samples being taken; striking similarities in messages and imagery; and numerous confirmations of the "Oz Factor" as well as reports of fog or mists surrounding cars. "The question is, How much mental manipulation are we dealing with?" Hall asks.

During the question period Dr. John Miller, the Los Angeles–area emergency-room physician, suggests that the skin scraping is usually done for bacterial or fungal searching. It may be performed to determine genetic types for the acquisition of DNA, he says, "but it is not a good source."

The next speaker is Richard Haines, whose presentation is "Multiple Abduction Evidence: What Is Really Needed?"

Haines is a dynamic, wiry little bald man with a meticulously trimmed mustache, wire-rimmed glasses, and the neat, precise manner of speech and dress of a retired British army major.

"A multiple abduction," Haines announces, "is two or more people who claim to be taken at the same time to the same place. Reliable evidence from two or more people to corroborate the event is needed." He describes one of his own cases, that of two twenty-two-year-old women who first met in 1974 and had known each other for one year before they were both abducted. They then remained friends for seven months after the event.

He explains the three-stage hypnosis process he has formulated in order to reduce as much as possible any contamination of the information obtained from a subject because of an investigator's bias. The first stage commences once a subject's deep trance has been achieved and tested. Haines then suggests the subject, "Tell me everything you see, feel, and hear about the event." He then sits back and listens without interrupting.

At the beginning of stage two Haines asks his subject, "Tell me everything you see, hear, and feel, *plus* everything you say out loud in conversation, what you hear back, and what you're thinking." Again, he sits back and listens.

At the start of the third stage, Haines has the subject go through the event a third time, but adds, "This time, I'm going with you and I'll be able to talk with you." It is during this stage that Haines asks questions in order to elicit information that, he hopes, will clarify or fill out the story.

Haines reports he used his three-stage hypnosis process on the two women subjects, hypnotizing them separately so that neither would be aware what the other had said. When he came to the third stage, he tells us, he had a list of 103 questions.

Independently, the women described the aliens as without expressions on their faces, with no hair, tiny holes that looked like noses, mouths that they did not use, and little half-inch openings for ears that were shaped like the letter *k*. Furthermore, there was a 67 percent match on their descriptions of what had taken place. "Incidentally," Haines adds, "they did not say they were taken into a UFO. They said they were taken underground."

Someone asks, "Could these two young women's shared vision have been a folie à deux?"—a psychiatric term to describe a shared paranoid disorder or an induced psychotic disorder. In a folie à deux a delusion develops in an individual who is in a close relationship with a second person with an already established delusion. The first individual's delusion is similar in content to the second's.[7]

John E. Mack denies that such could have been the case in Richard Haines's two subjects. Their shared abduction scenario could not have been a folie à deux in that "highly detailed, objective, descriptive, corroborative evidence was provided."

John Carpenter, the next presenter, agrees with Haines. "Independent interviewing and hypnotic regression of multiple witnesses to a UFO close encounter," he tells us, "are essential steps toward establishing a credible account with minimal opportunity for contamination, suggestion, or influential interactions. The separate hypnotic investigation of two or more participants greatly decreases the likelihood that imagination, delusion, or confabulation—the replacement of fact with fantasy in memory—serve as explanations for these encounters.

"In a November 1989 incident," Carpenter continues, "two women were driving in a remote area of western Kansas when they encountered a UFO and lost two hours of time. They experienced anxiety, insomnia, irritability, and bewilderment as a result of that night. Neither woman claimed any knowledge or interest in UFOs at all. They initially believed that they never left their car nor observed anything further. Hypnotic regressions, performed independently, revealed abduction scenarios with at least forty direct correlations between their recalled accounts."

Carpenter's detailed report of this incident was published in the *Journal of UFO Studies,* the publication of the J. Allen Hynek Center for UFO Studies (CUFOS). It is worth looking at in some detail here. In the report he refers to the two women as "Susan" and "Jennifer." (Susan, we now know from her panel appearance at the conference, is actually the abductee who changed her name to "Star.")

" 'Susan,' " Carpenter wrote, "is a 42-year-old businesswoman married to an engineer with two children ages 17 and 21. . . . She states that she has never given the subject of UFOs any attention and had not read any books on the subject. 'Susan' appears to be an honest . . . candid woman with no psychological problem or history of such difficulties. . . . 'Jennifer' is a 49-year-old widow with two grown stepchildren, ages 33 and 35. A college graduate with an MSW degree, she works as a freelance photographer. . . . She is somewhat shy and reserved but yet independent and adventuresome. She stated that she has not read any books or seen any movies concerning the subject of UFOs. . . . She is perceptive in noting small details and will keep thorough little journals at times."[8]

The two women were administered three objective psychological tests by CUFOS. Neither showed any overt signs of pathology or psychological problems as measured by the Minnesota Multiphasic Personality Inventory (MMPI). Both had low to moderate scores on the Index of Childhood Memory and Imagination (ICMI), which measures a tendency toward fantasy-prone behavior and thought. On the Creative Imagination Scale, which measures hypnotic suggestibility, Susan's score indicated a moderate tendency toward suggestibility; Jennifer had a score near the top of the range, meaning she would be a good hypnotic subject and potentially quite suggestible.

According to Carpenter's CUFOS report,

On November 6, 1989, these two women were on the road, pleasantly driving home to St. Louis from a conference in Aspen, Colorado. Jennifer was faithfully documenting in her log and had just noted it was 11:40 p.m. as they pulled out of a gas station in Flagler, Colorado. They had decided they would drive to Goodland, Kansas, before stopping for the night. Susan had been averaging 75–80 mph on Interstate 70; Goodland was 72 miles away.

Shortly after leaving Flagler, they caught sight of a bright object ahead of them in the east and slightly to the south but very high in the sky. They noted that it was fairly stationary but always stayed in the same location in relation to their car despite noting that the moon changed position in relation to their car and the object. They clearly observed flashing, colored lights on the object and occasional little movements. Then they both noted the rather sudden appearance of many smaller green lights near the brighter UFO.

While Susan drove, Jennifer kept her eyes on the skies for nearly an hour. Several times they pulled off the road briefly and dimmed all their lights so that they both could get a better view. During the last time they did this, Susan noted that the car clock indicated the time was 12:40 a.m. Suddenly they both saw a ball of light descend to within a hundred feet of their vehicle, hovering over a field ahead and to their right. Below this ball of light appeared a V-shaped "cone" of soft, "fluffy" white light reaching toward the ground with colored rays of pastel pink, blue, and lavender. These beams seemed to establish the edges of the "cone" and crisscross slightly at the bottom point. The women performed a "reality check" at this point by verbalizing to each other what they were seeing, and they reported the same visual details. They also both noted "black waves" through the lower portions of the windshields—reminiscent of heat waves on the horizon of a desert highway. They felt the excitement and rush of adrenaline, only to next remember that they were pulling back onto the road and feeling strikingly different. Now they felt similar feelings of exhaustion, irritability, and a preference for silence and solitude—quite an amazing and sudden transition in a matter of what seemed to be only seconds in time.[9]

The two women arrived in Goodland, Kansas, according to what they initially told Carpenter, "just minutes later." Susan noted the time and Jennifer documented it in her notebook as being 2:30 a.m. Once in their motel room, Carpenter reported, they noticed "startling changes in their physical appearance that matched their irritable feelings and fatigue." Jennifer's cheeks were red and flushed; Susan was pale, "like death warmed over," she later said.

The more prosaic and routine explanations for their alleged UFO observance were sought. Astronomer Walter N. Webb was able to discount their possibly having confused sightings of Venus, Jupiter, Saturn, or Mars with a UFO due to those planets' movements at that time of the month. Although the Taurid meteor shower had reached its peak four days prior to the women's experience, it "would not," Carpenter noted, "account for the hovering 'soft white ball,'" though "it could seem to describe the 'light hurtling out of the sky' at them. But then," Carpenter continued, "meteors are not known to stop in mid-air a hundred feet away and display a 'cone' of pastel light beams toward the ground. The witnesses had enough time to draw each other's attention to it, take turns describing it to each other, and observe simultaneously the 'black wavy lines' around the car."

That the object's "bright flashing lights" might have been due to atmospheric conditions refracting distant light can also be discounted due to the remoteness of the Kansas area from which they viewed it. And although "autokinesis" (the apparent motion of an object due to the small, involuntary movements of one's eyes) must be considered, both women are adamant that "the bright UFO was not a star, and that it paced their car, appearing in the same location through the windshield, despite the changing angle of the car in relation to the moon and other reference points."

It wasn't until the morning following their UFO encounter that the women discovered that although they believed they had driven three hours, they had used up only an hour's worth of gas. Susan and Jennifer subsequently checked their road map and noticed they had traveled but seventy-two miles in that three hours' time.

Upon their return to St. Louis both women continued to feel anxious and irritable. Susan, because of the UFO sighting and her determination to resolve the puzzle of the two hours of missing time, contacted a friend interested in UFOs, who in turn put her in touch with the state director of the Missouri Mutual UFO Network (MUFON). The MUFON state director alerted Carpenter.

On November 12, 1989, five days after the encounter, Carpenter began interviewing Susan. He tape-recorded her conscious recollection and then performed a one-hour hypnotic exploration into her period of amnesia.

"Susan was nervous, curious, cautious, and determined at the start of her session," Carpenter wrote, then continued:

> The major aspects of her experience were recovered, but the flow of details indicated a need for more time and further investigation to fully document what seemed like memories. The need for absolute secrecy and no communication with Jennifer was explained and strictly emphasized. . . . Susan indicated that she would have no difficulty maintaining her silence because she and Jennifer were only acquaintances living miles apart with no regular communication or routine contact with each other.[10]

Carpenter next contacted Jennifer and invited her to participate. She, too, was curious about what had happened, but maintained that upon seeing the UFO she had neither left their car nor seen anything further. Nevertheless, she met with Carpenter on November 24, twelve days after his initial session with Susan, and just seventeen days after the two women's encounter with the UFO. Susan was also present at this time.

At that meeting, Carpenter reported, Jennifer confirmed that "Susan had not revealed any information whatsoever." Afterwards, Carpenter asked Susan to go into another room and he put Jennifer through two and a half hours of clinical hypnosis, during which she was able to "break through the veil of amnesia to recall a wealth of detail." She, too, was then asked to segregate herself from Susan.

At that point Susan was brought back into the treatment room and placed under hypnosis for approximately an hour and a half. "Although she reiterated the same basic recollections," Carpenter wrote, "Susan had much more time to notice additional details and explore other aspects of her experience."[11]

In *On Stolen Time,* his summary of the UFO abduction mystery, Bullard wrote, "Few investigators have looked closely at the order of events in abductions, yet comparison demonstrates a striking consistency of form among the reports and thereby provides valuable evidence for a coherent phenomenon. . . .

"No case includes every possibility," Bullard continued,

> but a case qualifies as correct if everything it does possess follows the prescribed order. A notable majority of cases (84 percent of 193 detailed scenarios) conforms to this pattern. The reason for this order belongs within the phenomenon itself and begs for an explanation. A calculation of the probabilities for these arrangements happening by chance alone reaches one in tens of thousands, if not more. Anyone who would dismiss abduction stories as products of random chance might also be interested in purchasing a bridge in Brooklyn.[12]

If one compares Bullard's detailed "model" for an abduction scenario to Susan and Jennifer's tape-recorded, hypnotically recalled accounts, a striking number of similarities occur:

Both witnesses, under hypnosis, first saw the UFO in the distance—the prelude to what Bullard refers to as the "capture."

> JENNIFER: "I see this bright light—but it's not moving like a plane. . . . It *is* moving just a little bit . . . to the side and down a little bit . . . colored lights, too—the changing of lights. . . ."

> SUSAN: "It has the white light—in front of it. On the back and sides, it keeps flashing colors. . . . It's making little movements. . . . It's like oval . . . lights around the front. . . ."[13]

Both saw a fluctuation in the UFO's glow:

> JENNIFER: "[The UFO] would change intensity."

SUSAN: "I can see the UFO getting brighter! . . . Oh, it's much brighter! It's much closer!"[14]

Both saw numerous little green lights moving around the UFO. And as the UFO approached and hovered nearby, Susan and Jennifer both saw "black wavy lines" visible around the windshield of their car and observed a "cone" or "V" of pastel-colored light rays one hundred feet away.

JENNIFER: "This cone . . . white—soft like clouds with white behind it— all around . . . and streaks of colored light coming downward . . . like purple and blue and white and pink . . . crossing at the bottom like—like beams . . . like sunrays in a way . . . at the bottom of the 'V' or cone."

SUSAN: "There's a red ball of light . . . coming out of the sky. . . . These two color lines are coming out of it simultaneously from each side . . . and they look like a 'V'—and they form a 'V' down to the Earth."

JENNIFER: "This cone . . . was real close to us . . . like a hundred feet or so. . . . It was close over on the righthand side."

SUSAN: "Close . . . close, uh, maybe a hundred feet."[15]

Both women consciously claimed that following this initial sighting of the UFO they had proceeded on their trip without interruption, and that only subsequently did they realize that they were unable to account for two hours of their time.

Under hypnosis both women recalled that after they had observed the cone-shaped beam of light, they were "captured." Susan saw two Beings approach the car. One instructed her to stop the engine and reassured her that they were "friends." She found herself unable to react while both she and Jennifer were levitated out of the car in sitting positions.

Both women recalled being escorted by the two Beings and floating up into the night sky toward the round craft as their car grew smaller beneath them. Neither witness can recall exactly how they got inside; neither recalls any doorway.

JENNIFER: "I *do* seem to see the car from outside. . . . I'm behind it, looking down at an angle . . . above the right side of the roof. . . . I'm higher than just a little bit ago! . . . I see a pinhead of where the car was—it's real tiny now!"

SUSAN: "[The car is] way down there. . . . It's real small . . . the more I look at it the tinier it gets. It looks like I'm seeing [the UFO] from, uh, like I'm in the sky. It's like . . . like we don't weigh much. It's more like we're floating!"[16]

Both women enter the craft and realize they are inside a small, round room with geometrically shaped windows and a reddish glow.

> JENNIFER: "I see some windows . . . different shapes . . . one's round . . . like a panel in between each of these. Another one is like . . . a square . . . then a panel . . . kind of looking through a window that's not . . . flat, but curved. A triangular window . . ."

> SUSAN: "There's some windows . . . different shapes . . . like squares all together. . . . There's panels . . . rectangle windows—sideways. It changes shapes—"

> JENNIFER: "[In the first room] there's a span of orangy-red color—kind of diffuse. . . . There's a kind of glowing . . . um, white—not single light, but kind of an area that goes around like so. And it glows—kind of like red—sometimes burgundy—with some white . . . it changes."

> SUSAN: "There's some pink light coming from somewhere . . . the rest of the light looks white."

> JENNIFER: "Wherever I am . . . it's round like a ring. . . . There's no corners in this room. It's round . . . not like a round ball, not oval—kind of like frisbee round."

> SUSAN: "[The room] is more like a circle! It's more round."[17]

Through the craft's windows, both women see stars and a blue Earth-like planet.

> JENNIFER: "I'm looking out the windows . . . it's like, oh, like Earth . . . it's not so far away that I can't distinguish some lights and . . . we're high—we're high!"

> SUSAN: "I can see—looking out one of the windows . . . a bluish-like, ink-blue globe of some sort outside the window . . . like pictures you might see of planets . . . it's not a picture! . . . a deep blue. It looks bluish. It's real pretty."[18]

Both women experienced the second stage of Bullard's model scenario: the "examination." They recalled being taken into a large operating amphitheater–like room. Both recalled—from their different perspectives—Jennifer having been placed on a table under a bright light and her being calmed by a touch or gesture of a Being's hand. Both report that Jennifer remained dressed.

> JENNIFER: "There's some tall columns that go from the floor upward. . . . I'm lying on a table. . . . I can see the pole above . . . and the bright light above—right in the center."

SUSAN: "There's a column that comes down—real close to the table."

JENNIFER: "A panel of lights light up. . . . It's as if they're getting data from their panel of what looks like very sophisticated equipment—kind of all one moulding . . . it's all smooth . . . lots of different colored lights. . . ."

SUSAN: "There's some instrument-looking things—like panels . . . some cabinet-things . . . built into the wall."

JENNIFER: "[The large room is] kind of an auditorium—like oval-shaped . . . seats that go, oh, six or eight levels, and they all look alike on each side observing us."

SUSAN: "Oh! I'm in a *big* room—a big oval shape with a domed ceiling with windows up high . . . like a cathedral but not ornate . . . tiers of seats . . . and there's a lot of smaller [Beings] now!"

Each woman recalled seeing Beings.

JENNIFER: "I see something moving, but I don't know what it is. . . . It has arms and legs . . . they have one-color suits; the hands or gloves . . . are white. . . ."

SUSAN: "I don't really see clothing. It looks like everything molds together. . . . They're *not* naked . . . off-whitish. . . ."[19]

Each woman similarly described the Beings' bodies and heads as those of pale Small Grays. They both similarly described how the Beings moved.

JENNIFER: "Those things move around—almost like a floating action . . . but a controlled weightlessness—like, like they *glide* . . . they just glide!"

SUSAN: "They slide . . . very smooth and graceful."[20]

Both women similarly recalled the Beings' eyes, noses, and mouths.

JENNIFER: "The eyes are kinda big but they don't look like our eyes, black . . . elongated on each side—but narrowing down . . . smaller, going toward the ears. . . . It's wider toward the middle, and then it narrows down . . . almost like teardrops. . . . The bulbous area (nearest the nose)—kind of narrows down toward the outside . . . dark . . . all one color."

SUSAN: "It has huge eyes. They are really dark . . . huge eyes . . . slanted eyes. No eyelids . . . don't blink . . . real intense. Huge and slanted—real slanted—they stand out in contrast to the white (face). . . . The eyes are enormous and take over the face. . . ."

JENNIFER: "I see a space between the two eyes . . . but not a nose like our noses. Kind of smooth-like . . . no nose form per se . . . kind of a curved smooth area. . . ."

SUSAN: "No, not a nose . . . the eyes predominate the face. . . . The nose is flat as if it isn't even there."

JENNIFER: "I don't see mouths like ours at all. It looks almost mechanical . . . I don't see it open."

SUSAN: "I don't see tongues and teeth—the mouth doesn't open at all . . . I don't see them using their mouth!"[21]

They gave similar descriptions of the Beings' hands and fingers.

JENNIFER: "The hands or gloves are white . . . looks like about three or four fingers—all white. . . . They're long fingers . . . seems like four long fingers."

SUSAN: "The fingers are real long . . . and they're slender . . . they are more adaptable, more flexible. . . . They're not soft—they're, uh, like bony-hard."[22]

Both women described the Beings as having no hair. They similarly described being reassured and calmed both telepathically and by touch.

JENNIFER: "It's as if they were assuring us . . . we should not be afraid. They're not going to hurt us."

SUSAN: "They seem to be communicating . . . that they mean us no harm. . . . I don't think they talked. I *know* they're communicating. They don't *say* anything. It's not coming out of their mouth. I don't know if they even have a mouth! I *feel* them communicating."

JENNIFER: "They came over and patted my hand. *That* made me feel comfortable. . . . I feel warmth going into my hands. . . ."

SUSAN: "They try to calm me . . . somebody keeps rubbing my head—with those hands. They pass this hand over Jennifer's forehead area . . . which seems to either calm her or sedate her."[23]

Jennifer is placed on the examining table; she cannot see Susan from where she is, but Susan can see her.

SUSAN: "[Jennifer is] lying on a table—covered with some white type of material . . . a narrow table."

JENNIFER: "I—I don't see her [Susan]. I think I'm looking around for Susan—and I just don't see her at all."

SUSAN (in response to Carpenter's question "Can Jennifer see you from where she is lying?"): "I don't think so. I'm sitting [in] . . . looks like a lawnchair—white metal?"

JENNIFER (while on the table): "These figures are—one's moving around over here. The others—one's on my right . . . one's kind of like over here—in the back a little bit, and one is over on the left a little bit. . . . I can see them coming forward and looking down at me. . . ."

SUSAN: "It seems like there was somebody with this instrument-looking thing. Then there was—behind Jennifer's head—there was like three people standing there . . . behind her head."[24]

With the "preparation" stage of the examination completed, the exam moves forward into its second stage, the "manual" phase. Both women see some sort of preoccupation with Jennifer's fingers and hands. Jennifer recalls some form of electrodes/wires attached to her fingers. Both witnesses recall computerlike panels with blinking lights, etc., and Jennifer's ankles held by some sort of restraints.

JENNIFER: "Something's around my ankles like a strap—but not to tie me down. It's a strap. It's like something goes completely around each ankle."

SUSAN: "There are these little, um, they look like, um, stirrups . . . they're at the end of the table and her legs can just like kind of fit in them . . . maybe so she won't kick. Her feet are in these things."[25]

According to Bullard's model, the medical-examination scenario might then include "specimen taking," during which samples might be taken of blood, sperm, eggs, or hair, followed by a "reproductive exam," in which the sexual organs might be probed or examined. Neither Jennifer nor Susan reported or recalled any such activities taking place. However, Bullard's model scenario's next stage did take place: while Jennifer appeared sedated, Susan clearly observed the implantation of a tiny object up Jennifer's nostril with a dental-pick-like device. Jennifer reported severe nosebleeds afterwards.

SUSAN: "She's real quiet—she's not moving—I don't know if they use some anesthesia (Being had passed hand over Jennifer's forehead) . . . some kind of operation. . . . They have some type of implant thing . . . put it in the left side of her nose . . . looks like one of those things a dentist uses—a pick or something. . . . I think it was some type of operation. . . . She's been having her nose bleeding. When they are finished, they help her sit up. She's coughing or bleeding or something."[26]

According to Bullard's model sequence, following the completion of the physical examination, a "conference" period would then take place. But,

Carpenter noted, both Jennifer and Susan reported that most of the telepathic messages actually occurred during Jennifer's exam. Jennifer did hear
some noises apparently originating from the vicinity of the Beings.

> JENNIFER: "I think I asked, 'What are you doing to me?'—that they
> need to have more information about what my chemistry is all
> about. . . . Something was being *energized* through my system when
> they were taking all these tests, taking information from me—from my
> body chemistry."

> SUSAN: "They're working for the advancement . . . something about ge-
> netic coding . . . within beings. . . . Many beings have particular genetic
> codings that allow for our cooperation in what they're doing . . . some-
> thing that has been in us since our conception . . . something that we al-
> lowed. . . . It was a collective agreement . . . from other planes, other
> levels of existence. It was an agreement we had before our birth . . . and it
> is for the advancement of the species and the advancement of planet
> Earth. . . . It seems like they have this information that is transferred tele-
> pathically, working with us and through us! There is a telepathic link.
> They can work with us telepathically, now. . . ."[27]

Both women recalled then being taken to at least two of the craft's
rooms, which they remembered distinctly and in considerable detail—including, Carpenter points out, a memorable window view of an "inky-blue"
celestial object.

In keeping with the familiar scenario, the women were then returned to
Earth.

> JENNIFER: "It's as if we're just kind of descending . . . we're floating
> through the sky . . . then gently come down to earth."

> SUSAN: "One of the aliens does something with his hand—a movement
> with his hands . . . and we seem to be on our way back to the car . . . we
> don't fall . . . come back faster."

> JENNIFER: "They let us out to the right of the car. It was close to the car—
> just about where we saw the cone [of light] to begin with. . . ."

> SUSAN: "Two came with us. Two . . . and we get back into the
> car. . . . They are like seeing that we get into the car. . . ."

> JENNIFER: "Seemed like [I started to forget] once we got in—back in the
> car—like a dream, it disappeared. . . . Oh, it seems *real!* I—I was somewhere
> I've never been before—nor have I ever seen anything like this before!"

> SUSAN: "They are seeing that we get in the car. . . . They put their hands
> over—wave their hands over our foreheads, and we don't remember."[28]

In the final stage of Bullard's model scenario the abductee may suffer or notice physical effects, vague or unexplained anxiety, phobic responses, nightmares, flashbacks, insomnia, changes in personality—sometimes pursuing new interests or more satisfying work. Also, other UFO experiences may be reported, along with the remembrance of earlier incidents in one's life. An awareness may occur that other family members are involved, perhaps triggering recollections from them that they may have kept hidden or discounted for years.

"Susan," Carpenter reported, "experienced anxiety, restlessness, and exhaustion while Jennifer had nosebleeds, insomnia and red, flushed cheeks. After the amnesia was dissolved, Susan spent the next year changing jobs and pursuing new satisfying interests." (You will recall that Susan, now "Star," became a massage therapist.)

"During Susan's hypnosis she recalled an incident just three weeks earlier," Carpenter's report continued. "During the twelve months that followed the November 7 encounter, both women reported further incidents. Susan's daughter explored a peculiar bedroom memory under hypnosis with this author and uncovered a remarkably detailed experience matching the 'abduction scenario.' "[29]

The significance of this case, according to Carpenter, is that "two mature, highly credible women—apparently unfamiliar with any UFO-related data—reported a UFO encounter within 100 feet of their car. Neither woman," Carpenter continued,

> could consciously account for nearly two hours of time. Both adamantly claimed independently that they *never* left their car or saw anything else. Separate hypnosis sessions released two elaborate stories that produced many similar details of an abduction aboard an alien craft. At least 40 correlations could be found among descriptions of the creatures, craft interior, behaviors, procedures, and general scenario. Not only did the details match each other between their accounts but other details echoed both published and unpublished research data.[30]

In 1990, a year after her experience, Star, at Carpenter's request, addressed a large gathering of people interested in exploring the phenomenon. "UFOs were not in my consciousness," she told them. "It's not that I was a complete skeptic, it's just that it was nothing that ever interested me. I wasn't *into* UFOs! And since I've had the experience, I've had so many people say to me that they wish it had happened to them. And my response is, 'Then *why* did it happen to me?'

"I was never interested in it," Star continued. "I never read a book. It's like a year ago I had tunnel vision. It's almost like I lived in a little box. So when people are skeptical of the UFO phenomenon, I *understand!* I was there! I know exactly where they're coming from. But it is a type of tunnel vision. It might actually cause you to break out of your preconceived ideas about who we are and where we're going and what we're all about if you allow for anything other than what you can see, touch, and feel on this planet. I can honestly say that, because I have grown from it. I think that I am a much better person for having had my little world shattered—and for opening up new possibilities of what this life might be all about."[31]

Following Carpenter's presentation, the conference breaks for lunch.

In his commentary published with the results of the Roper Poll, John Carpenter compared the difficulty the outside community has with accepting that there might be anything to these abduction reports with the initial doubt and disbelief with which the first reports of family incest and child sexual abuse were received until, he wrote, "the growing number of reports finally forced the consideration of these issues by the mental health community."[32] Another parallel might be the skepticism with which the first reports of the Epstein-Barr syndrome (chronic fatigue) were greeted.

"Scattered psychological testing all over the United States seems to support the clinical impressions that the vast majority reporting UFO abduction experiences are basically healthy and free of psychopathology," Carpenter wrote. "Creativity and confabulation," his commentary continued,

> would produce a wide variety of individualized scenarios and details, reflecting one's unique background. Similarly, dreams may be alike in general themes but quite different in their specific details, characteristic of the individual and his life situations. Data collected from many researchers produce striking similarity in abduction theme, procedure, behavior, bizarreness, order of events, etc. Significant correlations are being found among written symbols observed, insignias on uniforms, anatomical detail, and other small and precise details which remain unpublished and, therefore, unavailable to the public.[33]

The question arises as to whether individuals might subconsciously develop similar abduction scenarios through their exposure to publications, movies, or television shows and documentaries. But, as Carpenter points out, a great many of the "abductees" had no prior exposure to abduction-related stories and no prior interest in the subject whatsoever. "Most would tell you," Carpenter wrote, "they have been quite happy in their lives and did *not* want this unexpected intrusion. When simple folks from rural areas with no television, and small children who cannot read, begin to recite the same familiar abduction scenario, how can one account for the supposed media influence?"[34]

The question also arises as to what role hypnosis or the hypnotist himself might play in influencing the outcome. But, as Carpenter reports, nearly one-fourth of all UFO abduction cases are consciously recalled without the use of hypnosis, and yet these accounts "correlate just as well as with those experiences retrieved from amnesiac period." Carpenter admits he has deliberately attempted to "lead individuals with direct hypnotic suggestions into sensible and credible directions but find consistent resistance to follow my lead. Instead, the person relates his/her own bizarre experience which then matches the accounts of others without the subject even realizing this."[35]

Information gained through the aid of hypnosis is certainly questionable and controversial in court cases, Carpenter tells us; but hypnosis does seem to pierce the amnesiac barrier in abduction victims and can bring them genuine relief.

There yet remains, however, the nagging worry that these abduction accounts might be hoaxes. But, as Carpenter has pointed out, fewer than 5 percent of all UFO reports have been statistically documented as hoaxes. And he asks the telling questions "What purpose is there to a hoax if the individual is fearful of telling others and avoidant of publicity? How could a farmer in Kansas construct the exact same lies as a businessman in New York or an artist in Paris? And for what obscure purpose?"[36]

It is clear that among the abductees I have spoken with here at the M I T conference, the last thing in the world they seem to want is any form of publicity. They absolutely do *not* want their names to be made public. What they *do* want is to be taken seriously, and they want someone to help them understand and make sense of what they believe is happening to them.

I have lunch that Monday afternoon with Carol and Alice. We are talking in general terms about the conference, and Alice is saying, "I'm still trying to approach this thing in a very rational, logical—as much as it can be rational and logical—way. Trying to detect some patterns to this, trying to find out what's going on."

"A lot of what we thought were childhood memories, for instance, we had forced into little boxes," Carol explains. "And we'd held on to that until little by little, as this conference has drawn on, those things have been taken out of the boxes and thrown away."

"Like what?" I asked her.

"The scars are part of it," Carol says. "The man with the cowboy hat. That was my last holdout. The man with the four-foot Stetson."

"What man in a four-foot Stetson?" I asked.

"It's a long story," Carol says, and emits a harsh little bark of laughter.

"It's a Being Carol saw," Alice explains.

"I didn't tell everything in last night's presentation," Carol says. "But last March 8 I had this weird experience with what at first I thought was a naked man in a four-foot Stetson hat. And this morning I was sitting on the bench outside during the coffee break—Alice was right next to me, and on the other side was one of the therapists, Joe Nyman. I asked Joe if he had ever heard of an incident where an encounter was with a Tall Gray Being, big, I mean six feet or so, wearing a cowboy hat. And he goes, 'Oh, yeah. A man with a big cowboy hat, a big Stetson? Oh yeah, we've had those.' And he said there were different kinds of costumes—"

"The clown, for kids," Alice interjects.

"Right," Carol says. "Orange hair for kids so the kids would think they were talking to a clown. And we heard at this conference from our own investigator about a new experiencer who had a similar man with a cowboy hat."

Carol and Alice begin talking about childhood memories, the odd little bits and pieces they had retained which had returned as flashbacks. Carol tells me about the flashback that had occurred during her presentation at the conference the night before: the memory of being a child frantically trying to keep the bright light from entering the closet. "The only reason I knew I was a child and approximately how old I was was because I knew that house I was in. So at least I could place it in a time period."

"But what's so frustrating about one of Carol's flashbacks," Alice says, "is that it's all in bits and pieces. It's just one little piece with nothing to connect it to."

"There's no one else there in the flashback I can recognize: 'That's so-and-so, it happened at such-and-such,' " Carol says. She is gazing through the restaurant window at the street outside. "It's like looking at a parking meter in space," she says, "just one parking meter, and based on that parking meter you're trying to reconstruct in your memory the city block surrounding it."

"And sometimes," Alice adds, "you don't even know what city it was in."

The first speaker after lunch is Budd Hopkins, whose presentation, "A Doubly Witnessed Abduction," is the account of a woman he calls Linda Cortile, who was abducted from her New York City apartment at 3:15 in the morning in late November 1989. It is the episode he alluded to yesterday at breakfast.

"Accompanied by three aliens," Hopkins reports, "Linda was floated out of a window twelve stories above the ground, then up into a hovering UFO. The event was witnessed by two security agents and the senior political figure they were guarding, as well as by a woman driving across the Brooklyn Bridge.

"The importance of this case is virtually immeasurable," Hopkins points out, "as it powerfully supports both the objective reality of UFO abductions and the accuracy of regressive hypnosis as employed with this abductee."

According to Hopkins, the two security men were driving the political official along South Street near the Brooklyn Bridge beneath the FDR Drive in Manhattan when their car's electrical system inexplicably cut out and they coasted to a stop. They could detect a reddish-orange glow through their car's windshield. At first, the security agent Hopkins calls Dan thought the glow was the rising sun; but almost immediately he realized he was facing not east but due west. Peering up through the windshield, Dan and his partner, "Richard," saw a fifty-foot-wide, oval-shaped object with rotating colored lights hovering above a fifteen-story apartment building at the street corner about five hundred feet ahead.

Richard pulled a pair of binoculars out of the car's glove compartment, and, as he watched, the craft—now making a barely audible low humming sound—descended until it was level with the top of the apartment building. All sound then stopped. A bright beam of blue-white light shot out from the bottom of the craft, and then, to the horror of the three men in the car, they saw a woman in a white nightgown float out of a window on the apartment building's twelfth floor, accompanied by three small creatures with big heads.

"My God!" Dan cried. "We've got to stop them!"

"How are we going to do that?" Richard asked. "Shoot them?"

The woman, escorted by the three Small Beings, hovered briefly in midair; they then ascended the blue-white beam of light and disappeared through an opening in the bottom of the spacecraft. A moment later, the light flickered out; the disc again emitted a reddish-orange glow, rose slowly upwards, then passed over the FDR Drive and the Brooklyn Bridge and dove into the East River, presumably carrying Linda Cortile within it!

My immediate impulse upon hearing this story is to laugh, to make jokes about it, to turn it into one of Bob Newhart's old comedy routines: "Now, let me see if I've got this straight, Mrs. Cortile. First you were floated by three small gray Beings through your window . . . then up a beam of light and into a . . . I see, a hovering alien spacecraft. . . . Uh-huh. . . . And in this spacecraft these beings did *what?* . . . They *stole your eggs?* Uh, why do you think they would want to do a thing like that, Mrs. Cortile? . . . Uh-huh, I see. Because they wanted to *breed* with you." But there is nothing funny about this story to Linda Cortile.

At the time of this abduction Linda was already seeing Budd Hopkins. She had initially contacted him seven months earlier, in April 1989, after reading his book *Intruders,* in which he described a woman abductee, "Kathy Davis," who had had some mysterious nose surgery and suspected that the Beings had implanted some sort of device there. Linda, too, believed she had had surgery in her nose she could not account for. For fourteen years she had carried a scar high up inside her nose, a scar positively identified by a doctor she had consulted as being a scalpel cut. But neither she nor her family had any memory of Linda having had any operations other than one for an impacted wisdom tooth and, several years later, an episiotomy following the birth of her first son.

In addition to the inexplicable nose surgery, there were strange, fragmentary memories of episodes that had taken place when Linda was a child and, later, a twenty-year-old. And so when Linda went to consult Hopkins, she assumed that together they would just look into these previous experiences. She was now, after all, a married woman in her early forties with two children, and nothing had happened for years.

The morning after the abduction, however, she awoke with conscious memories of the onset of paralysis the night before and the presence of Small Gray Beings in her bedroom. She recalled having cried out to her husband in bed beside her to wake up, but he wouldn't or couldn't. And then her memory ceased. She immediately telephoned Budd Hopkins, telling him, "I think something happened last night."

Three days later, Hopkins did a hypnotic regression session with Linda, and the abduction story emerged. With the aid of hypnosis she was able to recall how the Beings had led her from her bedroom, which overlooked her building's courtyard, to the living room, whose window looked out onto the street and beyond to a tiny strip of the East River. She then remembered being floated out of that window and up into the awaiting craft.

It wasn't until fourteen months later, in February 1991, that Hopkins heard for the first time from Richard, who, along with Dan and the senior political figure they were guarding, had witnessed Linda's abduction from their stalled car.

"Please respect our credibility at work," Richard wrote Hopkins. "We cannot let our identities be made public." He expressed his shock at what he had seen, adding, "This whole situation flies in the face of everything I've believed or knew about." He wrote of the stages of anger, fear, and embarrassment he had passed through. "The manner they took her drove us nuts! What could we do to help her? Who was she? Was she one of them?"

Hopkins thought Richard's question "Was she one of them?" a particularly interesting reaction. "It's a measure of how much they pushed the whole thing away," he later told me, "to assume—at least on one level—that maybe she's one of them. It's almost as if they're saying, 'I don't want to think she's a human being and we should have done something.' It's easier to think of her as part of the whole business."

The agents, of course, had no way of knowing that Hopkins was already aware of the abduction and that the woman they had seen was Linda Cortile. Hopkins immediately warned Linda that the men might visit her and that if they did so, she was not to share with them any details whatsoever of what she remembered. She was instead to tell them that it was extremely important they contact Hopkins himself. "At the very least," he told Linda, "try to get them to record a statement."

Hopkins's purpose was to acquire independent, uncontaminated confirmation of the details of the incident.

Not long afterwards Dan and Richard, identifying themselves as police officers, did visit Linda at her apartment.

Dan, who had been staring at Linda, sat down on the couch. "My God," he said, putting his head in his hands, "it's really her!"

"Thank God you're alive," Richard said as he embraced Linda. He had tears in his eyes. "We couldn't do anything to help you."

They told Linda how they had witnessed through binoculars what had happened.

If seeing Linda in person unsettled the security agents, hearing them confirm the details of her abduction had an even more devastating effect on Linda herself.

Several months after the M.I.T. conference, I was able to meet Linda at Budd Hopkins's New York studio. Leaning against the white wall of the stairway down into Hopkins's studio is *Mahler's Castle,* a large three-panel painting he completed in 1972. The more Hopkins looked at this painting, the more he was struck that what he had created was not a castle but a *temple;* and eventually he was doing a whole series of temple, altar, and guardian sculptures and paintings. Several of the guardian pieces, brightly lit by track spots, were displayed on the studio's plain white brick walls. Opposite the paintings was a cozy nook containing a soft couch covered in a black fabric. Books and periodicals spilled out of a series of shelves framing the couch. Linda Cortile, a small woman, was seated when I arrived. I told her I thought her story was "astonishing."

Linda speaks with a Brooklyn accent. "This stuff *is* hard to swallow," she said with a faint smile. "I used to be one of those people who would sit on my couch and watch other abductees like myself on TV and laugh at them!"

"Because you didn't want to believe it?"

"I put a *lot* of effort into disbelieving this!" she said. "I couldn't believe this was happening."

"What did you think was?" I asked.

"Well, when I was a child we thought there were ghosts in the house. We didn't really believe in ghosts, but things were walking through our apartment. At one point my mother said they came right *through* the walls! So what else could they be? My mother had the priest come every two weeks to bless the house. He'd walk around with his cross and holy water, and it didn't help! And then finally I was married and moved out of the house— and it kept happening anyway! I was in a different apartment in a different borough, and it was still happening!"

I asked Linda how much conscious recollection she had of the witnessed abduction.

"I remember getting into bed for the night," she said. "It was about three in the morning. I couldn't have been in bed more than five minutes when I felt a presence in my room. I wasn't asleep. I had just shut my eyes and I felt there was someone in our bedroom besides my husband and myself; and then I started to feel a numbness going from my toes up."

"Is this different from the numbness one normally feels as one falls asleep?"

"Absolutely," she said. "You know when you hit your funnybone and you get that tingly sensation up your arm? Well, that's what it feels like, only you can't move! Or when your leg falls asleep and it feels so heavy? But at least you can lift your leg and bang it so it wakes up? Well, the difference is you can't do that. You can't lift your legs."

"Are you sure that your memories emerging through hypnosis are real memories?" I asked. "Is there any way that these memories could be being manufactured by Budd?"

"When I saw those creatures in my room in November 1989, I was awake, I wasn't asleep," Linda said firmly. "I wasn't in any twilight sleep. I hadn't been sleeping yet. And I saw them with my own eyes. They were in my room! And not only did it scare the hell out of me, it confirmed that what I had been seeing under hypnosis was no dream!"

"But didn't your husband in bed beside you see them?"

"He wouldn't wake up! He wouldn't wake up no matter what I did! See, my husband snores real loud—sometimes to the point I can't sleep and I'll sleep on the sofa bed in the living room and I'll shut the bedroom door and

I'll still be able to hear him. So it was pretty unusual that I couldn't wake him up and that he wasn't snoring, either. I *knew* something was wrong. That paralysis was coming, from my toes up. It was dead quiet, And when I opened my eyes and saw those creatures, I knew immediately what they were; I recognized them from hypnosis.

"It wasn't just what I saw that bothered me," Linda continued, "it was the *confirmation* of what I was seeing under hypnosis! And I didn't want to *believe* this was happening to me, but it was. This wasn't hypnosis; this wasn't a dream; I wasn't sleeping. I saw those creatures with my own eyes this time. They exist! So what happens to the skepticism you used to have?" she asked. "What do you do with it? I mean, now you're sort of just hanging by a *hair* of skepticism instead of a rope! So I was saying to myself, 'Maybe I'm crazy. Maybe I'm just seeing things.' But that was the hair, you know?

"I mean, it's better to be crazy, to be mentally ill, because there's treatment for it," Linda explained. "There's a possibility it's going to be cured. But with this alien-abduction stuff, it doesn't stop. You can't stop it. So after November 1989, I was just trying to get over the fact that I had seen these things. I had accepted the possibility that I was crazy because I was still hanging on to that little hair of skepticism. And then," Linda said, "in February 1991, Budd received that first letter from that security agent, Richard, and . . . well, the hair broke."

Since that first communication from Richard, Hopkins has received numerous letters, tape-recorded statements, and drawings from the two security agents attesting to what they saw, plus confirmation from the "senior political figure."

After that meeting with Linda the agents started spying on her. "We watch her not to feel crazy," Richard wrote Hopkins. "When I see her, I tremble. It's real. The whole situation is real. It wasn't 'interesting' or 'exciting,' I thought it was terrifying."

In July 1991, five months after Richard had initially contacted Budd Hopkins, Hopkins received a letter from a sixty-year-old upstate New York woman who had been driving across the Brooklyn Bridge toward Manhattan at 3:15 that same November morning. Suddenly the lights on the Brooklyn Bridge had flickered and gone out and the electrical systems in her car and the few other cars about her malfunctioned and the cars coasted to a stop.

Ahead, clearly visible from where she was stalled on the bridge, was an orange-red disc hovering over Linda Cortile's building. The woman saw the disc's color change and the blue-white light shine down upon the side of Linda's apartment building.

"My God!" a woman in a car behind her screamed. "There are people floating in the air!"

In her letter to Hopkins the upstate New York woman explained that the reason she had decided to contact him was that two months earlier, in May, she had watched a CBS television show called *Visitors from the Unknown,* an abduction story. "From that evening on," she wrote Hopkins, "I thought about what I saw in New York City about a year and half ago. I spoke about it only once," her letter continued,

> and was made to feel ridiculous. I've never spoken of it again. In fact, I've never travelled back to New York City after what I saw and I never will again for any reason. . . . I do wish to remain anonymous. My family and friends do not take too kindly to the UFO subject. I have firsthand experience and I refuse to be made into a fool. It has taken me two months to build up the courage to write you this letter and draw the enclosed drawings. I don't want to be involved with these unnatural goings on; however, I must know if you know what's going on in New York City and if it happens often.
>
> One evening [and here she gives the date of Linda's abduction] I attended a retirement party in Brooklyn for my sickly boss. Unfortunately, she has since passed away. The party lasted until the early hours of the next morning. My boss invited me to stay at her house for the night, but I was anxious to get home. I drove to the Brooklyn Bridge with the intention of crossing over to the Manhattan side.
>
> Words can't express what I saw that morning up on the bridge. I can't begin to explain it verbally. You would have had to have seen it yourself. Enclosed you will find three drawings. After you finish looking through this little package I've managed to send you, you may think I'm crazy. If I am, so were those other people sitting in their cars up there on the bridge with me that morning. If you don't think I'm crazy and if you have questions I can only say *I saw!* And I *know* what I saw!

Drawing 1 shows the orange-red disc above Linda's building and the blue-white light shining down on the building's side. "I saw a building on fire; I was shocked to see what it really was!" the woman wrote. "The lights were so bright I had to shield my eyes. I was frightened and found this aircraft very threatening."

Drawing 2 shows the position and posture of Linda and the three Beings as they first appeared. "They came out of a window one right after another. There were six windows on that side of the building. I purposely counted them. It was from the second window on the left. There was enough light for thousands of people to see what was happening. I'll bet you dollars to doughnuts that thousands *did* see what happened from other areas of the city. The things that came out the window, I didn't know what they were. . . ."

Drawing 3 shows the position and posture of Linda and the three Beings as they ascended into the disc.

> As they rise up to the spacecraft. I didn't want to look. I was petrified, but something made me look. It wasn't until then that I realized there were four children standing up in mid-air. Yes, *in mid-air!* While I watched I could hear the screams of people parked in the cars behind me. Their screams were from horror. Please excuse the stick figures I drew in this drawing, but this is honestly how I saw three of the children. It was obvious that these three children were rickets-stricken. Their heads were so large in comparison with the normal girl-child standing in the air with them. I don't know what gender the three sickly children were, but I could see that the normal child was a girl child because she was wearing a white . . . nightgown. She was taller than the others. Perhaps she was a little bit older. Their next movement was when they all moved up closer to the craft, then they quickly whisked straight up into the object, underneath it, and disappeared.
>
> The aircraft quickly rose up above the building and flew away at a very high speed. It flew behind the building drawn on the right. It passed over a highway or drive below, then proceeded to climb higher over the center of the bridge. I was parked more towards the Manhattan side. I watched in horror. I don't know where it went from there because I had to look up to see but there's a bridge platform above and I couldn't see any more. I do know that when this aircraft passed over the bridge my clothing clung to me and my body hair stood up. The clinging sensation went away after the object went away and my car started up again.

Since the woman had not securely closed her car door, the first thing that happened after the disc had passed overhead was that the car's dome light suddenly came back on, startling her.

She concluded her letter to Hopkins writing:

> Mr. Hopkins, I wanted to talk to these people parked behind me; I was very shaken up. I could have used some calming down, but they were much too upset themselves and I couldn't communicate with them. Some of them were running around their cars with their hands on their heads yelling!
>
> Are you aware of what is going on in that dreadful city? Is anyone putting a stop to this?

Hopkins immediately contacted the woman and carried out detailed personal interviews with her. In order to evaluate her effectiveness as a witness he would deliberately get the sequence of some of the events wrong, or try to lead her into altering her descriptions, but she wouldn't change her story. She insisted upon what she had seen.

According to Hopkins, the details in the woman's letter and drawings, as well as those that later emerged during his interviews with her, matched exactly those particulars given by the men in the car stalled on South Street and by Linda herself. As Hopkins later told me, "There is absolutely no doubt in my mind that this woman saw what she saw. There just isn't!"

As if this witness's confirmation of Linda Cortile's abduction story were not bizarre enough, there is this additional corroboration: an entirely separate abduction incident evidently took place that same night at that same hour farther uptown in Manhattan, and a second woman abductee reportedly witnessed a reddish-orange disc flying down the East River from roughly where Linda Cortile's apartment and the Brooklyn Bridge stand.

Hopkins's presentation of the Linda Cortile story at the M.I.T. conference does not make the sort of stir I would expect. I later learn that this was not the first time most of them had heard the story.

John Miller, the soft-spoken Los Angeles–area emergency physician, rises next to speak on the "Lack of Proof for the Missing Embryo/Fetus Syndrome (ME/FS)."

Although ME/FS is a phenomenon widely reported by both Budd Hopkins and David Jacobs in their books, Miller is not convinced it exists. Jacobs, for example, writes in *Secret Life:*

> The problem of unplanned or inexplicable pregnancy is one of the most frequent physical after-effects of abduction experiences. Usually the woman feels pregnant and has all the outward signs of being pregnant. She is puzzled and disturbed because she has either not engaged in sex or has been very careful with proper birth control. She has blood tests and the gynecologist positively verifies the pregnancy. Typically, between the discovery of the pregnancy and the end of the first trimester, the woman suddenly finds herself not pregnant. She has no miscarriage, no extra-heavy bleeding or discharge. The fetus is simply gone, with no evidence of the rare phenomenon of non-twin "absorption," in which physicians theorize that a nonviable fetus can be absorbed into the woman's body.
>
> During the first trimester the woman may decide to terminate the pregnancy. At the appointment, the physician begins the procedure and is stunned to find that there is no fetus in the uterus. . . . The "Missing Fetus Syndrome" has happened to abductees enough times that it is now considered one of the more common effects of the abduction experience.[37]

"Missing embryo and/or fetus syndrome (ME/FS) stories now seem to be reported frequently by female abductees," Miller begins. "By now we should have some medically well-documented cases of this, but we don't. Proof of a case of ME/FS has proved entirely elusive." Miller points out that any ME/FS case that is not based on medical records cannot be considered "proven" and suggests that although obtaining medical records may be considered a "formidable obstacle" to non-M.D. investigators, it really isn't all that difficult if the patient will sign a consent for her records' release.

"The problems of proving a case of ME/FS go far beyond mere lack of medical records," Miller says. "Although a witness may sincerely believe that she has experienced ME/FS, there is ample opportunity for confusion, especially in cases of pregnancy that 'disappear' in the first twelve to sixteen weeks."

Miller places a transparency upon the projector:

Medical Causes for Apparent Disappearing Pregnancies

1. Blighted Ovum
2. Spontaneous Abortion (Miscarriage)
3. Missed Abortion
4. Hydatidiform Mole
5. Secondary Amenorrhea
6. Pseudocyesis (False Pregnancy)

"Items 1, 2, and 3 are very common," Miller says. "I see all of them in my emergency department on a virtually daily basis. Items 4, 5, and 6 are not as frequently seen."

Miller explains that a "blighted ovum" is a pregnancy in which an embryo has degenerated or been absent from the start. But since placental tissue secretes the beta-hCG hormone assayed when a modern urine or blood test for pregnancy is performed, "a positive pregnancy test," Miller points out, "does not in and of itself mean that a fetus is, or *ever was,* present."

When the products of a spontaneous abortion, or miscarriage, are examined, an embryo or fetus is very often absent; therefore, Miller explains, "it is not mysterious to find no fetus in this material," either.

As for a "missed abortion," the term used, Miller tells us, "when a pregnancy dies but is not aborted, it is unclear why some nonviable pregnancies do not progress to spontaneous abortion, but some cases of missed pregnancy can be carried five months or longer. Thus, it is possible to have a 'pregnancy' of more than five months' duration but ultimately have a 'missing fetus.' " Therefore, Miller reports, there is nothing mysterious about the absence of a fetus in cases involving an abortion or miscarriage of a pregnancy that because of abnormal development lasted many months. There may be nothing mysterious to Dr. Miller, but I can't help wondering if there's no spontaneous abortion and the "pregnancy" continues, what's happened to the fetus?

There's no time to ask. Miller is already explaining that with a "hydatidform mole" which occurs in perhaps one of out fifteen hundred pregnancies, a fertilized egg degenerates for unknown reasons into a rapidly growing mass of grape-like tissue that also secretes the beta-hCG hormone. "Thus a witness could report a positive pregnancy test and an enlarging uterus," Miller points out, "but only 'abnormal' tissue is found by doctors." In other words, a "missing fetus."

"Secondary amenorrhea" is the medical term for a woman not having her period for six months or more due to a number of possible medical causes other than pregnancy. "Milder, self-limited forms of this problem," Miller notes, "are extremely common. It is well known that a woman may miss several cycles for a variety of known or unknown reasons. . . . She could miss four or five periods without any anomalous forces at work."

"Pseudocyesis," or false pregnancy, occurs in about one in five thousand general-obstetrics cases. "The patient may have all of the presumptive signs of pregnancy including a 'full term'–appearing abdomen," Miller explains, "but with a small uterus and a negative pregnancy test. These patients frequently assume all features of the expectant-mother role and are bitterly disappointed when no baby ensues. The patient will often stubbornly, illogically insist she is, or was, pregnant despite being presented with the strongest possible evidence to the contrary.

"Of course," Miller continues, "none of these medical causes for apparent disappearing pregnancies account for the UFO/alien complaints that seem narrowly specific and fairly consistent from case to case in the missing fetus and/or embryo syndrome. But so far, these cases of alleged ME/FS have a will-o'-the-wisp quality to them."

Miller tells of a case he is reviewing in which a seven-month fetus allegedly disappeared overnight—"a startling event," he calls it. But based on the medical records he has obtained, it appears that this was a case of false pregnancy.

"So what would it take to *prove* an alleged missing embryo and/or fetus syndrome case to be genuinely anomalous?" Miller asks. The answer, he tells us, would entail interviews with a witness to establish her credibility; access to, and a review of, the patient's complete medical records, records of reasonable quality generated by practitioners of recognized competence; and, with the witness's permission, interviews with the physician or physicians involved. If the case should then still appear to be truly anomalous, Miller suggests, the final stage should be a review of the case by a "non–ufologically involved board-certified obstetrician and/or gynecologist, who should be kept blinded to any attendant ufologic allegations in the case to avoid the possibility of the introduction of bias into any opinion rendered." This, Miller adds, would of course eliminate a physician such as himself from taking part in the final proof process.

"Since we don't feel comfortable advancing a case as truly anomalous without disinterested third-party expert opinion," Miller says, "it should be clear that we don't feel that any non-M.D. researcher can successfully claim to have proven such a case on his own. It is disturbing to see these cases written about as some sort of established physical reality."

Miller concludes by stating that in his abstract published in advance of the conference he called for any attendees with proof of a case of missing fetus syndrome to bring that proof to the conference, and that although "this did not happen, some interesting leads requiring further follow-up were obtained." But the bottom line of Miller's presentation is that no clear and convincing evidence of the missing fetus syndrome alleged by Dave Jacobs exists.

"Clear and convincing evidence" is, in fact, the bane of this conference. I am hopeful that Jenny Randles, the next presenter, will provide some, since according to the program her talk is to be "Abduction Study Where Entity Was Photographed."

"On December 1, 1987," Randles tells us, "a retired police officer observed a figure in a streambed and went after it. . . ."

I am smiling as I take notes. "Retired police officer," "figure in a streambed": Randles already has the opening of a quintessential British mystery, which she then tops by adding that the officer paused to photograph the creature just before it "shambled behind a rock outcrop" to its parked flying saucer. That "shambled" is a nice touch, I think—part Bigfoot, part Quasimodo.

"When the officer got to the outcrop," Randles is saying, "he witnessed a classic UFO departure. Whereupon he returned to his car."

However, Randles reports, once back in his car, the officer discovered that (1) his watch was not working, (2) there was a one-and-a-half-hour "discrepancy," or period of missing time, and (3) his compass was 180 degrees off. He subsequently had his compass examined, and test results indicated it had been exposed to "a pulse magnetic field." Also tested were the rocks upon which the saucer had allegedly rested; but here, on the other hand, no anomaly was found.

Randles puts the photograph on the projector. It is a blurry black-and-white picture of *something* thirty yards or so ahead of the photographer in what we have been told is a streambed. "Three different analyses of the photograph agree it shows something four and a half feet tall, gray, with a large head and nonhuman proportions," Randles tells us. "Unfortunately the 400 ASA film used is too grainy to blow up for detail."

Pfui, as Nero Wolfe would say. The quality of the photograph is so poor it could be anything. It could even be, as the official British government explanation went, "an insurance salesman riding his bicycle." Why is it, with all the 35 mm auto-focus cameras and hand-held video cameras people now own, there are still no *clear and convincing* photographs of UFOs, much less alien Beings?

During the lunch break I talk with Linda Moulton Howe, a film and television documentary maker specializing in topics involving science, medicine, and the environment. She is, however, attending the conference as a presenter, not as a journalist. I ask her, too, what she really thinks is going on.

"I would have to start with how I got into this in the first place," she tells me. She explains how in 1979, she had already been the special projects director at the Denver CBS affiliate for three years, doing a series of documentaries and live television shows on environmental issues. Prior to coming to Denver she had written and produced a Boston-based syndicated medical program. Therefore, in September 1979, when reports of strange, bloodless animal mutilations began to appear in United States, Australian, and Canadian newspapers—accounts of a steer's ear, eye, or tongue taken, its genital and rectal tissue excised with cookie-cutter-clean precision, its jaw stripped of flesh—she was able to approach the story with a journalistic background in both medical and environmental hard-science-related subjects.

Initially she believed some government agency was taking tissue in this strange manner to examine it for environmental contamination. But as she researched the story, as she interviewed both the ranchers upon whose animals these mutilations had been performed and the law-enforcement officials to whom these ranchers had reported, environmental contamination was not what they wanted to talk to her about. They wanted to speak instead of the football-field-sized glowing orange discs they had seen over their pastures, or the cones of light shining down from something invisible in the sky onto their field where a mutilated animal would sometimes subsequently be found. And the more she looked into the story, the more she entered what she refers to as "a hall of mirrors with a quicksand floor."

The day after *A Strange Harvest,* Linda's television program on the mysterious animal mutilations, was broadcast, her Denver television station logged over three hundred telephone calls before they quit counting. Mail poured in for Linda, some with drawings; people wrote, "I've never told anyone about this before, but . . ." and they would recount their own mutilation stories, tell of their own encounters with strange craft and lights.

"And so, in a way—and I know this is a long answer to your question," Linda tells me—"I'm still at the end of some of those ripples that started with that film."

At the same time, Linda was doing documentaries and stories on other subjects: a Solar Max repair story for *MacNeil-Lehrer,* several projects for UNICEF on child-survival efforts in Africa and other places. "I had deliberately pulled myself back into this world we have to live in and the problems it has," Linda tells me. "But there was always this parallel track!

"Everybody here at the conference has the same experience," she explains. "It's like you're in two worlds. You make a living in what is the normal social paradigm we live in: the world in which for almost half a century now the UFO phenomenon has made occasional headlines, there have even been occasional photographs, and it has received a lot of play in the tabloids. But it is still a world in which the normal social paradigm has said the UFO phenomenon doesn't exist.

"But then for those of us who, one way or another, got into this quicksand, we come home and enter this other world because there are all these messages on our telephone answering machine: somebody reporting a cattle mutilation in Kansas, someone else reporting the sighting of a disc over a pasture. Or you get a call from somebody who woke up with a triangle of small marks on their leg, some bruises on their arm, and they're troubled and disconcerted, and suddenly you're in the abduction category. And in the abduction phenomenon, in spite of the controversy on hypnosis, you *do* have eyewitness encounters, broad-daylight eyewitness testimony. A rancher in Texas, out rounding up some cows, encounters two four-foot-tall, grayish-green creatures with big, black, slanted eyes carrying a calf. It scares him to death!" she tells me. "He runs away, comes back three days later with his wife and one of his sons, and they find the calf mutilated."

"How do you know about this?" I ask.

"I've *talked* with the son and the rancher!" Linda replies. "Or there's a husband and wife in Missouri—you can talk to them—who in July 1983 watched two small, white-skinned, silver-suited Beings with a cow down in a pasture somehow float this cow into some kind of cone-shaped craft and disappear."

"I could talk to them?" I ask.

"I can give you their names and addresses—these are people who *would* talk to you. They shared binoculars and argued over who would get to use them while they watched this strange event."

"Linda, you have a solid scientific background, and you don't seem off-the-wall, right?"

"I'm *not!*" she says, laughing.

"But what you're telling me *is!*"

"I know. You feel this has to be science fiction! But there are people—some of them here at this conference, others like the people out in Missouri and Texas—who've had *broad daylight* encounters with something that's *not* human! But to the paradigm we're living in, it's divided by this invisible line: it doesn't count. That's the odd thing about this phenomenon," she says. "We're dealing with the investigation of something which, as long as it is said it doesn't exist, it takes extraordinary evidence to prove it to anyone. And that is the dilemma for all us."

"But you're asking for an enormous leap of faith," I say. "If these cattle mutilations were being done by coyotes, we'd all be wonderfully able to accept that. But when you're saying that organs are removed without any blood, that the edges of the incisions are cookie-cutter-smooth, and that little gray men with big heads are carrying these cattle up beams of light into cone-shaped flying saucers, you've got to admit that requires quite an astonishing leap!"

"I know! I *know!*" Linda says. "I've *been* there. I've been exactly where you are. Denial. We're all in denial."

"So how did you get 'here' from 'there'?"

"It's the steady drip," she says, "the steady drip of letters and phone calls. And then you get invited to a conference as I was, to present my *Strange Harvest* documentary, and you get more feedback. And when you hear the abductees, how they struggle with this on a second-by-second, minute-by-minute, hour-by-hour basis because they're living and dealing with this intimately . . .

"I mean, I *know!* I know exactly what this conference must be like for you!" she continues. "It absolutely must be comparable to the way it was during any great revolutionary paradigm shift—whether it was Galilean, or Copernican, or Darwinian. We're in the middle of it! We're literally in the chaos of redefinition of what we are as a species in relation to the universe. If you go outside this conference, if you move into the new literature in quantum physics—Michael Talbot's *The Holographic Universe,* or John Gribbin's *In Search of Schrödinger's Cat* and *Time Warps*—you're hearing the same kind of stuff. *The Holographic Universe,* I was amazed to see, even has a chapter relating to the UFO phenomenon. But what Talbot and Gribbin and all these others are trying also to wrestle with is where theoretical math is taking us: that there has to be other dimensions and what we perceive as a solid reality is basically a quantum wave function—meaning, in theoretical physics and in a holographic universe, your briefcase next to you and my hand are like interference patters. They are mass/energy exchanges."

"What does this mean?" I ask.

"It means, theoretically, we may be getting close to this new definition of the universe. But until this story is accessible and has some impact on everybody's daily life, what else can you expect but indifference, if not ridicule? I, personally, have gone through enormous walls of disbelief and fear, and a lot of other things," Linda tells me. "*But,* what I've begun to realize in my own step-by-step process is this: depending on the evolution of the information, my perspective keeps changing. I think what's going on could be one thing one year and another thing the next. And because of that, I've become very cautious about saying that I think what's happening is negative, or I think it's positive, or I think it's anything in between—blue, yellow, purple. All I can say is, we're dealing with another intelligence."

"As in 'extraterrestrial'? From another planet?" I ask.

"I don't know *where* it is from!" she says. "I don't know exactly what the intent might be. But in the overall picture of the human impact you do begin to get a perspective—and so do the abductees I know. However, when you hit this new, like you have, you can't achieve any perspective. It's day-to-day. That's where your reactions are. But I've lived in this long enough now to see that an abductee who was absolutely traumatized in 1980, who used the words 'I was raped'—the abductee was male, by the way," she says, adding, "this is based on absolute fact—this same abductee twelve years later has embraced the notion that he is dealing with an advanced intelligence who is trying to guide this human species up out of a blind, myopic muck.

"In April 1983," Linda continues, "I was working on the development stage of a documentary for HBO. They had screened *A Strange Harvest* and asked if I would do an hour that went beyond the animal mutilation story; so I was working on a project with the title *UFOs: The E.T. Factor.* I spoke with Peter Gerston, the attorney who had done all the Freedom of Information Act filings against the National Security Agency, the Central Intelligence Agency, the Department of Defense Intelligence Agency, and a whole squad of other government acronyms, concerning suppressed, hidden, classified information that the intelligence community and our government had on UFOs. Anyway, in April 1983 I was sitting in this AFOSI [Air Force Office of Special Investigations] office at Kirtland Air Force Base outside Albuquerque with a special agent. . . ."

Linda pauses for a moment, then says, "I'm trying to speak as a journalist to a journalist, and the only way to deal with this complicated story is to look at its evolution by decades." She starts talking about the single- and multiple-eyewitness sightings of lights and discs in the sky during the late 1940s and how the modern age of the flying saucer had started with Kenneth Arnold's sighting on June 24, 1947.

A Marine Corps transport aircraft had been missing for several days in the Cascade Mountains area, where Arnold, an experienced Boise, Idaho, air rescue pilot, was flying his small private plane en route to Yakima, Washington. Arnold was keeping his eyes open for wreckage when he was startled by "a tremendously bright flash." Seconds later he spotted its cause: nine brilliant objects in loose formation racing over Mount Rainier.

Arnold estimated the nine objects' speed to be an amazing 1,700 mph, a figure he later lowered to the still—for those days—astonishing speed of 1,350 mph. (Arnold's sighting took place nearly four months before Captain Charles E. "Chuck" Yeager became the first man to "break the sound barrier" when he flew the Bell X-1 rocket-engined aircraft to 700 mph at 43,000 feet.)

Upon landing at Yakima, Arnold told the ground crew what he had seen. And when he continued on to Pendleton, Washington, his story had already preceded him, and skeptical newsmen were on hand when he arrived. But Arnold's solid reputation—not only was he a successful businessman and experienced, licensed air-rescue and mountain pilot, he was also a deputy U.S. marshal—forced them to pay attention.

"They were like no aircraft I had ever seen before," Arnold said. "I observed the objects plainly as they flipped and flashed along against the snow and sky." Arnold reported the objects he saw had *wings*. It was only later, as a result of Arnold's attempt to describe to reporters how the craft had flown with an undulating motion, "like a saucer would if you skipped it across water," that the press phrase "flying saucer" came into existence.[38]

Arnold's was by no means the first sighting of unidentified flying objects, nor was it even the first reported; but the wide publicity he received, and his credibility and courage in speaking out about what he had witnessed, encouraged others, hitherto fearful of ridicule, to come forward with accounts of their sightings, too. More important, perhaps, is the fact that Arnold's story gave birth to the term "flying saucer" as a means of describing something strange and anomalous that was clearly artificial, machinelike, and possibly otherworldly in the sky.

Arnold's sighting, of course, led to various explanations: he had seen the reflection of his instrument panel on his cockpit window; he had become slightly snowblind from searching for the downed aircraft; he had stared at the sun too long; he had seen mirages over the mountains. But there were some 850 reported UFO sightings in 1947, the peak occurring one month after Arnold's encounter. The press had attempted to report such stories objectively, but as the accounts grew more and more fantastic, as hoaxes were uncovered, and since no one had, so far as the media knew, come up with clear and convincing evidence that flying saucers existed, the journalists' natural skepticism emerged and translated itself into ridicule. Inevitably, one of their targets became Kenneth Arnold himself.

Arnold reacted bitterly: "Call me Einstein or Flash Gordon or just a screwball," he said. "I'm absolutely certain of what I saw! But, believe me, if I ever see again a phenomenon of that sort in the sky, even if it's a one-story building, I won't say a word about it!"[39]

On January 7, 1948, a second headline episode occurred. A flight of four Kentucky Air National Guard propeller-driven F-51 Mustang fighter aircraft were returning to Godman Air Force Base near Fort Knox when witnesses in Louisville reported a cone-shaped silvery object some three hundred feet in diameter moving in a southerly direction overhead. Fort Knox personnel observed the object as well; and after determining that it was not an aircraft or weather balloon, Godman flight controllers radioed the incoming F-51s to check it out. One of them, short on fuel, had to land; but the other three, led by Captain Thomas Mantell, climbed to intercept.

Mantell, in an attempt to reach the object, pulled ahead of his wingman and climbed until he sighted it. "Object traveling at half my speed and directly ahead of me and above," he radioed Godman. "I'm going in to take a closer look." Moments later, Mantell reported, "It's above me . . . it appears metallic and *tremendous* in size."

Despite the fact that his F-51 was not equipped with oxygen for high-altitude flight, Mantell decided to risk climbing to twenty thousand feet in the hopes of overtaking the strange craft. He lost consciousness in the thin air; his fighter plane stalled, spun, and fell out of the sky. Mantell was killed in the crash.

The story of the first military officer to be officially listed as having been lost in pursuit of a flying saucer received wide coverage. Rumors circulated that Mantell's body had been found bullet-ridden, or disfigured by unearthly radiation burns, or that he had been struck down by an alien spacecraft. The Air Force explanation at the time was that Mantell had been chasing the planet Venus. Three years later the Navy announced that a secret, high-altitude Skyhook reconnaissance balloon had been in the area and that Mantell had probably died trying to reach it. It is a plausible explanation.

In July 1952, a series of sensational sightings occurred in the Washington area. On July 10 a mysterious light "too bright to be a lighted balloon and too slow to be a big meteor" was reported by a National Airlines crew over Quantico, Virginia, just south of the capital. On July 13 another strange object climbed directly beneath a second airliner about sixty miles south of Washington, hovered off to its left for a few minutes, and then, when the airliner's pilot turned on his landing lights, accelerated up and away at tremendous speed. On July 14, eight UFOs were reported near Newport News, Virginia, by the crew of a PanAm flight; witnesses on the ground saw a UFO in the same area the following day.

Four days later, at 11:40 p.m. on July 19, radarscopes at Washington National Airport picked up seven UFOs southeast of Andrews Air Force Base. According to Edward J. Ruppelt, the former head of the Air Force Project Blue Book (the special organization established to investigate UFO reports, to which astronomer J. Allen Hynek was then serving as a consultant), the radars involved were a long-range (one-hundred-mile) radar in the Air Route Traffic Control (ARTC) section used to control all aircraft approaching Washington, and a shorter-range radar at the control tower at National Airport used to control aircraft in the immediate vicinity of the airport.

Bolling Air Force Base is just east of National Airport across the Potomac River; and ten miles further east, in almost a direct line with National and Bolling, lies Andrews, which also has a short-range radar. All of these airfields were linked together by an intercom system. According to Ruppelt's account:

> When a new shift took over at the ARTC radar room at National Airport, the air traffic was light so only one man was watching the radarscope. The senior traffic controller and the six other traffic controllers on shift were out of the room at 11:40 p.m. when the man watching the radar scope noticed a group of seven targets appear. From their position on the scope he knew that they were east and just a little south of Andrews AFB. In a way the targets looked like a formation of slow airplanes, but no formations were due in the area. As he watched, the targets loafed along at 100 to 130 miles an hour; then in an apparent sudden burst of speed, two of them streaked out of radar range. These were no airplanes, the man thought, so he let out a yell for the senior controller. The senior controller took one look at the scope and called in two more of the men. They all agreed these were no airplanes. The targets could be caused by a malfunction in the radar, they thought, so a technician was called in—the set was in perfect working order.
>
> The senior controller then called the control tower at National Airport; they reported they also had unidentified targets on their scopes. So did Andrews. And both of the other radars reported the same slow speeds followed by a sudden burst of speed. One target was clocked at 7,000 miles an hour. By now the targets had moved into every sector of the scope and had flown through the prohibited flying areas over the White House and the Capitol.
>
> Several times during the night the targets passed close to commercial airliners in the area and on two occasions the pilots of the airlines saw lights they couldn't identify, and the lights were in the same spots where

the radars showed the UFOs to be. Other pilots to whom the ARTC radar man talked on the radio didn't see anything odd, at least that's what they said, but the senior controller knew airline pilots and knew that they were very reluctant to report UFOs.

The first sighting of a UFO by an airline pilot took place shortly after midnight, when an ARTC controller called the pilot of a Capital Airlines flight just taking off from National. The controller asked the pilot to keep watch for unusual lights—or anything. Soon after the pilot cleared the traffic pattern, and while ARTC was still in contact with him, he suddenly yelled, "There's one—off to the right—and there it goes." The controller had been watching the scope, and a target that had been off to the right of the Capitaliner was gone.

During the next fourteen minutes this pilot reported six more identical lights.

About two hours later another pilot, approaching National Airport from the south, excitedly called the control tower to report that a light was following him at "eight o'clock level." The tower checked their radarscope and there was a target behind and to the left of the airliner. The ARTC radar also had the airliner and the UFO target. The UFO tagged along behind and to the left of the airliner until it was within four miles of touchdown on the runway. When the pilot reported the light was leaving, the two radarscopes showed that the target was pulling away from the airliner.

The clincher came in the wee hours of the morning, when an ARTC traffic controller called the control tower at Andrews AFB and told the tower operators that ARTC had a target just south of their tower, directly over the Andrews Radio range station. The tower operators looked and there was a "huge, fiery-orange sphere" hovering in the sky directly over their range station.[10]

At 10:30 p.m. on July 26, the following weekend, Washington National Airport's ARTC again detected slow-moving unidentified targets on its twenty-four-inch long-range radarscope. The objects, moving in an arc from Herndon, Virginia, to Andrews Air Force Base, were carefully tracked; each target was represented by a plastic marker placed next to the blip. When each target had been noted, an ARTC controller called the short-range-radar operators at National's tower and at Andrews. They, too, had been tracking the same targets.

At 11:30 p.m. two F-94 jet fighters were scrambled from New Castle County Air Force Base in Delaware. All civilian air traffic was ordered to clear the area as the jets moved in. As soon as the fighters had been vectored to where the objects were being tracked, the targets disappeared from the radarscopes. Visibility was excellent; the jets systematically searched the areas of the last radar plots, but neither visual nor radar sightings occurred, and the jets returned to base. Although the objects were no longer visible to the pilots or radar operators, witnesses in the Newport News, Virginia, area began calling nearby Langley Air Force Base to report a mysterious light that was "rotating and giving off strange colors." A few minutes later, Langley tower operators themselves sighted either the same or a similar light and called Air Defense Command for an interceptor.

Another F-94 was scrambled and visually guided toward the strange light by Langley tower radar operators. The fighter pilot observed the light himself and headed toward it. But then, the pilot reported, as he approached the light it suddenly disappeared, "like somebody turning off a light bulb." He had, however, been able to gain a radar lock on the invisible object for a couple of minutes before contact was lost.

Air Defense controllers subsequently guided the interceptors toward one group of lights after another. The pilots were able to get close enough to visually confirm the presence of lighted objects; but each time a jet tried to approach, the UFO, as if playing tag, sped away. One UFO, however, remained in place. The pilot confirmed the presence of a light exactly where the ARTC radar reported it to be; he cut in his F-94's afterburner, chased after it, and was more successful than he might have wished, since at one point he reported to the ground controllers that lights were surrounding his plane and nervously asked what he should do. Before the controllers had a chance to respond, those lights, too, disappeared.

The obvious question is, Could those radar targets have been created by the weather? A mild temperature inversion can cause a false target reading. But the radar operators at Washington National, Andrews, and Langley were experienced. False returns caused by inversions are not uncommon, and over the years those operators had seen every type of radar return, real or false, that exists. Every operator in the radar rooms was firmly convinced the targets on their screens were caused by radar waves bouncing back from solid, metallic objects. There were weather-induced targets on their screens, too, they said; but they were easily identified as such. In addition, there had been the visual confirmations.

The visual sightings of the unidentified flying objects over Washington by witnesses both in the air and on the ground, combined with the radar trackings, created headlines throughout the country and even temporarily drove coverage of the Democratic National Convention off the front pages of many newspapers. The Washington sightings were the most sensational UFO event since the Mantell tragedy four years earlier.[41]

UFO reports and inquiries pouring into the Pentagon and the Blue Book Project so tied up the Pentagon's phones that the nation's military nerve center was dangerously compromised. In order to allay fears and combat rumors about UFOs, the Pentagon rushed to hold a press conference. And on July 29, three days after the second series of Washington sightings, Major General John A. Samford, the Air Force's chief of intelligence, in an hour-and-twenty-minute briefing before a large gathering of reporters, summarized the Air Force's view by stating that the so-called flying saucers did not constitute a menace to the United States; that none of the several thousand saucer reports checked by the Air Force in the last six years had indicated the existence of any solid flying object except in those cases where the witness had observed a United States aircraft or missile and mistaken it for a UFO; that the United States had nothing in its weaponry, either existing or in development, capable of unlimited speed and without mass—characteristics attributed to many UFOs; and that the vast majority of reports could be attributed to natural phenomena or tricks to the eye.

A large portion of the briefing time was spent explaining how temperature inversion under certain conditions could create reflections of light causing false target images on both radar screens and the human eye. Not invited to attend the briefing were Major Dewey Fournet, the Pentagon's chief source of information during the Blue Book Project, and the Navy radar expert who had been present in the radar room with Fournet during the sightings three days before. Both men firmly rejected the temperature-inversion hypothesis.

During Linda Moulton Howe's review of the UFO phenomenon she mentions some of the other classic sightings from the 1940s and 1950s. One was the Chiles-Whitted sighting on July 24, 1948. Two experienced Eastern Airlines crew members, pilot Clarence S. Chiles and his co-pilot, John B. Whitted, en route from Houston to Atlanta, encountered a one-hundred-foot-long, wingless, finless, cigar-shaped object with two rows of large, square windows that emanated a bright, glowing light from within. On a seeming collision course with the UFO, Chiles threw his DC-3 airliner into a tight left-hand banking turn, and the object, with a forty-foot orange-red flame flashing from its tail, shot past not more than seven hundred feet away.

Another sighting was the famous "Lubbock Lights." These sightings commenced the night of August 25, 1951, and were witnessed by an Atomic Energy Commission executive and his wife from their Lubbock, Texas, backyard and simultaneously observed by four respected Texas scientists from their vantage point in another part of town. The object (or objects) was perceived as approximately three dozen bluish lights. It had the appearance of a giant flying wing as it twice moved across the night skies. Several hundred people in the area witnessed the same phenomenon over the next several days. On August 31, Carl Hart Jr. photographed the lights, but photo analysis could prove neither that Hart's still pictures were real or that they were a hoax.

There existed also two motion-picture films of alleged UFOs. At 11:10 a.m. on July 2, 1950, Warrant Officer Delbert C. Newhouse, a veteran Navy photographer, shot about thirty feet of film of ten or twelve strange, silvery objects in the sky near Tremonton, Utah. As the objects flew in a westerly direction, one of them veered off from the main group and reversed its course. After a thousand hours of investigation of the Newhouse film, the Navy Photographic Interpretation Laboratory concluded that the objects filmed were neither aircraft, birds, balloons, nor reflections and were in fact "self-luminous." The Robertson Panel—five distinguished nonmilitary scientists convened by the CIA in 1952 to analyze Project Blue Book data—concluded otherwise: they decided the objects were a formation of birds reflecting the strong desert sunlight.

At 11:25 a.m. on August 15, 1960, in Great Falls, Montana, Nicholas Mariana shot nearly twenty seconds of film of two disc-shaped objects as they moved across the sky. On some of the 250 frames the objects are seen passing behind the girders of a water tower, which gave film analysts an opportunity to measure the objects' approximate altitude, speed, azimuth, distance, and size. It was also a sequence difficult to have faked. Mariana admitted that he had seen two jet fighters on their final approach to a nearby Air Force base just prior to his sighting of the objects, but insisted he knew the difference between the jets and the objects. The Robertson Panel decided Mariana did not know the difference—that he had filmed the jets.

"All of a sudden in the 1960s came the 'contactee syndrome,'" Linda Moulton Howe is telling me. "People were reporting contact with these blond beings warning of nuclear war or various environmental catastrophes."

"Would that have been 'Professor' George Adamski, 'Dr.' Daniel Fry, Truman Bethurum, and people like that?" I ask.

"Well, they were in the 1950s," she says, "and they were dismissed pretty much whole cloth by the society at large."

"Do you dismiss them?"

"The people I know who knew these people don't, but that's a whole other story. A sidebar," Linda says. "Go to the early sixties: in 1961, the Betty and Barney Hill abduction. Suddenly abductions are starting, but they don't get reported until five years later. This same decade, you have animal mutilations making worldwide press, starting for the first time in the United States and Canada in 1967, and the Zamora and Dexter-Hillsdale sightings. . . ."

The Zamora sighting is one of the most puzzling. On April 24, 1964, at 5:45 p.m., near Socorro, New Mexico, Deputy Marshal Lonnie Zamora was pursuing a speeding motorist through hilly desert terrain when he heard a loud noise and saw bluish-orange flames off to his right, near where he knew a dynamite shack to be. Zamora abandoned the chase and drove over to investigate.

The mysterious flame was still visible when he turned off U.S. Highway 85 onto a gravel access road. The flame was funnel-shaped and appeared to be lowering itself to the ground. Zamora drove up a steep hill and upon reaching the top saw the object for the first time. It rested on the ground some 150 yards away. Zamora thought it was an overturned white car. He also saw two figures in what he assumed were overalls "very close to the object. One of these persons," he reported, "seemed to turn and look straight at my car and seemed startled—seemed to quickly jump. . . ."

Zamora radioed his headquarters that he was proceeding to the car wreck and drove forward until he was about a hundred feet from the object. Closer now, Zamora could see that it was twelve to fifteen feet long, constructed of something "like aluminum—whitish against the mesa background," and appeared "oval in shape," without doors or windows. Zamora radioed that he was leaving his car to investigate. He had scarcely stepped out when he heard three "loud thumps, like someone shutting a door," followed by "a very loud roar," and again observed bluish flame under the object. Thinking the object, whatever it was, was about to explode, Zamora ran panicked back to his car—ran, in fact, *into* it, with enough force to knock off his glasses. As the roaring noise increased, Zamora scooped up his glasses, put them back on, and, shielding his face with his arms, chanced glancing back long enough to see that the object was rising slowly into the air. As the object came level with him, Zamora was able to observe a red "insignia" on its side: a vertical arrow sandwiched between a horizontal line and an arc. He scrambled past his car to the reverse slope of the small hill upon which he had parked and dove behind it. The roaring sound gave way to a high-pitched whine, and when Zamora risked looking again, the object was about twenty feet in the air and moving rapidly away from him into the wind. It soon disappeared from view.

Zamora quickly returned to his car and radioed his report; then he went down to the slight depression in which the object had rested. There he found several spots where greasewood bushes were still burning and "landing pod" indentations in the ground. Several minutes later, when a sheriff arrived on the scene, he found Zamora pale and visibly shaken. The sheriff, too, saw the smoldering brush and indentations, and subsequently a gas station attendant reported that a customer had spoken of seeing a mysterious oval-shaped object flying toward the area just before Zamora had sighted it.

Major Hector Quintanilla, Ruppelt's replacement as Project Blue Book chief, was in charge of the Zamora sighting investigation. He later called it "probably the best-documented case in the Air Force files." J. Allen Hynek was so impressed with the case he returned several times to the site in his official capacity as Blue Book's chief scientific consultant to sift the ground for clues, collect samples of the soil, and investigate Zamora's character. "It is my opinion that a *real, physical* event occurred on the outskirts of Socorro that afternoon," Hynek concluded.[42]

The Dexter-Hillsdale sightings, too, created a furor. On March 20, 1966, near Dexter, Michigan, farmer Frank Mannor and his son watched a car-sized, football-shaped object with a central porthole and pulsating lights at each end of its brown quilted surface rise from a swampy area on his farm, hover several minutes at a thousand feet, then depart. The following day, eighty-seven women students at Hillsdale College in Hillsdale, Michigan, their dean, and a civil defense director all claimed to have watched for *four hours* a glowing football-shaped object hovering above a swampy area several hundred yards from the women's dormitory. At one point the object flew directly toward the dormitory, then retreated. On another occasion the object appeared to "dodge an airport beacon light." Its glow would diminish when police cars approached, and it "brightened when the cars left."

The Michigan sightings made nearly every newspaper. Even *The New York Times*—which normally declined to run a "flying saucer" story—gave it several inches. Major Quintanilla sent Dr. Hynek to Michigan to investigate.

"By the time I arrived," Hynek later wrote, "the situation was so charged with emotion that it was impossible to do any really serious investigating. I had to fight my way through reporters to interview witnesses. Police were madly chasing stars they thought to be flying saucers. People believed space ships were all over the area."

Hynek spent a week interviewing witnesses; he even pulled on a pair of hip boots to wade through farmer Frank Mannor's swamp. Pressure mounted for an explanation, and on March 27, Hynek held the largest press conference in the Detroit Press Club's history. Hynek later described the gathering of television reporters, newspapermen, photographers, and others, all "clamoring for a single, spectacular explanation of the sightings," as "a circus."

Hynek said he provided "what I thought at the time to be the only explanation possible. . . . I made the statement it was 'swamp gas,' " the phenomenon caused by decaying vegetation that has spontaneously ignited, creating a faint glow. "And even though I went on to emphasize I couldn't prove it in a court of law, that that was the full explanation. . . . Well," Hynek later said, "the press picked up the words 'swamp gas' even before I had finished the conference and that was all you heard or read about in the media for weeks."[43]

Hynek's "swamp gas" explanation was met with ridicule, hostility, and increased suspicion that the government was engaged in a cover-up.

A Gallup poll taken just prior to the Dexter-Hillsdale events showed that 96 percent of the people surveyed were aware of flying saucers; that 46 percent thought them real, 29 percent imaginary; and that 5 percent thought they had seen one themselves—a figure that, applied to the population in general, would mean that by 1966 approximately nine million Americans already believed they had actually sighted a UFO.

In the 1970s two close encounters in particular made news: the Pascagoula case in 1973 and the Travis Walton "abduction" in 1975.

The Pascagoula incident involved two men, nineteen-year-old Calvin Parker and forty-two-year-old Charles Hickson, both of Gautier, Mississippi, who were fishing in the Pascagoula River when they heard a buzzing noise behind them. Both turned and were terrified to see a ten-foot-wide, eight-foot-high, glowing egg-shaped object with blue lights at its front hovering just above the ground about forty feet from the riverbank. As the men, frozen with fright, watched, a door appeared in the object, and three strange Beings floated just above the river towards them.

The Beings had legs but did not use them. They were about five feet tall, had bullet-shaped heads without necks, slits for mouths, and where their noses or ears would be, they had thin, conical objects sticking out, like carrots from a snowman's head. They had no eyes, gray, wrinkled skin, round feet, and clawlike hands. Two of the Beings seized Hickson; when the third grabbed Parker, the teenager fainted with fright. Hickson claimed that when the Beings placed their hands under his arms, his body became numb, and that then they floated him into a brightly lit room in the UFO's interior, where he was subjected to a medical examination with an eyelike device which, like Hickson himself, was floating in midair. At the end of the examination, the Beings simply left Hickson floating, paralyzed but for his eyes, and went to examine Parker, who, Hickson believed, was in another room. Twenty minutes after Hickson had first observed the UFO, he was floated back outside and released. He found Parker weeping and praying on the ground near him. Moments later, the object rose straight up and shot out of sight.

Expecting only ridicule if they were to tell anyone what had happened, Hickson and Parker initially decided to keep quiet; but then, because they felt the government might want, or *ought,* to know about it, they telephoned Kessler Air Force Base in Biloxi. A sergeant there told them to contact the sheriff. But uncertain about the reception their bizarre story might get from the local law, they drove to the local newspaper office to speak with a reporter. When they found the office closed, Hickson and Parker felt they had no alternative but to talk to the sheriff.

The sheriff, after listening to their story, put Hickson and Parker in a room wired for sound in the belief that if the two men were left alone, they would reveal their hoax; of course, they did not. The local press reported their tale; the wire services picked it up; and within several days the Pascagoula close encounter was major news all over the country. The Aerial Phenomena Research Organization (APRO), founded in 1952, sent University of California engineering professor James Harder to Mississippi to investigate; J. Allen Hynek, representing the Air Force, also arrived. Together they interviewed the witnesses. Harder hypnotized Hickson but had to terminate the session when Hickson became too frightened to continue.

Hickson and Parker both subsequently passed lie detector tests. Hynek and Harder believed the two men's story. And Hynek was later quoted as saying, "There was definitely something here that was not terrestrial."[44]

The Travis Walton case is even more bizarre: On November 5, 1975, twenty-two-year-old Travis Walton had, with his six companions, finished thinning trees on Mogollon Rim, ten miles south of Heber, Arizona. They were driving home in their truck when they saw a glowing object hovering approximately fifteen feet above the ground off to the side of the road. They stopped the truck and Walton jumped out to get a closer look. As he approached, a beam of light flashed from the UFO and struck Walton so hard in the chest he was flung backwards ten feet and lay on the ground unconscious. His panicked companions sped off in the truck. As they fled they saw the UFO lift off and fly away. Subsequently they calmed down enough to return and look for Walton; but he was nowhere to be found.

According to Walton when he regained consciousness, he was inside the UFO lying on a metal table being observed by three small aliens with large hairless heads, chalk-white skin, huge oval eyes, and tiny slit mouths. A different alien, one who, Walton said, looked like a normal human being, later led him out of the UFO into a hangarlike structure containing a number of other alien craft. Several other human-looking aliens met him there and brought him to a second table upon which they stretched him out. A mask was lowered over his face and Walton blacked out. When he came to he was lying by the side of a road near Heber watching a UFO climb straight up into the sky above.

Walton, who thought he had been gone only a few hours, discovered he had been missing for five days.

"By the time of the Travis Walton case," Linda was telling me, "animal mutilations were being reported worldwide. They were occurring three cases per county per *day* in some Colorado sheriffs' offices and other places! Animals still warm to the touch with this same cookie-cutter stuff. And then something else happened: Jimmy Carter became President in 1976. He had been elected talking about his own experience of a UFO sighting shared with his son and had said when he became President, he would open up the government files on UFOs. But then, when he did become President, an extraordinary thing happened. He had been in office only a few months—I don't remember precisely how long now—and everything concerning UFOs was officially transferred to the National Security Agency.*

"Then in '79 there was another flurry of animal mutilations, which was when I first became involved in the story," Linda continues. "I made *A Strange Harvest* and was trying to grapple with that part. And that documentary led, in 1983, to *UFOs: The E.T. Factor,* the HBO project which I started telling you about before I began all this backtracking. And that led

---

* A report of Carter's account of his UFO sighting and subsequent efforts to make the government's UFO information public appears in British author Timothy Good's investigative book *Above Top Secret: The Worldwide UFO Cover-Up:*

> During his election campaign in 1976, Jimmy Carter revealed that he had seen a UFO at Leary, Georgia, in 1969, together with witnesses prior to giving a speech at the local Lions Club. "It was the darndest thing I've ever seen," he told reporters. "It was big, it was very bright, it changed colors, and it was about the size of the moon. We watched it for ten minutes, but none of us could figure out what it was. One thing's for sure: I'll never make fun of people who say they've seen unidentified objects in the sky."
>
> Carter's sighting has been ridiculed by skeptics such as Philip Klass and Robert Sheaffer. While there appear to be legitimate grounds for disputing the date of the incident, Sheaffer's verdict that the UFO was nothing more exotic than the planet Venus is not tenable. As a graduate in nuclear physics who served as a line officer on U.S. Navy nuclear submarines, Carter would not have been fooled by anything so prosaic as Venus, and in any case he described the UFO as being about the same size as the moon.
>
> "If I become President," Carter vowed, "I'll make every piece of information this country has about UFO sightings available to the public and the scientists." Although President Carter did all he could to fulfill his election pledge, he was

to my being in the Air Force Office of Special Investigations out at Kirtland Air Force Base.

"My original reason for going to Kirtland was to get witnesses and information about an alleged landing of an alien craft at Ellsworth Air Force Base in South Dakota in 1977," Linda tells me. "It's a long story. . . ."

It is alleged that around 9:30 p.m. on November 16, 1977, a "saucer-shaped object" landed approximately fifty yards beyond the fence surrounding an Ellsworth missile silo. Air Force security was alerted when an "inner zone alert" was triggered *beneath* the 150-ton hardened concrete block atop the silo. The alarm indicated someone or something had entered the underground chamber. Two airmen were sent to investigate.

According to the supposedly "official" report Linda later makes available to me:

> . . . Upon arrival (2134hrs) at Site #L-9, LSAT, JENKINS & RAEKE, dis-mounted the SAT vehicle to make a check at the site fence line. At this time RAEKE observed a bright light shining vertically upwards from the rear of the fence line at L-9. (There is a small hill approximately 50 yards behind L-9). JENKINS stayed with the SAT vehicle and RAEKE proceeded to the source of the light to investigate. As RAEKE approached the crest of the hill, he observed an individual dressed in a glowing green metallic uniform and wearing a helmet with visor. RAEKE immediately challenged the individual; however, the individual refused to stop and kept walking toward the rear fence line at L-9. RAEKE aimed his M-16 rifle at the intruder and ordered him to stop. The intruder turned toward RAEKE and aimed an object at RAEKE which emitted a bright flash of intense light. The flash of light struck RAEKE's M-16 rifle, disintegrating the weapon, and causing second and third degree burns to RAEKE'S

---

thwarted, and it was clear that NASA had a hand in blocking his attempts to re-open investigations. When Carter's science adviser, Dr. Frank Press, wrote to NASA Administrator Dr. Robert Frosch in February 1977 suggesting that NASA should become the "focal point for the UFO question," Dr. Frosch replied that although he was prepared to continue responding to public inquiries, he proposed that "NASA take no step to establish a research activity in this area or to convene a symposium on this subject."

In a letter from Colonel Charles Senn, Chief of the Air Force Community Relations Division, to Lieutenant General Duward Crow of NASA, dated 1 September 1977, Colonel Senn made the following astonishing statement, "*I sincerely hope that you are successful in preventing a reopening of UFO investigations*" [Good's italics]. So it is clear that NASA (as well as the Air Force and almost certainly the CIA and National Security Agency) was anxious to ensure that the President's election pledge remained unfulfilled.[45]

hands. RAEKE immediately took cover and concealment and radioed the situation to JENKINS, who in turn radioed a 10-13 distress call to Lima control. JENKINS responded to RAEKE'S position and carried RAEKE back to the SAT vehicle. JENKINS then returned to the rear fence line to stand guard. JENKINS observed two intruders dressed in the same uniforms walk through the rear fence line of L-9. JENKINS challenged the two individuals but they refused to stop. JENKINS aimed and fired two rounds from his M-16 rifle. One bullet struck one intruder in the back and one bullet struck one intruder in the helmet. Both intruders fell to the ground, however, approximately 15 seconds later both returned to an upright position and fired several flashes of light at JENKINS. JENKINS took cover and the light missed JENKINS. The two intruders returned to the east side of the hill and disappeared. JENKINS followed the two and observed them go inside a saucer-shaped object approximately 20′ in diameter and 20′ thick. The object emitted a glowing greenish light. Once the intruders were inside, the object climbed vertically upwards and disappeared over the eastern horizon. FAF #1 arrived at the site at 2230 hrs and set up a security perimeter. Site Survey Teams arrived at the site (0120hrs) and took radiation readings which measured from 1.7 to 2.9 roentgens. Missile maintenance examined the missile and warhead and found the nuclear components missing from the warhead.[46]

"I thought the meeting with this AFOSI agent inside Kirtland would last about fifteen minutes—'Here's something to check out and I'll be on my way,' " Linda was saying. "He began by telling me, 'That *Strange Harvest* documentary you did upset some people in Washington. They don't want UFOs and animal mutilations connected together in the public's mind.' Later, he reached into a drawer, took out a plain envelope containing some letter-sized stationery, and said, 'My superiors have asked me to show this to you. You can't take notes. You can ask me questions.' He handed the papers to me and said, 'I want you to move from that chair you're sitting in,' and motioned me to one in the middle of this big office, saying, 'Eyes can see through windows.'

"I was completely confused by what was going on," Linda continues. "When I looked down at the paper, what it said was, 'Briefing Paper for the President of the United States on the Subject of Identified Aerial Vehicles (IAVs)'—*IAVs*," Linda says with a little laugh, "not UFOs! To make a long story short, it was all about our government's retrieval of crashed discs and alien bodies, dead and alive. An alien—they discussed it as an 'extraterrestrial biological entity,' or EBE—had been taken to Los Alamos in 1949 from a crash in New Mexico. According to the briefing paper, the government learned a lot about that alien civilization."

"Was this the Roswell, New Mexico crash?" I ask.

"There were two different crashes at Roswell," Linda says, "one in 1947 and one in 1949.* This was supposedly the 1949 one. Six creatures were found, five dead and one alive. The bodies were described as gray-colored, with both reptilian and insect characteristics, about three feet to four and a half feet tall. Long arms, four long 'fingers,' no opposable thumb, clawlike nails with webbing between fingers. Instead of a nose and ears, there were only holes. An Air Force major took responsibility for the live one and had it transported to the Los Alamos Laboratory north of Albuquerque. According to the paper I read, the creature lived at Los Alamos until June 18, 1952, when it died of unknown causes."

I was speechless.

"The paper began with a summary about crashes of silver discs in the southwestern United States," Linda continues. "My memory says the first

---

* Ufologists consider the 1947 Roswell crash the most thoroughly investigated, authenticated, and enduring evidence of the government's conspiracy to prevent the public from learning the truth about UFOs. Believers in this "cover-up of cover-ups" insist that the remains of a "flying disc" were recovered on a rancher's land near Roswell; that the government was holding the bodies of aliens retrieved from the crash in Hangar 18 at the then-named Wright Field near Dayton, Ohio; that incredibly strong, lightweight structural materials recovered from the saucer were being examined; and that the ranchers upon whose land the saucer debris was found were warned not to speak about what they had seen under penalty of death. Books written about that crash include Charles Berlitz and William L. Moore's *The Roswell Incident,* Kevin Randle and Donald R. Schmitt's *The U.F.O. Crash at Roswell,* George Eberhardt's *The Roswell Report,* and Stanton T. Friedman and Don Berliner's *The Crash at Corona.* The incident also spawned numerous articles and a television drama.

Early in 1994, in reaction to continuing insistence that a cover-up existed, Representative Steven H. Schiff of New Mexico asked the General Accounting Office—the investigative arm of Congress—to urge the Pentagon to declassify documents relating to Roswell. In response, Secretary of the Air Force Sheila E. Widnall ordered that the Air Force investigation and report be as thorough as possible. The results of that investigation were reported in a box on the front page of *The New York Times* in late September that same year. According to the *Times:* "The wreckage, quickly whisked away by the Air Force, was part of an airborne system for atomic-age spying" called Project Mogul. Balloon-launched, its purpose was "to search high in the atmosphere for weak reverberations from nuclear blasts half a world away. The debris, found near Roswell, N.M., was a smashed part of the program's balloon's sensors, and of most consequence to the growth of spaceship theories, radar reflectors made of thin metal foil.

"At the time, the Air Force said the wreckage was that of a weather balloon, a white lie," the *Times* piece continued. "But over the decades, the incident grew to mythic dimensions among flying-saucer cultists, who spun slim evidence into weighty charges. . . . On Sept. 8, after an eight-month investigation, the Air Force issued a report and a number of thick appendices that to all appearances deflate the conspiracy theory once and for all. Of course, ardent flying-saucer fans contend that the cover-up continues."[47]

date was 1946. Other dates included 1947 and 1949 and some in the early 1950s. In addition to the two Roswell crashes, some others I remember listed were one in Aztec, New Mexico; one in Kingman, Arizona; and a crash south of Texas in northern Mexico. According to the paper, our radar interfered with the aliens' guidance system. But this is the bottom line: this is a planet in which there has been some kind of other intelligence involved for eons. And then in 1988, '89, '90, and '91 came the crop circles."

"You mean those patterns in the English wheat fields?"

"Not just England," Linda corrects me. "By 1990 some two thousand of these crop circle formations had been formed, and I don't think people understand we are talking about worldwide activity in more than a dozen countries! Last summer soil samples were taken from beneath some of these circles in England, in Medina, New York, and from Vancouver, British Columbia. A biophysicist in Michigan examined cell pits in the plants and found they had separated in such a fashion that the only biological explanation was that heat of some sort had been applied from the outside quite rapidly. The Oak Ridge, Tennessee nuclear lab did analyses on two soil samples—a limited amount, we all acknowledge that, but they have confirmed three isotope changes in the soil of two of those formations, and—"

"What do those changes signify?" I ask.

"It would be like if you tried to jump on a piece of coal to turn it into a diamond. When you change the subatomic structure of atoms, that's where you get into isotope changes. So when there were isotope changes in the soil in England, it's inexplicable in any easy way. It's as one of the nuclear design engineers said: you would have to have a portable cyclotron or fusion reactor and be able to control and focus it in order to cause that kind of isotope changes. And the investigators trying to understand this whole, giant UFO puzzle were looking at the crop circle phenomenon and asking, 'Are the crop circles building up to direct communication from the intelligence involved with this planet?' There've already been thirty-seven new crop circles this summer, probably more of them by now. And the people who are studying this phenomenon closely are convinced it's some other intelligence.

"So the whole mood of the field, from my perspective, shifted somehow when this crop circle phenomenon came in," Linda continues. "It's a subtle and odd thing, but it's as if the whole picture got wider, even though there's no verifiable direct connection. There's no 'I can show you a photograph of a silver disc making a crop circle.' Nobody has that. But somehow crop circles entered this picture as being part of the UFO mystery. What *may* be happening before the decade is out is that the crop circles and all are building up to finally meeting another consciousness from somewhere else in the universe."

"So you're saying they're not just circles?"

"No. Those who have studied the formations say the designs have a musical quality as well as a mathematical one. The February 1 *Science News* cover story is 'Geometric Harvest.' It reports that of the eighteen crop circles studied by Gerald Hawkins, the British astronomer formerly with the Smithsonian Astrophysical Observatory in Cambridge, Massachusetts, Hawkins discovered in eleven of them 'ratios of small whole numbers that precisely match the ratios defining the diatonic scale.' In other words, he found that these ratios produce the eight notes of an octave in the musical scale played on the white keys of a piano: do-re-mi-fa-so-la-ti-do."

"That was the first surprise," Hawkins said, according to the piece I later read in *Science News*. The existence of those ratios, the article continued, "prompted Hawkins to begin looking for geometrical relationships among the circles, rings and lines of particularly distinctive patterns that had been recorded in the fields. Their creation had to involve more than blind luck, he insists."

Based on his study of the geometric relationships of the patterns left in these fields, Hawkins was able to discover four new geometric theorems. He then realized, *Science News* reported, "that his four original theorems, derived from crop circle patterns, were really special cases of a single, more general theorem. 'I found underlying principles—a common thread—that applied to everything which led me to the fifth theorem,' [Hawkins] says."

The piece continued: "Remarkably, [Hawkins] could find none of these theorems in the works of Euclid, the ancient Greek geometer who established the basic rules and techniques of what is known as Euclidean geometry. He was also surprised at his failure to find the crop-circle theorems in any of the mathematical textbooks and references, ancient and modern, that he consulted.

" 'They really are not there,' Hawkins says. 'I found nothing close. I don't know where else to go.' "[48]

Although Hawkins does not entirely reject the possibility that the crop circles are the work of hoaxers such as David Chorley and Douglas Bower, the two elderly English landscape painters who admitted creating a number of the wheat-field patterns that puzzled southern England during the last decade, he argues that the hoaxers would have "had to know a tremendous lot of old-fashioned geometry."

As the *Science News* piece pointed out: "The hoaxers apparently had the requisite knowledge not only to prove a Euclidean theorem, but also to conceive of an original theorem in the first place—a far more challenging task. To show how difficult such a task can be Hawkins often playfully refuses to divulge his fifth theorem, inviting anyone interested to come up with the theorem itself before trying to prove it.

" 'It's a good test,' he says. 'It's easy to prove the theorem but so difficult to conceive it.' "[49]

Gerald Hawkins is not new to controversy. In his 1965 book *Stonehenge Decoded,* written with John B. White, Hawkins had proposed that the immense and mysterious Neolithic circle of stones in Salisbury was a sophisticated moon and sun observatory capable of predicting solstices and eclipses. His theory, Hawkins subsequently wrote, "was reviewed harshly: 'Tendentious, arrogant, slipshod and unconvincing,' 'meretricious persuasion,' 'literary giftwrapping,' 'moonshine.' "[50] But his Stonehenge hypothesis appears to be holding up. It will be interesting to see if his crop circle theories do as well.

"If in the crop circles there are mathematical components and musical components—both are quite the same, really," Linda is saying—"then some linguists are suggesting that what we are building up to is that an intelligence from somewhere else is communicating at literally a grass-roots level. It's bypassing political structure, it's bypassing governmental censorship. It is going to the broad earth itself to lay down some kind of communication and language."[51]

We talk a little about the various factions represented at the M.I.T. conference and how, as Linda says, there is emerging a "tension between the intuitive investigators and the demanding academicians.

"The academics are demanding hard physical evidence and scientific methods of experimentation," she says. "And it's way past time. I'm very grateful that the professionals are getting involved. But there's a whole group who's been at it for thirty years. And they already have a certain kind of intuitive understanding of certain elements of this phenomenon that can't be demonstrated or proven. It's just the sheer critical mass of information they have accumulated. And it's this same critical mass that makes this phenomenon now okay for the scientists and academics to investigate.

"But along with the rigorousness of the scientific method, which is vital," Linda says, "you start having people putting things into boxes. A lot of the abductees and the investigators feel that the boxes being drawn are too narrow. In defense of those who are narrowing the boxes, their argument is that you have to share with the public the core data, meaning only that which is the most repetitive, because all the other, more anomalous data is too far out and people won't accept it. But to those of us who are trying to grasp the biggest picture possible of what's happening, if you draw the boxes too narrowly, you could be excluding some of the key insights. And that's what's been happening. There are all of those asking for a bigger picture, who are insisting that there aren't *just* 3½-to-4-foot Grays with huge, black, slanted eyes, but rather that it's an extremely complicated picture."

Linda tells me of a Colorado deputy sheriff who went out on a cattle-mutilation investigation and came upon a mysterious glowing red rectangle in a forest of trees. "He was terrified!" she says. "He went back into town to get another deputy, drives back out, and now both men see a forest of trees with a glowing red rectangle and they don't know what to make of it."

"The glowing red rectangle was within the trees?" I ask.

"Yes! And they're scared to death! They return to town, and the next morning this Colorado deputy sheriff, haunted by what he had seen, drives back out to the site again. There are the tire marks of where they had stopped and everything, but there's not a single tree."

"What was there?"

"Nothing!" Linda says. "It had all been created. Remember the word they've used in this conference, 'staging'? It had all been staged. This is a huge other part of the complexity of this. Over and over again, in case after case—and it doesn't matter whether you're talking with the captain of a jet airliner at thirty thousand feet, or a farmer on the ground, or a housewife in her kitchen, or a reporter driving on a freeway who sees this enormous *Close Encounters of the Third Kind* lighted-chandelier kind of 'mother ship' in the sky—I mean, these are *real* things. This reporter in Colorado saw something so gigantic he thought the world was coming to an end. For those of us who have been in this long enough, when you've heard enough stories about a string of boxcars on a railroad track that suddenly go straight up in the air; or a helicopter that makes no sound but which suddenly turns into a disc; or a little biplane that moves into the fog and comes out a disc; or oil barrels in Texas that rise, vertically, straight up—"

"These are all phenomena that have been reported?"

"Yes! Absolutely. It's *staging!* There's something about this phenomenon at every level that seems to be creating theater—or is disguising itself in some way. And to jump back for a moment to this alleged briefing paper I was shown at Kirtland Air Force Base—if the implications of that paper were pointing in any direction that was true, it implies that this alien phenomenon isn't just a twentieth-century phenomenon, but that these ETs have come at various intervals in the earth's history to manipulate DNA in already existing terrestrial primates and perhaps in other life forms as well."

"How far back are you talking about?"

"To the best of my memory, the time intervals for the DNA manipulation specifically listed in the briefing paper were 25,000, 15,000, 5,000, and 2,500 years ago. And what this means is, it's not just a twentieth-century phenomenon—which none of us knows for sure—but rather it's millennia, and that maybe we are somebody's experiment."

"How about you, Linda?" I say. "You haven't been abducted, or had any experiences of this sort, yourself?"

She shakes her head no.

"So, in other words, you're just like me—only you're twelve years farther down the line."

"That's right!" she says.

The afternoon's sessions concentrate on the general psychological profile of the abductees. This, I think, should be interesting, because if there *is* some sort of psychological explanation for this abduction phenomenon, the initial indications of it should become apparent here.

Mark Rodeghier, the director of investigations for CUFOS, is up. Rodeghier, as the conference's first presenter, established the ground rules for considering whether an abduction had or had not taken place.

Rodeghier reports that psychological and demographic data was collected from thirty-two individuals who met the CUFOS criteria for an abduction experience. Of that sample, women outnumbered the men three to one. The group was 94 percent Caucasian; the median age was thirty-eight; the average education was at least two years of college. Forty-two percent of the abductees were Protestant, 21 percent had no religious affiliation, and 37 percent were presumably scattered among the world's other religions. Fifty-eight percent of the abductees were married; they averaged 1.9 children and 3.1 siblings. The bulk of them experienced their first abductions between 1970 and 1979.

Given the Index of Childhood Memory and Imagination (ICMI) for fantasy-prone individuals, the group tested at 24.0 on a 0–52 scale. The population norm is between 20 and 23. They tested 25.2 for hypnotic suggestibility; the population norm is 20.8. Of that test group, Rodeghier says, five of the individuals had scores above the standard cutoff point. In other words, the abductees examined were very slightly more fantasy-prone and more hypnosis-suggestible than the norm.

About 20 percent of the sample experienced vivid images and/or sounds when falling asleep or waking up.

The results of the Minnesota Multiphasic Personality Inventory (MMPI), designed to measure various neurotic or pathologic character aspects of a personality, indicated that the sample's mean scores fell essentially within the normal range for a group of adults. The MMPI is well-respected within the field if one is trying to get at individuals' more conscious behavior rather than unconscious intentions and impulses. It would reveal, for example, if an individual is prone to lying.

Rodeghier reports the study's conclusion: the sample abductees as a group tended not to be significantly more fantasy-prone nor have a significantly higher level of suggestibility than the population norm. Furthermore, the sample as a whole did not contain overt pathologies. A cluster analysis of the primary MMPI scales, however, revealed two well-defined groups of abductees; they were labeled Clusters I and II. The Cluster II individuals had higher scores on most MMPI primary scales and markedly higher scores on the Keane Post-Traumatic Stress Disorder Subscale. Cluster II individuals also reported more loneliness as adults, less happiness throughout their lives, more problems sleeping, and a greater incidence of sexual abuse as children.

I lean over and ask one of the psychologists seated next to me, "Who are the Cluster IIs?"

"The crazies," he says with a thin smile.

Joanne Bruno and Eric Jacobson, two Boston-area psychologists, report next on their study of individuals who had contacted the Massachusetts branch of the Mutual UFO Network (Mass-MUFON) because they suspected they had had abduction experiences and wanted hypnosis. The abductees had been referred to Bruno and Jacobson by Mass-MUFON, who were interested in determining how common those individuals' narrative features were, and the incidence of psychiatric disorders.

Bruno and Jacobson were looking for any factors in these individuals' lives or backgrounds that could be connected to their abduction experiences. It was simply a study of their abduction narratives coupled with a compilation of their medical and life histories. The two psychologists' preliminary impression, they report, was that there was no evidence of any psychological or organic reasons for these abductees' experiences. However, they did note that a "significant proportion" of the abductees reported a "lifetime of odd dissociative episodes" which did not appear to fit any pattern of those dissociative disorders normally encountered. Some provided "classic abduction narratives"; but there was a second group, which the psychologists referred to as the "florid" types, who, while they may have had an abduction experience, also reported having supernatural experiences including telepathic communication with aliens and ghosts.

The "florid" types, Bruno and Jacobson tell us, are highly hypnotic-suggestive, prone to trancelike states and dissociative disorders. Some simply had strange stories: the woman who remembered from her childhood a large, gray, stone rabbit beside her crib, but recalled nothing else mysterious. One "florid" told the psychologists a long story complete with numerous details about his life as the "mascot of an alien family who had raised him as a kid." He was diagnosed a schizophrenic. Another "florid," a woman, reported that prior to experiencing a week-long abduction, she had been fasting and had lost both her job and her lover. She believed she was being recruited by astronauts. Medical tests indicated she had a thyroid disorder, and the two psychologists determined she was suffering from a thyroid psychosis.

In other words, some people who do "present" with abduction narratives ("present" being, again, the psychiatric term for the general impression the individual gives) actually do suffer from identifiable psychiatric disorders. These are Rodeghier's Cluster II "crazies."

"It is very important, for a number of reasons, that we acknowledge and systematically explore this," Jacobson and Bruno tell us. "Among these reasons are: (1) Our critics will immediately point it out; the individuals' disorders will be verifiable; and our failure to acknowledge this will weaken our case that most abduction narrators do not suffer from any identifiable psychiatric disorder. (2) It is irresponsible for us to imply that people who present abduction narratives never need help for major psychiatric disorders. And (3) any study of human problems benefits tremendously from the development of differential diagnoses of cases, and our claim that we can identify 'real' abductees would be powerfully strengthened if we were able to demonstrate our ability to systematically differentiate those abduction narrators who are suffering a mental disorder from those who are not."

What they are saying makes sense: even if 80 percent of the individuals coming forward with abduction narratives are Cluster II "crazies," there are still 20 percent whose claims should be taken seriously enough to be scientifically pursued.

"This is an issue which is itself diagnostic of us and our claim to be doing some kind of objective research," the psychologists say. "To shy away from this issue would be a sign that one is interested in insulating an ideology about the abduction experience from contact with challenging facts. And that, of course, is how to promote a cult, not how to do science."

The question is raised that since there are some people who do have major psychological problems, "how do we differentiate between genuine abduction cases and psychiatric cases who use abduction as a shield?" Is the abductee telling the truth or not? How can one tell if an individual's abduction memory is a "screen memory" for something else. Some memories may in fact be cover-ups for sexual abuse as a child. And this can initially be difficult to determine. The three common themes in abductions—being chosen, bodily invasion, and amnesia—the psychologists point out, are all comparable to symptoms of childhood sexual abuse.

Jacobson and Bruno conclude their presentation by pointing out that since traumatized people lose their trust in humanity, spiritual missions can restore meaning to a distressed individual's life. Abductees may become "cosmic citizens"—a symptom of their postabduction awareness that a sense of mission is a way of restoring meaning. A significant number of abductees, it is noted, have turned to careers in such fields as education, holistic medicine, and religion.

Jo Stone-Carmen, an Arizona psychologist, reports next on her study of abductees with conscious recall. The subjects were asked to describe themselves; what were their five major fears? Their answers included being harmed, being alone, heights, UFOs, being disabled, control issues, insects, and water.

Where did they feel safe? For the most part, they indicated, the answer was nowhere. One said, "With God or in the grave." Another said, "On top of a mountain with all the trees chopped down and I could see for miles in every direction."

Asked if they had irrational thoughts, one answered, "I don't. But if I had one, it would be about UFOs and aliens."

Fifty percent of the abductees with conscious recall studied by Stone-Carmen suffered from Post-Traumatic Stress Disorder (PTSD); their symptoms were avoidance, sleep disturbance, fear of being alone, not feeling safe, low self-esteem, and flashbacks.

Stone-Carmen reports that thirteen out of twenty-three abduction experiencers in one study had attempted suicide—a figure 57 percent higher than that for the general population. Some correlation obviously exists between abduction experiences and attempts on one's life, she tells us, but its meaning is not fully understood, and further study is needed.

No mention is made of how this alarming statistic speaks to the danger of untrained therapists dealing with abductees. But one psychologist in the lecture hall stands to plead that we remember "we are dealing with fragile persons."

Not surprisingly, a substantial number of the abductees in the study showed low self-esteem, higher vigilance, and guardedness. Such wariness in dealing with the outside may be a function of social dynamics, Stone-Carmen explains, in that abductees, like alcoholics, suffer the heavy burden of keeping their problem secret.

Dr. Donald Johnson, a New Jersey psychologist, reports that his study group had average IQs, were no more suspicious or naive than the population norm, tended to be more open, and that authenticity was important to them. Johnson's study group were considerably more intuitive and feeling than the general population, but he concedes, "If aliens are interested in studying human emotions, it would be natural that they would select those who were more in touch with their feelings."

His closing remarks are important: "None of us studying abductee groups can be sure we are studying a truly random group," he says. "Therefore the scientific basis for these studies may be questionable. It is still in a rudimentary stage. We have to ask ourselves, 'Is what we are seeing a result of abduction, or is it a precondition?' "

We break for dinner at La Groceria, a small, loud Italian restaurant within walking distance of the M.I.T. campus. I am at a table with David Cherniack of the Canadian Broadcasting Company; Karen Wesolowski of the *Atlantic Monthly;* and Dr. James Harder, the University of California engineering professor who, as a consultant to the Aerial Phenomena Research Organization (APRO), was sent to investigate the Pascagoula case in 1973 and the Travis Walton case in 1975.

Dr. Harder is one of the old-timers in the UFO field. At a July 1968 House Science and Astronautics Committee hearing attended also by astronomer Carl Sagan, Project Blue Book advisor J. Allen Hynek, and astronautics engineer Robert M. Baker, Harder did not hesitate to state his belief that "on the basis of the data and the ordinary rules of evidence as would be applied in civil or criminal courts, the physical reality of UFOs has been proved beyond a reasonable doubt." The objects, he testified, were "interplanetary," and their propulsion system was based upon "an application of gravitational fields that we do not understand."[52]

It's approximately eight p.m. when we reassemble in the lecture hall and hear Budd Hopkins suggest that "if the number of abductees we're dealing with have a lower number of sexual-abuse complaints than the general public, then we could say they were screening sexual abuse behind abductions. But 35 percent responded yes to the question 'Did you ever experience sexual abuse, including fondling, oral sex, or intercourse, as a child?' "—a figure considerably higher than that given for the general population, which is approximately 20 to 25 percent.

The next speaker is Richard J. Boylan, Ph.D., a handsome, silver-haired, Sacramento-based psychologist and licensed clinical social worker. Boylan disagrees that the nature of the alien encounter and abduction experience necessarily entails psychological trauma for the subject. Although Hopkins and Jacobs report that as a result of alien abductions their subjects experienced, in Boylan's words, "severe fear, panic, chronic anxiety, and often a syndrome consistent with post-traumatic stress disorder," others, such as California clinical psychologist Edith Fiore and Boylan himself, have "noticed a contrasting pattern: subjects whose experiences combined fear—fear of the unknown rather than the menacing—with uplifting feelings and a sense of expanded consciousness or cosmic perspective."

Boylan places a transparency on the overhead projector:

Psychological Characteristics of CE-IVs and Resultant Emotions

a. Encounter with startling stranger(s) = fear

b. Unusual communication mode (telepathy) = uneasiness

c. Sudden entrance of ETs = fear

d. Loss of self-control, movement = fear

e. Penetration of contactee's mind = intrusion

f. Experiences "violating" physical laws = disorientation

g. Other family members involved in CE-IV = anxiety

h. Intrusive involuntary examination or erotic/breeding procedures = resentment

i. Exposure to worrisome mental scenarios = anxiety

j. Message that ETs will return = uncertainty

k. Memory suppression/fragmentation = disorientation

l. Exposure to advanced technology = curiosity

m. Exposure to advanced Beings = awe

n. Exposure to ET lofty principles = respectfulness

Boylan runs through his list quickly, explaining that both the sequence and the responses have been discussed to some degree at this conference already, and moves on to those characteristics necessary to create post-traumatic stress disorder. "The trauma must entail unusual intentional harm or a disastrous incident," Boylan states. "The trauma is repeatedly re-experienced through anxious recollecting, dreams, flashbacks, or phobic reaction to reminders. . . . Psychic numbing occurs. . . . The individual may be anxious and suffer disrupted consciousness. . . . And finally, the symptoms endure longer than one month.

"Those elements necessary to create PTSD that are missing for most CE-Four experiencers," Boylan continues, "are the first, that the trauma entailed unusual intentional harm or a disastrous incident; and the third, psychic numbing." (I am struck that the "close encounter of the fourth kind" phenomenon is so familiar to this conference's attendees that Boylan's "CE-Four" abbreviation rolls as easily off his tongue and into our understanding as his "PTSD" abbreviation for post-traumatic stress disorder would at a convention of psychiatrists.) "The CE-Four paradox," Boylan tells us, "is that the abductees experience trauma without PTSD."

He explains that the hypothesis should be that the abductee syndrome would be similar to the childhood incest syndrome in that there would be the presence of trauma, the experience of intrusiveness, psychogenic amnesia, a recognized taboo against disclosure, and the onset of PTSD. But, Boylan points out, this hypothesis doesn't prove true. The CE-IV experience generally does not elicit PTSD because (1) the aliens "show an absence of malice"; (2) the abductees generally have "ambivalent feelings about the ETs: they are bizarre/intelligent, detached/advanced, etc."; (3) the "ETs communicate reassurances and important agenda"; (4) during the abduction "no great harm happens"; (5) the contactee, following an abduction experience, "generally becomes more mentally active"; and (6) he or she becomes "more attuned to society and/or nature."

For that "minority of contactees" who do experience PTSD, Boylan suggests alternative explanations. "The ETs' 'medical'/gynecological/urological procedures create a flashback to an earlier human sexual-molestation experience." Or, he says, the abductee's "involuntary transfer to the spacecraft flashes that individual back to a previous human kidnapping or 'confinement.' " Or it might be that the "controlling, intrusive ETs trigger a flashback to abusive or intrusive parental experiences."

What Boylan is saying is that "his" abductees do not suffer from PTSD because, for the most part, they see their experiences as benign: the Beings are not malicious, and not only does no harm stem from this contact, but in fact certain benefits may even accrue. If a few abductees do suffer PTSD, it is probably because the experience reminds them, on an unconscious level, of an earlier abusive experience suffered in childhood.

What is now taking place in this M.I.T. lecture hall is evident: the slow grinding away at the premise upon which this conference was seemingly based—i.e., the Hopkins/Jacobs/Bullard scenario for menacing abductions. The shifting tectonic plates are dividing the conference attendees into two distinct camps: those who believe there are "good" aliens and those who believe all aliens are manipulative and bad.

At last it is John Mack's turn to speak. In the book of abstracts prepared before the conference, Mack had outlined the basis for his talk as follows:

When we consider the hundreds of years of training and scientific socialization that has brought mental health professional and other clinicians to our present positivistic world-view it is not surprising that the original reaction to the stories of abductees is to presume that they and their reports comprise some individual or collective fantasy or lunacy. Psychosis; dream or dream state; physical, sexual or satanic ritual abuse; multiple personality; and some sort of strange dissociative state are among the categories

that have been offered to account for these unusual cases. Yet my own experience with evaluating and/or treating more than 40 abductees (the
process is really more like a co-investigation than therapy, although the
abductees generally derive benefit clinically) has confirmed what other investigators have found: *There has yet to be discovered convincing evidence
that anything else has occurred to account for an abductee's distress other than
what he or she says has happened* [my italics].

   This, of course, then becomes the starting point of a great mystery.
Abductees present as trauma cases. But since trauma is, by definition, the
result of an interaction between the person and events in the world, what
then has happened to them? In this paper I will review the impact of abductions upon the psyche, personal development and ongoing lives of
abductees. I will discuss the meaning, actual and potential, of this phenomenon for abductees themselves, the mental health and scientific community and the global culture.[53]

   But Mack, to my disappointment, tosses away his planned remarks and
opens instead by saying, "You can't get there from here without a shift in our
world-view—a world-view that contains a 'we're here and you're there' sense
of separateness in which the physical world is all that exists. Music, art, etc.,
are in the spirit world, but are they real? In other words," he says, speaking
very quickly, "we can't deal with something such as the abduction phenomenon that is so shattering to our literalist, materialist world-view and then
try to understand it from a literalist, materialist world-view!

   "The abduction phenomenon attacks our perception of reality," Mack
says excitedly, and speaks of alien beings "who, like Merry Tricksters, float
through walls, turn on and off television sets as a way of showing off their
technological superiority. Is it an intrusion into our space or some sort of
psychic phenomenon?" he asks.

   "Our materialist concept requires that we choose: are they in the spirit
world, or are they in the real world?" Mack continues. "When we open our
consciousness, we get information that is replicable. But we also get information about Beings, reptiles, etc. that belong in the spirit world. They are
like creatures from 'beyond,' like creatures of imagination. But for something that *should* exist in the spirit world, they seem to show up in the hard,
real world. That *traffic* is not supposed to be!

   "And so when that traffic occurs," Mack says, "it forces us to learn, to
expand our notions of reality. What it means is that we must rethink our
whole place in the cosmos!"

   Mack is interrupted by a standing ovation, which he ignores to add,
"The scientists today are becoming aware of the fact that we have not had
an adequate model to deal with the concept of world forces."

Someone mentions the "super-string theory"—that there might be as many as six or seven dimensions, not just the three we recognize—and suggests that it is necessary for us to recognize the expansion of our stage. Ann, the abductee who "dreamed" she had piloted a two-seater UFO and had swum through an ocean to a neon-green shore, says, "We aren't seeing all the strings."

Someone else asks, "Could there be multiple space/time dimensions collapsing into the abductee's consciousness?"

Mary, the Joe Nyman abductee who sat next to me at the conference on the first day, rises to say, "I anticipate with great pleasure working with the Gray aliens. I'm not left bereft by my experiences. I give them my cooperation and my body, and they give me their koan."

"For the first time in our history," says Marilyn Teare, the silver-haired California therapist, "we are *studying something that is studying us!*"

Gilda Moura, the Brazilian psychologist, agrees with John Mack. "The opening of the consciousness is what we need to do," she says.

Boylan, addressing the audience, asks, "Do you trust the aliens more than you trust the military?"

There is a chorus of yeses.

But Mack warns, "We are at a point where, as a result of this phenomenon, we have more cynicism toward our own establishment than we do toward the phenomenon. We should raise some flags before we say it is ultimately good without some evidence."

Mack's presentation ends; but while it was going on there was a new excitement in the room, almost a revival-meeting fervor.

David Hufford, a folklorist from Pennsylvania, speaks next, on "Sleep Paralysis and Bedroom Abductions."

Sleep paralysis, he explains, is that temporary paralysis which occurs immediately before or upon awakening. "However, the psychophysiology of sleep literature," he says, "grossly underestimates the prevalence of the experience and is totally lacking in phenomenological description. It is in the phenomenology of this event, and especially in the presence of a strange 'visitor,' that its anomalous nature lies.

"Also," he continues, "from the phenomenology it is clear that either (a) sleep paralysis is often involved in the early stages of an abduction, or (b) the similarity of the sleep paralysis and the 'abduction acquisition' experience constitutes a very high volume of noise in the abduction data. This statement is in no way intended to debunk or explain away any part of the abduction mystery," he insists. "At present 'sleep paralysis' is not an explanation, even though some of its neurophysiological mechanisms are known with reasonable confidence—rather that sleep paralysis itself is an anomaly on a par with abductions."

Having said that, Hufford describes a case he encountered in which, he tells us, "an abductee asked for proof that he was not dreaming. When he awoke a triangle had appeared on his chest. He felt no pain. It was not a burn. And it has not entirely faded even after eight or nine months." He places a photograph on the overhead projector. It shows a man with his shirt off. On his chest is a clearly defined equilateral triangle about four inches to each side.

He describes another subject who heard footsteps in his bedroom, then suddenly felt a weight on his bed, followed by the pressure of someone kneeling on his chest. He had a choking sensation, struggled against the weight, and succeeded in throwing it off. When he turned on his light, nothing was there.

What Hufford's subject was reporting was the frightening "Old Hag" phenomenon. While in Newfoundland, Hufford had investigated the "Old Hag" experience. Witnesses there described it as an actual event: a shadowy supernatural being attacked them in bed, paralyzing and nearly suffocating them. Hufford had assumed the "Old Hag" was merely a folk belief of witchcraft conforming to local traditions. But when he returned to Pennsylvania and presented his findings to his students, he was surprised that a number of them came forward to report strikingly similar experiences they had endured. There was no "Old Hag" folkloric tradition in these students' backgrounds; they did not even know what to call the phenomenon, and had been embarrassed to tell anyone of their experiences out of fear of ridicule.

Hufford then learned there was the same legend in Sweden, Denmark, Poland, Holland, Germany, and Iceland (in Iceland the hag is an ogress), describing this same distinct and unique set of events. And so it seemed to be a common cross-cultural experience—but, unlike most folkloric explanations for an anomaly, the "Old Hag" phenomenon was heavily based on experiences that had shaped the tradition, rather than vice versa.

Seventeen percent of the students Hufford surveyed "had a positive response to the 'Old Hag' scenario," he tells us. Of that 17 percent, 80 percent sensed a presence, saw and heard something, or only heard, or only saw, something. Hufford identifies the "Old Hag" experience as sleep paralysis combined with hypnagogic hallucination. ("Hypnagogic" refers to the state of drowsiness preceding sleep.) The paradox of the "Old Hag" experience— like the paradox of the abduction experience—is that there is no known source for the content of the trauma.

Someone from the audience, referring to the photograph of the man with the triangle on his chest, points out that the triangle is not a unique symbol, since it is a common alien insignia. Hufford laughs and says, "That's why I showed it. So you'd all know I was okay."

A therapist rises and says that he has just had a triangle show up on one of his subjects in the last few days.

An abductee reports that under regression she realized that the mark the aliens had put on her had been a mistake and that they had told her to put ice on it and it would go away.

A few months after the conference, I came across *Fire in the Brain* by Ronald K. Siegel, an associate research professor in the UCLA School of Medicine's Department of Psychiatry and Behavioral Sciences. Siegel, whose special area of research is hallucinations, was familiar with David Hufford's work. (Hufford's 1982 University of Pennsylvania Press publication on the "Old Hag" phenomenon, *The Terror That Comes in the Night,* is listed as a reference for Siegel's "Succubus" chapter in *Fire in the Brain.*) Siegel includes this graphic account of his own encounter with the Old Hag:

I was awakened by the sound of my bedroom door opening. I was on my side and able to see the luminescent dial of my alarm clock. It was 4:20 A.M. I heard footsteps approaching my bed, then heavy breathing. There seemed to be a murky presence in the room. I tried to throw off the covers and get up, but I was pinned to the bed. There was a weight on my chest. The more I struggled, the more I was unable to move. My heart was pounding. I strained to breathe.

The presence got closer, and I caught a whiff of a dusty odor. The smell seemed old, like something that had been kept in an attic too long. The air itself was dry and cool, reminding me of the inside of a cave.

Suddenly a shadow fell on the clock. *Omigod! This is no joke!* Something touched my neck and arm. A voice whispered in my ear. Each word was expelled from a mouth foul with tobacco. The language sounded strange, almost like English spoken backward. It didn't make any sense. Somehow the words gave rise to images in my mind: I saw rotting swamps full of toadstools, hideous reptiles, and other mephitic horrors. In my bedroom I could only see a shadow looming over my bed. I was terrified.

But I'm a scientist. I must see what it is. I suspected that it was a hallucination; either the type that occurs in the twilight just before falling asleep (hypnagogic hallucination) or the type that occurs just before awakening (hypnopompic hallucination). All I would have to do is either look at the image or touch it and it should vanish.

I signaled my muscles to move, but the presence immediately exerted all its weight on my chest. The weight spread through my body, gluing me to the bed. . . .

A hand grasped my arm and held it tightly. . . . The hand felt cold and dead. . . .

Then part of the mattress next to me caved in. Someone climbed onto the bed! The presence shifted its weight and straddled my body, folding itself along the curve of my back. I heard the bed start to creak. There was a texture of sexual intoxication and terror in the room.

Throughout it all, I was forced to listen to the intruder's interminable whispering. The voice sounded female. I *knew* it was evil. . . .

The intruder's heavy gelatinous body was crushing the life out of me. . . . I started to lose consciousness. Suddenly the voice stopped. I sensed the intruder moving slowly out of the room. Gradually the pressure on my chest eased. It was 4:30 A.M.

I sprang out of bed, grabbed a flashlight. . . .[54]

Siegel flashed the beam around his bedroom, found nothing, called out, "Who's there?"

Worried that the intruder had hidden somewhere in his house, he conducted a room-to-room search. He found no one, of course.

Siegel has spent his adult life researching hallucinations and learning how to distinguish them from reality. He has immersed himself in claustrophobic, water-filled sensory-isolation tanks and Vietnam-era-style "tiger cages." He has studied the effects of hallucinogenic drugs on laboratory animals, human patients, and eventually, so as to better understand their effects, himself. As he notes, hallucinations are not dependent upon "brains seething with drugs or sliced apart by schizophrenia. . . . Questions of sanity and scientific naivete aside, if the hallucination appears real enough, anyone could be fooled. After all, some hallucinations have all the sensory qualities of real perceptions including sights, sounds, tastes and smells. They appear just as concrete and 'out there' as real events."[55]

So who—or what—was Siegel's "Old Hag"? Siegel explains:

The best explanation for my succubus experience was that I was in a state of sleep paralysis *and* having a hypnopompic hallucination. The fact that I saw images of rotting swamps concomitant with awakening was a strong indication that some REM activity was continuing during the hypnopompic period. But why the specific succubus or incubus image? Jung believed it was a racial memory implanted in our genes eons ago when our ancestors awoke in a dark cave and panicked at the presence of a predator. Some contemporary psychiatrists believe it is a return to the frightening, looming shapes of the infant's perceptual world. While such explanations may account for the ubiquitous nature of the experience, it is likely that the general features of the succubus are suggested to the sleeper by specific physiological sensations. The brain tries to synthesize a meaningful explanation from this material.

What are these raw sensations, and how are they produced? Awakening in a state of sleep paralysis can cause the person to hyperventilate and experience feelings of tightness or heaviness in the chest. Hyperventilation, even in the form of sighing respirations, also diminishes the supply of oxygen to the brain. This can produce hyperacusis, whereby sounds seem especially loud. Simple background noises, ticking clocks, even one's own labored breathing can provide the seeds from which grow more complex auditory hallucinations such as opening doors, footsteps, and garbled voices. If the oxygen supply is sufficiently reduced, sexual pleasure centers in the brain may be affected for both men and women. . . .

Intense efforts to move against the paralysis increase awareness of the rigid muscles, the body lying in bed under the covers, and the perspiring skin. In the hypnopompic brain, the restraint can turn into pressure from a grasping hand, the covers become another body folding itself over the sleeper, and the sweat nurtures gelatinous sensations complete with odors. Even the movement of the mattress and creaking of the bed were probably the result of my own struggles, not the intruder's. Autonomic nervous system changes in cardiac activity, skin temperature, and skin resistance can make additional contributions to the tingling, sensations of cold, and strong emotional responses.

Lying in my bedroom inside this paralytic terror, my brain was alert to the most subtle stimuli. I couldn't move, but my brain was using all its sensory modalities to probe the environment with intense scrutiny. Minor stimuli, usually unnoticed, were perceived so acutely that the brain attached major significance to them. For example, barely detectable shadows are normal in my bedroom, where a streetlight can be seen from the window. Looking through fear-dilated pupils, it would be easy to see these amorphous shadows, like inkblots, evolve into looming shapes from the id. And the smell of cigarette smoke, which periodically invaded my bedroom from the apartment below, undoubtedly accounted for the perception of tobacco breath. The smoke usually entered via my bedroom window, which was always open a crack, just enough to let in the cool air I thought arrived with the looming shape.[56]

"You don't have to have a medieval mind to see a succubus emerge from all these data points," Siegel concludes. "One of the best 'fits' the brain can make of these sensations is that someone or something is sitting or lying on top of the body. Yet knowing all this will not necessarily dispel the perceived reality of the succubus or the accompanying paroxysm of terror."[57]

As David Hufford pointed out, the "Old Hag" phenomenon is crosscultural; and as Siegel wrote:

I was not the first to be terrorized by such an experience. Throughout history many people have reported attacks by the *same* intruder. I was right when I said she smelled old. The Babylonians called her Lilitu, demoness of the wind, who seduced men by night. The Jews called her Lilith, the hairy night creature. She was the succubus of ancient Rome who leaped upon the sleeper and rode him to love or death. Then, in the Middle Ages, she became the witch Lamia. Finally, in Old Germany, she was known as the *mare,* the old, ugly woman who sat on the chest of the sleeper and produced the evil dreams we now call night*mares.*[58]

So untold numbers of people, for untold numbers of years, from all over the world, have described in effect the same experience of a monstrous female form—old, hairy, evil-smelling—who, seemingly following the same sequence, mounts the individual's chest, crushing the breath from his body. It is a hallucinatory episode so vivid and real, it has quite literally scared some of its recipients to death.

I am struck by the parallels suggested by the seeming rigidity of the sequences in the "Old Hag" phenomenon and the rigidity of the sequences reported in the alien abduction phenomenon by investigators such as Dave Jacobs and Budd Hopkins. But then Gwen Dean, a California therapist, follows Hufford with a presentation containing even more striking comparisons: the parallels found in ritual abuse and abduction accounts.

"Although there is no satisfactory definition of ritual abuse," Dean begins, "there are striking similarities between accounts of ritual abuse and alien abductions." She throws a transparency on the overhead projector:

Abduction Accounts		*Ritual Abuse Accounts*
examining table	vs.	altar table
forced intercourse	vs.	ritual rape
scary eyes	vs.	scary eyes
babies important	vs.	babies important
out-of-body experience	vs.	out-of-body experience
wounds, scars, bruises	vs.	wounds, scars, bruises
amnesia	vs.	amnesia
observers	vs.	observers
fear of hypnosis	vs.	fear of hypnosis
forced against will	vs.	forced against will
feels like drugged	vs.	may be drugged
told you are special	vs.	told you are special
isolated from other humans	vs.	isolated from other humans
abducted at young ages	vs.	abducted at young ages

In all, Gwen Davis tells us, she was able to find some forty-four parallels. It is nearly ten p.m.; Davis tells us there will be more discussion of the parallels tomorrow morning.

The third day of the conference is over.

As I walk back across the Harvard Bridge to my hotel on the Boston side of the Charles River, I catch myself warily glancing up at the nighttime sky, half-expecting to see a glowing orange-red disc.

Alone in my hotel room I turn on the TV in time to catch the news. A large portion of the broadcast is devoted to the ongoing "Earth Summit," the popular name for the United Nations Conference on Environment and Development in progress in Rio de Janeiro. President George Bush, responding to criticism that the United States is failing to take a leadership role, answers that America's environmental record is "second to none," and he calls for an "action plan" to avert global warming.

I half-listen to the news as I go back over my three days of conference notes. I am again struck by the psychological profiles of the abductees: that there is no evidence of any psychological or organic reasons for their experiences, that they have average IQs, in fact are average in so many ways. The unavoidable conclusion seems to be that they are *ordinary* people who have had *extraordinary* experiences.

An item on the TV news catches my interest: the Vice President of the United States, observing a spelling bee in Trenton, New Jersey, wrongly advised a contestant to add an "e" to his spelling of "potato."

I think about the abductees I have spoken with: that as off-the-wall as the young Massachusetts housewife with her stories of "Zar" and of groups of worlds working together may have seemed, Pat, the midwestern dentist's wife who wrestled with an alien's arm, seemed dead-on. I think of Carol and Alice and their image of trying to locate a parking meter in space; I am moved by their obvious confusion and distress, the terror of Carol's flashback that drove her to seek refuge in a closet.

I think about Linda Moulton Howe. She is a respected journalist and documentary filmmaker, and yet she seems to believe in a government cover-up; in cattle being raised up beams of light into UFOs, where their organs are excised with laser efficiency; in crop circle patterns being an alien "grass-roots" attempt at communication. Linda started out as skeptical as I am about this phenomenon.

I realize *I don't know what to believe!* How does one explain the similarities in the abductees' stories—the consistency of detail, structure, scenario? What would prompt a woman to make up a story about an extraterrestrial creature trying on her high-heeled shoes? How does one explain Budd Hopkins's story of Linda Cortile being "floated" out of her twelfth-floor apartment building into a hovering UFO before two cars of witnesses who confirm her account? How does one explain John Carpenter's story of the two women abducted in Kansas who, separately and unrehearsed, tell such matching stories?

CHAPTER V

At the Conference

Day Four

Tuesday morning Dave Jacobs and I again have breakfast together at the Eliot Hotel. "The key thrust of UFO research in the past has been the UFO sightings," he tells me. "We knew everything there was to know about sightings. There have been studies on the ground, trace cases, approximately forty-eight gazillion multiple-witness sightings from unimpeachable sources. And the sightings take a certain style of research—legwork, talking to witnesses; the methodology has been all worked out. Consequently we have amassed evidence not unlike a sledgehammer between the eyes. It is massive, overwhelming evidence that UFOs exist.

"However, abduction research requires different methodology," he continues. "It is intensely personal as opposed to confirmation of sightings. And the approach to the source is close to that of therapists. It often requires hypnosis; but hypnosis has a myriad of problems. There are always accusations of confabulation, leading, distortions—Eddie Bullard is going to be talking about that this morning."

Jacobs explains some of his discovery techniques. "A red flag during an encounter narrative is 'I stopped the car and got out to take a look.' We generally know that's not *all* that happened. Under hypnosis the subject retells the story: 'I got out of the car . . . I got out of the car . . .' and you can hear increasing anxiety in his voice. You are talking to him in the present tense: 'You are getting out of the car and what is happening? What do you see?' And he starts telling you what he saw, and it is an abduction scenario."

J. Gordon Melton, a Santa Barbara, California theologian, is the morning's first presenter. His topic is "Religious Perspectives of Stories: Contactees to Abductees." He reviews the contactees' reception: how following their surfacing in the 1950s they were called hoaxers, frauds, fakes, and how "channeling," which had started with the contactees, led to the New Age movement.

"The overwhelming majority of contactees," he says, "were not seeking contact. In fact, when it occurred, it interrupted their lives."

The contactees were for the most part unchurched people, he tells us. It was not a religious quest, and yet spiritual messages emerged. "No ufologist was ready to accept them. Their accounts were dismissed as cult-religious speculation.

"Satanic ritual abuse stories and alien abduction stories," he continues, "emerged at approximately the same time. And there are a number of parallels. The format of retrieved memories is similar." Gwen Dean, the evening before, had come up with some forty-four parallels, I recalled.

Melton goes on to compare the impact of the ritual abuse and alien abduction stories: listen to enough of them, he says, and you become convinced the tellers are not lying. In both cases there are a large number of independent accounts; people are telling similar stories with similar details without knowing each other. Both stories have the same claims on the truth: "If what they're saying isn't true, where is the story/trauma coming from?" Both types of stories share the elusive nature of the causative: one cannot with any certainty get from the satanic abuse story back to the group responsible for the abuse, just as one cannot get from the abduction story back to the aliens. Both types of victims need support; there is a danger in mixing research and therapy.

"As we begin to speculate on the reasons for abductions," he says, "it is tempting to move into theology—and New Age theology at that, since the New Age has the occult at its very root."

Somebody suggests the distinguishing feature between contactees and abductees is that "contactees have a good time; abductees don't."

During the question period, seemingly out of the blue, John Mack asks, "What are the criteria for evaluating information from the cosmos?"

Eddie Bullard next compares abduction reports to folklore narrative. "Folklore is filled with beings that come from distant worlds," he says, and mentions the lore of fairies and how "diminutive supernatural beings are universal." He tells how fairies traditionally take people to subterranean kingdoms; how the "faerie mound" rises out of the ground; how time moves at a different rate with fairies; how they are always stealing children and women, and cross-breeding occurs. It is a comparison he went into in more detail in his report "Folkloric Dimensions of the UFO Phenomenon" for the *Journal of UFO Studies*. In that report Bullard pointed out that there have already been a number of comparative studies of the similarities between UFOs and older supernatural lore: "Jacques Vallee [*Passport to Mag-*

onia, 1969] noted that many phenomena of UFO close encounters correspond to the phenomena of fairy meetings," Bullard wrote. His report continued:

> The recognition of folkloric parallels to UFO events has become a staple element in the literature as researchers expand ever further on Vallee's pioneering work. The dwarfish occupants reported in most UFO landings have their parallels in the almost worldwide beliefs about diminutive supernatural beings. Physical and mental effects of close encounters such as mental time lapse, paralysis, or subsequent illness resemble effects of encounters with ghosts, fairies, and demons. Fear of kidnap by sorcerers in motor cars panicked Haitians in the 1940s, in a predecessor to the current UFO abduction epidemic. The floating effect reported by abductees compares with transvection phenomena among 17th-century witches; the bedroom intrusion of strange beings in the night [compares] with incubus visitation. Even vehicle stoppages attributed to electromagnetic interference by UFOs are nothing new, since supernatural beings often exerted similar effects on horses and even bicycles. . . .
>
> The bizarre, surreal abduction story has proved the richest hunting ground for folklore parallels. Comparison has focused on imagery motifs, narrative structure, and extended mythological patterns, most notably initiations and shamanic journeys. How closely folklore and UFO abductions parallel one another is perhaps best exemplified by shamanic initiation: while the candidate is sick or entranced, his soul leaves his body and meets two friendly companions. They accompany him into an underworld where unfriendly demons capture the candidate and tear him apart, then reassemble him with new knowledge and magical powers added. A rock crystal inserted into his head gives him power, and further inspection takes place in a domed cavern illuminated with a uniform but sourceless light. When the initiate returns he may have been unconscious for hours or days, and subsequently leads a changed life as a shaman, capable of healing, magic, and communion with the spirit world. Anyone familiar with abduction reports readily identifies the shamanic equivalents of time lapse, alien escorts, gruesome examination within the spaceship, and life-transforming aftermath. Even the implanted electrode and uniform lighting in the examination room compare motif for motif among Siberian and abduction stories alike.
>
> These similarities seem too impressive to dismiss as chance, and weighty with important clues about the ultimate nature of UFOs. Why aliens should act like fairies or demons makes no sense outside of discredited ancient-astronaut speculations, but a great deal of sense if UFO reports are subjective experiences or supernatural fictions adapted for a modern audience. So many parallels suggest as much.[1]

"The echo," Bullard tells us at the conference, "comes down to us through history: 'No one is ever safe. Someone is going to get you!'—and they do! When you're in bed, when you're driving your car at night."

Movies are another prime suspect as a possible source for abduction stories, Bullard says, since science fiction films such as *Invaders from Mars, Earth Versus the Flying Saucers,* and *Killers from Space* are shot through with abduction stories. There is a possibility that people are picking up these ideas and interpreting them, digesting them in abduction scenarios. ("Movies set a vivid precedent for the implant, domed room, dying planet, and procreation problems of the abductors," Bullard noted in his article. " *The UFO Incident,* a TV movie based on the [Barney and Betty] Hill case, aired shortly before Travis Walton reported his abduction experience, which in turn received nationwide attention as a news event. Coverage of abductions in various media, especially Whitley Strieber's case [Strieber's writing about his abduction experiences in his books *Communion* and *Transformation*], has familiarized a large segment of the population with this phenomenon."[2]) "The similarities are there," Bullard points out at the conference, "but are made only by extracting elements that are similar from only parts of the stories. Fairies, for example, never examine anyone!"

Someone rises to draw a wonderful parallel between abduction accounts and J. M. Barrie's *Peter Pan:* the never-aging figure who comes down from the sky and floats children out of their bedroom accompanied by a little ball of light: Tinker Bell.

John Mack says heatedly, "I'm surprised nobody in this group has gotten up to say what we are dealing with here is radically different and has no connection with folklore!"

Off to my right someone rises and says, "What we are dealing with is radically different and has no connection with folklore."

Eddie Bullard next discusses what he refers to as "The Overstated Danger of Hypnosis." I am particularly interested in this, since so many questions arise over the validity of information gained in this manner.

The issue is that hypnotism many times is the only means of access to an amnesiac abductee's experience. Something like 25 to 30 percent of the abductees have conscious memories of their abductions; and these memories, incomplete and confusing, may consist simply of small, shadowy figures at the foot of the bed, perhaps a strange medical examination while lying naked on a table, an image of a white-glowing circular room, recurring dreams of flying. It has become common procedure in UFO research to use hypnosis to reach the unconscious mind, where, presumably, the abductee's complete UFO experience would still be stored. Hypnosis has in fact been enormously successful in helping these individuals "recall" their experiences. However, the use of hypnosis is also the basis for much of the skepticism surrounding the validity of the abduction experience, since, as most debunkers hasten to point out, there is always the criticism that the hypnotist consciously or unconsciously influences the subject's response. Bullard is fully aware of this. "According to the universal expert opinion, hypnosis is no guaranteed way to the truth," he tells us. "They speak of the subject's susceptibility and suggestibility, role playing, following the lead of the hypnotist. Therefore, the subject is likely to confabulate fiction that is true, untrue, or partly true. Details may come out, but the witness cannot distinguish between truth and falsehood. Experts are unanimous in their discrediting of any hypnosis-based reality of what happened.

"But if that were so," Bullard asks, "wouldn't all of Sprinkle's subjects see easygoing aliens?* And wouldn't all of Hopkins's see dangerous aliens? Instead of what you would expect in taking samples, you get a reasonable mix.

"Hypnosis in some cases does produce a great deal of the account; but in many more cases, without hypnosis, the accounts still emerge with similarities that are striking." Bullard concludes, "Hypnosis is not a determining factor, but I'm sure we'll be hearing from the skeptics forever."

They will.

During the coffee break I take Mary, the Joe Nyman abductee, aside and ask if I might speak to her about her previous night's comment, "I anticipate with great pleasure working with the Gray aliens. I'm not left bereft by my experiences. I give them my cooperation and my body, and they give me their koan."

As we sit down facing each other on the lawn, she says, "I'd appreciate it if you're going to use my account that you would alter my name."

"Would you like to choose one?" I ask.

Mary thinks for a moment, then says, "I'll take 'Darlene.' "

"*Darlene?*" I ask, surprised. "Why 'Darlene'?"

She laughs and explains, "Because it is about as far from the kind of name I'd want for myself as possible."

* Dr. Leo Sprinkle, former professor in the University of Wyoming's counseling-psychology department, founded the Rocky Mountain Conference on UFO Investigation in 1980. In 1989, he was forced to resign his tenure when it became public knowledge that he claimed to have been abducted by aliens as a child. Sprinkle believes the alien encounters are transformative journeys aimed at ultimately turning us into "cosmic citizens."

Mary tells me she is a university graduate, a communications specialist now working abroad, and that her first conscious recollection of her experiences came three years earlier, during the summer of 1989.

"How many experiences have you had?" I ask. "Have you any way of knowing that, or when they began?"

Mary takes a deep breath and exhales. "They began in this life when I was a few hours old, and for all I know I've had hundreds," she says.

"When was the last one?"

"Two nights ago."

"*During the conference?*" I ask, although, in hindsight, I should not have been so surprised.

"Yes," she says. "It was nothing out of the ordinary for me. I arrived back at the motel where I was staying, and while preparing for bed I was overcome with a feeling of apprehension—which is usually an indication to me that something is going to happen."

I was reminded of Joe Nyman's earlier presentation on abductees' psychological stages during an abduction. The Boston-area abduction investigator had given as an example of the first stage a witness making excuses to leave a gathering. "She arrives home and . . . feels a sense of urgency," Nyman had said, "a sense that someone is coming or that something is going to happen. It is a premonition that something is going to happen in a very short time."

"What form did this apprehension take?" I ask Mary.

"It's the feeling of being watched. That somehow something is coming. Sometimes it's a feeling of anticipation, but more often I would call it a kind of low-key dread. 'Apprehension' is a good word for it," she continues, "but it's a nagging feeling in the pit of your stomach, like 'Okay, I've got to be prepared for it.' "

During the second stage, the transition of consciousness from one's normal waking state, Nyman had told us, the witness "notices the presence of lights in the room that become a figure," or lights outside.

When Mary turned off her bedside lamp, she saw lights shining in her motel bedroom window. She got up and discovered the source was a house across the street. Someone had switched on a porch light. Relieved, Mary climbed back into bed and lay there for a few minutes before she fell into what she readily identified as a hypnagogic state—the state of drowsiness preceding sleep.

"During that time," Mary tells me, "I heard voices conversing to each other somewhere near my head on the left side. I perceived lights moving in the room, and that's all the recollection I have."

"Nothing else happened?" During the third stage, according to Nyman, there takes place the psycho-physical imposition and interaction similar to the abduction sequences Dave Jacobs has written about and reported.

"I believe that *something* else happened," Mary says, "but I'm very successful at screening those experiences I'm not prepared to deal with."

"How is it possible? Can you just put them out of your mind?"

"Everybody has unconscious screening mechanisms: PTSD, the whole thing," Mary explains. "Everybody has a way of protecting themselves from the recall of experiences which demand to be integrated into their entire human being, but which their consciousness or their perception of external reality won't permit them to integrate easily or successfully. As a result, that unintegrated material remains in your unconscious mind. When it's ready to be dealt with, it will then emerge as a conscious memory, and at that point," Mary says, laughing knowingly, "you undergo a paradigm shift. . . .

"Conscious acknowledgment of this experience," she continues, "looking at it squarely and confronting your fears about it, effects a transformative change in your life. By that I mean it usually changes forever how you perceive your reality. Now, to undergo this kind of thing all the time is really intense, and it's not always beneficial. So I have a mechanism that just screens me from consciously acknowledging those parts of the experience that I'm not yet prepared to put into a conscious frame of reference."

"In other words, you're able to forget what you're not ready to remember?"

She looks at me with a communication specialist's impatience with oversimplification.

"How have your perceptions of reality changed?" I ask.

Mary laughs at my question. "I'm a well-adjusted person," she tells me. "I've *always been* a well-adjusted person. A bit of a loner, too; but I'm highly successful in my field, and I'm successful at presenting myself as a highly functioning human being. But before I became aware of these experiences in my life I would have described my 'reality' as being just about as strange as anybody's acid trip on any day of the week."

I am wondering if I heard her right. "Acid trip" seems an odd, sixties metaphor for Mary to have used.

"So this is just one more thing I have to deal with," she is saying. "Do you remember the abductee, Pat, who said it was kind of like trying to describe to a blind person what 'red' looks like?"

I nod.

"This is what I've lived with all my life!" Mary says. "I wish you could get inside my head and see it; it's fairly beautiful most of the time. But I see things I'm aware that other people are not capable of seeing. And I experience things that other people would attribute to my being under the influence of some kind of hallucinogenic substance, or whatever."

"Be specific now," I say. "What sort of things do you see?"

Mary takes a deep breath. She hesitates for a moment; then, looking beyond me over my left shoulder, she quietly says, "There's somebody standing by the tree over there."

"Some*body* is there right now?"

"Um-hm," she says, nodding.

I twist around to look. I see nothing but the M.I.T. campus and trees. I turn back to Mary. "You see somebody standing there, still?"

"Well, it's a shape. I can't see it clearly, but it's a shape."

To cover my own rising apprehension I ask, "Does what you see frighten you?"

"No." She runs her hand through the grass. "Disembodied Beings are real to me, so it doesn't frighten me."

"Why do you think that Being is standing by the tree?"

"I don't know! They're just standing there," she says with a tense little laugh. "I mean, what do you want me to tell you about it?"

"*They*'re just standing there? You mean there's more than one?" I turn around for a better look.

"This person—or whatever it is—is standing there."

"Can you describe what this person looks like?" I ask, turning back to Mary. "Obviously, I don't see it at all."

"I can't see it clearly," she says. "It's just a shape. It's just like a cloudy form." Seeing my puzzled expression, she gives me another little laugh.

"All right, then let's talk about what you were saying at the conference."

"Okay!" she says with obvious relief, and bursts out laughing again.

"You said that you anticipated with great pleasure working with the Gray Beings."

"Yes, I would say so," Mary replies thoughtfully. "The work I have done with them has had many positive and beneficial effects on my life. So even though the feeling that I have just prior to an experience might be called dread or apprehension, I'm aware that that's the biological response—the animal in me. I'm able to control my fear through my awareness that what I'm feeling is simply similar to that of a rabbit in the woods cowering in fear when a superior intelligence walks by. The rabbit can't tell whether that person has good intentions or not; all the rabbit can tell is that it's afraid. So I suppose the apprehension I have is simply the fear that has been programmed into my biology as a survival mechanism. But it can accelerate to blind panic if I allow it to.

"Bringing that fear under control," Mary says, darting a look over my shoulder, "has been my task for quite a long time. But the more I'm able to control my fear, the better my experiences are. And so, to answer your question, I do anticipate with pleasure working with them, because . . ." She pauses for a moment, then says with a sigh, "Because this has been a good thing for me."

She doesn't sound convinced. "Why has it been good?" I ask.

"The more control I have over these experiences—these experiences over which there is no control—the more empowered I am in my everyday experiences to control the gross matter that I have to deal with in consensus reality."

" 'Consensus reality'?"

"Yes. In what *you* would call reality."

I decide not to pursue this tack; instead I ask Mary to give me an example of a koan.

" 'What is the sound of one hand clapping?' " she responds.

"Well, yes," I say, "but what I was looking for was one the Beings had given you."

Mary thinks for a moment. "If I asked them when my daughter Sarah was a tiny baby how could I help Sarah deal with this experience, their reply would be something like, 'You must listen very carefully when she speaks to you.' This is a koan because, although to all practical intents and purposes Sarah is capable of communicating on only a crude level, she is still so young she can't tell me what's the matter. She can't communicate with me the way I can communicate with you. And so if she is undergoing an experience, I have to be listening not just with my physical senses but with something else as well. The koan has just challenged me to experience my relationship with my daughter on something other than a purely physical level."

"When, at the conference, you said you gave these beings your body and cooperation, what did you mean?"

"Well, I consented to this right from the beginning. I've had the experience of dual reference—some people call it confabulation. I don't care if it's confabulation or not—I know what I saw and I have to deal with that. I identify with these beings. That's not necessarily a bad thing."

She begins to speak about how, as part of Zen Buddhism, there's the practice of "identifying with deities" and expressing "compassion and understanding towards disembodied spirits" and how contact with the Beings "is not a new human experience. It's just in a different frame of reference, a more Western frame of reference, I guess," she says.

"I think what I meant, Mary, was on a more literal level. Have you given them your body?"

"Yes," she responds. "I said yes to this. Yes. On a literal level, yes. I work with them on a biological level as well as a spiritual level."

"Have they taken samples?"

"Yes."

"Eggs?"

"Yes, probably," she says matter-of-factly. "I've had a couple of experiences which would indicate to me that, yes, that's *exactly* what they've done."

"And you've also experienced the classic 'medical examination' Dave Jacobs writes about?"

"Yes, I've had those. The core experience for me," she says, "is very similar to everyone else's: the abduction, the spacecraft, the examination table, the sampling, the screen memories, *all* those things. Yes, I would say that that's a fairly ordinary experience for me as well."

"How ordinary?"

"It doesn't happen every time, with every experience. I like to think of it as the seventy-two-thousand-kilometer tune-up."

"Like maintenance?" I ask.

Mary smiles. "Yes, 'maintenance' is a good word for it."

The conference attendees are beginning to file back into the building. I have time for one more question. "Do you think there's some sort of grand design?"

Mary thinks for a moment. "If I'm looking at the grand design, I can't perceive it. Let me put it this way. Imagine taking a pin and punching a hole into a card and then holding that card up and squinting through the hole at the room you're in. That's how well we can perceive the grand design— that's how well I perceive it, anyway. The grand design is there, but I can't make it out."

"Do you have any hint as to what this grand design might be?"

Mary is getting restless; she doesn't want to be late when the conference resumes. "To learn not to fear," she says. "And to learn how to love."

When we return to the lecture hall, folklorist Eddie Bullard is discussing Kenneth Ring's "Imaginal Realm" hypothesis and Ring's Omega Project effort to test near-death experiences (NDEs) against abduction experiences. Ring believed experiencers of both these kinds of episodes were remarkably similar types of people; that often they reported a host of other extraordinary experiences throughout their lifetimes: psychic sensitivity, apparitional observations, and out-of-body experiences. Ring suspected something in common unites these people: the developmental pattern of their childhood showed similar degrees of stress and awareness of alternate realities.

According to Bullard, Ring traces extraordinary encounters to the "Imaginal Realm"—"imaginal" not in the sense of unreal or illusory, but as in an alternate reality that is objectively self-existing, with dimension, form, and a population of its own. The Imaginal Realm, Ring says, is as real and as rich as the sensory realm, but it is discernible only by people in alternate states of consciousness. To see it requires imaginal or psychospiritual senses. Bullard tells us that Ring believes people with "encounter-prone personalities" possess these senses in unusual degree and glimpse imaginal reality more often than "their less-gifted fellows."

"Like shamans, mystics and visionaries," Bullard continues, "they are aware of experiencing a purer, more coherent reality than the empirical or intellectual realm. A UFO abduction has the genuine, tangible properties of a physical experience, but the aliens derive from contact with *other*—rather than *outer*—space."

Ring suggests, according to Bullard, that imaginal experiences are somehow linked to our concern for the environment. Abductees and Near-Death Experiencers both report warnings about the fate of the earth and hints of disaster. "Aliens treat us as we treat the world," Bullard says. "They suggest we are going through our planet's near-death experience. Abductees stand at the forefront of an evolution of consciousness, a global transformation that is slowly gaining momentum, guided perhaps by external forces, or perhaps from within, but always working to break down the narrow confines of present consciousness and open it to a greater fullness. Abductees were the first to be shown this, and they are going to lead us out and show us the way. The shaman's journey and the UFO abduction are parts of the same process. They signal different ways of being in the world. Meanwhile the growing number of extraordinary experiences mark the emergence of a redemptive form of higher consciousness at a time of crisis for the earth and its inhabitants."

John Mack is on his feet. "I want to continue in my role as category smasher," he says. "I object to either / or–ness! Aliens can literally exist and come into our world, and we can have consciousness in different forms: matter one moment, particles the next."

Behind me some of Joe Nyman's subjects, Mary among them, are crying out, "Yes! *Yes!* YES!"

Michael Papagiannis, a darkly handsome Boston University astronomer, next discusses the "Probability of Extraterrestrial Life on Earth." He points out that "the universe is favorably predisposed to the origin of life and the advancement of civilization.

"The universe has a billion billion sunlike stars," he says. "Therefore, the possibility of life elsewhere is quite likely. The chemical composition of the Earth and the stars is alike."

Suddenly I am not listening. I am thinking that while astronomers with devices, optical and otherwise, are looking deeper and deeper into outer space, other scientists, also with devices, optical and otherwise, are looking deeper and deeper into inner space. The paradox, as former *Saturday Review* senior editor Susan Schiefelbein wrote in *The Incredible Machine,* is that these scientists are discovering that "within our bodies course the same elements that flame in the stars. Whether the story of life is told by a theologian who believes that creation was an act of God, or by a scientist who theorizes that it was a consequence of chemistry and physics, the result is the same: The stuff of stars had come alive. Inanimate chemicals have turned to living things that swallow, breathe, bud, blossom, think, dream."[3]

How, over those billions of years in our primordial oceans' chemical cauldron, did molecules fuse into chains that mixed and mingled in such astonishing, infinite variety that suddenly somehow—because of lightning? heat? ultraviolet light?—one of those chains became so utterly unlike any other it came *alive?*

The explanation for this, the late essayist and physician Lewis Thomas wrote, remains,

> the greatest puzzle of all, even something of an embarrassment. Somehow or other, everything around us today—all animals, ourselves, all plants, everything alive—can trace its ancestry back to the first manifestation of life, approximately 3.5 billion years ago. The first form of life was, if we read the paleontological record right, a single bacterial cell, our Ur-ancestor, whose progeny gave rise to what we now call the natural world. The genetic code of that first cell was replicated in all the cells that occupied the Earth for the next 2 billion years, and then the code was passed along to nucleated cells when they evolved, then to the earliest multicellular forms, then to the vertebrates some 600 million years ago, and then to our human forbears. The events that . . . [have taken] life all the way from a solitary microbial cell to the convolutions of the human brain and the self-consciousness of the human mind, should be sweeping us off our feet in amazement.[4]

It *is* amazing. More amazing, somehow, than the suggestion that there must inevitably be intelligent life on other planets as well.

Several months after the conference I have a conversation with Budd Hopkins in which he brings up Michael Swords, a professor at Western Michigan University, who I only then learn was with us at M.I.T. Swords, according to Hopkins, "has done a lot of work on the extraterrestrial hypothesis. Most scientists accept the idea that it is highly probable that there are planetary systems elsewhere and that many, many different kinds of suns in the universe would have such planetary systems. Furthermore, the odds of one planet in each of these systems existing in what they call the 'green belt,' meaning not too far away from their sun to be too cold, is highly likely.

"There are huge numbers of such suns," Hopkins continues, "and the SETI [Search for Extraterrestrial Intelligence] people accept all of this. But as a biologist, Swords point out that if you pour two elements together in Nebraska and the same two elements together in North Dakota, you're going to get the same result. The basic law of science is: Given the same set of circumstances, the same things happen. You get the same mixes. So the assumption is that since we know from meteors that the building blocks of life are prevalent, it's highly likely that life would develop.

"And what Swords points out," Hopkins says, "is that in accordance with Darwin's theory of natural selection, when something develops that is efficient, it is retained. Binocular vision, for example. It is present in octopi, insects, vertebrates, and so on, so it would not be unusual to think of binocular vision developing and being retained when life developed on other planets. Nor would it be unusual to think that other species would have their brain and eyes close together and high up, nor an opposable thumb. There are a number of biologists who have no interest whatsoever in UFOs, but who assume that if life *is* developing elsewhere, it might very often take a direction similar to the direction it has taken here.

"Now, the most interesting contribution Swords had made to this argument," Hopkins tells me, "has to do with breathing air. And although nobody thinks of these alien creatures breathing air the way we do—you don't see the chest move, you don't feel their breath, and so forth—they do have some sort of use for oxygen, apparently. Swords points out that if the atmosphere of a planet had too much oxygen, there would be lightning-caused wildfires burning out of control, and all kinds of other problems which would virtually destroy the possibility of life developing. And if the oxygen content of the planet's atmosphere is too low, fires won't burn. You have to have enough oxygen to be able to control fire, because without the use of fire, according to Swords, technology will not develop. So his theory is that intelligent life will develop on planets with a certain particular range of oxygen in their atmosphere. No more than such-and-such an amount, no less than so-and-so. And if this were so, then this would imply that it would be possible for visitors from one planet to breathe the air of another. It all has to do with the notion of fire. All these things are theoretical, of course, but they make a pretty strong point."

One point being that at least scientists are thinking about these things.

Michael Swords's "green belt" is what other astronomers refer to as a "continuously habitable zone," that narrow loop around a star in which an orbiting planet can retain water on its surface without it either freezing solid or boiling away. It is, of course, the zone in which our planet orbits the sun. But at the 1993 annual meeting of the American Association for the Advancement of Science, M.I.T. astrophysicist Jack Wisdom suggested that life on other planets might be a great deal rarer than we think. It is not enough for a planet to orbit in Swords's "green belt"; it must also have a stable axis of rotation.

James Trefil, Robinson Professor of Physics at George Mason University, attended Wisdom's lecture and, writing in the *Smithsonian* column "Phenomena, Comment and Notes," reported:

> Earth's axis of rotation is an imaginary line that goes through the North and South poles. At the moment, it is tilted at an angle of about 23.5 degrees from the vertical and describes a lazy circle in space every 26,000 years, much like the axis of a tilted, spinning top. This means that many present features of Earth's climate—the alternation of seasons between summer and winter, for example—have always been present.
>
> But the story on Mars is quite different. [Dr.] Wisdom and graduate student Jihad Tourma have found that the direction of its axis of rotation moves around in space—in effect, its north pole points all over the map. It seems that the other planets in the inner solar system don't have the kind of stable axis of rotation that Earth enjoys.
>
> Why doesn't Earth's axis flop around, too? The answer is simple according to a team of French scientists led by Jacques Laskar of the Bureau des Longitudes in Paris. Earth, unlike the other planets, has a moon that is large relative to itself. It appears that the force that the Moon exerts on earth—the same force that raises tides on the ocean—serves to stabilize the direction of our planet's axis of rotation. Without the moon, our own north pole would wobble around in space just as Mars' does.
>
> So what would Earth have been without the Moon? Think about this: the little 1-degree wobbles of Earth's axis are thought to be crucial in initiating and ending ice ages. If the tilt angle got to be 54 degrees or more, there would be actually more energy falling on the poles than on the Equator. Given the exquisite sensitivity of Earth's biosphere to small change, what would massive fluctuations like that do to the climate? It's not hard to imagine such changes wiping out all life on the planet.
>
> If this is the case, then our view of life in the galaxy may have to change dramatically. In order for intelligent life to evolve, a planet has to form in an orbit that . . . remains in the continuously habitable zone of its sun. But in addition, perhaps, *that planet has to have a large moon* [Trefil's italics].

How many such planets can there be in the galaxy? Our present best theory is that the Moon was formed as a result of a collision between the newly formed Earth and a large asteroid. Such collisions during the formation of planetary systems are surely unlikely, and my guess is that Earth could well be the only planet in the Milky Way that satisfies both requirements for life to develop.

If this is true, the conventional wisdom on extraterrestrials is wrong. The galaxy isn't teeming with intelligent life waiting to communicate with us. There may be no one out there.[5]

At the M.I.T. conference, Michael Papagiannis closes his presentation by stating, "UFO observations cannot be reproduced; therefore, there is no hard scientific evidence. However," he pointedly adds, "the absence of evidence is not *evidence of absence.*"

I am reminded of what people here at the conference refer to as the Fermi Paradox, after the nuclear physicist Enrico Fermi, who supposedly asked, "If they're there, why aren't they here?" In other words, if advanced extraterrestrial civilizations do exist on other planets, why haven't they already visited us?

Harvard physicist Paul Horowitz, like Fermi, is a skeptic. Before he is willing to believe in aliens, he tells us, he'd like to see a "cigarette lighter, a tailpipe, a piece of landing gear off a UFO. Something I can hold in my hands!" Something, perhaps, like the "talking" robot he built as a teenager and with which he won his Summit, New Jersey, high-school science fair. "What we have is very poor evidence of extraordinary events," Horowitz says, "and clear evidence of ordinary events."

Several years ago, in his early forties, Horowitz created a portable ultra-narrow-band signal detector, the most advanced such machine ever built—not that there then were all that many such machines. It is a device used in conjunction with a radio telescope to search for any extraterrestrial intelligent life's radio signals—a considerably cheaper and more effective way to conduct a search than sending out planetary probes.

There are a million sunlike stars within light-years (the distance light travels in a vacuum in one year: approximately 5,878,000,000,000 miles) of us, Horowitz points out; Proxima Centauri, the star closest to our sun, is four and a third light-years away. The Andromeda Galaxy, the nearest galaxy to our Milky Way, is two point two million light years distant from Earth. Using our current rocket technology, we could reach Proxima Centauri in 33,000 years; a visit to Andromeda would take fifteen *billion* years! Horowitz's premise—that it is more practical to fund SETI to search for extraterrestrial radio signals than to send rockets to explore—seems inarguable for the time being, even though, as philosopher Terence McKenna has pointed out, "to search for a radio signal from an extraterrestrial source is probably as culture-bound a presumption as to search the galaxy for a good Italian restaurant."*[6]

As the conference breaks for lunch, John Mack pauses at the doorway leading out of the lecture hall and is immediately surrounded by members of the media. At first he tries to duck their questioning. "I'd like to be the person at the eye of the storm," he tells them, "but wisdom is knowing who to talk to."

Someone calls out a question I do not hear. I do, however, catch Mack's response: "These symptoms are real to the experience of the psyche," he says. "But since we don't trust the psyche, we try to discredit the instrument of the psyche. In other words, we try to find out what's wrong with these people. We have to have an epistemology," he stresses, "that respects and includes the human psyche as an instrument of knowing. There is no evidence that these abductees' stories are based on information they are getting from each other. There has not been one *bit* of evidence presented that suggests this phenomenon is any different from what the abductees are saying it is. I trust they are knowing something really important here and that it is not a product of their minds."

"If it is not a product of their minds, what is it?" someone asks.

"I have no idea," Mack says.

"You must have an opinion," someone else insists.

For a brief instant the Harvard psychiatrist looks wounded. "I will not speak to that," he says, then feels a need to explain. "As long as we have an epistemology and an ontology that responds to cigarette lighters," Mack says, shaking his head at Horowitz's skepticism, "we don't have a legitimate reality that will permit my reality to be heard."

A reporter starts to ask, "How does your reality differ from—?" but his question is cut off by Mack's announcement that he will not continue on the record "at the risk of being thought cuckoo."

More questions are flung at him, and Mack holds both hands up, palms out. "No more," he says. "The best way to advance in this field, unless you

* On October 12, 1992, three and a half months after the M.I.T. conference, astronomers began the first comprehensive high-technology search for evidence of intelligent life elsewhere in the universe. No longer named Search for Extraterrestrial Intelligence (SETI), but the less acronymic High Resolution Microwave Survey, this investigation, employing newly developed electronics, more sensitive radio receivers, and the most powerful telescopes to monitor millions of microwave channels through radio-telescopes throughout the world, was symbolically commenced on the five hundredth anniversary of the day Columbus stumbled onto the New World. So far, no intelligent life on other worlds has been detected.

want to draw lightning to yourself, is you don't stand up in a field without trees holding a piece of metal over your head. I'm not looking to attract sound-bite backlash."

As Mack hastily makes his exit, one disgruntled journalist near me mutters, "If one of those higher beings conducted an interview with me and two physical scientists, it would all have far more potential and significance than anything we're hearing here!"

I would be inclined to agree with him but for the fact that, as John Mack has just so succinctly said, "there has not been one *bit* of evidence presented that suggests this phenomenon is any different from what the abductees are saying it is." And since what the abductees are saying is that *humans are being abducted by creatures from another world—or worlds—who are coming to our planet in UFOs,* what continues to hold my interest is why a respected Harvard professor of psychiatry would for one minute believe such a thing.

In the fall of 1989 a psychologist friend and colleague of John Mack offered to introduce him to Budd Hopkins. Mack, unfamiliar with either Hopkins's name or his work, asked who he was. The woman explained that he was a New York artist who worked with people who reported alien Beings had taken them aboard spaceships. Mack told her he was not interested: as he later explained, he assumed both Hopkins and his clients shared "some sort of delusion or other mental aberration."[7]

Several months later, on January 10, 1990, Mack was in New York on unrelated business and, more out of curiosity than anything else, he did visit Hopkins. He came away impressed with Hopkins's "sincerity, depth of knowledge, and deep concern for the abductees whom," Mack felt, "had often been incorrectly diagnosed and inappropriately served by mental health officials."[8]

What changed Mack's mind about Hopkins and his clients, he reported, was what has clearly affected so many others who have become acquainted with Hopkins's data: "The internal consistency of the detailed accounts by different individuals from various parts of the country who would have had no way to communicate with one another and whose stories had emerged only with difficulty, accompanied by distressing emotions."[9]

Shortly after that meeting with Hopkins, John Mack returned to the New York artist's studio and met for the first time with several abductees. The consistency of their narratives again impressed Mack: the similarity of the manner in which they were brought to and released from the spacecraft; their depictions of the aliens; the manner in which they described the interiors of the ships, themselves, and what had happened to them once they had been taken aboard. At this time there had been very little detailed information of this nature available from the media. Face-to-face with the abductees, Mack was also struck, he later reported, "by the absence of any obvious mental illness or emotional disturbance other than the traumatic sequelae of the abductions themselves. No obvious explanation that could account for the abduction reports was apparent then."[10]

Nor, judging by his doorway response at the conference, did Mack feel any obvious explanation had emerged since.

Hopkins, who already knew of abductees in the Boston area, asked Mack if he would be willing to see some of them himself. As much out of an awareness that those people required help and understanding of a more professional caliber than they were getting as from his conviction that the phenomenon "reflected a mystery of more than clinical interest," Mack agreed to take some of Hopkins's referrals.

"The first cases that were referred to me in the spring of 1990," Mack subsequently wrote, "confirmed what Hopkins, David Jacobs, Leo Sprinkle, John Carpenter, and other pioneers who were investigating the abduction phenomenon had already discovered. These individuals reported being taken against their wills, sometimes through the walls of their houses, and subjected to elaborate intrusive procedures which appeared to have a reproductive purpose. In a few cases they were actually observed by independent witnesses to be physically absent during the time of the abduction. These people," Mack continued, "suffered from no obvious psychiatric disorder, except the effects of traumatic experience, and were reporting with powerful emotion what to them were utterly real experiences. Furthermore these experiences were sometimes associated with UFO sightings by friends, family members, or others in the community, including media reporters and journalists, and frequently left physical traces on the individuals' bodies, such as cuts and small ulcers that would tend to heal rapidly and followed no apparent psychodynamically identifiable pattern as do, for example, religious stigmata."[11]

Two and a half years later, by the time the M.I.T. conference was being organized, Mack was being referred to individuals through others involved in the UFO abduction phenomenon. He was also counseling persons who, having heard him speak in public on the subject or having read of his interest in the phenomenon, had contacted him directly. For example, each time Mack appeared on the radio or television, or there was an article about him in, say, *Harvard Magazine* or the *Wall Street Journal,* he would receive telephone calls or correspondence from prospective cases in a segment of the population that otherwise might not have approached him. Still others, prompted by seeing Mack's credit line on the televised *Intruders* miniseries, made from Budd Hopkins's book, felt brave enough to contact him, too.

They came forward hesitantly, timidly, rationalizing that if this *Harvard* professor was willing to risk saying this phenomenon should be taken seriously, then they might at least hazard telling him about those childhood experiences their parents had dismissed as "just a bad dream" or "a nightmare" or the result of "too vivid an imagination" instead of anything real. These individuals, however, had always known those experiences hadn't been dreams; they had been *real.* But they hadn't wanted to say so, or hadn't been brave enough to say so, until this Harvard professor dared intimate that those experiences they were so afraid of might in fact be true.

They, too, were familiar with risk. In almost every instance, Mack learned, when these individuals had tried to share their experiences with someone in their workplaces or among their own families—*even* if some of those family members were abductees themselves—they were met with silence or ridicule. And, in the phrase some of the abductees had used at the M.I.T. conference, they had learned to "go underground" with what had happened to them.

Almost universally the abductees were afraid to come forward. Even Mack was surprised by the subterfuge he would sometimes have to submit to before an experiencer would speak with him. In one case, an abductee first wrote Mack a letter giving him a post-office box in a strange town in which the abductee did not live and instructed Mack to write him there. The letter was signed with an assumed name. Only when Mack seemed to satisfy the writer's need for anonymity did the experiencer permit open contact. And in Mack's experience, the more prominent the individual abductees might be—whether by their own definition or in terms of their communities—the more likely they were to want to disguise themselves to prevent any chance of public recognition.

Despite this reluctance, by May 1992 Mack had seen more than fifty "possible" abductees, thirty-eight of whom fulfilled the set of selection criteria set out by Mark Rodeghier, CUFOS's director of investigations, on the first day of the M.I.T. conference. Of those thirty-eight, twenty were female and eighteen were male. The adults ranged in age from nineteen to fifty-six years old; one of Mack's subject was a two-year-old boy. And even though Mack offered support and counseling to these individuals, he always felt that his role was "as much that of a co-investigator as a therapist."[12]

Small wonder that Mack, too, could be evasive. When the reporter at the conference asked Mack if the abduction phenomenon was not the product of the abductees' minds, then what was it, Mack had not been entirely honest when he had responded, "I have no idea."

Wisdom, as Mack said, is knowing who to talk to; and the cautiousness of his answer reflected his unwillingness to risk being thought cuckoo by those of the media gathering for "sound bites" at the lecture-room door. But one hint of Mack's ideas lay in his observation "We don't have a legitimate reality that will permit my reality to be heard."

He was suggesting that his reality was less limited than Horowitz's or the media's.

After lunch, Ron Westrum, a Michigan Ph.D., speaks about the "Social Dynamics of Abduction Reporting." He compares the acceptance process in the UFO arena to the skepticism and ridicule encountered in the late eighteenth and early nineteenth centuries by those who reported that meteorites fell to the earth from outer space.

On July 24, 1790, a number of meteorites fell near Agen, in southwestern France. The phenomenon was seen and documented by no fewer than three hundred people. Even though meteorite fragments were exhibited, Pierre Betholon, editor of the *Journal des Sciences Utiles,* after publishing his account of the event in 1791, dismissed the reports as groundless and physically impossible.

Early in the morning of December 14, 1807, a huge fireball swept over New England and crashed into the earth near the town of Weston, Connecticut. Benjamin Silliman, then professor of chemistry at Yale College, and college librarian James L. Kingsley collected many fragments of the meteorite, including a chunk weighing approximately two hundred pounds. When sample pieces from the Weston meteorite shower were brought to President Thomas Jefferson, he remained skeptical of their origin. The remark attributed to him, however, is probably apocryphal: "It is easier to believe that two Yankee professors would lie than stones fell from heaven."

It is, of course, also easier to believe that a Harvard professor would lie than that aliens are visiting Earth.

During the question period, Sacramento psychologist Richard J. Boylan rises. I am so stunned by his query's preface, "As an experiencer myself . . . ," I do not hear what his question is. I cannot recall Boylan having made any mention of his being an abductee before, and judging by the murmur in the lecture hall, no one else in the audience was aware of it, either. I make a note to speak with him as soon as possible.

McGill University's D. C. Donderi speaks next, on the need for "Scientific Intelligence Approach to Abduction Evidence." He throws up on the screen a slide of an AT&T advertisement from a then-current issue of *Scientific American* depicting golfers in a golf cart being floated up into a hovering UFO. In the text accompanying the illustration, AT&T, pushing its own cellular phones, asks whether at times such as this you would be willing to settle for a competitor's inferior model. It's a clever advertisement if one overlooks the fact that if all the reports of electromagnetic interference during close encounters is true, AT&T's cellular phone wouldn't be working, either. Donderi's point, however, is that the abduction phenomenon has by now been so desensitized it is has entered contemporary society's mainstream. More recent examples of the commercialization of the phenomenon are the Bud Lite beer television commercial of glowing little aliens with big heads (and bikinis and dark glasses!) dancing to a boom box, and the Colombian coffee print advertisement showing a photograph of a UFO over someone's house with the caption "We know why they're here." (Neither of these examples, however, is as mainstream as Cheney's *New Yorker* cartoon depicting four Small Grays carrying a man from his bed while his blasé wife asks, "You want me to tape *Murphy Brown* for you?")

Donderi is saying that the abduction experience does not stand alone, that its hypothesis "is made more plausible by the Close-Encounters-of-the-Third-Kind hypothesis, which, in turn, is made more plausible by the UFO hypothesis. First came the witness accounts," Donderi continues, "then came the multiple-witness accounts, and then came the corroborative accounts."

Donderi is engaging in what I have heard referred to at this conference as Bayesian analysis: If the first part is true (that UFOs exist), then the second part (that CE-III encounters exist) is probable; therefore the third part (that abductions are really taking place) is more probable still.*

But, Donderi asks, "what evidence do we see of time having changed the phenomenon? How can they be 'high-tech' aliens if they've used the same technology for forty years? We should talk to people who were abducted forty years ago!" More to the point, I think, is why these Beings should need to repeat, in effect, seemingly the same experiments for so long a period of time. It is a question even the most fervent believers in UFOs have difficulty answering.

At the conclusion of Donderi's presentation, John Mack rises to ask, "What does it mean that we don't come across cases from Africa and Asia? Is it because they don't deal so sharply with distinctions between the physical and the paranormal?"

I thought Bullard had said there *were* cases from Asia. I go back over my notes. Bullard listed one in Japan and three in China as "vaguely reported."

---

* "But there is a catch," journalist Keith Thompson has pointed out. "The converse of [the Bayesian] theory is necessarily invoked: If any aspect of the UFO phenomenon is not true, then any of the rest of the reported phenomenon also may not be true."[13]

But I like where Mack's question is leading: societies that do not make sharp distinctions between the real world and the spirit world might not see in the abduction phenomenon anything worth reporting.

During the afternoon break, following Donderi's presentation, I hurry out into the hallway to find Richard J. Boylan so that I might set up an appointment to talk to him about his being an abductee. I am told the Sacramento psychologist escaped the lecture hall and the building "in a very bad mood." Evidently I am not the only journalist who wants to speak with him. In the absence of Boylan, I seek out John G. Miller, the emergency-room physician who had addressed the conference the first day on the procedural differences between "alien" and "human" physical examinations. I admired Miller because he weighed the evidence for this phenomenon as thoughtfully and carefully as he might examine a patient. I further liked him because he seemed as confused by the abduction experience as I was.

When Miller and I are seated together on the lawn, I ask him the question that, by now, I am constantly asking myself: "What do you think is going on?"

"I don't have any fixed opinion," Miller replies. "How can a person have any firmly held belief about this when it's so mysterious? The opinions of the true believers are hard to swallow; and the opinions of the die-hard skeptics are not based on reality, either. There *is* some middle ground." He thinks for a moment, and then he says, "It's clear that this is some sort of powerful subjective experience. But I do not know what the objective reality is. It's as if the evidence leads us in both directions."

His involvement with the phenomenon, Miller tells me, came about because a fellow physician had so many patients reporting abduction-related complaints he couldn't handle them all. The doctor then had asked Miller if he would see two of his cases.

"The first one was just a very reasonable man who had a very strange story," Miller explains. "I didn't use hypnosis—I don't use hypnosis—but from what this man could recall of his childhood and growing up, he had had these experiences with these Beings. And," Miller adds pointedly, "he clearly was *not* mentally ill—at least not to my level of being able to evaluate it. He just wanted to tell me his story—not for money, not to become famous or anything else. He just needed to tell his story to somebody who would listen, that's all."

This same patient, Miller tells me, was subsequently examined by Dr. Jo Stone-Carmen, who had written her doctoral thesis on abductees. (The day before at the M.I.T. conference, Stone-Carmen reported in her presentation, "Abductees with Conscious Recall Are Different," on abductees' high vigilance and guardedness.) Using what she called a phenomenological approach to her study of abductees, Stone-Carmen administered Miller's patient a MMPI, along with several other tests designed to calibrate an individual's personality characteristics. They were the same tests she had given the subjects of her dissertation. Stone-Carmen was unable to find any evidence of psychopathology in Miller's patient.

"I guess the core of the mystery is the incredible stories coming from credible witnesses," Miller tells me. "And the fact that these incredible stories are reasonably consistent from witness to witness."

"Also, as you noted in the experiencer you sent to Jo Stone-Carmen, there is nothing to be gained for these witnesses by telling these stories," I say.

"Right," Miller says, nodding. "In fact, I've known a number of witnesses where it would be extremely detrimental for them to tell these stories. I've met witnesses in the Los Angeles area who are very highly placed in businesses and professions, for whom it would be utterly disastrous to come forward with these stories."

"Has anybody been hurt by these experiences?" I ask. "Temporary trauma, certainly, but have you found any physical evidence?"

"I would say a lot of people have been traumatized by them, because if they were free of trauma these people wouldn't be seeking help. I'm talking here about mental trauma. But physical trauma? I've heard the allegations, but, again, I just don't know."

"Dr. Miller, have you ever seen hard evidence of any kind with these people?"

"It depends on what kind of hard evidence you want," Miller replies.

"I guess like Paul Horowitz was saying at the conference—a cigarette lighter or a piece of landing gear from a UFO, or an implant."

"Well, one highly credible witness that I worked with in L.A. had an overnight change in the grass in her backyard in a pattern similar to what was reported by Budd Hopkins in one of his cases. The soil and the grass changed in a circular pattern behind their home. But what this means, I don't know. I mean, a skeptic would say, 'Well, what you've got is dry dirt and dry grass—big deal,' you know?"

Carol and Alice are sitting outside on the lawn, too. When Dr. Miller and I finish, I walk over and join them. I am relieved to see they are beginning to feel more comfortable with me and do not automatically stop talking about the conference when I am around. I ask if they are taking part in the next session, the abductees' panel discussion on how to handle the media. They are not.

When we reassemble in the lecture hall, the abductees want to talk about something else.

One woman abductee says, "There seems to be an investigative bias. They look for things in their investigations that support their theory and 'gray-box' what does not fit."

"We feel vulnerable and out of control, that we are victims," another female abductee tells us. "Give us control. Help us to gain confidence. Give us something to show us we aren't victims of anything but our own fears."

One of the men who has had experiences since childhood says that coming to this conference has been very good for him, that it has created an environment in which he has felt less alone. "I kept my mouth shut for forty years," he says, "and I appreciate your thoughtfulness. We—the experiencers, the investigators, the therapists—are all part of the same phenomenon. We are the human link. And we are as strong as our weakest skeptic and as weak as our strongest supporter. You have to be accepting and nonjudgmental of what we tell you. We are all part of a team. And the name of the team? Take the first the first letter of the word 'experiencer' and the first letter of the word 'therapist.' The name of the team is 'ET.' "

Richard Price, the abductee whose "implant" has been studied, says he feels "taken advantage of when people are writing about me." He suggests the establishment of a 1-800 telephone number so that experiencers can have a means of getting in touch with other members of a group.

Another man speaks softly of his difficulty in Maine "of trying to find someone to talk with. I wrote Budd Hopkins, who referred me to Joe Nyman. There needs to be a compendium of researchers that witnesses can go to," he says, then adds, "and investigators. Keep in mind that when we come to you, there are not many other places to go. And if I feel you are not prepared to listen to what I'm telling you right now because it's not part of your *agenda* . . ." he says, then scowls and shakes his head. "I've come up with things that have hit Joe [Nyman] in my sessions and he was willing to put his butt on the line and absorb it." He pauses for a moment, then says that he had intended to say something about what he thought was happening, but felt he had already taken up too much time. "In brief," he says, "I can remember sitting around with other bunches of experiencers and we all feel something really big is coming up. And what is coming up, I feel, has now started."

Virginia, the Boston-area abductee who is one of Joe Nyman's people, speaks next. Earlier we learned she has had bedroom visitations and, as a child, was introduced to her cloned sister by aliens in a "sky house." "People who are traumatized should not go on TV shows," she warns. "Instead it should be people who have more control. We all start off anxious, depressed, looking for people who will validate us. We all need a good therapist. Guidelines are needed for how a therapist should proceed with someone."

David Cherniack from the Canadian Broadcasting Company suggests that any experiencer contemplating going on TV should "watch your market" and avoid exploitive television programs.

There is no prearranged dinner for this, the final night of the conference. A group of us who have been covering it for various publications or programs have decided to eat together for an informal discussion of what we think. There is David Cherniack; Karen Wesolowski, the special projects manager for the *Atlantic Monthly;* Margaret West of National Public Radio in Washington; Steve Fishman, author of *A Bomb in the Brain,* who has been covering the conference for *Details;* and myself.

We gather together in the hallway outside the lecture room to decide where to eat, and suddenly there is Richard Boylan wandering past by himself, looking somewhat at loose ends. Despite his reported ill humor earlier, he seems both both grateful and pleased by our invitation to join us. And to my surprise, our discussion that evening is not about the conference but an off-the-record (later made on-the-record) account by Boylan of a "six-state grand tour of reported Southwest secret sites" he had taken in his Chevrolet S-10 Blazer ten weeks earlier, in April, which had further convinced him that the UFO phenomenon is the subject of a massive and long-lasting government cover-up.

During that "grand tour" Boylan had visited the Tonopah, Nevada, USAF Air Defense Command Headquarters; the Tonopah Test Range; and Areas 51 and S-4 at the northeast corner of Nellis Test Range (the Groom and Papoose Lakes bases). Boylan had then continued on to Archulete Peak, just north of Dulce, New Mexico, near the Colorado border; from there to the three huge Los Alamos National Laboratories, which stretch five miles by thirteen miles over most of Los Alamos County; and to Kirtland Air Force Base outside Albuquerque, which houses the Western Regional Headquarters of the Department of Energy (Strategic Defense Initiative), the Sandia National Laboratories, the Defense Nuclear Agency headquarters, and the DOE's National Atomic Museum. He stopped at Sunspot, New Mexico, where the National Solar Observatory is located atop Sacramento Peak along with the Army Sacramento Peak Frequency Surveillance Station. From Sunspot Boylan had proceeded to the National Radio Astronomy

Observatory's Very Large Array of twenty-seven huge eighty-two-foot-wide receiving dishes on the plains of San Augustin in New Mexico and eventually to the Northrop "saucer plant" near Lancaster, California.

Boylan made this trip because, he tells us during dinner, "for several years articles have been appearing about secret government bases where exotic space weapons and American-made saucers are built and tested. But the testimony about these sites and saucers was always 'off the record' or from 'sources who cannot be named.' So I was determined to go see for myself.

"I really see this whole controversy as having three legs, like a three-legged stool: the UFO phenomenon; the extraterrestrial-contact phenomenon; and the U.S. government cover-up phenomenon," Boylan explains. "And by 'cover-up' one might expand it to include armed response or Strategic Defense Initiative response. 'Cover-up/SDI' is the third leg of the stool. And during my trip I got both very large confirmation that they, the U.S. government, were a lot farther along with Star Wars weaponry and physics and ability to deliver the goods than I had earlier come to know even from anything I had seen published."

"Where had you seen things published?" I ask.

"In articles in the L.A. *Times,* various magazines such as *Aviation Week and Space Technology, Popular Mechanics, UFO Magazine,* and *MUFON Journal.* I found many useful leads in Howard Blum's excellent book, *Out There,* as well as Timothy Good's essential *Above Top Secret.* I also sifted out as best I could the information from the disinformation in William Hamilton III's *Cosmic Top Secret.* Are you familiar with that book?"

"I'm afraid not," I admit.

"On its back cover is a computer-enhanced photograph taken by Gary Schulz which quite clearly reveals a bright orange-colored glowing flying disc with a cupola on top. That was taken along the same Area 51 boundary of Nellis Air Force Base that I went to and saw much the same thing."

"You saw a disc there, too? Did you photograph it?" I ask.

"*Them,*" Boylan corrects me. "I saw more than one. But I couldn't photograph them from the distance I was. They would have looked like stars at best. They were too many miles out and I had too-inferior equipment. Schulz has a much better photo, and another guy, Issuro Isokawa, took a good photo, too. These guys have much better telephoto lenses on their cameras. . . . But it's not just the discs. It's the things I saw on this trip like the fact that we have fusion reactors—miniaturized, contained, self-sustaining—and have had them for a number of years. Seven years, anyway."

"Dr. Boylan," I say, "how would you recognize a miniaturized fusion reactor if you saw one?"

"I'm not sure I would," he replies, smiling. "I'm just taking the government's information at face value. They're the ones disclosing; I'm not deducing. You go to the National Atomic Museum in Albuquerque and very insightfully read every bit of every exhibit and remember everything you've read and put it together, you'll find a number of interesting things—among them that a hundred-trillion-volt electromagnetic pulse capability has now been achieved. Those are just flat-out announced bits of data they've put out.

"And then there's the Department of Energy facility out at Tonopah Test Range," Boylan continues, "and the extreme security at Kirtland Air Force Base out at Albuquerque, where they've got electrified fences and double-door personnel chambers you have to enter, keypunch a code, then pass through to get into the building. All those 'One Year, $10,000 Fine' warnings if you trespass, you know? All that apparatus of extreme military security on a so-called Department of Energy facility—a headquarters, no less, not even an operational lab. I was just impressed by how much information one can get on how far along we are in exotic weaponry even without a high security clearance. And then, seeing our saucers both made and test-flown at the construction site and then hard tested at the military proving grounds demonstrated to me that not only are there UFOs flying around and obviously crashed and retrieved, but that we've hijacked their technology, either on our own or with extraterrestrial help, and have our own primitive Piper Cub sort of UFO stuff in the air putzing around."

"You're saying the discs you saw were *our own* saucers?" I ask.

"Yeah," he says matter-of-factly. "There's no reason to believe such crudely flown vehicles would pop up from the ground at Area 51 as some sort of alien disinformation campaign."

I look at the others around the table. "Maybe you'd better start at the beginning," I say.

"At the beginning of what?" he asks.

"At the beginning of your trip."

Boylan tells us his first objective had been the tiny town of Tonopah, Nevada: "Gateway to Black Budget aerospace/SDI projects," he says, then adds, "Of course, Albuquerque is the other gateway; and if you draw a line between the two, most Black Budget aerospace/SDI projects, according to my research, are built, tested, and based between these two towns."

Boylan pulls out of his jacket pocket a packet of color snapshots and begins sorting through them. "Although Tonopah's economy is ostensibly based on mining," he is saying as he selects the photograph he wants, "it houses an Air Force Defense Command Headquarters." He slides the photograph of an anonymously governmental-looking building across the table to me. A sign on the building identifies it exactly as Boylan has said. "This is a paradox," he continues, "since Nellis Air Force Base, the nearest *official* U.S. Air Force facility, is 180 miles to the south—unless, of course, there is a secret USAF presence at the north end of Nevada, which there is."

He slides a second photo across. It shows a dull-blue school bus marked "Shuttle to Sandia."

"I also spotted this while I was in Tonopah, Nevada. This is very interesting, since the Sandia National Labs is two states away in Albuquerque, New Mexico—unless, of course, there is a secret Sandia presence nearby. Which there is.

"From Tonopah, I drove east fifteen miles on U.S. 6 to the turnoff for the Tonopah Test Range." He slid a third photograph across to me; it was of the Tonopah Test Range entrance sign, depicting a small Hawk-type solid-fuel ground-to-air rocket. "You will notice," Boylan is saying, "that the sign misleadingly gives the impression that they test small rockets there. But after driving twelve miles south on the entrance road, I came to a huge, sprawling base operated not by the Department of Defense but by Sandia National Laboratories for the DOE. And according to a Sandia National Labs public relations officer with whom I spoke, 'Sandia National Labs is AT&T.' In other words, AT&T is the corporation behind the application of physics research to Star Wars weapons. When AT&T 'reaches out and touches someone,' " he says with a wry smile, "it may be with one of their electromagnetic pulse weapons.

"By the front gate are thirty large, two-story buildings where test-range workers are quartered," he continues. "And through binoculars—seven-by-thirty-five-power—I could see downrange approximately five miles where an additional, equally large complex of buildings was located. Here, to the south and east, extend hundreds of square miles for operation testing of such DOE weapons as the electromagnetic pulse, particle beam, tactical nuclear, and laser devices. Strategic nuclear devices, by the way, are tested one hundred miles further south at the Nevada Test Site, another DOE facility, while the U.S.-made saucers are test-flown one hundred miles to the southeast, at Groom and Papoose Lakes bases."

The Tonopah Test Range guards wore desert camouflage "jumpsuits," Boylan tells us, "with a cryptic shoulder patch reading 'ASI-SWAT.' " He shows us a photograph of a convoy of military two-and-a-half-ton trucks being let through the gate. The lead trucks are already turning downrange.

"When I approached the main gate on foot," Boylan says, "the two guards were surly and aggressively poised. Their weapons looked like a fat, black cylindrical, oversized rifle stock about five inches in diameter and a yard long, but there was no barrel or muzzle at the end. And although I am familiar with the appearance of U.S. and international, military, police, and elite-unit weapons, I had never seen anything like these strange-looking weapons before. Not wanting to experience this weapon pointed any closer at me, I accepted their refusal to let me pass through, and retreated."

Boylan left Tonopah and drove eighty miles east on State Highway 375 to Rachel, a small Nevada community composed predominately of mobile homes for workers at Area 51 of the Nellis Air Force Base test range. Rachel's popular watering hole is the Little A "Le" Inn Bar and Restaurant, its walls cluttered with Air Force patches, UFO photographs, drawings, and souvenirs, and autographed photographs of UFO researchers and investigative journalists. According to Boylan, the bar's proprietor, Joe Travis, told him "of having a UFO come down once at night after closing and illuminate the entire interior of their restaurant."

Of all that Boylan has said so far, only the Little A "Le" Inn Bar seems significant to me. Despite the most rigid security procedures on a military or government installation, one generally has to look only as far as the bar favored by that installation's personnel to find evidence of what really goes on behind the installation's closely guarded gates. If the Tonopah Test Range is engaged only in missile research, then why so much interest in UFOs at the local pub?

Boylan next describes how he continued twenty-five miles southeast and, using U.S. Geodetic Survey maps and the directions given in Hamilton's *Cosmic Top Secret,* took the "turnoff marked by the infamous black mailbox" and carefully drove west on dirt roads towards the Groom Lake base. He was at that time still on Bureau of Land Management property, about five miles from the boundary of the military reservation and, therefore, Boylan says, in "a perfectly lawful area to be driving."

"I was heading towards Area 51 and I had USGS topographic maps so I knew exactly where I was," he continues. "I'd come off Highway 375, driving down there minding my own business, and came upon this unmarked Ford Bronco with a light bar on the roof parked just off the roadbed facing me. In it were two guys with camouflage jumpsuits without insignia on them. 'Well, it's a free country,' I figured. 'A couple of bozos can sit out here in their RV in the desert if they want to.' But as I went by them I noticed they had weapons. I wasn't totally naive," Boylan tells us. "I expected they might have been guards, though I wondered why they were so far out. And there were no markings designating their authority, if they had any. Still, I figured, 'They're there and I'm here, and I've still got five miles to play with before the game gets abrupt.' I mean, I was prepared for there to be a locked gate and upon my failure to produce adequate ID, I'd be told to turn around and go back. But that part of the game was not allowed to be played out.

"Not long after I passed them," Boylan says, "my left rear tire collapsed. I rolled to a stop, got out, and saw that the tire had a sidewall penetration. The tread was good; I hadn't driven over anything on the dirt road that could have caused a sidewall blowout; and I concluded that one of those two men had shot my tire out."

"They had *shot* at you?" I ask stupidly.

"At my tire," Boylan says. "About a minute later the camouflaged duo made a U-turn in their Bronco, came up behind me, and one of them got out and said, 'You having some trouble?' By that time, I had the jack out and was trying to change the tire for the spare and I said, 'Yes.'

"He said, 'Were you heading up there?,' nodding towards Area 51, and I said, 'Yes.'

"So he asked me if I had a security badge. I told him I didn't and he said, 'Well, then it's no use going there. You can't get through up ahead.'

" 'Why?' I said. 'You got a locked gate?'

"And he said, 'Yes.'

" 'Well,' I said, 'I guess I can't do it anyway. I've got to limp back to town and get a replacement tire. This tire's shot.'

" 'Yeah, it is,' he said. 'Too bad.' And he just kind of chuckled and got back into the Bronco and they drove back to their previous position."

"Where were they in relation to your Blazer when your tire went flat?" I ask.

"I was proceeding due west on the right-hand side of the dirt road. They were facing east a little off the roadbed on the south side of the road, positioned as if they were coming from the other direction and parked off-road a little bit. It happened shortly after I had passed them."

"How hot was it out there?"

"It was late afternoon, warm, but mild. Probably in the mid-eighties."

"And you said your tires were in good shape when you made this trip?"

"Oh, yeah—oh, yeah," Boylan says.

"I've had sidewall blowouts, too, without anyone shooting at me," I say. "Could your tire have exploded for another reason?"

"I know what you're talking about," Boylan says. "You go over something in the road and it snaps up and pierces the tire. I never ran over anything."

"But you must have been watching them in your rearview mirror as you continued past them," I say. "You didn't see them get out of the Bronco?"

"This happened right after I went past them. I was looking straight ahead. Frankly, I didn't want them to wave me down, so I was doing the eyes-straight-ahead maneuver."

"Could there be any explanation other than that they shot your tire?"

"Oh, I looked for other explanations," Boylan tells me, "but, frankly, I was reluctantly forced to come to that one in the absence of any other. And what with that clear kind of firm, somewhat menacing attitude those two, and those other two guards at the Tonopah Test Range, manifested . . ." Boylan finishes his sentence with a shrug.

"So what did you do?" I ask.

"I retreated," he says with a wry smile. "I waited until it was dark, and then I returned and prudently parked about a quarter-mile east of where I had last seen the Bronco and got out my binoculars. I remained there observing the ridge line of the Groom Range above Areas 51 and S-4 from about nine to ten-thirty p.m., during which time I saw three bright round lights come up from below the ridge line, presumably off the desert floor, or else scooting low from somewhere else, then rising vertically.

"I spotted the first one around nine-thirty," Boylan continues. "I saw a bright golden-orange round light rise up vertically from behind the Groom Range. The altitude of the range at that point is probably about twelve hundred feet or so. They're not very tall mountains. So this one cleared the mountains by about five hundred feet then leveled off and seemed to hover for several minutes, then drifted slowly south about a thousand feet. It gave off a very intense red-orange light, a very bright glowing that looked more like ionizing effects rather than any light on board shining out. It was like the craft's whole frame was just ionizing off an extremely intense light—in other words, the frame was the light-emitting body, not a light from on board. And then it descended slowly, vertically, behind the mountains.

"The object had the same color and shape and was viewed from the same direction as the object photographed by Gary Schulz, who had enlarged and computer-enhanced his photograph to reveal a flying disc with a cupola on top surrounded by an ionization haze of light. Schulz called it an HPAC—a 'human-powered alien craft,' " Boylan explains.

"Soon, a second brilliantly shining round object rose vertically and hovered about five hundred feet above the ridge line. This object was strobing and emitting a brilliant blue-white light, apparently from the skin of the craft. It then began a series of incredible, blindingly fast pendulum and zigzag and back-and-forth maneuvers at mere fraction-of-a-second intervals, covering, perhaps, nine hundred feet in a jump! It just astonished me that something could jump around so fast through all those turns and acute angles.

"After this dazzling aerobatics performance, it settled down to hovering for a while, then resumed to gyrations again. Both super-quick maneuvering episodes lasted over a minute each. Finally the object again hovered motionless, then began flying south, downrange, at a constant altitude and direction at about 80 mph. I tracked it through my binoculars for about thirty miles before it became indistinguishable from the star field.

"About a half hour after it had disappeared," Boylan continues, "a third brilliant round object, glowing with the same intense red-orange-gold color, rose above the Groom Range, hovered, drifted slowly, then began strobing. Next it began gliding downrange again at a constant altitude and at about 80 mph, but with somewhat irregularly spaced erratic jumps forward." Boylan pauses for a moment, then adds, "Another odd thing was that the appearance of this craft alternated between strobes: on one phase it was a bright, sharply defined orb of orange-gold light; on the alternate phase it was a smudgy golden sphere of light."

I ask Boylan: If these had been conventional machines like helicopters, would he have heard their engines?

"Oh, I think so. It was quiet enough. You could hear anything. For example, at one point in the evening while I was staked out, some little biplane went over way far away. You could hear it drone for what seemed like twenty minutes. As soon as it cleared the horizon, you could hear it all the way to the next horizon."

"And the flying objects you saw made no noise?"

"None," he says. "And the angles they did it at! There's no jet or helicopter or anything that could move that fast at those angles, correct itself, and go again in thirds of seconds. It would have just been torn apart! You couldn't have steered that fast. There was a bit of remote jumping where you didn't see the body of the craft in the meanwhile. I mean, it was here and it was there. It was *most* extraordinary!"

"You said earlier you believe these discs are our own—how did you put it?—'primitive Piper Cubs'? What makes you think that?"

"Well, these craft were navigated in a rather conservative and slow fashion and did not display the confident maneuvering and extremely rapid departure style so often reported for extraterrestrial UFOs. And so I concluded that these are either U.S.-manufactured discs at a primitive stage of technology, or at a primitive stage of pilot mastery. However, the extreme hyper-fast aerobatics-in-place performed by the second object indicates to me, at least, that inertial forces, and therefore gravity, have been overcome by these craft."

Boylan goes on and on. At Archulete Peak, just north of Dulce, New Mexico, "reported in Howard Blum's *Out There* as an underground base,"* he says, he "drove around the mesa and discovered a mysterious 'ranch' " that was supposedly a "beefalo-raising outfit. However," Boylan continues, "in the front yard of the ranch between the road and the two ranch buildings were four odd twenty-five-foot-high guard towers on stilts." He has a photograph of them. He concludes that "there appears more there than meets the eye."

From Archulete Peak Boylan proceeded to the huge Los Alamos National Laboratories, where, he tells us, "theoretical research having weapons applications is conducted for the Department of Energy by the University of California." He took photographs of the entrance gate, No Trespassing and radiation warning signs, and the laboratory's building T-10, containing the Center for Human Genome Studies as well as the HIV (AIDS) Database.

"Rather strange enterprises for a military weapons-oriented research complex to be involved in, rather than the National Institute of Health," Boylan comments. "One cannot help being reminded of the rumors that AIDS is a biological weapon gone amok. Even more curious is another building which houses the laboratories theoretical biology and biophysics studies."

---

* Howard Blum, a prize-winning former *New York Times* journalist, reported only that in 1981, a Dr. Paul Bennewitz, "an accomplished physicist . . . with a soft spot for UFOs," had become convinced that "two opposing forces of aliens had invaded the United States. The white aliens wanted intergalactic brotherhood; they came to this planet in peace. However, the malevolent group, the grays, were in control."

According to Bennewitz, Blum writes, "it was the grays who were responsible for the cattle mutilations, the human abductions, and the implanting of mind-control devices in humans. The government was not only aware of this, but had also negotiated a secret treaty with these invaders. The grays were granted the right to establish an underground base beneath Archulete Peak . . . and in return the military had received a shipment of extraterrestrial weapons. But then an atomic-powered spaceship crashed on Archulete Peak. The grays suspected sabotage. And, Bennewitz was convinced after decoding radio transmissions, the treaty was about to be broken. The angry grays were preparing for nothing short of total war."

Despite the fact that the government had been running a disinformation campaign against Bennewitz to "systematically confuse, discourage, and discredit" him, Blum does not suggest that there was any truth to Bennewitz's charges.[14]

Boylan slides across a photo of that building and amends his last statement, saying it may be "less curious if the rumor is true that the extraterrestrial corpses from the crashed UFO near Corona, New Mexico, were brought to Los Alamos for study."*

"Besides nukes and exotic biology," Boylan is saying, "the Los Alamos National Laboratories also researches military applications of intense magnetic fields at its National High Magnet Field Laboratory—a prerequisite to gravity/antigravity research. The theoretical weapons physics of Los Alamos is translated into actual working models of high-tech weapons at Sandia National Laboratories in Albuquerque. . . ."

Boylan then visited Kirtland Air Force Base southeast of Albuquerque, where he spotted the Southwest Regional Office of the DOE (he shows us a photo), the Sandia National Laboratories (photo), the Interservice Nu-

---

* The story of crashed flying saucers and alien bodies recovered by the military in secret is another one of those UFO conspiracy stories that will not go away. Skeptics dismiss such accounts out of hand for lack of hard evidence; but in two specific instances—the alleged crash at Roswell, New Mexico, on the night of July 2, 1947, and the alleged crash at Corona, New Mexico, six days later—there is some compelling anecdotal evidence. Indisputably, in the Roswell case, anomalous wreckage was found by William Brazel dispersed over a crash site three-quarters of a mile long by several hundred feet wide on an isolated ranch he managed about seventy-five miles north of Roswell. The military quickly investigated the crash, cordoned off the site, swept the ground clear of any peculiar debris, and loaded it aboard a B-29, which was ordered to transport it to Wright-Patterson Air Force Base (then Wright Field) near Dayton, Ohio, for examination. An initial press statement, authorized by the Roswell Field commander, Colonel William Blanchard, was released, announcing that the wreckage of a flying disc had been recovered. According to the account Timothy Good published in *Above Top Secret:*

> On arrival at an intermediate stop at Carswell Army Air Forces Base, Fort Worth, Texas (headquarters of the 8th Air Force) General Roger Ramey took charge and ordered [509th Bomb Group Staff intelligence officer Major Jesse] Marcel and others on the plane not to talk to reporters. A second press statement was issued which stated that the wreckage was nothing more than the remains of a weather balloon and its attached tinfoil radar target, and this was prominently displayed at the press conference. Meanwhile, the *real* [Good's italics] wreckage arrived at Wright Field under armed guard; Marcel returned to Roswell, and Brazel was held incommunicado for nearly a week while the crash site was stripped of every scrap of debris.
>
> A news leak via press wire from Albuquerque describing this fantastic story was interrupted and the radio station in question, and another, were warned not to continue the broadcast: "ATTENTION ALBUQUERQUE: CEASE TRANSMISSION. REPEAT. CEASE TRANSMISSION. NATIONAL SECURITY ITEM. DO NOT TRANSMIT. STAND BY . . ."[15]

clear Weapons School (photo), and the Department of Energy's National Atomic Museum (photo).

At the National Atomic Museum Boylan learned that the United States "now has hydrogen bombs downsized as small as a RV propane tank" and that for five years the United States has been "producing controlled, self-sustaining nuclear fusion, contained by a strong magnetic field," he says. "They use lasers to implode fissionable material and produce fusion. This is an inexhaustible and rather compact energy source," he explains, "and may be the power plant for the gravity-defying craft I saw at Area 51."

It was at the National Atomic Museum that Boylan learned that Sandia National Laboratories had, he said, achieved "advanced particle acceleration capabilities that can deliver a one-hundred-trillion-volt burst of ions using a lithium diode one inch thick." Sandia National Laboratories and its test ranges, he tells us, extend south and east of the DOE headquarters for over a hundred square miles and take up most of Kirtland Air Force Base. "Activities identified by sign," he reports, "include mostly weapons application research in nuclear, magnetic, solar, electromagnetic pulse, laser and particle beam energy. But the pièce de résistance of Star Wars weapons research applications I found was 'Project ARIES, the Advanced Research Electromagnetic Pulse (EMP) Simulator Site,' where a two-block-long device was built for the Defense Nuclear Agency by EG&G. Does that name mean anything to you?"

"EG&G? No," I say.

"It stands for Edgerton, Germhausen & Greer, a shadowy corporation involved—along with Wackenhut Corporation—in security for Areas 51 and S 4, Black Budget weapons operations like Project Aries, and in maintaining various nuclear facilities for the U.S. government. The electromagnetic pulse weapon consists of a block-and-a-half-long barrel horizontally supported on a nonconductive wooden trestle twenty-five feet high connected to a two-story tower which is connected, in turn, to an immense electrical apparatus with huge arms and massive connecting cables, looking like a gigantic Van de Graaff generator. The long-rumored electromagnetic pulse generator at last!"

There is no photo.

Boylan suggests that the 100-trillion-volt electromagnetic bursts were designed to overpower extraterrestrial UFOs, since such a device is clearly "overkill for a mere incoming ballistic missile."

Trying to find the proper road back from the solar weapons lab, Boylan tells us, he came upon "the famous Manzano Mountain Weapons Storage facility, an entire mountain tunneled into for storage of various high-security items such as nuclear weapons and, according to Timothy Good in *Above Top Secret,* retrieved UFOs."*

Boylan was impressed by Manzano's security. The entire complex, he tells us, "is surrounded by three separate high, razor-wire-tipped fences with bare-earth zones between, presumably with motion sensors embedded. Armed personnel in jeeps constantly patrol the area. At the northern end of Manzano is the notorious Coyote Canyon Test Site, where extremely classified Air Force, DOE, and Sandia National Laboratories research takes place. This is the area where USAF personnel spotted a UFO hovering low in 1979."†

"Peering partway into Coyote Canyon by binoculars," Boylan's dinnertable account of his tour continues, "I could see a strange metallic ball twenty feet high resting on the ground, sheltered by a flat tin roof above, supported by four poles surrounding the huge sphere. Its purpose is un-

---

* Good himself does not allege that retrieved UFOs are stored at Manzano. He merely quotes a late-1980 letter to the Aerial Phenomena Research Organization (APRO) from an unnamed airman stationed at Kirtland, who wrote in part: "I have heard rumors, but serious rumors, that the USAF has a crashed UFO stored in the Manzano Storage area. . . . This area is heavily guarded by USAF Security. I have spoken with two employees of Sandia Laboratories, who also store classified objects in Manzano, and they told me Sandia has examined several UFOs during the last 20 years. Parts of one that crashed near Roswell, N.M. . . . was examined by Sandia scientists. That is still being stored in Manzano." The letter writer explained that he had to remain anonymous because he was "a career airman with time remaining on active duty. I feel I would be threatened if I disclosed my name."[16]

† Actually, the sighting Boylan is referring to is one of a series that took place between August 8 and 22, 1980, according to Air Force Office of Special Investigations (AFOSI) complaint forms obtained through the Freedom of Information Act and paraphrased for Timothy Good by Major Ernest J. Edwards:

"August 8, three Security Policemen . . . on duty inside Manzano Weapons Storage Area sighted an unidentified light in the air that traveled from North to South over the Coyote Canyon area of the Department of Defense Restricted Test Range . . ." Interviewed by AFOSI investigators separately, the three Security Policemen independently confirmed that at approximately 11:30 p.m. they had observed that "a very bright light traveled with great speed and stopped suddenly in the sky over Coyote Canyon. The three first thought the object was a helicopter, however, after observing the strange aerial maneuvers (stop and go), they felt a helicopter couldn't have performed such skills. The light landed in the Coyote Canyon area. Sometime later, [the] three witnessed the light take off and leave proceeding straight up at a high speed and disappear . . ."

The following night, according to this same AFOSI complaint form, a Sandia Security Guard reported that twenty minutes past midnight, "he was driving East on the Coyote Canyon access road on a routine building check of an alarmed structure. As he approached the structure he observed a bright light near the

known." But then he goes on to say that "whatever the research at Coyote Canyon is, it has made the water in the area unfit to drink or even wash your hands in," and shows a photograph of a sign warning about the water.

From Coyote Canyon, Boylan proceeded south toward Alamogordo to the National Solar Observatory at Sunspot. The observatory, atop 9,200-foot-high Sacramento Peak, is used to monitor the effects of solar electromagnetic radiation and geophysical and geomagnetic disturbances, Boylan explains, on the operation of spacecraft and satellite stability. Boylan notes that beneath the entrance sign for the observatory is "an additional small sign which reads 'Umbra'—the National Security Agency's highest security classification.

"A thousand feet east of the NSO," Boylan continues, "is the Army Sacramento Peak Frequency Surveillance Station with its several signs forbidding entrance and warnings of severe penalties. This station monitors electromagnetic communications and telemetry on and over White Sands Missile Range, Holloman Air Force Base, and NASA's secret Johnson Space City complex. My remote viewer consultant noted underground facilities at the surveillance station and EM force generation, which may explain why there were no cricket or forest sounds near this electromagnetic intelligence facility. It's probably operated by the National Security A—"

"Dr. Boylan, I beg your pardon," I interrupt, "but who did you say noted these underground facilities?"

"My remote viewer consultant, Nancy Matz. She's a woman I consult with back in Sacramento. She also told me she had spotted several levels of excavated chambers in Archulete Mesa, but that there had been a great disturbance inside the mountain which caused some of the chambers to cave in on others."

"She was with you?"

"No, no. I consulted with her back in Sacramento. She's a *remote* viewer: a person who happens to have the psychic gift for remote viewing. In other words, she can in her mind go with you to places you've been and see things you've seen and some things you may have trouble remembering."

---

ground behind the structure. He also observed an object he first thought was a helicopter. But after driving closer, he observed a round disc-shaped object. He attempted to radio for a backup patrol but his radio would not work. As he approached the object on foot armed with a shotgun, the object took off in a vertical direction at a high rate of speed . . ."

And again, on August 22nd, three other security policemen saw "the same aerial phenomenon" as had been described by the previous witnesses: "Again the object landed in Coyote Canyon." The report continues: ". . . another Security Guard observed an object land near an alarmed structure during the first week of August, but did not report it until just recently for fear of harassment."[17]

"How does she do this?" I ask.

"Did you meet Stubblebine's protégé, the 'spook'—Dr. John what's-his-face—academic degree . . . John Alexander from PsyCorp at the conference?"

"I don't think so," I say.

"PsyCorp is a civilian version of the Army military intelligence psychological warfare section. Stubblebine, Alexander's boss, was reasonably forthcoming about what they were doing when they were in military intelligence. Blum's book [*Out There*] talks a bit about this, too, how they have guys who can sit in the Pentagon and through remote viewing spot a Soviet submarine submerged beneath the Atlantic and give you its correct longitude and latitude. Well, Stubblebine and Alexander have taken this little dog-and-pony show civilian-side, developed their own stable of remote viewers, and I can pretty much guarantee you that their main customer is still the Central Intelligence Agency. Anyway, my person is not of their stable, but just happens through the grace of whatever higher powers to have the gift independently. And when I ran my grand tour of the Southwest bases, she kind of had the ability to see what I saw and to pick up some additional details—some of which I have had interestingly corroborated, either by me or by others. So that's what I'm talking about here when I say she got a couple of these details, such as the excavated chambers, through remote viewing."

"Remote viewing," I say with a straight face.

Boylan explains that because of the tight security at Holloman Air Base, the White Sands Missile Range, and NASA's Johnson Space City, he was unable to "reconnoiter" them, so he proceeded to the National Radio Astronomy Observatory (NRAO) with its twenty-seven Very Large Array dish antennae arranged in a two-mile-long, one-mile-wide inverted T with all those dishes pointing at a low angle above the horizon due north.

"The stated purpose of this facility," Boylan tells us, "is to collect weak radio waves from celestial sources. In other words, they are supposedly only mapping the heavens by locating stars and energized gas fields in space which emit electromagnetic radiation in the radio frequency. However, as with other sites on this tour, the National Radio Astronomy Observatory is not your average boring observatory. Parked adjacent to the headquarters was an *Army* truck with NROA insignia, and two—*two!*—ambulances with NROA insignia, which leads me to deduce that the handful of astronomers working there must have a terrible occupational accident record!

"As you know," Boylan continues, "the United States will announce on October twelfth to coincide with the five hundredth birthday of Columbus's discovery of the New World, that it is turning on its radio telescopes to listen for intelligent transmissions from space. One could speculate that the purpose of this upcoming high-profile government announcement is to create the 'fig leaf' for 'uncovering' ET communications and the eventual open admission by the government of extraterrestrial-government contact.

"What is *not* speculation," Boylan says firmly, "is the evidence, including physical evidence that the government's NROA dishes are *also* being used to transmit superpowerful signals *into* space! Specifically, towards the direction just above the low north horizon. One clue came when I was having dinner at a restaurant near there next to four astronomers from NROA. One was complaining about trying to get time on a radio dish to do his research. But while I was at the observatory, all twenty-seven dishes were pointed *away* from the main part of the sky towards a low target or whatever to the north. Furthermore, a photograph of these dishes at the observatory headquarters again shows all the dishes pointed at the same low north angle. Why this persistent focus on one area of the sky when there is such competition for time on the dishes?

"Another clue is the location of the NROA on the plains of San Augustin," Boylan is saying, "a desolate, silent region deliberately chosen for its remoteness from cities with their radio stations and EM radiation. But it was not until I left the NROA that I obtained *physical* evidence. As I was about two miles out from the Very Large Array, with both my FM and CB radios on, both radios were simultaneously blanketed by the most intense screeching and howling I have ever heard! This excruciating noise continued for several minutes. I could not believe my ears. How could NROA permit such powerful electromagnetic signals to interfere with their listening to delicate radio signals from space? Finally I was forced to turn off my radios and did not turn them on again until I reached Pie Town, twenty-one miles to the northwest. When I turned both radios back on, I could still hear that deafening screech. It lasted another two minutes, then mercifully stopped. Afterwards both my FM radio and CB radio were functioning perfectly, and I never heard that noise again.

"Now as a result of what I *heard* I deduced that the NROA was not only receiving signals from space, but *sending* them! And given the rule that electromagnetic field strength diminishes algebraically with distance, the capacity to swamp both the CB and FM radios' frequencies at twenty-one miles indicated to me that the sending power from the NROA dishes is extraordinary, as would befit a signal intended to penetrate into space. My question is, whom is the government signaling? And why are they lying about the purpose of SETI?"

At Pie Town, Boylan explains, he went to check out the Very Large Baseline Array which is under construction. This huge radiotelescope complex is supposed to connect with radiotelescopes already in existence in Puerto Rico, West Virginia, and Hawaii to create an "antenna" with a "dish size" the equivalent of one-eighth of the globe, but the only construction he saw was large ten-foot-diameter pipes, the purpose of which he could not determine. "What's really going on at Pie Town," he tells us, "I cannot say. So I headed west to my final destination in California's Black Budget Palmdale-Lancaster region."

There, sixty miles north of Los Angeles, in the Tehachapi Mountains east of Edwards Air Force Base, Boylan came upon the Tejon Ranch, where the Northrop Aircraft Corporation, he says, "has its secret saucers works, according to researcher William Hamilton III in his book *Cosmic Top Secret.* Following Bill's directions, I proceeded seven miles west from Lancaster on Highway 138 to Road 190, then three miles north to the Kern County line. Bill was right. Staked out with binoculars between three and five a.m. on April fifteenth, I saw the same intensely burning bright-orange-gold craft being test-flown there that I had seen above Areas 51 and S-4. As I watched, four ultrabright orange-gold orbs rose and traversed a brief one-and-a-half-mile test loop. At intervals of about a half-hour, each orb took off and plied its course. The first three took off from what appeared to be the southwest hangar area of the Northrop complex. The fourth took off from the northeast staging area. On the ground, each craft was not glowing at first, but appeared in the full moonlight like a parked airliner frame with backlit porthole windows. I estimate that the width of the craft was about fifty feet.

"As each began to rise," Boylan continues, "it began glowing intensely all over its frame, as though the frame itself—or perhaps an ionizing field around the frame—were emitting light. The intensity of this light increased proportionally to the power demand required to rise vertically above the ground to an altitude of about two hundred feet over the Northrop plant. At this altitude, and at maximum brightness, the craft hovered, then slowly began to glide at about 15 mph in a southwest direction for a mile and a half, stopped, then swung around, revealing its round bottom side, which emitted an even more intense light. Each craft would then cross back to the staging area, hover, then descend vertically to the ground. Once on the ground, each stopped emitting the bright light except for the dim, backlit portholes.

"The fourth craft," Boylan says, "made its loop in a northeasterly direction. Each of these flights appeared to be very brief and cautious 'test runs' to make sure that the craft actually flew before shipping them off to Area S-4 for full field testing prior to joining the growing fleet of U.S. saucers."

"So what do you make of all this?" I ask. "I mean, at your most paranoid moments what does what you saw mean?"

"I'm not so sure I'm the one who's paranoid," he said.

"Who is?"

"The government, or why else would our Strategic Defense Initiative funding have increased by 33 percent in each of the last three years while there has been a dramatic drop in the Soviet missile threat as the USSR has fallen apart? Are you familiar with Leonard Stringfield's comment that Star Wars, ostensibly conceived as a defensive system against Russian missile attacks, may have had from its beginning a defensive UFO connection? The Union of Concerned Scientists has insisted that there is no rationale for a SDI system as large as what has been proposed by either Congress or the Bush administration. This suggests to me that SDI has a different agenda than stopping Russian missiles, and that agenda is, I believe, a weapons countermeasures capability against extraterrestrials and their UFOs."

"What sort of 'countermeasures' are you talking about?" I ask.

"Countermeasures like those I saw on my six-state grand tour," Boylan replies. "Nuclear, laser, electromagnetic pulse, and particle beam weapons. Look, NASA itself inadvertently provided documentary evidence of this when the astronauts aboard the *Discovery* space shuttle transmitted a live video feed to earth of footage of a UFO crossing just above the Earth's atmosphere. On this tape you see a UFO sailing along a straight line, and then, suddenly, it makes a ninety-degree turn to the right and accelerates off into deeper space just as a shaped-pulse high-energy beam streaks up from Earth to exactly the spot where the UFO would have been had it not, a millisecond before, radically altered its course. This videotape was shown on NBC's *Hard Copy* program on June 5, 1992. Get a copy of it and see for yourself!"

"But if it's a video of what you say it is, why did it never make the evening news?"

"Because, of course, NASA says what one sees on the film as a UFO is nothing more than a piece of ice or water. That it isn't a UFO at all."

"So who *does* say it's a UFO?"

"Well, when it was shown on *Hard Copy*, *UFO Magazine*'s contributing editor Don Ecker said it looked to him like a Star Wars weapon shooting at a UFO above earth's atmosphere. And, from my research, it looks that way to me. This assembling of a fleet of U.S. saucers in Nevada appears to me to be part of a related effort to develop our capacity to wage combat with extraterrestrial UFOs on technologically similar terms. So my question is this: Is the U.S. government's aggressive and—to use your word—paranoid Star Wars Initiative response the one we want made in our name to visits by intelligent life from other planets? Is this the way we want eighty *billion* of our tax dollars used? Eighty billion, incidentally, is SDI budget for 1993 to 2005.

As Edmund Burke once stated, all that is necessary for evil to prevail is for enough good men and women to do nothing."

"What do you suggest we do?" I ask.

"Demand of our elected representatives that the so-called Black Budget be opened to full congressional and public scrutiny and debate. This means *all* the intelligence budgets, particularly the National Security Agency, the Central Intelligence Agency, the Defense Intelligence Agency. And finally, we need to demand that Congress pass legislation outlawing and invalidating the practice of secret Executive Orders by the President with no accountability, such as Truman's classified Executive Order of September 24, 1947, establishing MJ-12 and hiding extraterrestrial contact from the American people."

Time out.

The story behind the MJ-12 documents is a curious one. A little after noon on December 11, 1984, Jaime Shandera, a forty-five-year-old Los Angeles film producer with a background in documentaries for Time-Life and RKO General and only a limited interest in UFOs, was sitting alone in his home killing time prior to a lunch meeting when he heard his screen door open and the sound of an object being forced through the mail slot in his front door. When he got up to investigate, he discovered a bulky 8½-by-11-inch brown envelope sealed with tape lying on his floor. Shandera's name and address were neatly typed on a label affixed to the envelope; there was no return address. When Shandera opened the large envelope he discovered there was a smaller brown envelope, also sealed with tape, within it; and within the brown envelope, a white one. Within the white envelope was a canister containing a roll of exposed but undeveloped Tri-X 35 mm film. Shandera replaced the film in its canister, the canister in the largest of the envelopes, and hurried off to his lunch date. Coincidentally, the person he was meeting was Bill Moore, the writer who, four years earlier, had co-authored with Charles Berlitz (author of the 1974 best-seller *The Bermuda Triangle*) *The Roswell Incident*, an investigation into the alleged 1947 New Mexico saucer crash. According to Berlitz and Moore, the bodies of aliens were found in the wreckage—a momentous discovery that had almost immediately been concealed by the government of the United States.

Moore was waiting at the restaurant when Shandera arrived. Moore and Shandera's connection was that they had met to discuss the possibility of together making a fictional film based on UFO investigator and nuclear physicist Stanton Friedman's continuing research into the Roswell crash. Although the film never got beyond the discussion stage, Moore and Shandera remained friends. Furthermore, in the course of that friendship, Shandera had apparently been drawn into Moore's small coterie of believers in a government cover-up conspiracy. At the restaurant, Shandera told Moore of the mysterious roll of film, and, not bothering with lunch, the two men excitedly rushed out of the restaurant to Moore's house to inspect it. Although neither Moore nor Shandera had much darkroom experience, they managed to print up some contact sheets and hang them from one of Moore's living-room curtains to dry.

The contact sheets revealed seven pages of a typewritten document. The first words Moore was able to make out were those rubber-stamped at the top of each of the pages: "TOP SECRET / MAJIC / EYES ONLY."

Moore, unwilling to relinquish the glass for an instant to Shandera, excitedly raced through the cover page identifying the material as a briefing document on "Operation Majestic-12" prepared for President-elect Dwight D. Eisenhower, to be delivered on November 18, 1952. There followed the warning that the document contained "information essential to the national security of the United States;" and that "EYES ONLY access" was "strictly limited to those possessing Majestic-12 clearance level." The second page contained the list of members of the Majestic-12 committee. But it was the third page that Moore found the most stunning.

Following a brief review of Kenneth Arnold's famous "flying saucers" sighting, and the note in passing that of the hundreds of subsequent sightings that had been reported, many were by "highly credible military and civilian sources," and that "there were several unsuccessful attempts to utilize aircraft in efforts to pursue reported discs in flight," the third page went on to state:

> In spite of these efforts, little of substance was learned about the objects until a local rancher reported that one had crashed in a remote region of New Mexico located approximately seventy-five miles northwest of Roswell Army Air Base (now Walker Field).
>
> On 07 July, 1947, a secret operation was begun to assure recovery of the wreckage of this object for scientific study. During the course of this operation, aerial reconnaissance discovered that four small human-like beings had apparently ejected from the craft at some point before it exploded. These had fallen to earth about two miles east of the wreckage site. All four were dead and badly decomposed due to action by predators and exposure to the elements during the approximately one week time period which had elapsed before their discovery. A special scientific team took charge of removing these bodies for study. (See Attachment "C".) The wreckage of the craft was also removed to several different locations. (See Attachment "B".) Civilian and military witnesses in the area were de-

briefed and news reporters were given the effective cover story that the object had been a misguided weather balloon.[18]

Here, to Moore's astonishment, was a purported top-secret government document reporting that the remains of *four alien creatures* had been found and recovered two miles east of the wreckage of a crashed *flying saucer!* Not surprisingly, Moore's reaction to the documents was to ask himself, "Are these for real?"[19] It is the same question that has haunted everyone who has studied these documents since.

The validity of the MJ-12 documents, like the validity of the crashed saucer reports, is one of those pernicious questions that cannot be satisfactorily answered without hard evidence. However, because these documents provide the backbone for the credibility of many of the government cover-up conspiracy charges, they are worth looking into.

The documents, allegedly prepared for a briefing to be given President-elect Eisenhower by former CIA director Roscoe Hillenkoetter, identify Majestic-12 as a "TOP SECRET Research and Development/Intelligence operation responsible directly and only to the President of the United States." (Majestic-12 is also variously referred to in UFO literature as Majic-12, Majority-12, Majesty, MAJI [Majestic, or Majority, Agency for Joint Intelligence], MAJIC [a security classification meaning MAJI-Controlled], and the Country Club.[20])

"Operations of the project," the briefing papers state, "are carried out under control of the Majestic-12 (Majic-12) Group which was established by special, classified executive order of President Truman on 24 September 1947," a date that would place it two months after the alleged Roswell saucer crash:

> upon recommendation by Dr. Vannevar Bush and Secretary James Forrestal. (See Attachment 'A.') Members of the Majestic-12 Group were designated as follows:
>
> > Adm. Roscoe H. Hillenkoetter
> > Dr. Vannevar Bush
> > Secy. James V. Forrestal
> > Gen. Nathan F. Twining
> > Gen. Hoyt B. Vandenberg
> > Dr. Detlev Bronk
> > Dr. Jerome Hunsaker
> > Mr. Sidney W. Souers
> > Mr. Gordon Gray
> > Dr. Donald Menzel
> > Gen. Robert M. Montague
> > Dr. Lloyd V. Berkner

The death of Secretary Forrestal on 22 May, 1949, created a vacancy which remained unfilled until 01 August, 1950, upon which date Gen. Walter B. Smith was designated as permanent replacement.[21]

Who were these men, and why might they have been chosen for this group?

Heading the list is *Admiral Roscoe H. Hillenkoetter.* In 1947 Rear Admiral Hillenkoetter was Truman's first director of the Central Intelligence Agency, which, most likely only coincidentally, had been newly created the same month as Majestic-12. In 1956, four years after this document was allegedly written, the National Investigations Committee on Aerial Phenomena (NICAP) was founded by former Navy physicist Thomas Townsend Brown. Hillenkoetter joined NICAP's board of directors following his retirement from the Navy in June 1957. During his tenure as a director, Timothy Good reports, Hillenkoetter "made a number of extraordinary statements attesting to the reality and seriousness of the UFO phenomenon. He was convinced that UFOs were unknown objects operating under intelligent control and that 'the Air Force is still censoring UFO sightings. Hundreds of authentic reports written by veteran pilots and other technically trained observers have been ridiculed or explained away as mistakes, delusions or hoaxes. . . . It is imperative that we learn where UFOs come from and what their purpose is. The public has a right to know.' "[22] Hillenkoetter would have been a natural choice to sit on a secret government panel investigating UFOs. But, of course, as the former senior avionics editor of *Aviation Week & Space Technology* and this country's now-leading UFO debunker, Philip Klass, has noted, a clever hoaxer would have known this.

Dr. Vannevar Bush, Truman's highly respected scientific advisor through World War II and the 1940s, would also have been a natural. In 1941 Dr. Bush had organized the National Defense Resources Council and, in 1943, the Office of Scientific Research and Development, which played a major role in creating the Manhattan Project, which led to the first atomic bomb. But in 1948 Dr. Bush had written Truman that it was his wish "ultimately to be free of governmental duties in order to return more completely to scientific matters," and to that end had already resigned from the Defense Research and Development Board, another government organization. Klass, aware of this correspondence, asks why Bush would then have remained four more years on Majic-12. The most reasonable response to that, I think, would be to ask in return: If Bush had any scientific curiosity whatsoever, how could he *not* have remained on Majic-12?

Timothy Good quotes a top-secret memorandum written by a "highly respected scientist," Wilbert B. Smith, a senior radio engineer with the

Canadian government Department of Transportation, to the Controller of Telecommunications, recommending that a Canadian research project be set up to study UFOs. In this memo, dated November 21, 1950, Smith wrote: "We believe we are on the track of something which may well prove to be the introduction to a new technology. The existence of a different technology is borne out by investigations which are being carried on at the present time in relation to flying saucers."[23]

Smith further reported that through discreet inquiries made at the Canadian embassy in Washington, he had learned:

a. The matter is the most highly classified subject in the United States government, rating higher even than the H-bomb.

b. Flying saucers exist.

c. Their modus operandi is unknown but concentrated effort is being made by *a small group headed by Doctor Vannevar Bush* [my italics].

d. The entire matter is considered by the United States authorities to be of tremendous significance.[24]

Not surprisingly, Good concludes that the "small group" Bush headed must have been Majestic-12. And because Smith's secret memorandum was released by the Canadian government, its authenticity, security classification, and content, Good suggests, significantly increase the chances that the Majic-12 document is genuine.

James V. Forrestal, the other individual upon whose recommendation then-President Harry S Truman had established the Majestic-12 Group, had served as Truman's under secretary of the navy from 1944 to 1947. In 1947, two months after the "Roswell crash," the National Security Act was enacted and Truman appointed Forrestal to the newly created cabinet position of secretary of defense, with the task of reorganizing and coordinating all the armed services.

Among the MJ-12 documents that fell into Moore's hands was the brief September 27, 1947, top-secret/eyes-only memorandum from President Truman to Forrestal authorizing the secretary of defense "to proceed with all due speed and caution" in setting up the Majestic-12 organization. The memo closes with the President expressing his "feeling that any future considerations relative to the ultimate disposition of this matter should rest solely with the Office of the President following appropriate discussions with yourself, Dr. Bush, and the Director of Central Intelligence."[25]

Five years later, in November 1952, at the time the Majestic-12 briefing document was supposedly written, the composition of the Majic-12 Group remained the same but for the replacement of Forrestal. In March 1949, as a result of a serious nervous breakdown, James Forrestal resigned from his position as secretary of defense. Two months later he committed suicide. His seat on Majic-12 remained empty until August 1950, when it was taken by *General Walter Bedell Smith,* Eisenhower's World War II chief of staff. Smith, at the time this briefing document was allegedly written, was serving as director of the CIA.

Fourth man on the list of members was *General Nathan F. Twining.* Although Twining subsequently became chief of staff of the United States Air Force in 1953, and chairman of the Joint Chiefs of Staff in 1957, at the time the Majic-12 Group was allegedly formed he was the commanding general of the Air Material Command based at Wright Field near Dayton—the field to which the remains of the crashed Roswell disc were reportedly taken just two months before Truman's Executive Order creating Majic-12 was signed.

There is also evidence that "due to a very sudden and important matter" Twining had cancelled an announced trip to the West Coast on July 8, 1947, the day the first press report of the retrieval of a crashed disc near Roswell was released by the public information officer at Roswell Field. William Moore, into whose hands these documents had so suspiciously fallen, was subsequently able to learn that although reporters at the time of the saucer crash were told that Twining, while out of the office, was still "probably in Washington, D.C.," the general, in fact, had flown to New Mexico, where he remained through July 10.[26] Ten weeks later, responding to a request by the chief of the Air Intelligence Requirements Division at the Pentagon for information regarding "flying discs," Twining replied in a secret memorandum:

It is the opinion that:

    a. The phenomenon reported is something real and not visionary or fictitious.

    b. There are objects probably approximating the shape of a disc, of such appreciable size as to appear to be as large as manmade aircraft.

    c. There is a possibility that some of the incidents may be caused by natural phenomena, such as meteors.

    d. The reported operating characteristics such as extreme rates of climb, maneuverability (particularly in roll) and action which must be considered *evasive* when sighted or contacted by friendly aircraft and radar, lend belief to the possibility that some of the objects are controlled manually, automatically, or remotely.

    e. The apparent common description of the objects is as follows:

        1. Metallic or light reflecting surface.

2. Absence of trail, except in a few instances when the object apparently was operating under high performance conditions.
3. Circular or elliptical in shape, flat on bottom and domed on top.
4. Several reports of well kept formation flights varying from three to nine objects.
5. Normally no associated sound, except in three instances a substantial rumbling roar was noted.
6. Level flight speeds normally above 300 knots are estimated.

Twining then suggests that "due consideration should be given" the possibility that the objects are our own, "the product of some high security project" he knew nothing about, or that "some foreign power has a form of propulsion, possibly nuclear, which is outside of our domestic knowledge." But then Twining also suggested that due consideration should be given to the fact that there was a "lack of physical evidence in the shape of crash recovered exhibits which would undeniably prove the existence of these objects."[27]

Skeptics have made much of the fact that Twining here was denying the existence of any UFO-crash-recovered materials despite the allegations that he had flown to New Mexico during the Roswell saucer recovery and was commanding general at the air base to which the materials were supposedly taken. But what else *could* Twining say? Even if he himself had physically handled wreckage from the Roswell crash, this memo, although written the day before the Majestic-12 Group was formed, would have to reflect Twining's knowledge that he was to be a member of this group and was forbidden to disclose information about the saucer retrieval to anyone outside of his fellow Majic-12 members and the President of the United States.

According to Klass, within weeks of the formation of the alleged Majestic-12 committee, Twining was transferred to head the Alaskan Command, which, if the remains of a crashed disc were being examined at his former headquarters, didn't seem to make sense. Why didn't Twining remain in charge of the investigation? And why wasn't his successor at Wright Field appointed to take Twining's place?

Before moving on, it is important to note that a significant aspect of Twining's memo was the recommendation that "Headquarters, Army Air Forces issue a directive assigning a priority, security classification, and Code Name for a detailed study of this [flying saucer] matter. . . ."[28] That study, undertaken two months later, in December 1947, led to the establishment of Project Sign, forerunner of Projects Grudge and Blue Book, the United States Air Force investigation into the UFO phenomenon for which J. Allen Hynek served as scientific consultant.

Fifth man was *General Hoyt S. Vandenberg,* Air Force chief of staff at the creation of Majic-12. Vandenberg had been the second director of the Central Intelligence Group from June 1946 through May 1947 prior to the creation of the Central Intelligence Agency. An Air Force chief with an intelligence background would be another natural choice for Majic-12. Klass argues that if General Vandenberg knew UFOs were real and a threat at the time of the outbreak of sightings over the nation's capital in the summer of 1952, why had the Air Force and he not taken the mysterious radar and visual sightings more seriously instead of dismissing them as "temperature inversion"? But what could the Air Force do against objects capable of outrunning, outclimbing, and outmaneuvering them but deny they exist? Admission of such vulnerability had frightening implications for national security—a conclusion seemingly reinforced by Vandenberg's actions four years earlier, the year after the alleged Roswell crash. At that time, the Air Technical Intelligence Center had reported in its classified "Estimate of the Situation" that they were of the opinion that UFOs were interplanetary. Vandenberg's response had been to order ATIC's Estimate burned.

Dr. Detlev Bronk, the sixth man on the Majic-12 list, was chairman of the National Research Council, a member of the Medical Advisory Board of the Atomic Energy Commission, and, like Vannevar Bush, a scientific adviser to President Truman. Dr. Bronk, an internationally respected physiologist and biophysicist whose research specialty was the transmission of nerve impulses to skeletal muscles and fibers and nerve physiology, allegedly performed the autopsies on the "four small, human-like beings" recovered from the crashed Roswell silver disc. Dr. Bronk, too, according to skeptic Philip Klass, would be a hoaxer's safe choice.

Coincidentally, perhaps, Dr. Bronk was a member of the Scientific Advisory Committee to the Brookhaven National Laboratory along with National Bureau of Standards director Dr. Edward Condon, who subsequently was director of the USAF-sponsored Scientific Study of Unidentified Flying Objects committee of a dozen or so scholars commissioned in 1966 to objectively examine the existing UFO evidence and make a recommendation as to whether further investigation was deemed necessary. The "Condon Report," as the final study became known when it was released in 1968, left practically everyone dissatisfied. The response of the M.I.T. conference's David M. Jacobs to the Condon Report is typical among ufologists: "Condon's flip attitude, his controversial managerial style, and internal disagreements over procedures and evidence," he wrote in *Secret Life,* "severely hampered the committee's investigation. In spite of the committee's serious split, Condon recommended in the 1968 final report that the Air Force give up UFO investigations because 'further extensive study of UFOs probably cannot be justified in the expectation that science will be advanced,' and UFOs do not 'pose a defense problem.' For Condon, the entire UFO affair was an enormous waste of time filled with hoaxes, bogus contactees, and weak-thinking UFO enthusiasts awash in the 'will to believe.' "[29] Based upon the Condon committee's recommendations, the Air Force's overt expression of interest in UFOs ended and its position continued to be that UFOs were a public fad.

Timothy Good notes that "rumors that the CIA was responsible for the biased negative conclusions of Dr. Condon have abounded" ever since his committee's report was made public, and points out, "There can be no denying the fact that Condon and some key members of his committee deliberately set out to convey to the public an image of scientific impartiality, while systematically debunking the subject."[30]

Good also mentions the interesting fact that while the committee was in the process of making its study, Dr. Condon asked UFO researcher Dr. James Harder "what he would do if he were responsible for a project report that might reflect a conclusion that UFOs were a manifestation of extraterrestrial intelligence." Harder made public his response in a bulletin of the Aerial Phenomena Research Organization: "I said I thought there would be other issues than the scientific ones, notably international repercussions and national security. [Dr. Condon] smiled the smile of a man who sees his own opinions reflected in the opinions of others and said that he had given the matter much thought, and had decided that if the answer was to be a positive finding of ETH [Extraterrestrial Hypothesis], he would not make the finding public, but would take the report, in his briefcase, to the President's Science Advisor, and have the decision made in Washington."[31] In other words, according to Harder, Condon would have taken the report to the President's science advisor Majic-12 committee member Detlev Bronk and such a positive finding would have been killed.

The problem I have with Harder's version of his conversation with Dr. Condon is the problem I have with Harder himself. My impression of Harder from the M.I.T. conference is that he does not make the most reliable source: he tends to see conspiracies wherever he looks.* But, in fairness, if I had been investigating this phenomenon as long as Harder has, I would probably be borderline paranoid, too.

---

* The opening day of the conference, when I first met James Harder, he asked me if I was any relation to Air Force Colonel Joseph Bryan, III. I said, "Yes, he's my father. Why?" Harder in effect responded that my father had been the CIA plant in NICAP responsible for that group's disintegration.

Timothy Good, too, goes to some length in *Above Top Secret* to link my father's CIA involvement with NICAP's demise. Anyone who knows anything about the history of

Seventh man on the Majic-12 list is *Dr. Jerome Hunsaker,* a former head of the Departments of Aeronautical Engineering and Mechanical Engineering at M.I.T. At the time of the creation of the MAJIC-12 Group, Hunsaker was chairman of the National Advisory Committee on Aerospace. Ufologists and skeptics alike are in agreement that Hunsaker's credentials would make him a logical choice for examining the remains of a crashed flying saucer.

Sidney W. Souers is eighth. From January through June 1946, he was Truman's first director of the Central Intelligence Group, the CIA's forerunner. In 1947, at the time when Majestic-12 was established, Souers became executive secretary of the National Security Council. He retired in 1950 but was retained as a special consultant to the President on security matters. Klass finds it suspicious that Souers, two years following his retirement, would have remained on Majic-12 and asks whether it wouldn't have made more sense to appoint his replacement at the NSC in his stead. I don't have any problems with Souers remaining on Majic 12; the fewer people involved in any so sensitive an investigative group, the more secure the group's findings.

More puzzling is the inclusion of the ninth man, *Gordon Gray.* At Majic-12's formation, Gray was only an assistant secretary of the army; he did not become the actual secretary of the army until 1949. Klass's investigation into Gray's background—Gray had been schooled as a lawyer and had spent the previous decade as a newspaper publisher—provided no hint, Klass felt, as to why Gray might have been a member of this group. But Klass apparently did not know that in postwar Washington, Gray's reputation as a gentleman with intelligence, reliability, and without political ties or debts would have made him an attractive addition to any secret, Executive-Ordered intelligence-gathering committee. Furthermore, his legal and journalistic training would have made Gray a good investigator. In 1950, Gray was appointed special assistant to President Truman on National Security Affairs, and in 1951, according to UFO investigator William Steinman, he was directing the Psychological Strategy Board, to which Majic-12 member and CIA director Walter Bedell Smith referred in a 1952 CIA memorandum on the psychological warfare implications of UFOs.[32]

NICAP knows that the group didn't need *anybody's* help in its disintegration; it simply self-destructed. And in the second place, while I was growing up, my father's unswerving, outspoken faith in the existence of UFOs, which he maintained until his death in 1993, was, I felt, somewhat of an embarrassment—the equivalent of lending undue credence to horoscopes or the healing powers of crystals. In any case, I do not believe it was the sort of public position an agent would take whose covert role was to smother interest in UFOs.

Dr. Donald Menzel, the tenth member, was chairman of Harvard's Department of Astronomy and head of the Harvard Observatory for Solar Research. Prior to Philip Klass, Menzel was this nation's foremost debunker of UFOs. By the time the Majic-12 briefing would have been given Eisenhower, Menzel was already known for his books and statements dismissing UFO sightings as being due in every case to poor observations of natural causes such as ice crystals, temperature inversions, fog, mist, planets, meteors, light reflections or refractions and the like, and manmade flying objects such as aircraft, rockets, and weather balloons. Menzel, who called UFOs "a frightening diversion in a jittery world," once characterized his debunking UFOs as having given him a reputation as "the man who shot Santa Claus."[33]

Klass, inheritor of Menzel's mantel, theorizes that the distinguished Harvard astronomer was listed as a Majic-12 member by the hoaxers responsible for the document as "punishment"—a way of suggesting Menzel was not only a fool but a liar. On the other hand, Menzel's appointment might only have reflected the desire to have a "house skeptic."

General Robert M. Montague, the eleventh member, was director of the Anti-Aircraft and Guided Missiles Branch of the U.S. Army Artillery School. He was also commanding general of the Atomic Energy Commission installation of Sandia Base in Albuquerque. If a saucer had actually crashed in New Mexico, he would have known. And if an operation were mounted to shoot these intruders out of the skies, he would have been in charge of organizing it.

The last man was scientist *Dr. Lloyd V. Berkner,* executive secretary of the Joint Research and Development Board under Dr. Vannevar Bush. Dr. Berkner also chaired the committee whose study led to the establishment of the Weapons System Evaluation Group. Berkner subsequently served on the "Robertson Panel," a civilian scientific advisory panel requested by the Eisenhower White House, chaired by Cal Tech mathematician Dr. H. P. Robertson and convened and funded by the CIA. The purpose of this panel was to study the Air Force's most tantalizing Project Blue Book UFO reports. The Robertson Panel met for only four days, January 14–17, 1953, reviewed just twenty-three cases, viewed some films, then drafted its classified final report. This paper, signed by Berkner, concluded that although there was no evidence that UFOs were a *direct* threat to national security, such phenomena could become a threat if the great mass of reported sightings were to continue. Unless such reports could be eliminated, or at least greatly diminished, the Robertson Panel noted, the accounts might create "morbid national psychology in which skillful hostile propaganda could induce hysterical behavior and harmful distrust of . . . authority." In an interesting perceptual shift, the panel made not the UFOs but the reports themselves the opponent. The panel's consequent recommendation was to create an aggressive public education program of "training and debunking" to result in a "marked reduction in reports" and the concomitant loss of public interest in UFOs.

Skeptic Philip Klass's response to Berkner's inclusion in Majic-12 membership was to wonder why so busy a scientist as Berkner, a Majestic-12 Group member privy to the real story, would take part in another time-consuming study and then sign his name to a report whose findings he knew to be untrue. In a perfect world, that would be a perfect question. But it is an imperfect world; I think it quite possible Berkner would lend both his time and his name to what Majic-12 and the President considered an important "disinformation" campaign.

Within the body of the Majic-12 briefing document was the information that the disc recovered from the Roswell crash was "most likely a short-range reconnaissance craft," a conclusion based on the disc's small size and its "lack of any identifiable provisions." The document further pointed out that based on Bronk's autopsy of the craft's four dead occupants, it was tentatively concluded that "although these creatures are human-like in appearance, the biological and evolutionary processes responsible for their development has apparently been quite different from those observed or postulated in homo sapiens. Dr. Bronk's team," the report continued, "has suggested the term 'Extra-terrestrial Biological Entities,' or 'EBEs,' be adopted as the standard term of reference for these creatures until such a time as a more definitive designation can be agreed upon."

According to the Majic-12 document, "numerous examples of what appear to be a form of writing were found in the wreckage." Attempts to decipher them were "largely unsuccessful." Unsuccessful, too, were attempts to discover how the disc was powered: "Research along these lines has been complicated by the complete absence of identifiable wings, propellers, jets or other conventional methods of propulsion and guidance, as well as a total lack of metallic wiring, vacuum tubes or similar recognizable electronic components. (See Attachment 'F.') It is assumed that the propulsion unit was completely destroyed by the explosion which caused the crash."

The briefing document explains how the need for "as much additional information as possible about these craft, their performance characteristics, and their purpose" led to the establishment of U.S. Air Force Project Sign in December 1947; and that in order to "preserve security, liaison between SIGN and Majestic-12 was limited to two individuals within the Intelligence Division of Air Material Command. . . . SIGN evolved into Project GRUDGE in December, 1948. The operation is currently being conducted under the Air Force code name BLUE BOOK, with liaison maintained through the Air Force officer who is head of the project."

The document continued: "On 06 December, 1950, a second object, probably of similar origin, impacted the earth at high speed in the El Indio–Guerrero area of the Texas-Mexican border after following a long trajectory through the atmosphere. By the time a search team arrived, what remained of the object had been almost totally incinerated. Such material as could be recovered was transported to the A.E.C. facility at Sandia, New Mexico, for study."

A *second* object had been recovered! But in all the literature I've come across in this field, I have seen no serious investigation into whether this report was real.

The final paragraph of the briefing document stresses that "implications for the National Security are of continuing importance" since "the motives and ultimate intentions of these visitors remain completely unknown." It refers to the "significant upsurge" in the wave of sightings beginning that May (1952) and continuing through the fall and how this increase "has caused considerable concern that new developments may be imminent." (The period referred to includes the sensational radar and visual sightings of "targets" over Washington, D.C., on two successive weekends in July; but by the time this briefing paper was allegedly written, the reported sightings had diminished to the normal number of four to five a week.) "It is for these reasons, as well as the obvious international and technological considerations and the ultimate need to avoid a public panic at all costs, that the Majestic-12 Group remains of the unanimous opinion that imposition of the strictest security precautions should continue without interruption into the new administration. At the same time," the document concludes, "contingency plan MJ-1949-04P/78 (Top Secret—Eyes Only) should be held in continued readiness should the need to make a public announcement present itself."[34]

So what are we to make of this document? If *it* is real, then flying saucers are real, and so is the crash near Roswell, New Mexico. If it *isn't* real, then we're back to square one.

Over the years there has been considerable nattering over the Majic-12 document's minutiae: the odd punctuation of its dates, for example—the comma after the month as in "18 November, 1952," which may or may not have been standard policy in those days. Skeptics have questioned the listing of the Majic-12 Group leader as "Admiral Roscoe H. Hillenkoetter" instead of "Admiral R. H. Killenkoetter," arguing that he so loathed his first name he would not have tolerated seeing it in print. And although each sheet is marked as "COPY *ONE* OF *ONE*," I find it curious that the pages are not numbered; my experience with highly classified papers in the late 1950s was that each page would note both its number and its location in the document, as in "PAGE *1* OF *18* PAGES."

panel's consequent recommendation was to create
cation program of "training and debunking" to res
in reports" and the concomitant loss of public inte

Skeptic Philip Klass's response to Berkner's in
bership was to wonder why so busy a scientist as Ber
member privy to the real story, would take part in
study and then sign his name to a report whose fi
true. In a perfect world, that would be a perfect qu
fect world; I think it quite possible Berkner would
name to what Majic-12 and the President considere
mation" campaign.

Within the body of the Majic-12 briefing do
tion that the disc recovered from the Roswell crash
range reconnaissance craft," a conclusion based on
its "lack of any identifiable provisions." The docu
that based on Bronk's autopsy of the craft's four de
tatively concluded that "although these creatures a
ance, the biological and evolutionary process
development has apparently been quite different
postulated in homo sapiens. Dr. Bronk's team," th
suggested the term 'Extra-terrestrial Biological
adopted as the standard term of reference for the
time as a more definitive designation can be agree

According to the Majic-12 document, "numer
pear to be a form of writing were found in the wr
cipher them were "largely unsuccessful." Unsucce
to discover how the disc was powered: "Research a
complicated by the complete absence of identifiab
or other conventional methods of propulsion and g
lack of metallic wiring, vacuum tubes or similar
components. (See Attachment 'F.') It is assumed
was completely destroyed by the explosion which

The briefing document explains how the need
information as possible about these craft, their per
and their purpose" led to the establishment of U.S
in December 1947; and that in order to "preserve
SIGN and Majestic-12 was limited to two indivi
gence Division of Air Material Command. . . . SI
GRUDGE in December, 1948. The operation is cu
under the Air Force code name BLUE BOOK,
through the Air Force officer who is head of the p

But these complaints pale before the single strongest argument against taking the Majestic-12 documents seriously: the manner in which they surfaced in the first place. They arrived on a roll of *undeveloped* 35 mm film sent in unmarked envelopes to a Los Angeles television documentary film producer who, conveniently and coincidentally, just *happened* to be having lunch that day with the co-author four years earlier of *The Roswell Incident,* a thin book alleging the crash of a flying saucer in New Mexico, the recovery of alien bodies from its wreckage, and a subsequent government cover-up of what had been found.

The Majestic-12 documents' confirmation of Moore's journalistic exposé provides him with the primary motive for having faked them: he had the most to gain from public disclosure of the document's contents. And yet Moore *didn't* disclose them; instead, he and Shandera spent the next two years keeping silent about their existence while they set about trying to establish their authenticity. And only then did they go public, in a press release that stated, "Based upon research and interviews conducted thus far . . . the document and its contents *appear* to be genuine. . . ."[35]

And that's the dilemma. The document *does* appear genuine. There is outside evidence that supports such a conclusion: the Canadian scientist's top-secret memorandum stating that "flying saucers exist," which alludes to the "concentrated effort . . . being made by a small group headed by Dr. Vannevar Bush" to gather material on them. There is the apparently authentic General Nathan Twining secret memo reporting that the UFO phenomenon is "something real and not visionary or fictitious." There is the unassailable logic of the membership of the Majestic-12 Group.

And then there is that curious "Briefing Paper for the President of the United States on the Subject of Identified Aerial Vehicles (IAVs)" Linda Moulton Howe reports was shown her during her April 1983 meeting with the Air Force Office of Special Investigations agent at Kirtland Air Force Base outside Albuquerque. In an October 1987 letter to the editor and publisher of *Just Cause,* Linda wrote of that briefing paper:

> There was no designation of a specific president nor do I remember a specific date. Agent Doty said he had been asked by his superiors to show me the briefing paper, that I could ask questions, but could not take notes. The content described a series of crashed UFO discs at Aztec and Roswell, New Mexico; Kingman, Arizona; and a crash in Mexico. Extraterrestrial bodies from the downed crafts were retrieved and taken to laboratories for examination. The paper also described information from direct contact with the "Grays" about their extraterrestrial intervention and manipulation of the human race's biological, sociological and religious evolution. The paper outlined the government's efforts since the 1940s to ascertain

the origin, nature and motives of the E.T.'s through project Sign, Grudge, Gleem, Pounce, Blue Book and others and concluded with a list of some current projects: Sigma (communication with E.T.s), Snowbird (E.T. craft technology and efforts to fly one), Aquarius (overall research and contact programs re: E.T.s)—and one "closed" project with name similar to Garnet which involved the E.T. connection with human evolution.[36]

Linda would not have made this story up.

Where does this leave us? With a big question mark. Because with Richard Boylan's account of his "six-state grand tour of reported Southwest secret sites" in mind, and his tale of having stealthily made his way across the desert toward Groom Lake and Area 51 at night, there is this tantalizing item from the November 1, 1993 "Periscope" section of *Newsweek:*

THE MYSTERY AT GROOM LAKE

Is the Air Force testing a new supersecret aircraft code-named "Aurora," at its Groom Lake facility in Nevada? The air force denies the existence of such a project. But *Newsweek* has learned that Air Force Secretary Sheila Widnall on Sept. 30 asked Interior Secretary Bruce Babbitt to close 3,900 acres of public land in Lincoln County, Nev., for the "safe and secure operations of activities on the Nellis Range."

Why? In recent months reporters and aviation buffs have stationed themselves on two hills on the land, which overlooks Nellis's top-secret Groom Lake facility. From there, peering through long-range lenses, they can see activities at Groom Lake, known inside the air force as Area 51. They say they've seen up to six Boeing 737 commuter jets a day flying workers in from Palmdale and Burbank, Calif., and from Las Vegas. And they report night flights of a craft that, judging from its lights, has extraordinary maneuverability.

Now Widnall has moved to shut down the Groom Lake bleachers. The hills are part of the 3,900-acre tract she's asked Babbitt to close off. An air force spokeswoman confirmed Widnall's request. At Interior, a spokeswoman said: "We gather the air force wants the land to create a visual barrier, a buffer to keep the public from looking into part of the Nellis Range the air force wants to keep secure."

Aviation expert Bill Sweetman, who's written a new book on the "Aurora" mystery, notes that the remote Groom Lake facility is so costly to operate that the air force generally uses other bases for its standard secret projects. "So what's going on at Groom Lake that Widnall has been persuaded she must hide?" he asks.[37]

Boylan would have us believe they are hiding flying saucers. And Linda Moulton Howe says they are—or were—being built under the name Project Snowbird.

After the dinner with Boylan, we drift back to our hotels. It is not until I am back in my room in the Eliot that I realize I never got around to questioning Boylan about his abduction! I had been to busy listening to his story to ask.

As I go back over my notes I come upon my favorite line of the day. It was from the person who compared an alien abduction to Peter Pan coming down from the sky to float the children out of their bedrooms accompanied by Tinker Bell, a little ball of light. It makes me think of J. M. Barrie's line in Act IV of *Peter Pan:* "Do you believe in fairies? . . . If you believe, clap your hands!"

What is the sound of one hand clapping, I wonder, *one small, gray-colored hand with three cartilaginous fingers and no opposable thumb?*

CHAPTER VI

At the Conference

Day Five

The first speaker Wednesday morning, June 17, this last day of the conference, is David Gotlib, M.D., a Canadian therapist and editor of the *Bulletin of Anomalous Experience,* a small publication that describes itself as "a networking newsletter about the UFO abduction phenomenon and related issues, for mental health professionals and interested scientists, [which tries to] 'comfortably tread the narrow path between the groves of academia and the dust and heat of the marketplace, inquiring and suggesting, not asserting or insisting.' " Dr. Gotlib's talk is titled "Ethical Issues in Dealing with the Abduction Experience."

"The data we are working on is subjective experience rather than objective evidence," Gotlib reminds us. "The problem is the lack of physical evidence." And it is because of this lack, he suggests, that a "backlash is in effect. Our primary goal is to help the experiencers. We need more mental health professionals."

Gotlib proposes that the motto of the group dealing with the abductees should be "Above all, do no harm."

"We must be able to demonstrate to our colleagues," he continues, "that what we are doing is reasonable, safe, and effective. We have precious little clinical evidence or clinical data to defend our work." And because of that, Gotlib warns, investigators and therapists dealing with the abductees run the risk of malpractice.

Gotlib sketches out a "worst-case scenario": "An abductee has a breakdown," he says. "A family member feels the intervention of an investigator is responsible for that breakdown and accuses him of being guilty of negligence. An investigator must realize that an abductee is vulnerable." Legal action would open up a Pandora's box, Gotlib says. "Think of the media leaping on this story. If there *is* a government cover-up, such a story would provide them with a chance to destroy the movement. It would be disastrous for the witnesses, the therapists, and the investigators."

Gotlib concludes with the observation "It's high time we came up with a set of standards."

There is a good comment from one of the audience drawing a parallel between the dangers of treating abductees and current cases of therapists who while treating ritual abuse victims have been accused by members of the victims' families of having been responsible for presenting the idea of abuse into the victims' minds. He is referring to the false memory syndrome.

Dr. Stuart Appelle, who's with the Department of Psychology at the State University of New York's Brockport campus, agrees with Gotlib that a set of standards is needed, but points out that these standards already exist. "I've got a message," he tells the conference attendees. "Many investigators in ufology are not acting professionally. There *are* standards for professional researchers, and they are not following these standards. Dealing with human subjects is not a simple issue, so there have been guidelines that have been set up. And the way to enforce those guidelines is to ensure that: first, there is no funding for people who do not follow the guidelines; second, there is no publication for people who do not follow the guidelines; and third, there will be sanctions against people who do not follow the guidelines."

Appelle then throws a scare into those investigators associated with academia: "There exists a Federal Policy for Protection of Human Subjects document," he reports. "If you are associated with virtually *any* academic institution and you do not comply with these federal guidelines, you could create a situation in which the university would lose *all* funding for research."

Jenny Randles rises to point out that she published guidelines in her *Science of the UFOs* appendix ten years ago.

A panel of abductees provides the final presentation of the conference. They are to address us on "What Has and Hasn't Helped Me."

The first to speak is Mary, the communications specialist who, during yesterday's coffee break, had talked to me about giving the aliens her cooperation and her body and their giving her a koan in return. " 'Dual reference' was of immeasurable help to me to control my experiences," she says. "I have nothing to fear because we are all alike. Knowing this has helped me to control my fear."

Bob, an older male abductee from Maine, says, "As a youngster I was always looking out of the corners of my mind not knowing what was coming next. I was always stressed out. Every time I was in therapy and wanted to get into the realm of the unknown, the therapist would say, 'We're not going to talk about that. How do you feel about your parents?' Their attitude was, 'It's not a tangible reality, so it's not something we can deal with here.' "

He mentions his childhood dreams of a glowing blue light and suggests it might be helpful to have theologians brought into the abduction study, "because we're beginning to get into that now. The multiple appearances of the Virgin Mary, for example. A theologian might be handy as a reference person, because I think all of these incidents are interrelated."

John Mack rises to say, "You, the experiencers, are in charge of this product, not us."

One of the abductees suggests the implants are tracking devices, or pods that can be activated to promote change and growth.

An abductee mother of two children says, "My son was taken from his crib at eight weeks; my daughter was taken when she was six. They don't know how deeply I am involved. I think all this is a spiritual happening, but I want you therapists to be able to help my children when the memories begin to surface for them."

A male abductee in his thirties says, "Two years ago I finally got in touch with the right people. Support groups have been a great help for me."

The last abductee says, "I think the intentions of both the humans and the Beings should be studied very carefully."

There are some inconsequential closing comments by Dave Pritchard and John Mack and the conference is over.

We begin to file out; little groups gather together in the hallway or outside in the sunshine on the lawn. I search out Alice and Carol. They seem hesitant to leave, unwilling to separate from the support and understanding they have found here. We end up talking together and they agree to let me interview them this evening.

Alice and Carol come to my hotel room around six p.m. The refrigerator is stocked with snacks; I have picked up a bottle of vodka and one of white wine. I have set up my tape recorder and notes. After I make them each a drink they settle into the couch, their legs curled up beneath them.

CHAPTER VII

Postconference Interview

Carol and Alice in Boston

Carol Dedham eyes my tape recorder, then lights the first of the more than a dozen cigarettes she will smoke during the next three hours.

Alice Bartlett is a heavy smoker, too. Physically softer than Carol—less angular—she flips her long, straight, pale blond hair behind her shoulders and leans back into a corner of the couch. Neither of the women is wearing makeup other than a faint lipstick. As the light from the end table falls over Alice, I am again struck by how much she looks like Andrew Wyeth's portraits of the young Helga.

"Since we want to cover the whole story," I say, "I guess the best place to begin is with what is happening to you. What do you think is going on?"

Alice and Carol exchange looks; then Carol says, "We don't know! We don't know the source of the problems we've been having."

"What's happening is a lot of strange things we can't explain," Alice says. "A lot of things that just seem to make no sense in what we know as reality. It's very hard to tell whether what we're seeing, what we're feeling, what we're experiencing is something normal. Especially when you know in the back of your mind that it's *not* normal! That there's something going on that you just *can't* explain."

"You said it was very hard to tell if what you were seeing was real," I say. "What are you seeing?"

"It's *missing time!*" Carol says, suddenly anguished.

"I think you have to start with the missing time in December," Alice says, nodding.

"First of all, you have to understand that before *any* of this came about, before we started asking ourselves questions about any of this, we didn't *know* anything about this abduction stuff," Carol tells me. "We didn't know anything about any of what we even then considered 'weird junk' or 'strange stuff.' We were aware, of course, of UFOs—"

"We'd seen *Close Encounters of the Third Kind.*" Alice explains.

"Right," Carol says, "and it was all fascinating stuff. But then in September 1990 we had our first experience. That was when we saw lights out behind the house, and we went out onto the back deck to look at these strange lights that we thought were helicopters. . . ."

It was a Friday evening. Alice, Carol, and Alice's younger sister Grace were lingering over after-dinner coffee in the dining room of their farmhouse when they noticed, visible through the sliding glass doors that led from the dining room to the back deck, strange, brilliant-white lights in the nighttime sky. Leaving their coffee, the three women pushed back from the table and stepped out onto the deck to take a look.

High in the sky to the west, on a line between the tool shed and the horse barn, three bright white lights floated in a triangle. Off to the south, to the left of where the women were standing, were more lights. They weren't stars; the women were certain of that. Initially, they thought they might have been seeing helicopters with their spotlights on. Small Army bases dot that part of Maryland. But, Carol remembers thinking, if they were helicopters, they were behaving oddly.

As the women watched, the three white lights appeared to be approaching, though the light at the top of the triangle seemed to be lagging just a little behind.

For several minutes Carol and Alice and Grace watched the lights grow brighter and brighter, until they knew that if the lights were from helicopters, they would have been able to hear the rhythmic beating of rotor blades above the normal cacophony of that warm, autumnal country night. And then, abruptly, all the rural night sounds ceased. No longer did the women hear the ratcheting of cicadas and crickets, the call of the peepers, the distant barking of dogs, the muted creak and thump of the stallion stirring restlessly in the barn. In fact, as the lights became blindingly bright, the night fell absolutely still. They heard no sounds at all.

Suddenly, one of the points of light streaked away from the other two so swiftly it left a white track on the women's retinas.

"Whoa!" Carol cried. "Look at that! Look at *that!*"

"Did you see it? *Did you see it?*" Alice excitedly asked.

"I'm going out front!" Grace said. "I'm going to see where it went!" Alice's sister ran back through the dining room, the living room, and out the French doors that opened onto the front porch.

Later, describing this incident to me in my Boston hotel room, Carol tells me, "The light shot off to the northeast at such a tremendous speed that when it appeared to our right in a different place, it was as though it had left this trail of light behind it."

Carol remembers quickly checking to see if the other two lights had also moved. They hadn't. They remained in line above the barn and shed. She recalls watching the third light with Alice for a couple of minutes more, and then the light seemed to zoom away from them in a straight line and disappear. A moment later, Grace poked her head through the opening in the sliding glass doors leading out to the deck and reported, "There's nothing out front."

What was puzzling to Alice and Carol was that their memories of what they had witnessed did not match. Alice recalls there having been five lights, an additional two had been in a row to the left, to the west of the three in the triangle. Carol remembers Grace commenting on two lights that she had seen in the south. Alice recalls having watched the lights for a while and then, because she was getting cold (Carol recalls the evening was warm), going back into the house while Carol and Grace remained outside to watch. Carol says Alice stayed with her the entire time the lights were visible. Carol thinks they were visible for about five minutes; Alice thinks they were visible for half an hour. Alice does not recall Grace being outside at all.

What the two women did agree upon, however, was that they had never felt in any danger. Rather than being afraid, they had been excited, *thrilled* at seeing something that few people, they then believed, ever saw.

"When in September did this incident occur?" I ask.

"Early September," Alice says.

"Right after the Labor Day holiday," Carol adds.

"Were there other horses in the barn?"

"Not at night," Alice answers. "We only keep the stallion in at night."

"And you have two dogs? Isn't that right?" I ask.

"Yes," Carol says.

"While this was going on with the lights," I ask, "how did the dogs behave?"

Carol suddenly inhales sharply. Her whole body goes rigid, as if she were having a seizure. And then she doubles over, covering her face in her hands.

"Are you all right?" Alice asks, moving quickly to place her arm around Carol's shoulders.

Carol is hyperventilating, struggling for self-control. "I'm sorry!" she whispers.

I have no idea how to help Carol. I want to comfort her, but I am not sure my touching her right now wouldn't terrify her even more. She has burrowed into Alice's bosom like a frightened child. Suddenly Carol stiffens and again cries out. She is clearly terrified of what she is seeing.

Alice shoots me a look. "Flashback," she explains.

Carol is still whimpering, but she is regaining control. After a few moments she says, "Ohhhh, okay. Okay." And then, her voice a bit stronger, she adds, "It must be the city I'm in. These things have a horrible effect, I swear."

"It's okay," Alice says, quietly. "It's all right."

"Okay," Carol says even more strongly. And then, as if she were noticing my tape recorder for the first time, she forces a laugh and says, "Cut!"

Neither Alice nor I speak.

Carol struggles to breathe deeply and exhale slowly. "They scared Killer," she says.

"Who?" I ask.

"One of our dogs," Alice explains to me. She turns back to Carol and asks, "When?"

"I don't know," Carol says.

"What did you see?" Alice asks her.

"I can't breathe!" Carol protests. She is still trying to catch her breath. "We have one dog . . . I'm very attached to . . . Killer." Carol is forcing out her words between gasps for air. "She found us when she was about four to six weeks old . . . just ran across the yard . . . this tiny ball of white fur . . . adopted us . . . never left. We named her Killer because she lived off crickets. She was Cricket Killer until we shortened it. But I'm very attached to this dog and—and—" She again shakes her head as if to clear it. "And I don't know what I saw."

But Carol does know. And as the memory returns she begins once more to speak: "Killer was scared. And she was crying and she ran. . . . She ran around and . . ." Carol's voice is becoming shaky. "She ran around the house, the other side of the house. Around the back side of the kitchen. . . ." Carol is losing it again. She begins to cry; her voice rises, becomes squeaky: "Killer ran downstairs and she was whimpering and squealing. . . ." Carol is crying hard now. *And I don't know why!*

"It's okay," Alice says.

"This was not the same September 1990 incident with the three bright lights, the 'saucers'?" I ask. "Is this something entirely different?"

"*I don't know!*" Carol says.

"We didn't have Killer then," Alice says. "She came to us probably about two weeks after that saucer sighting." She turns back to Carol. "How big was Killer?" she asks. "Was this recent?"

"She was a *dog,*" Carol insists. "I mean, she was grown."

"This is why we don't trust memories!" Alice says. Her voice, too, is anguished. "We have no idea what's going on!" Her eyes, too, now fill with tears.

To the best of Carol's and Alice's recollection, after the September sighting of the triangular array of lights behind their farm, there had not been another UFO experience until fifteen months later: mid-December 1991.

On December 15, Carol had been to visit her parents in Hagerstown, about seventy miles west of the horse farm, and was driving Alice's aging Toyota back on a Sunday night. It was, again, about eight-thirty, very dark. And the night was warm enough for Carol to be driving coatless with her side window half-open. She was about a half-dozen miles from the entrance to their farm on Route 32, the two-lane blacktop road she normally took.

The road could be heavily traveled during some periods of the day, but at that hour on a Sunday evening Carol could expect only local traffic, and not much of that. That night, in fact, she had passed no cars on that stretch of state highway at all.

Carol had just come over a rise; there was an open field on her right, and the gravel driveways of a couple of houses set some distance back on either side of the road.

Just beyond the rise the road curves gradually to the right and cuts between twin groves of mixed pine and deciduous trees. As Carol approached the trees, she was startled to see three bright white lights in a row, visible through the tops of the pines on the left-hand side.

She wasn't frightened; she just thought, " *Wow!* It's them! They look like the same lights!"

Carol pulled to the side of the road next to the mailbox for one of the houses. She was thinking she ought to find somebody, go to one of the houses and get the people out so that they, too, could see the lights. But neither of the houses had any lights on—a detail that, for such an hour on a Sunday evening, would later strike her odd, although it did not make any impression on her at the time.

She put on the car's warning blinkers, rolled down her side window the rest of the way, and leaned out to get an unobstructed look across the road at the lights. Even though it was wintertime and the leaves of the deciduous trees had fallen, there were enough pines in the grove to prevent an unimpeded view. Still, the lights were so bright the whole area was lit up. Carol decided to leave the car to get closer.

She walked about thirty yards down the right-hand gravel shoulder of the road to where she knew a dirt country road cut to the left like a firebreak through the trees. From there, she felt, she would be able to see the lights clearly. Across from the dirt road, she stopped and turned to look. It was absolutely quiet. There were no night sounds at all.

The lights remained in a horizontal row over the trees. She was determined to discover what was causing them; she wanted to make out details, but she was blinded—the lights were so bright they hurt her eyes. Frustrated, she shielded her eyes with her hand and peered up through her fingers. Suddenly, as before, one of the lights shot away, this time straight over her head. Carol spun around to see where it had gone and discovered it was now above her. It was huge and hovering directly overhead, seemingly so close she could reach up and touch it. Its brightness illuminated everything.

Standing there alone on the gravel shoulder of the road, Carol couldn't understand why there weren't other people gathered around her looking up at this light, too. Why hadn't other cars come along and stopped? And why hadn't the inhabitants of the two houses come running out?

Carol tried to make out its details. She thought she could see two smaller blue lights on either side of main beam; and then she wondered if the remaining two bright white shining objects were still over the trees. As she turned back to look, she blinked. When she opened her eyes again, she was five miles away in Alice's Toyota, making the right-hand turn off Route 32 onto the road that leads to the farm.

She has no recollection whatsoever of what happened between the moment she looked away from the huge, brilliant object overhead and blinked and when she found herself turning onto the driveway to the farm. "I don't have an inkling!" she tells me that night in my Boston hotel. "Not a clue as to what happened in between. It's just a total blank to me, except that when I arrived at the farm I was completely disoriented and I felt like I wanted to throw up. My nose was running, my eyes were watery as though I had been crying for hours, and I had no idea what those reactions were from!"

Carol parked Alice's Toyota in the garage, got out, and made it as far as the laundry-room passageway between the garage and the house before she collapsed in front of Alice's sister Grace.

Grace quickly knelt on the linoleum next to Carol. "What *happened* to you? Are you all right? You're *bleeding!*"

"Bleeding?" Carol asked groggily. "Where?"

"Your *ears!* Your earlobes! Both of them! You're *bleeding!*"

Carol lifted her fingers to her ears. The fingertips of her left hand came away wet, those of her right spotted with blood. Her head ached; her eyes burned; she still felt disoriented, nauseous. When she held her fingertips before her eyes, her hands shook. While Grace ran off to get a washcloth and warm water to clean her off, Carol again touched her earlobes. There was something wrong with her earrings, but she wasn't sure what it was.

Grace was sponging off the blood when she noticed that Carol's earlobes were swollen and her earrings were in backwards. It looked, she later told Carol, as if someone had ripped the earrings out of Carol's ears and then tried to put them back in but had inserted them wrong.

"Where's Alice?" Carol asked.

"Asleep," Grace said.

"Asleep, why? What time is it?"

"A quarter to ten."

"*A quarter to ten?*" Carol said. "It *can't* be!"

She remembered she had noted it was 8:26 exactly when she made the turn onto Route 32, which led to their farm. From that turnoff to the farm was seven and a half miles. So it could not have been but a few minutes later that she came over the rise and saw the three bright lights above the trees— say, by then it was 8:32.

Carol had pulled off the road, parked, walked down the gravel shoulder to the cut made by the dirt road through the trees. And so it would have been 8:40 at the very latest when she stood looking up at the lights. She had not been there for more than a couple of minutes before the light on the right streaked away from the others and hovered overhead. She had then looked up at its bluish light for maybe another two minutes until she turned to see where the other two had gone. Therefore, it should have been between 8:50 and 9:00 when she made the turn into the farm. How could it now be a quarter to ten? Where had that three-quarters of an hour gone?

Grace helped Carol to stand and walked her to a soft chair in the living room. Once she saw that Carol was comfortable, she brought her a drink and sat down with her. From where Carol was sitting she could see the clock on the fireplace mantel. It was nearly ten.

"How are you feeling now?" Grace asked.

Carol shook her head. "I don't understand what happened. Something happened and I'm losing my mind. Somewhere between the time I turned onto Route 32 and pulled into here I lost forty-five minutes!"

The following morning, Carol told Alice only the barest details of what had occurred: that she had seen the lights again, that she had gotten home late, and that something strange had happened with her earrings.

"I was afraid she'd fire me!" Carol explained to me at the hotel. "I thought, Oh God, if she finds out I'm crazy I'll have no place to live!"

Seeing how upset Carol was, Alice had tried to make light of the incident. She told Carol that she had probably just misread the clock in the car—and as for the earrings, maybe Carol had slept on them wrong.

At that time neither of the women had made any connection between what had happened to Carol and the appearance of what they had believed were UFOs.

"It wasn't until the next incident," Alice said, "that we knew something was wrong. That was about two weeks later, on January second, this year."

"The day after New Year's, 1992," Carol said.

On that first evening of the new year Carol had driven into the nearest town with good restaurants for an early business dinner. She and Alice were in the process of establishing and incorporating a riding center for handicapped children. The tax structure had already been pretty well worked out, and now they were lining up the nonprofit organizations that would help sponsor and run it. Because the immediate postholiday period was normally slow on the horse farm, Carol and one of her business associates from the corporation had decided to take advantage of the break to mix business and pleasure: they would enjoy a leisurely dinner and afterwards go over the paperwork. Carol would sign what had to be signed, and that would be it.

That evening, when they had finished, Carol and the associate walked out of the restaurant together. "Where are you parked?" the woman asked Carol.

"Around back."

"I'm out front," the woman said. "Before you go, walk me to my car. I've got a Christmas present for you and Alice."

At her car, the woman pulled out a shoebox-sized package elaborately wrapped with expensive Christmas paper and a beautiful red ribbon and bow.

"My God!" Carol said when she felt how heavy the gift was. "What have you *got* in here?"

"It's just food," the woman laughed. "Brownies and fruitcake and cookies and fudge."

"This is so great!" Carol said, beaming. "It's so nice of you to remember us. Thank you very much!"

"You're very welcome," the woman said, and started to get into her car. "Oh, wait," she said. "Do you know what time it is?"

Carol started to push up the sleeve of her heavy black velvet jacket, then remembered she had left her watch back at the farm. But a waitress was leaving the restaurant, and Carol called out to her for the time.

"Eight-thirty, give or take," the waitress said.

Just before leaving the restaurant Carol opened a fresh pack of cigarettes and slid it into her cigarette case. Now she tapped one out, lit it, climbed into the club cab of the farm's big Ford F-150 pickup truck, and drove through town until she could get back on the four-lane highway that continued southeast about thirteen miles to the turnoff onto Route 91, the two-lane-blacktop back road to the farm. The truck had dual gas tanks; one of the tanks was empty, the other registered a quarter full. The truck had had about a half-tank of gas when Carol started out for the restaurant; so despite the fact that the Ford only got about eight miles to the gallon when it wasn't hauling the horse trailer or anything more than one passenger, she knew she had just enough gas to make it home.

After the turnoff onto Route 91, Carol paused at the blinking red traffic light marking the intersection with the little shopping center that had closed. Farther along, the 7-Eleven convenience store was all lit up, but there was nobody there. It struck her as curious that at nine on a Thursday night no one was at the 7-Eleven buying beer.

It also seemed a little odd that the two low ranch houses across from the convenience store were dark; not a light shone in the windows of either. Still, Carol didn't think it was anything to make a big deal of, and she continued another three-quarters of a mile up Route 91, where there was a slight incline before the road made a gentle bend to the right.

It was at the top of that hill, just when Carol started into the curve, that she again saw the three lights.

They were ahead of her, about thirty degrees above the horizon, a little bit to her left. This time Carol was scared. "Oh, God!" she half-sobbed aloud. "I know what this is! *I know what this is!*"

As she watched the three lights come closer, getting brighter, Carol blinked. Suddenly she was not on Route 91, as she had been, but on Route 32, going forty-five miles per hour through the slow curve to the right past the open field at the top of the hill just before the groves of pines where she had seen the three bright white lights through the trees two and a half weeks before.

In the blink of an eye she had found herself eight miles away on a different road heading in a totally different direction on the other side of the farm! And out of some sort of reflexive animal terror she floored the accelerator.

"I remember blinking and *there I was!* I can't describe what that feels like!" Carol tells me. "I was so scared! *So scared!* I hit the gas! Hit it *hard!* I must have been doing at least sixty-five down that road trying to get home as fast as I could."

Carol sped to the farm and pulled into the driveway. Alice's younger brother, Greg, was visiting for the holidays. He was standing at the back door of the farmhouse when he saw the Ford race in. He watched the pickup skid to a halt in a shower of gravel, saw Carol kick open the door, tumble out, and he hurried over to help. Not saying a word, Greg helped Carol to her feet and brought her into the little office in the back of the farmhouse by the kitchen and sat her down. Alice's sister Grace took one look at Carol and worriedly asked, "What happened?"

Carol was hyperventilating. Her whole body was shaking. "I don't know!" she panted. "I don't want to do this anymore. I'm going out of my mind! I'm *crazy!* We better do something with me. I'm going to wreck all the farm's vehicles, kill myself, or I'm going to kill somebody else!"

Alice's brother left Carol with Grace and went out to put the pickup truck into the garage. Carol's briefcase, her purse, and the Christmas gift the woman had given her were all on the floor of the cab, where they had fallen. Greg picked them up, took one more look around to see if there was anything else to bring in, and carried Carol's belongings back into the house.

"Here," he said, passing Carol her cigarette case.

Carol opened the case; the pack inside was empty. "I just filled it!" she said, surprised. "All my cigarettes are gone. They must have spilled out onto the floor."

"I cleaned out the truck," Greg said. "I got everything. There's nothing left on the truck floor. Your briefcase was there; it had come open. Your purse was on the floor, too, upside down. And so was the Christmas present. Everything was on the floor, as if you had come to a sudden stop."

"I did," Carol said. "When I pulled up to the garage."

"No, I saw you come in," Greg said. "You skidded. You would have had to have stopped faster than that. There's another thing: the truck smells funny."

" 'Funny'? How? In what way?" Grace asked.

"I don't know. It smells . . ." Greg thought for a moment. "It smells heavy. Sort of a dense, thick smell. I don't know how else to describe it."

"Where's Alice?" Carol asked.

"Asleep," Grace said.

Carol glanced up at the kitchen clock, then shut her eyes. It was ten-thirty. Somewhere, she now suddenly realized, she had again lost nearly three-quarters of an hour. She began to shake uncontrollably.

The next morning, while Alice was at her EPA job in Washington, Carol was idly watching Grace straighten up around the Christmas package from the business associate. It was then that Carol noticed that the ribbon and bow were missing, that the wrapping paper had been pulled up on one side, and that one corner of the package had been clumsily repaired with masking tape. The original package, she knew, hadn't had any masking tape on it at all.

"Grace, let me see that package for a moment," Carol said.

Originally the gift had looked as if "it had been wrapped by a pro," Carol tells me. "Now it was just gross-looking, like some two-year-old kid had gotten ahold of it and tried to wrap it, and all he had was masking tape."

Carol was staring at the masking tape, thinking, This was *not* here before! What is going on? And then she lifted the package and *it didn't weigh anything!* It was like picking up half a cup of water, she later says. Before, it had been dense, like a two-pound box of fudge; now it felt hollow on one side. A few minutes later, when Grace removed the wrapping paper and opened the box, Carol saw that it contained only a half-dozen cookies and a couple of brownies. Her business associate the night before had said the box had also contained fruitcake and fudge. Where had they gone?

Carol knew neither Greg nor Grace had been into the box; Alice would not have opened it before she left for work. Who had opened it? And who had rewrapped it and sealed it with masking tape? They didn't use masking tape on the farm.

Carol went out to the truck to see if by any chance someone had left a roll of masking tape there. She looked between and behind the bucket seats, in the side pockets, and in the glove compartment. There was no masking tape to be found. She was just sitting in the cab behind the steering wheel when she, too, noticed the odor still remaining inside the truck.

Sitting with Alice and me that night in the Boston hotel, Carol describes the truck's smell as being "like a greenhouse on a hot summer night that had been closed up. It didn't feel hot; it just had all that organic smell of heat and high humidity."

There was something else Carol checked. She turned on the ignition and looked at the fuel gauges. There was still just about a quarter of a tank of gas remaining. There was no way, she knew, that she could have driven around for forty-five minutes the night before and not burned up the gas.

The next morning, Saturday, Carol and Alice discussed both what had happened the previous Thursday night and the incident two and a half weeks before when she returned with her earlobes bleeding. That Saturday morning was the first time they thought there might be a connection between those two events and having seen the lights.

"I think what we need to do is call somebody," Alice said. "There are organizations who investigate unusual phenomena."

"Alice was just looking for straws in the sky," Carol later told me. "She was looking for an excuse for what was happening that did not mean that *I* had lost control, but rather that control had been *taken* from me. If she wanted to make a hundred phone calls to weird people and find a weird explanation that would take the responsibility away from me, let her do it. But

I knew in the end I was still going to have to deal with the fact that I was having a mental breakdown without any idea of why it was happening."

In the Washington phone book under "UFO" Alice found "UFO, Fund for Research" and dialed the number. Don Berliner answered the phone. In addition to being founder of the Fund for UFO Research, Berliner is a UFO investigator and a prolific author of articles and books on aviation and space topics. Alice explained what Carol was going through, and Berliner said there were some people around who had been dealing with this. "We think we know what has happened," he said. "Let me have them give your friend a call."

"I don't know if she'll be willing to talk to anybody about it," Alice told him. "But we need somebody's help."

When Alice told Carol that someone from the Fund for UFO Research would be calling back, Carol said, "Fine, I'll talk to them, but I have nothing to say. If you stick the phone in my ear and I have no choice I'm not going to be rude. I'll tell them what happened, and they'll tell me to go to a psychiatrist, and that will be the end of that."

When, a couple of hours later, the fund's researcher, Rob Swiatek, returned Alice's call, it wasn't the end of it at all. Instead, Swiatek opened what Alice referred to as "a Pandora's box."

Carol learned she wasn't the only one who had seen strange lights in the sky and then experienced what Swiatek referred to as an "abduction" along with an episode of "missing time."

Carol had never heard of the phrase "missing time," or the word "abduction" linked with a sense of displacement. "I had never heard of *any* of that stuff!" she later said. "I thought it was all weird."

"Oh, by the way," Swiatek said. "Did you save the wrapping paper? I'd like to take a look at it. And," he added, "your earrings—I want to look at them, too."

Saturdays could be busy at the horse farm. Weekend riders, clients who boarded horses, and various other people were continually passing through the house. Carol could hear Alice in the little office off the kitchen talking to the woman who came in on Saturdays to help out.

There was some wrapping paper in the dining room and Carol picked it up. She didn't see any masking tape on it, but she didn't bother to check if it the was the right paper, because she was thinking, what did it matter? None of this stuff is real anyway, she told herself, so who cares?

She started toward the kitchen on her way to the office so she could hand the Christmas wrapping paper to Alice to give to Swiatek, but as she entered the kitchen she suddenly felt a strange sensation, half-physical, half-emotional—a lightheadedness coupled with the premonition that she was about to remember something. She was walking past the refrigerator with the wrapping paper still in her hand when suddenly she wasn't in the kitchen anymore.

In her mind Carol wasn't in the kitchen; she wasn't anywhere on the farm. She was seated in a strange, enclosed space, and, she tells me, she was nude.

She was sitting crouched forward, her arms lying across her thighs, palms up. Something was pressing against the small of her back, holding her forward. It wasn't a board or a seat back; it felt more like a rod. It wasn't *pushing* her; it was just a steady pressure bracing her, holding her still. Carol didn't resist it. She didn't think she could resist it. She felt paralyzed.

She could not turn her head; she could move just her eyes, and only from side to side. Carol tried to see where she was. She didn't understand what was going on. She became aware how cold she was. It was the kind of cold that invaded her bones. She looked down at her arms and realized for the first time she was no longer wearing the long-sleeved black velvet jacket with the cuffs she had had on at the restaurant earlier that evening at dinner with the business associate who had given her the gaily wrapped Christmas gift of brownies, fruitcake, cookies, and fudge.

Suddenly Carol sensed she wasn't alone; someone else was there—maybe even more than one person. But she couldn't see. When she tried to look up, ahead of her, she saw only a dense, gray mist—except she knew it wasn't mist, because it didn't move. There was no breeze, no air to stir it. It just hung there like an impenetrable wall of cobwebs, and Carol felt trapped. She felt trapped and paralyzed and out of control. And then, when she detected a movement off to the right out of the corner of her eye, she felt scared.

She *knew* she was scared, she tells me, but until then she had never realized how scared she could be: straining to look to her right as far as she could, she saw those *hands* holding the Christmas package.

She saw those hands and her face screwed up, her throat tightened, and she started to lose it—because *they weren't HUMAN hands!*

They looked like a huge tree frog's hands, except the fingers were a dull, chocolate-charcoal brown! And they didn't have any *joints* in them.

Oh God, this is really crazy! Carol thought. And she started to cry, because she knew what she was seeing was *real*—that these were *real hands!* And Carol got the feeling that they were holding the Christmas package as if to say, "*Whoa!* What is *this?* This is the prettiest thing I've ever seen!"

It was, she explains to me, as if she were seeing a little child pick up something more beautiful than anything it had ever held before in its life.

And while Carol was watching those hands holding the package, she was thinking, What the hell *is* this? What is this *thing?* And she was still staring at those fingers, at the way they looked like they were made out of hose.

She couldn't see any knuckles; the fingers had no definition except for their somewhat spatulate tips. And there weren't but *three* fingers on either hand. Furthermore, there didn't seem to be a thumb. All Carol could see were the three brownish-gray fingers of the right hand curled two above and one below the lower right-hand corner of the Christmas package, and two fingers of the left hand cradling the bottom left corner of the box between them.

The *thing,* whatever it was, was holding the box out in front of itself as if to study it. It didn't tilt it or shake it from side to side. Carol could not see the creature's body, or its head or face. All Carol could see were its two three-fingered hands poking through the mist, holding the Christmas package, and she stopped breathing. She was thinking, I can't accept this! I don't know what this is! I *won't* accept it! But she could not stop staring at those hands.

The more Carol looked at the creature's hands, the more frightened she became. She knew she was beginning to panic, but she couldn't control it. Her eyes seemed fixed on the thing's tree-frog fingers and she was *terrified.* She was hyperventilating; she wanted to scream, she tells me—tried to scream, "What *are* you? What *is* this? What are you *doing?*" But no sound would come out.

Carol was telling herself, Don't look at those hands! Don't look! They'll go away if you don't look! But she couldn't stop staring at them. She couldn't even blink. She couldn't close her eyes. Instead she felt compelled to look at the creature's charcoal-brown hands out of the corners of her eyes and she was so frightened she had begun to tremble. She could feel her whole body shaking.

And then, toward her face out of the mist, there came another chocolate-brown three-fingered hand, and two of its flattened fingertips touched her eyelids, pressed them closed, and immediately Carol felt just fine.

All of a sudden she felt, Carol explains, exactly like she had in the sixties when she had smoked a little Acapulco Gold and would reach that stage in a high where everything in the world felt wonderful, but not yet funny—that point right before the giggles. Only now, she says, she wasn't sitting on a hilltop smoking marijuana with a bunch of friends; she was with strange creatures in an entirely strange place, bent forward, naked, with her arms across her lap, palms up, thinking, Why am I frightened? This isn't so bad. I feel fine. This is good. . . .

And then she felt someone shaking her and calling her name.

"I found Carol collapsed on the floor at the edge of the kitchen," Alice tells me at my Boston hotel. "It was like she was reliving all this stuff and all I could do was hold her."

"And I was going, 'What? What? What?' " Carol says.

She leans forward to tap a cigarette out of her case, takes her time lighting it, drawing in the smoke, then exhales slowly as she sits back again in
the couch. "That was the end of the memory, or the flashback, or whatever
it was," she tells me, adding, "I didn't know what it was! All I knew was that
something had happened, or that I had had this memory of something happening—only it wasn't a *memory.* I was actually reliving it. I wasn't *remembering* it happening, I was going through the whole event—whatever that
event was. . . .

"It felt like it was happening for the first time," Carol continues. "But I
wondered if maybe the flashback was a memory of what happened during
the time lapse when I was in the truck on January second, because I think
the wrapping paper is what stimulated the flashback—if it was a flashback.
But what was comical about the whole thing—if it could ever be termed
'comical'—was that what had triggered the flashback was the wrong wrapping paper."

"It was not the same paper from the truck," Alice explains.

When Don Berliner and Rob Swiatek from the Fund for UFO Research
later examined the masking tape on the correct Christmas wrapping paper,
it did not differ in any way from tapes commonly available.

The following weekend, on Sunday morning, January 12, Carol awoke
in Pennsylvania with blood on her sheets. She had been invited to stay at a
large farm there to give a three-day seminar, conference, and clinic to approximately twenty-five horse people. Alice had not gone up with her. The
clinic was to end Sunday afternoon; Carol would spend one more night,
then drive back down to Maryland on Monday morning. Sunday morning
she awoke with her right hand bleeding, and when she washed it, she found
what resembled a burn between the base of her little finger and the wrist of
her right hand, and had no memory whatsoever of how she might have obtained the injury. Carol bandaged her hand, completed the horse clinic, and
returned as planned to Alice's farm.

For the next two weeks, according to Carol, the wound continued to
throb and sting; but it was only when she removed the bandage and saw a
black line forming a perfect triangle around the borders of the injury and,
just outside the black line, a thinner white line, which Carol worried might
indicate an infection, that she decided someone ought to take a look at it.

One of the horse farm's boarding clients, a registered nurse at the local
hospital, looked at Carol's wrist, twisting it back and forth under the light.
"It looks like a chemical burn of some kind," she said. "What did you *do* to
yourself? The strange thing is that the wound has a laser-sharp edge, like a
laser cut," the nurse explained. "Laser cuts make a perfectly smooth outline
that leave a black edge."

When, at the nurse's insistence, Carol showed her wrist to a doctor, the doctor said the wound could only have been caused by some very caustic material being applied to the end of a triangular object which was then pressed against Carol's hand long enough to burn through three layers of skin. He told Carol he could not understand how she could not know when or how it had happened. "I mean, it would have been *very* painful," the doctor told her. "Even if you were drugged you could not have slept through it."

"Well, it happened while I was sleeping," Carol replied. "And I did sleep through it."

In the middle of the night on February 12, a month after the Pennsylvania incident, Carol was wakened by the sensation of something pulling on her leg. The next morning she discovered a huge bruise on her right thigh and the livid prints of three fingers on her leg. She also had three fresh puncture wounds forming a new triangle on her right thumb. She had no idea what might have caused them.

The next incident occurred at about 7:20 p.m. on Sunday evening, March 8. Carol was again returning from her parents' house in Hagerstown at the wheel of Alice's small red Toyota. She had left Interstate 70 and was on Route 32 past the B&O railroad tracks, driving up a long incline on the other side of a small town with a country store, when the Toyota's dashboard warning lights flashed on, then off. The car's engine died, the power steering and headlights went out, and Carol had to muscle the darkened, powerless car toward the shoulder of the road, where there would be adequate clearance to be safe. She pulled the emergency brake, put the gears in neutral, and twisted the ignition key. There was no ignition, no starter grind, but the headlights came back on.

To conserve the battery, she turned off the headlights and put on the hazard warning flashers. At first she thought somebody would come by to help her, but then she noticed there was no other traffic on the road.

Carol got out of the car to peer under the hood. She didn't have a flashlight, and she couldn't really see anything well enough to know what to look for. So she left the hood up and went back into the car to wait. The only living creature she saw was a wild turkey. It came out of the brush, walked to the middle of the road, and just stood there looking at her for a few moments. The turkey then strolled to the other side of the road, where it remained.

About five minutes later, a white car came over the top of the hill from the opposite direction toward her; the car slowed as it passed, then continued on. Carol had been unable to see who was in the car, whether it was a man or a woman driving. She couldn't see through its windshield. But she could see that the wild turkey was still at the side of the road. A few minutes later, the white car came up behind her, slowed down as it passed her, then accelerated back up and over the hill.

"You *jerk!*" Carol angrily said to its driver.

When the white car came back over the hill a third time and slowed as it passed her, Carol grew apprehensive. She watched the car in her rearview mirror as it descended into the little town, pulled in by the country store, turned around, came back up the hill, and stopped on the shoulder behind her with its high beams on.

The car's headlights were so bright Carol had to tip the mirror down so she wouldn't be blinded. Then she locked the car doors just to be safe. The window on her side was cracked about an inch to let some air in; the other windows were shut tight. As she looked in the side-view mirror, she saw the silhouette of somebody getting out of the car. Whoever he was, he was tall, at least six feet. And he was wearing a Stetson hat that must have been at least four feet across. Whoa! she thought. That hat is *huge!*

She remembers the person coming up to her driver's side and asking, "Are you having car trouble? Is something wrong?"

"Yes," Carol told him, "my car died. I don't know what's wrong with it. It won't start."

He had a flashlight with him and went around to the front of the car. Carol could see him looking down at the engine, flashing the light around, and then he said, "Start the car."

Carol threw in the clutch, twisted the key in the ignition, and nothing happened. She tried again. Still nothing.

The figure in the huge hat came around to the passenger side and said something; Carol couldn't hear what he said, so she cracked the window on that side and asked him to repeat it. "I don't know what's wrong with it," he said. "Do you see that light up there?"

Carol looked across the road beyond him. Up the hill, through the trees, she could just make out a light. "Yes, I see it," she said.

"Well, go up to that house and make a phone call. They'll let you use the phone."

"Okay," she said. She thanked him for having at least made the effort to stop. And then she waited until he had gotten back into his white car and driven off. She remained in her car until she saw a truck coming over the hill toward her; then she quickly got out, locked the car's door, paused until she was sure the truck would see her, and crossed in front of it. She wasn't sure why she did that, but she thought it important to make sure the truck driver could see that there was a woman out there alone in case that weird fellow in the huge Stetson came back.

Usually Carol can see well in the dark; she possesses considerably better night vision than most. But that night, as she climbed the gravel driveway to the house, she could barely distinguish the side of the road from the trees, and she felt she was tripping all over her feet. She kept slipping on the loose gravel, stumbling in potholes as she walked and walked and walked up the seemingly endless driveway toward the light.

In the darkness she didn't see the automobile parked at the top of the drive and struck her leg on its bumper. She felt her way around to the car's other side and came to what seemed to be a narrow flight of steep stairs up the bank to the house.

Carol was leery of the steps; she worried that if she fell and hurt herself, it might be twenty-four hours before anyone would find her. Instead, she walked up the bank toward the bright yellow bug light above the back door. She knocked and was startled to have the door opened immediately by an elderly woman. Next to her stood a large black Labrador retriever wagging its tail.

Carol apologized for showing up at her door in the middle of the night and said, "I know this sounds like a terrible cliché, but my car has broken down. May I use your telephone?"

"Oh, you poor dear! What an awful thing!" the woman said. "Of course you can use the phone. Come in! Come in!"

Carol followed the old woman through what she could now see was an old log house, then up a narrow flight of stairs to the newer second-story addition containing the living room.

Alice answered the telephone on the third ring, and when Carol told her what had happened, Alice said she'd be there within twenty minutes to a half hour.

Carol thanked the old woman for letting her use the phone and followed her back down the cramped staircase to the back door. The woman had to wrestle the Lab to keep the dog from following Carol out. Carol closed the back door behind her, walked down the bank, and suddenly could see everything clearly. She assumed her eyes had merely adjusted to the dark; but then she noticed it took her just seconds to walk the length of the driveway back to Route 32 and her car. Now she could see the gravel, the potholes, the bushes on the other side of the ditch, and behind them the trees. From the bottom of the earthen ramp to the end of the drive could not have been more than fifty feet; and yet, when she was walking up to the house, the driveway had seemed a *mile*, at least!

Carol crossed to her car, slipped inside, and sat waiting for Alice to arrive.

Twenty minutes later Alice came over the top of the rise in the Ford pickup, passed Carol in the opposite direction, and continued down to the country store at the bottom of the hill to turn around. At the warehouse next to the country store Alice noticed a white car parked with someone standing beside it. And as she turned and paused before heading back out onto the road, the person got into his car and drove up behind her. She stopped, watching in her rearview mirror, waiting for him to pull around to see which way he was going to turn, right or left; but then, suddenly, he was no longer there. The car wasn't behind her anymore, and Alice had no idea how he could have simply disappeared.

On the way back to the farm Carol told Alice what had happened and how tired she was, adding, "God, it seems like midnight."

"It's only nine-thirty," Alice said; and Carol realized she was again missing time.

Retracing her trip, Carol figured it had been seven-thirty when she pulled off the interstate and maybe ten minutes later when the car went dead. "I couldn't have sat in that car more than fifteen minutes," she told Alice. "Which would have made it only about eight o'clock when the man in the big hat stopped by. I *wouldn't* have sat there for an *hour* and fifteen minutes. I mean, that's ludicrous! I'm not that stupid! I'd have gone out and found a phone even if I'd had to walk back down the hill to that country store!" Carol paused for a moment and asked herself, "Why *didn't* I? Why *didn't* I do that? There must have been a public phone."

"Because the man told you to make the call from that house," Alice said.

"But why didn't I go to that *store* and call?" she asked. "And how come, according to you, it was five past nine when I called?"

The next afternoon, Carol led a tow truck to where she'd left Alice's Toyota. She gave the mechanic the key so he could unlock the car and prepare it for towing. He opened the door, slid behind the steering wheel, and said, "*Whew!* Did you have a fire in here?"

It took a week and a half to fix the Toyota. As Alice later explained, "Its whole electrical system was fried."

It was then that Carol attempted to discover on her own what had happened. She had, in the past, done self-hypnosis for relaxation purposes and decided to hypnotize herself in Alice's presence to make herself remember what had taken place when the car's electrical system had shorted out.

Everything was just as Carol remembered it: the Toyota died, she pulled to the side of the road, looked under the hood, got back in the car; the white car went by once, twice, a third time, and then turned around and pulled up behind her with its high beams on. Carol looked into the side-view mirror. . . . Everything, so far, had been just as she had recalled. But now, when she looked at the man reflected in her mirror, he was *naked!* At least she *thought* he was naked.

"Here was this *naked man* with a *cowboy hat* standing in the middle of the road with the high beams on of his car," Carol explains to me in the Boston hotel, "and I'm going, This is *wild!* I'm in the middle of the road with a stalled car and a kook who's naked, and he's the *only one who bothered to stop!* What are my odds here?"

Carol remembered it was so funny she couldn't be scared. "He stopped by me and said, 'What's wrong?' and I said, 'The car won't start,' " her recollection continues. "All of that was the same, except I'm trying not to laugh! The whole time I'm thinking, God, don't laugh! If this man's crazy, he could kill you if you laugh! But I couldn't control it! I'm covering my mouth with my hand so he won't see me and he goes by and looks under the hood. He has his flashlight—or there's some kind of light he's shining around the engine. And I look at his body through the crack between the back of the raised hood and the top of the dashboard, and I don't see a bellybutton or—or *anything!* There are no physical features, but there aren't any clothes, either. And he's white. Like a real pale, shiny white. And then I heard the voice.

"I heard it say, 'Start the car,' " Carol continues. "Only the voice came from *inside* my head! Like it was somebody standing right at the back of my skull speaking into it. I snapped my head around to see if someone was behind me, but there was nobody there. I *knew* there wouldn't be anybody there. And so I heard this 'Start the car' only inside my head. It did not come from in front of the car. It couldn't have through the raised hood, all that glass and closed windows. It was almost an order, like 'Don't question this: *Start* the car, *now!*'

"I tried to start the car, and, of course, it wouldn't start. Just the way I remembered it," Carol says. "Nothing happened. And he walked around to the passenger side of the car and leaned over and looked in the window, and this was the first time I really *saw* him. He had this huge Stetson which I thought was gigantic—and it *was* gigantic. *But so was his head!*

"This fellow had a head the size of three basketballs put together inside a hat that *fit* him! It wasn't that his hat was big, it was his *head* that was big! All I could see was one side of his face illuminated by his car's high beams. His whole side was in deep shadow. And it looked like he had wraparound sunglasses on, like aviator's glasses. And there were wrinkles, deep furrows or something, right at the bridge of his nose, and these lines or tucks down his cheekbone. But the weirdest thing was that he had this mustache hanging down from this little grape of a nose, this thing with sort of a rounded knob at the end.

Despite her self-hypnosis, Carol couldn't remember anything about the walk from her stalled car to the house until, as she told me, she had a flashback during one of the regular Saturday-evening horse-related seminars held on the farm. She got about halfway through her presentation when suddenly she flashed back to the gravel driveway leading up to the half-log-cabin house:

There was somebody—or some*thing*—a little behind her, to her left, walking like a machine with short, little, mechanical steps: *thump-thump-thump-thump. . . .*

Carol had the sensation that he—or it—was there to escort her: to make certain she went where she was supposed to. She couldn't understand how its footsteps could be so regular while hers were so stumbling and erratic.

She looked up toward the end of the driveway, which now, she realized, wasn't that far. She saw a car parked at the top and a person standing by the car's left bumper—except he didn't really look like a person. He didn't because he was *glowing!*

It was as though he was backlit; only, Carol knew, there wasn't a light behind him. She could distinguish the car clearly enough to see that it was a maroon Chrysler K-car with blue-and-gray-striped cloth seat covers; but she could not make out the features of the person next to it, or any distinct outlines. She could tell he was short: no more than three and a half or four feet tall. She was looking straight at him and walking toward him as if she really wanted to go to him—even though she knew she *didn't.* And as she approached this small, glowing Being, he raised his right hand toward her. She could not see if there was anything in it. He pointed at her and she remembered nothing else.

Carol's flashback was videotaped. "All our seminars are videotaped," Carol explains, "so when you look at the videotape you can see that there's a brief break in my presentation. You see me bring my hand up to my eyes as if I've lost my train of thought. There's a short pause and then I continue with the seminar. If you hadn't known what was going on, you wouldn't have known what was going on. I don't think anybody noticed."

Carol subsequently drove back to the house near which the incident with the man in the Stetson had occurred. The house was really there, as was the steep bank beside it. Parked at the end of the short, gravel driveway was a maroon K-car with blue-and-gray-striped seat covers.

"What do you think actually happened?" I ask.

"This is the reverse of what I ever would have thought I'd say or think," Carol replies, "but my *logical* side, my rational side, tells me something happened to me on that road. And whoever, or *whatever* it was, thought a real good disguise to relax a horse person by would be to show up as a cowboy. My logical, rational side tells me that it was all set up for me to go up that particular driveway at that particular time, and I was either escorted into a flying saucer, or . . . or I was abducted." She pauses for a moment, then laughs. "That's what my *logical* side tells me happened. My *emotional* side says, 'Nyahhh! You're *crazy!* You imagined the whole thing.' "

Alice, reclining next to Carol on my Boston hotel room couch, pointedly asks, "What about the missing hour?"

Alice then describes her problems with electrical objects: the banks of streetlights that will blink out as she drives by; the illuminated overhead turnpike entrance and exit signs that go dark as she passes beneath them; store lights that shut off as she nears, or how televisions will malfunction, and radios hiss and crackle with static. Recently both her home and office computers have developed "lethal errors" when she attempts to use them.

"When I switched to the other computer at work," Alice tells me, "that one had the same problem: keyboard errors. While I was sitting there, we had an inexplicable power failure in that half of the station. Maintenance checked on it and said, 'This is weird, because it's a connected system where the whole work station should be either on or off.' And it wasn't. Only the back half was off. They finally fixed it after a couple of days. They had to take the work station apart because the wiring between the two halves of the work station had somehow gotten fried. And they'd never had that happen before."

I ask Alice what scared her most.

For a long moment she is silent. "I think what is really scaring me is not remembering, not knowing," she says, and begins to cry quietly. "Not knowing, but knowing somewhere in the back of my memory there's an awful lot of stuff. And I'm *afraid* of it! I think that's why I'm afraid of hypnosis."

Alice pauses to dry her eyes. "My memories aren't like Carol's. I have very few conscious memories," she explains. "In some ways Carol has validation: she *knows* what's going on. All I know is I have a lot of inexplicable things that seem to indicate, *yes,* I've been through things similiar to Carol. But instead of conscious memories all I have is fear."

"What makes you think you've been through things like Carol?" I ask.

"Scars. I have a couple of scars that I've always explained away. They could be 'scoop marks.' I don't have any conscious memories of missing time, but there have been many mornings when I've woken up where it's followed the conference pattern: you don't remember putting your nightgown on inside out, but when you wake up it's inside out; or you're upside down in the bed. They're just the sort of little things that lead me to think something might be there. I've never slept well. I always used to have nightmares when I was a kid, but I have no idea what they were about. I slept on the top bunk bed; my sister Grace slept on the bottom. Every so often my parents would find me on the floor because I had fallen out without waking up. And there were other things I used to explain away. . . ."

"Things that happened when you were a child?" I ask.

Alice nods. "I had an awful lot of nosebleeds."

"And do you now think these were caused by implants?"

"No, I think I was just a kid with bloody noses. But I used to wake up in the morning with fingerprints on my arms, two or three fingerprints on my upper arms. I bruise easily. I just assumed somebody grabbed me and I didn't remember it. And there would be bruises on my body that were big enough that I'd think, 'Gee, I really ought to be able to remember where I got that!' But I never could, and the bruising was another thing I used to just explain away."

"The nightmares, the bruises, the marks on your body all could be indications of physical abuse as a child," I say.

"Maybe it is," Alice says noncommittally. "Maybe that's a simpler explanation."

"What is your relationship with your family now?"

"My sister, Grace, and my brother, Greg, are staying with me now," Alice says. "My mother died of cancer several years ago. And my father lives in Florida."

"Are you close?"

"To my father?" Alice asks. She looks at me, trying to decide whether to answer, and then she says, "Not really."

I say nothing.

"I was a strange child," Alice says, then alternating between tears and a determination to be objective, she tells me about her childhood.

"I was always very different from most of my family," Alice explains. "My grandmother, my father's mother, never accepted me. She was convinced when I was brought home from the hospital that they'd mixed up the children. That there was no possibility I could be her grandchild. My father's side was dark, Germanic. My mother had brown eyes and dark hair. Both my brother and sister have dark eyes and dark hair; I'm blond and blue-eyed. But my mother had two sisters, one who was blond and the other a redhead. That was the Norwegian side of the family. And since in a lot of ways I look so much like my sister, the same build, and that whole side of the family . . . yes, I really know I'm my mother's child."

"Were you a happy child?"

"No," she says. I see her eyes fill with tears. "I felt abandoned as a child. I was convinced my parents didn't love me. My father was very authoritarian. He was career military. We always had more fun when he was gone, because he'd be abroad for a year or so. But then it was always 'Wait until your father gets home.' And we'd put on extra pairs of underwear and jeans because we knew we'd get beaten with a belt or a paddle. That was normal."

"So it was primarily physical abuse?" I ask.

Alice starts to say "Yes," then hesitates. She glances at Carol and then back at me. I get the impression she is deciding how far she should go.

What follows next is a confusing account of a fishing trip Alice took in Florida with her father when she was twelve and her suspicions that he had raped her on the banks of a canal. She reports matter-of-factly their not speaking afterwards, her coming home with blood in her underpants, and her father's evident puzzlement that she would never go fishing alone with him again.

Alice then immediately tells me of having been in love with "a guy in high school. We were going to get married and stuff. And my parents said, 'You go to college, then you get married. Have a life first!' And we broke up, of course. But senior year in high school we were talking about getting married, having a dozen kids, the whole bit. At one point I thought I was pregnant. My period was a couple of weeks late, and we sort of had a celebration when it finally came. And then some time later, when I was in college, I realized I hated children. I couldn't stand them! I can't be around them!" she says, and bursts into tears.

The link between children and Small Grays is an obvious one, and I am trying to figure out how to bring this up when Alice tells me about the curious dreams she and Carol had the same night about a month before the conference.

"It was very, very disturbing and, I guess, clinched what people had been talking about at the conference for me," Alice says. "Last month I dreamed I saw four little gray guys standing to my left. I realized they were the Grays and said, 'Oh, it's them.' I wasn't panicked. I felt maybe a little fear, nothing more. But it woke me. I looked at the clock. It was four-fifteen, and then I went back to sleep. The next morning, I mentioned my dream to Carol. And she asked me what time it had been, because, she said, she had had a strange dream, too—a dream within a dream, really. She dreamed she awoke from a dream and saw one gray guy peeking out from behind the dresser in the doorway of her bedroom. She knew it was a Gray, and then, in her dream, she went back to sleep and woke up again and—"

"This time I knew there were two gray guys in the room," Carol interrupts. "I sat up in bed and saw two of them standing at the end of my bed just watching me. I tried to call Alice, but I don't think I could do more than whisper her name a few times. They didn't come any closer, so eventually I became sleepy again and just lay back down. But when I awoke in the morning my alarm clock was blinking, which means the power had gone off some time during the night. Then I hit the button that recalls the clock's last registered time before the outage and it read four-fifteen."

"So it was the same time as mine," Alice says. "But what was so scary was that after I saw those four little gray guys I developed symptoms like I was pregnant."

About a week after the dream, Alice explains, her breasts became tender and enlarged. She was crampy, with twinges and aches in her ovaries and abdomen; she had lower back pain. Her period was not normal. "It came and went in two days with a lot of pain," Alice explains. "I finally went to a doctor. He was convinced I was pregnant; I had all the signs of it. He did a pregnancy test which came back negative. And then he did an ultrasound, CAT scans. I thought it was cancer," she says, smiling wryly. "Anything was preferable to being pregnant. But there was nothing there! But just after I had the ultrasound examination I started having another period, within sixteen days of the previous one. This time there were no cramps, no pain. Nothing. I don't know what's going on. I have these erotic dreams. I don't know what's causing it. Something's going on."

"Had you had sexual intercourse during those past months?" I ask.

"Only in my dreams," Alice says, smiling sadly. "But within the last two months I had a very erotic dream. *Including* penetration. And I was sore the next day. But I have no conscious memories of it! I don't know what happened."

Later I ask Carol and Alice what impact this conference has had on them.

"First of all, overload," Carol says. "It's been very intense."

"But wonderful," Alice adds. "It was the first time we could talk to other people, that we haven't had to be afraid of talking about all this. What really helped me the most is to find other people who experienced things similar to what I experienced. And we could sit down and *talk* about it! I mean, Carol and I weren't *alone* anymore. And for me, that was really, really good. But there were some scary things."

"Like what?" I ask.

"Some of the things they were discussing," Alice responds. "Some of the bits and pieces they brought out. Carol and I would sort of look at each other and go—"

" 'One more down the tubes,' " Carol finishes.

"One more what?"

"One more of our rational explanations for what had happened to us," Carol says. "We'd hear someone else talking about the same thing happening to somebody else and I'd go, 'Oh, shit!' "

"Like what?" I ask.

"I guess the first one down the tubes for me," Alice says, "was when Hopkins was talking about scars. And he said, 'Primarily they're on the long bones, the legs, below the knees; but there are a lot of people who have scars on their arms and even on their faces.' And I thought, Oh, shit, because I've had a sort of scoop mark on my face ever since I was a child, and I started thinking about the explanation for it when I was a little kid—"

"That explanation was crazy!" Carol interrupts, laughing.

"The explanation was that when I was little I had a pinwheel on a stick and I was standing out there in the wind and I put the base of the dowel holding the pinwheel to my face and let the pinwheel turn. And that was what had left the scar."

"Right," Carol says sarcastically. "And can you imagine doing that to yourself until it made a hole in your face and drew blood?"

"I want to get back to your feelings about the conference," I say. "What was it like for you the first day?"

"Scary," Alice says. "I was scared of new people, of new things I might learn. When I arrived here, I was still excited about learning what was going on and finding out more. I was being all very rational, all very logical, but that first day was real scary. A lot of it, I think, was because I didn't know anybody. Richard Hall was our only contact here. It was such a relief to see him!"

"He was more scared than we were," Carol says.

"Why was that?" I ask.

"Because, in some ways, this abduction stuff is new to him, too," Alice answers.

"I had a problem with Richard at the beginning of the conference," Carol says. "I told Alice the second day, Sunday, I said, 'Richard is *avoiding* me! Why is he avoiding me? He's the only person we've got here!' I really wanted his support for that panel we were on that night. And Alice goes, 'He's not avoiding you. You're being paranoid. I never saw him avoid you.' And I thought, 'Well, I'm going to talk to him, because I feel this need to get it out.' So I asked Richard outright, 'What's wrong? Why don't you want to talk to me?' And he apologized and said, 'In all honesty you scare me. You frighten me.'

"I said, 'What do you mean, I frighten you?' " Carol continues. " 'You're my support system! How can I frighten you?'

"And Richard said, 'Because I can't help you,' " Carol says. " 'It's too intense,' he told me. 'It scares me and I don't want to do the wrong thing.' But then he did come around. He came and talked to me whenever he saw me."

"When I saw Richard the first day, I felt very, very relieved," Alice tells me. "I knew there was someone here we could trust."

"What about the other abductees?" I ask.

"We had Virginia, of course," Alice says. "We had talked to her on the phone extensively before we got here. The rest of the people were all strangers. Some of the names we recognized; we'd read a lot of their books and stuff. But I have this problem with famous people. I don't stay around them. I don't deal with them. I'm sort of put off by their famousness."

"Who were the 'famous people'?" I ask.

"Budd Hopkins," Alice says. "Dave Jacobs. John Carpenter. Bruce Maccabee—"

"Who's Bruce Maccabee?" I ask.

"Maccabee is sort of a clearinghouse for tapes and films. He analyzes them and stuff," Carol explains. "But the famous people, almost to a man, weren't terribly interested in talking to us 'experiencers,' heaven forbid, directly. They would talk to our researchers, our psychologists—"

"Or their own experiencers," Alice says.

"Or their own group. But they would not talk to those of us not connected directly with them, *unless* we said something during the panel discussion that struck them in some way. And then," Carol says with a little laugh, "they'd beat down doors to get to us, whether we wanted to talk to them or not."

We speak for a while about the other abductees and how their experiences relate to Carol's and Alice's. Alice feels that most of them are at a different point than she is; that they accept elements of the phenomenon that she is not yet willing to believe are true for her. "I'm sorry," Alice tells me, "but I cannot believe these gray guys are doing good things, that they're the old Space Brothers and goodness and light and wonderful stuff. I don't have any trouble with *their* believing it, because it helps these experiencers cope. But no, I can't believe that."

"I'm like Alice," Carol says. "I don't think these other experiencers are wrong just because they believe what they do and I don't. It's just very hard for me to accept at this time."

Alice nods and says, "I think that's what a lot of the experiencers were asking for at the conference: 'Don't put all of us in the same box. And don't try to make us fit the same box.' I think there are several boxes around, and . . ." She pauses for a moment, then adds, "I was going to say that I think they're all valid. But I don't think some of them are."

I ask Alice what "box" she feels she fits in.

"I guess I'm still back with the 'nuts and bolts,' " she says, smiling. "With Budd Hopkins and Dave Jacobs. These gray guys are not benign. They're doing things to us against our will. And the most frightening thing ever is, we have no control."

"And I don't think we ever will," Carol adds.

"We won't," Alice says bitterly. "It doesn't matter what we do or think. They're going to do whatever they want anyway."

"And I think they're going to do it fairly soon. Oh! I didn't want to say that!" Carol says, putting her fingertips to her lips. "I didn't really mean to say it out loud. I don't know why I feel that, I just do. I've believed it strongly—even though I don't know what it is I believe—from the beginning: that we're building tremendous momentum for something spectacular. Spectacularly good or bad, I don't know. Something really monumental is about to happen, and I don't know if we experiencers/abductees are involved personally or not."

"I think it's part of their disinformation," Alice says quietly. "From the stuff I've read, they've done this to people for so long: 'Oh, yes, next week or next year is the year. That's when it's going to happen.' The aliens have lied every time."

"But it's not the kind of feeling where you're going to want to run out into the streets carrying a sign saying, 'The World Is Going to End Tomorrow,' " Carol says. "It's more a gut feeling that goes all the way inside you and says, 'Something is about to happen. You can't stop it.' "

"Does that worry you?" I ask.

"I don't get overexcited about it. It's just there. I can't make it go away."

"And you don't know where it comes from, or whether it's good or bad?" I ask.

"No," she says simply. "I'm not hearing 'voices.' It has never changed in intensity from the beginning."

"When was the beginning?"

"I got that first feeling after the initial car episode, when I came back with my earlobes bleeding and I thought I was having a nervous breakdown."

The three of us are quiet for a moment.

I break the silence, saying, "I guess what strikes me is the loneliness. You abductees are dealing with something that the rest of us don't understand. And not only do we not understand it, some of us feel hostile to what you're telling us. We don't want to hear it. We don't believe you, or we're unsympathetic to you, or we think you're crazy."

"We've always felt extremely sorry for the many people we know out there who are alone," Carol says. "People who are trying to deal with this and come home to an empty house or—"

"—a husband or wife—" Alice adds.

"—they can't talk to," Carol finishes. "A friend or roommate they can't talk to. They have no one to turn to, nowhere to turn. They think they're crazy! And it's so *hard* on them! We have each other," she says, looking to Alice, "Thank God for that! Even if we don't know what we have, we have each other."

"But sometimes even that's not enough," Alice says.

"No," Carol agrees, "sometimes it's not. Because sometimes we feed on each other's fears. We scare each other even when we try not to. Sometimes we are so logical, we fail to see. We close all the doors and say, 'I *refuse* to believe that! That's just *too* bizarre! So I won't accept it.' "

"Like what?" I ask.

"Like the black helicopters when they first showed up," Alice responds.

There have been accounts in various UFO periodicals of "black helicopters" occasionally being seen in areas where UFO encounters have allegedly taken place. Nobody is quite sure what the helicopters mean or what they are supposed to represent. They have no apparent markings, dark-tinted glass, and may or may not leave a prop wash. According to these reports, the helicopters fly low, harassing passes over the homes and properties of people who have had UFO experiences. Depending on the various theories, the "black helicopters" either are part of the government involvement in the UFO cover-up conspiracy or are UFOs themselves, taking the form of helicopters.

When black helicopters began appearing over Alice's horse farm, she didn't pay much attention to them. "We said, 'Oh, don't worry about it,' " Alice tells me, " 'We get overflights of all kinds of stuff all the time.' And that was okay until Mother's Day, when Carol was over at her parents' house in Hagerstown and her sister looked out the window and said, 'What's this black helicopter doing up here?' Well, sure enough, when Carol went out the kitchen to the backyard, where they were preparing a barbecue, here was this little black helicopter going back and forth a little bit over the house."

"And then it would stop," Carol says.

"What was its altitude?" I ask.

"Probably about five hundred feet," Carol answers. "It was loud! The windows were rattling. We watched it from the back deck. It would go across, then stop about two hundred yards away. It would sit and hover at about five hundred feet, just looking at us. Then it would move off, sit and hover; move back, sit and hover. Finally, we got tired of looking at it and we went into the house and it went away."

"That was the last time we saw them," Alice says. "Mother's Day. Almost the beginning of April."

"We need somebody to try and help us sort out all of this stuff," Alice says. "Someone we can trust, who will not give us some sort of mechanical 'Anything you think is real is real.' Bullshit! It *ain't* real! Some of this stuff *ain't* real! Help me sort it out!"

"I get panic attacks sometimes that are so bad," Carol says. "I sit there and I go, 'There's nothing to be afraid of. Nothing's going on. The house is fine. Everything's normal. Everything's good.' But I'm *still* having a panic attack and I can't make it go away. You can't talk to anybody. Alice can't help me. She tries. There are times when there's just nothing you can do for another person. You need somebody out there who knows how to deal with a panic attack, who has the background, but doesn't have the emotional attachment, because you can get so wrapped up in it. When Alice gets upset, I get upset. It's real hard to help somebody when you're as upset as they are."

"We just feed on each other," Alice explains. "Still, despite all we've said, we're not in all that bad a shape."

"Sometimes you just need a hug," Carol says. "Somebody to say, 'Good girl!' And sometimes, too, you just need somebody to kick you in the butt and say, 'Hey, lighten up!' I do that to myself; Alice does it to herself. We'll be riding along, put a tape in the car, turn it up full blast in the rear speakers, open the windows, and start singing, because sometimes you just need to lighten up!"

The following morning, Alice and Carol return to their horse farm, and I, too, drive home. Their trip to rural Maryland and mine to the old Connecticut shoreline town in which I live take about the length we think they should; there is no "missing time."

During the days immediately following the conference, I am struck by how my perception of the abduction phenomenon has changed: I no longer think it a joke. This is not to say I now believe UFOs and alien abductions are *real*—"real" in the sense of a reality subject to the physical laws of the universe as we know them—but rather that I feel something very mysterious is going on. And based as much on what has been presented at the conference as on the intelligence, dedication, and sanity of the majority of the presenters, I cannot reject out-of-hand the *possibility* that what is taking place isn't exactly what the abductees are saying is happening to them. And if that is so, the fact that no one has been able to pick up a tailpipe from a UFO does not mean UFOs do not exist. It means only UFOs might not have tailpipes. As Boston University astronomer Michael Papagiannis insisted, "The absence of evidence is not evidence of absence."

CHAPTER VIII

Postconference Interview

David E. Pritchard, Ph.D.

Two weeks after I left Carol and Alice, I speak with conference co-chairman Dave Pritchard. I am curious as to whether this M.I.T. physicist's perceptions, too, may have changed.

"I must say my own reaction to the conference and, well, putting it all together," Pritchard says cheerily, "is, I was just wanting to look at this thing with the hypothesis of simple extraterrestrials here with their super technology doing experiments. And it isn't that simple. I mean, it *can't* be that simple. In science, you always try to find some aspect of a complicated phenomenon that you can understand and explain. Just one little corner of it. I'm still considering whether it's worth trying to find that one little corner."

"I thought you had tried to do that with the implant," I say, "and come up with nothing—though that's not to say a negative finding is a bad thing in science."

"That's right. I mean, I guess if you were trying to support this extraterrestrial hypothesis, you could say I came up with nothing positive. But I also realized how much harder the whole thing is. That to identify something like that 'implant' you need an interdisciplinary team: biologists, chemists, material scientists—and gee whiz! that's not what I had at my disposal!"*

"But aren't you also suggesting the conference changed *your* perceptions of the phenomenon?"

* Some time after the M.I.T. conference, Dave Pritchard did get his wish: Two portions of Price's implant, designated "Price I" and "Price II," Pritchard reported, were examined "in collaboration with the pathology group in the Wellman Laboratories of Photo Medicine at Massachusetts General Hospital." The leader of the group, Dr. Tom Flotte, is a dermatologist who routinely examines medical samples.

Flotte's group utilized both light microscopic examination and transmission electron microscopy on the samples. What Pritchard at the conference had cautiously described as "three little appendages . . . approximately one-quarter the width of a human hair" found

"*Yes!*" he says. "I now see this thing as a much more complicated phenomenon. You know, when you go to a Dave Jacobs and Budd Hopkins conference, you only get that hard edge: the table exams, the uncaring alien. But when you actually start talking to these abductees, you realize they have a much more complicated relationship with these experiences and with the aliens than, for example, is portrayed in Jacobs's book. They have much more feelings of ambivalence.

"My wife, Andy, found a woman in this area who has a tremendous amount of conscious recollections," Pritchard continues. "And so this woman came by our house last night, and Joe Nyman was there. Joe was very intrigued, because usually, as you know, he uses hypnosis on his people. And this woman went through not only the whole scenario of the different kinds of aliens, but also the whole dual-reference business of feeling that she is part alien, of talking about the night she was conceived—I don't know how much you talked to Joe Nyman . . ."

"Not much," I say.

"Well, you remember he gave this very controversial paper on dual reference? And, actually, I tend to believe him, because I think he's very com-

---

sticking out from the implant, Flotte's examination revealed to be not alien antennae but cotton fibers, possibly from Price's underwear.

"All of the results obtained at MIT indicate that the Price artifact . . . is of terrestrial biological origin," Pritchard's update reported. "The MGH findings suggest a reasonable scenario for the formation of this artifact: successive layers of human tissue formed around some initial abnormality or trauma, occasionally accreting fibers of cotton from Price's underwear that became incorporated into this artifact as this tissue hardened."

Pritchard noted "several difficulties with the hypothesis that this artifact is the body's reaction to the foreign object that Price reported implanted in his body by aliens. Firstly," Pritchard continued,

> there is no sign of such an alien implant; neither cutting the artifact nor examining it under a light microscope revealed any evidence that even a small portion of it was of non-biological origin. The small amount of missing material . . . was indistinguishable from the immediately adjacent material which was analyzed. Furthermore, this missing central section has an area only about $\frac{1}{25}$ of the area of the period at the end of this sentence and could not be seen at a distance of several meters as Price reported seeing the implant prior to its insertion under his skin. Finally, if this small missing section were the actual alien implant, then the cotton fibers stuck in the accreted outer layers of the artifact must have become attached later on and were therefore not part of the original alien implant, failing to confirm the existence of the wires reported by Price. . . .

"From this perspective," Pritchard concluded, "the result of our investigation is clear: whatever probability you initially assigned to the hypothesis that Price's artifact was of alien manufacture must be substantially decreased."[1]

petent, very insightful. And also, he said, several people had come up to him after the conference and said, 'Yes, I feel that, too. I'm an experiencer and I definitely have those same feelings.' And this woman who was here last night also went through that whole dual-reference business of feeling she's here on a mission, that if the child abuse of her had gotten too great, maybe they would have taken her back or offered her that option—"

"Wait a minute!" I interrupt. "What was this about her child abuse?"

"Well, you know, there's a correlation between child sexual abuse and experiencers," Pritchard says.

"I thought that had been disproved at the conference," I say. "I thought we were told that child sexual abuse occurs among experiencers only to a slightly higher degree than it occurs in the general population; and that, therefore, that indicated the alien abduction scenario was not being used as some sort of screen memory for child abuse itself."

"No, I don't think that's the case," Pritchard tells me. He says he thinks I am right that this statement was made at the conference, but his impression now is that the percentage of experiencers who suffered child sexual abuse is considerably greater than the population norm of 25 percent. He reports a conversation he had with Joe Nyman, who said the percentage of his experiencers who had been abused was maybe 35 percent, which, according to Pritchard, Nyman said was "statistically within the norm." But included within that 35 percent, Nyman told Pritchard, were the first half of all the experiencers he had investigated, interviews carried out at a time when he was not asking about child sexual abuse, because he was not yet sensitive to that issue. Therefore, that first half's percentage was markedly less than 35 percent. Among his second half of interviews, conducted when, Nyman said, he had become more aware of child sexual abuse and was asking his subjects about it, the percentage of his respondents to the question of whether they had suffered child sexual abuse was much higher than 35 percent. Pritchard felt this indicated there was a positive correlation.

"In any event," Pritchard continues, "in the particular case of the woman who came to our house last night, she had had an abusive childhood, and the aliens sort of apologized for putting her in that family."

"They apologized to the woman?" I ask.

"Yes. And I've heard stories like that before," Pritchard tells me. "I've heard one in which the aliens said, 'If it's really too bad for you, we'll get you out of there.' What they meant, I don't know.

"What Joe's done," Pritchard explains, "is, he's found that by pushing on the issue of 'Why is this entity familiar to you?' he goes back to a time when these people feel at one with the aliens. The stories that several of the experiencers have told is the religious myth: the idea of the alien coming with the soul and the little lantern-like thing, and implanting this into the pregnant woman. This came up with the woman who was here last night—not quite the same image, but of being present at her night of conception and being able to describe the house and the night. That astounded her mother, she told us, because her mother and father had only lived in that house four months, and not when she herself had been born."

"Did she seem entirely credible to you?"

There is a pause, and then Pritchard laughs. "I don't know how to respond, you know? I have such a *willing* suspension of disbelief. When you talk to these people, they just blow you away! I mean, this is what I'm talking about in terms of the whole experience. It isn't: 'I saw a UFO and it was as wide as a house and only about fifty feet in the air. And I saw windows and aliens in it and several other people reported it.' That's a kind of objective report, and that's *not* what we're dealing with here. We're dealing with people who say they met with God and feel some unity with him in the context of their UFO experience."

Pritchard continues: "Well, I've always been an agnostic—sometimes, when I was younger, unpleasantly so. But if somebody like a physics colleague came up to me and said, 'I go to church. In fact, in these hard economic times recently, I've gone to early-morning Mass twice this week, and it's really helped me deal with some of this stress,' I wouldn't say to him, 'What the hell are you getting suckered into? That stuff is just a pile of superstition. What's your objective reality for believing any of that stuff? Get a good night's sleep and you'll feel better.' And so, when I talk to those experiencers I feel the same agnosticism I do when I might talk to some colleague who spoke to me about going to Mass. But all these experiencers *are* telling very similar tales."

"That's one of the disquieting aspects of this phenomenon," I say.

"And this woman last night hasn't had any contact with any investigators. She wasn't misled by Joe Nyman, she was just sitting there and telling him her story."

"Do you know what exposure she might have had to UFO books and films?"

"I don't," he says. "But the striking things to me were this Dual Reference business of her childhood, and this witnessing of the embryo implantation scene, which is not in any of the books or movies I know."

I guide our conversation back to how the conference had changed Pritchard's perceptions. He refers to what he calls his "horizons broadened" list. He repeated that he now realizes there is a lot more to the phenomenon than the "table procedures," and that the conference has made him more aware of how the experiences have changed the abductees' outlook on life.

On a more practical working level, he says, he has come to realize that abduction-phenomenon research "is a tremendously interdisciplinary field. We need not only more mental-health professionals, clinical and experimental psychologists, and scientists—and I was very happy that the theologians were at the meeting—but what comes out of the conference is there is not currently any physical analysis of implants, missing fetuses, trace materials that might be strongly suggestive of an alien presence or technology. I think at the core we really need volunteers from forensic labs, radiologists, chemists, material scientists to handle properly the small amount of evidence we have on hand."

Pritchard's realization that as many as 1 percent of the overall population—two and a quarter million citizens of the United States—might possibly be abductees has also broadened his horizons. He explains that he reached that figure in four ways. First was the Roper Poll discussed at the conference, which showed that, as Pritchard put it, "people respond positively to these somewhat ambiguous questions: 'Have you ever seen a ghost? A UFO? Awoken paralyzed in the night?' and so on. We know experiencers respond positively to those questions," Pritchard says, "but we don't know if people screened out by this will have a particularly high percentage of being found to be experiencers—except through the work of Joe Nyman, who has gone around and asked about forty people at work and found about three who he is certain are experiencers, and a couple more positives who didn't want to talk to him about it anymore."

Second, Nyman's figure of three to five out of forty may be, Pritchard feels, another indication of the percentage of the population who could be abductees, since, as he points out, "a lot of people, when they begin to suspect they might be experiencers, go through long periods of denial."

A third indication for Pritchard was the informal poll taken by the doctor friend of Los Angeles–area emergency physician John Miller, who, Miller reported at the conference, had found 3 abductee cases out of 250 patients he had interviewed in his office—"And this was a guy," Pritchard explains, "who was not particularly adept at finding the hidden ones. In other words, as you know in this business, about one-third remember their experiences consciously, a half need hypnosis to recover more than a fragment, and there's another sixth where hypnosis adds significantly more information. So, as a doctor interviewing patients, if you're not adept at discovering these people, you won't find those who are in denial and who are hidden."

Pritchard's fourth indication was, he tells me, "a guy who was an experiencer who drove a taxi in Washington, D.C., for four years and asked everyone he got into a conversation with about this phenomenon. His number for people who had seen UFOs was 10 percent, and his number for people who thought they had been aboard was 1 percent, which indicates it's an incredibly prevalent phenomenon.

"Now this actually means two things," Pritchard continues, "the good news and the bad news. I'll give you the bad news first: it means the two thousand cases we had represented at the conference are only the tip of the *tip* of the iceberg—namely, point-one percent of that hypothetical two million. And so you have to ask the question, 'Why did these people come forth and not the other 99.9 percent?' Therefore you have to suspect, as many at the conference kept shouting, that the polling samples we now have are incredibly biased by the selection.

"On the other hand," Pritchard goes on, "it means you can go out and find these people in the general population, because you can even go to the Roper Poll and find the 2 percent, or whatever it was, who had four positives to the key indicator questions and ask them. My guess is you'll find that something like half of them are experiencers. Maybe it won't be a half, it'll be more like a quarter; but certainly you'll find experiencers by that route."

Two percent, according to the Roper Poll, translated to 3.7 million Americans being "probably abductees"; a quarter of that—Pritchard's conservative figure—would still mean more than 900,000 Americans would qualify.

I can't help thinking Pritchard's statistical base is shaky: the inconclusive, ambiguous Roper Poll; Joe Nyman's questions of his co-workers; a California doctor who didn't know what he was looking for; and a gregarious cab driver in our nation's capital. But shaky data is precisely the problem with this whole UFO phenomenon. I wish I knew the circumstances under which scientist Aaron Wildowski said, "The plural of anecdote is data."

He *was* joking, wasn't he?

"The mental health people are in a bind," Pritchard is saying. "It wasn't something I was really aware of until Dave Gotlib, the Toronto physician, pointed it out: it seems the most effective therapy for these people is to not discuss whether the experience is real or not, but for the experiencers to try to figure out what they experienced and come to grips with it. But if you do that as a professional therapist, you are coming very close to the line of encouraging the patient in his delusions. Which, of course, you are not supposed to do. So how do you handle that one?"

"Very carefully, I would hope," I say.

CHAPTER IX

Postconference Interview

Richard J. Boylan, Ph.D.

A week after my conversation with Pritchard I hear from Richard J. Boylan, the Sacramento clinical psychologist with whom I had dinner the night before the conference ended, when he discussed "off the record" what he referred to as his "six-state grand tour of reported Southwest secret sites."

Boylan's brief letter to me read:

> My processing has proceeded to the point where I am prepared to be quoted on the record, for attribution. The facts of the M.I.T. conference and extraterrestrial contacts must get out.
>
> The ball is in your court.

I telephone him before he can change his mind.

Boylan, who is fifty-four, graduated in 1961 from a small private college in California with a B.A. in philosophy; in 1966, he received his first master's degree (a M.S.Ed. in educational administration from Fordham in New York); in 1977, he received his second (a M.S.W. from the University of California, Berkeley); and in 1984 he received his Ph.D. (in anthropological psychology, with clinical emphasis, from the University of California, Davis). He has been interested in UFOs ever since he was eight years old, in 1947, and saw the newspaper reports of Kenneth Arnold's sighting of nine brilliant objects skimming above Mount Rainier "like a saucer would if you skipped it over water."

By the time Boylan was a teenager, he had read every science-fiction book in the North Hollywood Public Library, which, he told me, was "a rather sizable collection in those days."

In 1975, when Boylan was thirty-six years old, he was hiking with a friend in the foothills near the coast north of San Francisco when he saw a flying disc. Boylan, at the time, was on a trail perhaps fifteen hundred feet above sea level. The object, he estimated, was another two thousand feet above them, almost straight overhead.

The disc was not going very fast when Boylan first sighted it. He and his hiking companion watched it for about thirty seconds, and then, when they next looked up, forty-five seconds later, it was gone.

"If I were to guess, it was maybe thirty feet wide," Boylan tells me. "It was very clearly not a manmade object: no fuselage, no wings, no tail, no helicopter rotor, exhaust, noise, or anything else. It was going against the wind, so it wasn't a weather balloon. You could see every foot of its external dimensions. It was a round, dull gray, metallic object—flattish round, not an orb, more like a disc. My friend saw it, too. We didn't know what to make of it. It was in view a good half-minute. And I said to myself and my hiking companion, 'What do you know! I bet we've just seen a flying saucer.' "

"Why are you so sure it was not a balloon?" I ask.

"Because it had occurred to me that that was one of the things the object could be, so I checked the prevailing wind patterns and the object was going exactly opposite to the wind. I'm very familiar with the prevailing winds off there, and the wind at that time was blowing in from the coast, from the west. The object was heading northwest, into the wind."

"You were on a hill," I point out. "Could there have been a thermal rising up the cliff, then arcing back?"

"No, these are very low foothills with soft contours."

"It couldn't have been the sun glinting off an intercontinental jet or a military craft that was so far away you couldn't see?"

"It wasn't way the hell up there," Boylan says. "There's enough water vapor in the air near the coast so a distant object's image would appear to shimmer and blur. I knew because of the relative sharpness of the outline of the object we were looking at that two thousand feet was a reasonable estimate of its distance above us."

Two thousand feet is not all that far. At that distance, one could readily distinguish, say, the individual wings of a biplane.

The sighting of the disc rekindled Boylan's interest in the UFO phenomenon, and in 1978 he moved to the foothills of the Sierras and joined a California MUFON branch as a consultant and part-time auxiliary investigator.

"Perhaps one thing of interest," Boylan tells me. "I was county mental health director at that point and was familiar with the other county department heads. The welfare head was ex–Air Force; his military assignment had been working the deep-space radar dishes for NORAD under Cheyenne Mountain. I interviewed him and he told me, 'You know, when I was working those dishes we saw stuff up there in space that wasn't ours and it wasn't the Russians', and it was going at speeds and altitudes and were sizes that weren't either of ours's stuff. So,' he said, 'when you ask me about UFOs I've got no argument with you, because I've seen stuff on the screens that clearly fits that description.' This is a NORAD deep-dish officer," Boylan emphasizes, "telling me that while applying their best official approach to scanning the area of space they were responsible for, they could not explain the stuff that was showing up on their screens and had concluded among themselves this was UFO traffic."

For the next couple of years Boylan continued to read the UFO literature and report back to MUFON what little he came across as an auxiliary investigator (the usual sightings of strange lights at night); but more and more his interest in UFOs was taking a backseat to his commitment to the pursuit of a doctoral degree.

In 1986, two years after he was awarded his Ph.D., Boylan again began to follow the UFO phenomenon, "but only," he tells me, "in a kind of hobby way." And then, near the end of that decade, as the first of what Boylan considered "somewhat scientifically respectable reports of extraterrestrial contact" emerged, Boylan became intensely interested in UFOs again.

"There had been a growing subset of the UFO literature about aliens landing, getting out, walking around, people spotting them, and even of aliens coming up to people and having alleged dialogues," Boylan says. "But, as you know, this stuff was really hard to nail down without any kind of independent proof. Also, I'd seen enough UFO investigations to realize that the investigators are often not the kind of people upon whose testimony you would want to hang somebody. So I really didn't know what to make of those reports, but it continued to pique my interest, because here it was beginning to show up in my own work." Just in the course of interviewing his own patients to obtain their personal histories, Boylan explains, he learned that three of them had themselves reported extraterrestrial contacts.

"One of the seminal events in getting somebody with some scientific credentials behind the extraterrestrial contact phenomenon was when Dr. Edith Fiore, a South Bay Area California clinical psychologist, put out her book *Encounters*, on the number of people she had run across in her own clinical practice who'd had extraterrestrial contacts," Boylan tells me. "Prior to that time, Dr. Leo Sprinkle was reporting on this in his own clinical work, too, at the University of Wyoming. Back then he had been sort of a voice in the wilderness, without any other scientifically credentialed people backing him up. When Dr. Fiore became the second Ph.D. psychologist reporting the same thing, I started to have to take it quite seriously, because now, on the face of it, there seemed to be a basis for evidence."

More recently, publication of David Jacobs's *Secret Life* further convinced Boylan that he had better "wake up and pay attention to this stuff." The result, Boylan says, was that in January 1992 he launched his own research project to determine for himself whether the extraterrestrial-contact phenomenon met his own "rigorous criteria of believability. Not that I disparage Edith Fiore or Dave Jacobs or Leo Sprinkle," he adds, "but my father was from Missouri, the Show Me state, and I guess I inherited a bit of that. I'm one of those guys who's got to be shown.

"When I hear with my own ears, when I have the individual sitting in front of me and I can evaluate for myself whether this person is a little loose around the edges or not, then I feel I have a much more firsthand sense of the credibility of the person's reporting," Boylan explains. "Plus, through a research project, I get the chance to compare one person's anecdotes with another's and see if there's some kind of consistency in the stories from people who wouldn't have any basis for knowing each other. That way I can begin to get a handle on the phenomenon."

By early July 1992, the time of our conversation, Boylan had interviewed forty-one possible abductees. Boylan's subjects reported the same sequence of alien contact, physical paralysis, and removal to a separate craft or locale for further examination and communication by Small Grays and other beings that Budd Hopkins's and Dave Jacobs's abductees had. But any further comparison between Boylan and those two investigators makes the Sacramento psychologist flinch; Hopkins and Jacobs, Boylan feels, found too many similarities.

"I think Hopkins and Jacobs are abduction-happy," Boylan tells me. "What I've heard from folks doesn't always represent extraction elsewhere. In some cases the dialogue takes place without extraction—in the bedroom, for example, if that's the place of contact. Or there's information exchange on site. If a person drives his car, stops, and gets out, you are not *necessarily* levitated up to a spacecraft and planked out on a table. That explicitly *has not* happened in a number of cases. So I think Jacobs et al. tend to oversystemize the experience. Nevertheless, I have found consistency—more so than people just fancifully inventing stories could be expected to come up with. Furthermore, I checked on whether these people have read the UFO literature. Some have, but many of them have not, so they could not have been contaminated by reading reports. And these individuals are relatively clean enough that I consider the consistency from these clean sources suggests the reporting of a real phenomenon with some relative inconsistencies from case to case."

In addition to the consistency in Boylan's subjects' descriptions of the Beings—the most frequent among them Boylan describes as "the three-and-a-half-foot, gray-skinned, large-cranial, all-black-pupil no-white-showing slant-eyed folks"—there was also Boylan's subjects' accounts of a specific instrument used often in personal examinations: a foot-long silver rod approximately the diameter of a pencil that is sometimes inserted into, and at other times glided over, the subject's body. "It's apparently either some kind of remote viewing or examining instrument with no wires attached which presumably telemeters information back," Boylan tells me. "Very often at one end of this rod there is a light, that end being the one inserted during examinations. This description, down to the detail of the light at the end and that end being inserted, has been reported to me by a number of individuals who positively don't know each other or the literature."

During those abductions that did not involve extraction, Boylan's subjects were usually lifted or floated through windows that were most often closed. While being levitated to a hovering craft, they reported, they were able to see the landscape receding below and the stars or clouds above; in other words, they were awake and able to view their environment from their perspective in midair. Boylan's abductees described the intense, brilliant light they were lifted up as being white with a bluish tint.

Boylan points out that not everybody he interviewed was 100 percent bona fide and that some did turn out to be in his estimate "delusional or extremely loose with their perceptions." Still, he says, "the vast, vast majority, certainly 90 percent plus, seem to be free of psychological problems that would be such as to create the likelihood that their accounts were the production of those problems rather than their actual experiences."

Boylan explains that if someone who had had a sighting that he or she had truthfully reported had come to see him not because of the sighting but because of, say, marital problems or depression, the sighting had nothing to do with that depression, nor would it be incorporated into a system to explain the marital problems. Instead, he says, they would be "just side-by-side events." However, the sort of psychological problem that might account for these experiences, he said, would be found in a subject who was a "flat-out liar. A borderline personality type. These are the kinds of folks who are extremely fragile in their grasp of themselves and their place in the world. They often tend to jump on bandwagons as a way of borrowing some sense of identity and individuality. I would look at an extreme personality disorder who reports this stuff with great caution, because they're poor discriminators of reality."

Other psychological problems might be paranoid schizophrenia or a person with delusional disorder. "This latter is a category that is rather tricky," Boylan explains, "because it represents an individual who has one area of delusion and everything else in their psychological makeup registers as normal. They seem to talk, function, and make sense fairly well across the whole spectrum of their lives except for one narrow, little category where they maintain their delusional system. And if such a person were to pick extraterrestrial contact as their pet delusional system, they're hard to distinguish from somebody who looks normal and is not delusional in reporting contact.

"I've run across a couple of such folks," Boylan continues. "They weren't your average broad-spectrum schizophrenics; they seem only to have a narrow delusional system around extraterrestrial contact, and they were *tough!* I did not pick it up on the first interview in one of them, and I had to keep talking a while until he had slipped enough to give me the clues that this was delusional and not factual reporting."

"Dr. Boylan," I say, "if you yourself were one of these persons with just this same sort of narrow delusional system, how would you know it?"

Boylan gives a startled laugh. "Uh . . . well . . . let's see, how would *I* know? That's a tough question." He pauses for a moment, then says, "Well, perhaps it's easier to start with someone else. I've found a couple of qualities in the delusional disorder person's reporting that are different from what I presume are the qualities of truthful reporters. The delusionals tend to come across with some grandiosity. In a somewhat self-important way, they will say, 'Doctor, let me sit you down and take a few minutes of your valuable time and tell you what the aliens told me.' They lack perspective on the fact that this is bizarre stuff and they need to slow down and reality-test with the person they're talking to about whether they're coming through believable or not. They're consumed by the material, the information they are carrying, and they don't have that kind of tentative, perplexed, inquiring, wondering, self-doubting-about-their-own-sanity quality that you tend to get with real reporting individuals.

"Another thing is that they tend to get into areas of interpretation that have some kind of specialness," Boylan continues. "In one person's case, the bottom line was that it was satanic evil at work rather than extraterrestrial visitation. They weren't really aliens, they were devils dressed as aliens, trying to fool people. In another case, the delusional person was seeing himself as the possessor of special information none of the other thousands of other contactees presumably had, and he was doing me a favor by bending my ear to pump his special stuff into it. The genuine contactees tend to talk about some sense of message, but it's partial and leaves them somewhat perplexed and anxious to compare notes with others. They have the sense that 'there's a larger picture out there of which I don't have the whole.' With the delusionals, it's 'I've got it all, folks, and let me take some of your precious time to educate you dumb bastards.'

"So, applying that criteria to myself," Boylan concludes, "you'll some-what have to judge for yourself how I come across to you using those two yardsticks."

Boylan's subjects range from a person who has been an experiencer since early childhood forty years ago to someone whose experiences took place within the last year. The passage of time, he feels, is less important to their ability to come to grips with their experience than their individual makeup.

"Some people have unusual internal resources and can do this on their own without professional help," Boylan says. "And some people really require some assistance to get perspective on it and what the phenomenon means." Boylan's assistance lies in helping these individuals gain perspective by edu-cating them as to how widespread (and covered up) the phenomenon is. He also comforts them that they are not alone, that other people have experi-enced the abduction phenomenon and survived with their psyches intact.

"Oddly enough, given the unusualness of it, I don't see it as a particu-larly hard-to-integrate phenomenon once you have the information to put it in the proper perspective," Boylan tells me. "But if these people are not unusually self-resourceful, or if they've been 'debriefed' by someone who's got a point of view that would shape them to continue to perceive the ex-perience as traumatic and violative and one that puts them at risk, then it can be difficult."

I ask Boylan how he perceived the experience.

He thinks for a moment and tells me that he was going to make a jok-ing reference to Christopher Columbus and the American Indians having their first meeting, but decided that it was not such a good metaphor, given the eventual outcome of that contact for the Indians. Instead, he says, he ba-sically sees it as a "collision of cultures, not across an ocean but across star systems, and often with people who only vaguely and analogously look human. The fact that the aliens are intelligent life and communicative be-comes quickly apparent to the contactees. And the fact that they come from a technologically, and in many cases philosophically, superior civilization becomes quite evident, too. As a result, there are both traumatic and uplift-ing elements to these encounters. In most cases contactees have not in any serious way been hurt. And once they get past the shock of dealing interra-cially, as it were, they have often had a high-quality communication ex-change and are left with a sense of special privilege to be among the first to have had these kind of contacts."

By putting the phenomenon in an anthropological context, Boylan tries to make the experience seem less bizarre. Such contacts, he explains to his subjects, are not unprecedented; they have happened to other people and can be interpreted simply as one race or culture meeting another.

"My favorite metaphor," he tells me, "is the Harvard anthropologist in a helicopter landing in the back rain forests of Brazil and getting out with his clipboard, video camera, and boom mike and tapping some stone-age Tupi Indian offshoot on the chest with a pencil and saying, 'Hey, whatever the hell your name is, what do you guys eat?' "

According to Boylan, his contactees respond well to this comparison. "It allows them to reinterpret their experience as not so much an assault by intent as an unprecedented experience that may feel assaultive until you can see where the Harvard anthropologist is coming from with his agenda, and they can extrapolate that to the extraterrestrial visitors. It takes a lot of the jumped-by-lizards highway-brigand elements out of it, and the people settle down and really start to attend more to the message content, the perspective changing and information exchange, which seems to be the burden of what the extraterrestrials have in mind when they contact. Only a minority of them seem to be mostly concerned with body samples."

"That's not the impression you get from Dave Jacobs's book," I say.

"No, it's like the Grays are sperm-and-ovum-hungry, doing intergalactic fertility-product harvesting," Boylan says. He pauses for a moment, then adds, "Well, I don't want to psychoanalyze Dr. Jacobs, but I find the extreme regularity in his accounts astounding. I have not run across anything like it in either psychological or anthropological literature, and I think those are the two literatures most relevant to this phenomenon."

I ask Boylan to move away from his contactees to his own personal extraterrestrial experience.

It occurred, he explains, following his visit to the National Radio Astronomy Observatory's Very Large Array near Alamogordo, New Mexico. He had left Alamogordo in his Chevy S-10 Blazer at about nine o'clock the night of April 12, he tells me, and had driven down to Las Cruces and across to Deming on Interstate 10. At Deming, he had turned north on U.S. 180 toward the Gila National Forest, where he intended to camp for the night. U.S. 180, a two-lane blacktop highway, cuts in a near-straight line for about forty-five miles through high desert in the middle of nowhere.

Boylan had his CB radio on as he drove and had been talking back and forth with truckers heading to and from Alamogordo on the interstate; but at Deming, when he turned north on the more isolated U.S. 180, the truck chatter died out and his radio fell silent as he had driven out of range. He had not, however, turned off his receiver.

At about 11:20 p.m. Boylan thought he heard a voice he presumed to be from his radio say, "Watch out for the Smokey," although he wasn't sure he had heard the "e" sound on the end. He assumed someone was just broadcasting a warning about the presence of a Highway Patrol car, the sort of warning he had heard earlier from the truckers; but he thought it strange because he hadn't seen another car for miles. Boylan was, at that time, doing something more than the legal 55 mph speed limit.

Keying his CB mike, Boylan asked, "Where's the Smokey?"

There was no answer; that was odd, too. Never before had Boylan heard someone broadcast a Smokey alert without following it up with more details as to where the patrol car was located.

By then Boylan was maybe fifteen miles north of the Deming turnoff, on a stretch of road that was gradually rising between some piñon forests. Suddenly he saw, visible in the high beams of his headlights, what he presumed to be smoke on the road ahead.

"Where's the fire?" Boylan asked into his CB. "Does anybody else see the smoke or the fire?"

Again, there was only silence; but by then Boylan had entered the cloud.

That was his last conscious memory until he emerged from the smoke cloud's other side.

Boylan then continued on to the Gila National Forest campsite, only faintly bothered by his encounter with the smoke. The following morning, however, the memory of the cloud was more troubling, because he didn't think it had been smoke and he didn't think it had been fog. And when, as he began to dress, he noticed what appeared to be a couple of scoop marks on the big toe of his right foot, "I began to weave things together," Boylan tells me, "and my suspicions began to grow. Then I did a time analysis and figured I had an hour or so of missing time. And the continued subjective sense of strangeness coming off this trip after I had gotten back, along with a physical kind of pineal-gland pressure behind the eyes and nose, made me suspect there might have been more to the content of this trip than I consciously remembered."

Boylan decided to have himself hypnotized to see if anything might have happened that he was unaware of. It was through hypnosis, he tells me, that "additional details of the vapor cloud entry and emergence came out."

As soon as Boylan had entered the cloud, he had slowed down, hung the CB microphone back on its bracket, and put both hands on the wheel. The smoke seemed to be floating off the hillside to his left, drifting across the road, and continuing down to his right. As he drove deeper into the cloud, it became so thick he could no longer distinguish the roadbed or see its white lines; so he came to a complete stop. He did not pull off onto the shoulder; instead, he was blocking the right lane of the road.

It was pitch dark except for the stars, and he believed he should have been able to detect an orange glow of flames; but he could not. Nor did the cloud have any odor, and so he was forced to conclude that whatever it was he had driven into, it wasn't smoke.

He also knew it wasn't fog. He was in a New Mexico desert in April, on a bone-dry night, and above the cloud the stars were out. The air was crystal-clear; there was no moisture to make fog out of. There was no body of water around. The road he had been driving was gradually rising, so he wasn't in any sort of pocket where moisture could collect. And there he was at a dead stop in the right-hand lane of a two-lane blacktop highway crossing a sere desert enveloped in what, in his car's headlights, appeared to be a grayish-white odorless cloud.

Boylan got out of his car to investigate.

Feeling somewhat disoriented, he crossed the left side of the road to the ditch beyond which the ground gently rose to the scattered piñon trees. He traversed the ditch and, not sure of the direction in which he was heading, began to climb. He had gone only as far as the first trees when he stopped to locate his bearings. When he tried to move again, he could not.

Boylan was paralyzed.

At the same time he sensed the approach of two "persons," who, taking their places on either side of him, firmly gripped his upper arms and guided him forward and to his left a short way to their craft.

"The funny thing about the hands," Boylan tells me, "was that the fingers were very long and not like human fingers feel. In other words, they didn't feel like a series of hard bones defining fingers; it was more of a cartilaginous interior with a padded, fleshy exterior. They were gripping me with two fingers on top, one on the bottom, which led me to deduce I was dealing with three-fingered persons. Possibly they had an opposable thumb that wasn't engaged, but I couldn't feel it. The fingers weren't much wider than a normal human finger; but they were longer and quite strong and having more of a contouring, cartilaginous feel and less of a flat bone chink-chink-chink kind of wraparound feel that articulated human bones do.

"I was conducted forward a ways—I can't tell you if I walked or glided," Boylan continues, "until we were close up to this landed metallic vehicle shaped somewhat like, well, sort of a cross between a saucer and a dirigible." The object was not shaped like a classic flying saucer: it was fatter than a disc, perhaps twelve feet at its thickest; it had no cupola and was approximately thirty to forty feet in length. Boylan thought its cross-section would look like a cigar that had been flattened on the bottom—although the details of its bottom were difficult to determine, since it was partially embedded in the desert sand, as if it had crash-landed.

In addition to the two Beings who guided Boylan to the object, there was a third, who had apparently been injured in the landing. A gray-white cloud was still escaping from the craft, and Boylan assumed that the vapor he saw was some sort of by-product of the crash.

A doorway opened along the side of the craft, and the two Beings led Boylan inside, placed him in a seat, and departed. It was not until he was alone in the craft's dimly lit interior, inhaling what seemed to be the sort of stale, recycled air one breathes on a transcontinental airline flight, that he realized he had no idea what the Beings looked like. He had time to wonder if, in his paralysis, they had remained out of his vision or whether at moments his eyes had been closed.

Some time later the two Beings returned, and Boylan was able to catch a glimpse of one of them. He caught sight only of the creature's face: an oval head; no nose to speak of; and black, inhumanly large, oval eyes. There was not enough light to see details of its mouth. And because he was seated he could not be sure of the Being's height. But he had the distinct impression that it was because the Beings were concerned that he might have been harmed by inhaling the vapor that they had brought him to their craft for an examination.

The Beings led Boylan into the next room and placed him in what felt, he thought, like an astronaut's chair might in a pulled-back position, so that he was reclining but not quite flat. His ankles seemed held in place as if by a force field, and then Boylan felt an intense pressure as though something was being pushed far up into his nose. As soon as the object had been implanted, Boylan's ankles were released and he was free to go.

Boylan recalls the outside air being cooler, brisker as he was floated horizontally back to his automobile. He entered the Blazer, sat there for a moment, and then he started its engine, accelerated to road speed, and emerged from the cloud into the black, starlit night.

"It was at that point that fully conscious recall resumed," Boylan tells me. "So everything from slowdown to speeding back up, but not quite to 55 mph, is a missing chunk from conscious memory. The details have been retrieved through hypnosis."

"When you entered the cloud, how far beyond your headlights could you see?" I ask.

"My memory stops right about at entry into the cloud," he explains. "If I'd had that much clarity of thought I would have pulled off the road as soon as I became aware I couldn't see very far ahead."

But he hadn't. And the image of his automobile hidden within a cloud blocking the right-hand lane for as much as one hour is a troubling one. "Is it inconceivable that you would abandon your car in the middle of a public highway for that long?" I ask.

"I would never dream of doing such a thing!" Boylan says. "I consider it one of the most dangerous things you could do. But, by the way, when I resumed driving, it was twenty miles before I encountered another car, and there were none behind me. It's as many people have reported: as if the highway had been interdicted on both sides for some ways, so there was no real danger of being driven into—not that *I* knew that," he added. "But ex post facto, it became clear that that was the situation, and for that reason it was not a miracle that my car was not plowed into."

The excessive pressure Boylan had first felt behind the top of his nose while seated in the craft lasted four or five days, along with something that was almost a headache. These physical traces, too, were factors that had led him to search through hypnosis for an answer to what had happened to him.

Boylan went to three different hypnotists. Two of them could not elicit much detail from him, and he subsequently learned that they had had their own encounter experiences. (This has led Boylan to hypothesize that if a therapist is blocked himself, he may not be much good at unblocking someone else.) Boylan's third hypnotist, a woman, "also has remote viewing capabilities," he tells me, "and was very successful at hypnotizing me and getting most of the details I've gotten."

"And you're confident that these details are *your* details and not something your hypnotist has led you into?" I ask.

"Yes," Boylan answers. "Leo Sprinkle also worked with me. Several hypnotists pulled little bits of details out, and these details are either congruent or weave well. They don't contradict each other. I wanted to be careful that she wasn't leading me. And I retained enough of my hypercritical faculty that I was kind of watching her line of questioning while she was running me through this. I am *convinced* this is my stuff and not hers."

"So what do you now think really happened to you on that road to the Gila National Forest?" I ask.

"I think I had an encounter with some non-Earthly folks whose craft was by the side of the road," Boylan says matter-of-factly. "They seemed very benign and left me none the worse for wear when I got back in my car and finished my journey."

I am silent.

"Subsequently," Boylan continues, "the other thing I got from this trip—and I suspect from that experience—is a real sense of urgency to get out the message about the government's secret saucer program and their very current Star Wars agenda. I'm beginning to think this urgent agenda to get this information out may be part of the message I got at their hands."

"Dr. Boylan," I ask, "why do you think they showed themselves to you?"

Boylan thinks for a moment. "Well, I can't be sure about that. I think, being in possession of the information I have, it certainly may not be a bad pick to pump me up to get the word out. Maybe I would have done that anyway—I don't know."

"Let me go back to that note you wrote me: 'My processing has proceeded to the point where I am prepared to be quoted on the record for attribution. The facts of the MIT conference and extraterrestrial contact must get out.' Your note suggests that sense of urgency you've already mentioned, but what do you consider 'the facts' that must be gotten out?"

"That the phenomenon of multiple extraterrestrial contacts of a generally benign one-civilization-communicating-with-another nature is important for us as a people to be aware of. And that we must integrate this phenomenon into our experience. The government has no business standing in the way of that or in trying to stop that from happening—not to get into all the unsavory methodologies they use. What is happening is an important part of our human history, and to say that somebody who would deprive us of our history is out of line is putting it mildly!"

"Where do you think these Beings come from?" I ask. " 'Extraterrestrial' implies from the stars, but the more I speak to people, the more I sense the current thinking is that they come less from the stars than they do from another dimension."

"Maybe," Boylan says. "I don't know. Maybe it's inner-dimensional. Maybe it looks inner-dimensional because if you bend space-time you can emerge in a spot that previously looked empty and *bang!* you're there. I suspect their mastery of physics makes Einstein look like Newton. My assumptions, and the messages they seem to give the contactees, are that they are from other star systems and we're sort of the Johnny-come-latelies of intelligent life. And if we clean up our act nuclear-wise and ecology-wise and in terms of international relations, maybe we'll be let into the club one of these days."

"I have one final question," I say. "How do you think your father with his Missouri 'Show Me' background would respond to all this you've been telling me?"

"Well, he died when I was rather young, so this is a bit of an extrapolation," Boylan said, and paused. "I think he'd run me through tight and serious questions, and if I survived that as well as I seem to be doing here, I think he'd say, 'Well, by gosh, maybe there is something to this.' "

CHAPTER X

Postconference Interview

Pat

On Wednesday, July 15, not quite a week after I spoke with Richard J. Boylan, I receive a telephone call from "Pat," the pretty, blond, midwestern experiencer who reported at the conference how her dentist husband had leapt out of bed in the middle of the night to grapple with one of the aliens. Pat wants to tell me about her most important experience: the time she was "pulled through the eyes of an alien."

Over the phone she explains that this incident happened four years before, while she was attending a retreat in the middle of Missouri. For four days Pat had been participating in encounter groups and meditating—"going inward," as she put it, "to find out who I was." On the last night of the retreat, after the meetings ended, there was to be a dance at the main lodge. The evening had started to get chilly and Pat decided to walk the couple hundred yards along the path through the trees back to her cabin to get a jacket.

As she walked in the moonlight she felt a gentle breeze and heard the leaves rustling. "I looked to my right and I knew something was there," Pat says, "but I wasn't afraid."

She next had the sensation of entering an invisible "tunnel." The air around her felt compressed and still, and two Small Gray Beings met her in the tunnel and escorted her toward what appeared to be a weatherbeaten, vertically planked wooden shed. As Pat approached the shed, however, she realized she could see partially *through* it.

"What had happened was they had put up what looked like a 3-D holograph," Pat tells me. "They had somehow been able to take an energy field and stabilize it into this specific image of a shed—and don't ask me *how* they do it," she adds, laughing, "but it appeared like some form of electricity stationed in space. It was quite dark, so I really couldn't see totally through it, but I knew it was like a veil of some sort."

The two Small Grays led Pat around to the back of the shed, where, she remembers, she looked up and saw the alien craft hovering just above her. The next thing Pat knew, she was inside the disc.

"How did you get into it?" I ask.

Pat thinks for a moment before replying. "I think I was floated up at an angle," she says. "My feet never touched the ground the whole time, so I can't be sure whether there was a ramp or not, I wasn't paying attention to my feet."

Within the craft, on Pat's left, was a table with some objects on it. She is certain the table did not hold a person. About six yards ahead of her, also to Pat's left, were her two Small Gray escorts, and next to them several robed, taller, square-shouldered, sandy-blond-haired, more human-looking, presumably hybrid Beings whose skin was a pale flesh color.

"Their eyes weren't bulbed and dark like a total pupil," Pat tells me. "They weren't bulging out and almond shaped. They were more like ours, maybe a little larger." Pat could not see their hands or feet because they were hidden by their robes.

The Small Grays, however, didn't seem to be wearing any clothes at all. They looked like "typical Grays," Pat tells me, "except that they were more white." One of them was white with a slight bluish tinge; the other seemed a bit purplish. Although Pat did not notice their hands or feet, she did notice that their arms seemed entirely pliable instead of bending at an elbow: "It was more like an octopus arm," Pat says, then adds, "without the suction cups, of course."

Although the hybrids were looking at Pat as she stood before them, she could not detect any expression on their faces. "If they were emotional," she tells me, "they were loving and benevolent. I could feel that. These Beings have progressed to where they show emotions through an energy you sense. You know beyond a shadow of a doubt their feelings because you're feeling them, too. When they're sad, you feel the sadness they are feeling."

The dominant figure in the room, however, was a very tall alien who, as Pat was escorted into the craft, had stood with his back toward her. According to Pat, the Small Grays presented her to him and he "slowly rotated to face me." She laughs a little self-consciously. "Most of these cases aren't dramatic," she says, "but I want to tell you, this experience gives me goose bumps every time I think about it. It was just very theatrical the way he slowly turned and looked at me."

He, too, was wearing a robe; but unlike the hybrids, this Tall Being was wearing a hood which framed his sharply pointed chin, his thin, slitlike mouth, and tiny bridge of a nose. The Tall Being's most striking feature, however, was his eyes: almond-shaped, huge, dominated by totally black, irisless pupils. His dark eyes made his pale complexion seem almost chalky white.

"The depth of those eyes was indescribable!" Pat says. "It was like look-ing up at the sky at night: totally dark. He slowly turned and looked at me, and his eyes engulfed my whole personality: everything I knew and remem-bered about life, all my feelings, all the love I had for people on this earth and my love for Earth itself. All those emotions came out, and he knew *who* I was, and *what* I was, and then all of a sudden my body began to shake.

"Every molecule began to shake so very, very fast," she continues, "that what happened next was like a silent explosion. My whole body just burst into a million different pieces of light!" Pat exclaims. "And I looked down at myself and I could see that I was much larger than I thought I had been. And I was so much *brighter!* It was like my soul had escaped my body. And then," she says, "he pulled me through his eyes and we were free—free of all the physics of this earth that limit us, free of the body that puts a wall around our souls. . . ."

Pat laughs a little sheepishly. "It was such a beautiful experience! Just *beautiful!* I just can't express how spiritual it was. All I can tell you is that the human body is one poor, poor, *poor* piece of machinery compared to the soul! And that's what we live in: the body. But if people could really see their souls . . ."

I ask Pat where she thinks these Beings came from.

"They never told me! I used to think about that and get anxious about it. But then I realized they never would tell me. And after I stopped being anxious over that question, they did tell me. The word 'owl' came to me, and 'the Dipper.' They told me to look in the Dipper. See, a lot of this I know I can't be making up, because I don't even know the meaning of some of the words they use with me," Pat says, laughing. "I have to look them up. And some of the places they tell me about, I'll get a star map or my astron-omy book out. Well, when they told me to look in the Dipper, I started looking through all my astronomy books and I found that there is an Owl Nebula in the middle of the Dipper. And see, I didn't know *any* of that."

I ask Pat how the Beings communicate with her, and she says, "On oc-casion, when you get into a certain state, right before you fall asleep, the communication comes in real clear. They will just talk to me—not with me being there with them, or them here with me; they will talk telepathically. And I'll hear these conversations, and sometimes I'll wake up with the memory and sometimes I won't. Other times it'll be a week later and then it all kind of bubbles up like . . . like bubbles from the bottom of a lake? And suddenly I'll remember, like, twenty minutes of a conversation in a tiny split second—or at least that's the way it seems to me, sometimes.

"Telepathy is just so, so important for people to understand," Pat con-tinues. "When telepathy is used by these ones I deal with, it's the purest form of communication. I want so much to get this across to you, because with telepathy there's no room for lies. There's no room for cheating. You know the person, every bit of them, so you feel perfectly comfortable around these people—I call them 'people' instead of 'aliens,' " Pat explains, "because that is something I want to get across. I don't want nonexperiencers to be afraid. I'd say be cautious, but don't turn away from the experience. The point is that both Budd Hopkins and David Jacobs after the conference said they would have to look at the other side of this peaceful thing. And I was so elated!" Pat says. "I was so happy! Because I thought I was just a small voice in a forest of trees and wouldn't be heard."

CHAPTER XI

Postconference Interview

John E. Mack, M.D.

The M.I.T. conference's Harvard co-chairman, John E. Mack, M.D., left Cambridge for Czechoslovakia immediately after the last day's final presentations to deliver a report on "The UFO Phenomenon: What Does It Mean for the Expansion of Human Consciousness?" at the International Transpersonal Association Conference, then being held in Prague. As a result, I made arrangements to speak with him as soon as it was convenient upon his return; by then, the M.I.T. conference had been over nearly a month.

The day before we are to meet, when I speak with Mack on the telephone to get directions to his house, I express my apprehension about certain investigators' stability.

"Well, if you're attracted to these kinds of edges, you're likely to have—what would I say?—spaces in your psyche?" Mack tells me. "It's hard to do this work from a place of clear-cut stability. It is tempting to equate the instability of the investigator with the invalidity of the phenomenon; and I've had to struggle with that a lot myself! I ask myself, 'Does my interest in this subject fulfill some need of mine? Is there some dimension of my own self that has allowed me to be persuaded of something that I shouldn't be persuaded of?' and so forth. Then every time I go back to working with the people themselves, I get yanked back to their seriousness, their earnestness. They're not like people conjuring up some make-believe."

I remind Mack of his comment at the conference that the abductees suffered from post-traumatic stress disorder, but what was the source?

"We'll talk about this tomorrow," Mack says, "but if you look at the history of Western philosophy and science and at Rick Tarnas's book *The Passions of the Western Mind,* its central theme is the dominance and control of nature so that we need not be terrified of it. And, of course, the outcome of that need for dominance is a dead planet, because the only way this planet will be totally controlled is by taking it over—which we seem to have done quite a lot of already. There's the point at which that process of controlling nature begins to overshoot, which I think is what is happening now with this beginning encounter with the unknown that begins to challenge not just the fact but the wisdom of control."

The destructiveness of the human need to control nature is a theme Mack turned to in the paper he presented at the Prague conference. There he suggested that the psychological forces behind this need stemmed from two dimensions of the human mind: *dualistic thinking* and *materialism.*

Dualistic thinking, he said in Prague, is the tendency to judge the world in extremes: good or evil, black or white. And the specific property of this dualistic thinking was what Mack referred to as the polarity of separateness. "We have extended our notions of separateness to such a degree that we experience ourselves as completely divorced from nature, including other human beings," Mack explained. "The consequence of this extreme separation is the exploitation of nature, the treatment of Earth as a thing which we have the right to use, and even destroy, for our purposes. We have also separated ourselves from one another to the degree that we can commit or risk genocide relatively casually. We do not include the other as part of ourselves."

The materialist viewpoint, Mack stated, included two domains: the material and the spiritual. "But the only reality that is truly accepted is the reality of things we can touch, physical substance. The spirit world is out there, subjectively felt, perhaps, but it does not really *exist* like physical reality."

Mack hypothesized that it was the "helplessness before the Black Death and other diseases, or the terror of the natural world and the need to master and dominate it," which gave rise to the "extreme development and exaggeration of dualism and materialism" philosophy in the West—"a worldview," Mack stated, "that has become incompatible with the survival of life on this planet."

In Prague, Mack called this worldview a "species arrogance, a monumental hubris," as a result of which, he reported, "we are now faced with a different set of circumstances, requiring a new psychology and a different science, whose epistemology is not restricted to sensory, empirical ways of knowing.

"We have lost our relationship to nature, including our own human nature," Mack maintained, "and with it the sense of the sacred, which, almost by definition, means a deep connection with nature, a reverence for the natural world as the highest expression of God's work."[1]

Our lost relationship with nature and our neglect of our spiritual senses is a theme Mack would return to again and again in our talk.

Mack and I meet at his home in a suburb of Boston on Thursday, July 16. I tell him I spoke with his conference co-chairman, Dave Pritchard, whose most conservative estimate of the number of individuals in this country who might be abductees was around 900,000. I ask Mack how many Americans he himself thinks might qualify.

Mack, like Pritchard, refers back to the different data sources Dr. John Miller's "envelope epidemiology" presentation had included at the M.I.T. conference and says that he doesn't have any better data than that. He does say, however, that he thinks it is better to be conservative and to point out that estimates vary wildly, "anywhere from low hundreds of thousands up to three-plus million, depending upon the criteria used." But then Mack makes the point that "one of the things that's important to keep in mind is the psychological triggering factor here.

"I see many people who would not qualify in a poll at a certain point in time because they would say, 'No, I am not an abductee,' " he explains. "And then we have an interview which triggers a memory; or they see something that triggers something; or they read an article; or they hear me or Budd Hopkins or somebody on the radio or TV, and they go, 'Oh, yeah! That's like what happened to me. . . .' And then they recall something. Therefore, the next time they would be polled they would move over from the no to the yes category.

At the Prague conference Mack had stated that "as many as hundreds of thousands and perhaps more than a million individuals in the United States alone may have undergone these [abduction] experiences. . . ."[2] I ask him whether he was saying that he felt that even conservatively, as many as a couple hundred thousand Americans might be abductees.

"Yes. I mean, I don't know what to make of this statistically," Mack answers. "There is a curious way in which this phenomenon tends to make a mockery of all our linear thinking." He pauses for a moment, then explains, "One of the things about this phenomenon that intrigues me as a psychologist and a person looking at human consciousness is that this whole phenomenon has a kind of power to shatter all our epistemological categories.

"Take, for example, the question of 'Is it real or not?' Or 'Is it real in the physical world?' And the answer, in terms of this UFO abduction phenomenon, is always yes and no. It ranges. Sometimes it shows up very hard-edged in our physical world, like in this Hopkins–Linda Cortile incident, with independent witnesses seeing the same thing. At such times it appears to fulfill the objective empirical criteria of knowledge derived from direct observation and practical experience and not theory. But at other times such knowledge is very elusive. Sometimes there are witnesses who actually observe the person to be not present during the abduction. I have examples of that in my own work, of an eight-year-old daughter of one of my abductee-clients who is awoken by something that upsets her at four or five in the morning. The child experiences that she's had something happen to herself. She gets up and goes in to find her mother, and the mother's missing from her room. The child's father is there. The covers on her mother's side of the bed are turned down, but the mother's not there. The mother subsequently told me she had had an abduction experience at that exact time that the child discovered her missing. So it's not just out-of-body, it's out-of-house!

"At other times," Mack continues, "a person can be experiencing the energy of an abduction, the sense that the Beings are present, they're being taken; but their body remains there and somebody sees that they're there. Now we don't know whether the observer, the witness, might have been so called switched-off during that time when they observed the person being there. So we don't know if the person is physically taken but appears to be still there because there was a lapse of awareness on the part of the observers. There is often this elusive quality about it." An example of this sort of abduction would be the one Keith Basterfield mentioned at the conference in which the Australian woman Maureen Puddy "fainted" while sitting in her car in the presence of two Melbourne UFO researchers and later described how, while apparently unconscious, she was brought inside an alien craft by an entity who first beckoned to her from outside her car and subsequently appeared with her inside the craft's round, windowless, doorless room.

"The physical-evidence area is filled with peril for everyone—not just the investigators but the skeptics as well. Because from my perspective as a psychiatrist," Mack says, "what I have to offer here is not a claim about a phenomenon operating in the physical world—that is not my area. In other words, I find the physical evidence *corroborative.* If somebody wakes up or emerges from an experience with a raw cut, or a scoop mark, or a bleeding area or bloody nose, or some physical sign, then that tends to give the phenomenon some crispness for me as a person living in this pretty high attachment to the physical world. But it's not the heart of my contribution, of what I have to offer. While such evidence tends to corroborate that this is a phenomenon that can show its impact in the physical world—and from the standpoint of mainstream Western science this physical corroboration would be where the main argument would lie—it's not the main argument for me."

"But isn't precisely this lack of hard physical evidence the main argument used to demonstrate the phenomenon's lack of credibility?" I ask.

"It might be the main argument on which somebody might want to take me on," Mack agrees. "But at this point in my work I would be foolish to enter into that argument. Because often what will happen is you'll have the investigators who are speaking at the level of the actuality of the experience and the power of it, with *some* corroborative physical evidence; and then you will get the official debunker coming in and arguing *entirely* on the basis of how robust the lack of physical evidences are for UFOs in terms of the *grossest* measurements of Western physical science. It's that sort of argument that *totally* disregards the complexity and strength of the experiential dimension and its utter inexplicability from the standpoint of psychology or even a psychosocial explanation. You probably heard Paul Horowitz near the end of the conference say he wouldn't believe in UFOs until a cigarette lighter drops from one." Mack smiles wryly and adds, "Of course the clever answer to him would be that the aliens gave up smoking several hundred thousand years ago, but nobody was quick enough, or bothered enough, to make it. But it's that level of physical argument that misses the entire *power* of the phenomenon."

I ask Mack if he was suggesting that the demand for hard evidence may in fact be irrelevant.

"Not irrelevant—it's confirming, supportive, corroborative," Mack replies. "I can't say it's irrelevant, it's *important.* If a Budd Hopkins, or a David Pritchard, or someone who is studying the pathology of wounds, can demonstrate that these wounds heal in a way that doesn't ordinarily occur in Western medicine or healing, that's very powerful! And more power to them to do that. And people *are* working on that. But that's not where my contribution is. If somebody says, 'Well, how do you know that this little scar that occurred after an abduction was from the abduction?' I can't *prove* that. But it's the company that it keeps. It's the case after case after case: a person wakes up and says, 'I didn't *have* that before. That cut came afterwards. . . .' " Mack pauses for a moment, then he says, "I'll give you a case of mine. A man wakes up from an abduction experience with a four-inch gash in his leg; it's down to the bone. He's going to go to the doctor, but it's healed by the end of the day—*so he says.* Okay, someone could say, 'Well, maybe he's lying.' But that's *my business!* I've spent forty years in psychiatry; I did forensic psychiatry. It's my job when somebody's putting me on, or lying, or has some ulterior motive, or distorting. That's where I do have some expertise—in the discrimination of mental states. There isn't any suggestion, to me, that these are people who have some motive to distort their experience or to lie or to self-aggrandize." Mack shrugs and says, "Now, you could say they were *mistaken.* That, you know, they *mistook* their own experience . . ." But the expression on Mack's face indicates he thinks that option unlikely.

"So what has most convinced you to take this phenomenon seriously?" I ask. "Is it—"

Mack leaps in, not waiting for me to finish my question. "Case after case after case of, on the whole, timid people—'timid' not necessarily by virtue of character, but timid about reporting these experiences—who come forward reluctantly—'reluctantly' because they want to be truthful with themselves about what they've been through, out of a certain integrity that they have, and also a concern that there is something buried in their experience, the residue of which continues to bother them. And finally they get up the nerve to come see somebody about it.

"I tend to see the ones for whom it's been harder, in some ways, to seek help than those whom Budd sees. That may be for complex reasons having to do with where he tends to be most in evidence," Mack explains. "Paradoxically in this case, people are often much more willing to see nonpsychiatrists than psychiatrists, because they do or don't want to be labeled psychiatric. I see quite a few people who *do* want to be labeled psychiatric: the university administrator who came to see me, for example; I mentioned him at the conference. I listened to his story, and I listened and I listened. He could see I was taking his story seriously, and I could see him becoming more and more distressed that I wasn't finding him crazy. And by the end of our session he said, 'Gee, Doc, I had hoped you would tell me I was nuts. Now I have to deal with the fact that what happened to me was real and that scares me. It scares me because I don't know how to deal with it. I don't know what all this is!'

"And so what has been most powerful to me is the *authenticity* of the people," Mack says, "the *believability* of the way they speak, the degree to which they are isolated from one another. . . ." He pauses for a moment, then points out that the abductees' isolation from one another has diminished in the last year as more abductees have come forward in response to increased media coverage of the phenomenon. However, he points out, the current lessening of isolation does not take away from the fact that prior to the expanded media attention, individuals who had not been in contact with each other and who were unfamiliar with accounts of the phenomenon in the media were reporting much the same specifics and details. And it is inconceivable to Mack, he says, "that these stories have been somehow concocted from bits and pieces of cultural flotsam and jetsam that is floating around. It doesn't have that character.

"So it's the *nature* of these people," Mack continues. "The fact that I've been a full-time psychiatrist for thirty-six years—and there's nothing in my psychiatric experience that could account for what I was learning from these people. That was the single most powerful thing for me: here were people otherwise quite ordinary, unremarkable, reporting with full sincerity and in a most authentic way these extraordinary experiences which they did not want to believe were so themselves. People with very good reality testing who, when pressured by me, when pressed about their stories, said, 'Doctor, I wish it weren't true. I'd love to be dislodged from believing this, because it shakes up everything I've ever thought.' "

So the first aspect of the phenomenon to impress John Mack, I make a note, is *the authenticity, believability, and nature of the abductees themselves.*

"Another thing: when you get close to the heart of the experience," Mack is saying, "when you go deeper with them, either with or without hypnosis, and get close to the core of the experience, you meet extremely powerful emotional resistances. You get very intense indicators of powerful, traumatic events. You get nightmares, psychosomatic changes, fearfulness, mistrust, suspiciousness. They have difficulty exposing themselves to situations where it might reoccur.

"They may have phobias of hospitals or needles," Mack continues, "not phobias like childhood fears, but phobias that are very concrete as adults of situations that, when explored, turn out to be related to actual experiences from the abduction phenomenon."

I remember John Carpenter the second day of the conference mentioning the woman who, as a very young child, had developed a phobia about her dolls; she had thought they moved at night. As a result, she had all her dolls destroyed. According to Carpenter, during a hypnotic regression she recalled being with hybrid children aboard a UFO. In keeping with what Mack had earlier said about the isolation of abductees, Carpenter's patient had never come across any accounts or heard stories about hybrid children prior to her own realization during hypnosis.

Mack describes the emotional intensity of the memories sometimes recovered by these people during hypnosis and how "when you get close to the reliving of these experiences, they will literally *scream* with terror and their whole body shakes." There is nothing, clinically, that could produce that sort of response, he emphasizes, "except the reliving of something that has been done to them. There is *no other condition* I know of that can elicit, bring forth, that kind of emotional expression. Then that leaves me with the question 'What was it that was done?' "

The second aspect, then, is *the emotional intensity of the abductees' recall as indicative of trauma.* The presence of this intensity leads Mack to ask, What was the trauma's source?

Mack tells of running through all the possibilities: Was it some other kind of trauma? Was it rape? Is the patient reliving a war experience? Is there any past history of childhood abuse? Did they suffer some terrible physical injury when they were a child that they had suppressed? Did somebody try to suffocate them? Did their mother or father try to kill them when they were a baby? "You sort through all the traumas that people can suffer that have a strong physical quality to them," Mack explains. "And not one case that I have investigated—nor, to my knowledge, that *anyone* has investigated, neither Budd, Dave, John Carpenter, or myself—no one has *ever* come up with another trauma or set of traumas that could account for that emotional state.

"That is the core of it," Mack said. "That and the fact that these descriptions of their experiences are very consistent both sequentially and factually down to the minute detail. *Not* that everyone's is identical; there are variations. The ships may differ in size, the nature of the instruments change, the shape of the doctor's head on the vessel changes. There are other characters they may see. *But the basic structure is exceedingly robust!* And it's important to note again that this sequential structure was established in the patients' minds before all the recent media flurries, because now, you could argue, there's been the television show *Intruders* and other things that these individuals could have been taking this structure from. But this was not true in the 1970s and 80s when this phenomenon was first being described."

Narrative consistency, therefore, is the third aspect of the phenomenon that has impressed John Mack.

The fourth aspect is the *absence of any kind of diagnosed mental illness that would account for it.* In his "Abduction Phenomenon: A Preliminary Report," within a section titled "Who Are the Abductees? Psychopathology and Personality," Mack noted:

> Few generalizations can be made at this time about this important question because of the paucity of research data and the unusual nature of the phenomenon. Several co-researchers have set the absence of gross psychopathology as a *precondition* for their inclusion of a case in their series. Nevertheless, none of the abductees with whom I have worked have revealed obvious psychopathology, such as schizophrenic psychosis, severe depression, or other major psychiatric disturbances, that could account for the reported experience. Indeed, what has struck me most has been the "ordinariness" of the population, including in my sample, for example, a restaurant owner, two musicians, secretaries, a writer, a prison guard, university students, and several housewives. Several demonstrated resentment, slight suspiciousness, a sense of victimization, and other post-traumatic symptomology. Most seemed burdened in their lives by their abduction experiences.
>
> Some . . . report troubled relationships in childhood with one or both parents, alcoholism in the family, and childhood or adolescent

abuse. Several report personal isolation, troubled adult relationships, and problems related to conceiving and bearing children and parenting. But in other cases these disturbances are not present. In some cases, attitudes toward sexuality and decisions relating to having or not having children seem to be affected by the abduction history. In no case so far have I found a way of tying the non-abduction aspects of these individuals' histories to their abduction stories, nor have I found convincing psychodynamic links between the specific narratives of the reported abduction experiences and other aspects of the personal histories or emotional lives of the abductees.[3]

(John Mack's Preliminary Report also contains some interesting documentation of the testing of abductees by psychologist Elizabeth Slater. Her findings were the result of a 1983 experiment in which she administered the WAIS-R [Wechsler Adult Intelligence Scale—Revised], BVMG [Bender Visual Motor Gestalt], figure drawing, and Rorschach tests and the TAT [Thematic Apperception Test] to nine individuals picked by Budd Hopkins. Slater was *not* told these persons were abductees:

"In her initial report, written before being told who the subjects were," Mack wrote,

Slater noted that the subjects were of above average intelligence and demonstrated "a considerable richness of inner life." She found some to be "eccentric" or "odd" with "spontaneity and originality in thought and feeling." The inner richness tied to a "risk of being overwhelmed by the urgency of their impulses." The subjects were "in a rather continual struggle to bind [their impulses] and keep them at bay." "Under stressful conditions," she noted, "at least six of nine showed a potential for more or less transient psychotic experiences involving a loss of reality testing along with confused and disordered thinking that can be bizarre, peculiar, or very primitive and emotionally charged." She also noted a degree of identity disturbance (especially sexual identity confusion and "self-inflation"), lowered self-esteem, relative egocentricity, and/or lack of emotional maturity and minor but frequent "boundary failures" on their figure drawings. One spoke specifically of "a sense of smallness and victimization in the face of overwhelming outer forces."

Slater also observed "some degree of impairment in interpersonal relationships," "problems in intimacy" for some, and "a certain mildly paranoid and distrusting streak in many of the subjects" together with hypervigilance, "a marked tendency to attend and be sensitive to nuance and fine detail," "leeriness and caution," and a "disposition towards wariness."

After Slater was told of the nine subjects' reported UFO abductions she reconsidered her report from that standpoint. "The first and most critical question," she noted, "is whether our subjects' reported experiences could be accounted for strictly on the basis of psychopathology, i.e. mental disorder. The answer is a firm no." "If the reported abductions were confabulated fantasy productions," she wrote, "they could only have come from pathological liars, paranoid schizophrenics and severely disturbed and extraordinarily rare hysteroid characters subject to fugue states and/or multiple personalities." "Not one of the subjects," she wrote, "based on test data, falls into any of these categories." None, she said, demonstrated "psychopathology by which they might have invented their reported experiences of abduction."

Slater then considered the possible impact of the reported abductions. "Such an unexpected, random and literally other-worldly experience as UFO abduction," she suggested, "during which the individual has absolutely no control over the outcome, constitutes a trauma of major proportions." She noted also the denial of "opportunity for even minimal forms of mastery" in association with the UFO experience and the "social stigmatization" and "alienation" the victims would encounter. She concluded that their interpersonal problems, damaged sense of identity and body image difficulties, emotional turmoil and anxiety and wariness were "the logical outcome of the invasive and injurious nature of the reported UFO experiences." In 1991 Slater told me she had previously considered herself to be a "reality-oriented, plodding person," but this study "extended my narrowness" and "changed my thinking around." She saw scars from incisions in several subjects and wondered "what is this all about?"[4])

The fifth aspect of the phenomenon that has impressed John Mack is the presence often of present *corroborative physical evidence*. As Mack noted in his Preliminary Report, "The physical features which accompany UFO sightings and landings such as changes in physical and chemical characteristics of the soil, are among the most interesting and compelling aspects of the phenomenon. They provide a seemingly objective corroboration of reports that are otherwise so bizarre as to defy our credulity. . . .

"Physical manifestations," he continued, "at times frighten abductees, who do not want to believe that their experiences are real, and at other times reassure them of their sanity."[5]

These physical manifestations, we were told at the conference, might take the form of nosebleeds, fresh cuts, or scoop marks upon returning to consciousness following a period of missing time or upon awakening— sometimes upside down in their beds, or on top of their covers, or in a different room entirely, or even outside their house. Experiencers might sometimes be surprised to find themselves fully or partially dressed, their clothing missing or carefully folded or, in rare cases, exchanged for someone else's. Another common physical manifestation was one experienced by Carol: the sudden realization, while driving, that she was miles away from where she had been traveling just a blink of an eye before.

To Mack, the "most disturbing and elusive of all" physical manifestations are the reports of missing fetuses. But, as both he and John Miller noted, although many fetus removals have been claimed, none have been documented.

A sixth aspect of the phenomenon is the existence in many cases of an *association with UFOs:* at the same time the individual is having his or her abduction experience, other people in the community are observing UFOs in the same area. These witnesses may be people the abductee is close to or whom the abductee does not know at all. (An example of the latter would be Linda Cortile's abduction from her twelfth-floor Manhattan apartment into a waiting UFO, witnessed by the international diplomat and the two security officers guarding him plus the older woman crossing the Brooklyn Bridge.) In short, as Mack wrote in his Preliminary Report, although "many abductions seem to occur independent of UFO sightings by the abductee or other witnesses, a close association between UFO encounters and abductions has been consistently observed."[6]

The seventh, and perhaps the most striking and inexplicable, aspect of the phenomenon is its *occurrence in very small children*—some as young as two years old—who report in the best language they know how of little men taking them up into the sky, or sticking things in them, or "biting" their noses. Abduction reports by small children can be of particular scientific interest, Mack notes in his report, because "small children may not have been exposed so much to media accounts or discussions within the family, or by peers or friends."

Describing a specific case of his involving a small child, John Mack writes:

> Jill and Mike Ward have told me troubling things concerning their three-year-old son, Ned. When Ned was 21 months old Jill went up to his room one night and found "his blanket was all screwed up, as is typical. He was laying on it, and so I couldn't straighten the blanket out. The next time I went up to check on him his blanket was perfect. It was laying out over him beautifully as if someone had smoothed it over him." Mike "does not get up with babies . . . and my daughter can't reach into the crib."
>
> When Ned was just two, Jill saw him talking to the alien face on the cover of [Whitley] Strieber's *Communion,* kissing it and calling it "Pi." A few months later after waking from a frightening dream, [Ned] told Jill, "I fly in the sky . . . to the spaceship." Asked who was in the spaceship, he responded, "a man . . . little man." Six weeks later the Wards' seven-year-old daughter came into her parents' bedroom at five a.m. to tell them that Ned had come in to see her with a lot of blood on his face and coming out of one nostril. They also found blood on his pillow case and a scabbed-

over incision mark on the back of his head. When Jill asked him if anyone had been in his room Ned said, "Little man come through window.
Man bited me on the nose."

When Ned was two years and seven months old I interviewed him
with Jill. He was a lively, warm and outgoing child. I asked him to identify the cards in the Hopkins Image Recognition Test (HIRT) which contains ten cards devised by Budd Hopkins to explore children's abduction
experiences. They consist of ten large black ink drawings from faces that
would be familiar to children—a boy, a girl, Santa Claus, a policeman, a
clown, Batman, a Ninja Turtle, a witch, a skeleton and a typical alien. Ned
alertly identified each card correctly and matter-of-factly. When I showed
him the alien card Ned said, "I write it on the board."

Jill said they had done "a doodle like this" together on a blackboard.

I asked if he had "ever seen this guy."

"I open door, I drive the spaceship," Ned said. He said it was "that
man's. That man's spaceship." He seemed to be getting uneasy and said, "I
have my blankie. I put my thumb in my mouth."

After talking casually about where he had seen some of the other figures, I returned to the alien card and asked, "Where did you see this guy?"
and whether or not he liked him.

"I don't like him," he said.

"What does he do?" I asked.

My assistant, who had been present, noted "up to this point Ned has
been generally talkative and attentive, giving unsolicited information.
Now he often doesn't answer at all, or only after long silences."

JM: Is he nice or is he scary?

Ned: He's scary.

JM: [Tries to calm and reassure him, then:] Does he come into your
room sometimes?

Ned: Yeah. I have a big sword, now hit him out of my room." [gets
excited as he talks about fighting.] . . . I have my blankie, put my thumb
in my mouth. I were very tired.

JM: You get tired when he comes?

Ned: Yeah.

JM: And you put your thumb in your mouth?

Ned: Yeah. The guy breaks my window. I can't fix it anymore.

Ned becomes increasingly silent and edges across his chair to his
mother and sits in her lap. "A man came in my room," Ned said. "Man
has big flashlight to my eyes." After this Ned told of how "He hurt me."
("Where?") "On neck." He said, "I don't want to cry." Then he said, "I
feel better."

Ned tells Mack about how he likes to watch *Star Trek* and fights back
against the man. "A man run after me, I run faster," he says.[7]

Soon after, the child came into Mack's lap to be comforted.

"Parents can, of course, influence their children's experience," Mack's report noted. "Nevertheless, for a theory of the abduction phenomenon to be complete we must find a way to account for the emotionally intense and seemingly authentic detailed experiences of children as young as Ned whose exposure to outside sources of information has been limited."[8]

Any conventional explanation for the abduction phenomenon, Mack tells me, would have to provide an answer for what he refers to as the "whole package":

> The authenticity, believability, and nature of the abductees
> The emotional intensity of the abductees' recall as indicative of trauma
> The narrative consistencies of the abductees' stories
> The absence of any kind of diagnosed mental illness in the abductees
>   that would account for their experiences
> The corroborative physical evidence
> The phenomenon's close association with UFO sightings
> The reports of abduction occurrences by and among very small children.

"To my knowledge nobody who is skeptical or questioning has come up with an explanation that even *begins* to account for this syndrome from some other, more conventional source," Mack explains. "I'm a little careful where I present this and in what context. I didn't start to go public on this until I had seen enough cases myself that I said—like you said to me—'Something is going on!'

"Now, I'm not saying it's *extraterrestrial*," Mack continues. "Because, again, I think that this has a way of making you question your categories. 'Extraterrestrial' means it exists in the *physical world* the way we know it; it just doesn't happen to be from this planet—it's from another planet. It's physically out there. And I don't know that way of structuring it in terms of the physical world as we know it is going to help us very much.

"I'm very careful in the language I use about this," Mack says. "I can only say it shows up in our world in very powerful, vivid, physical terms affecting people very powerfully. But I don't know what the source of these experiences is. I don't know where this comes from. I have no way of knowing.

"Now, people say, 'Well, maybe it comes from some dimension beyond space-time,'" Mack continues. "Or 'Somehow they've developed a physics that has mastered the problem of moving around in the galaxy'—if they do, in fact, reside on some other star in our physical galaxy as we know it. But that's not an area I feel I can talk about. The one and only thing that I've really stayed with is the same thing you said, which is that my material says that something is going on here that is affecting these people powerfully, which I cannot account for in the physical world that I've grown to believe was reality. So," he says, leaning back, "this phenomenon is stretching my notions of what's real."

I ask Mack what possible psychological disorder could adversaries among his peers come up with that might explain any part of this phenomenon.

"The psychiatrists? Well, the main argument is that somehow this syndrome is related to dissociation. Dissociation is a big, big thing in psychiatric literature. And what psychiatrists arguing this never quite come to grips with is (a) the source of the trauma, (b) the mental content that results from dissociation, which is nothing more than a time-honored coping mechanism.

"Dissociation is by and large a defense device," Mack explains. "In other words, something happens to you." He leans forward, clasping his hands together in front of his chest. "You're traumatized in some way; somebody does something. You're overwhelmed by a rape experience or a sexual experience. And your psyche cannot tolerate the anxiety, the terror, the rage, the overwhelming traumatic nature of this. So, rather than experience this in an ego-shattering, fragmenting, horrible way, a split occurs. The content is put off there someplace," he says, gesturing with right hand off to that side. "It's *dissociated.*

"Part of the psyche is left to deal with the trauma: defend it, ward it off, avoid it, repress it—whatever the particular style of the particular person's avoidance structures are. It's over here," he says, again gesturing with his right hand, now a fist, "leaving some of the psyche," he says, opening his left hand in front of his body, "free to go on as best it can with its own life.

"Now this material will intrude from time to time, through nervousness, bad dreams, difficulty in human relationships, through certain intrusive fantasies, whatever," Mack continues. "But that's what dissociation is: it's a way of coping with something that the ego cannot stand. And when you treat people, you try to give them the strength to reopen that closed cabinet," he says, unclenching his right fist, "and take a new look at what's there.

"Now," he says, "to go from understanding that mechanism to saying that dissociation as a mechanism created the *content* of the experience is an altogether different matter. In other words, that's a leap which goes far beyond attributing the phenomenon to dissociation.

"Let's again take the two parts of the psyche," Mack says, now holding his left hand palm up in front of him, his right hand palm up to the side.

"The part that is present," he says, his left hand rising and falling as if he were trying to estimate the weight of an invisible object in his palm, "and the part that is dissociated," and he makes the same gesture with his right. "In the part that's present, you will have vague memories, fears, nightmares, some content which will bear some symbolic, perhaps, relation to this over here—" he glances at his right hand—"but it will not contain the full memory, because that's the effect of dissociation: to have only hints and dreams and nervousness, anxiety, and some symptoms. You could have some body symptoms, or phobic fears of going to hospitals if there was a trauma in a hospital, and so on. That's the job of dissociation: to keep the trauma out of consciousness.

"Now as you do the work and you uncover what was back here," he says, looking again at his right palm, "what you'll get eventually is closer and closer approximations to the actual memory of what happened, still with some distortion. It may be that at first you'll get monsters in a dream instead of the man who did the rape. But little by little—and the person may never get the actual memory of what literally happened—you'll get various distortions of the trauma: somebody tried to choke the person, or surgery as a child, whatever it may be. But I don't know of *any* work on dissociation where you get the invention of a completely false, complex, highly articulated, sophisticated narrative that bears *no* relationship to *any* of the actual experiences that led to the dissociation! 'Dissociation' is a structural term; it's not a content term. So you'd have to add to dissociation some mechanism of invention of a narrative."

After a pause to make sure I am following him, Mack continues: "Now, abductees *do* demonstrate dissociative mechanisms. I mean, you can see it happen. The fact that I need to use nonordinary states of consciousness—hypnosis or whatever—to recover the memory *by definition* means that they dissociated off. Otherwise they'd just talk to me like you and I are talking, and they would remember everything that way. So the very fact that I have to *use* a way of accessing memory, to bring them back that part of themselves with the memory that was warded off, means they did dissociate, but they dissociated *as a response to something that occurred!* It does not address what occurred, and *that* remains the mystery: What is the source of whatever it was that requires that they ward this off and not remember?"

I ask Mack why he thinks there is such resistance within the psychiatric and scientific community to even the possibility that the source of the trauma is what the abductees are saying. He momentarily deflects my question to tell me that in the 1960s, when he began research for his Pulitzer Prize–winning psychoanalytic biography of T. E. Lawrence, the reputation of the charismatic Lawrence of Arabia was "somewhat of a buffoon, a

Rudolph Valentino, *Desert Sands* and flowing robes" individual. The debunker mentality, Mack explained, existed about Lawrence in those days as much as it exists today concerning the alien abduction–UFO phenomenon.

"Liddell Hart was one of T. E. Lawrence's first biographers and knew him well," Mack continued. "Hart said you could measure almost scientifically how people regarded Lawrence according to how well they knew him. The ones that simply formed their opinion of Lawrence from the general scuttlebutt tended to be debunking, or argued about him from the standpoint of their own ideology: what they thought about the Middle East, or whatever. But the closer they came to actually knowing Lawrence and his work, the deeper their respect for him was. And Hart's observation held up. In other words, in the ten years I was doing research on T. E. Lawrence, I never met anyone who really *knew* T. E. Lawrence, who knew what he'd said and what he'd done, who didn't think very highly of him. And the debunkers were *always* the ones who had some political axe to grind, or had never known him, or who had just seen the popular statements about him.

"Well," Mack says, "it's the same thing with the abduction phenomenon. There are those who start out as atheists, nonbelievers. They reject it. But the people who get close to it, who see the cases, who study the materials, who listen to me carefully, or hear tapes I play, or read papers I've written, or in any way allow the material *to come into them,* they become agnostics. And eventually, if they stay with it, some of them come to the place which is really an advanced place, which is, 'I don't know what it is. Something's going on. It's interesting. It's scary.' But they truly suspend judgment." Mack pauses for a moment, then says, "The furthest you can go at this point is to say *there's an authentic mystery here.* And that is, I think, as far as anyone *ought* to go. But that's a powerful, powerful place to come to at this point.

"Now, most of the people who really are familiar with what I'm doing in any depth are with me on that. The ones that say 'Poor John! What's happened to John?' are like the Lawrence people—they have not studied the material. In a funny way, I've kind of moved away from trying to persuade the mainstream culture of the validity of this phenomenon," Mack continues. "I think it's time we grew up as a species and moved on to say 'Okay, there's something going on here.' Let's not just debate 'Is it real? Is it not real?' It's okay to ask 'What do you mean by real?' but let's move on to 'Something's going on here,' like you said, and look at 'What does this really mean for us?' 'What does it mean for our cosmology?' 'What does it mean for psychiatrists clinically in terms of our categories?' 'What does it mean for us in terms of our relationships to the ecology and to the environmental crisis?' 'What does this mean in terms of domains of reality?'

"Do they come from our physical reality?" Mack asks. "Or does it mean that somehow we have to change our categories of reality? I talk to Dave Pritchard about this all the time. Can he account for this within our space-time physical technology? Or do we have to put that aside?" Mack pauses for a moment, then shrugs. "There's a guy, Jack Sarfatti, out in California who says there's some kind of black time hole they come through from beyond space-time," Mack said. "They've mastered travel in and out of our space-time universe. I don't know anything about this. But we have to ask ourselves what this phenomenon means in terms of who we are in the cosmos. If we are not, as in Tom Wolfe's *Bonfire of the Vanities,* 'Masters of the Universe,' what does this do to our perceptions of ourselves if some other creatures can come in and, without our having any choice, overcome our wills and do with us as they wish?"

In his Preliminary Report, Mack referred to the phenomenon as a "kind of fourth blow to our collective egoism, following those of Copernicus, Darwin and Freud," in that it might lead us to realize, "Not only are we not physically at the center of the universe, transcending other life forms, and rational members of our psyche. We are not even the preeminent or dominant intelligence in the cosmos, in control of our psychological and physical existences. It appears that we can be 'invaded' or taken over, if not literally by other creatures, then by some other form of being or consciousness that seems to be able to do with us what it will for a purpose we cannot yet fathom."[9]

"What does this realization do to the species arrogance that is our hallmark as being the most important creatures?" Mack asks me.

I mention the briefing paper Linda Moulton Howe told me about, with its suggestion that these Beings have been genetically engineering us for tens of thousands of years in order that we might achieve what importance we have achieved.

"Right," Mack says. "I don't know that we have been tinkered with, but there is this kind of either literal interspecies breeding or some technology and information that is being injected into our brains that makes us experience it like that. What does this mean, that we're in this relationship? If there is this powerful connection of energies—and I won't even say 'species,' because that presumes it's real and from a taxonomy that's like ours—but if there is some kind of energy from some source we don't understand connecting with us, other beings, or other intelligence, what does this mean? Some people experience it as purely traumatic.

"And there's another interesting dimension to this," Mack continues, "which Budd Hopkins and Dave Jacobs and I argue about all the time, which is that I'm struck by the fact that there seems to be a kind of matching of the investigator with the experiencer. So what may be the archetypal structure of an abduction to Dave Jacobs may not be the uniform experience of, say, Joe Nyman or John Mack or someone else. And the experiencers seem to pick out the investigator who will fit their experience."

"Could you have that backwards?" I ask.

"Yes," Mack says amiably.

"It seems to me that Jacobs, Hopkins, and Nyman may pull out of their experiencers what they want to see."

"People said that of them at the conference; I can't say that," Mack responds. "I respect what they do a great deal. But the fact is, I had an experience in which twenty people were sitting around in my living room, and there was one woman there whom Budd had brought here one night when he was staying to do some work with her, and then she came to my support group the next month. I invited her.

"Each person in the group was talking about what they had been through in their own personal investigations of their experiences, the trauma of the thing, but that they had moved to another level. They had become very aware of the ego-shattering experience of having to rediscover our place in the universe; that there's some deeper purpose to this, some larger design, and that it doesn't really avail us or help us to think in terms of good guys or bad guys. And they're talking this way; and, you know, I participate in that kind of talk. And this woman who was in Budd's group was saying, 'I don't understand this! I mean, I've been victimized and traumatized and you're all talking about it as though there were some redeeming elements in this?' She didn't come back.

"Some of the investigators and I'm not saying Budd or Dave," Mack is quick to add, "—want to have it both ways: They want to treat this as a literal phenomenon of hybridization and genetics in our physical world. They want to treat it as literally physical: they're *real* and they're *aliens*. But in treating this phenomenon in that manner, they're not really looking at the shattering implications of this for the nature of our reality, or the fact that this means we're in a relationship that has some meaning beyond this.

"In other words," Mack says, "I don't see how, on the one hand, you can say this phenomenon shatters our notions of physical reality and then treat it entirely literally in terms of our physical reality." Mack pauses for a moment, then adds, "This isn't just my speculations. This is what happens with Harry, whom you saw at the conference. During regression this guy is *screaming* and *shaking* on my bed up there—it's terrible—'I'll *kill* you! *Fuck* you! Get *off* me!' " Mack says, moaning and pantomiming Harry's struggles to push the Beings away from himself. "And afterwards he'll say, 'But I'll tell you, John, the trauma of what they do with my body—the taking of the sperm samples, the paralysis, all that trauma—that's not what the big ter-ror's all about. The big terror is about the shattering of my reality view if I acknowledge that these creatures are real!'

"Often the last thing these abductees want to do," Mack continues, "is look in the Being's eyes. They know if they look, then they will have to ac-knowledge the presence, because the energy connection is so intense they can no longer deny the actuality of them. And then they have to admit there's some force, some power, some energy, some Beings—whatever it is!—that is completely inconsistent with the construction of reality they've maintained. It's as if it shatters their reality.

"And I'm more and more coming to think—and this relates to your question about the resistance in the culture—if you really face up to this story, this is a BIG story. If this is true, if *something important is really going on here* and this is not just psychological, but rather some kind of connec-tion with energy, Beings, whatever, in the physical world outside ourselves, or in some kind of consciousness which we've never understood which would stretch our notions of what 'consciousness' is, then this puts a big hole in the Western worldview.

"And you know there is nothing people are more attached to," Mack continues, "than their view of what is real, of what exists, and how the world is constructed. You begin to challenge that, and that is terrifying to people. And that's why I think the resistance exists.

"Maybe this Western scientific worldview was meant to protect us against our vulnerability to the kind of terrifying superstitions that led sev-enteenth-century clergymen to burn witches," he says. "Or the belief in witches themselves. Or those demons we so feared who brought us plagues, the Black Death. Or perhaps it was merely a recognition of our helplessness in the face of the physical world that the Western scientific/philosophical enterprise was meant to get mastery of. So the threat embodied in any ac-knowledgment of the possibility that this phenomenon might be true is seen as somehow reopening us to the dangers of superstition, medieval demons, witchcraft, and all of that. But I don't think it's that at all. I think it's as if we've escaped into rationality with Western science. We've 'mastered the universe.' And here we're back helpless in the face of creatures that we can't even declare to be our imagination at this point."

"Now," I say, "can you tie this in to what you were talking to me about on the telephone yesterday—the Western concept of controlling nature and Rick Tarnas's *The Passions of the Western Mind?*"

"Yes!" he says excitedly. "I have great respect for Western science. It has created miracles in getting rid of diseases. It has enabled us to feed people who would otherwise be starving. It has created opportunities for us to better know one another through advances in transportation, electronic communication, thereby enriching our lives. We are able to stay warm and dry at night and safe from savage animals. So the physical triumphs of science are palpable and enlist enormous respect. They have required a certain intellectual mastery over nature; and that mastery is Western science's great achievement. But, as I've said, there is a certain species arrogance in this dominance of nature and in the intellectual cognitive schools that have led us to be able to do that. It is this arrogance," Mack insists, "that has put us out of balance with nature."

"And do you see this UFO–alien abduction phenomenon as playing a role in correcting this imbalance?" I asked.

"I'm not saying that this phenomenon is somehow intelligently created to right that balance," Mack replies. "But it does seem to curiously operate counter to such an arrogance in that here's a situation where, clearly, we are *not* masters of nature. We are *not* in control. And it's very interesting that just at a time when we seem to be on the verge of ending life as we know it on this planet through our toxins and destruction of the rain forest and pollution of the seas, that a phenomenon such as this should occur which, in a sense, demonstrates to the direct experiencers—and indirectly to the indirect experiencers—that we are *not* in fact in control. So," Mack concludes, "were we to allow this phenomenon to be noticed, it does have the potential effect to shatter this kind of species arrogance."

I ask Mack the obvious question: If these Beings feel such an urgency to halt our destruction of our planet, why don't they intercede in a way that would be both meaningful and unequivocal?

"I'm not saying it's the *Beings* who sense the urgency," Mack answers. "It may be that the whole thing has some—I don't know, it's hard to think of it as . . ." His voice trails off.

I ask if he is suggesting the concept of the universe as a huge living organism of which the Earth is but one small part.

"It *could* be," Mack replies. "If you are a living organism and I am, and the Earth, in a sense, has some kind of organismic quality, it may be that there is some sort of divine scheme. I mean, we've so cut ourselves off from any sense of a divine design that we wouldn't know it if it were there! People talk about God in church, but they don't really believe there's any divine design. It's like with Joan of Arc: it's okay to have rules about God, as long as you don't experience conversations directly with God. They've burned people for that!

"Well, it's okay to mouth platitudes about God in churches," Mack continues, "but to actually experience a robust intelligence operating with some stake in the fate of this earth . . . I mean, Thomas Berry, the progressive Catholic theologian, has talked about the Earth being the finest example of God's creation; but we're cut off from any sense of a spiritual design or a design beyond our own material world.

"I was raised as the strictest of materialists," Mack explains. "I believed we were kind of alone in this meaningless universe on this sometimes verdant rock with these animals and vegetables around, and we were here to make the best of it, and when we're dead, we're dead. So this phenomenon has got me very agitated, sort of puzzled."

"But if there is a sense of urgency about the ecological disasters we are wreaking on this planet, why," I again ask, "don't 'they' come to somebody who can make some quick differences?"

"Well, this is an interesting question," Mack says. "I've thought a lot about that: how, first of all, information itself is a mystery. Jacques Vallee said he doesn't necessarily believe the abduction stories because it doesn't make any sense that they would need to abduct that many people to do those experiments on. But that presumes he knows what they're doing when they do these experiments.

"We *don't know* what they're doing!" Mack points out. "They may be studying energy systems of cells in ways we don't even have the slightest notion how. . . . It could be William Blake's line about seeing a world in a grain of sand. I mean, we don't know what the cosmos contains in the way of cells. We just have the grossest kinds of ways of measuring things with electromagnetic whatevers. So we really don't have any idea what they're doing when they monitor our brains or do these experiments with us. And if you think about how information evolves in the universe, you realize we really don't know much about that, either. Things evolve—we would argue why—it's not as if God had intervened directly in the affairs of mankind. That, again, would be a rather childlike religious view, it seems to me, because after all, nobody stopped the Holocaust, and nobody has stopped the great famines, plagues, and terrible suffering on the planet.

"It may be that, for reasons we can't fathom, the destruction of the Earth is not to be permitted," Mack says. "And the agency of the correction may be ourselves. In other words, it may be *our* transformation that is occurring here. It may not be that *they* are doing anything! It may be that somehow this reality is entering our minds and souls in some way and that it is we who are changing things or are to halt the destruction. That's what the experiencers report is going on. This is what *they* come to. And these people are not necessarily politically or philosophically sophisticated at all. That's what's so interesting! They are very ordinary people. As one of them said to me, 'It's like the butterflies coming back to stop the caterpillars that are denuding the bushes.'

"I'm far from being able to translate this phenomenon into a global, political, or spiritual change," Mack tells me. "But just staying with it from its closer-in, purely scientific and philosophical implications, it's very interesting in terms of our notions of what exists in the cosmos. First of all, I think our whole notion of 'us' and 'them' is all wrong anyway—the idea that 'out there . . .' Again, it's the Western view that there's an Out There that's going to affect us In Here rather than that there's an inner connection of our evolving psyches and the outside world. I fall into this trap myself—this dualism. I think the whole notion of 'extraterrestrial' is a notion of dualistic thinking anyway. *We* are extraterrestrial in a sense: our psyches are not confined to Earth." Mack pauses for a moment, then adds, "Maybe it's even wrong to ask, 'Is this outside ourselves or inside ourselves?' The very category of outside and inside is challenged by this phenomenon. Maybe the whole thing is the technological display of something from some other source."

In his Preliminary Report, Mack attempted to explore some of the challenges of the extraterrestrial hypothesis: "Almost as if by a process of elimination many investigators, at least in the United States, have come to the conclusion that UFOs are spacecraft navigated by extraterrestrials and that these beings exist in our material reality and perform the abductions," he wrote, then noted that "as [Thomas E.] Bullard has written, this hypothesis 'squares with shared experience better than with personal fantasy or cultural learning. . . . Never mind the whys and wherefores, the extraterrestrial explanation works. It satisfies believers with a systematic, internally rational account of the abduction phenomenon all for the price of buying a single premise: alien origins.' [David] Jacobs seems to be correct when he states, 'no significant body of thought has come about that presents evidence that anything else is happening other than what the abductees have stated.'

"Yet," Mack continues,

there are problems with the extraterrestrial hypothesis as well, especially as literally formulated. We are hard pressed to explain such phenomena as human beings being passed through walls and doors while potential witnesses are "switched off," or abductees taken on and off the craft without people (other than other abductees) seeing them come and go. Also, it is difficult to conceive of where the UFO occupants might reside when they are not invading earth air space, how they could live on any of the inhospitable planets in our solar system, how they could get here from distant stars or galaxies, or why the beings are so human-like and the procedures they perform so much like our medical/surgical procedures. Also, if these are, literally, extraterrestrial craft and beings, why is solid information so sparse? Further, why have we not seen better photographs of UFOs landing, for instance, in populated areas, and none of the beings themselves? Why, with the possible exception of the controversial Roswell incident do we have no artifacts that confirm an alien presence? And where are the hybrid babies being raised, or, for that matter, the crafts themselves when the abductees are undergoing their experiences?

Any theory, then, faces virtually irreconcilable contradictions. If the abduction phenomenon is considered from the standpoint of the psyche, we are faced with extremely bizarre material reported sincerely by otherwise sane people, and we cannot account thereby for the accompanying physical manifestations. On the other hand, a literal extraterrestrial hypothesis stretches our notions of the physical universe and its properties to and beyond conventionally accepted limits of reality. Faced with this dilemma some ufologists, especially Jacques Vallee and Karl Brunstein, are writing of the penetration into our reality by parallel worlds, even other universes. Vallee, for example, now states, "I believe that the UFO phenomenon represents evidence for other dimensions beyond *spacetime;* the UFOs may not come from ordinary space, but from a multiverse which is all around us. . . ."

"Interestingly, the abductees, themselves, who," Mack pointed out,

are often scientifically unsophisticated and largely unfamiliar with such writings, speak, including under hypnosis, of the sense that they have of the penetration into their consciousness of other dimensions beyond our familiar space/time reality. Many of the abductees I have met with have the sense of the operation of some other intelligence beyond our own which they feel is responsible for breeding new life forms, changing their own consciousness and affecting basic human notions of reality. Harry, for example, says, "When we witness their coming it is like scrim [a piece of fabric used in a theater to create the illusion of a solid wall or backdrop], or a movie screen. When they arrive you are looking at ordinary reality as a movie screen. When they come it is like someone shines a bright light behind the movie screen and obliterates the scene. What we perceive as the movie screen, what we call reality, they burn through, proving its only a construct, a version of reality."[10]

I ask Mack if, regardless of whether the extraterrestrial hypothesis is sound or not, he believes a government conspiracy exists to prevent the public from learning more about the UFO phenomenon.

He thinks for a moment, and then he says, "My view of the government is this: I imagine if I were a top Air Force general, say, and it's my job to protect the skies, Star Wars, whatever, and here I'm faced with a technology that can run circles around any technology that we have—*literally* run circles around it, move in and out of our air space, flip on and off the radar screen (and you've seen those time-exposure films where there are eighteen zigzagging streaks and in a second they're gone) and they're taking people out of their bedrooms—if that is, in fact, literally happening, and we're totally helpless—as this Air Force general, I've got to somehow present this information to the President. And the President asks, 'General So-and-So, what can we do about it?'

" 'With our present technology, sir,' I tell the President, 'there's not a damn thing we can do about it. And what's more, they're constantly trying to get information. What should I do?'

" 'Well, let's see,' the President says. 'Obviously we can't announce that there are extraterrestrials in these funny craft and they go in and out of our air space, and they're taking our people and there's nothing we can do, *but we're working on it!* You know? People would panic!' So—I'm still talking in the role of President," Mack says—"so the President would say, 'You can't acknowledge it as real, so we'll have to deny it.'

"As a result, the government's in a quandary," Mack says. "On the one hand, they have to deny it, and on the other hand, they have to block people's access to what information they do have—which is what creates the sense of a conspiracy." Mack shrugs, then adds, "But I think it's as simple as the way I just explained it: the government doesn't understand it any better than you or I do; there's no protection from this, so they can't do their jobs. And if your job is defense and you can't do anything . . ."

Mack confesses he feels somewhat sympathetic to the government. "If it were my job to protect our air space and I couldn't do it any better than that, I wouldn't admit it, either, you know? Sometime I'd like to talk to you about the politics of ontology and who decides what's real in a given culture. It's really a very small percentage of the population who determines this. It's similar to when the Church took over from the pagan beliefs of Europe. Although the Church became the official religion, the people went on believing whatever they had believed privately. It's sort of like that now: 70 to 80 percent of the people may believe in UFOs, but the scientific community says they don't exist. So they don't exist. It's assumed that that is a response to an empirical question, but I think a lot of this is also a political question."

"Hence the resistance?" I ask.

"Resistance has to do with the fact that a culture becomes deeply committed to a point of view, a way of seeing the world. And we've cut ourselves off from so much of the spirit world. . . . Did I give you the Rilke quote?"

Mack passes a page over to me:

That is at bottom the only courage that is demanded of us: to have the courage for the most strange, the most singular and the most inexplicable that we may encounter. That mankind has in this sense been cowardly has done life endless harm; the experiences that are called "visions," the whole so-called "spirit-world," death and all those things that are so closely akin to us, have by daily parrying been so crowded out of life that the senses by which we could have grasped them are atrophied. To say nothing of God.

—Rainer Maria Rilke[11]

"If you were God and you were trying to reach the Western mind," Mack says, "you could not reach it with anything other than that which shows up in conventional physical reality, because we don't have the senses to know anything else. What Rilke says there is that those senses have atrophied, those senses through which every people—including us before the seventeenth century—have known spirit realities, realities beyond the material. We've lost those senses and have paid such a price for our being 'masters of the physical universe' we've lost most of what we are, our God-given capabilities. And it's ironic that this rather crude, harsh intrusion of the abduction phenomenon into our senses is forcing certain people, the abductees, to open up to additional realities with great terror. But if *they* have such terror, imagine the nonexperiencers, who, when confronted by this phenomenon, respond 'It's nonsense!' because they have no means of relating this to their notions of reality. They don't because it doesn't fit!"

CHAPTER XII

Postconference Interview

John G. Miller, M.D.

On July 27, I hear from John G. Miller, the Los Angeles–area board-certified emergency physician, whom I last spoke with out on the lawn during the afternoon of the fourth day of the M.I.T. conference. At that time he said that while it was clear to him that the abduction phenomenon represented "some sort of powerful subjective experience," its "objective reality" still wasn't clear. Now, over month later, our conversation seems to pick up where our previous one left off. We are discussing Budd Hopkins's report on Linda Cortile's doubly witnessed abduction from her twelfth-floor New York apartment, and Miller expresses suspicion that that account may be "too good to be true."

However, despite his doubts about the Cortile incident, Miller is not prepared to disregard Hopkins's findings entirely: "Although Budd has his own firmly held beliefs about what is going on, which colors his data-collection process somewhat," Miller tells me, "I still found independently, in cases I investigated without hypnosis, the same specific complaints among patients who, at least to my knowledge, had no prior contamination from the Hopkins/Jacobs line of UFO-Beings kinds of stuff."

"What sort of complaints did you find?" I ask.

"Well, for example, when I first heard from one of my patients of being floated up out of their bed and through a solid window and then lifted up towards a UFO, I just assumed I was hearing something that was totally unique and probably some sort of out-of-body experience," Miller replies. "I later found out that Hopkins had heard of this many times, and that there are many others of my patients' specific allegations that Hopkins has also observed.

"I guess what I'm trying to say," Miller continues, "is from case to case my patients' complaints tend to confirm at least the sort of specific complaints that Hopkins elicited and recorded, as well as some that he hasn't. In other words, Hopkins and I have talked about some things that are not in his books that he's heard about and I've heard in my cases. There are these symbols, for example, that have come up in his work that witnesses have seen and described. I won't discuss what these symbols are, because they haven't been published, but they aren't something a person would make up. They are unique and unusual symbols."

The symbols Miller is referring to are a form of writing that many witnesses have observed within the craft. I have seen Budd Hopkins's scrapbook containing the various witnesses' attempts to reproduce that "writing." I will not describe it here because of Hopkins's use of it as a form of verification of a witness's experience. Suffice it to say it resembles no form of writing, real or imagined, that someone fantasizing such an experience might create.

Miller is also struck that his patients, too, report the same specific absences of food preparation facilities, sleeping quarters, bathrooms, and imaginative decor that other investigators reported at the conference. "Just think what human fantasy could do with alien kitchens and bathrooms, for example," Miller says with a little laugh. "We Americans are obsessed with kitchens and bathrooms! My wife and I just remodeled our house and replaced the kitchens and bathrooms in the house and guest house at great expense. And after it was all done—it looks great, by the way—I thought back and said to myself, Damn! We just tore out kitchens and baths that were better than those available to 98 percent of the world's population! And yet, hell no, it wasn't good enough for us. We had bought into this whole cultural obsession that the kitchen has to look like something out of *Good Housekeeping*. And yet you find this obsession absent from these abductees' stories.

"To me," Miller continues, "the absences of things such as that are at least as important as what is present: How many fingers do the Beings have? Do they have fingernails or not? It's like looking at an X-ray: many times you look for what's *not* there rather than what is. It's a trick that radiologists and every physician has to learn a little of. And in evaluating this phenomenon, although I know this seems a little odd, you're looking for what's not there, too. So if you think about it, if these stories are the products of human imagination, why don't we have these extravagant kitchens and bathrooms, for example?" Miller laughs softly again. "Think how wonderfully bizarre fantasized alien kitchens and bathrooms could be!"

"And what they could tell us about the Beings' anatomies," I add. "I mean, since they don't appear to have genitals, there wouldn't be much of a need for standard urinals."

"You know, in my paper on alien medical procedures, I mentioned that their examinations really shortchange the cardiopulmonary system, which is central to Western patients, certainly Americans," Miller says. "If, as a physician, you see anyone for any sort of complaint that has an internal-medicine flavor to it, if you don't pro forma listen to their heart and lungs with a stethoscope—even though you *know* it's not likely to be contributory—the patients will perceive they weren't examined at all. And yet, as I said at the conference, when you hear these stories of alien exams, the cardiopulmonary examination is of very low conspicuousness, if present at all. I was kind of shocked by how different the human and alleged alien examinations are; and yet, I also think there are some similarities."

Miller pauses for a moment, then adds, "I don't think I emphasized that well enough in my paper."

Miller mentions the parallels between taking skin samples and how examining a patient's fingernails might show indications of a disease. "The whole phenomenon is so bizarre, isn't it?" he says. "Mysteries exist. I guess that's the bottom line: *Mysteries do exist!*"

CHAPTER XIII

Postconference Interview

Carol and Alice at Their Horse Farm

In late October, I drive down to Maryland to speak with Carol and Alice again. During the four months that have passed since I saw them in Boston, Carol has had three "vivid dream" episodes (one of which she apparently shared with Alice) and two alleged alien UFO abductions, occurring one right after the other around Labor Day weekend. Further, she is now able to recall a mysterious earlier UFO sighting and encounter, and has discovered that her four-year-old granddaughter has had another presumably alien-related experience.

Alice is tending the horses when I arrive, so I sit with Carol at the farmhouse's dining-room table. It was from that table two years earlier, in September 1990, that Carol and Alice and Alice's sister Grace first saw the triangle of three strange, brilliant white lights in the nighttime sky and believed they were witnessing UFOs.

The second incident took place fifteen months later, on December 15, 1991. That was the episode in which Carol, returning at about 8:30 p.m. from visiting her parents in Hagerstown, again saw three bright lights, now in a horizontal line visible through the tops of some trees. Carol stopped, got out of the car, and walked forward for a better look. The next thing she recalled was being five miles away making the turn into the horse farm's driveway. She arrived at the farm nauseous, disoriented, frightened, and missing time. When Alice's sister came to comfort her, she discovered that Carol's earlobes were swollen and bleeding and that her earrings had been put in backwards.

The previously unrecalled sighting and encounter, Carol tells me that afternoon in Maryland, took place on December 10, 1991, just five days before the episode with the earrings. For eight months Carol had had no memory of it. But then, six weeks after the conference at M.I.T., Carol was driving Alice and UFO researcher Richard Hall back from Frederick on Interstate 70 toward the farm when suddenly, inexplicably, she turned off onto the Hoods

Mill Road exit ramp, put on the brakes, and brought the car to a stop. Hall was in the passenger seat next to Carol; Alice was seated in the back.

"Why'd you pull off here?" Alice asked Carol. "It's the next exit we always take."

Carol didn't answer. She was sitting as if in a trance, her hands still gripping the steering wheel.

"Carol!" Alice said, a little louder. "What are you doing?"

Still dazed, Carol put the car in gear and slowly pulled back onto the road. As she was continuing up the ramp, she became aware of Alice shouting in her ear, "WHERE ARE YOU GOING, CAROL? WHERE ARE YOU GOING?"

"*What?* I'm going to Hoods Mill!" Carol responded. And then she thought for a moment. I'm going to *Hoods Mill?* Why am I going to Hoods Mill? she asked herself. She snapped out of it and drove without further incident back to the farm.

Later, both Carol and Alice had the same idea: they wanted to return to Hoods Mill to see if that would trigger a recollection of what that episode had been all about.

Alice drove; Carol gave her directions. At the top of the Hoods Mill ramp Carol thought she remembered having made a right turn off the exit at dusk one afternoon and then a left at the next road she had come to. She told Alice to do the same. This second road, she recalled, had seemed narrow and overgrown; and what had started out as gravel gave way to dirt. Soon, driving the same road in daylight with Alice, Carol recalled that after passing a brick house on the dirt road she had rounded a curve and her headlights had illuminated a mailbox supported by a welded chain. "It should be just around this corner," Carol told Alice.

Alice made the turn and the mailbox was there.

"And past this," Carol said, "we make a left turn onto another dirt road."

Carol wasn't sure if the road she had turned onto on that previous half-remembered journey had been someone's driveway or not. She recalled only having driven a couple hundred yards further on to where an opening in the thick brush was used by farm vehicles for access to the fields. Alice and Carol found the opening and turned in. Directly in front of them was a field of tall corn. To the left was a long, narrow, faded-barn-red, vertically sided outbuilding, its tin roof brown with rust. Behind it, a tall white silo rose like a rocket on its launcher amid the corn. And to the left of the shed stood a dilapidated, open, one-story cattle shed.

Returning to the site that afternoon with Alice, Carol was surprised to see the outbuilding; in her memory she had thought it someone's house.

And there had not been any corn in the field then; instead, there had been what Carol later believed was a giant UFO.

What follows is a reconstruction of what happened the night she had that encounter. It is based on Carol's conscious recall, flashbacks, and a hypnotic-regression session, directed by Budd Hopkins in New York, I attend a month after my Maryland visit.

Late afternoon, December 10, 1991: Carol was returning from a visit to her parents in Hagerstown when, instead of taking the Sykesville Road exit off Interstate 70, as she usually did, she felt compelled to take the exit just before it.

A moment later, half angry with herself and half anxious, Carol realized she was lost. She knew only that she had never been on this road before and that she was going in exactly the wrong direction. It was dusk, and she could see the lights of an occasional house set back from the narrow blacktop road, some open fields; and then she passed a larger house with lights that bordered its driveway all the way from where it entered the road up to the garage. It looked to Carol like an airport runway.

There was a gravel road to her left and she took it, thinking she could find a place to pull off and back around. All she would then have to do was drive back to the narrow blacktop road, turn right, go back to the interstate interchange, and from there home to the farm. But when, after turning around, she reached the blacktop road again, instead of turning right she turned left. "Damn!" Carol said aloud. "What am I doing?"

There was another road ahead, Carol saw, and she decided to turn around there instead. She turned onto this road, the car bouncing from the bumps and ruts. She was becoming increasingly apprehensive. The road did not appear to have been recently used; both sides were covered with a dense growth. It was now only one lane wide, and narrowing; grass grew between the two tracks. What kind of road is this? Carol asked herself.

There were no more houses, no driveways to pull into. She leaned forward, peering deeper into the gathering gloom. Ahead, through the brush and trees, she saw a glow. There's a house up there, Carol thought. Got a lot of lights on it . . . out in the middle of nowhere! Weird!

As Carol approached the lighted area, she slowed the car to a crawl. Whatever the source of the light was, it was partially obscured by the silo Carol could now see off to the side of the road. It's huge! she thought wonderingly. What is it? It looks like a big building or something. The huge structure's exterior skin glowed like an enormous light bulb, illuminating the field beyond the object, even the hills farther back. And now Carol saw that there was a second, smaller, fish-shaped object suspended in midair off to the large object's right side; it was gently bobbing up and down as if rocked by a breeze. This smaller object gave off no light. It appeared to be charcoal-colored, made of a dull, unpolished metal. As Carol looked at it, first its nose would rise up and then its tail. Nose. Tail. Nose. Tail. Carol couldn't understand how this smaller object could be just floating in midair.

And then she saw there were people silhouetted by the larger structure's bright light. They were clustered together close to the right side of the glowing object as if transfixed, maybe a half-dozen of them in all. There was a man in a denim jacket and jeans holding a child by its hand; he was clasping a second, younger child against his chest. Next to him was a woman, and there were several other men standing nearby. It was difficult to tell from their silhouettes how old the other men were; they could have been adolescents.

Except for one man in a baseball cap off to the right of the group, all of them were looking at the huge, brilliantly glowing structure. The man in the baseball cap was facing the others. Carol wondered why he wasn't looking at the strange, lighted object, too.

The people seemed not to have noticed Carol's arrival. She considered calling to them, attracting their attention.

She wondered if the large glowing object was some sort of piece of machinery—a big, industrial, manufacturing-plant type of thing—and that maybe these people, for one reason or another, were working with it. But then she could see that the object was resting on a heavy landing gear; two metallic-looking retractible braces appeared to have come down from cavities beneath the thing, whatever it was, and locked into place. And there were windows visible at that end of the object which projected beyond the silo. The windows were recessed from their tops so that if someone was standing behind them he could look down. But there wasn't anybody standing behind them. If there had been, Carol thought, she would have seen them, because the light behind the windows was even brighter than the object's glowing surface.

It *was* some sort of building. It had to be. Carol was sure of that now.

The structure was at least two stories tall, flat on its top and sides, and oblong-shaped, like a cigar. She could see that it stretched back beyond the silo to the rear. Suddenly Carol thought maybe it wasn't such a good idea to let the people notice her. She was frightened that she might have stumbled upon some sort of secret *thing*. She didn't think she was supposed to be seeing this.

And now she noticed how warm she was. It was uncomfortably hot in the light. Cautiously she began to back away from her car, out of the light.

She kept moving backwards until she could hear the crunch of the dirt road beneath her feet.

Behind the outbuilding there was a low, flat cattle shed. Carol decided to sneak into the shed for a closer look. As soon as she had climbed over the gate, crossed the corral, and was under the shed's eaves out of the light, it was cooler. There were feed stalls with chicken wire closing them off. The light from the glowing object was so bright that where it shone through missing boards or holes in the shed's planking it threw dark shadows of chicken-wire pattern on the dirt floor. She crept closer to the wall on the other side of which the brilliant object rested. She could see through a crack one of the enormous braces it was resting on. What is this thing? she thought. Looks like a great big . . . banana. A giant tube . . . Got a rim around it. Like a platform or something . . . Can't see in the windows. Lots of light in there.

A humming, throbbing sound began to fill the cattle shed until the noise was painfully loud. Get out! Carol told herself. Get away from that noise!

Carol hurriedly backed out of the cattle shed. She climbed over the gate and crossed the road to the opposite bank, where she could squat hidden by bushes and small trees and watch.

From where she crouched Carol could still see the top of the structure. While she watched, a light came on toward the end of the object farthest from the silo. The light began to pulse. Its intensity seemed to follow the same throbbing sequence as the sound coming from behind the cattle shed. The light began to blink faster and faster, flicker brighter and brighter, and the throbbing noise grew louder and steadier, until, it seemed to Carol, the light was a brilliant, constant strobe white and the sound a loud, unwavering hum. She covered her eyes with her hands to keep out the light—and then, suddenly, the light was gone. The noise was gone. Carol opened her eyes and the object, too, had disappeared.

I must be going crazy! Carol thought. What *was* that thing? Nothing that big moves that fast!

Now Carol was beginning to realize that what she had been looking at had not been a building after all. But if it wasn't a building, what could it have been?

Carol emerged from her hiding place and stepped out onto the road. But there was nothing there. The people, too, had disappeared. Frightened, Carol climbed back into her car and hurried home.

Later, at the hypnotic regression session I attend in Budd Hopkins's Canal Street studio in New York, Budd remarks to Carol while she is still under hypnosis, "It's sort of a surprise that the thing left and you don't remember seeing it leave."

"Well, I didn't see it go!" Carol insists.

"It was a big thing. . . ." Budd says questioningly.

"I was covering my eyes," Carol explains, "but I didn't have them *that* covered. It couldn't have gone that fast."

"Here's what I'm going to do, Carol. In just a minute I'm going to wake you up," Budd says gently. "But before I do that, I want you to know that whatever memories were connected with how that thing left, or where the people went, or why it was so warm, or what caused the humming—all those things are pieces of memory still inside your mind, in your unconscious. And when you want them to come out, and it's time for them to come out, you'll remember if you saw the thing leave. You *must* have seen it leave," Budd insists, "because *it* was there, and *you* were there, and then all of a sudden you're still there and it's *not*. So you must have seen it leave. You must know more about it than you've remembered so far.

"So, whenever you want to remember that," Budd continues, "whether it's tonight, or tomorrow, or the next few days, weeks, or whatever, when it's time for you to remember, you'll allow those memories to come back, and you'll make sense of all this which so far doesn't make much sense."

That regression session takes place near the end of November 1992; after that, no further memories of this incident surface. Nor does Carol come up with any answer to why she was "called" to that place.

On Saturday, September 5, at the start of Labor Day weekend, seven weeks before I visit Carol and Alice in Maryland, Carol had another incident in which she seemed to have been "called" to a specific place. When I speak with her in Maryland, she has already dealt with this experience through an earlier hypnosis session with Budd Hopkins. Its significance, she tells me, is that it was "the first memory that I had after hypnosis of being on board. Of being levitated up and dropped back down."

This account, too, is a compilation of Carol's conscious and retrieved memories:

The episode began on a misty, drizzly, dark afternoon some time around two. Carol had been on her way to spend the weekend with her parents. She would leave her parents' house on Labor Day, Monday, and spend that night camping by herself in a log cabin across the border in a West Virginia state park. Alice was planning to join her at the cabin the following day.

"I would normally go straight down to Sykesville Road to Interstate 70 and head up to Hagerstown that way," Carol tells me as we sit at the dining-room table, "but that Saturday afternoon I turned right onto Route 26. And then I turned left onto a gravel road and I went maybe fifteen yards.

I stopped just to the right of the road without going into the ditch, got out of the car, and I saw ahead of me the little figure of someone. It was very foggy. I have yet to remember or to actually see that figure," Carol continued. "I don't want to, I guess."

"Could it have been a Small Gray?" I ask.

"Yes, I thought he was," Carol says. "But when Budd asked me to focus on him, I couldn't do it. I don't think I was ready at that point to do that. It was sort of like I would then have had to accept that something had really happened. And it seemed to be a sort of holdout."

I ask, "Could seeing this figure have been the result of your car's headlights projecting your shadow ahead of you on the fog?"

"I didn't have the headlights on," Carol answers. "I had on the parking lights."

When Carol got out of her car, the figure was standing on the off side of the ditch next to the fence, and she started walking in his direction. Suddenly, when she had approached within several yards of him, they both began to float upwards together at about a thirty-degree angle into the air, with the Being in front of her. As they rose, they were both tilted forward enough that Carol, looking straight ahead, was in fact peering down through the fog at the tops of the trees bordering the road. The rate of ascent was fast enough to make Carol nauseous. She tried to close her eyes but couldn't; she couldn't even blink.

Her arms and legs hung down limply. They felt heavy, as if they were being dragged up by her torso. She did retain some movement of her head, she discovered, and to keep herself from feeling vertiginous, she bent her head backwards as far as she could and rolled her eyes upwards. That's when she saw an object huge and very dark overhead, "like a black cloud," she tells me.

"Was it *like* a cloud, or *was* it a cloud?" I ask.

"I don't think it was a cloud, because I didn't notice it until we were close enough for me to see this dark thing and we just went up into it. It was enormous, maybe one hundred feet across. And it felt solid. There weren't any lights. There was no beam of light atop of me that I could tell. No shadows. We went up through this black opening, and the floor just sort of closed. There wasn't any door. There was no sign that there had ever been anything there like a door or something. So if there was a cloud, whatever I was on now was inside this cloud. It was just black, and because it was so foggy and misty I couldn't detect any sharp edges."

Inside the craft, Carol was still floating in the air, but at least she was vertical. And then an invisible force pivoted her around so that she was facing in the opposite direction.

The Small Gray was gone, and now she was alone across from what she assumed was some sort of wall, which gave off a very bright white light. But the light was diffused, as if it were shining through gauze.

Floating about ten inches off the floor directly in front of Carol, like a fancy room divider between herself and the wall, was a five-foot-high, three-foot-wide, matte-looking charcoal-gray block. The top of the block was level with the top of Carol's head. On the floor, just in front of the block, there was a plate with a raised symbol on it. To Carol, the symbol looked like the tracings of some sort of heart monitor or brain waves. There was nothing else to see in the room but the floor plate, the floating block, and the wall.

Carol still felt sick to her stomach, but now she was also feeling cold, terribly cold.

The next thing Carol knew she was being moved forward until her chest was touching the charcoal-gray block and she was floating directly over the plate in the floor. The moment her body touched the block, the block dipped down slightly, then tilted up in such a way that it scooped Carol onto it.

The block, like the room she was in, was icy cold. She was lying face-down, she told me, her right eye, cheekbone, and corner of her mouth squashed uncomfortably upon the block's frigid surface. And since she could not move, there was no way for her to make herself more comfortable.

"Were you still dressed?" I ask.

"Yes," she says, "but I wasn't alone anymore. The first thing I noticed was a figure standing to my left, sort of toward the head of this table thing. There was another figure near him. Gray skintight uniforms, everything monotone. I didn't see any decorations, belt buckles, sign of rank. There was just this usual gray crap. I couldn't see their faces because, suddenly, this silvery-white stuff came down over me."

A metallic-colored material had floated down over Carol, covering her like a sheet from her head to her feet. Except, she knew, it wasn't a sheet, it had descended much more gradually, more airily than it would have had it been cloth. And then, bit by bit, the material began to mold itself to Carol's body. For a moment she panicked. She thought she was going to suffocate, that she was being entombed in this icy material as it tightened over the back of her head, the left side of her face, her arms, her back and legs, her hands and feet.

She had no idea what the material was; she couldn't see it; but it seemed almost alive, spongy-soft. She could feel it still slowly constricting about her form. And then, suddenly, she was flipped over so that the material was beneath her and the "table" directly overhead. Carol had only a moment to realize she was being supported by the material before the matte-gray block shot upwards and disappeared into the ceiling. It retreated too fast even for Carol to see where it went. She couldn't look straight up anyway; the material, where it had come down over her, still covered half her face.

Carol had been on her stomach on the block when the material had enrobed her, her hands palms-up at her sides. Now that she was on her back, her palms were down, covered by the material. The Being who had been on her left was now on her right. He was, from what Carol could see of him, a Tall Gray: he had a very long, thin face with a pointed chin and what would have been high, broad cheekbones if, in fact, his body had had bones. His large, black, oval eyes were nonreflective, with no visible pupils. He moved closer to her and somehow made the material rotate Carol's right hand palm-up so that her thumb was extended and exposed. He was holding what looked like a double-barreled syringe. Carol subsequently came to think of this Tall Gray as a "Doctor Being."

"A needle came out of each cylinder," Carol told me. "And each cylinder was fed by a tube. There was some sort of yellow-gold liquid in the syringes and he injected it into me here on my thumb."

Carol holds her hand out to me. The faint mark of a double puncture wound is still visible in the meat of her right thumb.

"The holes are scarring up now," she says. "But he injected all of this yellow-gold fluid through those needles into my thumb and it hurt like hell! I couldn't speak, but in my head I was thinking, It hurts! It hurts! Why are you doing this? STOP doing this!

The needles were short, V-shaped, only about a third of an inch long. Carol could feel the initial prick of the needle's point; the tearing apart of the skin so that the wider portion of the needle could enter; then a fierce burning sensation as the fluid was pushed in. Everything about the procedure hurt, and Carol remembers tears trickling down the bridge of her nose.

This doesn't hurt, the Tall Gray told her telepathically.

It does *hurt!* Carol responded in her mind.

This does not hurt, the Doctor Being repeated. *I've never hurt you.*

It hurts! she protested again. *Take the hurt away any way you have to do it. Just make it stop.*

The Tall Gray put his hand on Carol's forehead and repeated, *This does not hurt.* And the pain was gone.

Carol realized it was power of suggestion, but she didn't care.

Is that better? the Doctor Being asked Carol. *How do you feel?*

I'll feel better when I leave.

Carol sensed the needles being removed, but she could not see where the syringes were taken. The Tall Being leaned forward over her, close enough to make her uncomfortable. He seemed to be studying her, and then, suddenly, she heard him tell her she could go.

"It was sort of like, 'You're dismissed now,' " Carol tells me. "It was almost unexpected."

I ask Carol, "When the Tall Being was giving you that injection and said, 'I've never hurt you,' did you feel you had seen him before?"

"Oh, yes," she said matter-of-factly.

"You recognized him?"

"It's not so much that you recognize him as there's the feeling that you've been in other situations with the same Being," she explains. "The Tall Grays don't look any different. They don't have characteristic features; one doesn't have a longer nose or larger mouth than another. It isn't something you *see;* it's something you feel. And I *felt* I should know him."

"When he touched your head, what did his hand look like?" I ask.

"Boneless, prehensile-like. He had four fingers, no thumbs. His head was broader than it was high, but the face was very long. A real long chin. The mouth literally a slit. I've never seen their mouths move, ever. And the head is set on this tiny little neck! I don't know how they keep their heads on. He was much taller than a Small Gray. I'm five-ten and he came up to my chin. Unlike the Tall Grays, the Small Grays have three fingers like little sausages attached to this long, thin hand like a bone. And they're *little.* Their shape is somewhat different. Their faces are a bit rounder. Some have pointed chins; some don't. They have rounded chins—"

We are interrupted by Alice coming back with one of their horse barn boarders. Neither Alice nor Carol wants anyone to know about their abduction experiences. They never talk about them when anyone else is around.

Later, when Carol can resume her story, she tells me that after the Doctor Being gave her the injections and told her she could go, the material that had been moulded to her body loosened. It seemed to tilt down and then she felt the material roll up beneath her and, like a bather bobbing in an ocean wave, she was pushed out until she was again standing—floating, really—upright just above the floor.

By then the Small Gray had reappeared and placed himself in front of Carol.

"Do you think he was your initial escort?" I ask her. "The one who had met you on the road?"

"I guess so," she says, then laughs, "but they all look alike to me. He just got in front of me and we started moving."

"What does this movement feel like?" I ask.

"You don't feel yourself moving. You don't realize it," she says. "There's no vertigo. It's not like when you go up to or down from one of their craft.

It's like being on roller skates, like your entire body is in a pocket and the whole pocket is moved, so you don't feel the passage of air or anything else."

"Is it like one of those airport moving walkways?"

"No, because the walkways are moving under you and you have to adjust your body's balance to keep from falling backwards. This doesn't happen here. You wouldn't feel you were moving at all except that you're passing from one place to another."

"Where did the Small Gray lead you?"

"To that spot in the floor," Carol replies.

And then, suddenly, the floor disappeared beneath her and Carol was standing by herself over an open hole three hundred feet in the air and she began to slowly fall. The tops of the trees seemed to be gradually floating up to meet her. She was dropped back onto the road close to where she had been taken from; but either because she was weak or because she hadn't used her muscles in some time, her knees buckled when she landed, and she collapsed backwards onto the wet gravel. Carol sat there in the middle of the road for a moment; then she pushed herself back up to her feet, walked to her car, and, without any memory of the abduction she had just experienced, continued on to her parents' Hagerstown house.

Carol would not have been suspicious that anything strange had happened to herself at all but for the fact that when she arrived in Hagerstown the seat of her blue jeans was wet. And just after she sat down with her parents at the dining-room table and glanced up at the kitchen clock, she asked if the clock was right. Carol's father gave her a quizzical look and said, "Yes, why?"

"It just seems later than it ought to be," Carol said. "I must have left late." At the time she still thought that was the reason; what else could explain the missing hour and a half of time?

But then her mother took Carol's hand, rolled it over, and, looking at it, asked, "What happened to your thumb?"

Carol looked down at the wound on her thumb for the first time; she had not noticed it before.

"There were two very large holes open in the middle like punctures in the fleshy part of my thumb below the joint," Carol tells me. "And around each one of the holes there was a white, puffy rim. It looked like a snake bite. There wasn't any blood; it wasn't sore. It didn't bother me at all. But I had no idea where the holes had come from. So I told my mother things just happen on a farm, that I did things to myself all the time, and since it didn't hurt that I was probably okay.

"But my parents insisted on putting some medication on it: first-aid cream, a Band-Aid. And my father kept asking me if there was something wrong—had anything happened? But since at the time I didn't know of anything, I said no, that I was just tired."

Carol was not particularly hungry, either. She tried to eat some dinner and about an hour afterwards broke out in a rash that covered her from her knees to the top of her head. She looked as if she had chicken pox, but she knew she didn't because she had had it as a child. It wasn't a poison ivy rash, either; she didn't itch, and she hadn't gotten poison ivy in years. She didn't feel bad; the rash was just there.

Carol's father wanted her to see a doctor; but because it was Labor Day weekend Carol knew a doctor would be difficult to find.

Twenty-four hours later, by Sunday evening, the rash was gone.

Monday morning, Carol and her parents decided to leave ahead of time in two cars for the West Virginia state park so that they could have an early dinner together in the lodge. They arrived at the park around three-thirty, but discovered dinner would not be served for another hour and a half. Carol's parents did not want to wait around that long and so they made sandwiches out of some of Carol's supplies and ate them at a picnic table by the lodge. Afterwards, Carol picked up the key to her log cabin, and her parents followed her up the hill in their car to the cabin she had reserved so they could help her unload the food and camping equipment she had brought for her stay.

In addition to a double bed, the cabin's single room was furnished with a desk and chair, a dresser, a small kitchen area, and a drop-leaf table with two more chairs. The table had been placed in front of the hearth of the massive stone fireplace that dominated the room. A door in that corner of the cabin led to a small shedlike bathroom with its toilet, shower, and sink. There was no reason to believe that Carol and upon her arrival the following day, Alice—would be anything but very comfortable in it. And yet, as soon as Carol and her parents approached the cabin carrying their first load, Carol's mother refused to go inside. It was only after considerable cajoling that Carol was able to persuade her mother to enter the one room; and once there, her mother refused to stay alone. She told Carol she was afraid. "This is not a good place," Carol's mother said. "There is something bad here."

Such a comment was out of character; Carol's mother was very practical. And yet here she was terrified to remain alone anywhere near that cabin while her daughter and husband walked the ten yards down the path to where Carol's car was parked to pick up another load.

Father and daughter were finally able to convince Carol's mother to sit in one of the front-porch rockers. From that chair Carol's mother could see husband and daughter at all times. And although Carol's mother didn't want to remain alone, she acquiesced. But the moment the last supplies had been brought in from the car, Carol's mother rose and said she wanted to leave. "I want to get *out* of here!" she insisted. "And that's *it!* I'm ready to go, and you, Carol, you should leave, too. I don't think you ought to stay here by yourself."

"I won't be by myself," Carol told her mother. "Alice will be here with me tomorrow. And besides, I *like* this cabin. I don't have any bad feelings about this place at all!"

"Carol, come with me a moment," her father called to her from the side of the cabin. "We need to find a scrap of wood to shim up the refrigerator."

The shim, Carol knew, was just an excuse to get her alone. And once she and her father were out of her mother's hearing, Carol's father said that he, too, would rather Carol didn't stay in that cabin by herself overnight.

"But *why?*" Carol asked.

"Because there *is* something wrong with this place," her father said. "I don't want you here. Not in this particular cabin. The holiday is over. Every other cabin is vacant. We can find you another one."

"I don't want *another* cabin," Carol told him. "I like *this* one."

Carol's father knew better than to try to change his daughter's mind. He and Carol's mother left immediately thereafter, and Carol tried to put their uneasiness about the cabin out of mind. But her father's apprehension disturbed Carol more than her mother's. Carol's father, too, had had some strange experiences. That second night of the M.I.T. conference Carol, as part of the abductee panel, reported the mysterious 1954 stalled-station-wagon/missing-time episode she had shared with him as a child while en route to his business meeting in Doylestown, Pennsylvania. And there had been, she knew, other odd experiences as well.

Carol's father's earliest experience had occurred in 1930, when he was twelve years old. He had gone down to the beach with his older brother to skip stones in the surf. They had been playing together for less than an hour when Carol's father bent over to pick up a particularly interesting seashell. When he had straightened up, everything about him was hazy and his brother was gone. Carol's father wandered the beach looking for his older brother for what had seemed to him only a few moments, then turned to look behind him. His older brother was there. He was there and equally frightened and upset, because he, also, had bent down to pick up a shell, and when he had straightened up, Carol's father suddenly seemed to have disappeared, too.

Neither of the boys would have thought much about this incident had it not been for the fact that when they returned home, instead of having been absent a little more than an hour as they had thought, they learned they had been gone three times that long. What's more, when they hadn't gotten back on time, their mother had called the police, who had thoroughly searched the beach the boys had been playing on and reported back they were nowhere to be seen.

According to Carol, her father's second experience occurred in 1932, when he was fourteen, again in the company of his brother. The two boys had been on a hiking trip with friends when, around two-thirty, they all decided to race to the top of the mountain pass. In order to beat the others, Carol's father and his brother chose a side path through the woods they thought only they knew about. That path should have brought them to the top in about a half-hour: by three o'clock. But when the two boys reached the top of the pass it was dark, somewhere around eight-thirty. Their friends had all reached the top hours before and had been out searching for them through the woods, calling for them. The brothers had not heard or seen the others. Carol's father has no idea how they reached the top of the pass in the dark, or what had taken them so long. Neither he nor his brother ever had any memory of what happened during that missing time.

The third incident was the disappearance of Carol's grandfather in 1939. "My father was a young man then," Carol tells me that afternoon in Maryland. "He was not married yet. He and his older brother and sister were home for some kind of holiday dinner and right in the middle of the dinner, while they were all sitting at the table, my grandfather pushed back his chair and said, 'I'm going to get a pack of cigarettes.'

"Everybody just stared at him," Carol explains. "First of all, he didn't smoke. So everyone was thinking, What's going on here? Why's he doing this? Then they thought he was up to something funny, that maybe he had a surprise of some kind. But it was the middle of dinner! And he looked kind of dazed when he stood up. Anyway, he left, got into his car, drove away—and no one ever saw him again!"

I asked Carol, "Is there any reason to think he might just have been fed up with his family and his life and decided to go out on his own?"

"No!" Carol says firmly. "He was a concert violinist. He probably had twenty-five students. He was a very dedicated musician; had been all his life. He was honored in the community; he seemed to have been quite a good father. That was the last time my father saw his father. His car was later found parked in front of the grocery store in town, but no evidence was ever discovered of where he went. He had essentially vanished, and he was declared legally dead eight or nine years later."

"Did your father sense there were any problems in your grandparents' marriage?" I ask.

"No."

"He never witnessed any arguments or scenes?"

"Not that he knows about," Carol replies. "He said his parents proba-bly weren't any different from any other couple at that time in terms of the man ruling the roost. But my father said he wasn't a bully; he didn't seem to be a domineering or inconsiderate husband. My grandfather seemed gen-uinely very fond of my grandmother. They spent a lot of time together. They had a ritual where they would sit together out on the porch every night and talk about what had happened during the day. He did not drink and, as I said, he did not smoke. As far as I know, he did not carouse. It was a very small community!

"He was busy all the time," Carol continues. "But he did have long spells where he would disappear for two or three hours and come back very upset, very tired. So there were periods where he was missing, but my father doesn't seem to know the details of much of that—or he doesn't remember, because it happened when my father was very young."

If, as was suggested at the M.I.T. conference, the abduction phenome-non is generational, then perhaps both Carol's father and her grandfather were abductees, too. This, of course, leads to concerns about Carol's son and granddaughter.

Back at the conference, as part of the abductee panel Sunday night, Carol showed the Magic Marker picture of the "flying machine" her four-year-old granddaughter, Stacy, had drawn, which included Stacy's sketch of Nu, the little Gray Being who sometimes took her up in the craft. Carol had also told us that Stacy hadn't wanted Carol to say anything about Nu to her parents. "Mommy and Daddy don't like him," Stacy had said. "And when I put my drawings of Nu on my wall, Daddy takes them down."

In the middle of August, about ten weeks before my trip to the horse farm, Carol, visiting her granddaughter, saw Stacy playing with an imagi-nary ball about the size of a soccer ball. Carol says she asked the child if the ball was invisible.

"Sort of," Stacy answered. And then, according to Carol, the child ex-plained it was "like a ball, but made out of light," that the ball "could make doors and windows open and close, and holes in solid walls big enough for her to walk through," and that these holes "would close up after she and the ball went through them."

Carol asked Stacy who had given her the ball to play with. The child glanced uneasily at her mother, seemingly hesitant to say anything about it in front of her, so Carol did not press. The following afternoon, however, when they were alone, Carol again asked her granddaughter where the ball had come from. According to Carol, Stacy said some of Nu's friends had given it to her, but that she could only play with it when Nu's friends were around.

(I do not learn about Carol's son's—Stacy's father's—childhood experiences until Carol mentions them after the hypnotic-regression session a month later at Budd Hopkins's studio.)

That first evening at the West Virginia state park, Carol's parents drove off, leaving her alone in her cabin high up the hill, at around five-thirty; it was still light out. Carol built herself a fire, more to get rid of the humidity in the cabin than because she was cold. She tried to eat something but still didn't have much of an appetite. She sat out on the porch and drank a couple of cups of coffee while watching the moon rise; then she went to bed around ten-thirty and slept soundly. In other words, despite her parents' concerns, Carol had no problems that first night alone in the cabin.

The following morning, the Tuesday after Labor Day, Carol awoke around seven-thirty, lounged in bed for a while, then arose and dressed. Carol doesn't wear a brassiere, so she simply pulled on her long-sleeved yellow T-shirt, white cotton panties, blue jeans, and a pair of comfortable shoes. She had eaten practically nothing for the past twenty-four hours but still was not hungry. She made herself a pot of coffee and carried her cup out to the rocker on the front porch to wait for Alice's arrival.

It was a bright, cloud-free, late-summer day. She had scarcely sat down when she was startled by the appearance of a strange, huge, yellow insect. The bug, whatever it was, had two buzzing wings spanning about six inches and an oval, three-inch-long body covered by plush, golden, beelike fur—except, unlike a bee's coat, there were no dark stripes. The insect's eyes were at the front of its head beneath its two antennae. It had suddenly come around the side of the cabin to the porch and hovered, buzzing, directly in front of and very close to Carol's face. It scared the daylights out of her. It remained there but a moment; then, in a swift, darting motion, moved to the side of Carol's face and hovered there. It then darted to the opposite side of Carol's face and hovered; switched to the back of her head and hovered; and returned in front of her again.

The insect always hovered buzzing directly facing Carol and very close to her head, but it never touched her. Then it would fly away for a few moments and come back. By nine o'clock that morning, Carol had grown comfortable enough with her insect companion to nickname it "Goldie." She never did discover what kind of insect it was. But because she had never seen one like it before, Carol assumed Goldie must have been blown in by a storm.

Goldie was not the only wildlife Carol saw that morning while she sat waiting for Alice to appear. Because the park was virtually empty except for herself and the occasional passing park ranger, Carol was able to see deer and bobcats, too.

Carol had expected Alice to drive out after feeding the horses and arrive around noon. Alice would spend the night and then, because of her job in Washington, leave early the next morning. But when, by three o'clock that Tuesday afternoon, Alice still had not appeared, Carol was growing restless.

The skies were darkening as thick storm clouds moved in. There was a deep growl of thunder in the distance. Carol now suspected Alice would not be coming, that some problem had arisen with the horses or the farm; but Carol didn't dare go down to the lodge to telephone, because Alice might choose that moment to arrive and would have no idea where to find her.

Carol decided to take a short walk on the park road that fed all the cabins. That way she would be within hearing distance of any car that came up. Her cabin, she confirmed, was the only one occupied. She did not stay out long. The thunder was coming closer, and when it started to rain, Carol went back to her porch to wait out the storm.

It poured steadily for about an hour while Carol sat in the rocker and watched. And afterwards, when the rain let up, there was ground fog.

Another cabin was situated on the slope of the hill several hundred feet above and to the right of Carol's. It was on the other side of the one-way park road that looped around the cabin area. From where Carol was sitting, she had been able to look through the side of her porch up that slope and see that cabin and any cars that came along the road. But a fog cloud had settled very low to the ground. It was so dense Carol could no longer make out the road or the neighboring cabin.

As Carol watched, the fog began to drift slowly down the hill toward her. Something about the cloud alarmed her. There was no swirling of the mist; it never quite touched the ground; and it didn't seem to change shape at all. It just came closer and closer. Carol rose from the rocker and stood at the side of the porch to watch the cloud more closely. It was now about four-thirty in the afternoon; the storm had passed, so the light was good. Therefore, the moment two thin, short gray legs became clearly visible at the bottom of the cloud, Carol panicked and ran inside the cabin.

Her first thought was to lock the Beings out; but then Carol realized, That's stupid! You can't "lock" them out! Instead she grabbed her car keys from the hook behind the cabin's front door and raced outside. Her plan was to get into her car and drive away. It didn't matter to her whether her idea made any sense or not; she just wanted to *do* something. She couldn't just sit back and allow them to take her.

Keys in hand, Carol leaped off the porch and ran down the path towards her car. She managed a quick glance over her shoulder and saw there were now two Beings for sure and, she thought, maybe a third emerging from the mist.

Three Small Grays were now floating down the hill at Carol single-file. There was no movement of their arms or legs. They were slowly gliding down, like skiers: knees and ankles locked.

Carol, at a dead run, made it to the bottom of the path and the gravel pull-off where her car was parked, its nose practically butting up against her cabin's neatly stacked firewood supply. She hurried to the driver's side, slid in, and jammed the key in the ignition. The car started immediately. She gunned the motor once and looked up.

The three Small Grays were now in front of her, between the woodpile and her car, only a few feet away. For an instant she considered putting the car's automatic transmission into drive and running over them; but then she thought, No, get away! Get out of here!

She shifted into reverse and, in a spray of gravel, backed out onto the one-lane road down to the lodge. Just as she reached the road she glanced back at the Small Grays again. The one in front had raised his arm and was pointing at the front end of Carol's car. She had but a moment to think, Oh, crap!, before she heard a snapping sound and her car popped out of gear.

She was still coasting backwards onto the park road, so Carol put her foot on the brake as she struggled to get the car back into reverse. The shift lever slid through the gears as if through butter; it met with no resistance of any kind. She didn't know what to do. Without gears she could not move the car forward or backward. Her car was stalled in the middle of the park road; she could not drive her car at all.

Carol looked back through the windshield at the Grays. The one in front was raising his arm again, and Carol lifted her hands from the steering wheel. *Please don't do anything more to the car,* she thought. She had just put 650 dollars' worth of repairs into her car the week before.

"I'm getting out," she said aloud to the Beings. "I'll come with you if you don't hurt my car."

She left the car in the road and pocketed her keys. "I won't resist or run away," she told them, "but I've got to remember this abduction. Please, this is one I need to remember."

The next thing Carol recalls is following a Small Gray back up the path, the other two behind her. She was not walking; both Carol and the Beings were floating. And then, suddenly, she was inside their ship.

She does not remember whether she entered the fog bank, or how she was brought inside the craft; she remembers only that the space she was in was like the insides of a marshmallow—except it wasn't soft. Still, the white, curved interior wall was rounded and seamless; there were no corners or sharp edges, no windows or doors. A bright, misty white light flowed evenly across the interior's smooth surfaces, but Carol could not see where it was coming from.

The three Small Grays floated Carol to a reclining chair and seated her in it. As the chair accepted her weight, it molded itself to her form. The chair, Carol realized, would have been extremely comfortable had its surfaces not been so cold.

Carol strained to look about her. She wanted to see everything, but the only part of her body she could move was her eyes; she could not move her head at all. There was nothing to look at except that blank, curving, seamless wall. The three Small Grays had moved out of Carol's line of sight and she was all alone—until three Tall Grays appeared at her right.

They all had large, black, nonreflective oval eyes that seemed covered by a film. Carol could not make out any pupils or change in coloration. She wondered if the film was some sort of goggle or protective covering. The light was so bright she could have used a pair of dark glasses herself.

One of the Tall Grays approached Carol until he was standing close enough to touch her. The other two remained standing a yard or so behind him to her right. She did not feel particularly frightened. She was at that point where she was resigned to letting them do whatever they wanted. Go ahead, she was thinking, I don't care what you do because I'm going to remember every single bit of it.

As the Tall Gray leaned over Carol, looking down at her, and she looked back up at him, she had the feeling that she was supposed to know who he was; that she was supposed to respond to him in some way. It was like a little itch in the back of her mind saying to her, You're supposed to do something here. But at the same time she was thinking, I don't want to. I don't want to.

Later, she realized she was supposed to have recognized him from the previous abduction, the one that had taken place on Saturday, just three days before. He was the Doctor Being who had given her the injections. But at this time she still had no recall of Saturday's abduction. She had no conscious memories of anything the "Doctor" had ever done to her, so she had no idea who he was. Instead she was thinking, Who are you guys? What the hell is going on here? Why am I here?

That was when, in her head, she heard the Tall Gray say, *You will be changed.*

What?! Carol exclaimed.

We have to do these things. It's important that we do these things, the Doctor Being said. *I'm going to explain this to you. You will understand.*

No, I don't understand! Carol thought. *Why do you have to do these things? Because it's important.*

Why is it important? Carol asked.

You don't need to know, the Doctor Being replied.

"The Beings just don't tell you anything," Carol explains to me that afternoon in Maryland. "They answer questions with more questions, or their answers don't relate in any way to your questions, or they refuse to answer you at all.

"It's a form of arrogance," she continues. "As if they were saying, 'You're a tool of some kind for some purpose. We're going to use that tool. And when we're through with it, we'll put it away, or throw it away, or whatever. We don't have to explain to the tool why we're using it.' It's a very arrogant response to all the questions, worries, and concerns you have when you're confronted with all this strangeness.

"Your feelings make no difference to them whatsoever," Carol says. "Although they sometimes do strange things, like putting their hands on your forehead to ease your pain and then asking 'Are you feeling better now?' But it's like some sort of taped response. It's not because they're concerned; it's because in order to deal with this social animal, us, they have to get our cooperation at some point without a lot of resistance. So they pretend to care."

The Doctor Being would not answer Carol's questions. She learned from him only that they had to do some things and that it was important. And then he turned back toward the other two Tall Grays—Carol came to think of them as "Techs," as in "Technicians"— and nodded once. One of the Techs immediately came forward. He was carrying a single-cylinder tube-fed syringe out of which projected a long, thin needle. Because Carol could move only her eyes, she could not see where the tube emerging from the top of the syringe led.

Carol's outstretched arms were resting palms-up on the arms of the reclining chair. The Doctor Being moved back as the Tech floated up against the right side of Carol's chair. He pushed up the sleeves of her yellow T-shirt and injected a rust-colored fluid into her upper right arm just beneath her smallpox vaccination scar. He then disappeared behind her and reappeared on her left side carrying a different, double-cylindered, double-needled, double-tube-fed syringe.

The fluid in one tube was golden, the other yellow. The needles, she later tells me, were longer and thinner than the ones the Doctor Being had used on her the Saturday before. And although Carol felt a prick as the needles entered and a stinging sensation when the fluids were injected, the shot was nowhere near as painful as the one given her with the wide double needles in the meat of her thumb. By comparison, she says, she hardly felt the injections in her upper arms. But she could see the liquids coursing through the tubes, and the injection seemed to go on and on and on.

After this second injection the Tech momentarily disappeared again and reappeared back on her right side carrying a third syringe.

Oh, no! Oh, God! Carol thought. Somewhere in the back of her mind she recognized this syringe: it was the big, double-barreled one with the thick needles. The Tech carefully lined up the syringe's twin needles over the previous punctures in her thumb. The injection was less painful than Carol thought it would be. The holes were already there; the needles had only to break through the thin scabs. Still, it hurt, and she told them so.

No, it doesn't, the Doctor Being said.

The Tech completed his job, moved out of view, then returned with the second Tech.

May we remove your clothes? they asked.

What? Carol asked, surprised. *No! No, I don't think so! I don't want you to. It's cold!*

They paid no attention to her.

The chair Carol was sitting in gently pitched her forward and the Techs, one on each side of her, reached behind Carol and pulled her shirt over her head. They then removed her white canvas shoes. Next came her blue jeans. She could feel their fingers undoing the jeans' button fly, and then their hands at its waistband. She could feel the fingers of the Tech on her right side against her flesh because he had mistakenly grasped the waistband of her underpants along with her jeans. Perhaps because Carol's body temperature was warmer, the Being's fingers seemed cool. But it wasn't their temperature that surprised her; it was their texture: like leather strips rubbing against skin.

The Tech realized his error and, like the Tech on Carol's left side, seized only the waist of her jeans. Together the two Tall Grays tugged her blue jeans over her hips and off. It was when the Techs removed her underpants that Carol got mad. *You can't do this!* she thought.

Yes, we can, the Doctor Being replied.

She was angry, embarrassed to be naked before the Beings, and she was cold. By this time one of the Techs had returned with a fourth syringe. It had only one large cylinder, but there were two long, thick, vicious-looking needles spaced about three-quarters of an inch apart. The Tech leaned forward and plunged both needles into Carol's stomach just at the bottom rim of her belly button and began injecting a reddish-orange fluid into her abdomen. The pain was continuous and so intense she was screaming inside her head, *THIS HURTS! THIS HURTS!* And she could hear the Doctor Being saying, *This does not hurt.*

It does! Carol sent back. *THIS HURTS!*

The Doctor Being placed his fingertips on Carol's forehead and the pain was gone. Carol's gratitude and relief was so immediate and profound she knew she would do whatever he asked if it meant keeping that pain away.

It wasn't supposed to hurt, the Tall Gray Doctor told her. *It shouldn't have hurt.*

Well, it did, Carol replied.

I've never hurt you before, the Doctor Being said.

It was at that moment that Carol realized that she had probably known this Tall Gray a long time. Her understanding of this was not on any conscious level. She still did not yet, for example, recall her abduction of three days before, or any of her previous abductions. She knew only that an ongoing, extended relationship existed between this Tall Gray Doctor Being and herself.

The Tech was removing the needles from her navel. Although there was no pain, she could feel the pull of the needles coming out. And then there was the nausea—not from the injections, Carol thinks, but as an aftermath of the pain.

Now we have to test you, the Doctor Being said. He and the two Tall Gray Techs left Carol alone in the chair. She remained there naked, her legs slightly apart, wondering why she was no longer cold. She tried to move her head to look around, but she was still paralyzed; the only muscles she could move were those of her eyes and, if she really concentrated and struggled, her eyelids.

The Beings were gone long enough for Carol to think she might even have dozed off. But then the Doctor Being returned with one of the Techs, who was carrying yet another syringe. Although this syringe, like the others, had a single cylinder and a tube leading Carol could not see where, it appeared to have some sort of small cup or funnel device instead of a needle, and the cylinder was empty.

The Doctor Being stood at Carol's right shoulder as the Tech, standing at Carol's right side, leaned across her and took her left arm. It was the first time she had seen his hands. His fingers were wrapped around the syringe like a vine, and Carol was too amazed to worry what he might do to her. She was thinking, Wow! They don't have any bones! There are no joints!

The Tech placed the cup end of the syringe against the big vein on the inside of Carol's left arm and applied a slight pressure. She felt the prick of a needle as it broke through her skin. But something went wrong. She experienced a burning sensation and the cup fell off and the syringe seemed to pop up in front of her face. She could see the needle with her blood on it. And then the Doctor Being moved into her line of sight and she saw him look at the Tech, and instantly the Tech was against the far wall. He seemed to have been flung back by the Doctor's eyes. But it had all happened so fast Carol wasn't sure she had even witnessed it.

The other Tech came forward with a replacement syringe. He pressed it on top of Carol's vein, there was a slight *phfut!* and she could see her blood filling the syringe, then flowing up through the tube. Only a small sample was taken, and then the needle was withdrawn and the blood specimen carried away.

When the Doctor came back to Carol she asked him, *Why did you take my blood?*

We have to, the Being responded telepathically.

Why do you have to? Carol asked.

It's not important that you know.

It IS important that I know! Carol told him. *You took my blood!*

The Being looked at her, then said, *We have to see if everything's okay.*

Why do you have to see? Carol asked. *What needs to be okay? What are you doing to me?*

Why do you need to know? the Doctor Being demanded with what Carol sensed was a bit of frustration. *Why do you need to know these things? You don't need to know this!*

What do you need my blood for? Carol asked. *What were all those other shots? What are you doing—?*

The Being cut Carol off. *You will be changed,* he told her. *You are changing.*

Carol did not understand what he was talking about. *What do you mean, 'changing'?* she asked. *What will I be changed into?*

You are changed, the Being said.

CHANGED TO WHAT? Carol thought more forcefully.

The Being repeated, *You are changed!*

Carol was convinced she didn't understand him. She wasn't surprised that she wasn't getting an answer, but she didn't know what he was talking about. And suddenly the Doctor Being said, *You will only eat cow things.*

Laughing inside, Carol thought, Now I know I'm not understanding what he's saying to me!

Hearing that, the Being repeated, *You will only eat cow things!*

Human beings cannot eat just cow, Carol protested. She was not normally even a red-meat eater; she preferred chicken. *We have to have other things in our diet. We cannot subsist on just cow!*

You can, the Being answered. *You are changed.*

"It was a there-isn't-any-room-for-argument remark," Carol tells me at the dining table of the horse farm. "When the Beings make a strong remark, or they're being adamant, you hear it differently. It's like you don't hear individual words so much as you hear everything all at once. That's why I thought I was misinterpreting what he was saying to me."

"So you don't get a 'sentence,' you get the idea?"

"Yes, you get the gist of it. So I figured I was just misunderstanding him. But when there's no room for argument, when they don't want to hear any more, or when they're beginning to get that little edge to their demeanor, it comes out sharp in your head. It doesn't show on them, because they have no facial expressions, but it comes out in your head as though there are little exclamation points on things. And so his last comment, that I must eat cow because I was changed, came out very strong. And I knew it wouldn't do me any good to argue. I decided instead to ask him about the horses."

"What horses?" I ask Carol.

A month before, Carol had had a dream so vivid and detailed, she says, she wasn't sure it hadn't been real. And when her memories of the dream didn't dissipate with time, she decided to write them down.

According to Carol, she does not recall how in her dream she arrived inside the alien craft, but once inside she was brought naked to a chair similar to the one she occupied while being given the injections by the Techs. As she approached the chair she saw, slightly behind it and to its right, a rectangular white box with rounded corners and a black, glassy top. On the box were two different symbols: at its front, a violet-colored representation of what looked a little like a winged garden hoe; on its side, a pink, double-winged, eaglelike figure on a black metallic background. Carol had never seen such symbols before and did not know if they meant anything. She was not, in fact, sure she hadn't entirely imagined them, since she saw them for only a brief moment as she approached the chair. She was much more curious about the chair, because there was a closed panel grafted to its back, out of which came cables.

The craft's interior was illuminated by a large tube of continuous white light attached to the ceiling. Beneath the light, along the wall where one might expect portholes, were picture-window-like frames containing not glass but some sort of slats. The slats, arranged in a regular interval around the interior of the craft, were constantly in motion. Carol has no idea of their function. They weren't what attracted her attention; what surprised Carol was the way the chair molded its icy surface to her body and that directly in front of her there was a wire mesh cage containing four very young horses.

One foal appeared distressed; a second seemed only a little anxious; a third looked curious; and the fourth looked simply bored.

At Carol's side stood a Small Gray who kept telling her, *Look at the horses. Look at the horses.* Out of the corner of her eye she could see the Gray's hands moving across the marshmallowy box's black glass top. She could not see what he was doing, only that each hand had four fingers and no thumb.

In obedience to the Small Gray, Carol kept looking at the young foals. Outwardly they appeared identical: they were brown with no markings and between three and four months old. The only thing odd about them, she told me, was their feet: instead of hooves, they had pads—soft, round, flexible pads that flattened and spread when they put their weight on them.

I think of other abductees' accounts of having been taken to a desert-like wasteland with a dying red sun and ask Carol if these foals' feet would be better suited to a soft, sandy surface than a hoof.

"Yes!" she says. "As soon as I saw them they reminded me of camels' feet, except there were no toes."

"Could the foals have been a holographic projection?"

"I don't know," she says. "They looked real."

The foals *looked* real, she tells me, but they made no sound nor gave off any odor—plus, they had these strange pads for feet. And that is why, Carol explained, when she could not get the Doctor Being to tell her how she was changing or why she could only eat "cow things," she asked him about horses: she had wanted to discover if her dream had been real.

The Doctor's response was the same as mine. *What horses?* he asked.

Do you have horses here? On this ship? Carol asked.

We do not have horses here, the Being responded telepathically.

Okay, Carol thought, *do you know about horses?*

Horses, yes, he said. *What about horses?*

Well, about their feet, Carol said. And when the Being did not respond in any way, she added, *Their hooves?*

Yes, he said. *Horses are changed.*

Here we go again! Carol thought. "Horses are changed." "People are changed." She wondered how she could make the Being understand that what she wanted to know was how did their horses' feet look. *Our horses,* Carol said to him, *the horses where I'm from, have hard feet. Their hooves are hard.*

No, no, no, the Doctor Being told Carol. *Horses have changed.*

Are their FEET changed?

Horses have changed.

Carol felt she wasn't getting anywhere. But then the Doctor Being glided out of sight and returned a moment later bearing a thin, square, translucent viewing screen measuring about eighteen inches square.

I will show you horses, the Being said.

Finally! Carol thought excitedly. Here's something I can relate to!

The Being lifted the screen until it was in front of Carol and then released it. The screen remained floating motionless in midair. It displayed a sharp color image of dozens of mature, brown horses moving about—just brown horses. There were no grays, no pintos, no chestnuts, no bays. The horses had no markings, no distinguishing blazes, white socks, or black legs. And there was nothing else in the image to help determine their size. The background seemed to have been totally whited out. All Carol could see was dozens of identical tiny brown horses with dark brown manes moving about, criss-crossing in front of each other, turning around. No horses entered the screen from the left or right; none left the screen, as one would expect were a camera in a fixed spot filming a wandering herd. As if penned in by the boundaries of the image, the horses simply milled about—and Carol couldn't see their feet!

These are horses, the Being said.

Yes, I KNOW that, Carol replied. *But I can't see their feet!*

Why do you want to see their feet? the Being asked.

Carol again tried to explain that the horses she had seen in her dream had pads instead of hooves.

No, no, no, no, the Being said. *Horses are changed. Horses are forever changed.*

No they're not! Carol insisted. *Our horses still have hooves.*

The Tall Gray's arm shot up and he plucked the screen out of the air and disappeared with it behind Carol. A moment later he returned with another screen identical to the first.

Cows, the Being said.

The image this time was of dozens of cows milling about. They were black and white, splotchy, like Holsteins—except, unlike Holsteins, these cows had two large, flexible tubes hanging down from their sides. One tube emerged low on their ribs just behind their front legs; the other came out higher up just in front of the cows' hind legs. The tubes, about twice the diameter of a soda can, were gray, ribbed like dryer hoses, and sealed at the end with some sort of black cap. Carol was concentrating on the tubes, trying to see if they grew out of the cows or if they had been surgically added. *Do all the cattle have these tubes?* she asked.

Cows are changed, the Doctor Being said. *Cows are changed. Horses are changed. People are changed.* And he snatched this second screen out of the air, too. From behind her she could hear him say, *You must only eat cow things.*

Here we go again, Carol thought.

You must only eat cow things, he repeated.

I can't ONLY eat cow things! Carol responded angrily.

The Doctor Being shot around her chair until he was hovering right beside Carol. He leaned forward over Carol so that his body was horizontal and tipped his head so that it was vertical at a ninety-degree angle from his neck. He pushed his face into Carol's so close that if he had had a nose it would have bumped hers and she would have felt his breath. But the Tall Gray had no nose as such, only a slight bump between two open holes in his face that may or may not have been nostrils, and there was no breath to feel. Nor was there any odor. She could not even sense a change in temperature.

The Doctor Being's face was directly opposite Carol's and she was peering straight into his huge, oval, nonreflective black eyes. She wanted to flinch, pull back, look away, close her eyes, but she couldn't. She felt helpless and frightened as the Being looked so deeply into her eyes that he seemed to be seeing through her. She has no idea how long he stared at her; it was as though time had stopped. She is not sure she even remained conscious. She knows only that the link between herself and the Being was so intense that when the Tall Gray broke the connection and departed from the room she was left with a headache.

The Doctor Being returned moments later with the two Tall Gray Technicians. *You are not to act crazy,* the Doctor told Carol.

Okay, Carol answered, *I won't act crazy.*

You are not to be crazy.

I won't be crazy, she thought, *but this whole experience, the pictures, the cows, is insane!*

You are not to think you are crazy, the Doctor told her.

Yes, Carol said.

And once again the Being told her, *You must eat only cow things.*

And then it seemed to Carol he was finished with her and that the Techs were going to dress her.

The two Techs had no problem getting Carol into her T-shirt, but her blue jeans were more difficult. Without bothering with Carol's white cotton panties, they managed to pull the jeans up over her knees, but they were having trouble sliding them over her hips.

Carol asked, *May I dress myself?*

The Techs backed away, taking her jeans with them; the Doctor joined them off to Carol's left side. Although she could hear none of what was being said, she could tell from their bobbing heads that the discussion the

Beings were having was animated. And then one of the Techs brought Carol's blue jeans back and dropped them at her feet.

You can dress yourself, the Doctor Being said.

Carol tried to sit up. She tensed her stomach muscles but nothing happened. She couldn't move. The Doctor Being raised his arm and made a downward gesture as if ordering a dog to sit. Carol did not know what he meant. He repeated the motion, and Carol realized he was trying to tell her to push down with her legs. She pressed down as hard as she could and the chair tipped forward, thrusting her out.

"I was up!" Carol tells me. "It was wonderful! I was standing and moving very slowly. Everything was as if in slow motion. If I'd had to hurry, I don't think I could have.

"I got my jeans on and my shoes," Carol continues, "and I still wasn't on the ground! I was still floating just above it. It's the strangest feeling, because it feels like your shoes are touching something, but you don't see anything touching the bottom of your feet."

"What were the Beings doing while you dressed?" I ask.

"They became very agitated, very worried that I . . . ." Carol pauses for a moment, remembering. "I wouldn't say that they were frightened, but they seemed concerned that maybe permitting me to move wasn't such a good idea. I was led out by this one Tech who came about up to my chin, which means he was maybe five feet tall. He was only about eighteen inches in front of me, and I was looking at the back of his head, trying to remember what he looked like. I was trying to see if I could detect a seam on the back of his uniform. But there were no seams. There weren't any shoulder blades or a spinal cord, either, there was nothing that stood out. No visible definition of any kind. He had sloping shoulders; not particularly wide, but now narrow either. . . . And his neck came right up to the back of his head. He was just weird-looking from behind: this real large head sitting like a daffodil on a stem, and there was no hair, veins, or anything on the head. . . ."

The Tall Gray Tech led Carol towards the wall. The second Tech and the Doctor Being followed behind her. A panel she had not noticed before suddenly lifted and disappeared into the ceiling, and the four of them floated through the opening into a brilliantly illuminated white corridor. Carol heard an airy swish as the panel dropped back down and vacuum-sealed behind them—at least she thinks it was the sound of the panel closing behind her. She couldn't turn to look. And besides, she was distracted by the long row of identical two-and-a-half-foot square boxes aligned along the corridor's left-hand wall.

Look at the boxes, the Doctor Being was telling her.

To Carol, the boxes looked like giant marshmallows: rounded corners, white, and without any visible markings.

Look at the boxes, the doctor repeated.

There were at least twenty-five of them, all the same size, all perfect cubes. They were not touching each other; instead, the boxes were spaced evenly the length of the corridor.

Remember the boxes, the Being told her.

Carol continued to fix her eyes on the boxes as she floated past them down the corridor. At the end of the corridor there was one last box identical to all the others.

Look at the box, the Being told her.

Carol did as he ordered, and the next instant, she was walking alone back down the hill to her West Virginia state park log cabin.

"I don't remember coming out of the ship; I don't remember a door or a hatch opening, or floating down from above. I don't remember *any* of that," Carol tells me. "I had no idea what time it was, because I didn't know anything had happened. The whole incident had been erased the instant I was back on the hill. I remember I tried to eat dinner. I remember before that sitting on the porch after the storm, watching the ground fog and playing with Goldie. It was getting dark and I was a little worried about Alice, because she hadn't arrived and I figured she wasn't going to. And I wondered what I had done all day. I remember thinking, Oh, hell, the whole day's gone! I'd lost an entire day. I remember going into the cabin and making hot dogs and baked beans and a cup of coffee—and then I threw up.

"I didn't think anything of it," Carol tells me. "I didn't at that time have any recall of the Doctor Tall Gray telling me, 'You must only eat cow things.' So I never made that link. I just thought only that what I had eaten didn't agree with me. And around nine-thirty or ten o'clock I got undressed and went to bed, still unaware that anything at all had happened to me at that point."

"When did you discover that your underpants were missing?" I ask.

Carol laughs. "Actually, it was not until the next morning, Wednesday, when everything came back. It was something I didn't think about, which was odd. Because with those jeans, if I don't wear panties underneath I slice myself in two!"

Wednesday morning Carol awoke in the log cabin's double bed with Goldie clinging to the outside of the window screen over the headboard. The huge, strange insect had presumably stayed there all night. Carol climbed out of bed, looked at the window screen, and said, "Good morning, Goldie." And Goldie flew around the cabin to the porch to wait for Carol to step outside.

When Carol went to brush her teeth, she discovered there was no water. She tried the shower and the kitchen faucet, but they were dry, too. Since none of the other cabins in her area were occupied, she decided to drive down to the lodge to report that the water was off.

Carol dressed, picked up her car keys, grabbed her purse, and went out the screen door, with Goldie practically in her ear. As she walked down the path she was surprised to see her car in the middle of the road. What's it doing there? she asked herself. She wondered if, during the night, it had slipped out of gear and rolled backwards down the slight hill into the road.

At the end of the path, the instant she touched the car's door handle the entire abduction incident of the previous day returned in her mind.

"Everything just came back all at one time!" she tells me. "It was like being hit over the head with a stick!"

It rained around three-thirty or four o'clock, just as it had rained the afternoon before. Carol had been sitting on her porch waiting for the rain to stop. By five or so it was only drizzling, and Carol looked over her shoulder up the hill behind her to the neighboring cabin on the other side of the road. It was misty, but otherwise she could see objects clearly. Standing in the grass in front of one of the unoccupied cabins was a figure who looked like a Gray.

At that distance she couldn't be sure whether it was a Small Gray or a Tall Gray, but it was definitely one of the Gray Beings, and she was suddenly afraid they were coming back for her again. But then, in her head, she heard the Gray say, *Do not be crazy. Do not think crazy.*

Carol, relieved that she wasn't going to be taken, thought, *Fine. I won't be crazy.* And, while Carol was looking at him, the Being disappeared. And that was the end of it—in a manner of speaking.

One morning a week later, back with Alice at the farm, Carol awoke in pain with two more fresh punctures just below her belly button. A clear fluid was leaking from the holes. And a week after that she awoke with blood on her arm and spots of blood coming from her belly's double puncture wounds. Furthermore, every time she accidentally ate something that was not a beef or dairy product, she broke out in a rash and suffered severe stomach cramps.

On September 21, a month before my visit to the horse farm, Carol was hypnotized by Budd Hopkins in Washington. Along with filling in some of the blanks in her memory of the state park abduction episode, the session gave Hopkins an opportunity to attempt to countermand the Being's "You must only eat cow things" order. Afterwards, Carol, Alice, Hopkins, and

Dick Hall all went out to dinner together. Carol was looking forward to having something other than beef. At the restaurant, she was so sure that the "deprogramming" had worked that she ordered one of her favorite appetizers: clam chowder. She managed one sip of chowder and immediately doubled over with severe stomach cramps.

"The cramps were so painful, I couldn't function," Carol tells me. "I couldn't eat. I couldn't sit at the table. I was suffering so much I made everybody's dinner miserable. I had cramps the entire drive home, all that night, and the next morning a rash appeared."

I spend the second day of my trip to the horse farm visiting with the two women the Maryland scenes where Carol's abductions had taken place. The landscape and buildings are as she described them; there is nothing out of the ordinary about the abduction sites at all. Granted, it is a warm, bright, sunny day and not a dark, misty night; but still I find it difficult to believe that anything so strange as Carol described could happen among such lovely open fields and rolling hills.

When we return to the farm, Carol goes off to tend the horses and I sit down with Alice. Since the middle of July, Alice tells me, she had been increasingly tormented by headaches. She was convinced they were caused by her eyes. Alice is nearsighted, but her prescription had improved from a -4.75 to a -4.00 in nine months, and within a few more months to a -3.75. In July, when her headaches became too prevalent to ignore, Alice went to see her eye doctor. Her eyeglass prescription was then at -3.50.

Because Carol, too, had reported recent improvements in her vision, and attributed it to her abductions, Alice was concerned that the changes in her eyesight might indicate that something similar was happening to her. But Alice, who had never had any flashbacks or conscious memories of an alien contact, was too analytical to accept without more proof that any such thing as encounters with alien beings might actually be occurring to her, too.

According to Alice, in the three months since her July visit to the ophthalmologist, her eyes improved to -3.25 and then to -3.00; but her headaches haven't gone away.

I ask Alice if the change in her vision couldn't be attributed to normal aging. "As we get older, we become more farsighted, and this can happen quite quickly," I say.

"It could be," Alice says. "Maybe that is what's happening. I don't know. But from what the doctors told me, my eyes were supposed to be getting worse, not better."

"Do you have difficulty focusing?"

"Not anymore. And I've also given up my reading glasses. I don't need them anymore."

"Are you suggesting that your eyes are improving because of your abductions, too?"

"Possibly."

Dave Jacobs has identified among abductees what he calls the "tunnel effect": a phenomenon in which abductees, or those who think they might be, begin explaining everyday occurrences as being the result of alien intervention. It is the same effect experienced by victims of a household robbery who will then attribute every creak and thump in their houses at night to prowlers. Carol and Alice are both women in their forties, the age at which farsightedness begins to hit. The changes in their vision do not seem otherworldly to me.

I ask Alice whether there were any other indications that led her to believe she might have been abducted.

"No," she answers, "I've just had a lot of things I've always explained away before, things like you and I have talked about—scars in the right places on my body that I've never paid attention to. Some Missing-Time episodes that I hadn't really thought of before; I just figured I'd read the clock wrong. But now I'm convinced they really are Missing Times."

"What Missing-Time episodes are you referring to here?" I ask.

"I guess the one that is most compelling to me happened a year ago in July," Alice replies. "I was visiting a bunch of colleges down south for work: Georgia, Alabama, Florida, Tennessee, and so on. I flew into Nashville and drove down to Huntsville, Alabama. They said it should take an hour and a half to get to Huntsville; it was all open highways. But it took me three. I thought I was just driving slow or something. . . ."

"Could they have been wrong at Nashville about the length of time it would take to get to Huntsville?" I ask.

"No, because then, when I came back to Nashville from Huntsville, it took me only an hour and a half on the same roads with the same traffic." Alice brushes her long blond hair back from her forehead. "I still don't know about that one," she says.

"And you think there were other Missing-Time episodes that same trip?"

"Yes. The worst one was when I was in Tuskegee, in Alabama," Alice says. "I'd spent the day there with people in the college and I had to drive down to Tallahassee for meetings the next morning. They said it took three, maybe four hours to get there. I left Tuskegee around four-thirty that afternoon.

"The next clear image I have about that trip was driving through this small town in Georgia," Alice continues, "and just outside the town I got picked up for speeding. I was going 85 mph, but the police officer said I'd slowed down as I passed him, so he gave me a ticket for going 78. And he said, 'Where are you headed?' I said, 'To Tallahassee.' And at the time I felt sort of disoriented, sick, as if I was getting the flu. When he gave me the ticket it was already seven-thirty p.m. I had been driving for three hours, but I was probably only a hundred miles out of Tuskegee!

"I finally got down to Tallahassee after ten-thirty that night," Alice says. "I checked into the hotel and went straight to my room. I still wasn't feel-ing well. I took a cold shower—which is unusual for me—and went right to bed. The next day I still felt sort of sick, too. Not throwing-up sick, just an uneasy stomach like you get with the flu, which is what I thought it was at the time. But the point is, it took me close to six and a half hours to get to Tallahassee, and it should only have been a three-to-four-hour trip. I have no idea what happened in between, but I think *something* did."

"Other than the Missing Time, what makes you think that?" I ask.

"The way I was feeling," Alice replies. "Disoriented. Sick to my stom-ach. It was just uncharacteristic behavior for me. Yes, I speed when I drive, but not, usually, that much. Also, the police officer wrote on the ticket that there was 'moderate traffic.' I didn't recall seeing another car for what had seemed like hours. But I had the feeling that the reason why I was speeding was because I just wasn't getting there. It was taking too long for me to get to Tallahassee.

"And, of course," Alice adds, "this was before I knew anything about this alien-abduction stuff. But the more I think back on it, the more I think yes, something happened."

A month later I meet Alice and Carol at Budd Hopkins's New York stu-dio, where Alice, under hypnosis, provides an explanation for why her drive to Tallahassee took so long: she stopped to give birth to a half-alien baby.

CHAPTER XIV

Postconference Interview

Carol and Alice—First Hypnosis Session
at Budd Hopkins's Studio

On Friday, November 20, I arrive at Budd Hopkins's Canal Street studio ahead of Alice and Carol, who are taking the train up from Washington. While Budd and I wait for the two women to appear, we speak a bit about Carol's experience at the West Virginia state park. I mention that I think it curious Carol returned from that episode missing her underpants; but Budd assures me that the loss of such an article of clothing is not uncommon at all, that he has had other cases of women abductees who returned without their underpants, or, even stranger, wearing the wrong underpants—meaning someone else's. He also tells me that Linda Cortile once awoke from an experience wearing her pajama tops on her legs, and when she got out of bed and tried to walk, she tripped on the sleeves and fell.

I ask Budd if he has any suspicions that the abduction phenomenon may be being caused by something other than extraterrestrials.

"Well, when I say 'extraterrestrials,' that's a blanket term to cover whatever it is out there that's not from here," he replies. "People get into these huge arguments about 'interdimensionals' or 'meta-terrestrials.' There's been every damn thing. I think I've told you about the remark of the man who said he didn't believe they could be extraterrestrials because they weren't 'doing the sort of things extraterrestrials would do.' That's one of the great lines," Budd says, laughing. "I think as soon as the man uttered it he realized how absurd it was to say a thing like that. So when I say 'extraterrestrial,' it's a blanket term to cover whatever this is. But I'm absolutely convinced that this is *not* self-generated—although there may be people for whom it is. With Carol I don't have any doubt. I don't know what to say about Alice except that the chances are, considering everything else, it is not self-generated with her, either.

"One thing is the self-doubt people present who are coming up with this stuff," Budd continues. "If someone has a delusion . . . Take a paranoid, for example. A paranoid is wrapped in certainty. He *knows* what's going on: 'The CIA is coming in every night and pumping poison gas under the door.' A paranoid doesn't ask, 'Am I making this up?' They don't admit the remotest possibility they are wrong. But everybody that comes to us is saying, 'Can this be real? Is this what's happening to me? It sounds so crazy!' It's the initial response: 'I know it's real, and yet I can't accept that it's real.' 'I know it's happening, and yet I'm filled with doubt about it.' 'It's crazy! How can it be real?'

"You see, the basic underlying thing is always going to be the people's need to deny because *this is just too crazy*—this just can't be! When you think about it: People floating through walls . . . I mean, how the hell does somebody get floated out of a twelfth-floor apartment up a beam of light?"

I tell Budd about Carol's granddaughter, Stacy, and the lighted ball that enables the child to pass through walls.

"Well, we've certainly got dozens and dozens and dozens of cases of those," he says. "But, see, once you admit the physics of this on any level— that one can float through a closed window, that a craft can go thousands of miles per hour and stop on a dime without apparently decelerating—once you allow these things, then you've really got no floor under you in terms of conventional physics. It just doesn't work to say, 'That's impossible.' The *whole damn thing* is impossible!"

Budd tells me about his conversation with J. Allen Hynek. One morning, as the two men had breakfast together, Hopkins described a case of his and told Hynek, "You know, I live every day of my life as if none of this were true." According to Budd, Hynek responded, "Oh! I live every day of *my* life as if none of this were true, too. How could we get through a day with it fixed firmly in your mind that it's really going on?"

Budd's doorbell rings. Carol and Alice have arrived.

For the first thirty minutes Budd and the two women discuss what to investigate. Budd decides he will hypnotize Carol first. The event he wants to explore is the one that triggered her flashback at the conference: why had she hidden in the closet as a child?

"I think that's something we ought to try to go into, because it's going back to when things start," Budd tells her. "Sometimes when you get back to the very beginning of things, it sort of establishes a pattern that then makes a lot of other stuff fall into place and make sense."

Carol is apprehensive. She tells Budd she is afraid that if she remembers an early incident, then "all the rest of it is going to come rushing back all at one time, and I'm going to explode from all of this."

"No, listen," Budd tells her, "all the way through this there's been a sense that even though you have remembered a lot of things that came in a rush from here and there, you still haven't had so much stuff come at you that it's been overwhelming."

"Except in West Virginia," Carol says. "That was almost—"

"That's partly because you remembered it all, too," Budd tells her.

"Well, yes, all at one time," Carol says. "I was mentioning to Alice why it took touching the car's door handle for it to come back. And I began to think it was something the Beings did. They gave me that as a catalyst because if I had remembered it from the time when I came back, I would have been alone in that cabin, isolated, two and a half miles from the next individual, with no way of getting off the mountain at night. And it would have been too much to deal with."

"Well, chalk one up for some consideration on their part," Budd says wryly.

"I don't know if it was consideration or just saving my sanity for some other purpose," Carol says.

She reports to Budd that by the time she was telling me of her West Virginia episodes, she had already begun to feel detached from them, as though they had happened to a second party or even a third party; but while coming back from hypnosis it had seemed very real. She can still *feel* it, she explains. But now that she has gotten farther from the experience, specific incidents and their sequence have become, she says, "real, real fuzzy."

Budd tells her there were three or four explanations for this: "(a) that it was deeply traumatic; (b) you're in an altered state when it happens; (c) you're remembering it vividly through hypnosis, which is already another altered state; and (d) there's a powerful need to deny."

"I still go back and say that probably didn't happen," Carol tells him. She thinks for a moment, then asks, "If you had to pick between what you consciously remember, what comes out under hypnosis, what you remember later, and what you relate down the road, which would be the most accurate?"

"Of course I tend to feel hypnotic recollections are very strong and real," Budd replies, "because the state you're in under hypnosis is very akin to the state you're in when it happens."

John Mack would agree. In an informal talk given before Interface, the Holistic Education Center in Cambridge, five months later, he says:

There's a lot of controversy around hypnosis: Is it accurate? Do people report memories correctly? The research on this shows that the accuracy of memory increases according to how salient the matter is under discussion.

In other words, if it's something that vitally affects the person—a trauma, a rape, abuse—and it's reported with affect, with emotion, hypnosis fleshes out what they otherwise can remember. Where hypnosis is *not* accurate is where the matter is not of significance to that person. That might be in the courtroom, for instance, where somebody is being asked to report whether a car came in from the left or the right, or who was driving. There they were a witness, but it was not of vital importance; and they feel they have to come up with something. But where it is something as central to the well-being of an individual as this abduction phenomenon is, I have no reason to doubt what is reported. And people who do this work, who use hypnosis in this, are careful to be very open ended, and not lead the witness.

Hypnosis, for reasons that we don't entirely understand, seems uniquely capable of undoing the amnesia that occurs in the abductions— an amnesia which seems to have two dimensions to it. The first is the repression that ordinarily occurs in people when there is something that is disturbing and traumatic. Here the psyche will dissociate, put the experience out of consciousness so the individual can go on functioning. Many of the abductees have had these experiences throughout their lives. It is a lifelong phenomenon when one gets to know the full story in any given case. The repression protects the person. . . . But there is another element to this amnesia; and that is that every person at some point will report that the aliens forbid them to report it, told them not to remember, that there's some switching-off of memory which is imposed. And hypnosis seems almost to fit just like a template, perfectly, to undo the repression, the forgotten elements, and to bring back memories.[1]

Of John Mack's then sixty-nine cases, he had done between one and seven hypnosis sessions on forty of them.

Prior to hypnotizing Carol, Budd Hopkins wants to make certain he understands who would have been in the house with Carol when she had had her childhood closet experiences. Carol says her eighteen-month-younger sister, Mary, and her parents would have been there.

Budd establishes that the closet in which the incidents took place was in the second-floor bedroom Carol and Mary shared. She remembers there were children's clothes on the hangers and a shelf above the closet rod which held boxes and sweaters. "The closet was not real big," Carol says.

Budd asks Carol if she ever went into the closet to play.

"No, that's where I went for safety," Carol replies. She tells how her father remembers mornings when he would find her asleep in the closet with all the clothes taken down from the hangers and wrapped around her. "He told me he was constantly digging me out of piles of clothes and hangers," Carol says. "I felt the closet was a very safe place."

"The feeling was that you were protecting yourself against the light, is that right?" Budd asks.

"I don't remember ever being frightened by something you could see except for the light," Carol replies. "I was afraid that if the light touched me, 'they' could do something—whatever that was. I can't even verbalize what it was. I was safe only if I could keep the light from touching me, so I would try to block it out."

"I think this closet incident would be a good thing to look into," Budd says.

Carol sort of shrugs, then nods her assent.

Budd and Carol discuss what should be Carol's "safe place" during the hypnosis regression session, that place in her mind to which Budd can take her if the recalled events become too frightening and she needs to retreat.

Carol says that when she does "relaxation," she visualizes a "round room that's underground. I take a ladder down and it has curtains that cover the windows. And there's a big, long comfortable sofa and I sit down on the sofa and I have a little button. And when I want to look at something I can push the button and open the drapes; and when I don't want to look at it I push the button and close the drapes. That seems to feel pretty safe, and it doesn't exist."

Budd thinks for a moment, then says, "I don't like some of the implications of that: the round room and buttons and reclining. . . ." Carol's "safe place" bears too many similarities to the interior of a disc. "How about a garden?" he asks her.

"I love rose gardens," Carol says.

"Okay," Budd says. "Let's have a rose garden with a hedge around it on a very sunny day."

There is some discussion of the garden and what other problems might arise. Budd tells of the woman who went to a New Age hypnotist "because she was trying to explore some stuff. And she started into this abduction experience, her car stopped, she was terrified and everything else, and she was getting so scared. And the hypnotist, using an old formula, said, 'You're safe! You're surrounded by white light!' "

Carol and Alice laugh. The New Age hypnotist's image, of course, is the classic prelude to an abduction. Budd's point is that unless the hypnotist is thoroughly briefed by the subject, he might inadvertently bring something into the session he doesn't mean to.

After a short break Carol lies down on Budd's black couch, her head resting on a pillow, her body covered by a soft, pink wool blanket. The lights in the studio have been dimmed. Budd is sitting in a hard wooden chair at Carol's head; Alice, who has pulled out some knitting, is sitting cross-legged on the floor by Carol's feet. I am seated at Budd's right shoulder, a position from which I can see and hear Carol's responses clearly.

Budd asks Carol when she graduated from high school. She answers that it was in 1964 and tells him the name and location of the school she attended.

Budd makes a note on the yellow pad he holds on his lap. "Okay, just to begin this process as before," he says, "it's going to be very easy. You've done this before and know what it's like. I just want you to get that feeling, Carol, of going down into yourself. Into your own mind and body, away from the outside. The sense that you have when you go to bed at night of closing off the outside world and going down into yourself. It's a very safe, comfortable feeling of being down into yourself and away from the outside. I want you to feel the comfort of the bed under you, the couch, starting at your heels. You can feel the way the bed supports your feet; and, higher, you can feel the curvature of the calves of your legs. You can feel the way the couch curves up around each of your legs, supporting your lower legs and higher at your thighs. . . ."

Budd is leaning forward, cupping his chin in his hand. His voice is low; he is speaking slowly as he talks Carol's body down, moving her deeper and deeper into a hypnotic sleep.

"In your thighs, your upper legs," he is saying, "you are feeling that wonderful soothing flow of warmth and peace; your whole body is feeling comfortable"—on "comfortable" his tone rises to a slightly higher note—"and relaxed," he says; on "relaxed" the tone lowers again. "Feeling peaceful [rising] . . . relaxed [lowering]." The two notes rise and fall like Carol's chest as she breathes.

Not quite ten minutes later, when he is certain that Carol is "asleep," Budd "takes" her into her safe place, the rose garden. "It is a sunny summer morning, the roses are in full bloom," he tells her. "I want you to see yourself in this garden. You're just enjoying this incredibly blue sky, the warmth of the sun on your skin, the fragrance of those roses. It's just so unbelievably beautiful. And you can hear the sounds of the bees, the insects, the birds. That wonderful sense of humming, the sounds of nature, alive. Alive like you . . ."

There is silence broken only by the click of Alice's knitting needles.

After another couple of minutes Budd tells Carol that he wants her to know that she can go back to that "beautiful, secluded, fragrant, wonderful rose garden any other time you wish and would like to be in a beautiful, special place. But right now I just want you to feel your body relaxing even more deeply. I want you just to enjoy that sense of your body resting, your body at peace. Enjoying that sense of calm, the quiet of the room, your whole body feeling comfortable . . . relaxed . . .

"Peaceful . . . relaxed.

"And in this very relaxed state, with your mind extremely alert, I want you to go back in time, back a lot of years ago, back to the time that you were a very, very little girl, living in that first house in—" Budd pauses and looks down at his notes—"in Cornwall, Maryland. I want you to see yourself in front of a mirror as a *very* little girl. A little girl of three or four or so. Living in that house. Sharing a room with Mary. A little girl.

"I want you to see in the mirror how little you are, how small and innocent," Budd continues. "Again you can look into your face, your eyes, and see the playfulness and fun a little girl has. And at the same time there's some undercurrent in her face, because not everything is right. Other things are there, as with any child. You can see in your eyes and your face other things that are not calming. . . .

"And as we gaze at that image of yourself in the mirror, looking at yourself, I want you to get the feeling of going into your house. You're going upstairs to your room. Everything is big. The steps look steep and big because you're so little. You go to your bedroom, the room you share with Mary, and as you look in the doorway on this sunny day, you can see how the room is arranged, and," Budd now instructs Carol, "you can speak whenever you like.

"As you look into your room," Budd tells Carol, "I want you to manage to answer some questions about it. As you look, do you see one bed there? Or are there two beds?"

"Two," Carol says.

I am struck by her voice. It is that of a four-year-old girl!

"Are these bunk beds?" Budd asks her.

"No."

"They're two little twin beds done separately?"

"Yes," she says very quietly.

"How many windows are there in the room?"

"There are two together."

"Two windows together," Budd says. "Now, is there a closet in the room?"

"Um-hm."

"And as you're standing in the doorway," Budd says, "you're so little, a little girl looking at the room, is the closet to your left, to your right, or is it ahead of you?"

Carol thinks for a moment. "It's on that side," she says in her little-girl voice, making a jerky motion to her left. At the chronological age Carol now is in her mind, she does not yet know her left from her right.

"It's on the left side. Okay," Budd says. "Now as you go into the room and you can see the closet, you can see Mary's bed, and you can see your bed, let's allow it to start getting dark in the room. It's starting to get onto nighttime, because at night a little girl like you has to go to bed. Mary has to go to bed. . . ."

Budd pauses to give Carol time to make the transition to night in her mind.

"I want you to get the feeling of getting into your bed," Budd continues. "Your mommy and dad come in to make sure you're in bed, tucked in. And then there's that time when you're alone in the room, Mary is there, and it's very, very quiet in the room, and at some point, Carol, there's going to be something that's going to startle you or frighten you. We know that because we know you went to the closet for safety. We don't yet know what it is that startles you. Perhaps you had a bad dream. Perhaps you heard a noise you can't understand. But you know what it is that's frightening you, that's going to drive you to trying to hide. So you're lying in bed, and what's going to happen is I'm going to count to three, because whatever dream or memory or whatever it is, everything has a beginning, a first moment when you sense that something is different. Something's going to change here. And you're going to sense it. . . .

"My hand is going to come down on your hand, on your right hand through the blanket. And that's a signal," Budd instructs. "When you feel the warmth of my hand, you'll know it's okay, that you're safe and with me. And it will be okay to remember what that was that was frightening the little girl at that time.

"So, one, we're at the edge of that memory, that very beginning . . ." Budd tells her.

"Two, my hand is coming down on your hand now. . . ." Budd rests his hand gently on top of Carol's. And as he touches her he says, "Three!"

Carol does not speak. Her head tosses restlessly back and forth on the pillow. Her breath quickens, then quickens some more. She is almost panting now.

"Tell me what's happening," Budd says gently. "You're all right. . . . Feel my hand. . . . You're okay."

"AYYYIIEEEEE!" Carol's scream is so loud we all jump. "DADDY!"

"It's all right," Budd says, trying to reassure her. "You're safe. My hand's on yours now. Do you feel my hand?"

"*Daddy?* DADDY?" Her voice is quavering with fear.

"Can you feel my hand on yours, Carol?" he asks gently. "Do you feel my hand?"

"Ohhhhhh! Ohhhhh! *Daddy?*"

"It's okay. Daddy's going to come. Your daddy's going to come," Budd says. "What are you seeing? Why are you calling your daddy?"

"The *cats* are coming in!" Carol replies, panicked.

"Tell me what's happening."

"The *cats* are back! . . . *Daddy?*" Carol cries out. *"Ohhhhhhh!"*

"Well, you can tell Daddy all about that when he comes," Budd says gently. "But instead of your Daddy, just tell me right now. What are the cats like?"

Carol is too frightened to answer.

"Hold my hand. Feel my hand." Budd says soothingly. "Tell me about the cats."

"They're in the window," she says.

"The cats are in the window?" Budd asks. "What do they look like? Do they have big whiskers?"

Carol moans and clutches Budd's pink blanket to her face.

Not for one moment does Budd believe that "cats" are what Carol is really seeing.

"Big, long whiskers?" Budd repeats. "They're not going to hurt you. We're not going to let them hurt you. We're just remembering this. Tell me about the cats."

Carol still cannot answer.

"Carol, tell me about the cats," Budd says more insistently. "Feel my hand. I'm right here with you. Tell me about the cats. Do they have long whiskers, these cats?"

"No. They're just cats," she says in her little-girl voice. "Looking in the window."

"Okay, now here's what I want," Budd tells her. "I want you to take a deep breath. Take a deep breath, Carol. Take a deep breath. Just feel yourself relax, take a deep breath just to relax. . . ."

Carol takes a deep breath, then another.

"That's good. Deep breaths," Budd says. "Feel my hand? Feel my hand on yours? Okay. Now just rest. . . ."

Carol's breath slows, and as she brings herself back under control, Budd says, "So the cats are looking in the window. Now you're a very, very observant and smart little girl, and you're going to be safe here. Tell me, is there one cat? Two cats? How many cats are there?"

Carol's breath begins to quicken again.

"You can peek," Budd tells her. "You don't have to let them know you're looking. You just open your eyelids a tiny, little bit, and you can see just through your eyelids. They don't know you're looking."

Her head tosses on the pillow.

"How many cats are there? Take a look. Through your eyelids. Just open a little bit."

Carol mumbles something.

"Hmmm? I'm sorry?" Budd asks.

"I don't want to look at them," Carol says.

"Okay, here's what you're going to do. You're not going to look. You're just going to close your eyes, okay? Just close your eyes. Now I want you to tell me how your body feels. Be just a little girl lying there in bed, and this has been scary. How does your body feel? Tense? Relaxed? How does your body feel?"

"Co-ld," she says in her little-girl voice.

"You feel cold? What are you wearing? Do you have enough blankets on you?"

"It's summertime. It's hot."

"It's summertime. It's hot. But you feel cold?"

"Feel cold," Carol says. "My pink nightgown on."

"Okay, you have your pink nightgown on and you're cold. But how do your arms and legs feel?"

Carol pauses, thinking; then, still in a little girl's voice, but with a hint of frustration, she responds, "I don't know!"

"You just lie there," Budd says gently. "You're going to keep your eyes closed and you're just going to listen. I know it's very scary, but we know that everything was fine in the morning and you were safe." Budd pauses, then asks, "What's happening? Do you hear anything? Or what do you sense?"

"They're at the window," Carol says, very frightened, "an'—an'—and I can't wake Mary up!"

"Do you call to her?"

Carol replies in a very small, scared, broken voice, "I *yelled* to her!"

"Did you yell real loud?"

"I—I—I yelled real loud," she says between little gasps of breath, "an— an—and my daddy won't come."

"Well, your daddy eventually does come," Budd reassures her. "You see Daddy eventually. It may not be until morning, we don't know, but you'll see Daddy eventually."

"Why won't anybody wake up?" Carol pitifully asks.

"Where do you think the cats are now?" Budd asks her.

"Inside!"

"Inside? Where are they inside in relation to you?"

"They're *inside the window!*" Carol replies, clearly terrified.

"So they came in," Budd says. "Are they little cats or big cats?"

"*Big* cats!"

"Are they down on all fours?" Budd asks.

"I don't knowwww!" She does not want to look.

"But you know they're big cats. They shouldn't be here, should they?"

"No!" she says firmly. "They came in!"

"Why don't you just say something to those cats right now. What do you want to say to those cats?" Budd asks her.

"*Go away!*" Carol says. "GO AWAY!"

"We know they finally do go away," Budd says reassuringly. "We know that happens. But let's see now, they're inside the window? Now let's just see what's happening."

Carol makes little grunting noises, "Unh—unh—unh—it's bright in here. All this light coming in the window!"

"This light coming in the window, is it from a streetlight outside?"

"No! Nooo!" she insists. "There's no streetlight out there! There shouldn't be a light out there! It's coming in the window, *and,*" she says, her voice rising again in terror, "*it's gonna hurt me!*" She is whimpering with fright.

"Carol, do you know how, when they make movies, they have those big cameras that can go up in the air and look down and you can see a whole big scene?" Budd asks her. "Have you ever seen that?"

She shakes her head no. Carol, as the four-year-old she now is under hypnosis, has no idea what Budd is talking about.

"Okay, we'll come back to that another time," Budd says agreeably. "But right now let's look at the light. Is the light colored? Or is it white? You have a very good power of observation."

"Buh-lew," Carol says in her little-girl voice.

"It's blue light, okay," Budd says. "Now, is there any sound? Do you hear anything? Do the cats meow or talk to you or something?" Budd asks.

"*No,*" she says insistently.

"Do you talk to them?"

"NO!" Carol's breath is quickening. She is getting scared again.

"Feel my hand, feel my hand," Budd says soothingly. "Now let's take another nice deep breath. A real deep breath."

Carol inhales deeply.

"Oh, that's good. Fill your lungs. Feel your lungs fill up with air and relax. That's good, just relax. Just relax. . . . It's very scary, it's very scary, but we know in the morning everything's okay. . . ." He waits for Carol to calm down. "So, what's going to happen with these cats?" he asks her. "We know they left, they leave in the morning, but before they leave let's see what they do."

"I don't want tooo," Carol says, near tears.

"Well, I don't want you to have to look at them," Budd says. "Let's just sense—tell me how your body feels?"

"Scared," she answers very quietly.

"Your body feels scared. . . . You know," Budd says, "sometimes cats jump up on the bed and—"

"*Dad-dyyyy?*" Carol calls out and bursts into tears.

"Your daddy's there in the morning. Right now this is very difficult to go through. He comes in the morning, and, you know, when you wake up in the morning, are the cats there, or are they gone?"

"They're gone," Carol answers, still crying.

"Remember that," he tells her. "It's just very scary right now. So let's just see what happens. . . ."

"They're putting something in my ear-r-r!" Carol protests and cries out with pain.

"They're putting something in your ear?" Budd asks.

"In my ear!" Carol wails. "He stuck something in my *ear!* And it h-hurts!"

"Okay, now listen to me, when I count to three that ear thing will be all over. *One* . . . you feel it in your ear . . . *two* . . . now, *three!* It's all over. The ear thing is over—whatever that is that the cat put in, the cat's leaving. The cat took it out—whatever it is." Budd pauses for a moment, then says, "Now, let's get rid of those cats. Do you want to get rid of those cats?"

"Yes!" Carol says, snuffling.

"Do they go back through the window? Is that how they get out?"

"*I don't know!*" she says in a tiny voice.

"They're gone. We're rid of those cats. What happens when they leave?"

"I go in the closet."

"You go in the closet."

"And then I wake up."

"You wake up inside the closet? Does it feel better in the closet?"

"Yes!" Carol says, crying. Then she adds, "They'll take *her,* Mary, next time!"

"Well, you go in the closet. We're not going to worry about Mary right now. We're going to worry about Carol right now. So little Carol goes into the closet there, does she? Does she make a little bed in there? What does she do?"

"Pulls all the clothes down onto the floor," she says, still crying, "and pushes them into the door." Her breath is ragged.

"Does the little girl go to sleep in there eventually?" Budd asks her.

"No. I don't fall asleep. Gotta watch the door."

"You mean the door to the closet?"

Carol nods yes.

"Now, let's just move this ahead," Budd instructs her. "See, with all memories and dreams it gets to be morning again. Morning always comes, the sun always comes up. It feels better as the sun comes up. Let's take another easy, deep breath. . . . Fill the lungs. . . ."

Carol inhales deeply.

"Oh, that's a good deep breath, a real deep breath," Budd tells her. "Feeling much better now, clothes are all around you, you're feeling safe now. You're feeling safe in there behind the door as long as you've got your own little place. Feeling safer, feeling safer . . ."

Carol is breathing more regularly now.

"Okay, morning comes and the sun comes up," Budd continues. "The sun comes up, and is your dad going to come in? . . . Does he come in and find you in the morning?"

"Yes," Carol answers in a tiny voice.

"Does your mom?"

"My mom comes in when Mary is crying."

"Mary's crying?" Budd asks. "Why is Mary crying?"

Carol whispers, "Because I'm not *there*."

"I can understand that," Budd says. "So your mommy comes in. . . . I bet you're glad to see her, aren't you!"

"No!" she says firmly.

"No? Why not?" Budd asks, surprised. "Because you want to see your dad?"

"I want Daddy!" Carol says, sniffling. "It's awfully cold!"

"Why don't you want to see your mommy?"

"Because she doesn't come!" she says insistently, fighting back her tears; then, more quietly now, she repeats, "She doesn't come!"

"I see," Budd says. "If you had something you could say to your mom right now, what would you say to her? Let's say that right now you can say something to your mommy—what would you like to say?"

In a tone that is half angry, half hurt, Carol says quietly, "How come you never help me?"

"That's a good thing to say," Budd tells her.

Louder, more accusingly, Carol again asks, "*How come you never help me?*" And she again bursts into tears.

"It's upsetting that she didn't help you, isn't it?" Budd asks.

"She never comes when the cats come," she says, her voice quavering. "She *doesn't come!*" she sobs.

"Maybe sometimes the cats keep your mommy or your daddy from coming in," Budd reassures her gently. "That can happen. That can happen sometimes."

"My *daddy* comes," Carol says accusingly. "My mommy *never* comes."

"Okay," Budd says soothingly. "Okay. . . . Now, I want the sun to come up and it's nice and bright in your room. You come out of the closet, what does your mom say to you?"

After a pause, Carol says, "My mommy asks, 'What are you doing?' "

"And what do you say to your mommy?"

"That it's still cold."

"You don't tell her about the cats?" he asks.

"No," she says, and again her tone is somewhat accusing. "She doesn't know about the cats."

"Well, why don't you tell her about the cats?"

"Because she can't help me," Carol says matter-of-factly.

"But maybe if you did tell her, she'd be able to help you next time," Budd says, then asks, "Did you tell your daddy about the cats?"

"Yes, I tell my daddy."

I have an idea. I pass Budd a note on which I have written, "Ask Carol if her father was there when the cats came." Budd reads my note and nods, saying, "Okay." Then he turns back to Carol and says, "Let me hold your hand. Now I want you to take a very deep breath again, a very deep breath. Feel your lungs expanding. That's it. Just relax. A nice deep breath. A nice deep breath. You're very relaxed. A nice deep breath." He pauses for a moment, then asks her, "Does your ear still hurt after the cats did something?"

"A little bit," she replies.

"Okay, you're just very relaxed. I want you to see the sun coming in the window. It's a nice day outside. It's summer, isn't it? Do you go out and have some fun and play today?"

"No," she whispers. "It's raining out," she says.

"It's raining out?" Budd asks, surprised.

"Can't go outside."

"Well, it's going to be sunny some other day," Budd says, smiling. "Okay, you're just very, very relaxed now. Let's have a very easy, deep breath. Just relax. Just feel a very easy deep breath. . . .

"Let's move up now through that time you were in high school . . . you're getting older . . . that time when you were getting ready to graduate from high school and moving right up to the way you are today. There's still one thing I'd like to ask about from that time when you were a little girl, just looking back from the present, from as you are now as an adult: Do you think when the cats came in that your daddy was there at all? Was your daddy ever there?"

"Sometimes," Carol answers, now in an entirely normal grown-up voice.

"He *was* there sometimes when the cats came?" Budd asks again. "Do you think he saw the cats?"

"Yes," she whispers.

"How did he look when he saw the cats? Did he talk to you?"

"Noooo," she replies, still in a whisper.

"How did he look when you looked at him?" Budd asks. "Was he sitting down?"

"Standing in the doorway." Her voice remains adult.

"Was he smiling? What kind of expression did he have on his face?"

"I don't know," Carol says, thinking. "He didn't have any expression."

"Do you think he actually saw the cats?"

"Yes."

"When they were near him, how big were the cats? Did they come up to your daddy's knees? Were they taller?"

"Up to his ribs."

"They came up to his ribs," Budd says, nodding. "Did they have short fur or long fur?"

"They didn't have *any* fur."

Budd looks backwards over his shoulder at me as if to say "Gotcha!" Then he turns back to Carol and asks, "Did you ever see your daddy leave with the cats? Did they ever talk and go out together? Go down the stairs or anything? Or did they just stay in the room together?"

There is a long pause while Carol thinks over her answer. "He'd take me out with him," she says. "He'd pick me up out of my bed. . . ."

"Okay," Budd says. "And what happened when he picked you up?"

"We'd just walk out."

"Did he speak to you and tell you where you were going?"

"No."

"Did you say anything to him?" Budd asks. "About what was happening?"

"I couldn't say anything," Carol answers as if her inability to speak should have been taken for granted.

"And when you walked out, where did you walk to? Down the stairs?"

"No, he'd carry me. He'd be walking through—" she says and stops.

"And when he was walking, let's see where you go."

"We just walk—" she starts to say and stops again. "We walk—we just walk out—" Carol catches her breath.

"Walk out into the hallway?"

"Noooo!" Her voice is tightening up; she begins to breathe faster.

"In which direction do you go?"

"Just *out!*" Carol says insistently. "Out through the *window!*"

"Okay, you go out the window," Budd says calmly, gently. "And the cats—are they with you?"

Carol does not answer. Instead she exhales sharply: "*Whew!*"

"What's outside the window when you go out? Is there a tree out there? What's right out there?"

Carol, in her father's arms, is floated through her second-story bedroom window over the roof of the back porch. Father and daughter glide down to the ground between the house and the garage, where a large spacecraft is waiting. The Small Grays, who Carol's screen memory had led her to believe were cats, enter the craft first; four-year-old Carol and her father follow. Carol's father lowers her until her feet touch the ground. As she is being lowered, Carol is looking at her father, and she is frightened and upset to see that he is crying.

There are other humans in the craft. Carol sees a number of children of varying ages, some in pajamas, others in daytime clothing; she does not recognize any of them. She does not believe they are from her neighborhood. There's one little girl who looks a bit like her sister, Mary, except that unlike Mary, she has brown curly hair and is wearing "shorty pajamas," not a nightgown. The children are just standing silently in place, as though waiting for something to happen.

There are not as many grown-ups as there are children. Carol thinks they might be the children's parents; she is not sure. The adults also are in varying styles of dress—and undress: one of the women, Carol sees, is naked; she feels embarrassed for her.

The adults, too, are standing around, not talking. If there are any Beings present at this time, Carol does not see them.

The only furniture in the room to which they've been brought are several white ironing-board-shaped tables. Like all the tables reported by abductees, the tables in this craft are of one piece, molded in such a way that the central pedestal supporting them appears to flow into the floor. The tabletops are empty.

While Carol looks on, some of the grown-ups and children leave the room. Anxiously, Carol notices that they do not come back. She wants to ask her father where they have gone, but she cannot speak. And then it is their turn.

Carol and her father are floated along a circular corridor with a railing that leads to a large, high-ceilinged room. In the center of the space stands a row of tall transparent tubes; they rise like Plexiglas elevators from the floor, too high up for Carol to see their tops. One by one each child is placed within a tube. When it is Carol's turn, she can see her father through the transparent wall outside the tube. He is again weeping; they would not let him enter with her. And then, while she is standing alone in her pink night-gown within the tube, it begins to snow—except it isn't snow. The substance showering down on her is dry and warm; and instead of sticking to her, the flakes pass through her nightgown and her body. The shower stops and a Being telepathically tells her to close her eyes.

I don't want to close my eyes! Carol protests.

Close your eyes!

It begins to snow again, a different substance.

Ow! It stings! It burns! Carol cries in her mind.

Close your eyes! Close your eyes!

She closes her eyes and the burning sensation goes away. This second substance has a lemony smell and leaves her feeling sticky.

You can go now, she is told. Carol opens her eyes and sees her father again. He does not look so frightened now.

Carol and her father are directed around the bank of elevator-like tubes to the far end of the large room, then along another corridor with a railing until they reach an exit tunnel, through which she can see perhaps a score of other adults and children departing the craft. When Carol and her father step back outside, it is cold and dark and misty. Her ear hurts, and when she tries to walk she feels stiff and clumsy.

Carol and her father climb the steps to the back porch and door to the house and walk inside. Her father takes her upstairs to her bedroom, where Mary lies in her bed, still asleep.

As if by mutual agreement, Carol's father leads Carol to her closet, and once she is inside her safe place, he closes the door. Immediately Carol begins to feverishly stuff clothing into the chinks and cracks in the closet door.

After Carol's hypnosis we are sitting around Budd's studio having a drink and some crackers. Carol is recalling how her father carried her into the spacecraft. "I just remember when he leaned over to put me down he was real stiff in the legs. In other words, he didn't take a step forward or bend. He just put me down so that we were nose to nose, and I saw *tears* in his eyes, which made *me* cry."

Budd turns to me and says, "You see, everything about that account rings absolutely true for what a four-year-old kid and her helpless father would have done had this happened. I mean, there isn't a false note there."

I tell him the part I find particularly chilling is the "cats" looking through the window even though Carol was on the second floor. Carol shudders at the memory. "Why don't I hate cats?" she asks. "I love cats! I think they're wonderful creatures."

"Because they weren't cats!" Alice and Budd say together.

"Yes, but if I thought of them as cats," Carol says, "why wouldn't I forever be associating cats with something that terrified me? Like my son, John, loves cats, but he's been terrorized by what he thinks are cats staring at him through the window."

"Cats were staring through the window at John, too?" I ask.

I did not know that Budd and Carol, during that earlier hypnosis session in Washington, looked into memories Carol had of John's nightmares when he was four years old and he and Carol were living in Savannah. She remembered hearing her son scream; thinking he was having a bad dream, she crossed the hall to his room. "There're all these cats around the house!" the little boy cried to his mother. "We have to chase the cats away!"

Carol tried to explain to John that because there was latticework around the bottom of the house, cats liked to go in there to get cool and to have kittens. She explained that there was not much she could do about that; she didn't want to kill them or set traps. She asked John why the cats so bothered him.

"Because they jump up on the windowsill at night," he replied, "and they scare me. They peer in at me through the windows, stare at me all night long, and it keeps me up."

Carol couldn't understand why the cats were such a big problem. It just seemed silly to her at the time. But years later she still remembered how her four-year-old son would wake up in the middle of the night crying that the cats were looking at him through the window.

Under hypnosis with Budd, she was able to recall going to her son's bedroom, that it had been brightly lit, and that she had seen the same "cats" in his bedroom that had been in hers as a little girl. She remembered trying to enter her son's bedroom but being unable to pass beyond the doorway. John was sitting on the side of his bed screaming, "*The cats! The CATS! Get rid of the cats!*"

The little boy was crying hysterically, but he couldn't move off of his bed, and Carol could not move toward him. And then in her head she heard one of the "cats" say, *Tell him you can go with him.*

She told John that it was okay, that she would be with him. And the two of them were floated across the bed and through the window. Going through the closed window, Carol said, "felt like passing through sheer curtains, but there was not a solid feel to it. It was more like a heavy mist."

On board the craft John was put on a table that was too small for him; and so, while Carol watched, the Grays floated him to a larger table.

The Doctor Being whom Carol had most recently seen during her West Virginia state park abduction was standing at her right.

Why are you doing this to my son? she asked him.

I want to examine him, the Being replied.

I don't want you to hurt him, she said. *I want to take him home now. But he's not yours!*

Yes, he is, Carol insisted. *He's MINE!*

He's only partly yours, the Doctor told her. *He's ours.*

The Beings took blood and skin samples from John and then permitted the little boy and his mother to return home.

The next morning, when she asked John about the nightmare, he replied that he hated the house because of all the cats.

Carol told him they would get rid of the cats.

"The cats are always having to take stuff back," John said.

"How do you know that?" Carol asked.

"Because," the four-year-old answered, "I'll have to go back there and stay someday, and I don't want to go."

"Oh, that sounds silly!" Carol said.

"It *sounds* silly," John agreed, then added matter-of-factly, "but it's true."

John's daughter is Stacy, the little four-year-old whose drawing of the spaceship in which she traveled with her friend Nu Carol had shown at the conference.

CHAPTER XV

Postconference Interview

Brenda, Erica, Terry, and Linda Cortile— Abductee Support Group Meeting at Budd Hopkins's Studio

Budd Hopkins has arranged for Carol and Alice and I to attend one of his support group meetings after dinner that Friday evening. Present are several other women who have come to Budd for help in understanding and dealing with their abduction experiences; among them Linda Cortile.

I recognize another member of the support group from the conference: Brenda, the commercial artist who went public about her experiences on several television shows and sells "alien T-shirts" of her own design. She is forty, with dark, touseled hair and an attractive, somewhat pouty face.

According to Brenda, when she was twenty she was abducted from the rooftop of her Bronx home and brought by a sixty-foot-diameter circular disc to its underground base in the Southwest. When parked at the base, half of the disc was hidden beneath the surface of a lake; the other half was buried beneath the sand. The entrance to the base was through a camouflaged shed near the edge of the lake. The shed, in turn, led to a tunnel which descended to a hangar for the craft. While at the base, Brenda tells us, she saw hybrids, Grays, and Nordics. The Grays and the Nordics, she noticed, did not communicate with each other at all.

Erica is another of Budd's abductees. She is in her early thirties, has black, curly hair, a fine-featured, pretty face, and works as a designer in a fashionable New York clothing store. Erica believes her family—not just her direct line but uncles and cousins as well—has been involved in abductions for generations.

Not long ago, in her Eighty-fifth Street apartment, Erica tells us, she had an abduction experience after which she had a faint conscious recall of having embraced her eighty-seven-year-old grandfather, even though at that time he was supposedly in Florida. So several days after the abduction she telephoned him and asked if "anything weird" had happened to him that week. According to Erica, her grandfather said, "Why are you asking me that?"

"Well, Tuesday morning," Erica asked, "did anything happen?"

"Yes!" he said. "I was having a dream where I saw three grotesque creatures. It was like I was watching television."

"Gramps, what did they look like?"

"They looked Asiatic," he said. "They had big, slanting eyes."

Erica asked him exactly when this dream had occurred. It coincided with the time of her abduction.

"So, I'm pretty sure it's been happening to him," Erica says, "because he told me when he was a little boy he had had a lot of weird experiences that had been telepathic and all that."

Brenda tells us she met a woman abductee in Florida who reported that in 1888, her great-great-great-grandfather, while living in Texas, had been returning home along a dirt road, shotgun in hand, from a visit to his fiancée's isolated prairie home and had seen a bright light moving toward him in the sky. According to the story, he had continued walking as the light came closer and closer, and then the next thing he knew he was sitting on a rock a dozen yards from where he had been, and his shotgun had been fired.

"Now, today we would understand it as a UFO story," Brenda said. "But back then, they probably thought it was the spirit world or something."

There are seven women in all attending the support group meeting: in addition to Carol and Alice, Erica and Brenda, and Linda Cortile, there are two others. Because those two seem a little hesitant to have me there, I ask them what it is like dealing with someone who is sympathetic but doesn't necessarily *believe* them.

Erica answers instead. "It doesn't bother me if you don't believe me," she says. "I'm going through this, and I have my friends around me who are going through this. We have each other. What bothers me is that every day at work I walk by one of the self-help offices on the way to the bathroom—one of those offices where if you need help with AIDS, or this or that, there are counselors. But there's nobody there for us. When we get abducted, there are no 911 calls we can make. I feel like we're ostracized. We're like silent victims, because we can't really outwardly discuss what we're going through. And when you're on the subway and you're looking at those help posters for drugs or alcoholism—'When you're ready to get off your high horse, come see us'—well, there's nobody we can see except Budd. Budd's our lifeline, because he brings people together in our support group meetings, where we can talk."

Terry, one of the two women who have not yet spoken, nods at what Erica is saying. "There's a tremendous sense of betrayal involved," Terry adds.

"Why 'betrayal'?" I ask.

"Because for the rest of your life you're left with the feeling that there's nothing out there that is safe," Terry replies. "There's no one you can trust, and there's nowhere you can go. As Erica said, there's no abductee hotline, and unless you're one of the lucky ones who end up in a support group like this, you're just *out there alone*."

"All we have is each other," Brenda agrees. "And you have to try to keep supporting each other no matter how difficult it is. You have to stay tight as a group, because you also have to understand how to deal with it when new people come in, so we can help them. And there's going to be new people all the time."

"Okay," I say, "let me try to come at this from a different direction. When did you begin to suspect that what was happening to you wasn't a fantasy, a hallucination, a dream, or any of a number of those excuses one presumably makes to oneself rather than believe what is really going on? What convinced you it was real?"

"When I saw the aliens consciously for the first time," Linda Cortile answers. "When I saw them in my room at the foot of my bed. Before that, as far as I was concerned, you always have the doubt that no matter how good you may think hypnosis is, there's the possibility that past dreams were coming out, and that that was why I was seeing all those weird creatures. But in 1989, that time when I saw with my own eyes the aliens standing at the foot of my bed, I wasn't asleep. I know what I saw. They were *there!* It was real."

"I had physical traces of an abduction," Brenda says, "but that didn't make it real. I had flashbacks of seeing Grays, but that didn't make it real. None of the memories that I had made it real. What made it real for me was abductee Betty Andreasson describing in her book the shoes the aliens had put on her feet. They were made of some sort of clear element, glass or plastic of some kind, and were three inches high. And the same shoes were put on me! They had some way of staying on your foot; I don't know if it was a strap or something. But Andreasson described this as some way of monitoring you around the ship, and that's exactly what they had put on my feet. When I later read this in her book, I burst into tears. It was the sort of small detail that makes you think, My God, how can two people have the exact same image?"

Erica had a similar experience. She dreamed she was back in her house with her father when the living-room door swung open and standing in the lower left-hand corner of the doorway was a little white gorilla. It was a dream so vivid she compared it to watching a movie. After a hypnotic regression session with Budd, she began to have flashbacks, one after another, in a constant stream, all involving her father. So in an attempt to come to some sort of understanding about what had happened, Erica went to visit her father in Brooklyn. Her father, surprised to see her, asked Erica what she was doing home.

"Dad," Erica said, "I had a dream and you were in it. We were in the living room, and the door swung open—"

"And the living room door swung open—" her father was saying.

"—and standing in the left-hand corner," Erica and her father said simultaneously, "was a little white gorilla."

The two of them just stared at each other. How can this be? Erica was thinking.

"How could that be?" her father asked.

Erica is positive that she and her father could not have had the same dream.

But what made the abduction experience especially real to Erica was a physical trace. Erica has a condition because of which cuts do not heal properly; she scars easily. The year before, she cut her thumb badly enough that she was rushed to St. Vincent's Hospital, where the wound was stitched up. And although the doctor, at the time, was very pleased with the suturing job he had done, the resulting scar became coarse and puckered. Shortly thereafter, according to Erica, she was abducted from her Manhattan apartment. She remembers being on a table in an alien craft, where the Beings, she tells us, "cut open my leg and it was bleeding. I was conscious, and I saw this with my own eyes: The creature put his hand over my leg and the red stuff inside the cut was absorbed, and the white stuff, the plasma, was left on his fingertips. I was looking at this as if in shock, and then the wound in my leg kind of sealed up.

"When I awoke the next morning," Erica continues, "there was a very fine, hairline scar on my leg. And this kind of scar wasn't possible! All my life since I was a baby I have had scars: from falling downstairs, from falling off my bicycle on concrete. So when I saw this smooth, thin scar on my leg I went into an immediate panic, because I *knew* there was no way a scar could be like that on *my* leg, since I don't heal that way! Therefore I knew the experience had to have been real. And then you have to deal with this. You *know* you were taken in the middle of the night. But there's no one to turn to. It's very hard!"

Recently Erica went to a dermatologist and asked him if there was anything he could do about the coarse scar on her thumb. He said he couldn't, that that was the way the scar was going to look. So she showed him the hairline scar on her leg and asked, "Well, what about this?"

"That's a *very* good job!" he said admiringly. "Who did that?"

What could she tell him?

Toward the end of the support group meeting, Brenda tells us about an incident that occurred only a month before. She was sitting alone at an outdoor café near Battery Park City one evening when, she says, she saw a Small Gray approaching her. The Being's form was hazy, silhouetted as if backlit. Not until the Gray reached her table did he become completely visible. Then he told her, *We have to go.*

"Okay," Brenda said.

She rose from her table to follow the Being and suddenly found herself being flown over the Hudson River. It was dark, cold; they were flying very fast, and in the moonlight she could barely make out the waves of the river far below. The black water terrified her. Twenty years earlier, she had been in a boat on the Hudson at night with friends. They had all been smoking pot and thought it would be fun to take a swim. So she had jumped overboard with the others and had immediately panicked when she went under. She surfaced like a cat who'd been tossed in a pond: clawing and howling to get back into the boat. Flying over the Hudson in the dark brought back the memory of having been momentarily trapped beneath that black water, and, frightened, she clung to the Small Gray to keep from falling.

According to Brenda, the Being guided her to a huge, unlit UFO hovering high over the river. She did not even see the craft until she was directly underneath it, and could discern its large, dark shape above her, and within that darkness, a somewhat lighter open inner circle of gray. The Being, with Brenda still clinging to him, was sucked up into the interior of the ship, and once they were inside, there was light enough for her to look at the alien who had been holding her.

"I just sort of patted him," Brenda tells us, "like, 'Oh, thank God! I thought I was going to fall into that river!' I was much more afraid of the water than that alien, because I knew he didn't represent my death as much as the water did. So even though I should have blamed him for abducting me, I was very grateful he had helped me across the water. Of course, when I went through the ship a little bit, and other things happened, a few of the other Grays I resented; but this particular one . . ." Brenda pauses for a moment, remembering, and then she adds, "The fact that I would *like* this Gray was very uncharacteristic."

—————

CHAPTER XVI

Postconference Interview

Carol and Alice—Second Hypnosis Session
at Budd Hopkins's Studio

Saturday morning, in preparation for her hypnosis session with Budd, Alice explains the background of her Tallahassee trip, the one in which she appeared to have missing time.

Alice tells Budd how she spent the night before the trip in a motel outside Tuskegee, Alabama, then the next morning had met with the dean, various professors, and students of the Tuskegee Institute. She did not finish until around four, and left for Tallahassee about four-thirty. They had told her at the college the trip would take three, maybe four hours.

Alice was stopped for speeding just after going through a small town in Georgia. She had been doing 85 mph. "There was nobody on the highway and I was late," she explained.

She said she thought it was around seven-thirty when she was stopped by the cop and around ten-thirty when she checked into the motel. The three-to-four-hour journey to Tallahassee had taken roughly six hours, although, as Alice pointed out, it had not all been driving. She thinks she may have stopped at a fast-food restaurant on the edge of Tallahassee.

"So we do have a time problem," Budd says, and makes a note.

"Unless they were talking superhighways and I took backroads," Alice says. "That's what I assumed was the explanation at the time."

"Yes, but if you were cruising along at eighty-five, you certainly weren't lingering on the back country roads. 'Dawdling' does not spring to the lips as a description of your driving to Florida," Budd says with a smile.

Alice checked into the hotel in Tallahassee and took a cold shower. It was an odd thing for her to do, she admitted, but she thought she was doing it because, as she said, she "just felt so horrible."

"Why not a warm shower?" Budd asks.

"I don't know."

"When was the last time you took a cold shower?"

"Never," Alice replies. "I was just so hot. The motel was hot. And the whole next day I felt weird, half sick to my stomach." She was convinced, she explains, that she was coming down with the flu.

Alice had felt very disoriented when she checked in. She had pushed the elevator button to take a ride up to her floor, but the elevator door had seemed to open and shut too fast for her to get in. The next time the door slid open, she pushed her briefcase in to hold it, and the closing door crushed the briefcase. She had a sense that she wasn't moving quickly enough, she says, that "everything was in slow motion."

There follows a discussion of what else Alice might like to look into during the hypnosis session. She reports that she had nightmares as a child, but no idea of what they were about.

Alice speaks about her childhood: how she felt abandoned, that her parents didn't love her, and how at night she would cry herself to sleep. She talks about her very authoritarian career-military father who would beat her with a belt or paddle.

"Were there any fears or phobias that got focused when you were little?" Budd asks.

And Alice answers, "None."

I thought Alice would disclose her suspicions that her father had raped her during a fishing trip when she was twelve, but she doesn't mention it.

"What about fears or phobias now?" Budd asks.

"Children," she says. "Small ones. Once they get bigger, it's okay." ("When I was in college, I realized I hated children," Alice told me that last night in Boston. "I couldn't stand them! I can't be around them!")

"If someone handed you a two-month-old baby to hold, what would happen?" Budd asks.

Alice sighs. "I don't think I'd drop it, but I wouldn't take it."

"You couldn't handle it, okay," Budd says, making a note on his yellow pad. "Let's say some friend hands you a baby to hold wrapped up—for whatever reason, maybe to put money into a parking meter. But, looking at the baby, what would be your feelings?"

Without hesitation Alice answers, "Revulsion. Fear."

"Did you ever think you were pregnant?"

"Besides last summer, only once or twice," she says. "Once in high school I thought I was pregnant. My period was a couple of weeks late, and we sort of had a celebration when it finally came. And I remember one time, probably ten years ago, when I went through that again and I thought, Oh my God, I'm pregnant! I can't handle this. I could have been pregnant, but

I wasn't. That's when I went and got my tubes tied. I said I'm not even going to take the chance of that anymore.

"But what's weird," Alice continues, "is I always thought it would be neat to be pregnant, to go through the experience, because I wanted to have the experience. *But I didn't want the baby when it came out!* I just thought it would be neat to find out what pregnancy would be like."

"You've never had an abortion?" Budd asks.

"Never. Why?"

"Because people would say ambivalent feelings about a child could come from deliberately having an abortion or something like that," Budd explains.

"No, that's absolutely clear that never happened," Alice says firmly.

Budd makes a note. "Let's get specific about the babies—children," he says. "You start with a newborn little baby and range through its really help-less times, then a year old, then it walks, and at two years it starts to talk and then up through school. Is there any period here where the revulsion is stronger than other periods?"

"When they're about that high," Alice says, holding her hand about three feet above the floor.

"So that would be like a two-and-a-half-year-old?"

"Walking around," Alice says, and shudders. "There's a day-care center in our building, and the children get on the elevator with me sometimes."

"So 'toddler' would be more accurate," Budd notes. "How about a new-born?"

"It's not as bad."

"I'd really like to look into this phobia, because when you have something this powerful," Budd says, "it can cause all kinds of problems in the real world, because you're going to run into friends with babies."

"I know," Alice says. "I avoid them. If my friends have kids, I still—"

"You do well with Stacy," Carol interjects.

"She's bigger," Alice explains. After a child reaches about four and a half feet tall, Alice tells us, she seems to be able to handle his or her presence. But when Stacy was small, Alice would have to get out of the house. Even now, when the neighbors' little children come to the horse farm, Alice escapes.

Budd asks Alice, "When you have that sense of revulsion and fear, do you think of yourself in any way different from what you are now? Do you see yourself as another child? When you have that shock and fear, does it flash into anything in your life that suddenly you're a little kid, a twelve-year-old girl, a teenager or anything?"

"No," Alice says. "In fact, when I was going with this guy in high school, senior year, we were talking about getting married, having a dozen kids, the whole marriage bit, and doing everything you're supposed to. And I was okay with that. But at some point in college . . ."

"So you didn't have it when you were little?"

"No," Alice says. "It came after high school."

Alice explains that in college she studied experimental psychology because she thought she wanted to work with mentally and physically disturbed children. She actually did work with disturbed children for about six months, then found she couldn't do it any longer. She just became too upset.

Thinking that there may be a possible link between working with disturbed children and the onset of her phobia, Budd asks which were the most memorable of the children she encountered. Alice said one was a fourteen-year-old girl with a five-year-old's mentality. Alice and other students would go to the parents' house to work with the child. They would have her crawl, patterning her to try to open up the neural pathways.

Another was an autistic child who was "completely blank," Alice says. "There was just no reaching her. She was probably four or five."

And then there was a third child, who, Alice says, was "sort of autistic but also violent. She was also four or five, but tiny—and very strong. When she went into one of her violent fits, it took several people to hold her down."

Budd asks Alice to imagine the first autistic child in the studio with us, "What would she be doing?"

The child would be "curled up in the corner," Alice says. "She would be facing out but totally absorbed."

"Did you feel sorry for her, or afraid of her?" Budd asks.

"I don't know about then, but right now what I'm feeling is that she was safe," Alice replies.

"Because she was closed off?"

"Yes." Alice thinks for a moment, then says, "I did some strange stuff when I was in college. We had encounter groups, and I remember one of the things we decided to play is that someone would be an autistic child. The rest would draw him out and get him back into stuff. I got to be the autistic child. It was so *safe*," Alice says, and she begins to cry. "I didn't want to come out! I eventually did, of course, but it felt so very safe."

"So, in a certain sense, you envied that child?" Budd asks.

"Yes."

Alice explains that the little girl was safe because she always had someone there to take care of her, to try to draw her out, to get her to communicate; but, Alice tells us, she quit working with the child because she became too emotionally involved.

Budd determines that Alice's hesitation about holding a child has nothing to do with her fear of being an inadequate protector. "I just don't want the child close to me," Alice explains.

"Because they might do what?" I ask.

"I don't know."

Budd makes a note on his yellow pad, then asks Alice, "What do you think about when you think of the child being revolting?"

"Just that I've just got to get away," Alice replies.

"It's the child in totality," Budd says, making another note. "In your worst-case scenario, how does the child behave?"

"The child clings to me. Grabs me around the legs."

"Do several children up the ante of fear more than just one?"

"Yes. If there were like six, I'd . . ." Alice's voice trails off, and she shudders again.

"If a child grabbed you around the legs, could you just reach down and pull the child's arms off you? What would you do?"

"I'd run away."

"But what if the child were hanging on?" Budd asks.

Alice looks stricken. "I'd kick him away. I'd try not to hurt him, but . . ."

Budd takes some more notes, then asks Alice if there is anything she would like to ask him.

"No. I trust you," she says, then adds, "But I'm scared."

"I know," Budd says gently. "Just assume at the outset that all sorts of horrible things are going to emerge, and tell yourself, 'Okay, screw it. So we have a lot of horrible stuff and then we have lunch.' So start out with the assumption 'Okay, what am I going to learn? I'm going to learn I got picked up, and this and that happened.' You've read the books. . . ."

"I've read them all," Alice says, nodding.

"So just imagine that the very worst you've ever read happened. So what? Here you are still."

"Yes, that's what I keep telling myself."

"Okay," Budd says.

It is decided that Alice's safe place, like Carol's, will be a rose garden. Budd urges Alice to avoid trying to analyze what would take place under hypnosis. He tells her to "be a reporter, not a pundit."

The studio lights are dimmed; Alice is settled onto the black couch, covered with the blanket, and made comfortable.

The hypnosis session begins. Ten minutes later Alice is comfortable, relaxed . . . peaceful, relaxed. For the next few moments Budd takes her into the safe place: "I want you to smell the beautiful air filled with the odor of the roses. I want you to feel the warmth of the sun on your skin, the gentle breeze that keeps you at a perfect temperature. I want you to look up at the clear, blue sky. I just want you to enjoy with all of your senses that beautiful, beautiful rose garden, just for the next few moments, in silence. . . ."

After a long pause Budd tells Alice they will return to that rose garden at another time. And then he puts her into deeper and deeper sleep. "You're feeling comfortable . . . relaxed," he tells her. "You're feeling peaceful . . . relaxed. . . ."

Budd takes Alice back to Florida in her mind. "And in this very relaxed state, with your mind so alert and so clear," he tells her, "you can see yourself as you were a little over a year ago in the summer when you were on your drive around the South visiting colleges. You've got that rental car and you've been at Tuskegee. It's getting on late in the day, in the afternoon, and it's time to go. . . ."

Budd allows Alice time to reach that time and place in her memory, and then he says, "I want you to get the feeling of being in your car now, of getting in your car. Things are packed in the back and you're all set and you start off. It's late afternoon; you get the feeling of the hum of the engine of the car, driving along, heading to Tallahassee.

"You're driving along, and various things happen on this trip," Budd tells her. "There are various interruptions, things that were unexpected. We know at one point there's a police officer. So there are some things that happened.

"I want you to get the feeling of driving on," Budd repeats, then asks Alice to describe what the landscape looks like. "You can speak whenever you like," he tells her.

"It's farms," Alice says in almost a whisper. "And it's very poor. It's peanut fields . . . peanut fields. There're some flat fields."

"Just look out the window as you drive along. . . ."

"Trees. Peach trees . . ."

"As you drive along, everything looks kind of typical, but maybe at some point you notice something that seems a little different. See if you notice anything different. It could be any number of things. . . ."

After a pause Alice says softly, "It's just boring."

"Boring? Uh-hm," Budd says, smiling over his shoulder at me. "Just keep looking as you drive along. . . . We know for sure there was at least one surprise on this trip. If there's one surprise, there could be more surprises. Something that breaks the monotony. I'm going to count to three now, and my hand is going to come down on your hand, and it will feel safe and it will feel nice. When I count to three, you'll get that first inkling of some kind of surprise or shock. My hand's coming down on yours.

"One," Budd says. "You're driving along . . . something's going to interrupt the monotony. . . . Two, right on the edge now . . . three!"

There is a long silence, and then Alice whispers, "It's like a crown of light. . . ." And a moment later she adds, "Like fire."

"Like a fire, um-hm," Budd says. "Keep looking at it."

"Like a gas stove burner," Alice whispers.

"Is this off in a field somewhere?" Budd asks.

There is wonder in Alice's voice as she answers, "Yes!"

"Where is it in the field?"

"I don't know—it's on my right."

"Um-hm. Just keep looking at it."

After a brief pause, Alice says, "Gone."

"It's gone? Do you mean you passed it by?"

"No, it just went away."

"Is there any traffic on the road?" Budd asks her. "Other people who might notice things?"

"No," Alice says. "I'm all alone."

"Do you see road signs, or where you are?"

"Stop sign," she says. "I turn right."

There is another long pause, and Budd says, "You're just driving along—let's just see what you see. Just report what you're seeing. A little town?"

"No. Nut trees. Big trees."

"How're you feeling?" Budd asks her.

"Pretty good," Alice responds.

"Bored, maybe?"

"Yes, it's a long drive."

"A long drive," Budd repeats. "And you're driving along. . . . How's the car performing? Are you having any car trouble?"

"It's okay," she says, then adds matter-of-factly, "I have a feeling it's stopped."

"What's stopped?" Budd asks, leaning forward closer to Alice.

"The *car.* I can't see it. I just feel it. . . ."

"Did it stop with a jerk, or did it just slow down gradually?"

"Gradually."

"All of your senses are extremely alert. Your sense of feeling—"

"*Cold!*" Alice says, shivering.

"You're cold? Is the air conditioner on in the car?"

"I don't think so," Alice says with a sigh.

"Tell me what you're feeling," Budd says. "Your body is very, very aware of anything it feels. It felt a little cold. . . ."

After a moment Alice whispers, "Waiting."

"Waiting? And how are you waiting?"

"I'm sitting there."

"Is the car moving or stopped?"

"It's stopped."

"Have you pulled off the side of the road, or are you in one of the lanes?"

"Sort of half in the lane and half on the shoulder."

"Is this the main route you were on when you made the right turn?"

"No," Alice says. "It's a little road."

"Why did you make your right turn at the stop sign?" Budd asks.

His question doesn't seem to concern Alice. "I just turned right," she explains.

"Is this a smaller route than the one you were on?"

"Yes."

"So, you're just kind of waiting," Budd says. "Now, I'm going to put my hand back on your hand. My hand's coming down, and that's a sign that it's okay to go along with this and see what you're waiting for. Whoever or whatever you're waiting for is going to show up. Or it won't show up, it won't happen, in which case you'll just leave," Budd tells her.

Alice inhales sharply.

"What's happening?" Budd asks.

"There's somebody at the window!" Alice says, surprised.

"At the window of your car? Um-hm. Is this on the driver's side?"

"Yes."

"Okay. A quick glimpse. Just as though your eyelids don't even completely open. When I count to three just through your eyelids a quick little look and see who's there. One, getting ready to take a quick look . . . two . . . three! Quick look and close your eyes. Who's at the window?"

"I don't know!" Alice says, concentrating. "It's a long face."

"A long face," Budd repeats. "Um-hm."

Alice's breath quickens. "It's not a person!" she says tensely.

"Tell me about the person."

Alice inhales sharply and cries out.

"You're okay," Budd says soothingly. "You're with me. Feel my hands. Tighten up on my hands when you need to. Tell me what's happening, Alice. You're just a reporter. You're just going to look. It was a long time ago. Tell me what's happening."

After a slight pause she says, "I'm supposed to go with him."

"Does he tell you that?"

"No. I just *know*."

Alice takes a deep breath and exhales.

"Now this is the South," Budd says. "You could have been seeing a lot of black people. Is this a black person?"

"No," Alice whispers. "This one's gray."

"Gray. Right," Budd says without emotion. "So, let's just see now. Do you lock the door of the car?"

"No."

"What do you do?"

"I get out. . . ." Alice whispers. And then, with an exasperated sigh, she asks, "*Why am I doing this?*"

"Let's worry about that later," Budd tells her. "When you get out, what do you see around you?"

"Lots of trees. . . . They're *big* trees. They're not peach trees. They're big."

"When you get out do you stand next to this person?" Budd asks her.

"Yes."

"Is he a big person?"

"Yes," she says, again inhaling deeply. "But we sort of float away!" Alice exhales slowly.

"Let's allow that floating feeling to happen."

"That's *weird!*" Alice says with a mixture of apprehension and wonder. "It's . . . it's *nice!*"

"Where are you floating to? Let's see where you are going."

"I don't know," Alice says. "I'm upright."

"Okay, let's see where you float to."

"Octagon! Sharp sides. Each corner. *Ooooh!*" she cries. "There are lights there."

"On the thing that looked like a gas light?" Budd asks.

"Yes. Like a gas burner. . . . There's a thing on the bottom," she says and pauses. "A whole octagon! With a hole."

"Do you mean there's a hole in the middle of the octagon?"

"*Yes!*" Alice says with wonderment. "But it's like a flange down there."

"Just make your eyes a camera and look at it. So, what happens next?"

"We go straight up," Alice whispers. "Inside . . ."

There is a pause.

"What's happening?" Budd asks her.

"Just standing there."

"Where are you standing?"

"White room—*ooooh!*"

"What's happening?"

"Squiggles."

"What do you mean, 'squiggles'?"

"On the wall or something. Squiggles. Like on a black screen."

"Anything present except squiggles?"

"Softness," Alice whispers.

"You can draw that for me later."

"You can't draw softness," Alice tells him.

"Well, you can draw the squiggles."

"Okay," she says pleasantly.

"Are you alone in this room?" Budd asks. "Or is the person with you who took you in?"

"Yes, sort of," she says, and she begins breathing anxiously. "Eyes."

"What?"

"*Eyes!* More eyes . . ."

There is another long pause.

"Where do you see these eyes now?" Budd asks her.

"Around."

"Um-hm," Budd says. He is leaning forward over Alice, cupping his chin in his hand.

"Shorter eyes . . ." she says.

"Are there a lot of people standing around looking at you?"

Alice takes a deep breath. "Yes," she responds. "There're three or four of them," she says, exhaling.

"Let's see," Budd says. "Are they standing there facing you, or are they to the left or the right?"

"There's one over there," Alice says, pointing to her left side, "and there's two over there." She points over her left shoulder.

"Okay, we're going to get a sense of what they're going to do," Budd says. "Did anybody tell you what this was all about? Do you ask them what's happening?"

"Why'd you do this?" Alice asks, apparently of the aliens.

"What did they say?"

"We need you." Alice responds. Then she asks, whispering, "*Why?*" Her tone of voice becomes both exasperated and sad: "You don't need to know!"

There is a long pause and then Alice asks, seemingly of the aliens, "Can I go home now?"

"You want to go 'home' now—you mean back to the car?" Budd asks.

A huge sigh escapes Alice's lips. "Wherever," she says. "They don't think so. So I can't."

There is a pause.

"What's happening?" Budd asks her. "Are you still standing there?"

"I'm lying down."

"Um-hm."

"Weird," she says, then cries out in surprise, "Ooooooh! That's a strange-looking one."

"What's that one look like?" Budd asks.

"He looks more like a dragonfly. Something above his eyes," she says, and sighs.

"Does he have wings?"

"No. He doesn't have wings. . . . He looks mad."

"He looks mad," Budd repeats. "Does he say anything to make you think that?"

"Nooo," Alice whispers.

"Okay, this is what I want you to do now while whatever this all is is happening. I don't want you to look. I want you to keep your eyes closed and not look at anybody. But I want you to know, Alice, that your body is extremely sensitive; it has its own memories that can feel, for instance, the surface that you're lying on. What that surface feels like. Your body can feel the sense of the fabric, whatever's next to your skin—clothing, a T-shirt, whatever you're wearing. What are you wearing?"

"Nothing."

"Nothing," Budd repeats in a flat tone.

"*It's cold!*" Alice says, and shivers.

Alice curls up on her right side, burrowing into the blanket.

"Your body remembers exactly what it felt," Budd says gently. "You're lying there, and you're cold, and you don't have anything on. This is what we're going to do. We're going to start with your feet and we're going to move up from your feet systematically through your whole body and see what your body's memories are. Starting with your feet. What do your feet feel? Concentrate your attention down there; let's see if your feet feel different in any way. If they feel any of those things or if they feel normal."

"My heels are cold," Alice says, taking another deep breath.

Budd gradually focuses Alice's attention away from her feet to her ankles, to her calves, her knees, her thighs. "Okay," he says, "Now, being very systematic, you're lying there and we're moving up to your female parts, to your genitals. What do you feel in that area that feels different in any way? Or does that part of your body feel normal?"

"It feels tight," Alice says. She is still lying on her right side, facing Budd. "Cramps," she says, almost wonderingly. "*Ooooooh!*" She draws her knees up to her chest in pain. "*Owwwww!*"

"Is this pain in your abdomen, or is this down lower?"

"Down lower," Alice says, now writhing in pain.

"In your genital area and all that?"

"Yessss!" she hisses in obvious discomfort. *"Cramps!"*

"Now your body has very, very good memories and can sense what's happening," Budd tells her. "It can sense what's causing this sort of feeling. What are you sensing in that part of your body?"

"Pain," Alice cries. "Pain! . . . Oh! *Ohhhh! OhhhHHHH!"*

"Pain. Inside you?"

Alice is moaning in agony.

"Okay, we're going to turn that pain down," Budd says soothingly. "That pain volume is set up pretty high. It's a volume control, and it's set way up at a seven on that pain. And we're going to put a hand on that volume button and turn it down now to a six . . . turning it down . . . it's easing off. Turning it down to a five . . . it's still present, it's still definitely there, but it's easing off. Down to a four now . . . turning it down . . ."

When Budd reaches two, Alice sighs with relief.

"Now, when this is happening," Budd continues, "is there any movement involved, or is it still? What does it seem like? What would cause something like this?"

"Owwww! Terrible pain," Alice says and cries out again.

"Let's keep that dial turned down now. We're not going to let that come back up. But it's still present. What would you do to duplicate that effect?"

"Ohhhhhh," Alice moans.

"You said this was the vaginal area—would it seem that there's something inside you? Or is this something on the outside? What kind of—?"

"No, it's like everything was just squeezed into a little tiny knot!" Alice groans.

"As if there's pressure again from the outside?"

"Yes . . . outside, but inside, too."

"Is it steady, or is it intermittent? Does it come and go?"

"It comes and goes."

"Is it connected to a feeling of some kind of movement?" Budd asks. "Or is it just a still presence that's affecting things?"

Suddenly we hear Alice's horrified whisper: *"Oh, my God!"*

"Is it happening again?" Budd asks worriedly.

Alice has burst into tears; she cannot answer.

"Tell me what you're feeling now," Budd says gently. "You're okay—my hand is on your head now. Feel the warmth of my hand on your forehead. It feels much better. Just tell me what's happening. Tell me like a good, clear reporter—tell me what's happening."

"I feel like I just had a baby!" Alice cries, her voice breaking.

"You feel like you just had a baby."

"I wasn't pregnant!" she sobs.

"It's okay. You're okay now," Budd says gently. "Feel my hand; my hand's on your forehead. Feel it? That feels much better. What was that feeling like? Did you feel that something passed through you?"

"*Yesss!*" Tears are streaming down Alice's cheeks.

"Something came from the inside and went out?"

"Yesss. The pain's gone."

"Good," Budd says. "Now, just to quickly—"

"*That can't be!*" Alice cries in disbelief.

I look over at Carol; she, too, is in tears.

"Don't worry about that," Budd says calmly. "Let's not even worry. We don't know what this experience is, and we're not going to try to guess. This is what I want you to do: Probably at the time, you opened your eyes just a little bit to just glance down and see what was happening. When you glance down, do you see anything? Just let yourself look down in that direction and see if you see anything."

"It's tiny. It's very tiny," Alice says, with a hint of revulsion.

"How tiny is it?" Budd asks.

"About the size of a pear . . . Ohhhh!"

"And what happens to this pearlike thing which you're seeing?"

"They're taking it away," she says, so matter-of-factly I am surprised.

"Do you at any time look at it as it's being taken away?" Budd asks her. "Can you see what it seems to resemble?"

"It's pink and wrinkled," Alice whispers.

"Does it have appendages? I mean, you feel like you had a baby. Does it look like it has—?"

"It's very short. Real short . . . little. Tiny."

"Do you hear any tiny cries from the—?"

"No."

"Okay. So it's taken out. Now, how do you feel? Do you feel some relaxation that it's gone? You feel much better that it's gone?"

"*Yes!*" Alice says with obvious relief.

"Okay. Good. . . . Do they say anything to you about this?"

After the slightest of pauses, Alice answers, "They say it's theirs."

"It's theirs?" Budd repeats. "Do they say that to you?"

"Yes."

"Do you ask how this came about? What do you say to them?"

"I say, 'How can it be? . . . Where did it come from?' "

"Alice, this is what I want you to do for me right now," Budd says. "Let's just float slowly away from that experience, and this is what I want you to do, because your body is extremely sensitive with its own memories. Let's go back some months before this. I want you to feel your body very, very subtly and intensely. If you were pregnant at some point—we don't know whether you were—but if you were, your body is going to know that a seed was inserted into it somehow to produce that baby.

"There are different ways it could have occurred," Budd continues. "Through intercourse, the normal way—a penis. People can be artificially inseminated; all kinds of things can happen. Only *your* body remembers whether it ever felt anything like this in the months prior. I want you to concentrate all your attention down to the sexual parts of your body. I'm going to count to three, and in those months or even weeks before this happens, your body is going to remember if it ever felt anything connected with this.

"One," Budd says, "concentrating your attention down to that part of your body . . . two, right on the edge . . . three . . ."

"Tube," Alice says immediately. "A long tube like Dr. Fulton uses." Fulton is their local vet.

"A long tube?"

"Yes."

"Where are you when this tube is being used?"

Alice pauses, thinking. "I don't know," she says. "Some place white."

"Are you by yourself, or is there a doctor there with you?"

"No. Just them."

"Just them," Budd repeats.

"Ohhh! *Why are they doing this?*" Alice asks, surprised. "*Oooooh!*"

"Does it hurt?"

"It's weird."

"What's the diameter of this tube? If you start with the diameter of a pencil, is it that diameter or is it bigger?"

"Littler."

"Littler," Budd repeats. "Thinner."

"It's flexible . . . clear," Alice says, more in wonder than in discomfort.

"Is it attached to something on the other end?"

"Like a syringe. There's white stuff in the syringe," Alice says. "I guess it's sperm."

"This is what I want you to do: Somehow or other you were brought to that place and this was done to you. I want you to back up in time as if you were backing up a movie. Memories are extremely clear. Let's move back. Where are you?"

"I'm in the barn," Alice says, then corrects herself. "No, I'm in a field. Pulling weeds! *Oh, God!*"

"What's happening?"

"I'm pulling weeds in the field. It's summer. The weeds are low."

"Where is this field?" Budd asks.

"It's the log cabin field," Alice says, referring to a field on the horse farm in which the ruins of an old cabin remain. "They're in the field. It's a little spaceship."

"How big is it?"

"About the same size as a station wagon. Maybe twenty feet long," she replies. "They walk up to me. I have to go with them."

"Do you try to run away?"

"No," she says, then suddenly smiles. "We're floating toward the ship. It's neat!"

"Who is with you?" Budd asks.

"There are three of them. One on each side and one in the front."

The Beings bring Alice into the craft, which appears to contain just one large, round, white room. In the middle of the room is a table.

"I have to get on the table," Alice explains. "I don't think I want to do this anymore," she says worriedly, as if speaking to the aliens, "Can't we just not do this anymore?" There is a brief pause, and then she cries out, shaking her head, "*No!*"

"What's happening?" Budd asks.

"Oh, I'm tired. They won't let me walk out!"

Alice is laid out on the table, naked.

"They've got that tube again!" she says, frightened.

"Is it like the tube before?" Budd asks.

"*Yes.* They put it *in* me!" she whispers.

"How far?"

"About six inches." Alice cries out in pain and curls up. "It goes into the fallopian tubes," she says. "OWWW! *It hurts!*"

The tube is inserted past the cervix, into her left fallopian tube.

"Have they done this to you before?" Budd asks.

"YES!" Alice answers and bursts into tears.

"How old were you when they did it the first time?"

"I was just a kid!" she cries, outraged and hurt. "I was twelve! Oh God, I hate you!" she says to the aliens. "Leave me alone! Go choose somebody else!"

"Where were you when this happened?"

"It was at night when I was fishing with my father," Alice replies. "On a canal."

Budd and I exchange looks.

"Who else was there?" he asks Alice.

"It was just me and my dad."

"What is your dad doing?"

"He's just standing there!" Alice replies angrily.

"Does he try to help you?"

"He can't," she says with a mixture of sorrow and resignation. "He can't protect me."

"What is he doing?"

"He's scared. He's just standing there. He can't move."

"How do you feel about your father?"

"I feel *hatred* for him!" Alice says, furious. "He can't protect me!"

Budd explains to her there was nothing her father could do, that he had been "paralyzed" by the aliens; and that instead of hating her father, she should direct her anger at the Beings. "What are the aliens doing to you?" he asks Alice.

"They hurt me," she says, beginning to cry again.

"Where do they hurt you?"

"It hurts me inside," she says, then cries out, "It's too big! I'm just a little kid!"

"Where is it inside?" Budd asks.

"It's in the vagina and it's big."

Budd establishes that the object is thicker than a pencil. He asks what she is feeling.

"It's like a tearing sensation," she sobs. "I'm bleeding from my vagina."

Under Budd's gentle questioning Alice reveals this entire episode is taking place on the banks of the canal in front of her father. "It's like we never left that place," Alice says. "They did it right there."

"Did your father see all this?"

"It was done in front of him, but I don't know if his eyes were open or closed."

Budd takes the still-hypnotized Alice back to her Tallahassee trip and asks her what happened after the Beings had taken the pear-sized baby away from her.

"After they took the baby away, they cleaned it up and me up."

"Do they show you the baby?" Budd asks.

Alice shudders. "I don't want to see it!" she says.

"Why don't you want to see it?"

"I hate babies! They're not *human!*" she says disgustedly. "They don't look right."

"Have you seen these babies at other times?"

"Oh, yes!"

"Tell me what they look like."

"They're not babies," Alice says. "They're just walking around. Thirty or forty of them. They have big heads. Fatter bodies than the gray guys. Some of them have little bits of blond hair."

"Do they say anything? Do they speak to you?"

"They make noises."

"What sort of noises?"

"They squeak."

"Why have they brought you to all these babies?" Budd asks.

"They want me to pick them up," she says, and makes a face. She is revolted. "*Ugh!* Someone gives me one! I have to hold it! 'I don't want to do this!' . . . I almost dropped it."

The encounter with the babies is so obviously distressing for Alice that Budd decides to move her out of that scene to one from her childhood when her father was stationed in England.

In past discussions Alice has seemingly recalled meeting a little girl with glasses and blond curly hair from—or in—Wisconsin. Budd Hopkins has a theory that the aliens assemble certain people together—that Alice and Carol's friendship, for example, rather than being recent and accidental, reflects his hypothesis that aliens had placed the two of them in contact with each other ever since they were little girls. Alice and Carol both sense they have known each other for a longer time than their current relationship would indicate; and each has memories of special "little girls" who were friends they saw only at odd times. Budd decides to pursue this theory with Alice.

That part of the session seems to me inconclusive. Under hypnosis, Alice tells of being nine years old and meeting with a little girl in the countryside. Budd asks Alice how she had gotten there.

"I floated there from a ship," Alice replies.

"How old is the little girl?"

"She's older than me. She's in the sixth grade, I'm in the fourth. . . . She tells me she has a gray dog."

"Do you see her dog?"

"It's not there."

I remember Carol's and Budd's exchange at the M.I.T. conference when Budd asked the abductee panel if they remembered any childhood experiences. Carol told of having had "an imaginary dog who took me for walks to places where children couldn't go." When Budd asked what color the dog had been, Carol, without thinking, had answered, "Gray," then exclaimed, "*Oh!*" The dog, Carol had realized, could have been a "screen memory" for a Small Gray.

Budd asks Alice if she had ever seen the little girl before.

"We know each other," Alice replies.

"How do you know each other?"

"We met when we were littler."

"How little?" Budd asks.

"I was in a playpen. She's outside. I'm inside."

"Where is the playpen?"

"It's inside something . . . a bedroom. There's a single bed. . . . She doesn't have her glasses on."

"Who else is in the room?"

"There are other little kids with dark hair sitting on the floor in a corner. They're just little ones. . . . Why aren't they locked up?"

"Locked up?" Budd asks.

"In a playpen like I am," Alice replies.

"Why are you in the playpen?"

"Because I get into trouble."

Budd asks Alice to describe the other children. One, she says, has a bib. Another is wearing diapers. One has shorts on and is wearing a little English cap. His shorts are part of a suit. Alice doesn't know whose bedroom this is and says they won't let her have toys, because "I throw them around and break them." Budd asks her to look closely at the children who are off to one side, and Alice suddenly recognizes them: "It's my brother and sister in the corner!" she says excitedly. "I think we're in England!"

Alice's sister Grace is only two. That means Alice is about three. "I don't know how to talk yet," Alice says, "but the nice little girl knows how to talk."

Budd tells Alice he is going to wake her up because that's a good memory. But before he can do that Alice bursts into tears. When Budd asks her why she is upset, she replies, "I feel guilty for my father."

Budd tells her she can now deal with her father in a different way and that relationships, as a result of what she has learned, are going to make a lot more sense.

He tells her she will be able to look at children now with a different eye and a different sense of understanding.

He then works on her headaches, tells her that "those emotions and feelings are going to come out," and when they do, gradually her headaches will fade. And that there is going to be an "easing off of all the terrible tensions and fears."

Budd begins counting backwards, five, four, three, two, one, the numbers becoming progressively louder. Alice, no longer hypnotized, lies there on the couch for a few minutes; then she stirs slightly and rubs her eyes as if awakening from a deep, restful sleep. She sits up, stretches, and looks around the darkened studio at us as though not sure where she is or who we are. A moment later she smiles and says, "*Whew!*"

Budd turns the lights back up, then speaks to Alice about her past counseling. He points out that her counseling tried to focus on what Alice thought was the problem: her alleged rape at age twelve by her father. Budd explains that everything she was saying and observing about the rape "was appropriate to the age" and that "decades of mistreatment have to be undone little by little. Now that it has been revealed as an alien-encounter experience," Budd says, "the trauma should fade. The proof is in the detoxification of the trauma."

Her alleged rape by her father, Budd explains, was not the problem. Her father had not caused the trauma, because he was not the source of the trauma.

"It's not a hidden memory," he tells Alice. "You were being treated for the wrong disease. The proof will be if there is a sense of relief. The headaches will ease off. Depression will ease off. There will be a sense of wholeness."

Alice does not look convinced. I ask her how she is feeling.

She smiles wryly. "I guess," she says, "I can't deny my contacts with the little gray shits anymore."

CHAPTER XVII

Postconference Interview

Carol and Alice—Third Hypnosis Session
at Budd Hopkins's Studio

After a break for lunch, Budd decides to hypnotize Carol again. He wants to look into the "vivid dream" she had the previous July 15—a dream in which Alice also was present. A "vivid dream"—also referred to as a "lucid dream"—is what Dr. Jayne Gackenbach defines as "a dream during which one knows one is dreaming when the dream is ongoing."[1]

Based as much on current research into dreams as on his own experience, theoretical physicist Fred Alan Wolf explains that the primary difference between an ordinary dream and a lucid dream is "the extreme sense of reality. . . . The major factor is the awareness that one is dreaming while the dream is progressing and the vivid details that one can remember after the dream. Upon awakening, the dreamer has immediate recall of the dream and the recall that during the dream one felt in control of the events of the dreaming entity.

"I use the word *entity*," Wolf explains, "because, although I know the entity is 'I,' it feels different from my normal waking persona in several ways. The awareness of being split into two conscious minds is the most striking difference. There is the sleeping person 'at home in bed' and there is the person experiencing the dream and knowing all along that he or she is in bed at home."[2]

On July 15, although Carol knew she was "dreaming," she also strongly suspected that what happened to her in her dream was real.

"The word 'dream,' or the idea of dreams, provides a good example of how a familiar term has to be looked at more carefully, even redefined," John Mack has observed. He continued:

> When abductees call their experiences "dreams," which they often do, close questioning can elicit that this may be a euphemism to cover what

they are sure cannot be that, namely an event from which there was no awakening in another dimension. On several occasions I have seen a look of distress, even tears, on the face of an abductee who is realizing that an experience that he or she had chosen, more comfortably, to consider a dream had occurred in some sort of fully "awake" (another word that might need to be redefined) or conscious state, however different this might be. The problem is complicated further by the fact that dreams are an important way that we normally process and integrate experiences during the night. Therefore, it is not surprising that, since abductions are themselves powerful and disturbing experiences, they may frequently give rise to true nightmares or dreams that recreate in modified form the abduction experience, even during the same night the experience occurred.[3]

Budd Hopkins wants to discover whether Carol's dream had any basis in "reality." One means by which he hopes to determine this is to see if any of the sequences Carol thinks she shared with Alice might be present in Alice's unconscious as well. However, to avoid "contamination," it is essential that Alice not be present when he discusses the dream with Carol. Alice is sent off to take a nap in a different room.

Once Alice is gone, Carol explains that in her dream she was standing on the back deck of the farmhouse when a flying saucer floated noiselessly overhead, paused briefly, then continued northwest.

Although it was evening, it was still light out. Carol tells us she remembered sensing that the craft wanted her and Alice to pursue it; the large disc would wag sideways, then dart off, leaving a trail of light they could follow. So Carol and Alice, in their nightgowns, ran together across the back pasture and through the woods after the light. Eventually the two women reached a large open field, where the craft was hovering quietly, waiting for them some fifty feet above the ground.

Carol's dream immediately cut to Alice and herself outside the "hangar" where a number of people had gathered. Some of them, Carol says, she knew from their Maryland horse community and others from the conference at M.I.T.

"Guards" wearing helmets and masks that seemed to provide them air escorted Carol and Alice through large metal double doors into an underground space cavernous enough, Carol says, to hold "several 727 jets." Within this hangar was a huge saucer tilted up at about a thirty-degree angle.

The disc, Carol tells Budd, "looked like the one we followed, only much bigger. Perhaps a little more oblong, with a fishtail flange at the end."

While Carol watched, four enormous caterpillar tractor vehicles, not unlike those used to trundle the space shuttles to their launch pads, were rolled up beneath the giant spacecraft, two in the front, two in the rear. The tops of the tracked vehicles then unfolded like a fire engine's aerial ladder to further lift and tilt the alien craft until it was resting at a forty-five-degree angle. It appeared, Carol thought, almost as though the huge saucer were being put on display.

On the other side of the hangar were perhaps a hundred people, many known to Carol and Alice. By now everyone had quieted down; they seemed almost subdued. Carol remembered wondering in her dream why all those people were there.

Far above them, the roof of the hangar had a slight dome shape similar to that of an observatory. As the aperture at the top of the hangar's dome slowly opened, Carol could hear bits of sod, falling from the roof, hitting the tilted spacecraft below.

Alice was frightened, Carol says. She kept grabbing Carol's sleeve until Carol became impatient and told her, "Just watch!"

By this time the dome of the hangar had opened all the way and Carol, looking up, was struck by how black the sky was. The hangar entrance's large steel double doors then clanged shut, the sound reverberating throughout the vast space. Everybody who was supposed to be there had, Carol felt, now been assembled.

At that point in her dream two of the helmeted, uniformed guards came to where she and Alice were standing. She knew the guards were human beneath the mask apparatuses and that the masks were "to protect *us,* not them." The guards escorted Carol and Alice across the hangar to where the other humans were standing. The guards did not carry guns; instead, according to Carol, they carried a rod-shaped, black electronic device which Carol assumed was for identifying the people there. They "put the calculators right up against you," Carol explains.

The guards gestured for the first group of five or six people to head toward the giant saucer. "When the people walked behind the caterpillars," Carol says, "you lost them, because the caterpillar treads were so tall they were hidden."

Alice and Carol were in the second group of five or six. The guard led them past the caterpillar treads to the rear of the craft. Each tread, Carol estimated, was well over eight feet tall and seventy-five feet long. Passing them, she says, she noticed "a rubber, acrid smell of burnt wiring." Despite their vast size, Carol was worried that the caterpillar supports might not be able to hold the huge craft up.

She recalls that as she and Alice passed beneath the disc, she looked up at some strange glassy globes that completely covered part of the underside of the craft. "They looked like crystal balls, only they were milky," Carol tells us.

She could see a door in the rear of the craft, but no ramp or steps leading up to it. She was still looking for the entryway when she saw the others in her group getting "sucked up" into the back of the giant disc. She had time only to wonder, How did they do that? And then, Carol says, she woke up.

Later, in her journal, Carol would write, "I awoke feeling very excited. I felt as if I had really been there, had actually touched the caterpillars. I could still feel the coldness of the metal and smell the grease and oil. It seemed real to me, rather than the memory of a vivid dream. I can still see the details of this craft to this day just as clearly as I saw it in my dream."

It is time for the hypnosis session to begin. Following a ten-minute break, Budd gets Carol settled on the couch and starts to put her under. After another ten minutes, Budd is telling Carol, "Throughout your whole body there is a soothing feeling of warmth from your head to your feet. Comfortable . . . relaxed . . . peaceful . . . relaxed . . . comfortable . . . relaxed . . . peaceful . . . relaxed . . . And in this very relaxed state, with your mind so alert . . ." Budd says, and sets the scene for Carol's July 15 dream. And then, once he has Carol standing on the back deck of the farm, he says, "You're going to see something when I count to three, something beginning to happen that's odd or different. One, something, whatever it is, is about to happen. . . . Two, it's right on the edge. . . . Three . . ."

Carol is breathing smoothly, deeply.

"What's happening, Carol?" Budd asks. "Tell me what is happening."

"I'm calling Killer to come back into the house," Carol says, and calls, "Killer! . . . Here, Killer!" She suddenly exhales sharply. "Whew! . . . Must be a plane. . . . It's no plane. . . . Ohhh, *neat!* NEAT! It's one of *them!*" She laughs happily. "Gotta call Alice. . . . Alice! ALICE! You won't believe this!" There is a pause, and Carol calls impatiently, "*Hurry up!*" She is breathing harder now. Even more impatiently, she calls out to Alice again: "Hurry UP! Look at this!"

There is a twenty-second pause and then Carol says, "You know what I think? I think it's one of *those!* Look how *big* it is! It's *huge!* It's like a fish."

"Where is Alice?" Budd asks her. "Is Alice with you now?"

"Yes. We're both on the porch."

"What is she wearing?"

"A pink nightgown. We're both wearing nightgowns."

"What do you have on your feet?"

"Nothing. We're both barefoot."

"Is it warm out? Cold out? What time of day is it, Carol?"

"It's night. It's cool. . . . You can't even see the stars, this thing is so bright! It has piece at the end like a fishtail. . . . *Ohhhhh!*"

"What's happening, Carol?"

There is an amused wonder in Carol's voice. "It's *showing off!* . . . Nobody would ever believe this! Come on, Alice, let's go! Hurry up!" There is a brief pause, and Carol again impatiently tells Alice, "*Come on!* We'll never get another chance like this! . . . Oh boy! *Look! Look! Look!*"

"What do you see, Carol?"

"It's kind of wagging at us. Hurry up! *Hurry up!* . . . Alice doesn't want to go," Carol explains angrily. "We're going to miss it. Pay attention, c'mon!"

"What is the craft doing?"

"It's waiting for us down there. Nobody will believe this! Maybe she—" Carol suddenly laughs. "So? Wipe it off!"

"What happened?"

"Alice stepped in manure," she says, still laughing. "She told *me* to watch out for the manure, and *she* stepped in it!" And then, impatient with Alice again: "Hurry *up!* Come *on!* Look at it up there! *Geez!*" she says in an awed tone.

"You've got to quit smoking!" Carol tells Alice. "It's over *there!* See that dark spot over there? See the stars? You've *got* to come!" Carol insists. "I'm not going to go by myself."

There is a pause. "Alice! Listen to me!" Carol says. "We're *supposed* to go. We *have* to go."

"So what?" Carol snaps. "You're not being rational, okay?"

Budd asks Carol what Alice is saying.

"She says it's cold," Carol answers, but then she is speaking to Alice again: "It's not *that* cold! That's really *dumb!*" There is a pause, and Carol asks in a sharp voice, "When are we ever going to get to do this? We got an *invitation!* What do you want, to have it written in gold?

"You're being a baby, okay?" Carol says impatiently. And then her voice softens: "I won't make you do anything more."

There is a long pause, and then Carol says sadly, "I'm sorry. I have to go. *I have to go!*" She begins to cry. "It's important, Alice. *Please* understand. Please come with me—*please?*" Carol pleads. "We always go together."

There is another long silence, and then Budd asks, "What's happening now, Carol?"

She does not answer.

"Where are you right now?"

"Nowhere," she says in a flat voice.

"Where's Alice?"

"She's not here."

There is something in Carol's tone that makes Budd lean closer to her. "Where is she, then?"

"I can't tell you that," Carol says nervously, guardedly.

"Can't tell me what?"

"I'm not supposed to talk about that." Carol says tensely. She is clearly under some sort of stress. I, too, lean forward. Something is going on here that Budd has not anticipated.

"Why can't you talk about it?" Budd asks quietly.

"It's just a dream."

"What aren't you supposed to talk about?"

"I can't say."

Budd looks over his shoulder at me. Neither of us thinks Carol is talking about the spacecraft incident anymore. "Who told you not to talk about it?" he asks. He is pressing her gently, trying to see where this might lead.

"*They* did," she says.

"You know you don't have to obey them if you don't want to, Carol," Budd tells her. "You can tell me what they wanted."

"Don't make me do it!" Carol says. She is becoming increasingly agitated. *"Don't make me do it!"*

Unsure of whether Carol is speaking to him or to the creatures, Budd waits for her to say more.

Suddenly Carol announces, "I want to go to the garden." She is referring to the rose garden, her "safe place."

"Why do you want to go to the garden?" Budd asks her.

"Because I can't talk about a dream. I can't talk about this."

"Why can't you talk about it, Carol?" He is still pressing her.

"Because it was a *secret!*"

"What was the secret?"

"That I was supposed to go," she says.

"Where?"

"Over there. And Alice was supposed to come with me. We're supposed to do all these things together."

Her response suggests to me that maybe she is still talking about chasing the UFO.

Budd decides to try a different tack. "How long have you had to do these things together?" he asks.

Carol tosses on the sofa. She is now extremely anxious. "I don't like this!"

"How long have you had to do these things together, Carol?" Budd repeats a little more insistently.

Carol bursts into tears. *"We were babies!"* she cries. "We were just little, tiny babies!"

"You and Alice?"

Carol nods yes. "I was holding her up. She could hardly sit up. We have to be together, take care of each other."

"How old is Alice?"

"She doesn't talk. She's just scared," she says. Her tears have stopped; she has brought herself back under control. "She doesn't know what they are."

"What *who* are, Carol?"

"They're on the floor. Like a tile floor. On the kitchen floor on a blanket."

"Are these other children?"

Carol nods yes.

"What do these children look like?"

"They don't have any color. They're not gray and they're not white."

"How old are you, Carol?" Budd asks gently.

"*I'm* four," Carol says. She has suddenly lapsed into a little girl's voice. "*She's* just a baby!"

"Are there any adults around?"

"There's a lady."

"What does she look like?" Budd asks.

"She's just a little person," Carol replies in her child voice. "She has funny hair."

"Funny hair? What kind of funny hair?"

"Stringy. Like she's going to go bald."

"What color is her hair?" Budd asks.

"Yellow," Carol says, the word sounding like "lell-o."

"Why is the little girl you're taking care of scared?"

After a moment, Carol answers, "She doesn't have a mommy."

"She doesn't have a mommy, so somebody has to be there?"

Carol has lapsed almost into baby talk. She takes little gasps of air between words. "Somebody [breath] to take care [breath] of her when she comes here [breath]. I take care of her."

"And how does she get there when she comes there?" Budd asks. "How do you get there when you come to this place?"

Carol's breathing is irregular because she's afraid of the answer. "We fly here," she says.

"You fly there? Where are you when you start the flight? Are you at home and they're out in the yard? Are you with your mommy and daddy?"

"I don't know," she says, and then nervously adds, "Sometimes I'm in the closet."

"You're in the closet? And you come out of the closet?"

"When I think they're all gone," she says, becoming agitated again.

"When you think they're all gone," Budd says. He sees that Carol has started hyperventilating. He puts his hand on hers to calm her and says reassuringly, "You're all right."

Carol puts her index finger to her lips.

"We've got to be quiet?" Budd asks.

Carol nods her head yes.

"Just tell me what you're feeling," Budd says.

"She's scared—*shhh!*" Carol whispers. "She wants her mommy."

"And you're going to be her mommy right now, sort of? You're going to be her little mommy?"

"Yes," she answers in a breathless, little girl's voice.

"It's okay, you calm her down. That's very good the way you calm her down," Budd says soothingly. "You know just what to do, don't you? It's nice the way you calm her down like that. She needs her mommy. Is she a pretty little girl? Little baby?"

"Yes."

"What color hair does she have?"

"She has yellow hair, too." Again, she pronounces it "lell-o."

"Now, let's see what's happening. This lady with the funny hair, does she say anything to you?"

"She doesn't talk," Carol answers matter-of-factly.

"What's she wearing, this lady? Does she have a dress on?"

"No. She has . . . she has—" Carol inhales sharply—"*loose skin!*"

"She has loose skin," Budd says calmly. "Um-hm."

"It's funny skin. She wears a thing over here—" she says, touching herself above her left breast—"like a pin?"

"What is on the pin?" Budd asks.

"I don't know what it is. Maybe it's her name."

"Does it have writing on it? Does it look like writing?"

"I don't know what it is," Carol responds, still speaking in a little girl's voice. "I don't see that before."

"Is it a picture of something?"

"No," Carol says, concentrating on the image in her mind. "But there's something there."

"Does she tell you you're going to have to take care of this little girl?"

"Yes," Carol says. And then, as if she were afraid she is going to be punished, she says, "I was going to do that anyway. I would have taken care of her anyway! I wasn't going to leave her all alone." Carol's mouth screws up and she begins again to cry. "She's just a baby!"

"She's just a baby and you're like a little mommy," Budd says. "And you can take care of her like a little mommy can."

"I will, okay," Carol says, still crying.

"You're a very, very good little girl, and you can take care of her fine."

Budd, understandably, decides to explore again his hypothesis that Alice and Carol have been linked together since childhood. "Let's move away from this, and let's see the next time you see her," he tells Carol. "The next time you see her, is she a little baby, too? Or is she a little older? Let's go to the very next time you see her."

Carol inhales sharply.

"What happened?"

"*Careful!*" Carol says. Her tone of voice is different now: older, angry.

"What's happening?"

"Sometimes she gets dumb," Carol says. Her tone is that of a disgusted preadolescent, a nine-year-old who considers herself an adult compared with the child she has been ordered to deal with.

"What does she do when she gets dumb?"

"*She pinched me!*"

"She pinched you? I bet that hurt!"

"It's going to hurt her, too!" Carol warns.

"How old she is now?"

"I don't know."

"Can she talk?"

"Yeah—sometimes she doesn't shut up!"

"What does she have on now?"

"A little dresslike thing. It's a sort of yellow . . . it's got white on it. White and yellow." When she says "yellow" we now hear the "y."

"Can she walk?"

"Yeah. Boy! She runs all the time! Can't hardly keep up with her."

"You really have to chase her around, don't you," Budd says sympathetically. "What's around the room? Let's look at the room she's running around in."

"There's other kids in there. I've seen them before."

"Tell me about those kids. What do they look like?"

"They're ugly," Carol says very quietly.

"They're what?"

"Ugly. Ugly kids," she says more loudly. "But you get used to it."

Her voice is still that of a nine-year-old.

"Now these little kids, do they look kind of like this little baby, like this little blond girl? Or do they look different from her?"

"What little blond girl?" Carol asks.

"What?" Budd asks, startled.

"What little blond girl?" she repeats. "My little blond girl?"

"Yes, the little girl you've taken care of," Budd says, relieved that they seem to be back on track. "Do they look like her, or are they different?"

"No, they're ugly. A.J.'s cute."

Budd and I exchange glances: *A.J.?*

"A.J.'s cute? Why do you call her 'A.J.'?" Budd asks. "What's that stand for?"

"I don't know. That's her name."

"Okay, so you call her A.J. What does she call you?"

Carol thinks for a moment. "She doesn't call me. She calls me Mommy sometimes."

"Because she thinks you're her mommy?"

"No! She doesn't really think that," she says, as if impatient with Budd's silliness. "She calls me Mommy because—I don't know why she does that."

"That's because you're taking care of her like a mommy."

"She makes me mad, though. If I were her real mommy, I'd spank her, 'cause she doesn't listen. She throws things all the time. She's always doing stuff."

"What does she tend to throw?"

"*Anything!* She throws everything you give her! You try to give her stuff and she throws it like it doesn't mean anything at all."

"Like a dolly?" Budd asks.

"She doesn't play with dolls. We don't play with dolls. Dolls are for babies," Carol says, but now her voice seems even younger. If Carol was a nine-year-old at the beginning of this sequence about A.J.'s behavior, she seems now to be five.

"She doesn't like dolls," Budd says. "What kind of things might she have to throw?"

"She'd have a block. They gave her one to look at."

"What does the block look like?"

"It's a block with colors on it. It's sort of soft. She's supposed to know what to do with that. *I* don't know what to do with it," Carol says, exasperatedly. "She wants me to help her do it and I don't know *how* to do it."

"How big is this box thing? Is it as big as a box of Kleenex?"

"No. It's like a . . . it's like a . . . a block of, like, letters?"

"Like when you have little blocks with the alphabet on them?" Budd asks.

"Yes, only it doesn't have any letters. It has colors."

"Colors on the side?"

"And she's supposed to do something with that. But I can't help her do that! I can't do *everything!*" she says, as if upset at the unfairness of it all. "She gets real mad, she throws everything! And then they get all upset with her, and then we all get in trouble because of that."

"When you get in trouble, what happens? Does the lady yell at you?"

"They don't yell. They don't do things like that. They take you and they put you somewhere else," she says, clearly upset at the thought. "So she has to be real good or they'll take her away from me."

"Um-hm," Budd says, nodding. "Now, when you say there are these other children there who are ugly, are there other children that aren't ugly, besides you and this little girl A.J.?"

"No. No."

"Just the two of you and then these ugly children?"

"Ugly. They're all ugly-looking children. They don't have regular things like us. . . ." Carol pauses for a moment, then adds in a tone both faintly sarcastic and superior, "And they're not *real smart*, either."

"Every now and then with children, you know, one of them will cry and another will laugh," Budd says. "Do you see some of them laugh or cry?"

"No. They don't do *anything*. You have to make them do things," she says; and now Carol's voice seems even younger than five. "*I* can make them do things, too," she says cockily.

"How do you do that?"

"I go over and pull their hair."

"Oh? You pull their hair?" Budd says, turning back to me with a smile. "What happens then?"

"Everybody gets mad. The lady comes and gets me and pulls me away."

"Does she say anything to you?"

"She just tells me not to do that anymore."

"I see. Are there games that you play with these children?"

"We're supposed to play with these blocks," she says, then adds, "If they don't want to play, you can't make them play." And then, in an angry and impatient tone of voice, she says, "Oh, quit, A.J.! That's enough!"

"That's A.J.? What's she doing now?"

"She's just being dumb! . . . *Quit it!*"

"Let's just jump ahead a little bit. I want you to be about fifteen," Budd tells her. "You're going to be an older girl—you're a teenager, you're in high school. You're fifteen or sixteen. Do you see A.J. in your high school?

Carol seems to be thinking. And when she speaks, her voice has become more mature. "No," she says.

"When's the last time you see her when she's little?"

Carol thinks back. "She was nine. She said she was nine."

"And where do you see her?"

"Ohh!" she says disgustedly.

"What happened?"

"Bugs!" Carol's voice has changed. She sounds like a young girl again. Budd's verb tense, his "where *do* you see her" rather than "where *did*," has apparently sent Carol back in time.

"Bugs flying around?" he asks. "Are you outside?"

"*Are* you," not "*were* you."

She inhales deeply. "Yeah," she says, exhaling. "*Geez,* it's hot!"

"Where are you?"

"In the woods. There's a field out here. . . . Where the hell *is* everybody, anyway?" Carol makes impatient little popping sounds with her lips: *puh-puh-puh-puh-puh.*

"So what are you now, about thirteen or fourteen?"

"No, I'm—" she sighs deeply—"I'm twelve years old. I'm going to be thirteen pretty soon."

"I see. Let's watch. I want you to see exactly the way A.J. comes. When you first see her."

"*Tch!*" she says with a twelve-year-old's exasperation; then she makes the little *puh-puh-puh-puh-puh* lip sounds again.

"Maybe she just comes walking up through the woods," Budd suggests. "Nyahhhhh."

"I want you to look and see where you see A.J. first."

"*Oh!*" Carol says in surprise. "Don't do that! . . . The witch!"

"What did she do?"

"She comes up behind me!" Carol says, irritated.

"So you didn't see her come?"

"I don't know where she came from," Carol says impatiently. "She comes up—why does she always do this!"

"What does she say?"

"Where have you been? Where have you been?" Carol asks A.J., still impatient. And then, almost singing, she says, "You better be *carefulll.* You better be *real carefullll.* I know what I'm *talkin'* about. . . . *Just be careful.* Don't do *anything* to make them mad. If you *do* anything, then it makes it *worse.* I know what I'm *talking* about, *listen* to meeee."

"What does she say to you this time?"

"She thinks it would be neat. It's *not* neat!" Carol tells Alice, then explains to Budd, "They're letting her hold those babies, and they're not neat, I'm telling youuu."

"What about the babies?" Budd asks. "I didn't understand this. She said *what* about the babies?"

"They let her hold the babies."

"They let A.J. hold the babies?"

"Yeah. *Dumb,* A.J.! I'm tellin' you. Don't let them do that. When they start letting you hold babies, I'm telling youuu, don't let them do thaat."

"Did they do that to you?" Budd asks.

"Oh, yeah," she says matter-of-factly. "Lots of times they did that."

"You had to hold the babies?"

"Yeah, I didn't like that any, either."

"What do the babies feel like?" Budd asks. And then to test Carol he tries to lead her, saying, "I bet they squirm around and cry, don't they?"

"No, they don't!" Carol replies with absolute certainty. "They don't do—it's like holding something *dead!* It's *disgusting!*"

"All babies squirm around," Budd insists.

"*These* don't," Carol says firmly. "They're just like those other little tiny ones that were always there. They don't do anything. They're like they're dead. I don't even think they're real! I don't know what they are, but they're not really like babies."

"Now, when you hold those babies—" Budd starts to say.

"God!" Carol says, as if repelled by the thought of holding one of those creatures.

"Are they heavy?" Budd continues. "They feel heavy for a little girl to hold, I bet."

Carol will not be led. "No, they don't weigh anything!" she says. "They're like paper."

"Like paper, um-hm. Now when you hold them, how are you supposed to hold them? On your shoulder?"

"No, you're supposed to hold them . . ." Her voice trails off.

"In your lap?"

"No, up close," she says uneasily. "And walk them. And one time they told me I was supposed to let the baby nurse. . . . I didn't want to do that."

"Did you think you had breasts that a baby could nurse at?"

"I know I could. I'd done that before."

Budd is as confused as I am over what age Carol now is in her mind.

"You know you could? Did you have milk for the babies?" he asks.

Carol whispers, "Yes."

"How did you know you had milk for the babies?"

"I know it was there. Bobby told me all about that."

"Who taught you all about that?"

"Bobby."

"Who's Bobby?" Budd asks.

"Bobby Murphy. He told me everything when I was eleven," Carol says.

"Um-hm. Do you go to school with Bobby?"

"Nooo, nooo!" Carol says, laughing. "Bobby has his sister, Maureen. And Maureen graduated last year. I mean, she's like *five years older* than I am."

"So he knew all about these things?" Budd asks.

"Yeah, and Maureen would help him, and . . . and I knew everything about that stuff."

I am thinking, Jesus, what are we getting into here?

"Did Bobby go to school, too?" Budd asks.

"Nooo!" Carol says, as though Budd's question were too silly to be taken seriously.

"Was he too young to go to school?"

"Oh, noooo! He's twenty-five!"

"He's *twenty-five?*" Budd asks, struggling to keep the surprise out of his voice. "Oh," he says, "Um-hm. . . . I want to ask you a very personal question: What's the first time a boy ever did something to you or did some stuff that had to do with sex? Was that Bobby? Or was that somebody else?"

"I don't like to talk about that," Carol whispers uneasily.

"Hmm?" Budd asks, not sure he heard her. "The very first boy."

"I don't like to talk about that," Carol says more firmly.

"You don't have to talk about it if you don't want to."

"Bobby was *good!* He was *nice* to me," Carol says, on the verge of tears. "He *never* hurt me. He gave me books to read, and he was very, very good to me."

"And he was trying to help you and teach you?" Budd asks sympathetically.

"He taught me *everything.* And he never hurt me. He never, never hurt me."

"Was it a bad boy who did something to you the first time?"

Carol can no longer hold back her tears. "It wasn't fair!" she sobs. "He just didn't know! . . . He just didn't know. He probably didn't know how old I was. . . . I was too young, I think."

"Was this a boy you went to school with?"

"No," Carol says, still crying.

"Where did you meet him?"

There is a pause, and Carol says, "In a bedroom." She stiffens suddenly, and I can hear her inhale sharply.

"It's okay, it's okay," Budd says gently.

"*He's very cold! He's very cold!*" Carol says, an edge of panic in her voice. "*Don't!*" she says as she feels Budd's hand touch her shoulder.

"I'm going to put this blanket over you," Budd says.

Frightened, Carol insists, "Tell him—tell him he's *cold!*"

"Let's pull the blanket over you, okay?" Budd arranged the blanket under Carol's chin and tucks it around her shoulders. "What are you on when he does something?" he asks.

Carol is tossing and turning under the blanket.

"Let me hold your hand," Budd says, taking Carol's hand in his. "I want you to hold my hand *real* hard."

Carol is panting with fear.

"Hold my hand real tight, okay?" Budd says, and Carol's hand grips his. "Just tell me where it is and who it is."

She is still afraid. "In a bedroom. In a bedroom. A bedroom," she cries.

"Who is he? Look at him. Let's just get a—"

"I don't *want* to look at him!" she says firmly. "I know what he looks like."

"What does he look like?"

Carol is still crying. She does not speak.

"What does he look like?" Budd asks again.

Tears stain her cheeks. "*I know who he is!*" she says, racked with sobs. "I've seen him before. Lots of times. *I know who he is!*" She struggles to catch her breath. "*Ungh!* He does things! He does things! And he always stands there and tells me, 'Everything is fine. Everything is fine. Everything is fine.' And it's *not* fine, because—" she says, and suddenly starts kicking and thrashing around on the sofa. "*Go away from me! Go away from me!*"

"Is he doing something to you?" Budd asks.

"He's right on top of me!" Carol replies. "*Go away!*" She is still struggling, trying to push this phantom weight off her body.

"Let me hold your hand—"

"Just go away!"

"Let me hold your hand," Budd says gently, soothingly. "This is me holding your hand now, Carol. Do you feel my hand? I want you to tighten on my hand, know it's my hand. Okay . . . what does he do to you?"

She does not speak.

"Is he somebody you know?" Budd asks.

"No. I mean, I know who he is but I don't know . . ."

"Does he have a name?"

"No, he doesn't have a name."

"What does he look like?"

"He looks like *them*," she says with revulsion. "All of *them*."

"What color hair does he have?"

"He doesn't—" Carol's breath is ragged; she struggles to have enough air to speak. "He doesn't have hair. He doesn't have hair anywhere. He's like rubber. He's cold. All the time he touches me he's cold. *Don't do that!*" she screams.

"What's he doing to you? Now I want you, Carol, to take a deep breath. Just rest a minute, take a real deep breath. . . . That's good. Take a real deep breath, a very deep breath, okay? . . . Are you warmer?"

"It hurts."

"What hurts?"

"Down there," she says.

"Down between your legs it hurts again? Is that where it hurts?"

She is silent but for her ragged breathing.

"Is it down in your female parts?" Budd asks. "Is that where it hurts?"

We cannot hear her answer.

"What did he do? Just tell me what he did," Budd says.

And in a voice so weary it suggests this happens all the time, she replies, "He made another baby."

"How does he do that?" Budd asks. "Does he have a penis he puts in you?"

"No . . . no."

"He doesn't do that. What does he do?"

"He gets over on top of me," she says, wearily still, "and he puts something he has—he puts it in down there and he gets on top of me and it just all goes in there. And then he takes that thing out and then it doesn't hurt anymore. It's no big deal."

Budd appears to be digesting what Carol told him, and then he says, "What I want you to do right now, just as if he's right in front of you this minute, I want you to tell him what you think about this."

"I don't want to look at him," Carol says.

"Let's look at him directly, not just indirectly," he says, squeezing Carol's hand. "Look at him. What would you like to say to him right now? You can say whatever you feel like saying. All of the things you've wanted to say and haven't said. Tell *him* what you'd like to say."

"I don't think I should do that," she says in an ominously quiet tone.

"Carol, this is *your* body and *your* mind. You can do what you want to—" Budd stops when he sees that she is crying hard again.

"They can do this any time they want to!" she sobs. "They can come and do stuff. They can come and put things in and take things out. *They can do anything they want!*"

"Speak to him directly," Budd says, leaning forward closer to Carol. "What if he says to you, 'I have your permission' . . . ?"

Carol's responds by savagely pounding the sofa with her fists. A cry of pure rage escapes her lips.

"Okay, okay, take a deep breath now, Carol," Budd says gently. "Take a real deep breath. You know he's lying when he says that. He's lying, isn't he. You know he's lying. Now, take a deep breath, just a deep breath. . . ."

Carol is still striking the sofa with her fists, but no longer as forcefully.

"Nobody has the right to do that to you," Budd continues. "Will you listen to me for a minute? Listen to what I'm going to say: Nobody has the right to do this to you. No one has the right to do anything to you that you don't give them permission for. And you didn't give him permission. So, he's stealing from you, and taking from you, and that's not right. You have every reason in the world to be angry. Every reason to say, 'Leave me alone! Don't do this to me any longer.' Every reason in the world to say, *'Don't ever do this to me again! Leave me alone!' "*

Carol has begun to calm.

"If you feel you want to be angry like you just were," Budd says, "the best, the healthiest thing in the world—"

Carol mumbles something, then says, "I fixed it."

"They can't do it now, can they?"

There is a pause, and in a much stronger voice Carol says, "They can't ever do that again." She evidently is referring to the tubal ligation she had a dozen years ago.

"Okay, feeling a little better?" Budd asks. "Take a deep breath. You fixed them! You showed them! You showed them! Do you have a right to your own body, Carol?"

"Yes," she says softly.

"You have a little granddaughter right now. "If she says to you, 'Grandma, people are trying to do things to me—should I let them?,' what would you say?"

"I don't know *what* I'd say!" Carol responds. She is crying again. *"You can't stop them!"*

"Wouldn't you say, 'It's okay to try to resist them'?"

"Yes!" she sobs.

"Then that's what you must do, too. You must try to resist them."

"I don't know *howwww!*" she wails.

"Say 'Try to resist,' " Budd insists. "That little girl has a right to her own body, her own life, doesn't she? And you're going to be able to tell her and help her feel she has the strength. See, you had nobody to help you when you were little, did you?"

"My daddy tried," she says sadly.

"Your daddy tried. But your granddaughter has somebody who can really help her, and that's you. You're going to be a big, big help in her life. And that's going to be one of the most wonderful things you can do in the future."

Budd sits back again and says, "Now I want you to take a very deep, relaxing breath," Budd tells her. "Just relax . . . just relax . . . just relax . . . just relax. . . . Let's go back to that other little girl, A.J., and the times you saw her. When was the first time you saw her when you were a woman, an adult?"

"I don't know if it's her . . ." Carol says uncertainly.

Carol tells of seeing two women, one of whom might have been Alice, in a Washington department store ten years earlier; the other woman might have been Alice's sister Grace. Alice would have been around thirty at the time. Carol thought she recognized her and had whispered, "A.J.? . . . A.J.?" The "Alice" woman had looked at her, but Carol doesn't think the woman recognized her. The next time Carol saw Alice was when she became Alice's farm manager ten years later. She says she thinks Alice is the same little girl she knew before; but, as with the woman in the department store, she isn't sure.

"Of course she looks older than she did when you met her as a little girl," Budd points out.

"Yes, but I didn't know I knew her as a little girl. I just thought I saw her somewhere before. It's very confusing!"

"Of course it's confusing," Budd says. "So we're now getting up to the present. Here's what let's do. Let's move back to that field where you were very exasperated because Alice was so slow, and she wouldn't come, and she stepped in the manure and everything."

"That's *her* fault!"

"That's her fault," Budd agrees. "And then there's something about—there's something you don't particularly want to talk about."

"Oh, boy!" she says reluctantly. "Do we have to do this again?"

"Yes. Let's just see what that was about."

"I don't know if I want to do this," Carol says nervously.

"Well, you've told me a lot about it. There's something about . . . is there something about . . . soldiers? What's this about soldiers?"

"They're not soldiers. They're guards."

"How do you meet these guards?"

"At the door in the tunnel."

"Where's this tunnel?"

"Underground! Underground!" she answers sharply, beginning to breathe more quickly. "We're underground! Oh, I don't like being down here! This is terrible! . . . It's cold as *hell* down here! OH!"

"How'd you get there, underground?"

"I don't know! I don't know. We're down underground. We're down here and Alice is *not happy!* She is definitely not happy. Not a happy camper!"

"Okay, not a happy camper. What's happening underground?"

"We have to walk into this big room like a hangar or something. Big, huge hangar," she sighs, a little shakily. There is a brief pause and then, "*Ohhh, boy!* Wow, it's sort of neat. . . . *I* think it's sort of neat; I don't think Alice thinks this is really neat at all. Oh, wellll, we're here now. Might as well keep going. . . . A guy puts something on me. Puts something on me."

"What's that he puts on you?"

"Some machine or something. I just know it's a machine. . . . And it makes my ear ring. My right ear. Buzzes or rings or, sort of, you know . . ."

Her breath has become a bit labored. "There's a bunch of people over in the corner."

"Let's look at the people. What do they look like?"

"Lot's of people. I know lots of people there. I think Alice knows people, too."

"That's very interesting," Budd says. "Let's look at those people and see who they are."

"Ohhhhh, there's Ruth, I haven't seen her in a hundred years. I don't remember her last name. I knew her a long, long time ago. I went to school with her. . . . And there's LuAnne Morris. Of course, she's not Lu Morris anymore. She was my best friend."

"Does she recognize you?"

"Yeah, and Jack's with her, too. Geez," she says with a little laugh, "I'm surprised Jack's here!" She laughs again and calls out, "Hey, Jack!"

Budd establishes that Jack is LuAnne's husband. He is wearing a blue short-sleeve shirt and slacks. LuAnne is in a red dress.

Carol is as excited at seeing LuAnne as if they had come upon each other at a boring cocktail party. "Wow! This is neat! This is wild! Why're you here?" she asks LuAnne.

"Do you know everybody there or just some of them?" Budd asks.

Carol tells us she does not know everybody; still, she seems surprised at how many of those assembled in the hangar she does know. Alice, too, appears to Carol to have found several friends.

Budd asks Carol if I am there. She says I'm not. Budd isn't there, either. Nor is Richard Hall, the former NICAP director, who befriended Alice and Carol in Maryland. "Let's look around and see if you know anybody else," Budd tells her. "Is Jane there?"

Jane is the government secretary with a high security clearance who, as a member of the M.I.T. abductee panel, expressed difficulty at leading "a life filled with secrets"—the one who asked, "How do you open a conversation with 'Oh, by the way, I was abducted by aliens'?" During an earlier break, Budd and I spoke about Jane. Evidently she has been having a very hard time. He mentioned that she had taken the commuter train to work the week before and had arrived at her office two hours late with her shirt on backwards. Lately, Jane has become so distressed, Budd told me, he is worried she might be suicidal.

Carol says Jane is there in the underground hangar, "but she's not talking to anybody."

"Let's look at Jane," Budd says. "What's Jane wearing?"

"She's wearing a blue sweater, and she's a got a blouse or something underneath the sweater, because it's got a collar on it. And she has on like a pair of culottes, knee socks . . . I can't see her feet. But she's sitting in a chair and has her feet tucked up underneath her—underneath the chair. And she's another not-a-happy-camper. She and Alice ought to get together. Jane is real upset. She doesn't look happy. I don't want to talk to her, because she gets so upset all the time. I think I'll stay away from her."

Budd asks if any other members of the abductee panel are there.

Carol appears to be looking around in her mind. "No," she says. She tells us she recognizes one woman she has met before, but cannot remember where she met her. Lansing and Amanda, a couple of women who boarded their horses at the farm, were there, too. "Oh boy!" Carol says, laughing. "This is really going to scare the crap out of Amanda! 'Hey, Amanda,' " she says softly. " 'Hey, Amanda, it's okay. Ohhh, see? That's scary, huh?' . . . I think Amanda's really scared," Carol tells us. "Lansing isn't. Lansing's all excited. She thinks everything is 'neat'! Lansing's like— well, you could die and she would still think it was 'neat,' but she's okay. . . . 'I know, Amanda, it's okay. It's okay.' Some people are upset, some people are scared and confused—*I don't know what's going on!*'" she says impatiently. "Why're you asking *me?*" Carol snorts in disgust. "I'm just here, okay? It's an invitation, right? You showed up, I showed up."

"What do the chairs look like that people are sitting on?" Budd asks her.

"They're metal folding chairs, but not too many people are sitting down."

"You said Jane was sitting down."

"Yeah, Jane's sitting down. She's like glued to the chair. Nobody's going to be moving Jane. They'll have to carry her! *Oh!*" Carol says excitedly, "Here they come! Here they come! *Here they come!* What *are* these guys? Boy, *neat!* I want one of those to ride in. Then I wouldn't get sawdust in my eyes in the arena."

"What are you referring to?" Budd asks.

"The guards' helmets," she says. "Covers the whole head and everything. I guess they can breathe in there." She asks one of them, "Geez, can you guys breathe in there?" And then, as if trying to catch the guards' attention, Carol calls out, *"Hey!"* She seems not to get a response and answers her question herself, saying, "I guess so. . . . Okay, then they're going to take some people. They pull out these things and point them at people, and then they pick some and they go over there to this thing. . . . *Ohhh*, stuff is falling out of the roof or something! 'The sky is falling!' " she says, and laughs to herself.

"What's falling?" Budd asks.

" 'The sky is falling,' " she repeats. "That's a fairy tale or a rhyme or something," she explains, making herself laugh again. And then, a moment later, Carol announces, "This is really a weird dream!"

The heavy steel hangar doors clang shut, and then, as the ceiling begins to open, the immense underground hangar space echoes and rumbles with the deep grinding sounds of heavy machinery. Grass and sorrel and rocks tumble from the lips of the aperture and drop into the huge underground space. Some debris strikes the tilted spacecraft.

When it is Carol's turn to be led to the giant UFO, she tells Budd, "I guess I want to go. I guess I do want to go. I'm curious," she says. "I really want to see what's in there." But then, sounding uncertain, she adds, "I—I just wonder if I get to come back. . . . I don't know if I get to come back."

She is worried that the group that was led into the spaceship ahead of her group has not reappeared. They were sucked up into the rear of the saucer and have not been seen again.

"There are so many people and they're all milling around," Carol says. "I see all these people I know and I try to talk to everybody, but I'm afraid I'll miss something, you know? I'm afraid if I talk to somebody I'll miss something. Something's going to happen. We're going to get to go now. Oh, c'mon!" she says impatiently. "It's *our* turn! It's *our* turn! C'mon! C'mon! C'mon! Look happy! Look happy! Look happy! It's just a dream," she says, and then, very softly, says again, "just a dream. . . ."

The guard guides Carol's group between the giant caterpillar treads, beneath the disc, and to its rear. "It's so *huge!*" she says in an awed tone. "*Nothing* is this big! Nothing in the whole world is this big. This is really a great dream!"

But while Carol is looking up at the milky glass orbs beneath the saucer, she is gripped by uncertainty again. "I don't think I want to do this," she tells us. "I think I've changed my mind."

"Maybe you don't have much choice," Budd suggests.

"Really I can—I can walk away from here. I don't have to do this," Carol says. "I can walk. They can't make me do this one. This is just, you know, this is just a dream. I don't have to do this." She exhales sharply: "*Whew!*"

"Do you want to go away from it?" Budd asks.

"Nooo," she says reluctantly. "I guess I can stand it. I'm so curious all the time! Why do I have to be so damn curious? It's probably going to kill me someday. Ohhh, crap! I'm going to go up inside it now."

It is Carol's turn to be sucked up into the craft; the quick ascent turns her stomach.

Budd asks her what the machine looks like inside.

"It's *absolutely huge!*" Carol replies. "It's like layers of stuff! There's holes around things, and tubes, and you can look up through pieces and there's an entire other section up there. Probably another one on top of that. It's like—

it's like a *city* in here!" There is a pause, then Carol exhales—"*Whew!*"—and says, "Wow, this is a big place!"

She tells us there are maybe thirty other people now inside the craft with her; but she is worried that she does not see Alice anywhere. "Oh, God, I hope Alice came," Carol says. "I don't want to do this by myself."

Jane isn't there, either. But Amanda and Lansing, the horse farm boarders, are, as are several other friends she recognized in the hangar. Nobody seems particularly happy, Carol tells us. They are all just standing around waiting. And then, like pieces of mail, they are sorted and transported to different sections of the huge ship.

Carol is among those sent single-file down a sloping, semicircular tunnel lit by fluorescent-like tubes within tubes. She has still not entirely recovered from the nausea she felt being sucked up into the craft, and now the motion of her descent affects her stomach again. She spots Lansing ahead of her and also a man she identifies as Rudd. Rudd is wearing only bedroom slippers and Jockey shorts.

"I always thought Rudd was built better than that," Carol remarks. She notices he has a scar on his leg.

"Where's his scar?" Budd asks.

"It's right here," Carol says, indicating the back of her left thigh. "It's a big scar. I wonder where he got that from. He's funny 'cause he keeps trying to hide it. Walks like this," she says, holding her hand behind her thigh. "Listen, if I were him I'd be walking like this," she says, shielding her crotch. "He's a nice guy. I like Rudd. I didn't see him before, but he's here."

"When you say 'better built,' do you mean more muscular?"

"No, just he looks pale like a chicken. But it doesn't matter what he looks like; it just surprises me."

Carol describes others with visible marks or scars. And then she tells us Erica from the support group is there, except that "she's not 'Erica,' she's somebody else."

"She doesn't look quite like Erica, you mean?" Budd asks.

"No, she looks like Erica."

"But she has a different name?"

"Yes. I don't call her Erica," Carol says.

Erica is wearing only a T-shirt, Carol reports, "but it's real short. She hasn't got anything on underneath it. I hate to tell her, but if she leans over she's in deep trouble."

Budd asks Carol if any of the other women from the support group are in the craft with her, and Carol says there is only Erica. "But it's not her name," Carol insists. "Her name is something else. When I see her I call her something else."

When Budd starts to say something, Carol interrupts, insisting, "I know it's her. I'd know her anywhere. I've seen her before."

"What do you call her?"

"Karen? . . . Carla? . . . Caroline? . . . It's something like that. It's got hard letters, like a Karen or a Carla or a Caro—*Catherine!* It's Catherine— I call her Catherine. I think that's her. It must be her. It looks just like her."

"Okay," Budd says, "so you go down this sort of incline. Is it long?"

"Yes. It takes a long time to get down there."

"Is there a railing to hold on to?"

"No, it doesn't matter. You just sort of—*plup!*—move to places."

"And when you get down there what happens?"

"There," it turns out, is a room with a strong, unpleasant odor—the smell, Carol tells us, "of burnt meat. We all have to come through there, and it smells real bad. *Whew!* I don't like this stink. It's terrible. Hope we're not for dinner!" Carol says with a short bark of laughter. Then she sighs, saying, "Oh, okay, over on one side there's, like, tray things, flat. I don't know what they are; they're like trays, only they aren't . . . they aren't . . ." She pauses, exasperated; she doesn't know how to describe them. "They're like . . . like . . . uh . . . metal trays, and they have these handlelike things on one side of them. I don't know what it looks like. It looks like *trays* on this thing that has handles. And there are lots of those of things—" she counts eight of them—"on the side over here, and we're standing up against where the wall, like, curves, up next to this tunnel thing that we came through. Ohh, *damn!* This smell's starting to get to me."

Carol shakes her head. "There's stuff on this one tray over here that looks familiar. There's this thing that has this itty-bitty little scissorlike thing on the end of it. It comes out of this tube altogether, and then by compressing something two little claw-things come out and hold things. And they take things out and put things in with it. Ohhhh," she says, suddenly nervous, "I know what they are! It's the stuff they use in the ears!"

She makes a worried little *plup-plup-plup-plup* sound with her lips. "Oh, I didn't come all this way for this!" she says, then laughs sarcastically. "Golden opportunity, right?"

"And then what happens?" Budd asks her.

"Okay, yeah, okay. We're going down past these things. I keep trying to look at the tray," she reports, "but after a while I can't see it. There's other stuff on there, I can't tell what they are. Oh, boy," she says, her voice suddenly shaky again, "we go past this stuff that has tables and things, and I know what those are tooooo."

"Is there anything on the tables?"

"No, there's nothing on the tables, but I know what they are," she says uneasily. "I've seen those tables before; they have these things, these boxes things. Box things. And they have stuff in these boxes. And they have things coming out of the box," she says, speaking quickly now, as if to get this part over with. "Boxes that have these long, hoselike things on them. Stuff they put down your stomach. . . . And there are things that come down from the ceiling. . . . Oh, *geez,* I hate these places!"

Carol tosses restlessly on the sofa. "They'll make us stop here," she complains. "I don't know why they're doing this. Why are we just doing this?" And then, a moment later: "Phew!" she says with relief. "We're going on by this thing and we go around, it's like levels. You move along and you're like going around and up a little incline and then you go around again and there's, like, another room. And it's like you can see everything. If you look at it right, you can see all these levels in there. . . .

"I don't want to go up in heeeere," Carol says, suddenly sounding worried again. "I shouldn't have come," she sighs. "I shouldn't have come. Oh, boy, that's really *dumb!* I'm such an idiot!" There is a little pause and she whispers, "Ohhhh, God . . ."

"What's happening?" Budd asks.

"I know where we're going," she says. "We're going to go up to the babies! They have baby everythings up here. They have baby babies, they have baby horses, they have baby kangaroos, baby mice, and they have baby-baby-baby—everything's *babies!*" She sighs. "There's lots of them, and we just go from one little baby place to another little baby place. God, it's like Universal Motherhood!"

"Are there grown-up kangaroos and mice?" Budd asks.

"No. None of those things! It's all baby things. Baby here, baby there. Baby everything. Everything is babies. Oh, God, I mean I like babies, okay? Babies are neat. It's okay about having babies. Babies are okay. But God, you can't have *everybody's* babies." She exhales wearily. "Ohhh, enough with the babies already. Enough with the babies! God, I don't want any more!"

Sensing Carol's exhaustion, Budd asks, "Would you like me to bring you back home now, Carol, and then we can come back to this tomorrow?"

"Yes," she says.

"I'm going to put my hand on your forehead and it's going to make your stomach feel much better," Budd tells her. He gently cups Carol's brow. "Feel my hand? We're going to take you home now. We're going to take you home and you're going to go up to bed. Up to bed and the evening's over. We're going to come back and pick it up tomorrow where we left off. . . . But right now we're going back to bed, feeling relaxed. Do you feel yourself back in bed at home? Back at your farmhouse, feeling better?"

"Ummmmmm," Carol says softly.

Budd tells her how relieved she will feel, that she will have a great sense of inner strength. He tells her that her body is going to feel at ease now; that she'll have a nice night's sleep; that she's come through whatever this dream memory was just fine; that she feels a sense of togetherness with all those people who are sharing these kinds of experiences. "But above all," he adds, "you'll have that sense of yourself as a survivor. Here you are at this point in your life, you've survived all these difficult things."

And then Budd brings her out.

"Five, you're starting to wake up," he tells her. "Four, you're waking up. . . . Three, you're almost awake." His voice becomes louder with each count. "Two. . . . One, fully awake."

Carol opens her eyes. The Saturday-night session has ended.

CHAPTER XVIII

Postconference Interview

Carol and Alice—Fourth Hypnosis Session
at Budd Hopkins's Studio

Alice is in tears when I arrive back at Budd's studio Sunday morning. She is still feeling overwhelmed with guilt at having blamed her father for her supposed rape during the fishing trip she took with him when she was twelve years old. But although as a result of the previous day's hypnotic regression session she is questioning her father's crime, she is still not entirely convinced that it was the alien who penetrated her. "One image has not yet replaced the other," she confesses. "Instead, there is a new image, a new scenario, *and* the old one."

Alice tells us that after the alleged rape her father could never understand why she would not go fishing with him again. She also reveals a subsequent terror of land crabs. After what happened on the sandy banks of that canal, she would not get out of the car if land crabs were around. Budd hypothesizes that a possible reason is that a land crab's eyes, like those of the alien rapist, are wide apart.

He tells Alice that this morning he would like to hypnotize her concerning Carol's July "dream" of the UFO in the underground hangar and the two women's "possible childhood linkages."

"The importance of this," Budd explains to me, "lies in the architecture of the acts: Carol and Alice knew each other as children and act as magnets for one another." It is symptomatic of his hypothesis that the aliens "are planning friendships or relationships" and that they bring people together as "part of a deepening plan. But," he adds, "part of the problem is, What does this mean in terms of relationships and control?"

Alice says she does not believe the "little gray shits," as she continually calls them, "are capable of *complete* control." She compares their ability to control humans to the amount of control humans have over their pets.

Carol agrees. "They can control the body," she says, "but not the mind." She gives as an example that although the Beings want female abductees to hold the babies, the women seem to have a choice.

Alice was not present when Budd hypnotized Carol about the dream, so I know Alice cannot have picked up any details of her "possible linkages" to Carol from that. And since in our extended conversations the two women have never conjectured about such a linkage, and since I have never come across any references to a "shared" childhood episode in either of their journals, I assume that any previous interest in or exploration of that topic would have to have been minimal, if present at all. As a result, I am not concerned that Alice may already have been contaminated should she be questioned about childhood linkages.

I am concerned, however, that Alice may already know so much about Carol's underground UFO dream that any supporting or corroborative information she gives under hypnosis would be suspect. I know, for example, that Alice and Carol constantly speak to each other about their experiences; and that Carol, in her journal, wrote a very detailed account of the appearance of the UFO, of having called Alice out of the house to see it, and of their race across the pastures after it. I know that Carol described their view of the huge craft in the underground hangar, and that friends and acquaintances were among the people gathered there with them. Therefore, the question I have is not *whether* Carol has spoken to Alice about the dream but rather *how much* she has told her.

However, Alice tells me she has never read Carol's journal; and that since Carol has spoken very little about the dream, she—Alice—did not "know a whole bunch. I knew Carol had gone to some underground place where there were a lot of other people, but she didn't say who. She told me she thought the underground thing was in the alfalfa field out back, and that was it."

If that is so, Alice would not know that while chasing after the saucer she, according to Carol's account, stepped in manure; nor would she know she and Carol had gone inside the craft—an act that reminds me of Dave Jacobs's aside to me at the M.I.T. conference, "It took twenty years to realize the UFOs might have an inside." And that in turn reminds me of NICAP's early ambivalence towards saucer sightings in general: if a witness reported more than one sighting of a UFO, he or she was no longer regarded as reliable. The reason was that seeing UFOs more than once was at that time as inconceivable as winning the lottery twice.

Budd makes Alice comfortable on the black couch, then slowly puts her under. Once he is sure she is "asleep," he says, "We want to go back to the summer, the warm months of the summer, when you and Carol were working hard at your place in Maryland. Everything is normal and nice. There's going to come a certain night, however, back in July, a particular night, you're upstairs getting ready for bed, and when I count to three, on that particular night you're going to hear Carol call to you. You're upstairs, not sure what this is all about, and she's going to call to you from downstairs in the evening after dinner. When I count to three, this very special evening you're upstairs getting ready for bed, you're going to hear Carol call.

"One, you're about to hear her call to you from downstairs on the porch or wherever. . . . Two. . . . Three. . . ."

Alice makes no sound. Her breathing seems deep and undisturbed.

"She's calling," Budd repeats. "Tell me what her voice sounds like. What she's saying to you."

"Scared," Alice whispers.

After a long pause, Budd asks, "And what do you do?"

"I run downstairs and out to the porch. . . . *Lights!*"

"You see lights?"

Alice sounds puzzled: "An upside-down blue ring . . . gas burner."

"The lights look like an upside-down gas burner, um-hm," Budd says, and makes a note. "Where do you see this upside-down gas burner?"

"Between the chicken coop and the ash tree . . . over the orchard."

"What's Carol saying to you?" Budd asks. "Let's listen to what she's saying."

"We're supposed to go," Alice says. "She's got my hand."

"Do you have your coat on?"

"No."

"What do you have on?"

"Blue nightgown."

"You said 'blue nightgown'?" Budd asks. In Carol's "dream" Alice's nightgown was pink.

"She's leading me off the porch," Alice says, then lapses into silence.

"Tell me what's happening. Where are you going?"

"Back towards the trees," she says, and sighs. "We're going behind the house, back towards the gate by the little pond. Towards the woods. I think it's overhead and we're following."

According to Carol, Alice had hung back, Carol had to keep telling Alice to hurry up. "Are you excited and eager to follow this?" Budd asks.

"Yeah. It's an adventure. It's exciting. . . . *Ooooh!*"

"What?"

"I stepped in something," Alice says.

"What kind of shoes do you have on?"

"I don't have any shoes on," Alice says. Carol had also reported they were barefoot.

"What did you step in?" Budd asks.

"Yech," she says disgustedly. "Something sort of squishy."

"What do you think it is?"

"I *hope* it's mud. I don't think it was, though, I'll tell you."

Alice scrapes the manure off with a stick and continues after Carol, who takes her hand and leads the way. The disc is far ahead of them—"over the mailman's house," Alice reports—and she, too, says it is light enough out to see.

There is another long pause, and Budd asks, "What's happening?"

"A mine shaft!" Alice says, surprised. "Timbers!"

Budd tries to pin down where the mine shaft might be. "Is it near the mailman's house, or where is it?"

Alice takes a deep breath. "There's woods around," she says. "Think it's beyond the mailman's house. The edge of his woods."

"Are you tired from going such a long distance?" Budd asks.

"No . . . uh-uh," Alice says. "More like children. I feel like skipping."

"You feel like skipping? Good. So this mineshaft—"

"Tracks! Goes down. Like for a little railroad car." Alice falls silent again.

"Why are you going down this mine shaft?" Budd asks.

"I don't know," Alice says. "Carol's leading."

"Is it tall enough to stand up in, or do you have to stoop?"

"Carol's stooping. I can walk upright."

"I bet it's kind of scary, isn't it, to go down the mine shaft at night like that with no flashlight?" It is a deliberately leading question.

"No," Alice says, not taking his lead.

"How do you see in this mine shaft?"

"The walls are green. And phosphorescent," she says, and sighs.

Budd waits for Alice to say more, but she does not speak. "What are you seeing?" he asks her. "What's happening? I bet it's a small, tight place, isn't it?" he asks, testing her again.

"No! *Big!*" Alice says firmly. "Clay floor. How can they get clay underground?"

The mine shaft entrance is new information. Carol did not know how she had arrived underground.

"I bet it's really dark," Budd says.

"No, there's lots of light."

Alice cannot determine where the light comes from; Carol did not mention the lighting at all. But since Carol could see across the width of the hangar, we can assume the space was well lit in her "dream," too. Carol said the interior had been large enough to contain "several 727 jets." Alice now says the space is "like two or three aircraft hangars" and that its walls are faced with smooth rock.

"Just look around," Budd tells her. "Let's just pause for a minute. I'm going to take your hand. You've come down here—feel my hand—we'll stay together, and give me just a very good look around this big room and see if you see any movement, or whatever. See if anybody else is there."

"It's weird," Alice says after a moment. "It's like there's Astroturf down there. There's people in brown steel folding chairs. Nobody's sitting down." Presumably, by that Alice means no one is sitting on the ground. Carol, too, saw people in metal folding chairs; one of them was Jane.

"Let's look at the people," Budd says. "Do you see anybody you know, for instance?"

"Most of them are strangers," Alice says, then adds, "Lansing and Amanda are there. And Lansing's little kids are there."

Carol, too, saw the two women horse boarders, but she did not mention the presence of Lansing's children. Amanda, according to Carol, appeared very frightened; Lansing seemed excited. When Budd asks Alice what the two women's facial expressions are, Alice says just that they seem relieved to know somebody, then says excitedly, *"Ohh! Tiffany is there!"*

"How do you know Tiffany? Who's Tiffany?"

Alice sighs and says, "We were in school together. In college. I haven't seen her in twenty years! There's a man with her. He has dark hair. . . . How'd she get here?"

Carol, too, had recognized a former schoolmate she had not seen in a long time.

Budd asks Alice how many people are down there with her.

"Oh, a hundred. Lots!" Alice says. "Lots. Big groups of people."

Carol, in her prehypnosis account of her dream, said there were about a hundred people present. Under hypnosis, however, she did not mention a specific number, she said only that there were "lots."

"Okay," Budd says, "let's look around and see if you see anybody else that you know."

Alice lets out her breath slowly while she "looks around." She identifies several people whose names are meaningless to us; none of them were mentioned by Carol.

Budd asks her to look around some more. He is trying to find more overlaps between Carol's and Alice's accounts.

Alice sighs again. "So many people . . ." She appears to be still searching. "Colin and Mary and Barbara and Diana should be there, but I don't see them."

These names, too, are meaningless. "You don't see them," Budd says. "We'll just go through some names, then. I'm just going to pick some names out of a hat. First of all, am I there?"

"No."

Further questioning reveals Alice does not see me, Richard Hall, or Jane, the conference abductee whose state of mind Budd was so worried about. Carol didn't see Budd, Richard Hall, or myself, either, but she saw Jane.

Budd asks Alice if she sees anyone from the support group we met with the other night. Carol had seen Erica, whom she knew by another name, "Catherine."

Alice does not see Erica, but she does see Terry, the support group member who had said she felt "a tremendous sense of betrayal" from her abductions.

"Terry's hair is longer," Alice tells us. "She's shorter, too; I thought she was taller."

Budd asks Alice to describe what Terry is wearing and then, in an effort to determine why Alice and Carol are not seeing the same people, he asks, "Are you still standing next to Carol, holding her hand?"

"Uh-uh . . . no. She's on the other side, talking to somebody."

"How far away is she? Ten feet?"

"No—fifty, a hundred feet."

"Do you think she has a different view of things?" Budd asks.

"Yes," Alice says.

Carol, too, reported having become separated from Alice.

"Now let's look through the crowd," Budd says. "Is everybody dressed in sort of casual clothes, or is somebody dressed oddly?"

Alice mentions a man in a business suit. She doesn't feel he belongs there.

"How about anybody without any clothes on?" Budd asks. Here he is searching for any reference to Rudd, the man Carol saw who was dressed only in his bedroom slippers and Jockey shorts.

"No, most everybody's got clothes on," Alice answers. There are children in pajamas, she says; she and Carol are in nightgowns; but most of the adults "have real clothes on—except that weird guy in the suit with a mustache."

"Are people talking to each other? Do you talk to people? For instance, do you talk to Tiffany, your old college friend?"

"Yes," Alice says.

"What does Tiffany say she's been doing since you seen her all these years?"

"She says she's a child's doctor, a pediatrician," Alice says. "When I knew her in Colorado she wasn't even in med school." Alice did know, however, that Tiffany at that time was intending to become a doctor.

"Did she tell you where she's living?"

After a pause Alice answers, "California."

"Did she say what town she's living in in California?"

"Sacramento," Alice says, then adds, "We didn't really have much time to talk." (Ten days after this session Alice is able to locate Tiffany and speak with her by telephone. Tiffany is living not in Sacramento but in Cleveland, and she is not a pediatrician but an anesthesiologist. She has never lived in Sacramento, and never left Ohio during the period Carol's dream took place.)

Like Carol, Alice senses that the people gathered in the underground hangar are apprehensive, subdued. Budd keeps asking her to look around, to try to see if she recognizes anyone else. He mentions some of the other women from the support group meeting: Brenda, Linda Cortile, Erica.

Alice does not see any of them. She does, however, see Pat, the M.I.T. conference abductee whose husband wrestled the alien to the ground.

Budd's next question seems to me to be leading. "I want you to look to see if there's anybody practically undressed," he says. "A man?"

"Yes!" Alice says, surprised. "He's got Jockey shorts on. Hairy chest. He's tall. He's got hair on his shoulders, too."

"Have you seen him before, or is he a stranger?"

"Don't know," Alice says. She appears to be trying to look at the man more closely. "Hmm," she says. "He's got slippers on his feet. That's weird."

Carol, too, saw Rudd wearing only Jockey shorts and bedroom slippers. She didn't notice him until she was inside the spacecraft. According to Carol, he had large scar on the back of his left thigh.

Budd asks Alice if the man in the slippers and Jockey shorts has any other distinguishing features besides hairy shoulders.

"He's got a big scar on the inside of his left calf, a long cut," she replies. "It's all puckered, like it's a real bad scar, about six inches long."

Budd shoots me a look. I half-expect him to whisper that old *Twilight Zone* line of Rod Serling's: "Coincidence? I don't think so. . . ." Alice and Carol *both* saw a man naked but for bedroom slippers and Jockey shorts, with a scar on his left leg. The fact that Carol saw the scar on the back of the man's thigh, and Alice saw it on his calf, is irrelevant. The two women might just have seen him from different angles; and if the injury was serious enough, it is not inconceivable that he would have been scarred on his thigh and calf both.

Alice, too, describes the man as being not well-built, but strong. But despite Budd's persistence, he cannot get Alice to identify the man as Rudd. We learn later that Alice does not know Rudd; he is a friend of Carol's, not hers.

"One last thing here, on the people," Budd says. "You said there were folding chairs. Brown?"

"Yes, they're on the Astroturf."

"Let's just look at the chairs and see if anybody's sitting in the chairs. Somebody may be sitting down."

"There are." There a brief pause, and Alice says, "There's a shaft of light from the top! Lots of light! It's nighttime, isn't it? Where's that light coming from?"

"Let's look at the people sitting down," Budd gently insists. Alice sighs. Despite Budd's hope that Alice will identify Jane, she does not recognize any of those seated on the folding chairs.

I am wondering whether Alice and Carol could be describing different incidents. Perhaps they made more than one trip to this place. I write down my question and pass it to Budd, who asks Alice, "Is this the first time you've ever been in this place? Does it seem familiar in any way? Or is it all new?"

"It seems familiar. . . . Different people, though," she says.

"You think you've been here more than once?"

"Yes."

Budd then asks Alice to just let her mind drift and "see if there's anybody else that—any other time or anywhere that you might have seen different people that you know. In other words, just concentrate on people you might know." He asks Alice if she thinks she might ever have seen me there some other time. No. Dick Hall? No. Budd? No. Jane? No. Brenda? No. "Okay," Budd says, "let's just move now back to this light. You know, you may remember things that will pop in your mind. You said there's a light shining down from up above? From the roof? Or where is it?"

"It looks like an opening," Alice says. "Like sunshine's coming in. Like a sunbeam."

Carol, too, described the dome opening; but rather than having seen any light, she had commented upon how black the sky was and described the bits of earth and rocks that were falling from the widening aperture onto the skin of the huge disc. Alice has not mentioned the presence of any spacecraft at all.

"What else is in this room?" Budd asks her. "We have the lights, we have the people, we have the rocks around the side, we have Astroturf, the folding chairs. Is there anything else in this room?"

"There's something coming out of the walls. Like half an arch? Like a runner in the middle, as though something's supposed to slide on it? It comes out of the wall. I don't know what it's for. It looks like it's trying to hold the wall up. Like a support . . ."

During the long pause that follows I am thinking that Alice's "half an arch" might be the forty-five-degree-angle-tilted spacecraft. "It's dark in the corners," Alice is saying. "It seems to go way back. All black . . ."

"Now, you come in there," Budd says, "and you and Carol kind of separated from each other a little bit, right? You said you were some distance apart. Now let's just see what's going to happen next. Every dream or fantasy or whatever has a sequence of events. So when I count to three, let's just move to the next event.

"One," Budd counts, "we're just getting ready for this story to move ahead. . . . Two. . . . Three!"

When Alice speaks, it is with a certain sense of wonder. "Most people are gone!"

"Where'd they go?" Budd asks. "Did you see them go someplace?"

"No." Alice pauses and then says, "Shaft."

"Do you see Carol? Is she right there with you?"

In Carol's account, by this time in the experience she and Alice had rendezvoused and were standing together in line.

"Yes," Alice says.

"So it's just you and Carol, and everybody else is gone?"

"Yes. There are six to eight other people around. . . . Tiffany is gone. . . ." And, then with a mixture of surprise and wonder, Alice says, "A green elevator shaft with *eyes?*"

Budd will not be distracted. He wants to know what happened to the people. "Before we get into that," he says, "let's move back a bit, because at some point, since you're in a big room and it's well lit and there's lots of people, at some point you're going to see what happens to those people. We know they leave, because they're not there."

"Have to line up. Have to line up," Alice says, then adds, "In groups. We march away."

"Each person?"

"No, a whole line of people," Alice says. Carol had told of being marched off to the craft a half-dozen or so at a time.

"Where are they marching?" Budd asks.

"To the left, around the edge, towards that arch thing. . . ."

Does she mean towards the huge disc?

"Is it possible that you march over there, too, since the other people are?" Budd asks. "Maybe you do, maybe you don't. We don't really know. What do you think? Did you ever march over there? . . . Maybe you don't. Maybe you just leave. But since other people are, maybe you are marched there, too."

Here again Budd's line of questioning seems to me to be dangerously close to leading. I can't help wondering if Alice is unconsciously shaping her answers to reflect what she thinks he wants to hear.

I am bothered that I do not find Alice's account as convincing as Carol's. But that may be a result of the differences in their personalities. Alice will speak of Carol's ability to "pick up more on details," whereas she herself "picks up more on patterns and feelings." Carol is visual; Alice is analytical. Carol's accounts are filled with intricate, subjective visual images and a strong narrative drive. Alice's account is more detached, interrupted by pauses and observations, as if she were standing back from the experience to evaluate its meaning or uncloak its illogical flaws.

Alice tells us that she and her group are marched "toward that elevator thing," then adds, "It's behind the arch. . . ." I am wondering if she means the disc's rear entrance, the opening through which the people, in Carol's account, were being levitated into the craft.

"So you go over to that elevator thing," Budd says. "Let's just see where you go now. Are you and Carol together, or are you separate?"

"No, we're together," Alice says. She mumbles something about having found Carol, then says, "Umm, weird. It's like we go into a black hole."

Maybe the arch isn't Alice's visual interpretation of the leading edge of the tilted spacecraft after all; and her "black hole" is not a portal leading into the craft. According to Alice's account, upon their arrival at the "black hole" opening, instead of being sucked up into the huge spaceship, she and Carol "tumble" *down* an incline, "sort of like feathers floating."

In Carol's account, shortly after she entered the craft, she and Alice were separated and Carol was moved down a sloping, semicircular tunnel that emerged into a room that smelled of "burnt meat." During the journey through the tunnel she saw Lansing ahead of her. Alice sees Lansing ahead of her, too. But instead of emerging from the inclined corridor into a space with a strong, unpleasant odor, Alice seems to end up again in the huge hangar—if, in fact, we correctly understood that to have been where she saw the metal folding chairs, all those people, and her friends.

"Since you moved on," Budd says, "it's obviously for some purpose. Let's see what you've moved on to."

"There's a . . . a *Close Encounters* ship!" Alice says, her voice filled with awe.

"What do you mean by 'a *Close Encounters* ship'?" Budd asks.

"It looks like a big one. Except it's not as big as the one in the movie. . . . I don't how they got it underground, my goodness!"

"Is it resting on the ground? Hovering? What is it's situation?"

"It's hovering," Alice says. "It doesn't make any noise. A few lights flashing."

"And what happens when you go into this room and this big thing is there? Incidentally, I didn't ask, but since we all know about these experiences, do you see any of those people around you associate with the UFOs? That aren't human?"

Alice thinks there may be some Beings over by the ship now, but says she's too far away to be sure. The "guards" whom Carol saw in a helmet-and-gas-mask combination, wear, in Alice's account, dark business suits, white shirts, ties—and are barefoot. "That's dumb!" Alice giggles.

"Sometimes people who are ushering have like a flashlight or some kind of thing to point directions," Budd tells her. "Do they carry anything, or are they just empty-handed?" He is looking for the rod-shaped electronic device Carol called a "calculator," which she assumed was used for identifying people.

Alice appears to be considering Budd's question. "I don't think they are carrying anything," she tells us. "They just say 'Follow me' and we go. Or they go. The one that led us didn't go down the tube."

"Let's look at the face of the one who led you. What's he look like?"

"He's got a pointed chin and—oh, *shit!* He does sort of have those eyes. . . . Not real bad. He's sort of got a face like a wolf."

"Does he have hair like a wolf?" Budd asks.

"No."

As her account continues, we learn from Alice that everyone is "just sort of milling around" and that there's some kind of gold urn topped by a round ball which they have to put their hands on. Alice thinks it reads their fingerprints. Alice then hears "metal clangs . . . echoes" and says she is beginning to get scared. She detects a slight odor of vinegar and attributes it to her fear.

"How about the other senses—anything else?" Budd asks. "Sense of touch? You've described putting your hand down on this urn. You said it was warm to the touch?"

"The ball was warm; the urn wasn't real cold—not as cold as it should have been. Oh! That's because of the ship! It's got heat near it."

"Can you just walk up to the ship? Could you bang on it with your fist if you wanted to?" Budd asks.

"I can't reach it. It's too tall. Might just be able to touch the bottom of it." In Carol's account the ship was hoisted out of reach on giant caterpillar-tracked carriers.

"That's what I meant. Do you think it's close enough to reach if you walked over to it?"

"Maybe on the bottom I could. It's too tall to touch its edge." She pauses, then suddenly says, "A door! Ramp. *Whoops!* There we go!"

"How are you going? Slow? Fast?"

"Floating. Fast. Just sort of pick you up and up you go . . . except you don't lose your balance."

I am thinking *this* must be where Alice is sucked up into the ship.

"So you float up fast into this. . . . Is Carol with you? Do you see her, too, going up?"

"I don't see her anymore."

In Carol's account, once inside the craft she did not see Alice, either, and worried that she was going to have to go through the experience alone.

"Okay," Budd says, "when you get up there, what do you see? Where are you? You don't see Carol, so you're sort of on your own now?"

"Yes." After a pause Alice says, "A spiral-like thing." She seems to be studying it. "A spring?" she says questioningly. I am wondering if the "spiral-like thing" could be the wedding-cake-like layered interior Carol saw.

And then Alice, surprised, tells us, "There are portholes and stars out there! This is dumb! Can't be!" The pause this time is longer. "Crab Nebula? How can that be?"

"Why do you say Crab Nebula?" Budd asks.

"That's supposedly what's there to the right."

"Is that something you recognize? Or is that something they tell you, or what?"

"They told me that. . . . Oh, damn," Alice says, "Jo's here."

"Joe?" Budd asks. "Who's Joe?"

"Jo," I learned when I visited the horse farm, is Alice's familiar entity: a Tall Gray Doctor Being similar to the one who keeps reappearing in Carol's experiences. Alice first became aware of Jo during a hypnotic regression session done with a Maryland psychologist in July in an attempt to rid herself of the increasingly painful headaches she had been suffering. Under hypnosis Alice at first saw mostly colors—the sort of thick red mist one might see through a microscope in a blood slide. But then that image suddenly went black and was replaced by a very dark blue, brilliant, metallic light. As soon as Alice saw the blue light, she started screaming and covered her eyes. Within the light she had seen a pair of big, black alien eyes right in front of her face. She next saw just the tops of four or five Small Grays' heads and their eyes and deduced she was lying down on a table. And then the Small Grays disappeared and Alice became very frightened, because all she now saw was the huge, wet oval eyes and pointed chin of the Doctor Being, so close to her face she cried out in alarm.

Before starting that hypnosis session Alice had discussed with the psychologist her presumption that her father had raped her. That is why when, during the hypnotic regression, the doctor first heard Alice's description of this tall figure whose eyes and chin were opposite hers, and observed Alice's growing apprehension, she assumed Alice was presenting some sort of screen memory of her childhood sexual trauma. As a result, when the doctor then asked Alice what the figure's name was, she fully expected Alice to speak her father's name. Instead, seemingly without hesitation, Alice answered, "Jo."

Joe? thought Carol, who was attending that session. She and the psychologist exchanged looks. Who the hell is Joe?

Alice's answer had taken even Alice by surprise. She remembers thinking even though still under hypnosis, "Joe"? How do you spell that? Is that J-O-E or just J-O?"

Jo, Alice explains to Budd, is "a Gray. One of the shits. . . . Why's he telling me this about the Crab Nebula?"

"What kind of room are you in?" Budd asks. "What kind of space? Big space? Little space?"

"I'm around in the front where the stars are," she says with a bemused smile.

"What's happening?" Budd asks.

Alice is looking at a strange new creature. Jo has been joined by a second Being with the sort of pointy ears worn by Leonard Nimoy as Spock. "Spock-ears," as Alice refers to him, is stationed in front of some sort of control panel behind Alice and to her left. "Why do you think they have you in that room with them?" Budd asks.

"They want to show me something," Alice responds with a sigh. She suddenly twists her head to the left.

"What are you looking at?" Budd asks. "Do you see something over there to your left?"

"Holes in the softness," she says. "Amorphous holes in the softness of the edge of the wall. It's all rippled, like the lips of a giant clam. And sometimes you can see into the holes. . . ." There is a long pause; then Alice takes a deep breath and exhales, "*Whewwww.*"

"What's happening?" Budd asks.

"Boobs," Alice says wonderingly. "Little ones. On somebody."

"Who are they on?" Budd asks.

"A very pale-skinned, bug-eyed . . ." Alice's voice trails off.

"But they have breasts?"

"Yes. They're little."

"Do they have nipples?"

"Yep. They're prominent. Very red. Like milk bottles."

Alice has lost me. The Being's nipples are prominent like very red milk bottles? What does this mean?

"Where'd this person come from?" Budd asks.

"I don't know. Out of the wall? Out of those holes in the soft wall?"

Alice tells us the Being is naked except for a cape crossed over "her" shoulders, leaving her breasts bare. "She" has no hair, nothing that might be female genitalia.

"Whoops!" Alice says. "She just got down on all fours and went away. Right out the door. That was weird. She just left! Don't know what it was."

"Did you see the feet going out the door?"

"Nope," Alice says, and then her tone of voice changes, as if she were speaking to someone else. "I don't want to sit in that chair," she says. "But I have to? Okay."

"So you sit in the chair?"

"Yes."

"Is this one of those metal folding chairs?"

"No, it's a soft white chair," Alice says. "Damn, I can't get up!" She falls silent again, then sighs and says, "Little balls."

"What?"

"Little balls. Yes, sort of like—" she makes a fluttering butterfly motion—"in front of the screen. . . . They're like light balls . . . balls of light," she says, and sighs again. "Do anything you want," she says with a hint of petulance. "I don't care. . . . I'll just sit here. Not going to do anything."

"Is your nightgown long enough to keep you warm?" Budd asks.

"It's gone," she says, and whispers as if to herself, "God, I want it on the right side out this time. Dumb shits."

"Do you want it right side out because sometimes it's put on wrong side out, is that it?"

"They're not too bright that way," Alice says, and heaves a big sigh. "Can I go home now? I'm bored. . . . I don't care. . . ." She seems to be talking to the Beings again. "You know, guys, this is getting pretty old!" she says with impatience. "If you're not going to do anything, let me go home. I got to go to work tomorrow! I need some sleep. Get on with the show, or send me home."

"Are these little lights still there bouncing around?" Budd asks.

"Nope, they're gone."

"Do you think these things were alive, or were they just lights? Or what were they, or do you know?"

Alice shakes her head. "They just *were*," she says. "They just were."

"So do they let you go home now? Or do you have something else in mind?"

"Yeah, I think I've got to sit there for a while. It's *boring!*"

"How do you feel sitting there with no clothes on?"

"I don't give a damn," Alice says, and heaves another big sigh.

"Well, let's see the next thing. Let's move this ahead to the next event," Budd says. "Obviously, you're sitting there and there's going to be something happening. It may just be that you get up and walk away, we don't know. When I count to three, we'll go to the next incident. . . .

"One," Budd counts, "you're sitting in the chair, about to move to what happens next. . . .

"Two," he says, "we're right on the edge now. . . .

"Three!"

There is silence. Alice's breathing is regular; her body is still. "Clouds," she says suddenly.

"*Clouds?*" Budd asks, barely containing his surprise.

"Volcano?" Alice says quizzically. "Oceans? . . . *Whoa!* We're going fast!"

Budd is confused. "Where do you see these things?" he asks.

"Weird, but true," Alice says, sounding almost chipper. "Just floating along."

"Now, let's look out of the corner of your eye, and let's see if you see any of the people."

"Yep," Alice says cheerily.

"Where are they?"

"One on each side."

"What are they doing?" Budd asks.

"They've got my hands. . . . God," she whispers with wonder in her voice, "this is like *Superman*. . . ." The image she has is the scene in the movie *Superman* in which Lois Lane is flown over moonlit Metropolis by Superman. "*Zooooommmm!*" she says.

"Are the men looking in your direction or away from you?"

"They're looking ahead. I can sort of look around, though. I mean, I get to look down. It's okay. It's sort of neat."

"Do you see cities? Roads?"

"Cities, yeah—New York City. But I've never seen it like this. They say it's New York City, though. . . ." After a brief pause she asks, "Why do we have to land here when I don't have any clothes on?" There is a trace of apprehension in her voice.

"Where are you landing?" Budd asks.

"Somewhere in New York."

It is here that Alice's account becomes the most dreamlike. The two Beings land with Alice at night in front of a large Manhattan building. There is nobody around to notice Alice is nude. She cannot identify the street she is on; but says the building has "dumbbell-shaped" glass on it and the number 21.

Alice and the two Beings enter the building, apparently by passing through its closed glass doors. Inside they are standing on a red carpet; there is a small banklike counter and velvet ropes suspended from stanchions and, beyond the ropes, stairs leading up. Alice deduces she's in the lobby of a theater.

There is no one in the theater except Alice and the two Beings. The three of them continue into the auditorium itself. Only the stage is lit.

As they float down to the stage Alice complains, "I don't have time to sit through a play. C'mon, guys, what is this?"

The stage is bare except for a prop rowboat. Only its bow half is visible, pointing from behind the curtain stage left.

"I don't want to go on stage!" Alice says impatiently, then, with a sigh, complies. "Okay," she says. There is a pause and Alice testily says, "Quit farting around and take me home!" There is a longer pause and Alice again sighs. "Supposed to meet somebody here," she explains.

"Let's move ahead to that," Budd says. "Do you recognize who you meet, or is this a stranger?"

"It's a stranger," Alice says, sounding both surprised and confused. It is as though she had expected to meet someone else. "He has a hat on—he has a coat on," she reports. And then, as if only just now realizing she is on a well-lit stage standing naked before him, she adds with obvious embarrassment, "*God, he's got clothes on!* This isn't fair!" But then she reports, "He doesn't care." And a moment later, "I thought I looked pretty good, too!"

"What does he say to you? What made you say that just now?"

"He looked at me," Alice says matter-of-factly.

"So you mean he looked at you like he was attracted to you?" Budd asks.

Alice nods yes. "God, he's good-looking," she says, then sighs. "I don't want to go away now."

The Grays apparently want Alice to leave, but now she doesn't want to. She is attracted to the stranger and would like to get to know him. She tells us the stranger's name is Derek, that he's in his mid-forties, over six feet tall, clean-shaven. He has sandy brown hair—almost, but not quite, blond. His speaking voice is trained, cultured, rich, as though he belonged in the theater. His accent is Continental.

"Does he look at you—after all, you're not dressed—does he look at you as if he's thinking erotic thoughts?" Budd asks.

"Yep," Alice says cheerily. "That's okay." She is silent, then says with a big sigh, "*Shit!* Another married one. Goddamn wedding ring on."

Alice is quite certain that she has never seen him before.

"Can you imagine what he might look like when he's . . ." Budd pauses, then says, "sixteen?"

"Ohhhh," Alice says disappointedly. "I thought you were going to say 'naked.' "

"Well, let's do that," Budd says.

"Yes. Sort of nice." She takes a deep breath. "Hmmmmm," she says.

"Do you see him naked, or are you just guessing?"

"Just guessing."

"Does he touch you?"

"He gives me a hug," Alice answers. "Tells me it's okay to go. We'll meet again. . . . How does he know that?"

Budd asks Alice to think of the stranger as a sixteen-year-old. Alice seems to be considering that, then says he has light blond hair, freckles, and is wearing a green-and-white-striped rugby shirt.

"Where are you?" Budd asks.

Without a moment's hesitation Alice responds, "England."

Alice tells us she has met him in the stands during a soccer practice. She does not even like soccer and wonders what she's doing there. She is now fourteen, but he's a lot older. "I think he thinks I'm just a kid," she says.

She believes they may have been kissing and hugging and that it felt good, but that it wasn't "serious like adults get serious," she says. "It was just kids and it felt good. Till it got scary, and then we ran away."

"Do you think you ever saw him earlier, when you were even younger?" Budd asks her. "As younger kids? . . . Maybe you did, maybe you didn't."

Alice says she doesn't know.

"Okay, we're going to move back to the theater and he is there and he's told you he's going to see you again, and the little gray guys are going to take you away. Is that what happens?"

"God, that's a neat feeling!" Alice exclaims. "Rising above the steps . . . ahhh, out the front door and up."

Budd again tries to ascertain where in New York Alice might be. But she cannot see any street markers or store names, no neon signs. There are cars parked along the street, but she cannot tell their age. "Cars are cars," she says, though she adds that she has the feeling there's an airport nearby.

Budd asks her if anything seems unusual about the street.

"Yeah," Alice says. "It seems so quiet! New York's supposed to be busy, busy, busy."

"Now, when they take you away, where do you go?" Budd asks. "You're flying along, where do you end up at the end of this flight?"

Alice seems to be looking around her. "In the woods," she finally says. "It's all pine trees."

"Are you still naked?"

"Yes," Alice says. And then she recognizes where she is. "Oh, my goodness!" she says. "That's the pine tree where I buried the foal. It's in the back of the property." Carol is nowhere around. Alice inhales sharply. "All of a sudden I got my nightgown back on."

"While you're standing in the field?"

"Yes, it just sort of appeared."

Alice walks back to the farmhouse, pausing only to say "hi" to the horses on the way back, and is surprised to discover that Carol is already in bed.

"I want you just to look at yourself, your body, your hands, your feet, knees," Budd says. "Is there anything . . . ?"

"My feet are dirty," Alice says, then says, "Oh, well, I'm tired. I'll go to bed anyway."

"Okay, just before I wake you up I want to set a little scene," Budd tells her. "A number of years ago, you were in a department store shopping. And when I count to three, you'll hear somebody calling to you very softly. You might be a little confused, but you'll hear somebody call you softly by a special name. You'll hear who's calling. So, one, you're in the store, this is a few years ago. . . . *Two,* you're about to hear some person calling to you. . . . Three."

Alice is silent. Budd is obviously trying to link Carol's account of possibly having recognized Alice, and maybe Grace, ten years ago in a Washington department store. According to Carol, at that time she had softly called to Alice, "A.J.? . . . A.J.?" But Alice hadn't answered.

"What are you hearing?" Budd asks.

Alice frowns. " 'Didi Kitten.' "

"What is that again?" Budd asks.

" 'Didi' and 'Kitten.' "

"What does that mean?"

Alice laughs. "I don't know, but there's somebody playing underneath the dresses over there. A little girl, in the store."

The little girl is about six years old. She is blond and is wearing saddle shoes and white cotton socks.

"And she says 'Didi Kitten'? What do you think that means?" Budd asks.

"Like she wants me to play," Alice says in a child's voice.

"She wants you to play. Is she calling you like you're a kitten?"

"Yes," Alice whispers.

"What's the 'Didi' mean?" Budd asks. "Is that just childish words, or does that mean something to you?"

"I don't know," Alice says, then explains, "My mother takes me away too quick."

"Okay," Budd says, "let's move this ahead now. Let's make you thirty or so. Let's put you again in the store in your thirties. In another store. Let's see if anybody whispers anything to you. . . . You may notice something; you may notice nothing. But you may unconsciously hear something, somebody whispering to you. Calling. It might not be 'Didi Kitten,' it might be.

It might be something else. We don't know. . . ." There is a long pause, and Budd says, "Maybe you just don't hear anything."

"I can't even find the store!" Alice says, frustrated. Her voice is normal again. "You sure I was in a store when I was thirty?"

Budd specifies that the store was in Washington, that Alice was between the ages of twenty-five and thirty-five, and, at my suggestion, adds Alice's sister Grace to the scenario to further narrow it down. "Okay," he says. "I'm going to put my hand in your hand. I want you to be in the store now with Grace, your sister. It's a while ago. Doesn't matter how old you are. You're a mature woman—anywhere from late twenties to late thirties, somewhere in there. You're in a store. . . . Somebody whispers something. . . ."

Alice is silent.

"What's the matter? You don't remember anything? That's okay."

Budd decides to end the session.

"So, five," he says, "you're starting to wake up. . . .

"Four," he says, his voice becoming louder and louder, "waking up. . . .

"Three, almost awake. . . .

"Two. . . .

"One," Budd says in a normal speaking tone. "Fully awake."

Alice's eyes are open. She remains quiet, as though she were surfacing from a deep sleep.

"Now, *that*," she says, "was a *weird* dream!"

Later, during the post-session discussion, Carol points out that as a child she had named all her stuffed toy kittens "Didi Kitten" and that she had saddle shoes and wore them all the time.

CHAPTER XIX

Postconference Interview

Carol and Alice—Fifth Hypnosis Session
at Budd Hopkins's Studio

After lunch on Sunday, Budd prepares to hypnotize Carol for a third time that weekend. They want to explore Carol's experiences of December 15, 1991, and January 2, 1992.

The December 15 episode was the one in which Carol, while driving Alice's car back from a visit to her parents' house, again saw three bright lights in the sky. Afterwards, she returned to the farm panicked, disoriented, nauseous, with her earlobes bleeding and her earrings in backwards. She was also missing time.

On January 2, Carol was returning from a business dinner in town with the friend's beautifully wrapped Christmas gift of brownies, fruitcake, cookies, and fudge on the seat of the farm's pickup truck beside her. When she arrived back at the farm the gift was minus half its contents and its wrapping paper was torn and masking-taped. Again she was panicked, disoriented, nauseous, and missing time.

Carol and I covered both these incidents that June night in my Boston hotel room after the M.I.T. conference; so I am already familiar with the details leading up to the alleged abductions.

Carol is made comfortable on Budd's black couch; the pink wool blanket is arranged around her for warmth. Budd is seated near her head, his yellow legal pad on his lap. I am in my customary spot just behind his right shoulder. Alice is curled up on a fluffy sleeping bag on the floor.

"Now, we'll go back to December 15, 1991," Budd is telling Carol. "You were coming back from Hagerstown. How far from home were you when you saw the lights?"

"From the main drag going through Mount Airy, I was on that route that leads to the farm," Carol says.

"So you'd already turned off Interstate 70 and were on Route 32 going northeast in Alice's red hatchback, and you stopped because you saw the lights?"

"Well, I pulled over just because I wanted to get a better look at them," Carol explains. "They didn't look like airplanes, and if they were airplanes, they were damn close to the ground. They didn't make any noise, though."

"Then this is the first conscious memory you had of a UFO thing?"

"It's the first time I associated anything that happened being related to the lights."

"That's what I mean," Budd says. "Okay, let's get started."

It is a quarter to four. By four, Carol is hypnotized and the session begins.

"I want you to go back to that December fifteenth incident, when you were making that drive home from seeing your family in Hagerstown," Budd says softly. "It's such a familiar drive—you've made it many, many times coming back from Hagerstown. It's evening. You're driving along in Alice's little red car, you're just driving along December fifteenth, kind of anxious to get home; the trip is getting a little tiring. It's nighttime, or getting there. You're driving along Route 32, you make the turn, you're driving back very close to the farm, you're going to look over to the side and you're going to see something odd. When I count to three, you'll see something strange. You don't know what it is exactly as you're driving along. . . ."

"One," Budd counts, "you're going to look up and see something odd. . . ."

"Two," he says, and pauses.

"Three!"

Carol is silent.

"Do you see something unusual that you don't understand exactly?" Budd asks her.

"My head hurts," she tells us.

"Your head hurts?"

Carol winces with pain, "*Ow!* Geez!"

"Does it hurt more on one side than the other?"

"Yes. . . . I've got to pull over," Carol says. She is in obvious agony.

"We're going to turn that pain down," Budd tells her.

"It's right there," Carol says. She touches herself just over her left eye.

Budd places his fingertips on the spot Carol indicated. He tells her he is turning the pain down like a volume button from a six to a five to a four to a three to a two, and as the numbers get lower, Carol responds with visible and audible relief.

"Now, when it stops," Budd says, "what happens?"

"I don't know," she answers. "I just put my head down."

"Against the steering wheel or something like that?"

"Yes. I must be tired. It hurts. . . ." She is breathing heavily, panting almost. "My ears are ringing. Must be a really bad headache or something. *Whew!* Can't drive like this. . . ."

"Where are you exactly?"

"I'm at the side of the road. I let the car stall or something," she says, then adds, "Not that I care."

"Did you feel it jump just before it stalled?"

"No," she says, still breathing hard. "My head hurts so bad I didn't notice. . . . *Whew!*"

"Is the dashboard lit up? Can you see to drive?"

"No. The lights aren't on. I probably turned them off." Carol winces with pain. "*Ohhh* . . . oh, boy!"

"Let's just turn that hurt down again. My hand is back on the dial—I can still turn it down a little bit. I want you to keep looking, see what you notice. Are you near a house? Are there trees? What is there?"

"There's a mailbox in front of the car. No name. It's got numbers on it, but I can't tell what they are. . . . *Whew!*" Carol exhales sharply and mumbles something like "Oh, I don't want to drive."

"What did you say?" Budd asks her.

"I need to go and I don't want to drive," she says. "There's nobody home anyway. All the lights are off, so I'm sitting in somebody's driveway or something." She pauses for a moment, then asks questioningly: "Streetlights? . . . Why are there streetlights up there? Oh, man, it hurts to look at them! They're so bright, it hurts my eyes!"

"Let's look away so it doesn't hurt your eyes," Budd tells her. "Just glance away. Lower your eyes. . . . So are these streetlights on their poles now?"

"I don't know, but they've got to be streetlights over there. . . . Ohh, awful bright!" Carol, on the couch, stiffens suddenly; then her whole body jumps, scaring us all. "WHAT? *What?*" she asks, very frightened. "Geez, don't scare me like that!" she says more calmly. "Oh—ow! Hurts. Hurts. I banged my head."

"What did you bang it on?" Budd asks.

"The steering wheel," she says, and then, as if talking to someone else, asks, "Whaddya want?" She sounds frightened again. "Oh, you scared me," she says. "You really scared me!"

"Who is this?" Budd asks. "Somebody stopped their car?"

Still frightened, Carol responds, "I don't know. I can't look. . . ." She is close to tears. "Oh God, what am I doing to myself?"

"Is it a neighbor? A policeman? What does that person say to you?"

"He's just there. The light's back there. I can't look because it hurts. I think I'm supposed to move. . . . Maybe I'm in his driveway or something?" Carol begins to cry. "I can't drive! I can't!" she whimpers. "My head hurts so bad! Please, just give me a minute, okay? I'll move in a minute!"

"Is the man's voice loud when he says to you you have to move?" Budd asks.

"Nooo. I just think that's what he wants me to do."

"Do you see him gesture to move the car with his hand?"

"No."

"So how do you know he wants you to move?"

"Because he's standing there," Carol explains shakily.

"Maybe he's trying to help you," Budd suggests.

"I can't," she says, and then there is another sharp intake of breath as her fear mounts. "How'd they do that?"

"Now, feel my hand here," Budd says, as he places his hand on hers. "Feel my hand on yours. You can tighten your hand on mine—"

"*It's them!*" Carol interrupts in a fierce, terrified whisper.

"You can tighten your hand if you want," Budd is saying. "It's what? Who?"

"It's THEM!" Carol says loudly. "They're *outside!*" She moans with fear.

"Who is 'them'?" Budd asks.

Carol repeats, "It's *them!* It's those guys! Outside! I still can't see them. I can't see. It hurts to look at them."

"Is that because of the bright lights?"

"Lights," she says, breathing hard. "Lights so bright. It's got—*ohhh*— it's got a thing on it. There's other ones over there . . . other lights over there. But they're not the same. I don't know if they're streetlights or not." Her voice is quavering with fear. She seems to be looking more closely at the scene playing out in her mind. "I don't think those are streetlights," she says, her breathing still labored. "Ohhh . . . blue stuff . . . feels like . . . a heat lamp or something . . . burns. . . . *Phew!*"

"Burns all the way through the glass of your window?" Budd asks.

"I'm not in the car," Carol tells him. "I'm outside of the car. I'm standing somewhere. I'm standing on this road. The light is really bright. It burns. . . . Oh, man! Feels like it's solid something. It's heavy."

"Do you see any other cars coming up and down the road that might see this, too?"

"No. It's dark. I can't see anything outside this thing. It's starting to burn my face. Feels real hot. *Owww,* burns there!" she says. *"Whew! Whew!"* She is panting from the heat. "Turn it off!" she tells them angrily. "Can't move. I can't move. . . . *Mmmff!*" She appears to be struggling with someone or something; her breathing rate accelerates.

"What's happening, Carol?" Budd asks gently.

She is panting now, lost in her vision.

"Carol," Budd says, "just tell me what's happening."

"I'm going up," she whispers. "Up somewhere . . . way up high."

"How'd you get way up high?"

"I don't know!" Carol says, and moans with fear.

"When you go way up high, where are you? When you stop moving?"

"I'm standing someplace," Carol says. "It's yellow in here."

"The surfaces are painted yellow?"

"I don't know—it feels yellow," Carol says. Her voice is steadier now, calmer, as she tries to explain. "It feels yellow, gold. . . . The light felt blue; this feels yellow. . . ." She is quiet for a moment, then again cries out in fear: *"Ohhh! . . .* Ohhhhh!"

"What's happening?" Budd asks.

"I want to do this myself," Carol insists. She is not talking to Budd.

"What is it you want to do yourself?"

"They're going to make me . . . go over there." Carol is breathing hard again, as though she cannot get enough air in her lungs. "I don't want to go over there because it's . . . it has those things."

"Where is it that they want you to go?"

"They want me to go over to those tables . . . to get on the table," Carol says. "I don't do that anymore. . . . It has things for the feet. . . . I don't have to do that anymore."

"What is it that has things for the feet?" Budd asks.

"Have to put your feet in there. . . . Round bars, and you have to put your feet in there and then they close on your feet."

"Okay, you take a look at that," Budd tells her, "because you're going to make a drawing for us later what that looks like."

"I don't have to do those anymore. I don't have to do that thing ever again," Carol says, and takes a deep breath. "I don't have to do this," she says again. Her voice is becoming increasingly tense. She is caught in her vision like a swimmer in an undertow. "I don't have to do this anymore!" It is not clear to whom she is speaking, but we assume she is arguing with the Beings. "I don't want to—" I cannot make out what it is she doesn't want to do. "I can do it," she says pleadingly, "I don't ever run away."

"What is it you can't do anymore?" Budd asks softly.

"I want to be able to move. I won't run away. *I want to be able to move myself!*" Carol sounds distressed at first, then resigned. "Oh, okay . . . okay . . . okay. I don't have to use those things," she says. "No, I'd really rather not!"

"You'd really rather not do what?" Budd asks.

"I don't want to turn my head."

"They want you to turn your head?"

"No, they just said *they* want to turn my head. . . . No, I don't really want to do that."

"Do what?" Budd asks.

"Because he's going to—" sharp inhale—"put that thing—" another sharp inhale—"in my ear. *Please don't put that thing in my ear!*" Carol cries out in pain. "They put something in my ear!" she whimpers, near tears. *"Please don't! I'll be good!"* She is pleading now. *"Please? . . . Please?"* She begins to cry. "I'll put my feet in there," she says, now crying hard. "I won't hurt anybody! Let me get up!"

Budd squeezes Carol's hand. "Feel my hand in yours. I'm right here with you," he tells her. "This has passed; we've been through this. This ended. What did they want you to put your feet in? I don't understand that."

Carol is crying so hard, it is difficult to understand her. Evidently, while she was lying on the table, the Beings wanted her to put her feet into devices similar to the stirrups a woman would rest her ankles in during a gynecological exam—except that once Carol's feet are in the Beings' restraints, she is powerless to remove them.

"Have you ever seen anything like this elsewhere?" Budd asks.

"Yes. All the time," she says. She is having difficulty catching her breath. "They put—they put my feet—in those things. They don't—let you—you can't take—they don't—let you—take your feet out."

"So do you put your feet in these things?"

"No! I don't want to do it!" Carol cries. "They said they didn't have to do that one now."

"Didn't they hurt your ear, though?"

"Yesssss!" she moans, still in tears.

"Did they do something to your ear?"

Carol does not answer.

"Feel my hand now," Budd says gently. "I want you to feel my hand. I want you to put your hand around my hand and I want you to tighten up on my hand. That lets you know I'm here with you. We're just looking back. This is all over. It's ended. We're looking back to last year. It's not quite a year ago. And so just right now as we look back, let's see what they're doing.

Just looking back . . . they did something to your ear. What's that feel like? What did they do?"

When Carol speaks, she is much quieter, calmer. "They stick a thing in my ear. . . . It hurts. . . . It just gives me pictures and stuff. . . ."

"What are the pictures it gives you?"

"Oceans and waves and things."

"Is that a nice picture?"

"No," she says.

"It doesn't make you feel good?"

"No, it doesn't do anything. It just doesn't look like real water . . . and he says it is. Just a pattern of things. I'm supposed to follow the pattern. . . . To where?" she asks, seemingly of the Being. "I don't know what that means, 'follow the pattern'—I don't know to where I'm supposed to follow it. . . . I just look at them."

"While you look at the pattern, let's look to your left and your right," Budd tells her. "Just out of the corner of your eye. Do you see anything to your left or your right?"

"I don't know. . . . I don't think my eyes are open."

"You're eyes aren't open?"

"Red colors. Red waves. Like blood," Carol says. "Not a real nice picture. And foamy stuff. Bubbles and foamy stuff. Looks like soap bubbles and whipped cream or something . . . not ocean foam. . . . It's the wrong kind of foam, guys," she tells the Beings.

And then, after a short pause, Carol announces, "I'm looking at a picture."

"What is the picture of?" Budd asks.

"Funny scenes."

Carol describes a heronlike cartoon bird with short, thick legs whose wings are on fire. She sees make-believe waves; a large, tailless mouse; and something that, she says, "looks sort of like a bear," except that it has "fingers instead of claws—short, stubby little fingers," very pale, tan, short fur, and narrow, pointed ears, like a cat's.

"It's not really a bear," Carol explains. "It's another one of their cartoons."

There is also something that, she says, is "supposed to be a baby bear, I guess. He's really ugly, too, because he doesn't have any hair . . . bald as a bat."

"A bald bear," Budd says, making a note.

"Must be a newborn or something. Can't fool me, 'tain't a bear . . ." Carol says; then, as if speaking to someone else, she adds, "Not particularly, no."

"What was that?" Budd asks.

"He wants to know if I want to hold the bear. . . . I don't think so," she tells the Being. Suddenly she cries out in pain, "OUCH! Careful!"

"What happened?" Budd asks.

"They moved that thing," Carol replies. "Take it out," she tells the Being, "or don't move it. . . . It just hurts when he moves it."

She is referring to whatever it was that was put in her left ear. As long as it is not moved she seems all right.

"Now we're back to water," Carol says. "Water water water everywhere and not a drop to drink. . . . May I go now?" she asks, and a moment later complains, "I don't *want* to hold the baby bear. It's *not* a baby bear. I don't know *what* it is. . . . No, I don't *want* to. You can't make me do that. . . ."

"What is it they want you to do?" Budd asks.

The Being again wants her to hold the baby bear, Carol explains. She tells him she doesn't want to and that it's "not real, anyway." But the Being evidently insists the bear *is* real. There is a moment of silence, and then Carol worriedly says, "Oh, *ohhhh,* they're going to take that thing out. I hate this part!"

"What thing are they taking out?" Budd asks her.

"They're going to take that thing out of myyy—" Carol takes a quick, deep breath—"EARRRR!" she says, exhaling loudly. *"Care-fullll!"*

Budd starts to say, "My hand's coming down—"

But Carol doesn't hear him. *"Care-fullll!"* she says tensely. She braces herself against the pain, then sags with relief. "Ohhhh, yeah, ohhhh," she says. "Thank you very much. Can I go now?" She heaves a big sigh. "Yeah, okay. . . . *Okay!*" she says more adamantly. *"Whew!"* And then, very quietly, she asks again, "Can I go now?"

"I'm sorry?" Budd says, not sure he heard her.

" 'Well, excuuuse meee,' " she says sarcastically, then cries out, *"Ouch!"* She flicks at something near her ear.

"What's happening?"

"Leave it alone!" Carol says with almost a giggle. "He's playing with my earrings. . . ."

"Who's playing with your earrings?"

"This guy over here. I don't know who he is. He's not mine. He's somebody else's."

"What's he look like?"

"I can't see him from here," Carol says, adding, "He's not talking to me, so he's not mine." There is a pause; then Carol says, "Give them back!"

"Did he take them off?"

"Took them off," she says. *"Give them back!"* she says more insistently.

"Just leave him alone," Budd says. "You'll get them back."

Carol takes a deep breath.

"Now what I want you to do as best you can is look around," Budd tells her. "You've seen this bear thing, and we've seen that there was somebody there fooling with your ears—let's look around and see if you can see anybody else."

"There's one, I know him. He's down on the left side behind the box," Carol says. "And there's a guy I know down on my right. . . . He's the one that talks to me."

"Any other people watching you there?"

"I don't see them. I'm in a little space this time. Not a big space."

There is a long pause, and then Carol makes a face. "Mmm, *yech!*"

"What's happening?"

"*Yech!*" she says again, her face screwed up with disgust. "They made me—*yech!*—taste this stuff."

"What stuff?"

"*Blyah!*" she says. She licks her lips and makes little sounds as if she were trying to get rid of something stuck to her palate. "Gross-tasting stuff!"

"What is the stuff?" Budd asks. "Something you want to eat there? Drink there?"

"No, they *give* you stuff," Carol tells him. "Stick it in your mouth."

"What does it taste like?"

"Shit," she says matter-of-factly, and makes another face. "*Yech!*"

She describes the substance as a thick liquid. She does not know what color it is, because she cannot see it before it is put in her mouth. Budd asks her if it has a name, and she says, "No, it's just 'Take this.' 'Eat this.' "

Whatever the substance is, Carol tells us, it makes her sick. It is not the first time they have given it to her, she tells us; she has been forced to swallow it often.

"What's it for?" Budd asks her.

"I don't know," Carol says. "They don't tell me. . . . It doesn't do any good to ask anyway. . . . I tried not to swallow it one time. But it made me sick when I couldn't swallow it and they made me swallow everything." She tells Budd that even though it had made her sick, they forced her to take more and keep it down. "I won't do that anymore!" Carol says firmly.

"Next time, if that happens," Budd tells her, "if you feel like it, you can throw up on them. That's okay to do."

"*Yuck!*" Carol says. "It's just really bad stuff. . . ." She is silent for a moment, then says, "Oh, c'mon. . . . May I go home now?" There is another brief pause, then she tells us, "I guess they're going to let me go home now. Goody! Goody-goody. Oh, goody. . . . Okay. . . . Yeah, yeah, yeah," she says, apparently to the Beings. "Yeah . . . okay." There is a trace of apprehension in her voice.

"What's happening?" Budd asks. "Is it just before they let you go?"

"They're trying to tell me my mother's over there," Carol says, now clearly nervous. "They're saying she wants me to hold the bear."

"Your mother wants you to hold the bear?"

"My mother's not there!" she tells the Being. "It's silly! I'm not going to hold the bear."

Budd asks, "Is this the same bear they showed you earlier?"

"I don't know," she says. "I can't see any bear."

"The bear you saw earlier, was it as big as a cat?"

"I don't know. I guess. I don't know," she says.

"Do they give a name to the bear?" Budd asks.

"No," she says, shaking her head. "Just 'a baby bear.' But it's not a baby bear. . . . Hmmm, yeahhh, okay," she says, and there is a sharp intake of breath.

" 'Okay' what?" Budd asks her.

"Oh, just going down there," she says with another quick inhale. "*Okay! Okay!* . . . Ohhhhh, one of these days they're going to drop me!"

"Going down where? How do you go down?"

"Going down the thing, that thick stuff—*ohhhh*," she moans. "Go down in this light. In this heavy thing. Thick stuff. And it just goes down and you just go with it."

"What do you see when you go down?"

"Nothing. It's just light. Everything is in light. And when you get down there it's hard . . . hard to get your feet. *Ohhhhh*," Carol moans, "I feel sick."

"Where are you now?"

"In the road."

"Where's your car?"

"Right behind me. . . . Got to get in. . . . I feel like I'm going to be sick," she says, clutching her stomach. "Oh, geez, I feel so sick! *I feel so sick!* Oh, wow! I've got to get home. Got-to-get-home. Got-to-get-home. Got-to-get-home," she chants. "*Whew!* Almost missed that one!"

"Missed what?" Budd asks.

"The turn. Almost missed the turn, going so fast. Got to slow down . . . slow down . . . I feel like I need to—oh, *God*," she says with increasing concern, "I have to throw up. *Whew!* Oh, boy. I have to stop! I have to throw up."

She emits a low moan, and Budd, realizing Carol really *is* about be sick, urgently tells her, "We're going to turn that nausea down! We're going to turn that nausea down!"

Carol, lying on the couch, gags.

"My hand's coming right over your head now. Feel my hand on your head. Okay? That's calming you down. You're not going to have to throw up now. You did then, but not now. You're okay now," Budd says, and Carol gags again. *"You don't have to throw up now,"* he says even more insistently. "That was *then*. In the past. *Now you're okay.* Feel my hand on your forehead. Now you're okay. . . ."

Carol's breathing slowly returns to normal.

"Yes," Budd says, "you're feeling better. We just want to get home. Let's just drive home in a real hurry. Do you see the lights of the house down there, driving along?"

"Yes."

Carol sees the farmhouse lights and pulls into the garage. "Just go inside! Go inside!" she tells herself.

Budd asks if Alice is awake; Carol says Alice is in bed. And then, speaking very quickly, nervously, she tells him that Alice's sister Grace "doesn't know what's wrong. Grace's all upset. Because something's wrong. . . . I don't know what's wrong," she says to Grace.

"I can't tell her what's wrong. I don't know what's wrong," she tells Budd, then, addressing Grace again, says, "Something's wrong. Don't feel good. I got—my ears are bleeding! I don't know what's wrong." There is rising panic in her voice. "*What's wrong?* I don't know what's happened! Something happened!"

"What does Grace say to you?" Budd asks.

"She doesn't know what's wrong," Carol says, and then to Grace she says, "It's okay. I just got scared for some reason. . . . Ohh, what's wrong with me? *I don't understand what's wrong!*" She stirs restlessly on the couch. "Something happened. What happened?" she asks agitatedly. "Something happened. Something . . . happened. I don't understand . . . what happened! I don't understand why I can't remember!"

"Okay," Budd says gently, "let's just go upstairs to bed and relax."

"I don't feel good," Carol moans.

"Feeling better? Getting into bed, just relaxing?"

"What happened to me?" Carol asks in a soft voice.

"Here's what I want you to do: Take two easy, deep breaths. Fill your lungs," he tells her.

Carol does what he asks.

"That's good. Just take another deep breath," Budd tells her. He gets Carol breathing deeply. "Ohhh, that's good, you're relaxed," he says. "Your body relaxes. . . . Your body relaxes. . . . Easy, deep breath. . . . Your body's relaxing. . . . Feeling sleepy. . . . Body's relaxing. . . . Feeling sleepy. . . .

"In just a few minutes now," he continues, "I'm going to wake you up. When you wake up, you'll remember everything you need to remember of this incident—things that maybe you haven't even mentioned. When you wake up, you'll feel a sense of relief. Those deep breaths have calmed your body. You won't be sick. You'll just wake up feeling a little tired, remembering the experience as you need to remember it."

Budd tells Carol that the emotion of tonight's experience is over and she is to put it behind her.

And then, with increasing volume, Budd tells her, "Five, you are starting to wake up. . . .

"Four, you're waking up. . . .

"Three, almost awake. . . .

"Two. . . ."

He pauses for a moment, then says, "One, fully awake."

For a minute or so, Carol just lies there with her eyes closed, not speaking, not moving. Then she opens her eyes and says, "I have an earache."

"Well, that will go away slowly," Budd tells her. "It's just a trace memory."

He looks down at Carol, who still hasn't tried to stir from the couch. "That wasn't too pleasant, was it?" he says.

"No," she says. She thinks about the experience for a moment, then pushes herself up into a sitting position. "I don't know what that baby bear was! Looked like a—I don't know *what* it looked like! They said it was a baby bear, but I know it wasn't a bear."

"Do you think you ever held the baby bear?" Budd asks.

"No, I didn't," she says firmly. "It was like a cartoon. How can you hold a cartoon? It was dumb."

Budd asks her about the Being who had been playing with her earrings.

"He took them out and he was playing with them! He was doing this," she says, jiggling her silver pendant earrings back and forth, "and pulling on them and yanking on them, and I'm going, '*Quit it!* What are you doing over there?' I think he was just playing with them like a child who had never seen anything like them before and was curious and wanted to examine them. Anyway, it was quite painful, the playing and jerking them and stuff."

Budd explains he didn't want to continue the hypnosis session to cover the January 2 Christmas-wrapping-paper incident because he didn't think Carol would have been up to it.

"It would have been too much," Carol agrees. "I was so sick to my stomach." She makes a face at the memory. "I have to describe something to you," she tells us. "When they give you this stuff, it's so foul—you're forced to swallow it, first of all; you can't help it. They stick it in your mouth; you *have* to swallow it. And when you swallow, it's so foul-tasting your throat closes up and your immediate response is to reject it, to vomit it up. But," she continues, "if you try to vomit it up, it's like they do something to you so that it forces your whole throat to open up and everything goes back down. It's like an involuntary reaction. And they make this happen by putting their hand over your mouth or something. They don't let you throw up. And your stomach is rolling all the time and boiling around and you feel God-awful.

"And you have those awful emotional swings!" Carol continues. "I get in there and first I'm scared. It's like this never happened before. And then you realize that, well, maybe it *has* happened before; but this part hasn't. Or maybe it happened, but it's somewhere else that it happened. And then you're in the middle of being afraid about something when they make you angry about something. And you go from being mad to something else: upset, or hurt, or emotionally injured. It just belts you around until you get tired and can't fight it anymore."

Budd asks her more about the thick liquid she was forced to swallow. She says she had no sense of its color, but it tasted "sort of pinkish." She says, "They just put it in your mouth. Either it's on the end of a finger or it's in a tube."

She describes the ankle restraint as an inverted U-shaped bar device that rose up from the end of the table and "falls over on the side of the foot to lock it in with the legs spread. It encloses the foot from behind, and that's it, you're not moving anywhere."

The cartoon images were "like watching a movie in the dark," she explains. "It was all-encompassing. Started with waves—supposed to be ocean waves? It was too thick, Jell-O-y, and moving too slow to be water. I got the impression that that was supposed to relax me. Which it sort of did. White noise. You sort of get hypnotized by the motion. And then I saw foam and stuff, different colors—red, then blue. Like a cartoon. Then blah grayish-brown, and stuff would bubble up from the bottom—it looked like somebody spilled whipped cream that was going watery. The image would start to be stupid, and then it would go away. The image would just go blank. It wouldn't go dark; it just goes blank. And then there was this birdlike thing with its wings on fire. Wings flapping, but they were on fire. And it looked like a cartoon. Fire looked real, but the bird didn't. I wasn't worried about the bird having its wings on fire because it wasn't a real bird."

"Carol, at the end when you are saying that you don't want to hold the bear, are you still with your eyes closed?" I ask.

"I was sitting up on the table," she says.

"So when they say your mother wants you to hold the bear—"

"It's not 'they,' " she corrects me. "It's one. There's only one who ever talks to me. He said, 'Your mother wants you to hold the baby bear.' And I said, 'I'm not holding the baby bear and that's not my mother. There's no mother. My mother's not here. There is no baby bear. I'm not holding a baby bear.'

"It was an image placed in my mind somehow," she explains. "There was nothing to judge its size by, because there was nothing next to it. The bear didn't have claws; it had stubby little fingers that it walked on like an ape. But it was built sort of like a bear, except that it had sharp, pointed ears sort of like a cat. But it did have a snout. . . ." She pauses, reflecting on the image, then adds, "And there was no way to know its sex."

"Did it have short hair? Long hair?" Budd asks.

"Real short hair. Downy. You could sort of see the skin through it. It was like they were trying to make a newborn cub; it was pinkish. The mother was a beige color, very pale."

"Did you smell an animal smell?" I ask.

"There wasn't any smell at all," Carol says.

It is apparent after some more discussion that there is nothing in Carol's background to suggest any reason for the bear image at all.

We never do cover the wrapping-paper incident that weekend. And the following morning, Carol and Alice take a train back to Washington and return to their farm. I drive back to my home in Connecticut.

So what does this all mean?

CHAPTER XX

Various Theories

Nothing exists except atoms and empty space; everything else is opinion.

—DEMOCRITUS,
362 B.C.

New opinions are always suspected, and usually opposed, without any other reason but because they are not already common.

—JOHN LOCKE,
An Essay Concerning Human Understanding,
1690

Reality? We don't got to show you no steeeeenking reality.

—Physicist NICK HERBERT,
in conversation, 1990

"The central paradox of human-alien interaction is the continuing unsolvability of the UFO phenomenon by conventional means and models, coupled with the continuing manifestations of the phenomenon in increasingly bizarre forms."[1] Thus Keith Thompson, the least tabloid and most scholarly of the phenomenon's journalists, sums up the dilemma confronting anyone attempting to write about this subject today.

The genesis of the debate over whether UFOs are extraterrestrial spacecraft or not lies in Kenneth Arnold's 1947 sighting of nine bright shining objects flying "like a saucer would if you skipped it across water."[2] And for nearly fifty years now, neither the believers nor the skeptics have budged much from their original points of view.

Believers still maintain that UFOs are physically real, solid, metallic-like craft piloted by superior creatures who, through their mastery of some form of advanced (as yet undiscovered by us) system of propulsion, are able to transport themselves through space from their galaxy to ours at velocities that defy the physical laws of the universe as we understand them. Furthermore, once on Earth, these craft are capable of performing such acrobatic shifts in direction and fantastic feats of acceleration and deceleration that were they composed of terrestrial materials, they would burn up or break up in our atmosphere and gravity.

Skeptics still say it's all hogwash. The immutable laws of physics dictate no material object can approach the speed of light; therefore, because of the vastness of our universe, no extraterrestrial beings could reach us without traveling tens of thousands of Earth years to get here.

The advent of the abduction phenomenon has served only to enlarge the debate to include such technological riddles as: How do these alien beings convey themselves and their human victims through solid roofs, windows, and walls? How are they able to levitate people up beams of light? How do they communicate telepathically? How are they able to find their victims again and again? And if tiny artificial objects are in fact being implanted in human bodies, what purpose do they serve?

In short, "What is going on?" and "What do they want from us?" have been added to "Where are they from?"

Initially, many attending the M.I.T. conference seemed satisfied that what is going on is nothing more or less than what the experiencers have been saying is going on: Human beings are being abducted by alien creatures into UFOs, where medical procedures are being performed on them prior to their being returned to Earth. And what these beings want from us is our participation, willing or not, in a breeding program, the result of which is the creation of hybrid alien/human offspring.

The skeptics demand hard evidence; the believers show them blurry photographs, landing trace scorch marks, puncture wounds, scoop marks, scars.

Philip J. Klass, publisher of the *Skeptics U.F.O. Newsletter* (and the media's official skeptic), thinks all abductees are "people seeking celebrity status . . . little nobodies."[3]

Professor of psychiatry John E. Mack, M.D. (the media's latest official "Harvard crazy": Timothy Leary *cum* Wilhelm Reich) emphasizes the remarkable lengths to which abductees go to protect their anonymity.

Clearly, *whatever* is happening to the abductees, it is something that defies conventional explanations.

Of course I have reservations about the origins of Carol's and Alice's abduction accounts; of course there were moments when I felt Budd Hopkins might have been "leading" them; of course the stories they were telling were so foreign to my concept of "reality" that I did not believe there was any way they could be true. And yet . . .

And yet as I watched Carol and Alice under hypnosis flail about and pound Budd Hopkins's couch in rage and frustration, heard them cry out in terror, weep in sorrow, as I witnessed the two reliving their abduction episodes, their emotions appeared entirely genuine to me.

In his 1987 book, *Intruders,* Budd Hopkins admitted his own "belief system" had been sorely strained by the abduction cases he had been investigating. "Our minds can only go so far," he wrote, "and then a kind of self-imposed censorship takes over."[4]

But no amount of self-imposed censorship can dissipate what John E. Mack referred to as the "authenticity, believability, and nature" of the abductees themselves. "That was the single most powerful thing for me," he told me in Boston. "Here were people otherwise quite ordinary, unremarkable, reporting with full sincerity and in a most authentic way these extraordinary experiences which they did not want to believe were so."

Critics of the phenomenon will attribute the abductee's story to his or her desire to please the hypnotist by telling him what he wants to hear. But that suggestion, Mack points out, "fails to take into account how disturbing abductions are to the experiencers and how intense the resistance is to bringing what they have gone through back into consciousness, or to accepting the reality of what they have gone through at all. . . . Furthermore, abductees are particularly unsuggestible," Mack insists. "To meet the above criticisms I and other investigators have tried repeatedly to trick abductees by suggesting specific elements—hair on the aliens, corners in the rooms on the ships, for example. Proponents of the controversial 'false memory syndrome' as an explanation for abduction memories need to account for this."[5]

In addition any theory that attempts to explain the abduction phenomenon must still account for what Mack refers to as its "five basic dimensions":

1. The high degree of consistency of detailed abduction accounts, reported with emotion appropriate to actual experiences, told by apparently reliable observers.

2. The absence of psychiatric illness or other apparent psychological or emotional factors that could account for what is being reported.

3. The physical changes and lesions affecting the bodies of the experiencers, which follow no evident psychodynamic pattern.

4. The association with UFOs witnessed independently by others while abductions are taking place (which the abductee may not see).

5. The reports of abductions by children as young as two or three years of age.[6]

Budd Hopkins quotes a letter he received from a young Minnesota woman who experienced abductions as a child and adult. The intelligence and articulateness with which she was able to summarize her experience seems typical of abductees:

> For most of us it began with the memories. Though some of us recalled parts or all of our experiences, it was more common for us to seek them out where they were—buried in a form of amnesia. Often we did this through hypnosis, which was, for many of us, a new experience. And what mixed feelings we had as we faced those memories! Almost without exception we felt terrified as we relived these traumatic events, a sense of being overwhelmed by their impact. But there was also disbelief. *This can't be real. I must be dreaming. This isn't happening.* Thus began the vacillation and self-doubt, the alternating periods of skepticism and belief as we tried to incorporate our memories into our sense of who we are and what we know. We often felt crazy; we continued our search for the "real" explanation. We tried to figure out what was wrong with us that these images were surfacing. *Why is my mind doing this to me?*
>
> And there was the problem of talking about our experiences with others. Many of our friends were skeptics, of course, and though it hurt us not to be believed, what could we expect? We were still skeptics ourselves at times, or probably had been in the past. The responses we got from others mirrored our own. The people we talked to believed us and doubted us, they were confused and looked for other explanations just as we had. Many were rigid in their denial of even the slightest possibility of abductions, and whatever words they used the underlying message was certainly clear, *I know better than you what is real and what isn't. I'm right and you're wrong.* We felt caught in the prison of a vicious circle that seemed to be imposed on us as abductees by a skeptical society:
>
> *Why do you believe you were abducted?*
> *You believe it because you're crazy.*
> *How do we know you're crazy?*
> *Because you believe you were abducted!*
>
> Our own belief was less an intellectual process than an experiential one, and what finally dawned on us was that others had no proof the abductions *weren't* real.

Her letter concluded, "Nothing in life had prepared us for these experiences, and it all seemed impossible to comprehend."[7]

"Precisely because the UFO vision seems absurd to ordinary, non-initiated consciousness," Thompson points out, "the experience (and the one who had had it) will be ridiculed by the collective. With feelings of rejection as insult added to the injury of the reality shattering UFO experience, the UFO initiate is tempted to relieve the feeling of being rendered *less than* ordinary by pretending to be *super*-ordinary, sometimes taking on the role of a cosmic prophet who has glimpsed the new cosmic horizon."[8]

But, as Thompson noted in *Angels and Aliens: UFOs and the Mythic Imagination,* his erudite examination of the UFO phenomenon, the aliens stopped at *Communion* author Whitley Strieber's house "not because they intended to anoint him avatar of the New Age, nor even to urge him to write a best-selling confessional account of his experiences,"[9] but, according to Strieber, because they saw a light burning in his living-room window.

So much for Strieber's ego.

Still, many of the abductees feel they have been chosen, singled out for some unknown purpose to perform some unexpressed function. Both Carol and Alice, under hypnosis, sensed that their bodies had been used for alien procreation. And John Mack now appears to agree with Budd Hopkins and David Jacobs when he writes in *Abduction* (1994) that the "abduction phenomenon is in some central way involved in a breeding program in the creation of alien/hybrid offspring."[10] But, Mack goes on to suggest, "for most abductees the hybridization has occurred simultaneously with an enlightenment imparted by the alien beings that has brought home forcibly to them the failure of the human experiment in its present form." He continues:

> Abduction experiencers come to feel deeply that the death of human beings and countless other species will occur on a vast scale if we continue on our present course and that some sort of new life-form must evolve if the human biological and spiritual essence is to be preserved.
>
> Investigators who perceive the UFO abduction phenomenon from an adversarial perspective, tend to interpret its meaning one-sidedly. The aliens are using us, the argument goes, for their own purposes, replenishing their genetic stock at our expense after some sort of holocaust on their own planet. If they make us feel that there is something worthwhile about this whole process, this is the result of deception. I would not say that the aliens never resort to deception to hide their purposes, but the above argument is, in my view, too narrow or linear an interpretation.
>
> My own impression is that we may be witnessing something far more complex, namely an awkward joining of two species, engineered by an intelligence we are unable to fathom, for a purpose that serves both our goals with difficulties for each. I base this view on the evidence presented by the abductees themselves.[11]

John Mack's abductees have spoken of aliens "breaking through from another dimension," as he reported, "through a 'slit' or 'crack' in some sort of barrier, entering our world from 'beyond the veil.' " And Mack now believes that "consciousness expansion and personal transformation is a basic aspect of the abduction phenomenon. I have come to this conclusion from noting in case after case the extent to which the information communicated by alien beings to experiencers is fundamentally *about* the need for a change in human consciousness and our relationship to the earth and one another."[12]

And it is the abductees' repeatedly voiced recognition of this insistent need for a change that causes many of the more open-minded scholars and investigators in the UFO movement to perceive the alien-abduction phenomenon as some sort of evolutionary prod—"as much of a prod to our next level of consciousness," Thompson suggests, "as rapidly blooming sexual urges are a prod to a teen-ager's move from childhood to adolescence. Both represent a death of a previous naive way of being. The privilege of being young—a young person, a young planet, a young soul—is believing we can remain innocent forever."[13]

Anne, an abductee, told John Mack, "Something else is interested in us that we don't want to know about. This is happening. It's not just a happy little dream where you can feel like you're important. This is really a responsibility, and things that you don't want to see happen are going to happen."[14]

Virtually all of Mack's abductees, he writes, "have demonstrated a commitment to changing their relationship to the earth, of living more gently on it or in greater harmony with the other creatures that live here."[15] Such a commitment, of course, is hardly new. And alien-generated concerns over our destruction of the planet had surfaced as a parallel communication at the M.I.T. conference, I knew; but it was not until after the conference that I learned there were those in the UFO movement who had been insisting that the conservation of our planet has been the *primary* consideration of our alien visitors and that both this message and its messengers have been around for a long, long time.

"Whatever the visitors are," Whitley Strieber writes in *Transformation,* his 1988 sequel to *Communion,* "I suspect they have been responsible for much paranormal phenomena, ranging from the appearance of gods, angels, fairies, ghosts, and miraculous beings to the landing of UFOs in the backyards of America." And then—in a hypothesis whose breathtaking leap echoes the top-secret presidential-briefing-paper information Linda Moulton Howe gleaned from her interview with the Air Force security officer at Kirtland Air Force Base—Strieber continues:

> It may be, that what happened to Mohammed in his cave and to Christ in Egypt, to Buddha in his youth and to all of our great prophets and seers, was an exalted version of the same humble experience that causes a

flying saucer to traverse the sky or a visitor to appear in a bedroom or light to fill a circle of friends.

It should not be forgotten that the visitors—if I am right about them—represent the most powerful of all forces acting in human culture. They may *be* extraterrestrials managing the evolution of the human mind. Or they may represent the presence of mind on another level of being. Perhaps our fate is eventually to leave the physical world altogether and join them in that strange hyper-reality from which they seem to emerge.[16]

If we can accept the possibility that these Beings—whatever form they may take—have been in contact with us for tens of thousands of years, then we should not discard the possibility that, in Strieber's words, "we may very well be something different from what we believe ourselves to be, on this earth for reasons that may not yet be known to us, the understanding of which will be an immense challenge."[17]

"We can try to make the phenomenon fit the world as we have known it," John E. Mack writes, "jamming it into a kind of procrustean bed of consensus reality. Or we can acknowledge that the world might be other than we have known it. . . . I have spent countless hours trying to find alternative explanations that would not require the major shift in my worldview that I have had to face. But," Mack concludes, "no familiar theory or explanation has come even close to accounting for the basic features of the abduction phenomenon. In short, it is what it is, though the ultimate source of these experiences remains a mystery."[18]

The least demanding "shift in worldview" required by this phenomenon asks only that we extend those boundaries that we deem to be the limits of technology. In other words, just because UFOs and their occupants defy our laws of physics does not mean there are not further laws of physics we have not as yet discovered or do not as yet comprehend. Technology is constantly advancing; stunning scientific achievements, therefore, should not surprise us.*

Nor should the paradigm shift required by acknowledging that there might be other intelligent beings in the universe set us back on our heels. After all, who today could argue convincingly that our sun is the only ce-

---

* Although, of course, they sometimes do. History is filled with examples of what J. Allen Hynek called "temporal provincialism": In 1895, for example, Lord Kelvin, the British physicist, stated that "heavier-than-air flying machines are impossible." In 1923, Nobel Prize physicist Robert Millikan announced, "There is no likelihood that man can ever tap the power of the atom." And in 1932 University of Chicago astronomer Dr. F. R. Moulton expressed his opinion that "there is no hope for the fanciful idea of reaching the moon because of insurmountable barriers to escaping the earth's gravity."[19]

lestial object about which planets orbit, or that Earth is the only planet capable of sustaining life?

No, the shift demanded by the UFO phenomenon that *is* so difficult is the one that forces us to consider that there might exist simultaneous *other realities;* further, that it is during, or within, some sort of overlapping of these realities that alien abductions occur. And it is this hypothesis that sends us reeling backwards to confront the original question raised by the UFO phenomenon: Where do they come from?

Early ufologists were about evenly divided between those who concentrated their efforts on the discovery and analysis of "hard evidence"—the photographs, the landing traces, changes in soil composition, etc.—and those who focused upon eyewitness reports, close encounters of the third and fourth kinds.

But then in the 1960s there emerged a third group of ufologists who were part historians, part folklorists, part scholars, and maybe even part dreamers. They were the students of the phenomenon who had come to suspect that there might be parallels between contemporary UFO reports and accounts of human confrontations with mysterious beings since earliest times.

In this third group was Jacques Vallee, then a young French graduate student and computer scientist. Another member, I learned to my surprise, was longtime Air Force consultant J. Allen Hynek, with whom Vallee had become acquainted in 1960 while Hynek was teaching at Northwestern University. (Vallee is allegedly the real-life figure upon whom Steven Spielberg based the French-speaking UFO scientist, played by François Truffaut in *Close Encounters of the Third Kind.*)

In the mid-1960s Vallee wrote *Anatomy of a Phenomenon,* a book still considered one of the most sophisticated scientifically based explorations into the UFO phenomenon. In it he showed he was less interested in explaining UFOs than he was in analyzing them. Keith Thompson attributes Vallee's decision to turn away from mainstream UFO research's concentration on finding a simple, uncomplicated explanation for UFOs to an incident that occurred in 1961 while Vallee was working with the French Satellite Tracking Program, part of a worldwide research network that reported to the Smithsonian Astronomical Observatory. According to Thompson:

> One night [Vallee] and his coworkers tracked an elusive object that behaved abnormally for a satellite yet seemed not to be an airplane or a lighted balloon. Vallee felt the excitement of knowing he and his colleagues were *on* to something. But before they could feed their data on this object into the computer for analysis, their supervisor confiscated and erased the tape. The object no longer existed, for all intents and purposes.

For Vallee, the unknown (and now forever lost) object on the radar screen immediately paled in significance compared to the deliberate suppression of scientific evidence he had just witnessed. It was in trying to understand the reflexive action of his supervisor—who saw himself as a scientist no less than Vallee and his colleagues saw themselves as scientists—that Vallee became truly interested in the UFO phenomenon. As his study continued, he came to believe "that one should not try to prove that UFOs constitute a new phenomenon of an unknown, possibly artificial nature before one has made an attempt to understand why such violent reactions are provoked by the thought of . . . contact with our civilization by nonhuman knowledge for nonhuman purposes, possibly prompted by nonhuman emotions and perceptions."

In 1969, Vallee the consummate scientist surprised many of his colleagues with his suggestion that UFOs may not be a "scientific" problem after all, for "modern science rules over a narrow universe, one particular variation on an infinite theme." Likewise, Vallee said, "ufology has become such a narrow field of specialization that the experts have no time left for the general culture." He called on his colleagues to join him in moving beyond the limited—and increasingly obsessional—concern with whether UFOs are extraterrestrial in origin, and to begin probing the UFO phenomenon's impact on culture and our collective psyches.[20]

Vallee's call to look in other directions was an outgrowth of ideas he had shared with, among others, J. Allen Hynek, who later explained, "It began to seem to us that rather than being 'extraterrestrial' in any simple sense, UFOs could well be part of the same larger intelligence which has shaped the tapestry of religion and mythology since the dawn of human consciousness."[21]

In his two books *Passport to Magonia* (1969) and *Dimensions: A Casebook of Alien Contact* (1988), Jacques Vallee moved beyond discussing the international history of UFOs to analyze the world's anthropological, religious, folkloric, mythic, and literary fables, those "larger mechanisms," as Thompson calls them, "that generate religious visions, mystical raptures, appearances by supernatural creatures, and flying saucers—all relying on the same processes and mechanisms, all sharing similar characteristics and effects on the human observer, *depending on the predominant belief structure of a given culture* [Thompson's italics].[22]

In other words, observers would see what their times and environment prepared them to believe they might see. Take, for example, Ezekiel's Old Testament vision:

And I looked, and behold, a whirlwind came out of the north, a great cloud, and a fire infolding itself, and a brightness was about it, and out of the midst thereof as the colour of amber, out of the midst of the fire.

Also out of the midst thereof, came the likeness of four living creatures. And this was their appearance, they had the likeness of a man.

And every one had four faces, and every one had four wings.

And their feet were straight feet; and the sole of their feet was like the
sole of a calf's foot; and they sparkled like the colour of burnished brass.[23]

An admirer of Spielberg's *Close Encounters of the Third Kind* might see
the same vision and report:

I looked up at the churning lightning-filled clouds to the north and saw
a huge, bright, fiery-orange, rotating object emerge; it was the *mother
ship!* Four smaller scout craft emerged from the Mother ship. They were
star-shaped: like a man with his arms and legs outstretched. Each craft
had four windows and four wings. Their landing gear pointed straight
down, then flattened out into pads. The craft had a polished metallic appearance. . . .

With a little imagination, Ezekiel's vision can be interpreted to mean
that he saw, in addition to the huge mother ship and small starships, some
large, cupolated discs with windows spaced above their rotating rims; that
when the craft moved, they made deep, resonant noises, but when hovering
they made no sound; and that throughout the period these discs and scout
craft were darting about, the huge, towering mother ship remained high
above them—the bright orange light shining from its interior so brilliant,
Ezekiel tells us, he collapsed in awe:

And he said unto me, Son of man, stand upon thy feet, and I will speak
unto thee.

And the spirit entered into me when he spake unto me, and set me
upon my feet, that I heard him that spake unto me.

Then the spirit took me up, and I heard behind me a voice of great
rushing. . . .

I heard also the noise of the wings of the living creatures that touched
one another, and the noise of the wheels over against them, and a noise of
a great rushing.

So the spirit lifted me up, and took me away. . . .[24]

The beings spoke to Ezekiel telepathically, telling him to stand up and
to not be afraid. And then they abducted him.

In 1830 an American wrote of the religious vision he himself had experienced: "I saw a pillar of light exactly over my head, above the brightness
of the sun, which descended gradually until it fell upon me. When the light
rested on me I saw two personages, whose brightness and glory defy all de-

scriptions, standing above me in the air. One of them spoke to me."[25] The experiencer, Joseph Smith, went on to found the Mormon Church.

During the Middle Ages, Western man persistently believed he was under the scrutiny of aerial Beings who lived in the skies. In his *Introduction to Plutarch's Lives,* A. H. Clough includes this account of the intercession by Agobard, the respected archbishop of Lyons, in behalf of three men and a woman who stood accused by a mob of having just landed in a "cloud-ship" from a legendary celestial region known as Magonia:

> One day, among other instances, it chanced at Lyons that three men and a woman were seen descending from . . . wonderfully constructed aerial ships, whose flying squadrons roved at the will of the Zephyrs. . . . The entire city gathered around them, crying out that they were magicians. . . . In vain the four innocents sought to vindicate themselves by saying that they were their own country-folk, and had been carried away a short time since by miraculous men who had shown them unheard-of marvels. . . . The frenzied populace paid no heed to their defense, and were on the point of casting them into the fire, when the worthy Agobard, Bishop of Lyons . . . came running at the noise, and having heard the accusations of the people and the defense of the accused, gravely pronounced that . . . it was not true that these men had fallen from the sky, and what they said they had seen there was impossible.[26]

During the battle between the Saxons and the Franks at Sigisburg in A.D., 776 fiery aerial phenomena appeared overhead in the shape of military shields.

In A.D. 1118 Emperor Constantine observed a fiery cross in the sky along with the message "In this sign you shall conquer."

German scholar Hartmann Schaeden in 1493 published an account of a remarkable fiery sphere he observed fly a straight line across the sky from south to east, then turn west directly toward the setting sun. (A contemporary illustration of this phenomenon depicted a cigar-shaped device surrounded by flames against a blue sky.)

Once in Nuremberg in 1561 and three times in Basel in 1566, numerous large black discs were observed in the sky. According to Swiss scholar Samuel Coccius, who witnessed the phenomenon: "Suddenly, they started racing towards the sun with great speed, with some turned toward each other as though in combat. Some were seen to turn fiery red and then they vanished."[27] Other witnesses reported observing large aerial cylinders out of which came spheres and discs that performed mock aerial battles.

Many of these sightings were witnessed by thousands who interpreted them as religious miracles or omens.

The first "mystery airship" was seen in November 1896 in the sky over California. During the next five months thousands of people told of having also observed dirigible-shaped craft beneath which some sort of illuminated passenger carriage seemed suspended. Witnesses also reported some of these strange craft carried colored or white lights; others were equipped with red or white searchlights. However, among the numerous mystery airship sightings reported over both urban and rural areas of this country's West and Midwest between November 1896 and May 1897, one that took place on the night of April 19, 1897, in Leroy, Kansas—given contemporary accounts of animal mutilations—is of particular note. That night Alexander Hamilton, a former congressman turned farmer, was awakened by sounds of disturbance among his cattle. He quickly dressed, went outside, and "to my utter astonishment," he subsequently reported, he observed "an airship descending over my cow lot."

Hamilton rushed back inside to awake his son and his hired man. The men hurriedly picked up axes and raced outside. Hamilton estimated that the "airship" was approximately three hundred feet long. As they watched, the craft descended until it was no more than thirty feet off the ground. Beneath the cigar-shaped airship's main structure the three men could clearly see "a carriage . . . made of glass or some other transparent substance."

"It was brightly lit within," Hamilton noted, "and everything was plainly visible." He then added that the glasslike undercarriage "was occupied by six of the strangest beings I ever saw. They were jabbering together but we could not understand a word they said. . . . Some noise attracted their attention," Hamilton continued, "and they turned a light directly on us."

Hamilton, his son, and the hired man next heard a buzzing sound like that of "a great turbine wheel," and the huge aerial device began to rise "lightly as a bird." The craft then stopped and hovered over one of Hamilton's heifers. The calf appeared caught in the cow-lot fence. When Hamilton went to rescue the young animal, he discovered the calf was tied to a cable that stretched from the airship. At that moment, the aerial craft, "heifer and all," Hamilton reported, "rose slowly, disappearing to the northwest."

The next day, a neighbor familiar with Hamilton's cattle brand brought him all that remained of the calf: its head, hide, and legs.

"I don't know whether they are angels or devils or what," Hamilton remarked, "but we all saw them . . . and," he added, "I don't want anything more to do with them."

An affidavit accompanying the news account of Alexander Hamilton's experience with the mystery airship was signed by eleven "prominent citizens," each of whom had known Hamilton for between fifteen and thirty years and was willing to attest to his confidence and belief in his statement being "true and correct."[28]

The last mystery airship sighting of that series took place on the morning of April 30, 1897, when one of the phantom machines was observed silently floating northeastward over Yonkers, New York, towards the Atlantic Ocean.

Although by the end of the nineteenth century enough had been learned about structures, streamlining, power plants, and control devices to construct powered balloons or airships that could be flown successfully, it was not until October 19, 1901, three years *after* the last mystery airship sighting, that a pilot of an airship or dirigible was capable of navigating a simple seven-mile round-trip course within thirty minutes.*

My point is that cross-country journeys of the sort suggested by the many mystery airship sightings were still not feasible.

Strange sightings continued. During World War II veteran fighter and bomber pilots and crews on both sides reported strange glowing balls of light that would pursue their aircraft, play tag with them, even fly formation off their wingtips; Allied pilots referred to them as "foo-fighters."

Later, between 1946 and 1958, thousands of people in the Scandinavian countries close to the Soviet Union observed "ghost rockets" streaking through the sky, or hovering overhead and then shooting off in a different direction.

"As with later flying saucer reports," Thompson points out, "the objects anticipated feats of technology not yet possible, although not beyond the range of imagination. This prompted some researchers to speculate that a vast paraphysical metaphenomenon lay behind all human visionary experiences, aimed at slowly and imperceptibly expanding human consciousness."[30]

Among the most striking modern visionary experiences was the famous "miracle at Fátima," which combined both aerial and religious phenomena. Keith Thompson describes it as follows:

> On May 13, 1917, three illiterate shepherd children, at work tending sheep outside Fátima, Portugal, were surprised by a bright flash in a nearby pasture called Cova de Ira, widely known as an old sacred place. Approach-

---

* This is the feat accomplished on that date by airship pioneer Alberto Santos-Dumont, when he piloted his balloon from the Aero Club at Saint-Cloud outside Paris around the Eiffel Tower and back within thirty minutes, thereby winning the prestigious Deutsch Prize.

Santos-Dumont, heir to a Brazilian coffee fortune, was celebrated for his flights about Paris in the early 1900s. "It was not uncommon to see his airship," writes historian John Toland, "sail down the Rue Washington and hover over his ornate apartment until a butler, standing on the steps, would haul him down."[29]

ing the pasture, they were caught in a luminosity that nearly blinded them. In the center of the blaze of light, they perceived a little woman who told them she was "from Heaven" and warned that worldwide suffering could be averted only if people [ceased] "offending God." The illuminated figure—who quickly became known as Our Lady—asked them to return to the same spot every month.

On June 13, the children returned. This time fifty witnesses watched as the three knelt in prayer and the oldest, ten-year-old Lucia, addressed an unseen entity whose answers were unheard by anyone other than Lucia and her two young companions. One witness reported hearing a faint voice or beelike buzzing. At the end of the dialogue, witnesses heard an explosion and saw a small cloud rise near a tree.

Forty-five hundred witnesses joined the three children near the same tree in the same pasture on July 13. This day several witnesses reported "a buzzing or humming sound, a decrease in the sun's glow and heat, a small whitish cloud about the tree of the apparitions, and a loud noise at the Lady's departure," writes Joseph Pelletier in his book *The Sun Danced at Fátima.*

On August 13, the crowd grew to 18,000, but the three children were not among them. They had been jailed by local officials eager to "put an end to this nonsense." Even so, those present in the field reported a clap of thunder followed by a bright flash and a cloud surrounding the same "magical" tree. One month later a crowd of 30,000 watched in astonishment as a globe of light appeared in plain view, advancing through the valley floor from east to west, coming to rest on the same tree.

Two deeply skeptical priests—who arrived expecting to find evidence only of contagious hysteria—reported that a white cloud formed around the tree as "falling flowers" descended from the sky and disappeared as witnesses reached to touch them.

The most amazing display occurred in Fátima on October 13, when 70,000 gathered in the pouring rain. Many came to keep faith with the prophecy of Our Lady, others to taunt what they saw as a display of vile medieval supernaturalism. Shortly after noon, thick gray clouds suddenly parted and rolled back like curtains of a stage, as a strange sweet fragrance filled the air. The sun appeared against the clear blue sky as a flat silver disc revolving on its own axis and sent forth shafts of red, violet, yellow and blue light in all directions. Suddenly the disc plunged erratically downward in zigzag fashion, causing thousands of witnesses—believers and disbelievers alike—to fall to their knees in public confession of their sins before the world ended.

The disc stopped short and began slowly rising into the sky in the same irregular way, disappearing into the sun, which stood once again fixed in its natural brilliance. The entire display lasted less than fifteen minutes. No less amazing was this fact, confirmed by the managing editor of Lisbon's largest daily newspaper: the streets and clothes of thousands of witnesses were no longer wet, even though heavy rains had fallen within the hour. Throughout the countryside, strange healings were reported.[31]

Thirteen years of scrupulous investigation later, the Catholic Church offered this evaluation of the Fátima sighting: "This phenomenon, which no astronomical observatory registered and which therefore was not natural, was witnessed by persons of all categories and of all social classes, believers and unbelievers, journalists of the principal Portuguese newspapers and even by persons some miles away. Facts which annul any explanation of collective illusion."[32]

What the 70,000* Fátima witnesses and the Catholic Church saw as a miracle Jacques Vallee sees as just one more aspect of the UFO phenomenon: "The final miracle had come at the culmination of a precise series of apparitions combined with contacts and messages that place it very clearly, in my opinion, in the perspective of the UFO phenomenon. Not only was a flying disc or globe consistently involved, but its motion, its falling-leaf trajectory, its light effects, the thunderclaps, the buzzing sounds, the strange fragrance, the fall of 'angel hair' [the flowerlike petals] that dissolves upon reaching the ground, the heat wave associated with the close approach of the disc—all of these are frequent parameters of UFO sightings everywhere. And so are the paralysis, the amnesia, the conversion, and the healings."[34]

Vallee's scholarship and research, like Keith Thompson's, are so evident that anyone trying to see in the UFO phenomenon something less one-dimensional than the argument "Are they real?" ends up reading and quoting him. John Mack, for example, who calls Vallee "perhaps the most comprehensive cross-cultural ufology investigator," devotes several pages in his *Abduction* to Vallee's discussion of the international history of UFO encounters, his description of "hundreds of sightings of strange sky-born objects and their occupants across time, continents and societies," and Vallee's citing of "the seemingly unexplainable presence of discs in the symbology of various civilizations—the Phoenicians and early Christians, for instance, associated them with communications between angels and God."[35]

Vallee also focuses upon the multitude of historic similarities worldwide among those creatures Mack refers to as "nonhuman, shape-shifting, aeri-

* The record for the largest number of witnesses to a single sighting of an unexplained aerial phenomenon is held by China, where one million persons in 1981 simultaneously saw a spiral-shaped UFO.[33]

ally adept beings" with "extraordinary powers" who have frequently appeared before humans in "thousands of different guises . . . to partake of and/or take away something belonging to humans, desiring to communicate with or simply play tricks on them."[36]

Eddie Bullard at the M.I.T. Conference addressed the parallels between the fairies of folklore and the Small Grays of UFOs. But the point of this, as Vallee explained, is not just that the "same power attributed to saucer people was once the exclusive property of fairies," but that "the UFO occupants, like the elves of old, are not extraterrestrials. They are denizens of another reality."[37]

Vallee muses whether "an advanced race somewhere in the universe and sometime in the future has been showing us three-dimensional space operas for the last two thousand years, in an attempt to guide our civilization. If so," he asks, "do they deserve our congratulations?" And he wonders:

> If they are not an advanced race from the future, are we dealing instead with a parallel universe, another dimension where there are other human races living, and where we may go at our expense, never to return to the present? Are these races only semihuman, so that in order to maintain contact with us, they need cross-breeding with men and women of our planet? Is this the origin of the many tales and legends where genetics plays a great role: the symbolism of the Virgin in occultism and religion, the fairy tales involving human midwives and changelings, the sexual overtones of the flying saucer reports, the biblical stories of intermarriage between the Lord's angels and terrestrial women, whose offspring were giants? From that mysterious universe, are higher beings projecting objects that can materialize and dematerialize at will? Are the UFOs "windows" rather than "objects"?
> There is nothing to support these assumptions, and yet, in view of the historical continuity of the phenomenon, alternatives are hard to find, unless we deny the reality of all the facts, as our peace of mind would indeed prefer.[38]

Mack proposes that even if we allow "for the time being that there is little knowledge about the domain from which the alien beings derive—perhaps not even language or concepts to describe it," we should grant "that *something* is going on that cannot be dismissed out of hand."[39]

If we do accept that, Mack maintains, we are then forced to acknowledge that "we are living in a vastly different universe from that which I, for one, was taught about at home and in school." In that more familiar universe, he points out, "the various spirit entities, God or Gods and other mythic beings that peoples throughout the world, including in our own culture, experience as altogether real have no objective reality. They are the subject matter of psychology and psychopathology, anthropology, religious study, and science fiction, the projection outward of the perceptions and images of the brain. If we make these entities real, it is through metaphor and symbol, as poets do so well."

But, Mack insists, "to acknowledge that the universe (or universes) contains other beings that have been able to enter our world and affect us as powerfully as the alien entities seem able to do would require an expansion of our notions of reality that all too radically undermine the Western scientific and philosophical ideology which Tulane philosopher Michael Zimmerman calls 'naturalistic humanism.' "[40]

This Western scientific and philosophical ideology, philosopher Richard Tarnas writes, is one whose "governing assumption" is that "any meaning the human mind perceives in the universe does not exist intrinsically in the universe but is projected on it by the human mind." The consequence of "this complete voiding of the cosmos, this absolute privileging of the human" is, Tarnas continues, the "ultimate anthropocentric projection, the most subtle yet prodigious form of human self-aggrandizement," indicative, he feels, of an intellectual "hubris of cosmic proportion."[41]

Paradoxically, as one moves deeper and deeper into the UFO phenomenon, one feels the need to move farther and farther away from the true/false debates believers and skeptics become enmeshed in. This is because such arguments deteriorate into discussions about what defines "real." Keith Thompson understandably shares this impatience: "Over the years," he reports, "nothing about the respective claims of UFO disciples and UFO debunkers has convinced me of the need to reach definitive conclusions about the ultimate nature and origins of this phenomenon.

"Instead," he continues, "I have watched with fascination as a persistent body of remarkable stories (or in UFO jargon, 'sighting reports') has given rise to provocative mythic horizons and imaginal realms."

Thompson contends that "these symbolic worlds are real, vital, and filled with significance *whether* or *not*," he argues, "any particular UFO was the planet Venus or a Venusian starship."[42]

John Mack's impatience, too, lurks just beneath the surface in his insistence that the physical reality of UFOs is not the important issue. "I am often asked why, if UFOs and abductions are real, the spaceships do not show up in more obvious form," he complains in *Abduction*. " 'Why don't they land on the White House lawn?' is the reigning cliche. The most popular answer to this question among those who take the phenomenon seriously is that the aliens do not *dare* to manifest themselves more directly.

Government leaders would panic, might attack them, and surely would not know how to avoid scaring the rest of us.

"I believe," Mack continues, a little less testily,

> that there is a better answer to this question. . . . The intelligence that appears to be at work here simply does not operate that way. It is subtler, and its method is to invite, to remind, to permeate our culture from the bottom up as well as the top down, and to open our consciousness in a way that avoids a conclusion that is different from the ways we traditionally require. It is an intelligence that provides enough evidence that something profoundly important is at work, but it does not offer the kinds of proof that would satisfy an exclusively empirical, rationalist way of knowing. It is for us to embrace the reality of the phenomenon and to take a step forward appreciating that we live in a universe different from the one in which we have been taught to believe.[43]

In his short book *Flying Saucers: A Modern Myth of Things Seen in the Sky*, published in 1959, Carl Jung wrote, "Something is seen, but one doesn't know what. It is difficult, if not impossible, to form any correct idea of these objects because they behave not like bodies but like weightless thoughts."[44] The eminent Swiss psychiatrist-philosopher, then eighty-four years old, wondered whether UFOs might not be "materialized psychisms"—actual physical or paraphysical objects created by the collective unconscious.

In February 1951 Jung wrote a friend of his inability to determine whether UFOs should be considered rumors related to mass hallucinations or actual facts. Jung explained that he found both options interesting, adding: "If it's a rumour, then the apparition of discs must be a symbol produced by the unconscious. We know what such a thing would mean seen from the psychological standpoint. If on the other hand it is a hard and concrete fact, we are surely confronted with something out of the way. . . . The phenomenon of the saucers might even be both, rumour as well as fact. . . . It's just too bad that we don't know enough about it."[45]

Jung did not mean "rumors" in the sense of uncorroborated hearsay; he meant them, Thompson explains, rather as " 'visionary rumors' of the same order as religious visions. Such visions are experienced in times of personal and collective distress or danger, or in response to 'vital psychic need,' Jung noted. Perhaps the collective unconscious was sending forth such visions, just as individuals experienced abnormal convictions, visions, and illusions at times of dissociation between conscious and unconscious attitudes.

"With a certain somberness," Thompson continues, "Jung noted that he was not pleased to conclude that the appearance of UFOs clearly indicated 'coming events which are in accord with the end of an era.' Such large-scale anomalies typically arise when wholesale changes are under way in the balance of forces in the collective unconscious—that vast repository of images and motifs common to the myths and dreams of peoples throughout the world, all connected as a complex matrix transcending time and space. Jung had no doubt that humanity was entering a time of profound transition. . . .

"The frequently reported round shape of the objects suggested to Jung the *mandala*," Thompson points out, "a recurring image of psychic totality found in mythologies throughout the world, with names such as the 'sun wheel' or 'magic circle.' UFOs might represent a mythological concept of the soul, which was said in ancient times to assume the form of a sphere. Jung found it interesting that an image expressing order, wholeness, and salvation should 'now take the form of an object, a technological construction,' to bypass the disadvantages of mythological associations in an age where magic had been supplanted by machines."[46]

The obsolescence of mythological symbols as questionable transmitters of psychic messages aside, the appearance of UFOs as "materialized psychisms" was what really interested Jung—which is not surprising. It was Jung's contention that there exists a collective unconscious within which—or out of which—certain basic, original primordial patterns or images emerge that are shared by all mankind. The basis for these universal patterns or images Jung called "archetypes."

Jung, Thompson explains, "originally conceived of archetypes as the deepest patterns of psychic functioning, the root patterns of instinctive behavior. He came to see archetypes as the immaterial potentials inherent in *all* structures, as fundamental to the existence of all living organisms. Eventually," Thompson notes, "the archetypes became in [Jung's] own words, 'the bridge to matter in general.' "[47]

It is the questioning of this relationship between mind and matter around which much of the current thinking about UFOs revolves. Philosophers, physicists, psychologists, neurologists, neurosurgeons, biochemists, researchers, scholars, folklorists, abductees, and journalists alike circle this issue like dogs circling a spot on the rug, searching for a warm and comfortable place where they might set their intellects down.

"The ultimate mystery facing us is how matter becomes conscious," writes theoretical physicist Fred Alan Wolf. "Simply put, we argue that we are made of matter, then how does that matter seemingly produce or create images and thoughts? Or even put more crudely, how does meat dream?"[48]

Jung hypothesized that there existed a realm of being between the physical and the psychical, what Wolf calls the "third reality," located "between the earthly mundane and the completely abstract world of concepts."[49] Others—among them Islamic scholar Henri Corbin, psychologist Kenneth Ring, folklorist Peter Rojcewicz, and physicist Werner Heisenberg—have referred to this third reality as the "Middle Realm" or "Imaginal Realm."

"The Imaginal Realm is real," Wolf asserts, "but not physical, and as such it is not unlike Jung's notion of the psychoid archetype and a related alchemical idea he calls the *unus mundus* (one world). It is a place where psyche and nature manifest with a dual aspect not resolving itself into either of its two aspects."[50] Rojcewicz, professor of humanities at New York's Juilliard School, explains this concept as follows:

> The psychoid nature of the unus mundus is a blurred-reality genre. The psychoid realm raises questions of perceptions and epistemology. In our materialist tradition we are trained to develop a monocular vision and see only the physical. If we happen to see a blurred-reality genre, that is, something in an ambiguous ontological state, most of us would likely see only the most conspicuous physical aspect of it. Some of us would fail to see anything at all. As far as we know about the process of perception, the brain intercedes from moment to moment, matching up and synthesizing what is occurring out there with what it has already recorded. Psychoid phenomena raise the question of whether or not an event takes place in an intermediate realm which doesn't manifest exclusively in a physical objective way or leave a trace.[51]

"Psychoid events," Wolf speculates, "are occurring in a realm of reality that does not fit into material physics. Yet, psychoid events have both a partial and temporary physical manifestation."[52]

Michael Grosso, an artist/philosopher/college professor well known for his UFO research, hypothesizes, according to Wolf, "that UFOs and other extraordinary phenomena are actually manifestations of a disturbance in the collective unconscious of the human species . . . caused by the violent impact of modern science on human life and the ecology of the earth."[53] Henry H. Price, professor of logic at Oxford and former president of Britain's Society for Psychical Research, expressed the opinion that every "idea" is inherently psychokinetic: in other words, it has the potential to materialize itself in some form. Grosso suggests that if our ideas are shared telepathically—even though we might be unaware we are sharing them— we would be creating group thought processes which might have increased psychokinetic potential. "This would imply," Wolf explains, "that a myth such as the UFO that was understood in a fictional sense might objectify

itself temporarily under certain circumstances in space and time and assume certain commonly physical characteristics." This concept "could
have some basis in the quantum physical idea of observer-created reality,"
Wolf thinks. "If more than one observer is involved some form of amplifi-
cation may occur wherein several people have the same or similar images
of an event."[54]

Grosso makes the point that we in the Western world are haunted by
our desire for a gentler age, but that because of the plethora of televised and
still pictures of abused, starving children, our unconscious minds are filled
with such images. The visual reports of the aliens, Grosso notes, are of similar life forms: fetal-like Beings often resembling the starving children with
sticklike arms, large heads, and bulging eyes one views in nations where
drought and famine and war have decimated the land. "Could this explain
the persistence and the similarity of the images of aliens as they appear to
us?" Wolf asks. "Are we witnessing something akin to a . . . survival dream
of the human species that manifests in some of us?"[55]

In *some* of us, but not *all* of us.

"Studies show that we often do not see something unless we truly believe
in it," Wolf writes. "Michael Grosso finds this interesting from a neurologi-
cal viewpoint; there may, however, be some percipients who encounter
UFOs simply because they possess a wider range of the visual field and have
different thresholds."

Psychologist Kenneth Ring in *The Omega Project: Near-Death Experiences, UFO Encounters, and Mind at Large* (1992), suggested that people who
have UFO (or Near-Death) experiences might be "encounter prone" and
that because of unusual experiences in their past, they might be more open
to such experiences in the future. "He in no way suggested that these individuals are less capable of coping with reality," Wolf emphasizes, "on the
contrary, that they are distinctive, spiritually sensitive, and possess visionary
psyches that may be signals of an evolutionary trend—a new stage of early
development." This new trend might be, Wolf continues, "the recognition
that mind is not confined to individual and separated persons, but is universal, singular, and beyond any conceptual limit we enforce, such as the notion of space-time confinement. Thus I am suggesting that Near-Death
Experiences (NDEs), UFO encounters, and a range of other imaginal realm
(IR) bleed-throughs into our normally seemingly separated minds are an
evolutionary trend leading us to a single one-mind experience of our SELF,
the whole universe and nothing else."[56]

British biochemist Rupert Sheldrake has proposed that when a new organic chemical is crystallized, "on the first occasion it may not crystalize at
all easily; but on subsequent occasions crystallization should occur more

and more easily as increasing numbers of past crystals contribute to its morphic field by 'morphic resonance.' "[57] Sheldrake reports this has been borne out in practice and hypothesizes that what this experiment suggests is the existence of an unconscious collective cumulative memory accessible to all nature. According to Sheldrake, individuals who do the London *Times* crossword puzzle at night, for example, do it more quickly than those who work it in the morning because through morphic resonance the answers have already entered the collective unconscious. If so, this might account for the similarity in abduction accounts.

UFO experiences are from the Imaginal Realm, Wolf speculates, and therefore have a different but "real" feeling to them as compared to ordinary experiences. "They are not the same as so-called solid-reality experiences that we commonly experience in everyday life," he explains, then adds: "I am also not saying they are fantasies or hallucinations." Wolf suggests a connection exists between Imaginal Realm experiences and certain experiences occurring both physiologically and psychologically in the dreaming brain. "The first piece of evidence that leads to this evolutionary conclusion," Wolf reports, "is one of the points Ring makes: the discontinuous character of UFO encounters and NDEs resembles that of similar phenomena in dreams."[58] Unquestionably there was a discontinuous character to Carol's and Alice's encounter narratives. They were—as Thompson remarked about UFO encounter events in general "typically surrealistic—dreamlike, fantastical, at once less and more than real."[59] Their narratives were interrupted by quick cuts: "Suddenly I was inside . . ." or "The next thing I knew . . ." or "I don't remember how I . . ."—the sort of rapid scene shifts common to our own dreams.

Ring emphasizes that it is important not to confuse the description of the experience with the experience itself. In other words, a person describing a UFO encounter will automatically impose upon that experience a linear, time-ordered sequence in an attempt to make sense of it. However, as Ring also makes clear, he is not saying UFO encounters *are* dreams as such; he is saying they are *like* dreams; similar, Ring states, to "dreams that one has *awakened into* and that, in some unknown way have come to interpenetrate ordinary reality, resulting in a kind of double vision, which, eventually, returns to normal. If these experiences are some [form] of dream [they] must be some sort of *collective dream* since many people are reporting similar, and similarly bizarre, encounters."[60]

Fred Alan Wolf also reports the interesting connection discovered by UFO researchers Paul Devereux and Michael Persinger between electrical activity in the brain and both NDEs and CE-IV experiences: "Devereux has found that people usually report observing unusual light phenomena,"

Wolf writes, near fault lines, power lines, transmitter towers, mountain peaks, isolated buildings, road and railway lines, and bodies of water including waterfalls. In many instances these lights seem to emerge from the ground and either swiftly dissolve or hover, sometimes touching down to the ground again and then rising several thousands of feet in the air. They have also been seen during daylight hours and appear metallic. Light phenomena also tend to reappear in certain regions of the world so often that local people have incorporated them into folklore and superstitions. Devereux believes that such light phenomena are characteristic of high-amplitude electromagnetic disturbances.[61]

UFO researcher Devereux and Michael Persinger, who is both a professor of psychology and a clinical neurophysiologist, believe, according to Wolf, that "UFO phenomena are natural occurrences producing high-amplitude electromagnetic pulses that are direct products of stress relief in tectonic plate movements of the earth's crust. Persinger's statistical studies show that seismic events are clearly related to UFO reports. In other words, during seismic events more UFO sightings will be reported."[62]

Let's, for a moment, say this is true. If Devereux and Persinger are correct, then, Wolf suggests, if a person is at the right distance—not too near and not too far—from a tectonic stress release and its resulting burst of electromagnetic energy, that person might see light phenomena typical of those reported during Close Encounters of the First and Second Kinds. And if, Wolf continues, the person "approaches the light or if he happens to be standing near enough to it, he may be close enough to the electromagnetic energy burst (EMEB) to feel its effects. These could include the raising of hair on the body and head, skin tingling, goose bumps, and other signs of nervous excitation. Following this line, deeper immersions could lead to brain disturbances resulting in psychological disturbances and hallucinatory images."[63]

This is not as farfetched as it might at first seem. The temporal lobe of the brain is particularly sensitive to electrical disturbances. Probably the most research bearing this out was done by the late neurosurgeon Wilder Penfield, who, Wolf reports, observed that "the temporal lobe has convolutions that are apparently new evolutionarily and are not committed to motor or sensory function. . . . During the initial learning stages of childhood some of these convolutions seem to be devoted to interpretation of present experience in terms of past experience. This part of the temporal lobe has today been labeled the *interpretive cortex.*

"During surgical procedures on patients suffering from temporal-lobe seizures (epileptic seizures caused by electrical discharges originating in the temporal lobe)," Wolf explains, "Penfield and his colleagues stumbled upon the fact that electrical stimulation of the interpretive areas of the cortex occasionally produced . . . 'dream states' or 'psychical seizures'. . . . It was clear to Penfield that these 'dream states' were not dreams. They were electrical activations of sequences of records laid down during the patient's earlier conscious experiences. The patient 'relived' all that he had been aware of during an earlier period of time. He was having a moving-picture 'flashback.' "[64]

In Penfield's paper *The Mystery of the Mind: A Critical Study of Consciousness and the Human Brain* (1975), the neurosurgeon described how vivid some of these "flashbacks" could be. Through the electrical stimulation of certain specific areas of a patient's temporal cortex, the subject might relive the whole range of human sensory experiences—tastes, smells, emotions, physical responses, and especially visual and auditory details—as though they were happening to the individual all over again. For example, one young male patient, Penfield noted, reported being at a small-town baseball field watching a child sneak under the fence to get in to see the game. Another patient relived the experience of being in a concert hall and being able to hear the contributions each of the different instruments made to the music.

Princeton psychologist Julian Jaynes disagrees that the basis for these flashbacks is past experiences. "These areas [of the patient's temporal cortex]," Jaynes writes, "are not the 'brain's record of auditory and visual experience,' nor are they its retrieval, but combinations and amalgamations of certain aspects of that experience. The evidence does not, I think, warrant the assertion that these areas 'play in adult lives some role in the subconscious recall of past experience, making it available for present interpretation.' Rather the data lead away from this, to hallucinations that distill particularly admonition experiences, and perhaps become embodied or rationalized into actual experiences in those patients who reported them on being questioned."[65]

Jaynes speculates that until late in the second millennium B.C. human consciousness did not exist; instead, early humans walked around in something like a "dream state" of trance unconsciousness, automatically obeying what they took to be the voices of gods. What was this state like? "Some of the fundamental, most characteristic, and most common symptoms of florid unmedicated schizophrenia," Jaynes writes, "are uniquely consistent with the description I have given . . . of the bicameral mind."[66] Consciousness, Jaynes suggests, was only *learned* three thousand years ago, distilled out of a cauldron of cataclysms and catastrophes partially created by this earlier hallucinatory mentality. (It is interesting to note that not until the end of the sixteenth century was madness considered a symptom of a malfunctioning brain rather than of having been "touched" by the gods.)

Michael Persinger reports in the *Journal of Near-Death Studies* that all of the major components of the near-death experience (including looking down at one's own body, flying, hearing hauntingly beautiful music, being drawn to a brilliant light, and a profound sense of meaning) can now be duplicated upon a patient in a laboratory by introducing a minimal amount of electrical current induction to his temporal lobe.

"Based on the above findings," Wolf concludes, "there seems to be no doubt that imaginal-realm experiences are produced by electrical disturbances in the temporal lobe. These can be induced by anomalous electromagnetic phenomena, such as those that accompany tectonic stress relief in the earth's crust and brain surgical procedures, and even under laboratory settings. But," he then asks, "what about you and me? What about so-called normal people who, through seemingly no fault of their own, experience such phenomena when no added electrical stimulation is present?"[67]

Persinger, Wolf reports, seems to agree with Kenneth Ring: some individuals may be "encounter prone." For whatever the reason or reasons, Wolf writes, these individuals may be "unusually sensitive to normal temporal-lobe electrical activity."[68]

Ring did a study of people who had had NDEs or some kind of UFO experience and, as a control group, people who had not but were interested in them. He discovered that the NDEers and UFOers were not more fantasy-prone—a finding borne out by researchers' reports at the M.I.T. conference. They were, however, more susceptible to alternate realities—and had been so since childhood.

Why would a child be more sensitive to alternate realities than to fantasies? What did these individuals, as children, have in common, Wolf asks, that would make them more prone to these kinds of experiences? "The answer," he tells us, "is disturbing and illuminating. There appears to be a high correlation between child abuse and imaginal realm sensitivity." And here Wolf again quotes psychologist Ring: "These children come," Ring reports, "not from the ranks of the fantasy-prone, but with histories of child abuse that include sexual and psychological trauma, neglect, and family dysfunctionality."[69]

Dave Jacobs disagrees. "What is astonishing, what is incredible," Jacobs told me, "is that although virtually all therapists immediately think that the abduction phenomenon is a screen memory for sexual abuse, they have never been able to produce one *single* case of this. They have not put forward even one case which unequivocally shows that abduction fantasies are caused by repressed memories of sexual abuse. If there is such a case, I want to see it. I want to see how it works and what its dynamics are."

John Mack disagrees, too. While acknowledging the associations made between sexual abuse and abductions, Mack expresses his belief that "errors related to the misremembering of traumatic experiences, or the reverse—traumatic experiences of one kind (abduction) opening the psyche to the recollection of traumas of another kind (sexual abuse)—can lead to falsely overstressing the association. I have worked with one woman, for example," Mack continues, "who went to a capable psychotherapist for presumed sexual abuse and incest-related problems. Several hypnosis sessions failed to reveal evidence of such events. But during one of her sessions she recalled a UFO that landed near her home when she was a six-year-old girl from which emerged typical alien beings who took her aboard the craft. For the first time, she experienced powerful emotions, especially fear, in the therapy hour. The therapist who referred the woman to me told me that he was 'clean,' i.e., was not directly familiar with the abduction phenomenon and did not suspect that she had such a history. There is not a single abduction case in my experience or that of other investigators that has turned out to have masked a history of sexual abuse or any other traumatic cause. But," Mack stresses, "the reverse has frequently occurred—that an abduction history has been revealed in cases investigated for sexual or other traumatic abuse."[70]

Sexual abuse in her case was a screen memory for an abduction.

But the role child abuse plays in susceptibility to alternate realities can't easily be resolved. Abused children tend to dissociate. "A family history of child abuse and trauma promotes dissociative response as a psychological defense," Wolf notes. "If you grew up in a home of unpredictable violence or sexual abuse or other forms of trauma, you would be motivated to tune out of the situation."[71] As Kenneth Ring explains, "They can do anything to your body but you, the '*real*' you inside, will go elsewhere. Once you learn to dissociate in response to the trauma, you are much more likely to become sensitive to alternate realities."[72]

Michael Persinger suggests that physical abuse may physically affect the brain in such a way that it becomes more sensitive to alternate realities. Perhaps this is what "encounter-prone" people are: people who, because they were abused as children, have brains responsive to stimuli others do not.

"To a frog with its simple eye, the world is a dim array of greys and blacks," Michael Murphy notes in *The Future of the Body*. And perhaps he is right to ask, "Are we like frogs in our limited sensorium, apprehending just part of the universe we inhabit? Are we as a species now awakening to the reality of multidimensional worlds in which matter undergoes subtle re-organizations in some sort of hyperspace? Is visionary experience analogous to the first breathings of early amphibians? Are we ourselves coming ashore to a 'larger earth'?"[73]

"I am struck by Murphy's analogy between the limited vision of the frog and the human being," Keith Thompson writes. "The visual apparatus of a frog, consisting of a mere handful of nerve cells, is rudimentary indeed when compared, say, with the structure of the human eye. The frog sees little more than indistinct shapes and forms, limited (as Murphy notes) to a gray-black hue. This is not to say the frog sees 'incorrectly,' " Thompson adds, "but rather *the frog sees what it can see according to its structure* [Thompson's italics], which is adequate for snaring insects with its tongue and—much of the time—eluding predators. We humans know there is 'more' to see, but the frog does not—at least so far as we can tell."

Thompson then speculates: "It is conceivable that we perceive UFOs and other 'anomalous' phenomena according to our predominant yet still-evolving psychospiritual 'structure.' Just as the frog is 'embedded' within a world of forms that it does not apprehend fully . . . what we humans term 'reality' may in fact be a limited spectrum of a much larger realm of possibilities, where what we call 'mind' and 'matter' have not yet distilled into the few dimensions that we can 'capture.'

"Ours may well be a 'world within worlds,' " Thompson muses. "In Michael Murphy's phrase, this earth may be embedded in a 'larger earth.' "[74]

Where does this leave us?

David Jacobs warns, "We must realize that the abduction phenomenon is too important to dismiss as the ravings of prevaricators or psychologically disturbed people. I hope the extraordinary lack of scientific concern to date does not in the long run prove to be a mistake with undreamed-of consequences."[75]

Budd Hopkins insists: "UFO abduction reports, because of their similarity of content and detail, must be accepted one of two ways: Either they represent some new and heretofore unrecognized and nearly universal psychological phenomenon—a theory which does not take into account the accompanying *physical evidence*—or they represent honest attempts to report real events."[76]

John Mack tells us that "no familiar theory or explanation has even come close to accounting for the basic features of the abduction phenomenon. In short, it is what it is, though its ultimate source remains a mystery."

Keith Thompson suggests it is "a prod to our next level of consciousness."

Whitley Strieber reports, "We may very well be something different from what we believe ourselves to be, on this earth for reasons that may not yet be known to us."

Carl Jung wrote that UFOs behaved "like weightless thoughts" and wondered whether they might be "materialized psychisms."

Michael Grosso thinks UFOs might be "manifestations of a disturbance in the collective unconscious caused by the impact of modern science on human life and the ecology of the earth," and that the strange physical characteristics of the Small Grays reflect our collective fear over what is happening to this planet's children.

Jacques Vallee asks whether UFOs are "windows" rather than "objects," then tells us the "UFO occupants are not extraterrestrials" but "denizens of another reality."

Peter Rojcewicz explains that "psychoid phenomena raise the question of whether or not an event takes place in an intermediate realm which doesn't manifest exclusively in a physical objective way or leave a trace."

Kenneth Ring calls that intermediate realm the "Imaginal Realm."

Fred Alan Wolf suggests that because "psychoid events have both a partial and temporal physical manifestation," they are "occurring in a realm of reality that does not fit into material physics" but does, however, fit into quantum physics, "which doesn't describe the realm of subjective experience or the realm of objective experience," but rather "the realm of imaginal experience that is potential material experience."[77]

John Mack says we must acknowledge that "the world might be other than we have known it." Vallee wonders whether "an advanced race somewhere in the universe and sometime in the future" has been attempting "to guide our civilization" and if not, asks, "Are we dealing instead with a parallel universe, another dimension where there are other human races living?" Whitley Strieber says the "visitors" are responsible for the paranormal phenomena.

Mack says the trauma caused by the phenomena is often mistakenly blamed on child abuse. Kenneth Ring says child abuse is responsible for the ability to perceive these phenomena; it has made such individuals more susceptible to alternate realities. He calls the experiencers "encounter prone" and suggests such persons' visionary psyches may be the first signs of an evolutionary stage in human development.

Wolf suggests that such "imaginal realm bleed-throughs into our normally seemingly separated minds are an evolutionary trend leading us to a single one-mind experience of our SELF, the whole universe and nothing else."

"The acknowledgement of [the alien beings'] existence, after the initial ontological shock," Mack writes, "is sometimes the first step in the opening of consciousness to a universe that is no longer simply material. Abductees come to appreciate that the universe is filled with intelligences and is itself intelligent. They develop a sense of awe before a mysterious cosmos that becomes sacred and ensouled. The sense of separation becomes an essential aspect of the evolution of the abductees' consciousness."[78]

Julian Jaynes reports, "From fossil evidence we know factually that the brain, particularly the frontal lobe in front of the central sulcus, was increasing with a rapidity that still astonishes the modern evolutionist."[79]

Wilder Penfield discovered that electrical stimulation of the interpretive area of the temporal lobe could produce "dream states" that were not dreams but vivid "moving-picture 'flashbacks' " to earlier experiences.

Fred Alan Wolf states, "there seems to be no doubt that imaginal-realm experiences are produced by electrical disturbances in the temporal lobe."

Michael Persinger reports that all of the major components of the Near-Death Experience can be duplicated upon a patient in a lab and notes that statistics show there will be more UFO sightings during seismic events.

When Václav Havel, president of the Czech Republic, received the Philadelphia Liberty Medal at Independence Hall on July 4, 1994, he referred to two specimens of postmodern science, the "anthropic cosmological principle," first set out by English physicist Brandon Carter in 1974, and the "Gaia Hypothesis,"* suggested by another Englishman, James Lovelock, two years earlier, in 1972.

The anthropic cosmological principle, Havel explained, "brings us to an idea, perhaps as old as humanity itself, that we are not at all just an accidental anomaly, the microscopic caprice of a tiny particle whirling in the endless depths of the universe. Instead, we are mysteriously connected to the universe, we are mirrored in it, just as the entire evolution of the universe is mirrored in us."

According to the Gaia Hypothesis, Havel continued, "we are parts of a greater whole. Our destiny is not dependent merely on what we do for ourselves but also on what we do for Gaia as a whole. If we endanger her, she will dispense with us, in the interests of a higher value—life itself."

Near the conclusion of his remarks Havel declared, "The only real hope of people today is probably a renewal of our certainty that we are rooted in the earth and, at the same time, the cosmos. This awareness endows us with the capacity for self-transcendence. Politicians at international forums may reiterate a thousand times that the basis of the new world order must be universal respect for human rights, but it will mean nothing as long as this im-

---

* "Gaia" is the Greek "Mother Earth."

perative does not derive from the respect of the miracle of Being, the miracle of the universe, the miracle of our own existence."[80]

Five weeks later, in response to Havel's speech, Nicholas Wade wrote in *The New York Times Magazine* that the trouble with the anthropic cosmological principle "is that it is closer to metaphysics than to physics. It invites you to think of a celestial clockmaker who designed the machinery and set the parameters just right for life to evolve. But unless someone finds a serial number stamped on the universe, it offers no way of proving the clockmaker's existence or seeking evidence of his purpose.

"Scientists have given the idea mixed reception," Wade continued,

The Princeton physicist Freeman Dyson has declared the principle "illuminating," his own take on it being that the universe is designed to make life possible but not too easy. On this reading, presumably, the transcendent value for humankind is simply to survive, for purposes to be revealed at a later time. The cosmologist Joseph Silk, on the other hand, has likened the anthropic principle to the satisfaction felt by a colony of fleas in a dog's pelt that everything in their world had been ordained just right for their existence, a theory that proved eminently tenable until the dog's mistress got a flea collar.

The trouble with the Gaia Hypothesis, Wade went on, is that "the idea quickly becomes mystical since it strongly implies a nice greenhouse with a thermostat and a kindly gardener who set the system in motion." Wade's skepticism is clear: "The anthropic principle and the Gaia hypothesis are both elegant ideas," he wrote,

expressed in scientific language by scientists who share Havel's yearning for a glimpse of transcendent purpose in the universe. But neither concept is a part of practical science because the very transcendent element that so attracts Havel also renders them untestable. Science is not revealed by introspection; it is a system of inquiry rooted in the empirical. It requires its theories to grow from established fact and to explain what is, not what might be.[81]

The dichotomy between *What is* and *what might be* is what powers the UFO phenomenon. It is the mystery that has intrigued me and so many others who remain on the outside; it is the conflict—if that is not too strong a word—that arose at M.I.T. and was best embodied by the differing points of view of its two chairmen.

In his closing remarks at the conference John Mack had asked us to look at the phenomenon with a "kind of philosophical, spiritual perspective. You all know the Vermont farmer that gave up trying to explain directions to the city slicker by saying, 'You just can't get there from here.' Well, we can't get there without a shift in our worldview."

Both at the conference and in our subsequent conversations Mack suggested that the data accumulating on the abduction phenomenon was so revolutionary that it was necessary for us to abandon our traditional scientific methods and adopt some other approach. "We are very vested in the materialist/dualist worldview," he had told us in his closing remarks. "Those of us in the scientific, economic establishment hang on tight to our familiar paradigm. Perhaps scientists hang on tighter than all the rest because our lives and work depend so much on an agreed upon set of assumptions about the universe. But now, really, we can stop fussing over whether we have got something real here. Instead, it may be time to expand our consciousness and reach out to embrace the extraordinary breadth and depth of power and meaning to the abduction phenomenon."

Pritchard disagrees. The phenomenon, he said in his closing remarks, is "an incredible problem that begs for a careful and multidisciplinary investigation. That has been the spirit of this conference, and that is the spirit that we must communicate to others outside this community." By example— such as his investigation into the Price "implant"—and by his words, Pritchard was declaring his faith in the scientific method.

"Being an active researcher in physics, especially Quantum Mechanics," Pritchard recently wrote me, "reaffirms this faith in the scientific approach. Philosophers could never convince a large majority (even of philosophers) that time and length can transform into each other or that reality doesn't exist until it is measured—but the scientific method has done this by finding theories that make quantitative predictions of the degree to which these things happen that agree with reproducible experiments. I don't think it is sensible to try new epistemologies on any phenomenon until the old reliable scientific method has been carefully and assiduously applied and come up empty—obviously not the case with abductions since this [was] the first truly scientific conference on the subject."[82]

In other words, Mack is to Pritchard as Havel is to Wade?

Several weeks after I had returned from attending Carol's and Alice's hypnosis sessions in Budd Hopkins's studio in New York, I was sitting on the back steps of my house looking up at the overcast late-afternoon sky. Suddenly, almost directly above me, I saw a flat, saucer-shaped object passing overhead. The disc, silhouetted against the thick, dull-gray cloud cover, was about the size of a dime held out at arm's length.

Because of the unbroken clouds and the failing light there was no way to determine the disc's altitude or volume; and since it was moving slowly and appeared to be following the prevailing wind patterns I assumed I was looking at a child's balloon. But, as I continued to watch, the disc rotated slightly and I saw the unmistakable metallic glint of its surface. And then as it turned even more I saw that the object wasn't round like a balloon at all! Two of its sides were distinctly flattened. I experienced a rush of excitement: I was finally seeing a UFO! But then I felt a slight puff of wind and the object soared upward.

What I was looking at, I realized, was one of those pillow-shaped, silvery, Mylar party balloons.

Prior to the Abduction Study Conference at M.I.T. it had never occurred to me that I might see a UFO. More significant, perhaps, I had never deliberately scanned the sky in search of one. Now, when I step outside at night and see lights moving against the stars, a part of me hopes that they will not *always* turn out to be airplanes.

If the conference, and my subsequent interviews and discussions with its participants and investigators, failed to provide me with "clear and convincing evidence" that these abductees experienced extraterrestrial visitations, I did come away a believer in the sincerity and merit of their quest. Like the abductees and their examiners, I am filled with wonder at their encounters. I envy them their experiences (some of them, anyway); I *want* them to be true. I want to believe that beings from other worlds—if they haven't visited us already—someday will.

I have come to admire Dave Pritchard, Budd Hopkins, and John Carpenter; Dave Jacobs, John Miller, and D. C. Donderi; Mark Rodeghier, Linda Moulton Howe, and all those other "presenters" and abductees at the M.I.T. Abduction Study Conference—the ghost of J. Allen Hynek included—to whom John Mack could also have been referring when he acknowledged at the conference's opening the "heroic, courageous—I won't quite say 'foolhardy,' but that was the word going through my head—work of Dave Pritchard in all of this. He has put himself on the line." They all put themselves on the line. They all were "taking a stand" and moving "science and human thought along."

I can't bring myself to judge them "foolhardy" either; I admire them far too much for that. I respect their conviction that the evidence is so compelling they have no choice but to risk not being taken seriously.

I am beginning to sound like Eliot Rosewater, Kurt Vonnegut's fictional multimillionaire, who crashes a science fiction writer's convention being held in a Milford, Pennsylvania, motel and drunkenly enthuses to the startled assembly, "I love you sons of bitches! . . . You're the only ones who'll talk about the *really* terrific changes going on, the only ones crazy enough to know that life is a space voyage, and not a short one either, but one that will last for billions of years. . . . You're the only ones zany enough to agonize over time and distances without limit, over mysteries that will never die."[83]

And yet what could be more important than the search for proof that there might, in fact, really be terrific changes going on; that we might, in fact, *not* be alone, that there might, in fact, exist *something* above and beyond the reality we can see?

Keith Thompson quotes the ancient Chinese aphorism "The fish is the last one to know that it lives in water" and goes on to explain:

> The fish takes for granted that the medium it knows is the True Element—indeed, the *only* element. Why should it imagine otherwise? But then, one day, a particular fish swims into a remote part of the lake and sees a strange object above. The fish has no name for what it sees from below, but we who are above would call the object a "bobber." Amazed, the fish returns to its school and tells what it has seen. The story is impressive, but the other fish are not so interested. After all, there is always fresh kelp to find, not to mention larger, hungry fish to avoid. News of such strange objects can only be a dangerous distraction to the overall affairs of the school.
>
> Over time, however, others see the bobber, and a robust set of legends grows. Then, on a particular day, a fish happens to swim too close to the object and gets "hooked." Suddenly this fish finds itself pulled *up* and *out*, into a vast and altogether amazing realm of *above* and *beyond*. Those who have snagged the fish and reeled it in, after analyzing the creature according to particular criteria, decide the fish is not a "keeper" and toss it back into the ocean. Bewildered, the fish makes it way back with an even more incredible tale to tell about another world—a very different kind of world—populated by the most marvelous of beings.
>
> Depending on how this news is revealed and received, the fish is deified, eaten, or simply isolated from the rest of the school, where it is left to muse aloud, "Water! We live and swim in *water!* I have just now seen that which is *not* water: I have glimpsed 'dry land,' and 'open sky.' Does anyone hear me? Does anyone *care?*"[84]

I care. And I am beholden to those people I met in the course of this book for having so richly populated the universe, our little "blue pond," and my imagination with "the most marvelous of beings"—be they Small Grays, Tall Grays, Nordic-types, reptilians, John Mack's aerially adept "Merry Tricksters," or Carl Jung's "materialized psychisms."

And whereas it might be foolhardy to admit I would *like to believe* there exist mutually unearthly creatures who might ask one Earthling woman to "eat only cow things" and ask another permission to try on her high-heeled shoes, I cannot honestly say I have come across any hard evidence of their presence.

Still, until someone comes forward with proof that such beings don't exist, I intend to continue keeping an eye out for their "bobbers"—and, yes, an open mind.

Zar would like that.

C. D. B. BRYAN
Guilford, Connecticut

Notes

BACKGROUND

1 Budd Hopkins, *Intruders: The Incredible Visitation at Copley Woods* (New York: Random House, 1987), p. 27.

2 David M. Jacobs, *Secret Life: Firsthand Accounts of UFO Abductions* (New York: Simon & Schuster, 1992), pp. 305–6.

3 John E. Mack, introduction to *Secret Life: Firsthand Accounts of UFO Abductions,* by David M. Jacobs (New York: Simon & Schuster, 1992), pp. 9–11.

4 J. Allen Hynek, *The UFO Experience: A Scientific Inquiry* (New York: Henry Regnery Co., 1972; Ballantine Books, 1974), p. 2. Page citations are to paperback edition.

5 Hynek's *Science* letter quoted in David M. Jacobs, *The UFO Controversy in America* (Bloomington, Ind.: Indiana University Press, 1975), p. 215.

6 Ibid.

7 Hynek, *The UFO Experience*, pp. 31–34.

8 Ibid., p. 11.

9 Quoted in Jacobs, *UFO Controversy,* p. 215.

10 Hynek, *The UFO Experience,* pp. 31–34.

11 Ibid., p. 34.

12 Thomas E. Bullard, "On Stolen Time: A Summary of a Comparative Study of the UFO Abduction Mystery" (Mt. Rainier, Md.: Fund for UFO Research, June 1987), p. 40.

13 Ibid., p. 13.

II. AT THE CONFERENCE: DAY ONE

1 John E. Mack, Introduction to *Secret Life: Firsthand Accounts of UFO Abductions,* by David M. Jacobs (New York: Simon & Schuster, 1992), p. 12.

2 Jacobs, pp. 95–96.

3 John S. Carpenter, commentary in "Unusual Personal Experiences: An Analysis of the Data from Three National Surveys," conducted by the Roper Organization (Las Vegas, Nev.: Bigelow Holding Corporation, 1992), p. 51.

III. AT THE CONFERENCE: DAY TWO

1 Carpenter, introduction to "Unusual Personal Experiences," p. 21.

2 Ibid., pp. 21–22.

3 Ibid., p. 25.

IV. AT THE CONFERENCE: DAY THREE

1 Louis Joseph Vance quoted in J. Bryan III, *Hodge Podge: A Commonplace Book* (New York: Atheneum, 1986), p. 47.

2 David M. Jacobs letter, in *Journal of UFO Studies* 3, quoted by Keith Basterfield in private correspondence with author.

3 Keith Basterfield, "Maureen Puddy: An Australian Abductee Physically Present During an Abduction." Private correspondence with author, May 1992, photocopy.

4 Ibid.

5 Ibid.

6 Keith Basterfield, private correspondence with author, 9 July 1992.

7 "Induced Psychotic Disorder (Shared Psychotic Disorder)," in *Desk Reference to the Diagnostic Criteria* (American Psychiatric Association), p. 123.

8 John S. Carpenter, "Double Abduction Case: Correlation of Hypnosis Data," *Journal of UFO Studies* (1991), pp. 91–92.

9 Ibid., pp. 92–93.

10 Ibid., p. 99.

11 Ibid., p. 100.

12 Thomas E. Bullard, *On Stolen Time: A Summary of a Comparative Study of the UFO Abduction Mystery* (Mt. Rainier, Md.: Fund for UFO Research, June 1987), p. 40.

13 Carpenter, "Double Abduction Case," p. 110.

14 Ibid., p. 110.

15 Ibid.

16 Ibid.

17 Ibid.

18 Ibid., p. 111.

19 Ibid.

20 Ibid.

21 Ibid., p. 112.

22 Ibid.

23 Ibid.

24 Ibid.

25 Ibid.

26 Ibid., p. 113.

27 Ibid.

28 Ibid.

29 Ibid., p. 108.

30 Ibid., p. 102.

31 Ibid., p. 102.

32 John S. Carpenter, commentary in "Unusual Personal Experiences: An Analysis of the Data from Three National Surveys," conducted by the Roper Organization (Las Vegas, Nev.: Bigelow Holding Corporation, 1992), p. 52.

33 Ibid.

34 Ibid.

35 Ibid.

36 Ibid.

37 David M. Jacobs, *Secret Life: Firsthand Accounts of UFO Abductions* (New York: Simon & Schuster, 1992), p. 246.

38 Kenneth Arnold, quoted in David C. Knight, ed., *UFOs: A Pictorial History from Antiquity to the Present* (New York: McGraw-Hill, 1979), pp. 31–33.

39 Ibid., p. 34.

40 Edward J. Ruppelt in Jay David, ed., *The Flying Saucer Reader* (New York: New American Library, 1967), pp. 17–25.

41 Ibid. p. 25; Jacobs, *UFO Controversy*, pp. 75–79.

42 Lonnie Zamora, Hector Quintanilla, and J. Allen Hynek quoted in Knight, *UFOs: A Pictorial History*, pp. 114–18.

43 Hynek quoted in Knight, *UFOs: A Pictorial History*, pp. 132–33.

44 Jacobs, *UFO Controversy*, pp. 278–79; and Knight, *UFOs: A Pictorial History*, pp. 178–79.

45 Timothy Good, *Above Top Secret: The Worldwide UFO Cover-Up* (New York: William Morrow & Co., 1988), p. 369.

46 Linda Moulton Howe, *An Alien Harvest* (Littleton, Colo.: Linda Moulton Howe Productions, 1989), p. 270.

47 William J. Broad, "Wreckage in the Desert Was Odd but Not Alien," *New York Times*, September 18, 1966, pp. 1A, 40A.

48 Gerald Hawkins, quoted in Ivars Peterson, "Geometric Harvest: Euclid's Crop Circles" *Science News* 141, no. 5, pp. 76–77.

49 Ibid., p. 77.

50 Gerald S. Hawkins, *Beyond Stonehenge* (New York: Harper & Row, 1973), p. 72.

51 Readers interested in a more detailed examination of the crop circle phenomenon should read Linda Moulton Howe's most recent book, *Glimpses of Other Realities: Volume I: Facts and Eyewitnesses* (Huntingdon Valley, Pa.: Linda Moulton Howe Productions, P.O. Box 538, Huntingdon Valley, PA 19006).

52 James Harder, quoted in Jacobs, *UFO Controversy*, p. 236.

53 John Mack, "What Is Psychologically Anomalous About Abductions: A Challenge for the Mental Health Field," in book of abstracts prepared for Abduction Study Conference by Andrea Pritchard (1992), p. IV-B, photocopy.

54 Ronald K. Siegel, *Fire in the Brain: Clinical Tales of Hallucination* (New York: Dutton, 1992), pp. 83–85.

55 Ibid., p. 6.

56 Ibid., pp. 88–90.

57 Ibid., p. 90.

58 Ibid., p. 87.

V. AT THE CONFERENCE: DAY FOUR

1 Thomas E. Bullard, "Folkloric Dimensions of the UFO Phenomenon," *Journal of UFO Studies* 3 (1991), pp. 17–18.

2 Ibid., p. 30.

3 Susan Schiefelbein, *The Incredible Machine* (Washington, D.C.: The National Geographic Society, 1986), p. 9.

4 Lewis Thomas, foreword to *The Incredible Machine*, p. 7.

5 James Trefil, "Phenomena, Comment and Notes," *Smithsonian* (July 1993), pp. 18–19.

6 Terence McKenna, quoted in John E. Mack, *Abduction: Human Encounters with Aliens* (New York: Charles Scribner's Sons, 1994), p. 410.

7 John E. Mack, "The Abduction Phenomenon: A Preliminary Report" (June 1992), p. 15, photocopy given to author.

8 Ibid.

9 Ibid., p. 16.

10 Ibid.

11 Mack, *Abduction*, p. 19.

12 Mack, "The Abduction Phenomenon," p. 16.

13 Keith Thompson, *Angels and Aliens: UFOs and the Mythic Imagination* (New York: Addison-Wesley, 1991), p. 63.

14 Howard Blum, *Out There* (New York: Pocket Books, 1990), p. 257.

15 Timothy Good, *Above Top Secret: The Worldwide UFO Cover-Up* (New York: William Morrow & Co., 1988), p. 255.

16 Unidentified Airman quoted in *Above Top Secret*, pp. 407–8.

17 Major Ernest J. Edwards quoted in Good, *Above Top Secret*, pp. 405–6.

18 Stanton J. Friedman and Don Berliner, *Crash at Corona* (New York: Paragon House, 1992), pp. 195–97.

19 William Moore, quoted in Blum, *Out There* (New York: Pocket Books, 1991), p. 268.

20 Linda Moulton Howe, *Alien Harvest*, p. 137.

21 Briefing Document, Operation Majestic 12, in Blum, *Out There*, p. 316.

22 Good, *Above Top Secret*, pp. 346–47.

23 Wilbert B. Smith, quoted in Good, *Above Top Secret*, p. 183.

24 Ibid., p. 478.

25 Harry S Truman, quoted in Good, *Above Top Secret*, p. 551.

26 William Moore, quoted in Good, *Above Top Secret*, p. 260.

27 Good, *Above Top Secret*, pp. 476–77.

28 Ibid., p. 478.

29 David M. Jacobs, *Secret Life: Firsthand Accounts of UFO Abductions* (New York: Simon & Schuster, 1992), p. 37.

30 Good, *Above Top Secret*, p. 346.

31 James Harder, quoted in Good, *Above Top Secret,* p. 346.

32 Good, *Above Top Secret,* p. 259.

33 Donald Menzel, quoted in David C. Knight, ed., *UFOs: A Pictorial History from Antiquity to the Present* (New York: McGraw-Hill, 1979), p. 91.

34 Good, *Above Top Secret,* pp. 545–50.

35 William Moore and Jaime Shandera in Blum, *Out There,* p. 270.

36 Howe, *An Alien Harvest,* p. 253.

37 "The Mystery at Groom Lake," "Periscope" in *Newsweek,* November 1, 1993, p. 4.

VIII. POSTCONFERENCE INTERVIEW: DAVID E. PRITCHARD, PH.D.

1 David E. Pritchard, "Post Conference Investigation and Updated Conclusions," in *Alien Discussions: Proceedings of the Abduction Study Conference* [in press], p. 295.

XI. POSTCONFERENCE INTERVIEW: JOHN E. MACK

1 John E. Mack, "The UFO Phenomenon: What Does It Mean for the Expansion of Human Consciousness?" (paper presented at the International Transpersonal Association Conference, Prague, Czechoslovakia, June 1992), pp. 3–5.

2 Ibid., pp. 1–2.

3 John E. Mack, "The Abduction Phenomenon: A Preliminary Report" (June 1992), pp. 4–5, photocopy.

4 Ibid., pp. 9–12.

5 Ibid., p. 40.

6 Ibid., p. 49.

7 Ibid., pp. 37–39.

8 Ibid., p. 50.

9 Ibid., pp. 59–60.

10 Ibid., pp. 55–56.

11 Rilke quote photocopied and given to author by Mack.

XIV. POSTCONFERENCE INTERVIEW: CAROL AND ALICE— FIRST HYPNOSIS SESSION AT BUDD HOPKINS'S STUDIO

1 John Mack, transcript of tape-recorded talk given at "Interface," Cambridge, Mass., April 23, 1993.

XVII. POSTCONFERENCE INTERVIEW: CAROL AND ALICE THIRD HYPNOSIS SESSION AT BUDD HOPKINS'S STUDIO

1 Dr. Jayne Gackenbach, "Frameworks for Understanding Lucid Dreaming: A Review," *Dreaming* 1, no. 2 (1991), p. 109.

2 Fred Alan Wolf, *The Dreaming Universe* (New York: Simon & Schuster, 1994), p. 192.

3 John E. Mack, *Abduction: Human Encounters with Aliens* (New York: Charles Scribner's Sons, 1994), p. 407.

XX. VARIOUS THEORIES

1 Keith Thompson, "The UFO Experience As a Crisis of Transformation," in *Spiritual Emergency,* edited by Stanislav and Christina Grof (1989), pp. 124–25, photocopy.

2 Kenneth Arnold, quoted in David C. Knight, ed., *UFOs: A Pictorial History from Antiquity to the Present* (New York: McGraw-Hill, 1979), p. 33.

3 Philip J. Klass, quoted in Stephen Rae, "John Mack," *New York Times Magazine,* March 20, 1993, p. 33.

4 Budd Hopkins, *Intruders: The Incredible Visitations at Copley Woods* (New York: Random House, 1987), p. 179.

5 John Mack, *Abduction: Human Encounters with Aliens* (New York: Charles Scribner's Sons, 1994), p. 25.

6 Ibid., p. 43.

7 Letter from young Minnesota woman in Hopkins, *Intruders,* pp. 197–98.

8 Thompson, "The UFO Experience," p. 132.

9 Ibid., p. 134.

10 Mack, *Abduction,* p. 415.

11 Ibid., pp. 415–16.

12 Ibid., p. 319.

13 Thompson, "The UFO Experience," p. 132.

14 Mack, *Abduction,* p. 417.

15 Mack, *Abduction,* p. 398.

16 Whitley Strieber, *Transformation: The Breakthrough* (New York: William Morrow & Co.), p. 236.

17 Whitley Strieber in Thompson, "The UFO Experience," p. 127.

18 Mack, *Abduction,* p. 400.

19 J. Bryan III, *Hodge Podge: A Commonplace Book* (New York: Atheneum, 1986), p. 200.

20 Keith Thompson, *Angels and Aliens,* p. 400.

21 J. Allen Hynek, quoted in Thompson, *Angels and Aliens,* p. 80.

22 Thompson, *Angels and Aliens,* p. 101.

23 Ezek. 1: 4–7.

24 Ezek. 2: 1–2; 3: 12–14.

25 Joseph Smith, quoted in Thompson, *Angels and Aliens,* p. 70.

26 A. H. Clough, *Introduction to Plutarch's Lives,* quoted in Thompson, *Angels and Aliens,* p. 120.

27 Samuel Coccius, quoted in Thompson, *Angels and Aliens,* p. 70.

28 Knight, *UFOs: A Pictorial History,* p. 25.

29 John Toland, quoted in J. Bryan III, *Hodge Podge Two: Another Commonplace Book* (New York: Atheneum, 1989), p. 10.

30 Thompson, *Angels and Aliens,* p. 70.

31 Ibid., pp. 152–54.

32 Quoted in Thompson, *Angels and Aliens,* 154–55.

33 H. Chiang, "UFO Sightings and Research in Modern China," in *MUFON 1993 International UFO Proceedings,* quoted in Mack, *Abduction,* p. 12.

34 Jacques Vallee, quoted in Thompson, *Angels and Aliens,* p. 154.

35 Ibid., p. 10.

36 Mack, *Abduction,* p. 10.

37 Vallee, quoted in Mack, *Abduction,* p. 96.

38 Jacques Vallee, *Dimensions: A Casebook of Alien Contact* (New York: Ballantine Books, 1988), pp. 143–44.

39 Mack, *Abduction,* p. 406.

40 Ibid., p. 406.

41 Richard Tarnas, quoted in Mack, *Abduction,* p. 420.

42 Thompson, *Angels and Aliens,* p. xi.

43 Mack, *Abduction,* p. 421.

44 Carl Jung, *Flying Saucers: A Modern Myth* (Princeton, N.J.: Princeton University Press, 1978), p. 6.

45 Jung, quoted in Thompson, *Angels and Aliens,* p. 42.

46 Thompson, *Angels and Aliens,* p. 43.

47 Ibid., p. 4.

48 Fred Alan Wolf, *The Dreaming Universe* (New York: Simon & Schuster, 1994), p. 43.

49 Ibid., p. 227.

50 Ibid., p. 226.

51 Ibid., pp. 227–28.

52 Ibid., p. 228.

53 Michael Grosso, quoted in Wolf, *The Dreaming Universe,* p. 224.

54 Wolf, *The Dreaming Universe,* p. 224.

55 Ibid., p. 225.

56 Ibid., p. 243.

57 Rupert Sheldrake, quoted in Stephen Clark's review of Sheldrake's *A New Science of Life* [London] *Times Literary Supplement,* March 12, 1982, p. 279.

58 Wolf, *The Dreaming Universe,* p. 244.

59 Thompson, *Angels and Aliens,* p. 39.

60 Kenneth Ring, quoted in Wolf, *The Dreaming Universe,* p. 244.

61 Wolf, *The Dreaming Universe,* pp. 246–47.

62 Ibid., p. 601.

63 Ibid., p. 63.

64 Ibid., pp. 247–48.

65 Julian Jaynes, *The Origin of Consciousness in the Breakdown of the Bicameral Mind* (New York: Houghton Mifflin, 1990), p. 112.

66 Ibid., p. 408.

67 Wolf, *The Dreaming Universe,* p. 248.

68 Ibid., p. 249.

69 Ibid.

70 Mack, *Abduction,* p. 70.

71 Wolf, *The Dreaming Universe,* p. 249.

72 Kenneth Ring, quoted in Wolf, *The Dreaming Universe,* pp. 249–50.

73 Michael Murphy, quoted in Thompson, *Angels and Aliens,* p. 227.

74 Thompson, *Angels and Aliens,* pp. 228–29.

75 David M. Jacobs, *Secret Life: Firsthand Accounts of UFO Abductions* (New York: Simon & Schuster, 1992), p. 317.

76 Hopkins, *Intruders,* p. 193.

77 Wolf, *The Dreaming Universe,* p. 230.

78 Mack, *Abduction,* p. 407.

79 Jaynes, *The Origin of Consciousness,* p. 134.

80 Václav Havel, "The New Measure of Man," *New York Times,* July 8, 1994, p. A27.

81 Nicholas Wade, "Method and Madness: A Fable for Fleas," *The New York Times Magazine,* August 14, 1994, p. 18.

82 David E. Pritchard, private correspondence with author, December 7, 1994.

83 Kurt Vonnegut, *God Bless You, Mr. Rosewater* (New York: Dell Publishing Company, 1970), p. 18.

84 Thompson, *Angels and Aliens,* pp. 229–30.

Bibliography

Adamski, G. *Inside the Space Ships.* New York: Abelard-Schulman, 1955.

Alexander, J. "Comparative Phenomenology of Near Death Experience," in *Alien Discussions: Proceedings of the Abduction Study Conference.* In press.

Appelle, S. "Federal Policy for the Protection of Human Subjects and Its Applicability to Abduction Research," in *Alien Discussions: Proceedings of the Abduction Study Conference.* In press.

Basterfield, K. "Abductions and Paranormal Phenomena," in *Alien Discussions: Proceedings of the Abduction Study Conference,* in press.

———. "Abductions: The Australian Experience," in *Alien Discussions: Proceedings of the Abduction Study Conference.* In press.

———. "Abductions: The Fantasy-Prone Hypothesis," *Alien Discussions: Proceedings of the Abduction Study Conference.* In press.

———. "Maureen Puddy: An Australian Abductee Physically Present During an Abduction." 1992. Photocopy.

Baird, J. C. *The Inner Limits of Outer Space.* Hanover, N.H.: Dartmouth University Press, 1987.

Bateson, G. *Mind and Nature: A Necessary Unity.* New York: E. P. Dutton, 1979.

Benson, T. "The Close Encounter: Initial Percipient/UFO Interaction," in *Alien Discussions: Proceedings of the Abduction Study Conference.* In press.

Blum, H. *Out There.* New York: Pocket Books, 1990.

Boylan, R. "Some Abductees Don't Have Post-Traumatic Stress Disorder," in *Alien Discussions: Proceedings of the Abduction Study Conference.* In press.

Bracewell, R. N. *The Galactic Club: Intelligent Life in Outer Space.* San Francisco: San Francisco Book Company, Inc., 1976.

Broad, W. J. "Wreckage in the Desert Was Odd but Not Alien." *The New York Times,* Sept. 18, 1966, pp. A1, 40.

Bryan, III, J. *Hodge Podge: A Commonplace Book.* New York: Atheneum, 1986.

———. *Hodge Podge Two. Another Commonplace Book,* New York: Atheneum, 1989.

Bullard, T. E. "Abduction Reports Compared With Folklore Narratives," in *Alien Discussions: Proceedings of the Abduction Study Conference.* In press.

———. "Folkloric Dimensions of the UFO Phenomenon." *Journal of UFO Studies* 3 (1991), pp. 1–57.

——. "Hypnosis and UFO Abductions: A Troubled Relationship." *Journal of UFO Studies* 1 (1989), pp. 3–40.

——. "Kenneth Ring's Imaginal World Hypothesis," in *Alien Discussions: Proceedings of the Abduction Study Conference.* In press.

——. "On Stolen Time: A Comparative Study of Abduction Reports." Mt. Rainier, Md.: Fund for UFO Research, 1987.

——. "On Stolen Time: A Comparative Study of Abduction Reports Update," in *Alien Discussions: Proceedings of the Abduction Study Conference.* In press.

——. "The Overstated Dangers of Hypnosis," in *Alien Discussions: Proceedings of the Abduction Study Conference.* In press.

——. "The Rarer Abduction Episodes," in *Alien Discussions: Proceedings of the Abduction Study Conference.* In press.

——. *UFO Abductions: The Measure of a Mystery.* Mt. Ranier, Md.: Fund for UFO Research.

——. "The Variety of Abduction Beings," in *Alien Discussions: Proceedings of the Abduction Study Conference.* In press.

——. "The Well-Ordered Abduction: Pattern or Mirage?" in *Alien Discussions: Proceedings of the Abduction Study Conference.* In press.

Cameron, G., and T. S. Crain. *UFOs, MJ-12 and the Government: A Report on Government Involvement in UFO Crash Retrievals.* Seguin, Tex.: Mutual UFO Network (MUFON), 1989.

Campbell, J. *The Hero with a Thousand Faces.* Princeton: Princeton University Press, 1949.

Carpenter, J. "Commentary," in *Unusual Personal Experiences. An Analysis of the Data from Three National Surveys.* Las Vegas, Nev.: Bigelow Holding Corp.

——. "Cures of Abductees' Ailments," in *Alien Discussions: Proceedings of the Abduction Study Conference.* In press.

——. "Double Abduction Case: Correlation of Abduction Data." *Journal of UFO Studies* 3 (1991), pp. 91–114.

——. "Investigating and Correlating Simultaneous Abductions," in *Alien Discussions: Proceedings of the Abduction Study Conference.* In press.

——. "Multiple Participant Abductions." Paper presented at the Seattle UFO Research Conference, 1993.

——. "Resolution of Phobias from UFO Data," in *Alien Discussions: Proceedings of the Abduction Study Conference.* In press.

——. "Therapist-Investigator Partnership," in *Alien Discussions: Proceedings of the Abduction Study Conference.* In press.

Chiang, H. "UFO Sightings and Research in Modern China," in *MUFON 1993 International UFO Symposium Proceedings.*

Clark, J. "Airships: Parts I, II." *International UFO Reporter* (1991). 1: 4–223; 2: 20–21, 23, 24.

Condon, E. U. *Scientific Study of Unidentified Flying Objects.* New York: Bantam Books, 1969.

Davenport, M. *Visitors from Time: The Secret of the UFOs.* Tigard, Ore.: Wildflower Press, 1992.

David, J., ed. *The Flying Saucer Reader.* New York: New American Library, 1967.

de Moura, G. "Abduction Phenomenon in Brazil," in *Alien Discussions: Proceedings of the Abduction Study Conference.* In press.

De Simone, D. "Investigation vs Therapy," in *Alien Discussions: Proceedings of the Abduction Study Conference.* In press.

Dean, G. "[Abduction] Comparisons with Ritual Abuse Accounts," in *Alien Discussions: Proceedings of the Abduction Study Conference.* In press.

Desk Reference to the Diagnostic Criteria from DSM-III-R. Washington, D.C.: American Psychiatric Association, 1987.

Donderi, D. C. "Validating the Roper Poll: A Scientific Approach to the Abduction Evidence," in *Alien Discussions: Proceedings of the Abduction Study Conference.* In press.

Doyle, Arthur Conan. *The Sign of Four.* London, 1890.

Emenegger, R. *UFO'S Past Present & Future.* New York: Ballantine Books, 1974.

Fowler, R. E. *The Allagash Abductions: Undeniable Evidence of Alien Intervention.* Tigard, Ore.: Wildflower Press, 1993.

———. *The Andreasson Affair,* Englewood Cliffs, N.J.: Prentice Hall, 1979.

———. *The Andreasson Affair, Phase Two.* Englewood Cliffs, N.J.: Prentice Hall, 1982.

Friedman, S., and Berliner, D. *Crash at Corona.* New York: Paragon House, 1994.

Fuller, J. G. *The Interrupted Journey.* New York: Dial Press, 1966.

Gackenbach, J. "Frameworks for Understanding Lucid Dreaming: A Review." *Dreaming* 1, no. 2 (1991).

Gallant, R. *Beyond Earth: The Search for Extraterrestrial Life.* New York: Four Winds Press, 1977.

Gotlib, D. "Ethical Issues in Dealing with the Abduction Issue," in *Alien Discussions: Proceedings of the Abduction Study Conference.* In press.

———. "Methodological Problems in Abduction Work to Date," in *Alien Discussions: Proceedings of the Abduction Study Conference.* In press.

Good, T. *Above Top Secret: The Worldwide UFO Coverup.* New York: William Morrow & Co., 1989.

Gordon, J. S. "The UFO Experience." *Atlantic Monthly* (August, 1991), pp. 82f.

Grosso, M. "Transcending the 'E.T.' Hypothesis." *California UFO* 3, no. 3 (1988), pp. 9–11.

———. "UFOs and the Myth of a New Age." *ReVISION* 11, no. 3. (1989).

Haines, R. "Multiple Abduction Evidence—What Is Really Needed?" in *Alien Discussions: Proceedings of the Abduction Study Conference.* In press.

———. "Novel Investigative Techniques," in *Alien Discussions: Proceedings of the Abduction Study Conference.* In press.

———. "Some Evidence for a Family Linkage," in *Alien Discussions: Proceedings of the Abduction Study Conference.* In press.

Hall, R. "Are Abduction Reports 'Mass Hysteria'?" in *Alien Discussions: Proceedings of the Abduction Study Conference.* In press.

Hamilton, W. F. *Cosmic Top Secret: America's Secret UFO Program.* New Brunswick, N.J.: Inner Light Publications, 1991.

Havel, V. "The New Measure of Man." Acceptance speech upon receiving the 1994 Philadelphia Liberty Medal; reprinted in *The New York Times,* July 8, 1994, p. A27.

Hawkins, G. *Beyond Stonehenge.* New York: Harper & Row, 1973.

Hopkins, B. "A Doubly Witnessed Abduction," in *Alien Discussions: Proceedings of the Abduction Study Conference.* In press.

————. "The Hopkins Image Recognition Test (HIRT) for Children," in *Alien Discussions: Proceedings of the Abduction Study Conference.* In press.

————. *Intruders: The Incredible Visitation at Copley Woods.* New York: Random House, 1987.

————. "The Linda Cortile Abduction Case. Parts I, II." *MUFON UFO Journal.* New York: Intruders Foundation.

————. *Missing Time: A Documented Study of UFO Abductions.* New York: Richard Marek Publishers, 1981.

Hopkins, B., D. Jacobs, and R. Westrum. *Unusual Personal Experiences: An Analysis of the Data from Three National Surveys.* Las Vegas, Nev.: Bigelow Holding Corporation, 1991.

Horowitz, P. "Radio Search for ET Intelligence," in *Alien Discussions: Proceedings of the Abduction Study Conference.* In press.

Howe, L. M. *An Alien Harvest.* Littleton, Colo.: Linda Moulton Howe Productions, 1989.

————. *Glimpses of Other Realities; Volume I: Facts and Eyewitnesses.* Huntingdon Valley, Pa.: Linda Moulton Howe Productions.

Hufford, D. "Sleep Paralysis and Bedroom Abductions," in *Alien Discussions: Proceedings of the Abduction Study Conference.* In press.

————. *The Terror That Comes in the Night.* Philadelphia: University of Pennsylvania Press, 1982.

Hynek, J. A. *The UFO Experience: A Scientific Inquiry.* New York: Ballantine Books, 1974.

————, and J. Vallee. *The Edge of Reality.* Chicago: Henry Regnery Co., 1975.

Jacobs, D. M. "Description of Aliens," in *Alien Discussions: Proceedings of the Abduction Study Conference.* In press.

————. *Secret Life: Firsthand Accounts of UFO Abductions.* New York: Simon & Schuster, 1992.

————. "Subsequent Procedures," in *Alien Discussions: Proceedings of the Abduction Study Conference.* In press.

————. "Table Procedures," in *Alien Discussions: Proceedings of the Abduction Study Conference.* In press.

————. *The UFO Controversy in America.* Bloomington, Ind.: Indiana University Press, 1975.

Jacobson, E., and J. Bruno. "Dissociative Disorders in Abductees," in *Alien Discussions: Proceedings of the Abduction Study Conference.* In press.

————. "Psychological Profiles of Abductees," in *Alien Discussions: Proceedings of the Abduction Study Conference.* In press.

Jaynes, J. *The Origin of Consciousness in the Breakdown of the Bicameral Mind.* Boston: Houghton Mifflin Co., 1976.

Jung, C. G. *Flying Saucers: A Modern Myth of Things Seen in the Sky.* New York: New American Library, 1959.

Klass, P. J. *UFO Abductions: A Dangerous Game.* Buffalo: Prometheus Press, 1989.

Knight, D. C. *UFOs: A Pictorial History from Antiquity to the Present.* New York: McGraw-Hill, 1979.

LaParl, B. "Brain Scan Anomalies of Two Abductees Claiming Implants," in *Alien Discussions: Proceedings of the Abduction Study Conference.* In press.

Mack, J. *Abduction: Human Encounters with Aliens.* New York: Charles Scribner's Sons, 1994.

———. "The Abduction Phenomenon, Preliminary Report." 1992. Photocopy.

———. "The UFO Phenomenon: What Does it Mean for the Expansion of Human Consciousness?" Paper delivered before the International Transpersonal Association Conference, Prague, Czechoslovakia, June 1992.

Miller, J. "Envelope Epidemiology," in *Alien Discussions: Proceedings of the Abduction Study Conference.* In press.

———. "Medical Procedural Differences: Alien vs. Human," in *Alien Discussions: Proceedings of the Abduction Study Conference.* In press.

———. "The Realization Event—An Important Historical Feature," in *Alien Discussions: Proceedings of the Abduction Study Conference.* In press.

———, and R. Neal. "Lack of Proof for Missing Fetus Syndrome," in *Alien Discussions: Proceedings of the Abduction Study Conference.* In press.

"The Mystery at Groom Lake." *Newsweek,* November 1, 1993, p. 4.

Nyman, J. "A Composite Encounter Model," in *Alien Discussions: Proceedings of the Abduction Study Conference.* In press.

———. "The Familiar Entity and Dual Reference," in *Alien Discussions: Proceedings of the Abduction Study Conference.* In press.

Papagiannis, M. "Probability of Extraterrestrial Life on Earth," in *Alien Discussions: Proceedings of the Abduction Study Conference.* In press.

Penfield, W. *The Mystery of the Mind: A Critical Study of Consciousness and the Human Brain.* Princeton: Princeton University Press, 1975.

Peterson, I. "Euclid's Crop Circles." *Science News,* 141, no. 5. (1992), pp. 76–7.

Pritchard, D. "Physical Evidence and the Reality of Some Abduction Phenomenon," in *Alien Discussions: Proceedings of the Abduction Study Conference.* In press.

———. "Terrestrial Search for Extraterrestrial Intelligence," in *Alien Discussions: Proceedings of the Abduction Study Conference.* In press.

Rae, Stephen. "John Mack: UFOs Land at Harvard." *New York Times Magazine,* March 20, 1994, pp. 33.

———. "UFOs Land at Harvard: John Mack's Abductees." *The New York Times Magazine,* March 20, 1994.

Randles, J. *Abduction: Over 200 Documented UFO Kidnappings.* London: Robert Hale, 1988.

———. "A Feature Analysis of Abduction Reports in Britain," in *Alien Discussions: Proceedings of the Abduction Study Conference.* In press.

———. "Imaginal vs Real Abductions," in *Alien Discussions: Proceedings of the Abduction Study Conference.* In press. 1995

———. "A Study of an Abduction Where the Entity Was Photographed," in *Alien Discussions: Proceedings of the Abduction Study Conference.* In press.

Ring, K. "Near Death and UFO Encounters as Shamanic Initiations: Some Conceptual and Evolutionary Implications." *ReVISION Journal* 11, no. 3 (1989).

———. "Near-Death Experiences: Implications for Human Evolution and Planetary Transformation." *ReVISION Journal* 8, no. 2 (1986).

———. *The Omega Project: Near Death Experiences, UFO Encounters, and Mind at Large.* New York: William Morrow & Co., 1992.

Rodeghier, M., J. Goodpaster, and S. Blatterbauer. "Psychosocial Characteristics of Abductees: Results from the CUFOS Abduction Project." *Journal of UFO Studies* 3 (1991), pp. 59–90.

Rodeghier, M. "Evidence for Abuse Among Abductees," in *Alien Discussions: Proceedings of the Abduction Study Conference.* In press.

———. "Psychosocial Characteristics of Abductees," in *Alien Discussions: Proceedings of the Abduction Study Conference.* In press.

———. "A Set of Selection Criteria for Abductees," in *Alien Discussions: Proceedings of the Abduction Study Conference.* In press.

Ruppelt, E. *The Report on Unidentified Flying Objects.* Garden City, N.J.: Doubleday, 1956.

Sagan, C. *The Dragons of Eden: Speculations on the Evolution of Human Intelligence.* New York: Ballantine Books, 1977.

Schuessler, J. "Vehicle Internal Systems," in *Alien Discussions: Proceedings of the Abduction Study Conference.* In press.

Sheldrake, R. "Morphic Resonance and Collective Memory." Paper presented at the International Transpersonal Association Conference, Prague, June 1992.

Siegel, R. K. *Fire in the Brain: Clinical Tales of Hallucination.* New York: E. P. Dutton, 1992.

Smith, Y. "Abductions of Children Ages 4–15," in *Alien Discussions: Proceedings of the Abduction Study Conference.* In press.

Stone-Carmen, J. "Abductees with Conscious Recall Are Different," in *Alien Discussions: Proceedings of the Abduction Study Conference.* In press.

———. "A Descriptive Study of People Reporting Abduction by Unidentified Flying Objects (UFOs)," in *Alien Discussions: Proceedings of the Abduction Study Conference.* In press.

Strieber, W. *Communion: A True Story.* New York: William Morrow & Co., 1987.

———. *Transformation: The Breakthrough.* New York: William Morrow & Co., 1988.

Stringfield, L. H. *UFO Crash/Retrievals: The Inner Sanctum.* Cincinnati, Ohio: Leonard H. Stringfield (privately printed).

Talbot, M. *The Holographic Universe.* New York: HarperCollins, 1991.

Teare, M. "California Therapist Ethical Standards," in *Alien Discussions: Proceedings of the Abduction Study Conference.* In press.

Thomas, L. Introduction to *The Incredible Machine.* Washington: National Geographic Society, 1986.

Thompson, K. *Angels and Aliens: UFOs and the Mythic Imagination.* New York: Addison-Wesley Publishing Company, 1991.

————. "The UFO Experience As a Crisis of Transformation," in *Spiritual Emergency,* edited by Stanislav & Christina Grof. 1989.

Trefil, J. "Phenomena, Comment, and Notes." *Smithsonian,* July 1993, pp. 18–19.

Vallee, J. *Dimensions: A Casebook of Alien Contact.* New York: Ballantine Books, 1988.

————. *Passport to Magonia.* Chicago: Henry Regnery Company, 1969.

Vonnegut, K. *God Bless You, Mr. Rosewater.* New York: Dell Publishing Co., 1970.

Wade, N. "Method and Madness: A Fable for Fleas." *The New York Times Magazine,* September 14, 1994, p. 18.

Walton, T. *The Walton Experience.* New York: Berkeley Books, 1978.

Westrum, R. "Social Dynamics of Abduction Reporting," in *Alien Discussions: Proceedings of the Abduction Study Conference.* In press.

Wolf, F. A. *The Dreaming Universe.* New York: Simon & Schuster, 1994.

————. *Taking the Quantum Leap: The New Physics for Nonscientists.* Rev. ed. New York: HarperCollins, 1989.

Wright, D. "The Need for Policing," in *Alien Discussions. Proceedings of the Abduction Study Conference.* In press.

* Anyone wishing the complete 600-plus-page illustrated *Alien Discussions: Proceedings of the Abduction Study Conference*—carefully edited, indexed, and updated by Andrea Pritchard, David E. Pritchard, John E. Mack, Pam Kasey, and Claudia Yapp—may obtain it by sending a check for $69.95 (which includes handling and postage within the United States) to Proceedings, P. O. Box 241, North Cambridge Post Office, Cambridge, MA 02140.

Index

PERMISSIONS ACKNOWLEDGMENTS

Grateful acknowledgment is made to the following for permission to reprint previously published material:

Addison-Wesley Publishing Company, Inc.: Excerpts from *Angels and Aliens: UFOs and the Mythic Imagination* (pp. xi, 44, 70, 99, 101, and 228) by Keith Thompson, copyright © 1991 by Keith Thompson. Reprinted by permission of Addison-Wesley Publishing Company, Inc.

Dutton Signet: Excerpts from *Fire in the Brain* by Ronald K. Siegel, Ph.D., copyright © 1992 by Ronald K. Siegel, Ph.D. Reprinted by permission of Dutton Signet, a division of Penguin Books USA Inc.

Budd Hopkins: Excerpts from *Intruders: The Incredible Visitations at Copley Woods* by Budd Hopkins (New York: Random House, Inc.), copyright © 1987 by Budd Hopkins. Reprinted by permission of Budd Hopkins.

Linda Moulton Howe: Excerpts from *An Alien Harvest* by Linda Moulton Howe (Huntington Valley, Penn.: Linda Moulton Howe Productions, 1989). Reprinted by permission of Linda Moulton Howe.

J. Allen Hynek Center for UFO Studies: Excerpts from "Double Abduction Case" by John S. Carpenter and from "Folkloric Dimensions of the UFO Phenomenon" by Thomas E. Bullard (*Journal of UFO Studies*, new series 3, 1991). Reprinted by permission of the J. Allen Hynek Center for UFO Studies.

David M. Jacobs: Excerpts from *Secret Life: Firsthand Acounts of UFO Abductions* by David M. Jacobs, Ph.D. (New York: Simon & Schuster, Inc., 1992). Reprinted by permission of David M. Jacobs.

The New York Times Company: Excerpts from "Method and Madness: A Fable for Fleas" by Nicholas Wade (*The New York Times*, August 14, 1994), copyright © 1994 by The New York Times Company. Reprinted by permission of The New York Times Company.

Science News: Excerpt from "Euclid's Crop Circles" by Ivars Peterson (*Science News*, Vol. 141, No. 5, February 1, 1992), copyright © 1992 by Science Service, Inc. Reprinted by permission of *Science News*, the weekly newsmagazine of science.

Charles Scribner's Sons and *Simon & Schuster Ltd.*: Excerpts from *Abduction: Human Encounters with Aliens* by John E. Mack, copyright © 1994 by John E. Mack, M.D. Rights in the United Kingdom administered by Simon & Schuster Ltd., London. Reprinted by permission of Scribner, and imprint of Simon & Schuster, Inc., and Simon & Schuster Ltd.

Fred Alan Wolf: Excerpts from *The Dreaming Universe* by Fred Alan Wolf, Ph.D. (New York: Simon & Schuster, Inc., 1993). Reprinted by permission of Fred Alan Wolf.

A NOTE ON THE TYPE

The text of this book was set in a modern rendering of the type first cut by Claude Garamond (c. 1480–1561). Garamond was a pupil of Geoffroy Tory and is believed to have based his letters on the Venetian models, although he introduced a number of important differences, and it is to him we owe the letter which we know as "old style." He gave to his letters a certain elegance and a feeling of movement that won for their creator an immediate reputation and the patronage of Francis I of France.

Composed by North Market Street Graphics,
Lancaster, Pennsylvania
Printed and bound by The Haddon Craftsmen,
Scranton, Pennsylvania
Designed by Cassandra J. Pappas